TADATOSHI FUJIMAKI

When I have to greet a big group of people, I get nervous, and my hands and voice start shaking like crazy. I asked a friend what I should do, and they said it happens because I want to give a good impression. I'm just too self-conscious. That comment shook me in a different way.

—2013

Tadatoshi Fujimaki was born on June 9, 1982, in Tokyo. He made his debut in 2007 in *Akamaru Jump* with *Kuroko's Basketball*, which was later serialized in *Weekly Shonen Jump*. *Kuroko's Basketball* quickly gained popularity and became an anime in Japan in 2012.

Kuroko's BASKETBALL

23 & 24

SHONEN JUMP Manga Edition
BY TADATOSHI FUJIMAKI

Translation/Caleb Cook
Touch-Up Art & Lettering/Snir Aharon
Design/Julian [JR] Robinson
Editor/John Bae

KUROKO NO BASUKE © 2008 by Tadatoshi Fujimaki
All rights reserved.
First published in Japan in 2008 by SHUEISHA Inc., Tokyo.
English translation rights arranged by SHUEISHA Inc.

Printed in Canada

Published by VIZ Media, LLC
P.O. Box 77010
San Francisco, CA 94107

10 9 8 7 6 5 4 3 2 1
First printing, June 2018

viz.com

shonenjump.com

SHONEN JUMP MANGA

Kuroko's BASKETBALL

23

UNDER A BLUE SKY

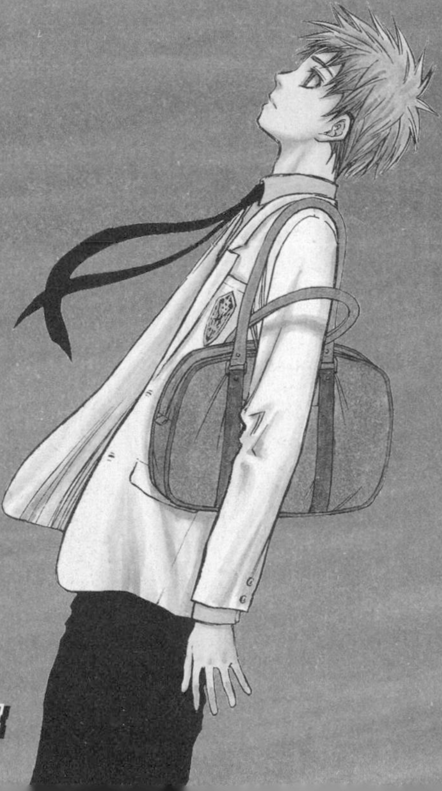

TADATOSHI FUJIMAKI

CHARACTERS

TAIGA KAGAMI

A first-year on Seirin High's basketball team. Though he's rough around the edges, he's a gifted player with a lot of potential. His goal is to beat the Miracle Generation.

TETSUYA KUROKO

A first-year on Seirin High's basketball team. Gifted with a natural lack of presence, he utilizes misdirection on the court to make nearly invisible passes.

TEPPEI KIYOSHI

A second-year on Seirin High's basketball team and the club's founder. He was hospitalized but returned shortly after Inter-High.

RIKO AIDA

A second-year and coach of the Seirin High basketball team.

JUNPEI HYUGA

A second-year on Seirin High's basketball team. As captain, he led his team to the Finals League last year despite only playing first-year players.

KUROKO'S BASKETBALL

RYOTA — **KISE**

One of the Miracle Generation. Any basketball move he sees, he can mimic in an instant.

SHINTARO — **MIDORIMA**

A first-year at Shutoku High, he's the top shooter of the Miracle Generation.

DAIKI — **AOMINE**

The ace of the Miracle Generation and Kuroko's former friend, he's now a first-year at To-oh Academy.

YUKIO — **KASAMATSU**

Kaijo's captain. As a second-year, his failure resulted in Kaijo's loss during the first game of Inter-High. His teammates implicitly trust him.

SEIJURO — **AKASHI**

Captain of the Miracle Generation during his time at Teiko Middle and the current leader of Rakuzan's ferocious team.

ATSUSHI — **MURASAKIBARA**

One of the Miracle Generation. A first-year on Yosen High's basketball team. He plays center, but he doesn't actually enjoy basketball all that much.

Teiko Middle School is an elite championship school whose basketball team once fielded five prodigies collectively known as "the Miracle Generation." But supporting those five was a phantom sixth man—Tetsuya Kuroko. Now Kuroko's a first-year high school student with zero presence who joins Seirin High's basketball club. Though his physical abilities and stats are well below average, Kuroko thrives on the court by making passes his opponents can't detect!

Aiming for the Winter Cup title, Seirin plays against To-Oh and Aomine in their first game of the tournament. In game four, they defeat Yosen and Murasakibara. In the first semifinal game, Rakuzan, led by Akashi and three of the five Uncrowned Generals, triumph over Shutoku and Midorima. Next up, it's Kaijo versus Seirin in the second game of the semifinals. Who will emerge as the winner in this all-out dogfight?!

STORY THUS FAR

TABLE OF CONTENTS

199TH QUARTER:

A TALL ORDER

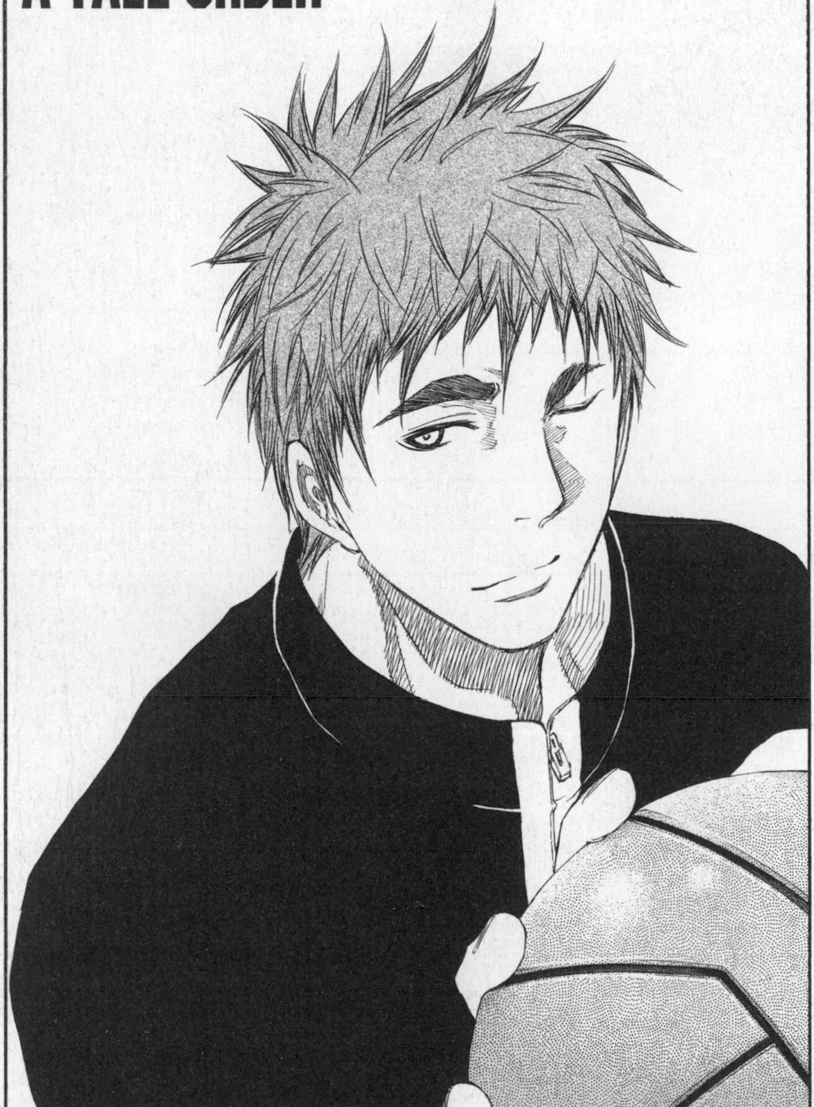

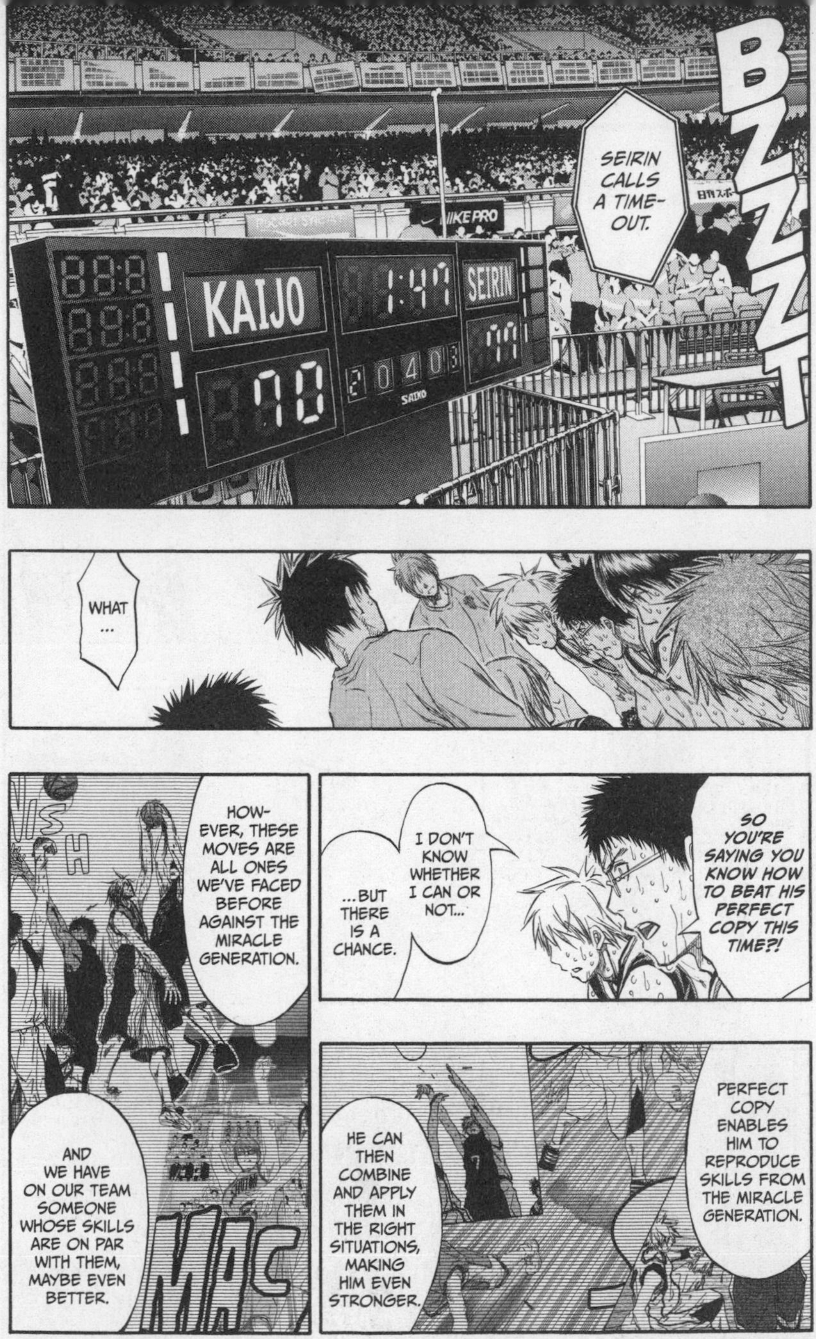
BZZZT
SEIRIN CALLS A TIME-OUT.
KAIJO
SEIRIN
WHAT ...
SO YOU'RE SAYING YOU KNOW HOW TO BEAT HIS PERFECT COPY THIS TIME?!
I DON'T KNOW WHETHER I CAN OR NOT...
...BUT THERE IS A CHANCE.
PERFECT COPY ENABLES HIM TO REPRODUCE SKILLS FROM THE MIRACLE GENERATION.
HE CAN THEN COMBINE AND APPLY THEM IN THE RIGHT SITUATIONS, MAKING HIM EVEN STRONGER.
HOW-EVER, THESE MOVES ARE ALL ONES WE'VE FACED BEFORE AGAINST THE MIRACLE GENERATION.
AND WE HAVE ON OUR TEAM SOMEONE WHOSE SKILLS ARE ON PAR WITH THEM, MAYBE EVEN BETTER.
MAC

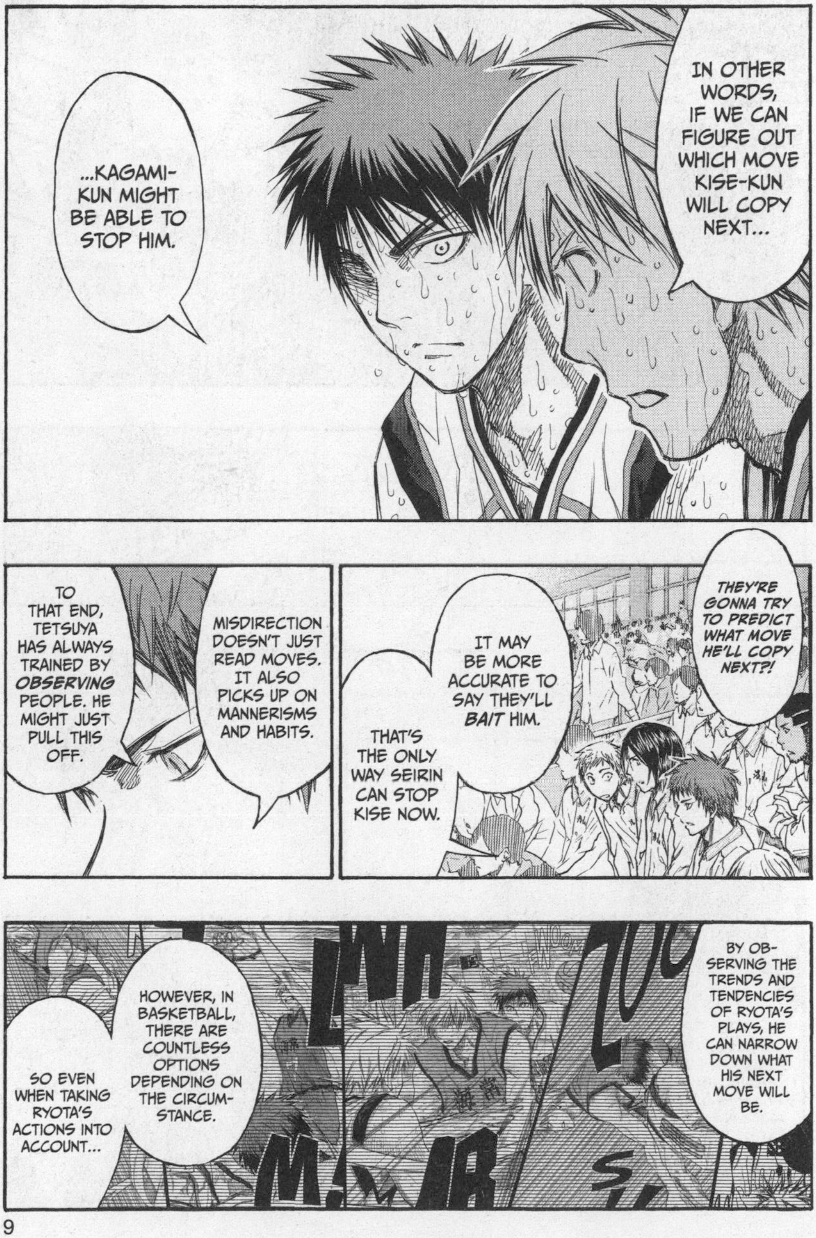
IN OTHER WORDS, IF WE CAN FIGURE OUT WHICH MOVE KISE-KUN WILL COPY NEXT...
...KAGAMI-KUN MIGHT BE ABLE TO STOP HIM.
THEY'RE GONNA TRY TO PREDICT WHAT MOVE HE'LL COPY NEXT?!
IT MAY BE MORE ACCURATE TO SAY THEY'LL *BAIT* HIM.
THAT'S THE ONLY WAY SEIRIN CAN STOP KISE NOW.
MISDIRECTION DOESN'T JUST READ MOVES. IT ALSO PICKS UP ON MANNERISMS AND HABITS.
TO THAT END, TETSUYA HAS ALWAYS TRAINED BY ***OBSERVING*** PEOPLE. HE MIGHT JUST PULL THIS OFF.
BY OB-SERVING THE TRENDS AND TENDENCIES OF RYOTA'S PLAYS, HE CAN NARROW DOWN WHAT HIS NEXT MOVE WILL BE.
HOWEVER, IN BASKETBALL, THERE ARE COUNTLESS OPTIONS DEPENDING ON THE CIRCUM-STANCE.
SO EVEN WHEN TAKING RYOTA'S ACTIONS INTO ACCOUNT...

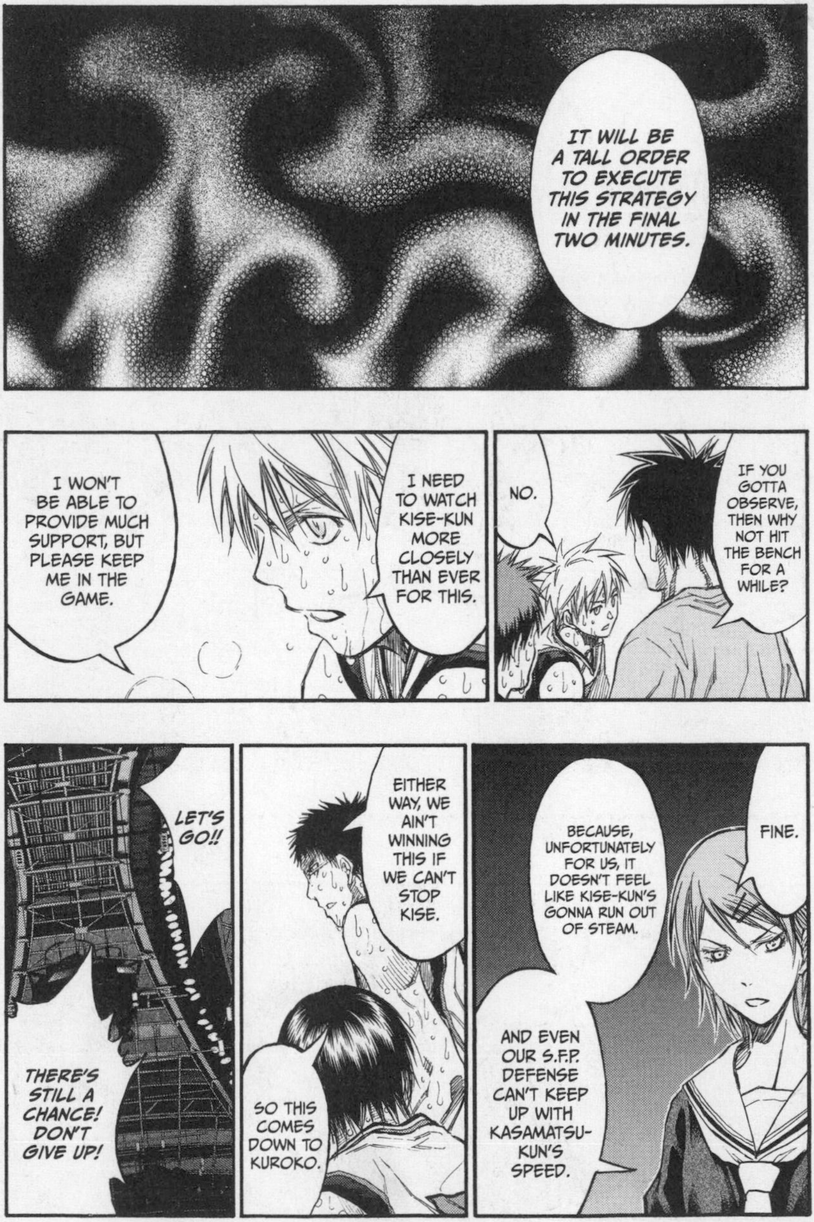
IT WILL BE A TALL ORDER TO EXECUTE THIS STRATEGY IN THE FINAL TWO MINUTES.
IF YOU GOTTA OBSERVE, THEN WHY NOT HIT THE BENCH FOR A WHILE?
NO.
I NEED TO WATCH KISE-KUN MORE CLOSELY THAN EVER FOR THIS.
I WON'T BE ABLE TO PROVIDE MUCH SUPPORT, BUT PLEASE KEEP ME IN THE GAME.
FINE.
BECAUSE, UNFORTUNATELY FOR US, IT DOESN'T FEEL LIKE KISE-KUN'S GONNA RUN OUT OF STEAM.
AND EVEN OUR S.F.P. DEFENSE CAN'T KEEP UP WITH KASAMATSU-KUN'S SPEED.
EITHER WAY, WE AIN'T WINNING THIS IF WE CAN'T STOP KISE.
SO THIS COMES DOWN TO KUROKO.
LET'S GO!!
THERE'S STILL A CHANCE! DON'T GIVE UP!

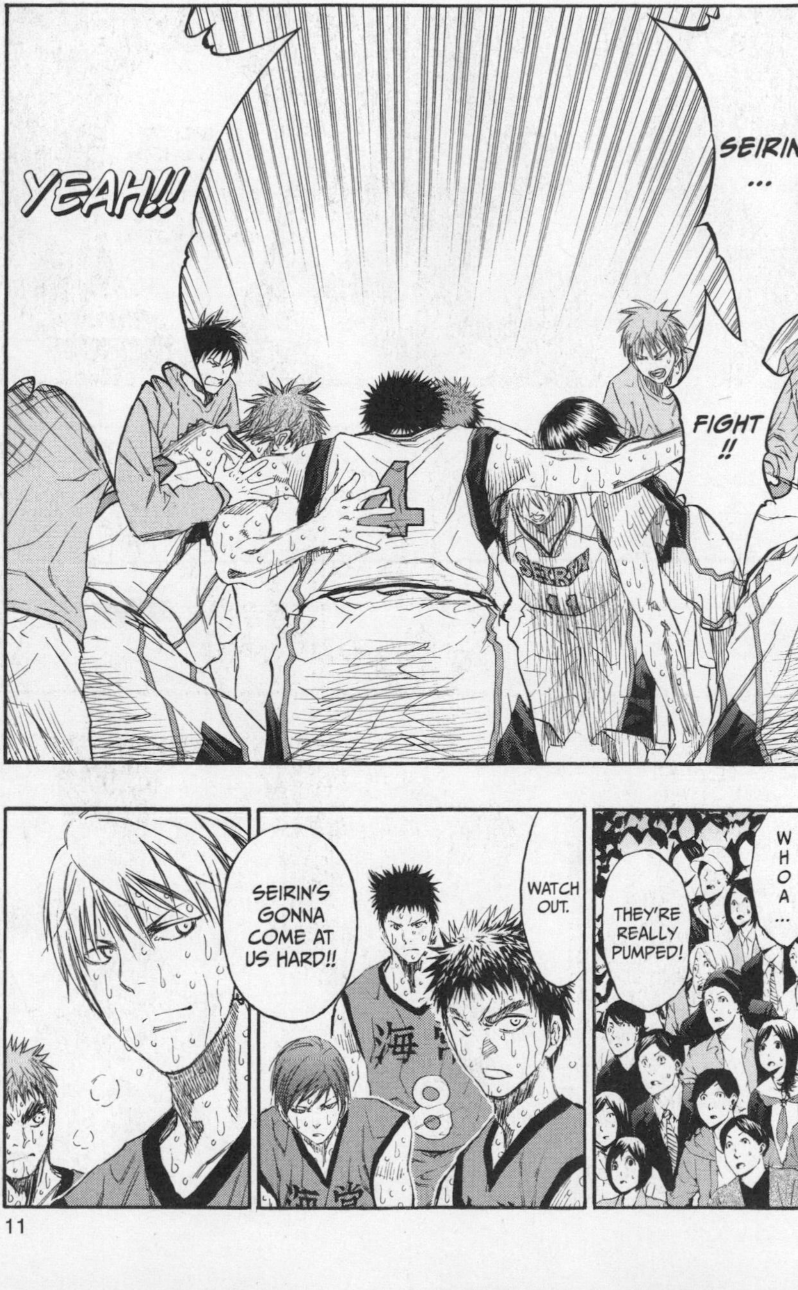
SEIRIN ...
FIGHT !!
YEAH!!
WHOA ...
THEY'RE REALLY PUMPED!
WATCH OUT.
SEIRIN'S GONNA COME AT US HARD!!

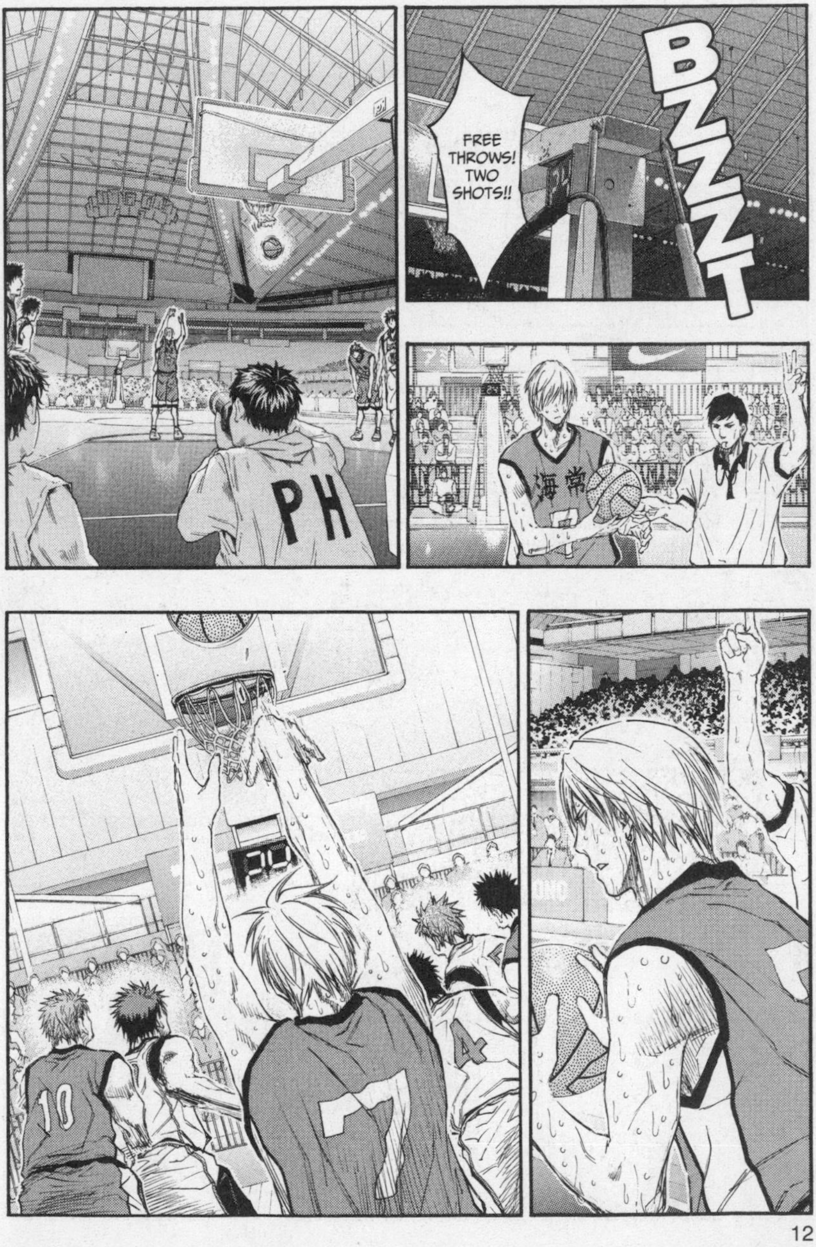
BZZZT
FREE THROWS! TWO SHOTS!!
PH

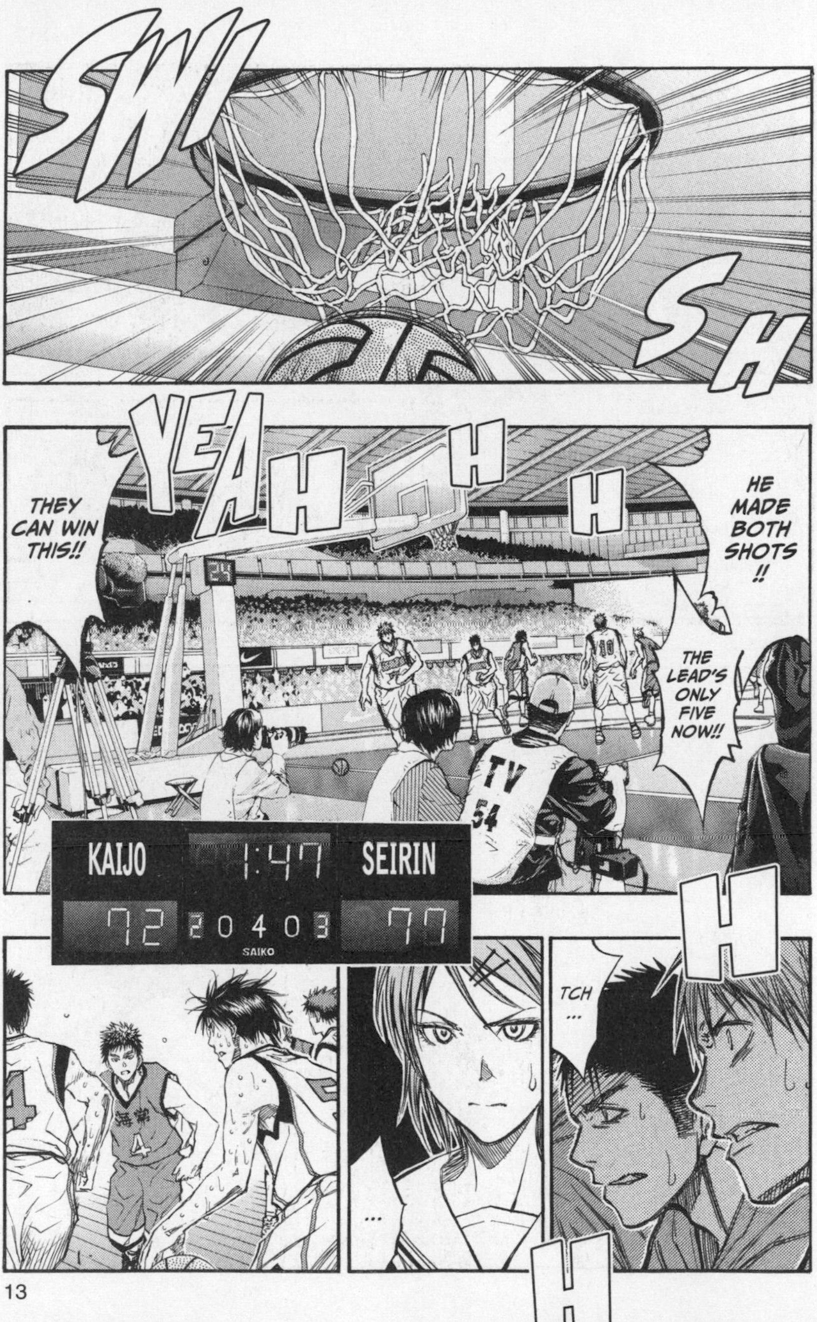
SWISH
YEAHHHH
HE MADE BOTH SHOTS!!
THE LEAD'S ONLY FIVE NOW!!
THEY CAN WIN THIS!!
KAIJO
1:47
SEIRIN
72
20403
77
SAIKO
HH
TCH...
...

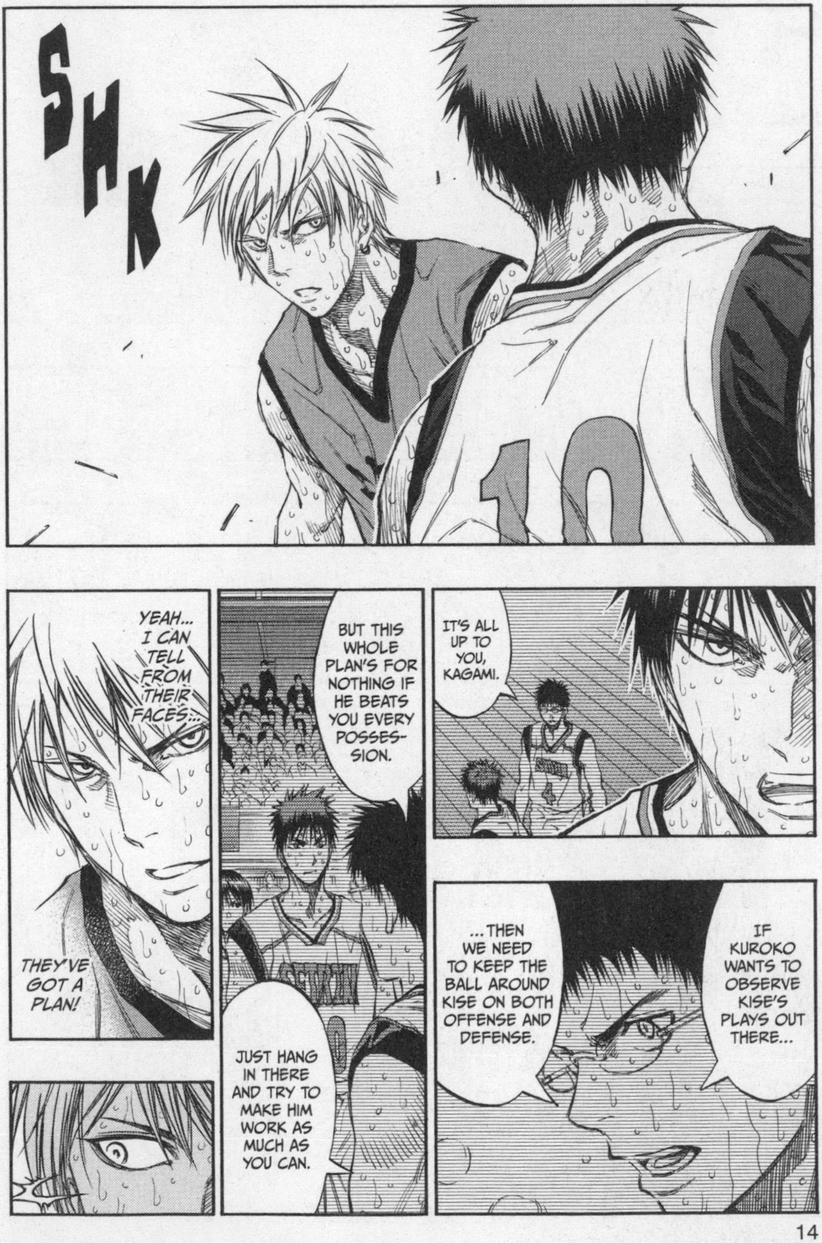
SHK
IT'S ALL UP TO YOU, KAGAMI.
IF KUROKO WANTS TO OBSERVE KISE'S PLAYS OUT THERE...
...THEN WE NEED TO KEEP THE BALL AROUND KISE ON BOTH OFFENSE AND DEFENSE.
BUT THIS WHOLE PLAN'S FOR NOTHING IF HE BEATS YOU EVERY POSSES-SION.
JUST HANG IN THERE AND TRY TO MAKE HIM WORK AS MUCH AS YOU CAN.
YEAH... I CAN TELL FROM THEIR FACES...
THEY'VE GOT A PLAN!

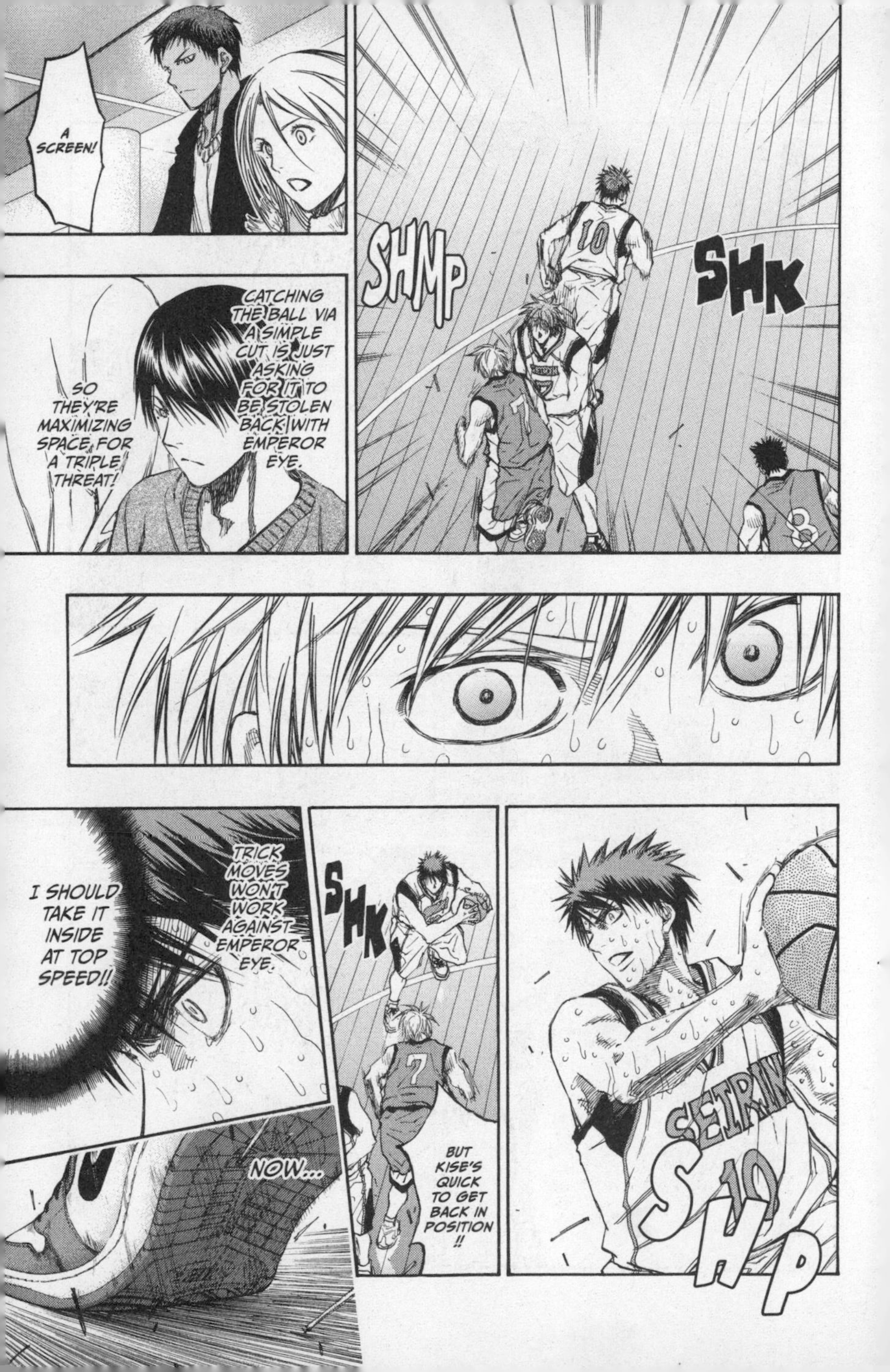
SHK
SHMP
A SCREEN!
CATCHING THE BALL VIA A SIMPLE CUT IS JUST ASKING FOR IT TO BE STOLEN BACK WITH EMPEROR EYE.
SO THEY'RE MAXIMIZING SPACE FOR A TRIPLE THREAT!
SHP
SHK
BUT KISE'S QUICK TO GET BACK IN POSITION!!
TRICK MOVES WON'T WORK AGAINST EMPEROR EYE.
I SHOULD TAKE IT INSIDE AT TOP SPEED!!
NOW...

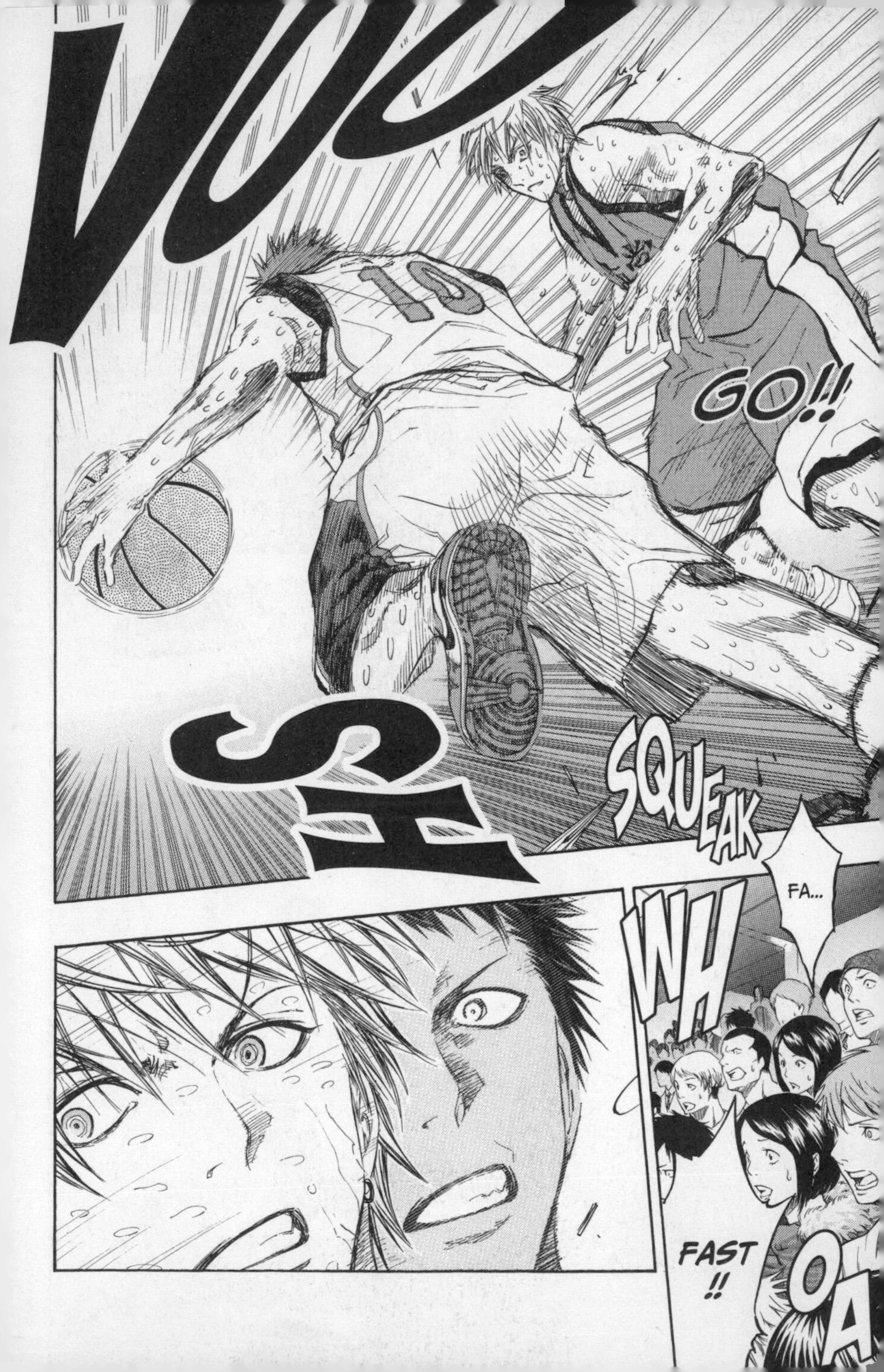
VUU
GO!!
SQUEAK
SH
WH
FA...
FAST!!
OA

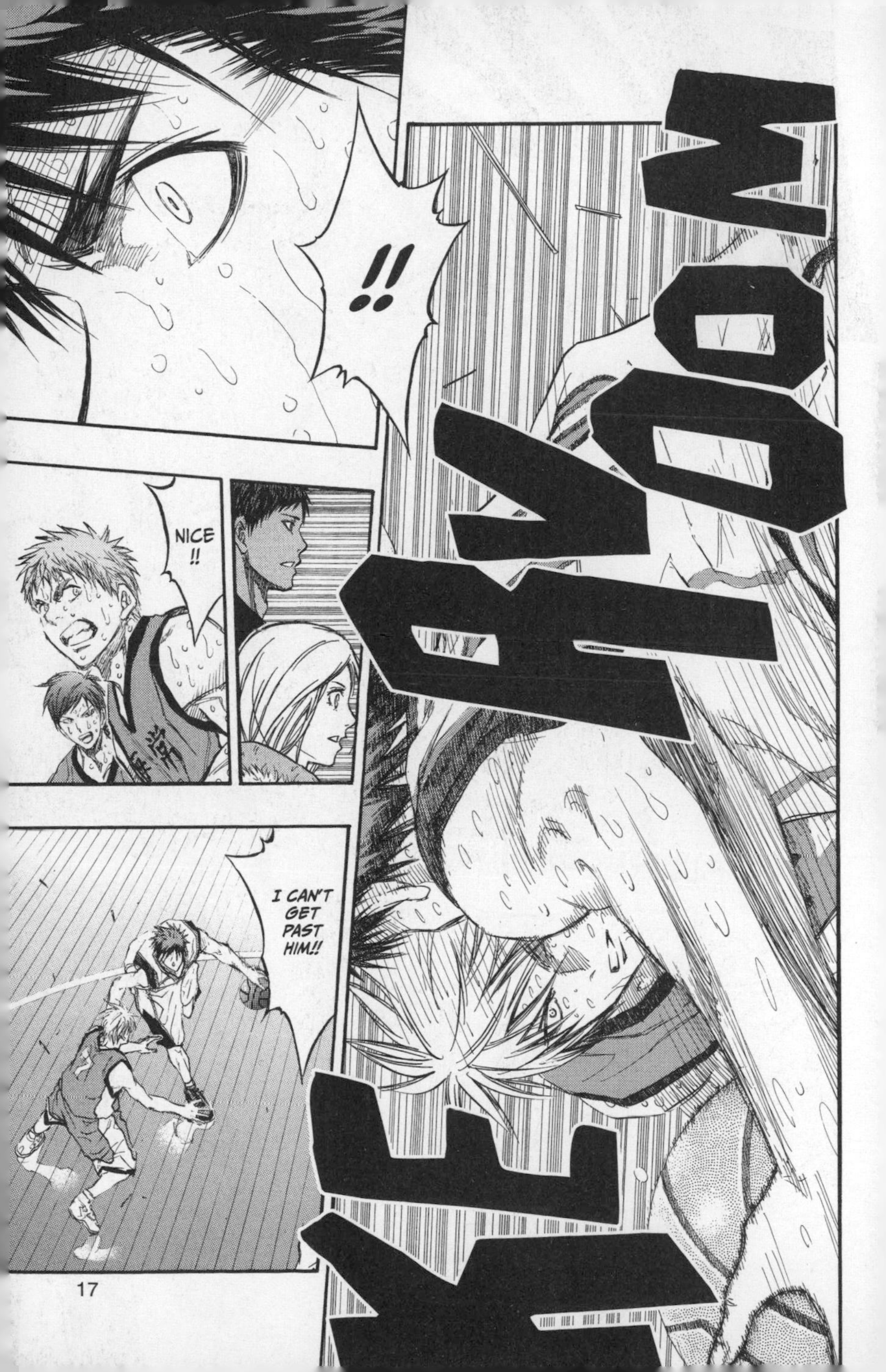
!!
NICE !!
I CAN'T GET PAST HIM!!

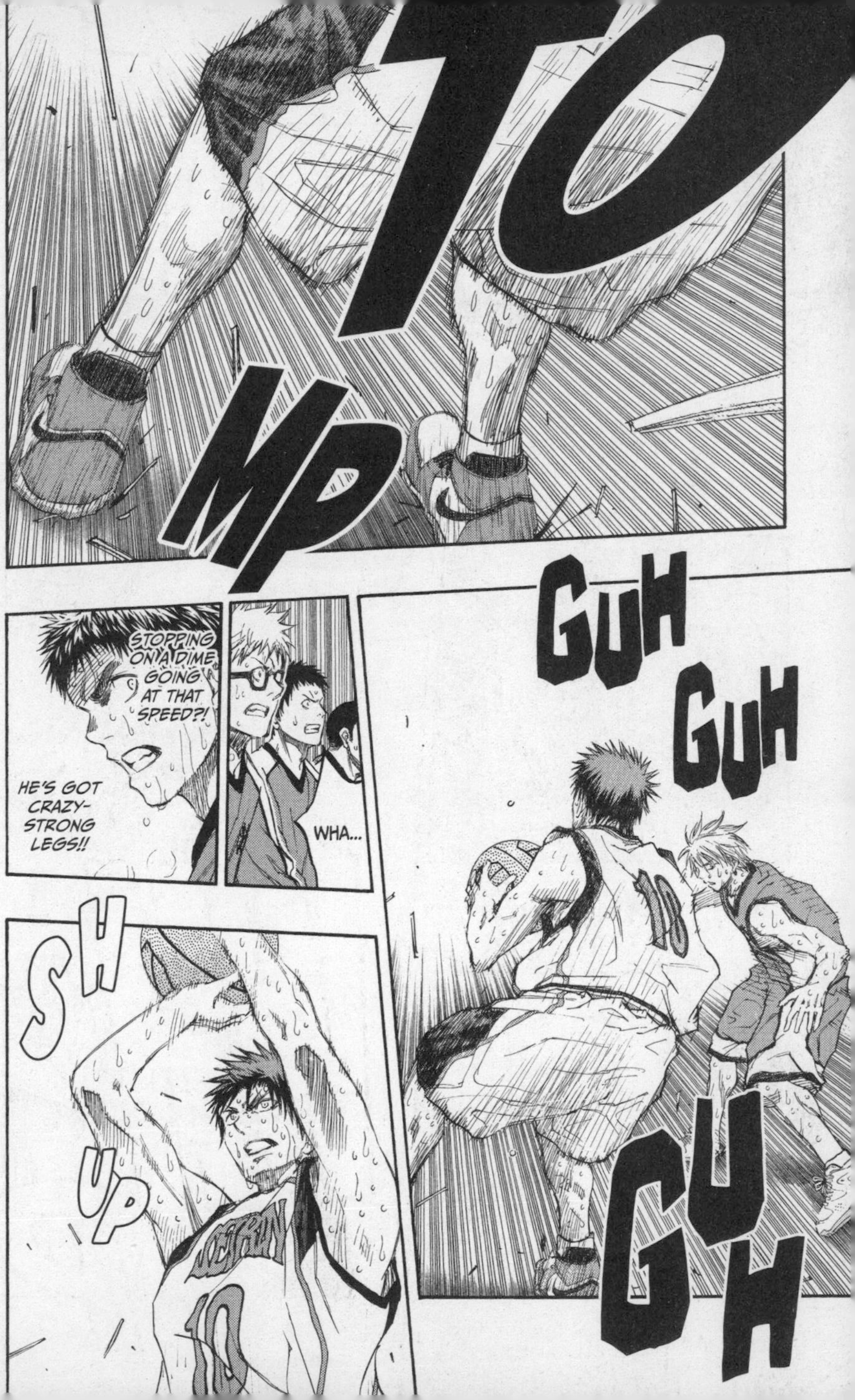
TOMP
GUH GUH
GUH GUH
WHA...
STOPPING ON A DIME GOING AT THAT SPEED?!
HE'S GOT CRAZY-STRONG LEGS!!
SHUP

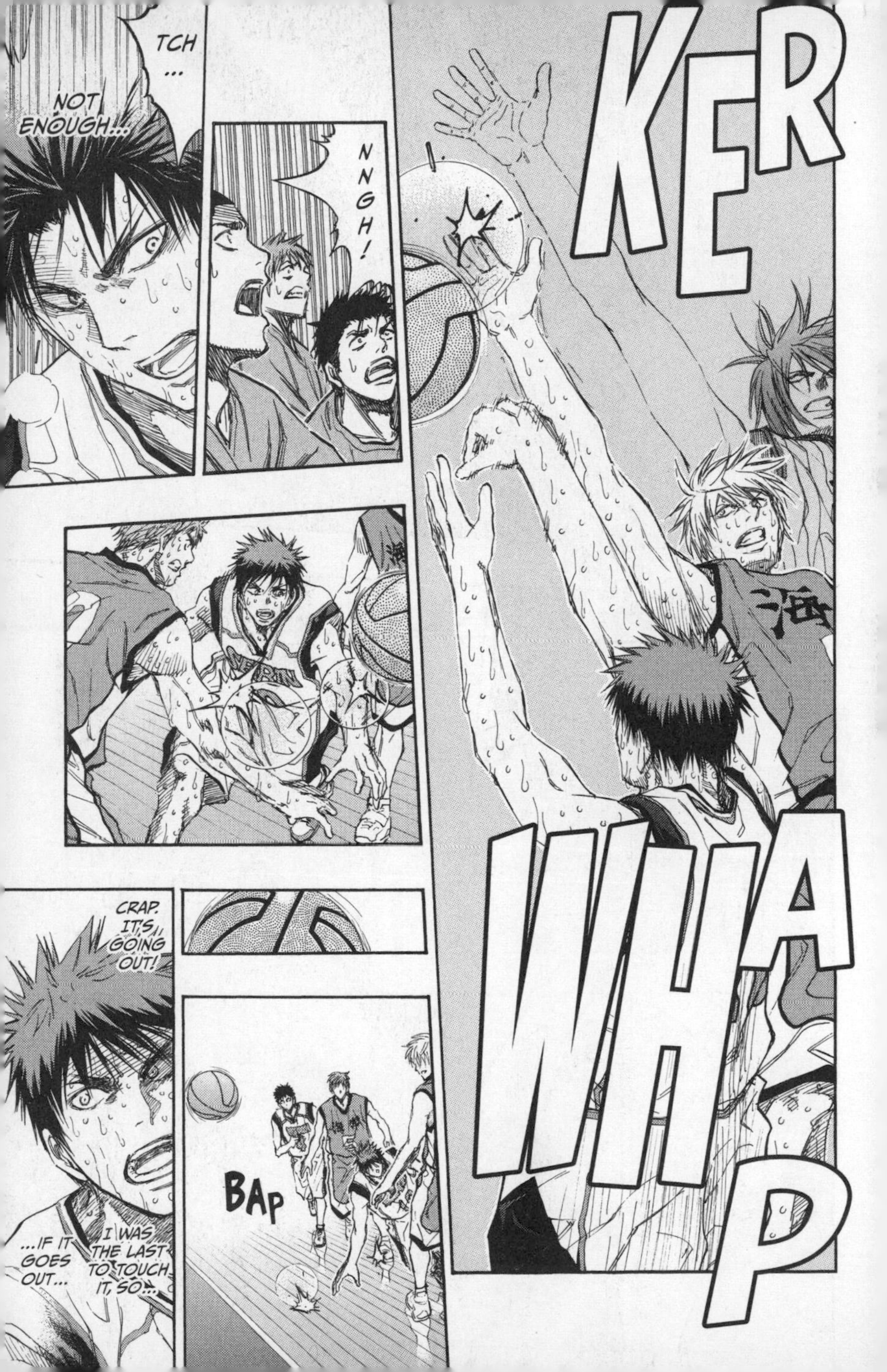
KER
WHAP
NNGH!
TCH...
NOT ENOUGH...
BAP
CRAP. IT'S GOING OUT!
I WAS THE LAST TO TOUCH IT, SO...
...IF IT GOES OUT...

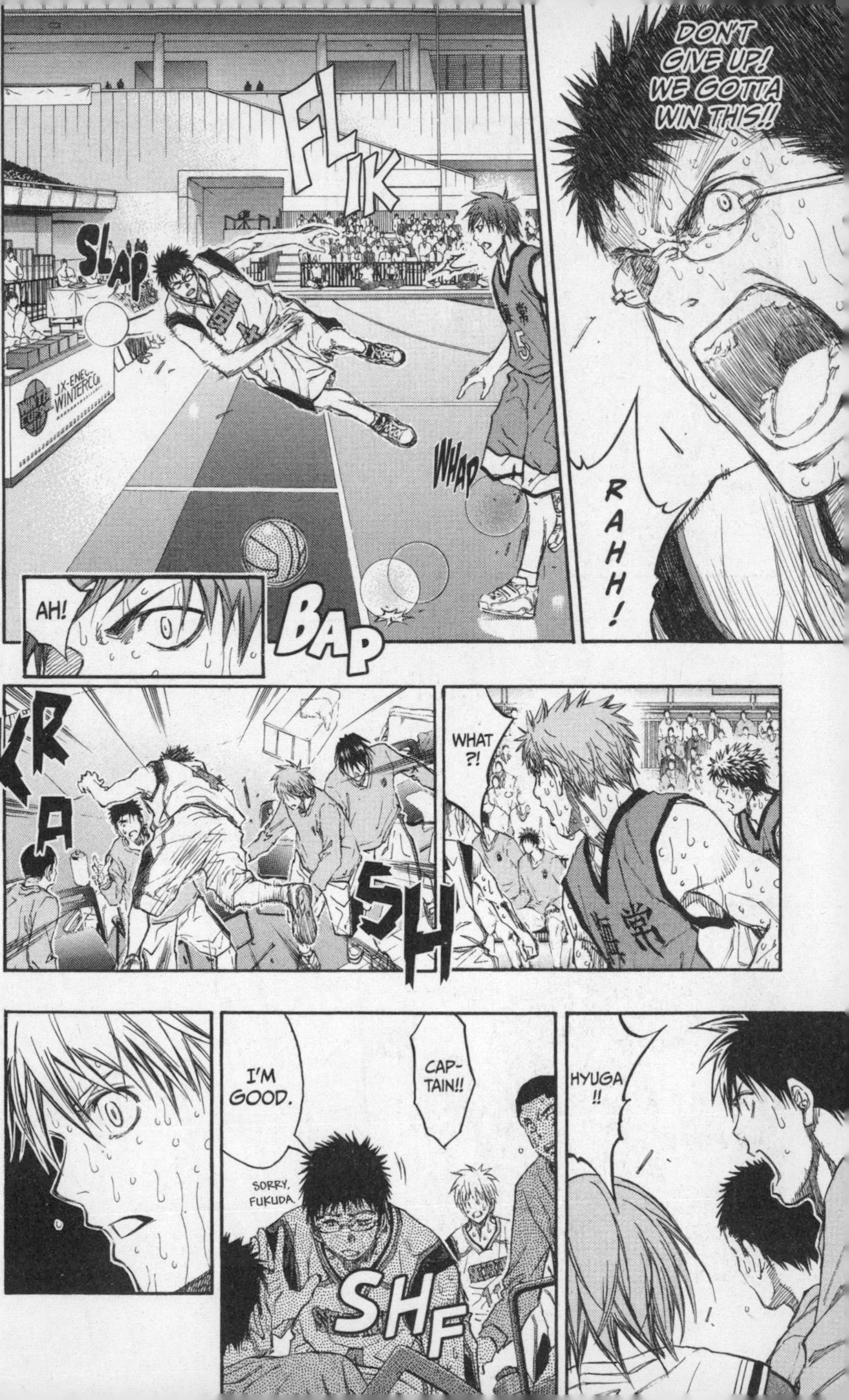
DON'T GIVE UP! WE GOTTA WIN THIS!!
RAHH!
FLIK
SLAP
WHAP
AH!
BAP
WHAT ?!
KRASH
HYUGA !!
CAP- TAIN!!
I'M GOOD.
SORRY, FUKUDA.
SHF

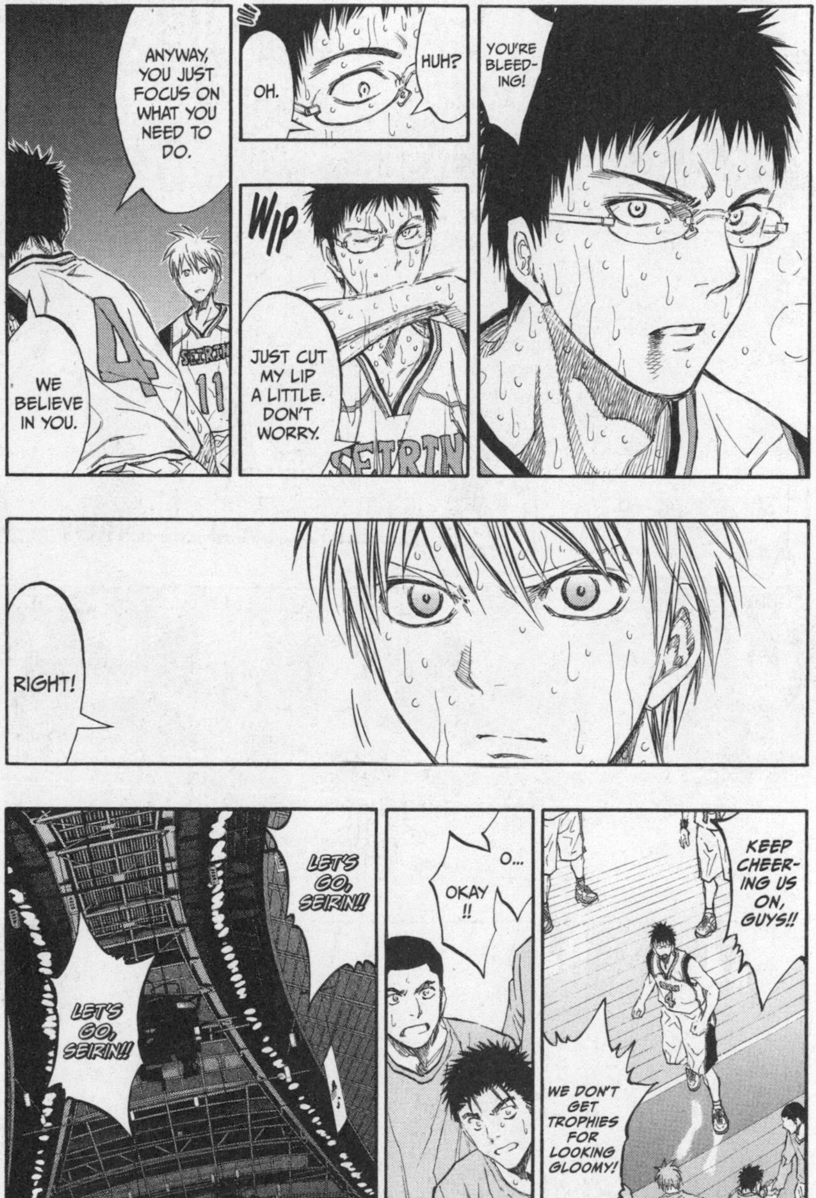
YOU'RE BLEEDING!
HUH?
OH.
WIP
JUST CUT MY LIP A LITTLE. DON'T WORRY.
ANYWAY, YOU JUST FOCUS ON WHAT YOU NEED TO DO.
WE BELIEVE IN YOU.
RIGHT!
KEEP CHEERING US ON, GUYS!!
WE DON'T GET TROPHIES FOR LOOKING GLOOMY!
O...
OKAY!!
LET'S GO, SEIRIN!!
LET'S GO, SEIRIN!!

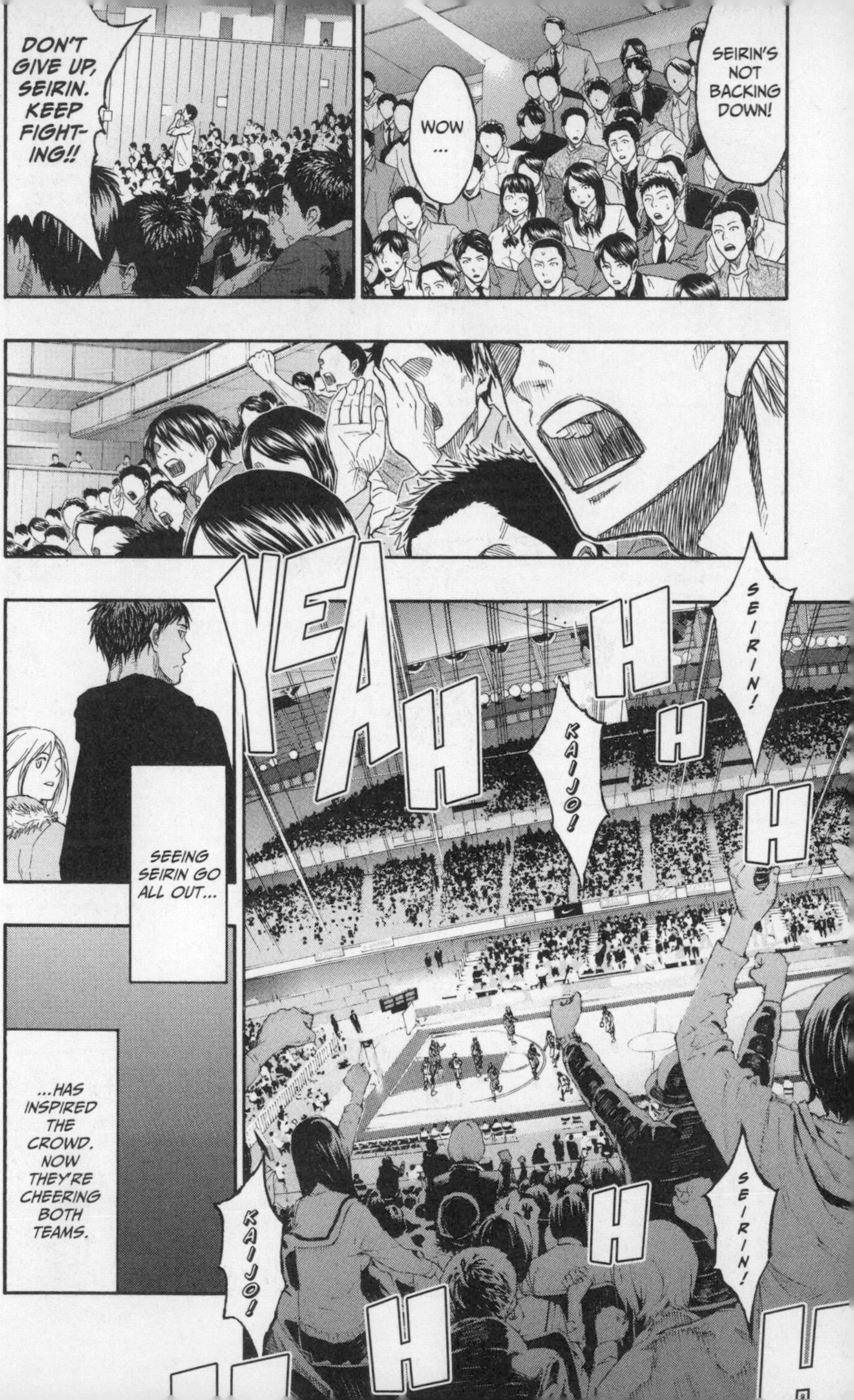
SEIRIN'S NOT BACKING DOWN!
WOW...
DON'T GIVE UP, SEIRIN. KEEP FIGHTING!!
YEAHHHHH
SEIRIN!
KAIJO!
SEEING SEIRIN GO ALL OUT...
...HAS INSPIRED THE CROWD. NOW THEY'RE CHEERING BOTH TEAMS.
SEIRIN!
KAIJO!
HHHH

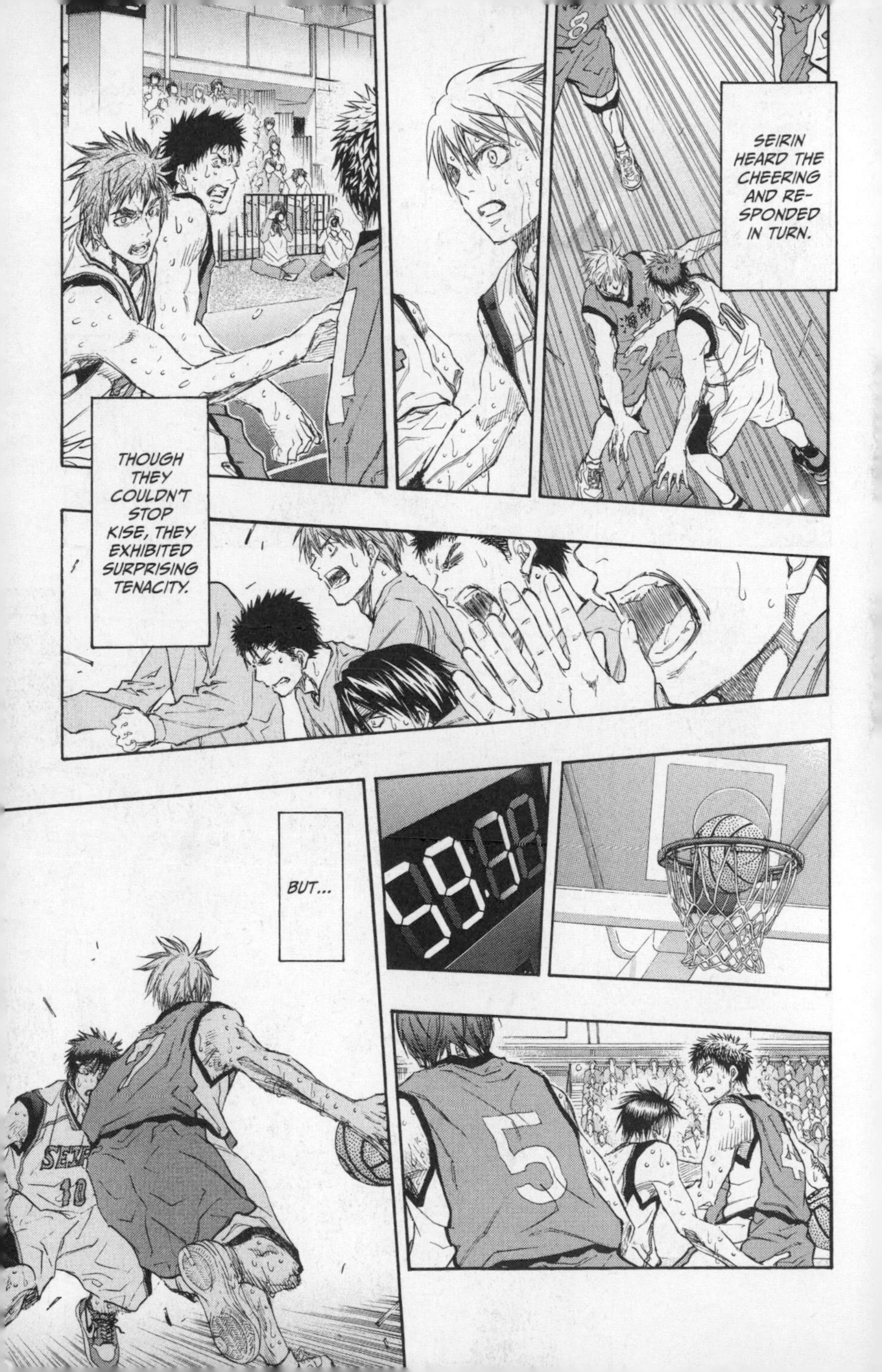
SEIRIN HEARD THE CHEERING AND RE-SPONDED IN TURN.
THOUGH THEY COULDN'T STOP KISE, THEY EXHIBITED SURPRISING TENACITY.
BUT...

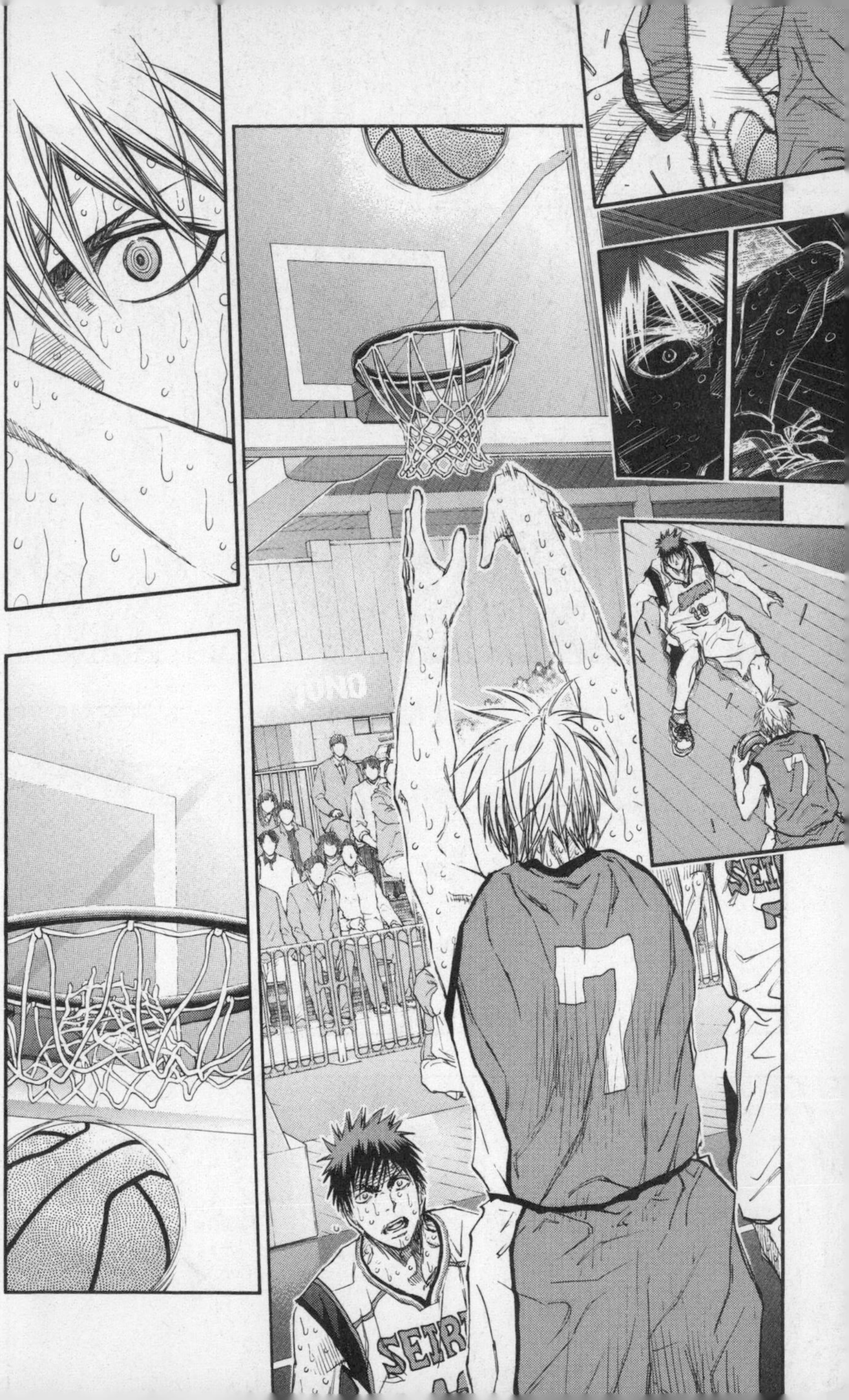

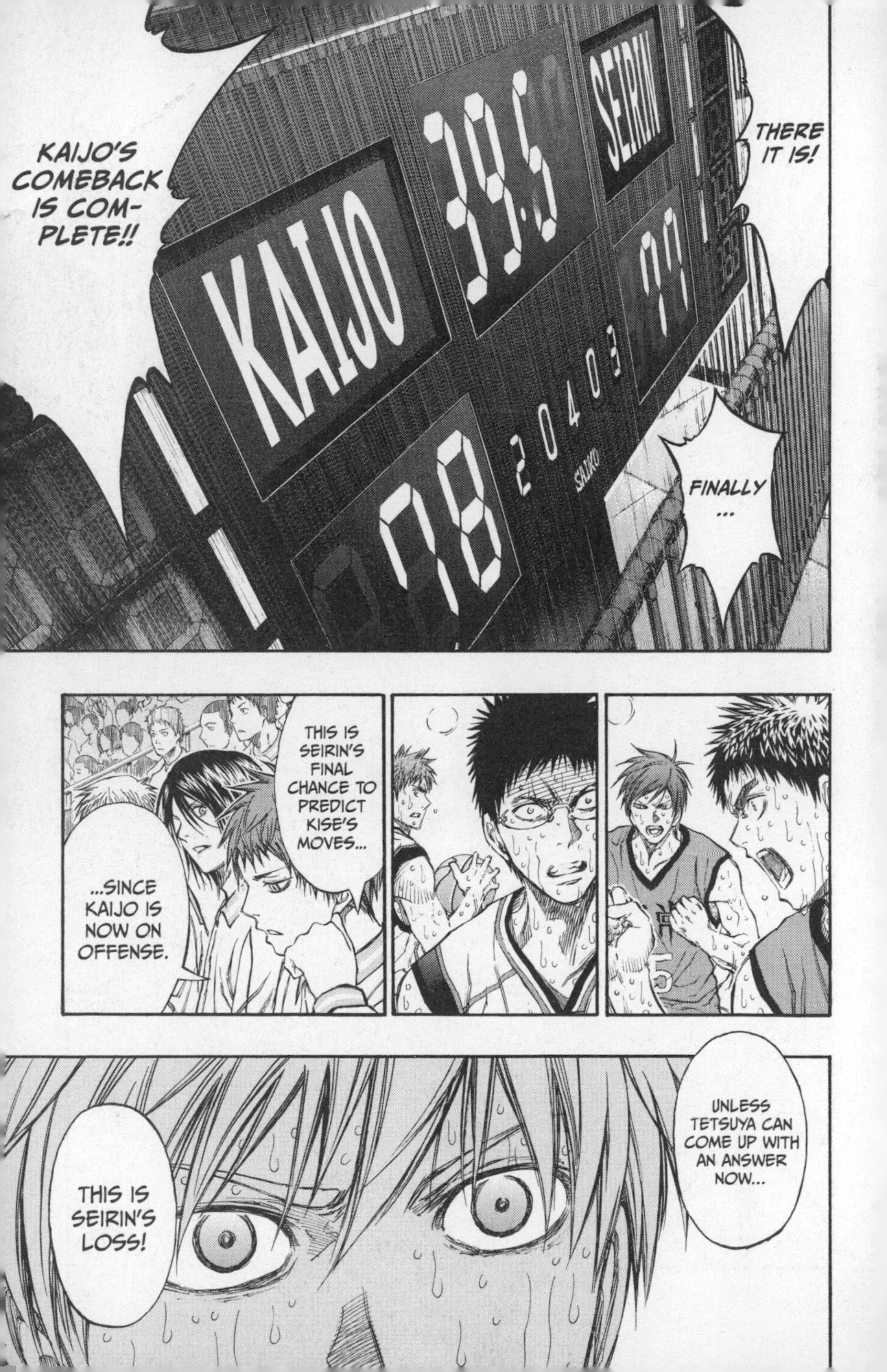
THERE IT IS!
FINALLY...
KAIJO
SEIRIN
KAIJO'S COMEBACK IS COMPLETE!!
THIS IS SEIRIN'S FINAL CHANCE TO PREDICT KISE'S MOVES...
...SINCE KAIJO IS NOW ON OFFENSE.
UNLESS TETSUYA CAN COME UP WITH AN ANSWER NOW...
THIS IS SEIRIN'S LOSS!

KUROKO'S BASKETBALL

Q&A

W/ HALFWAY-DECENT ANSWERS

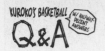

Q. **PLEASE LIST MURASAKIBARA-KUN'S TOP THREE FAVORITE FLAVORS OF SNACKS.**
(TOSHITADA MAKIFUJI from SHINAGAWA PREFECTURE)

A. 1) CREAM STEW
2) STONE-BOWL BIBIMBAP
3) SQUID-INK PASTA

KUROKO'S BASKETBALL BLOOPERS

TAKE 1

KRA
SH
SMOOCH
?!
BLARRRGHHHH!
SHAKE IT OFF.
HYUGA AND FUKU-DA!!

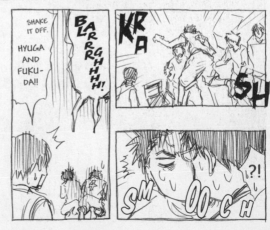

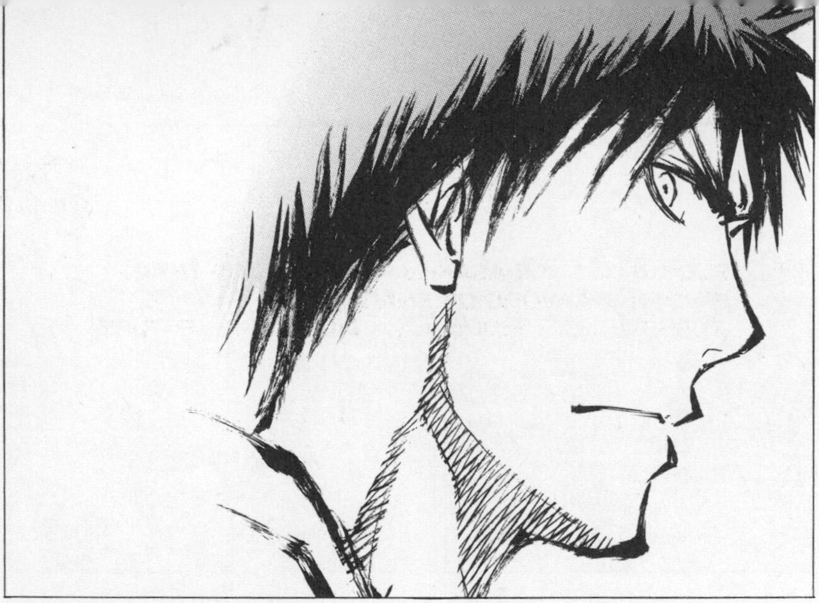

200TH QUARTER: THE ANSWER

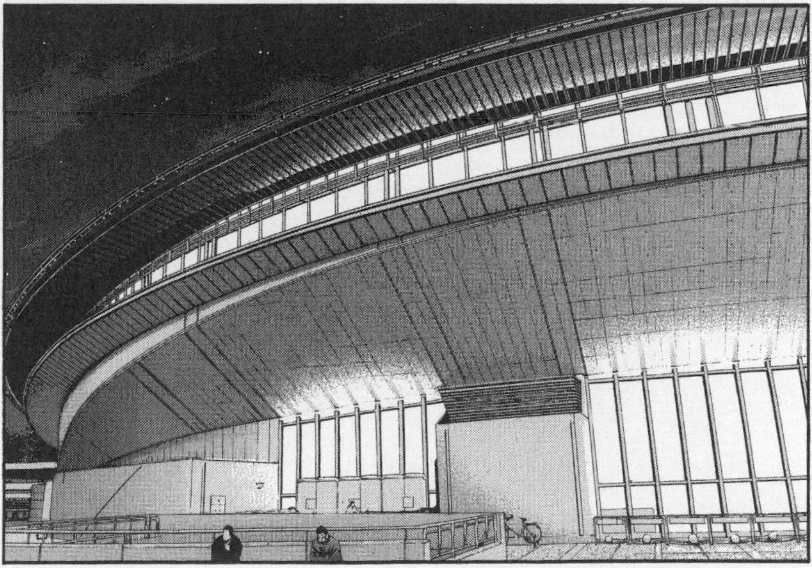

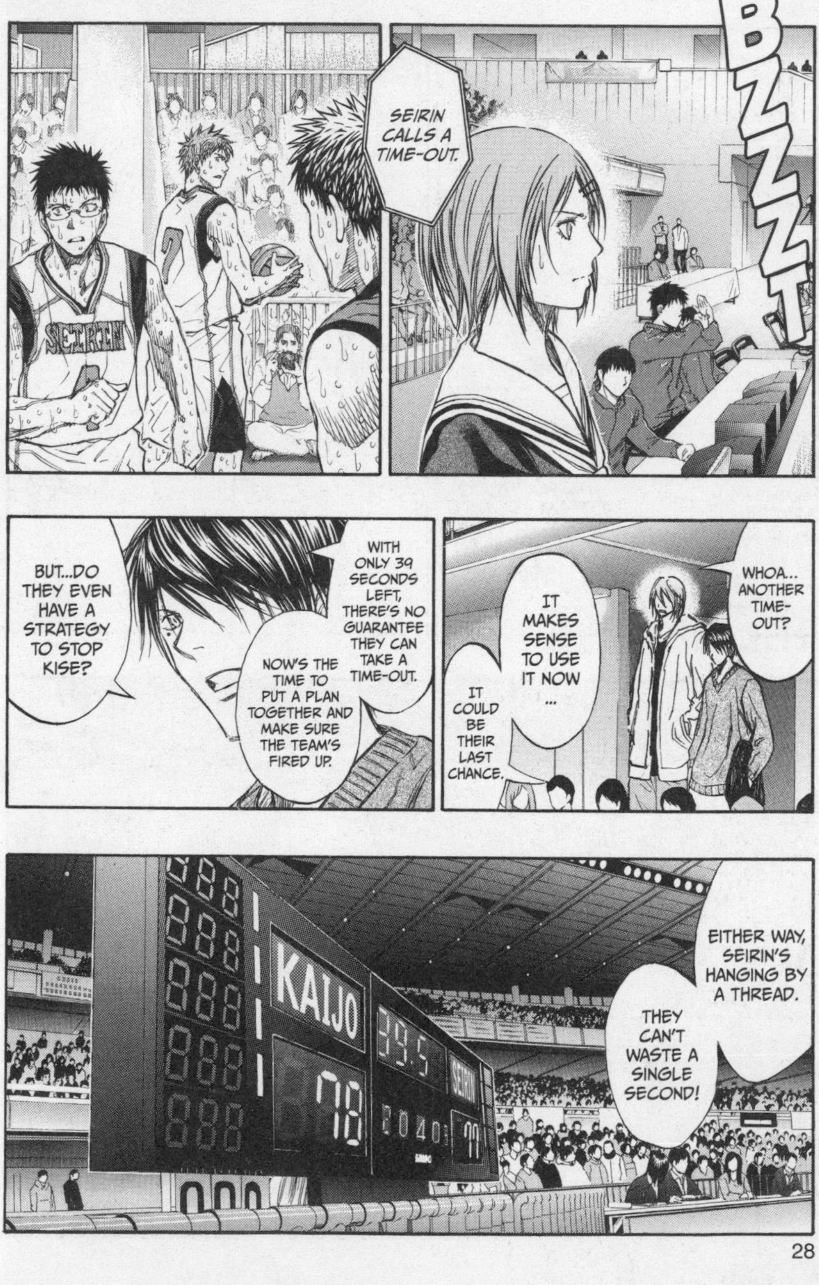
BZZZT
SEIRIN CALLS A TIME-OUT.
WHOA... ANOTHER TIME-OUT?
IT MAKES SENSE TO USE IT NOW...
IT COULD BE THEIR LAST CHANCE.
WITH ONLY 39 SECONDS LEFT, THERE'S NO GUARANTEE THEY CAN TAKE A TIME-OUT.
NOW'S THE TIME TO PUT A PLAN TOGETHER AND MAKE SURE THE TEAM'S FIRED UP.
BUT...DO THEY EVEN HAVE A STRATEGY TO STOP KISE?
EITHER WAY, SEIRIN'S HANGING BY A THREAD.
THEY CAN'T WASTE A SINGLE SECOND!
KAIJO

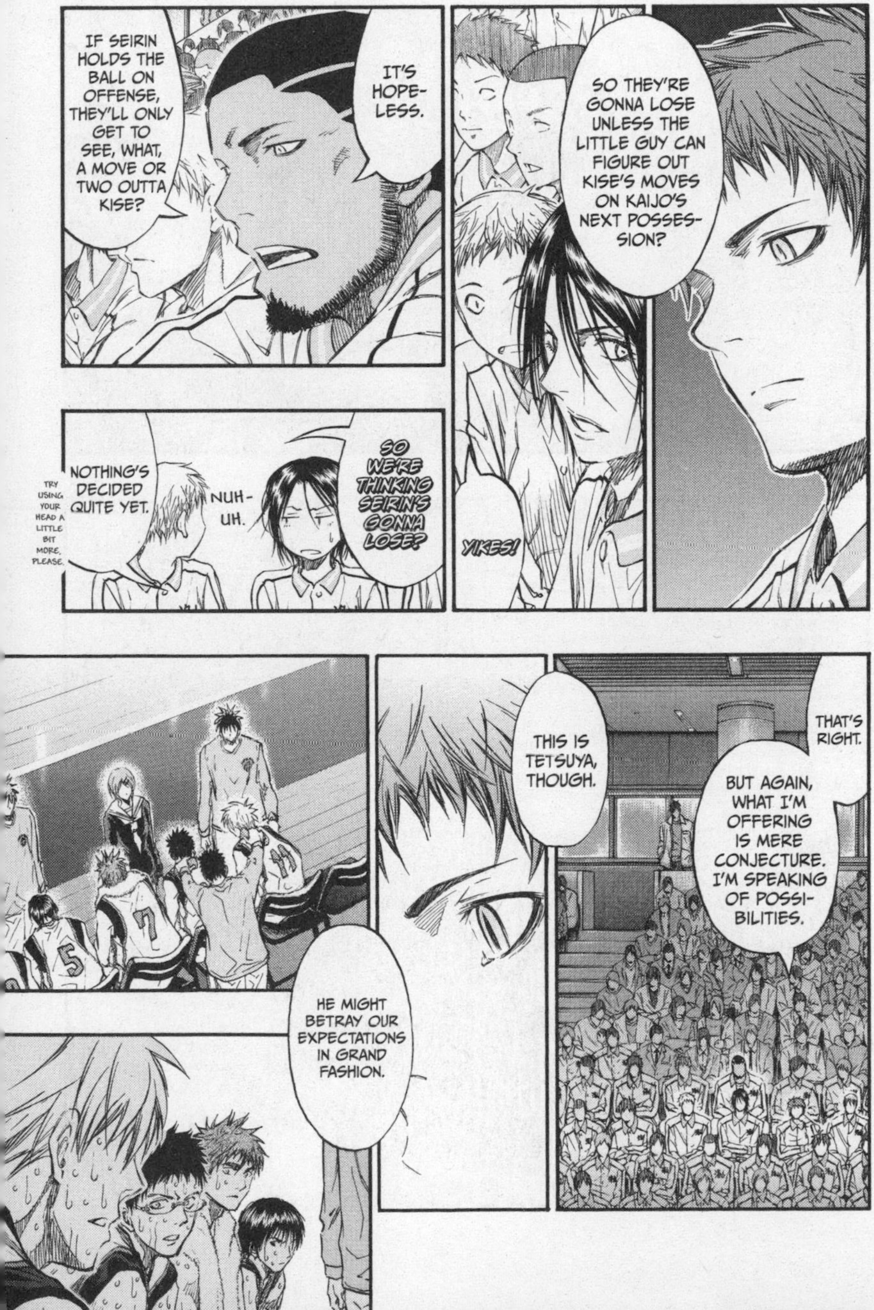
SO THEY'RE GONNA LOSE UNLESS THE LITTLE GUY CAN FIGURE OUT KISE'S MOVES ON KAIJO'S NEXT POSSESSION?
YIKES!
IF SEIRIN HOLDS THE BALL ON OFFENSE, THEY'LL ONLY GET TO SEE, WHAT, A MOVE OR TWO OUTTA KISE?
IT'S HOPELESS.
SO WE'RE THINKING SEIRIN'S GONNA LOSE?
NUH-UH.
NOTHING'S DECIDED QUITE YET.
TRY USING YOUR HEAD A LITTLE BIT MORE, PLEASE.
THAT'S RIGHT.
BUT AGAIN, WHAT I'M OFFERING IS MERE CONJECTURE. I'M SPEAKING OF POSSIBILITIES.
THIS IS TETSUYA, THOUGH.
HE MIGHT BETRAY OUR EXPECTATIONS IN GRAND FASHION.

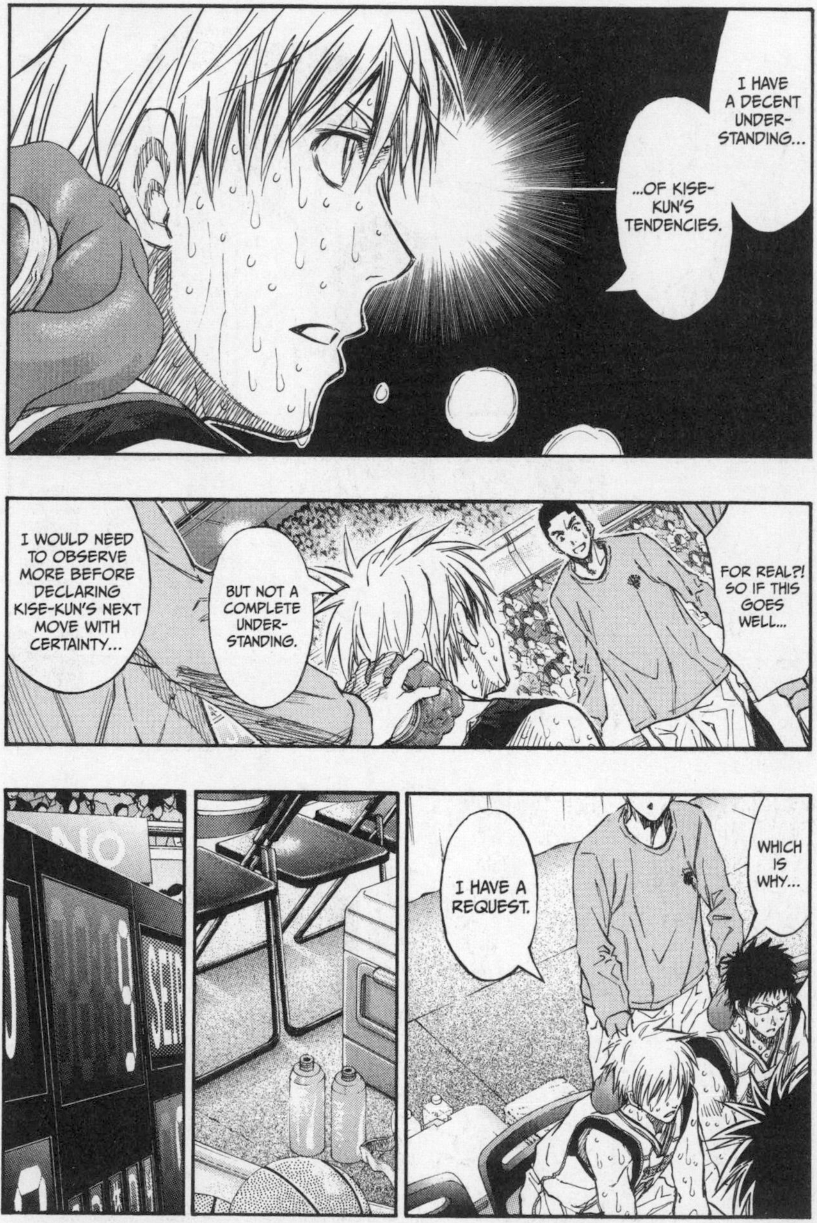
I HAVE A DECENT UNDER-STANDING...
...OF KISE-KUN'S TENDENCIES.
FOR REAL?! SO IF THIS GOES WELL...
BUT NOT A COMPLETE UNDER-STANDING.
I WOULD NEED TO OBSERVE MORE BEFORE DECLARING KISE-KUN'S NEXT MOVE WITH CERTAINTY...
WHICH IS WHY...
I HAVE A REQUEST.

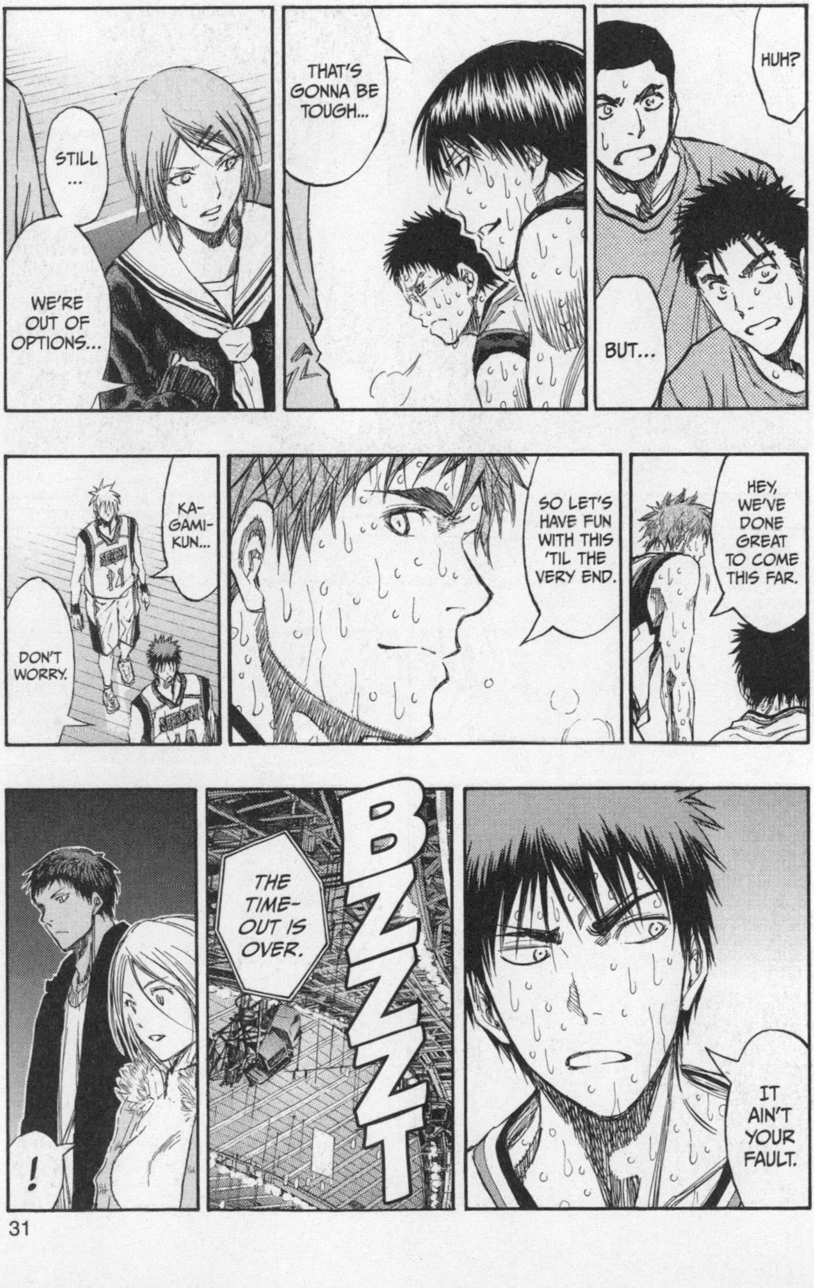
HUH?
BUT...
THAT'S GONNA BE TOUGH...
STILL ...
WE'RE OUT OF OPTIONS...
HEY, WE'VE DONE GREAT TO COME THIS FAR.
SO LET'S HAVE FUN WITH THIS 'TIL THE VERY END.
KAGAMI-KUN...
DON'T WORRY.
IT AIN'T YOUR FAULT.
BZZZT
THE TIME-OUT IS OVER.
!

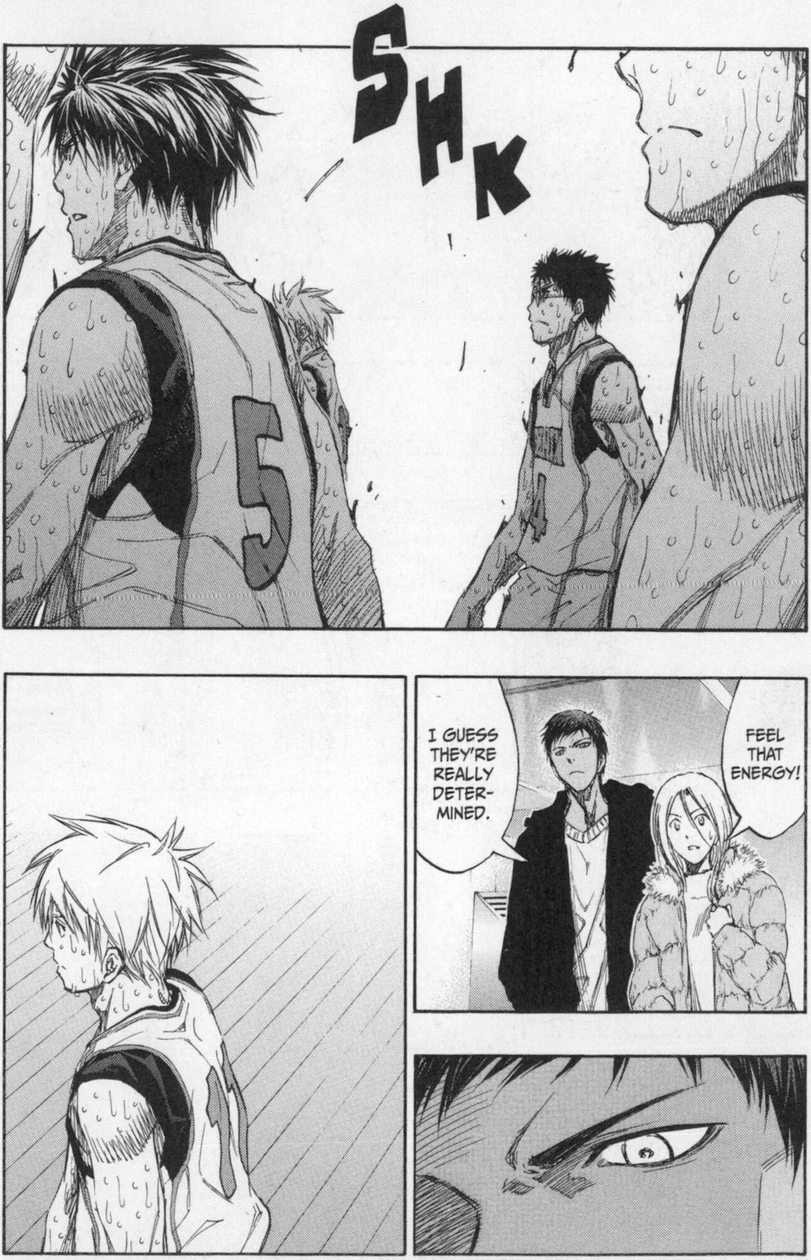
SHK
FEEL THAT ENERGY!
I GUESS THEY'RE REALLY DETER-MINED.

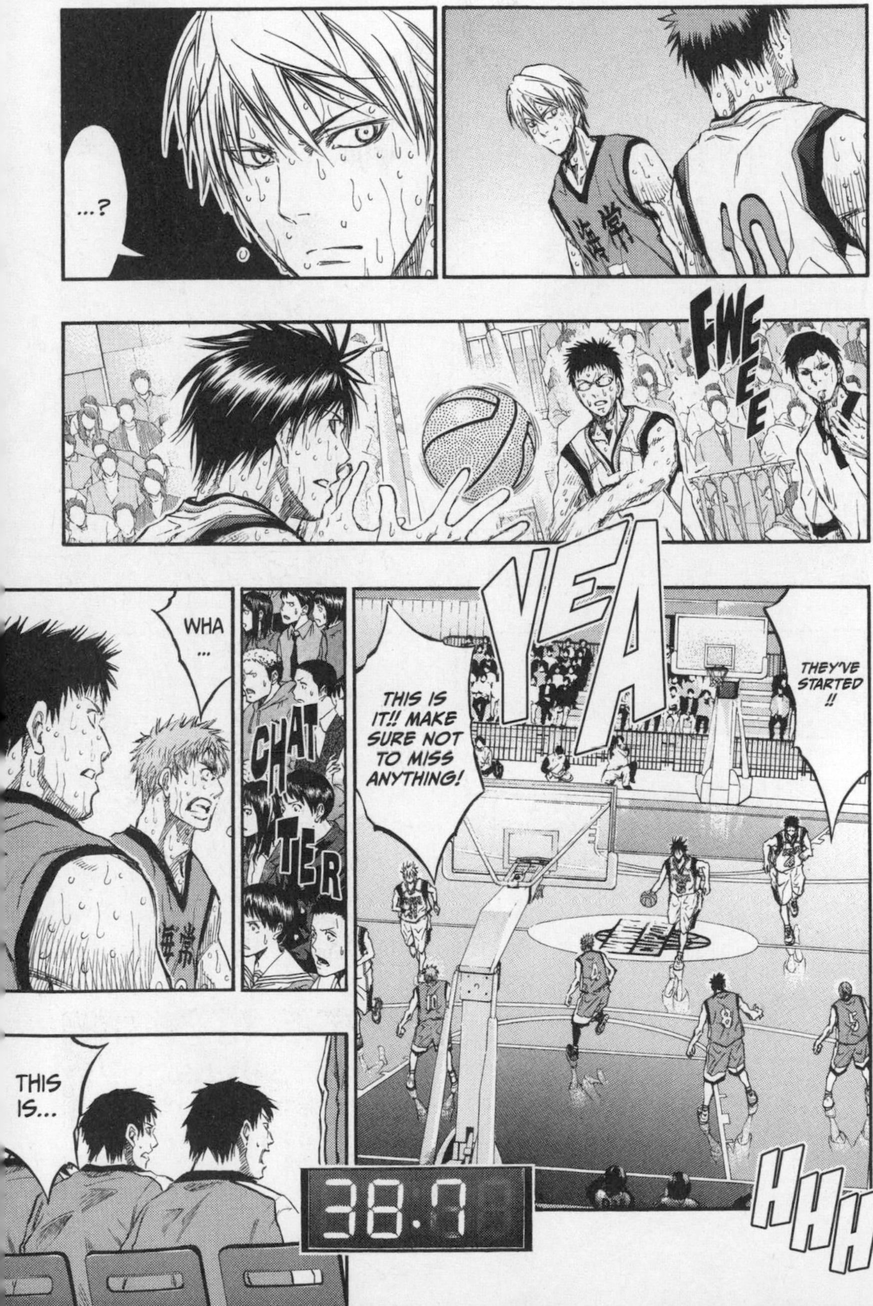
...?
FWEEE
YEA
THEY'VE STARTED !!
THIS IS IT!! MAKE SURE NOT TO MISS ANYTHING!
HHH
CHATTER
WHA ...
THIS IS...
38.7

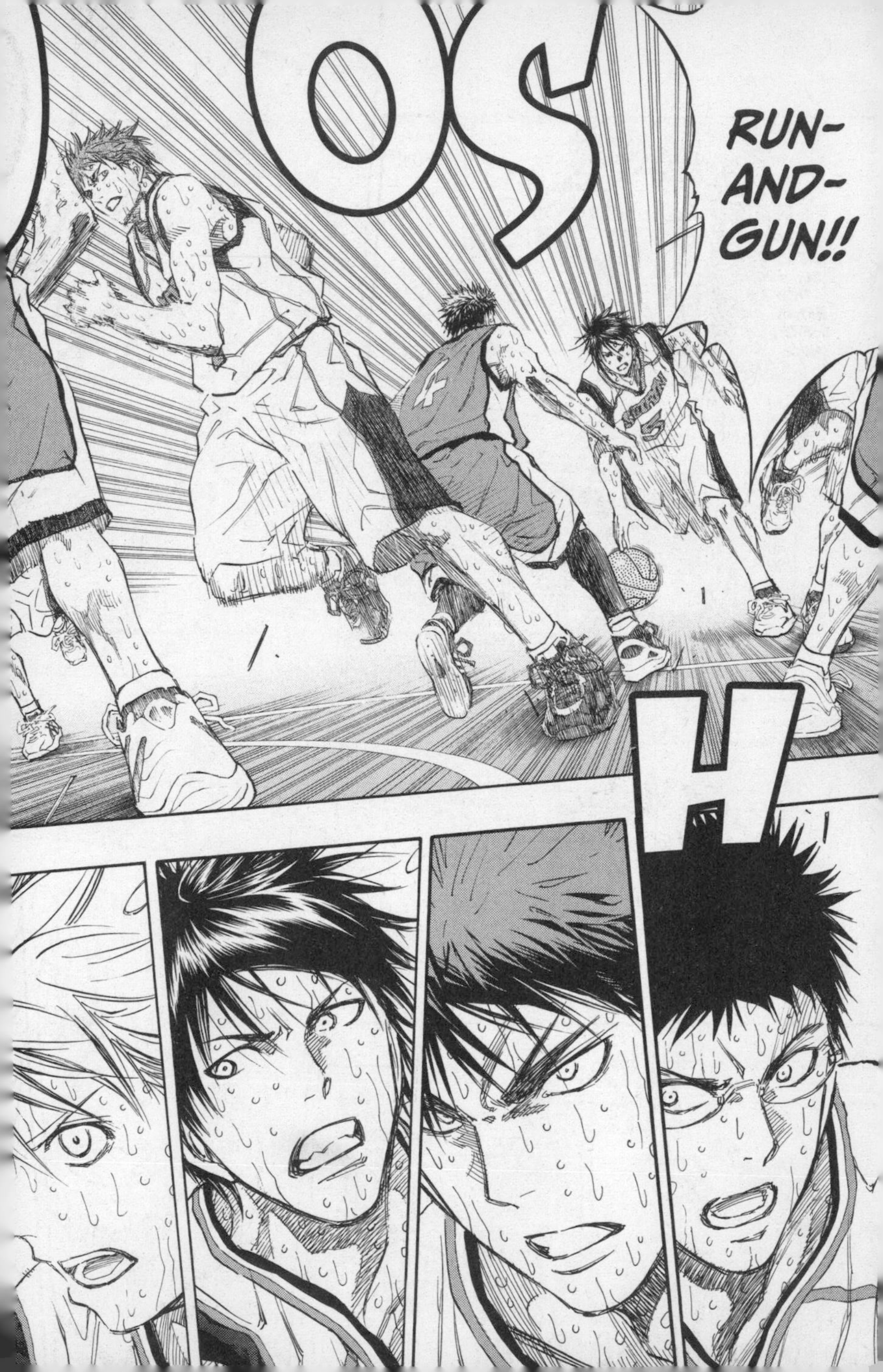
RUN-AND-GUN!!
OS
H

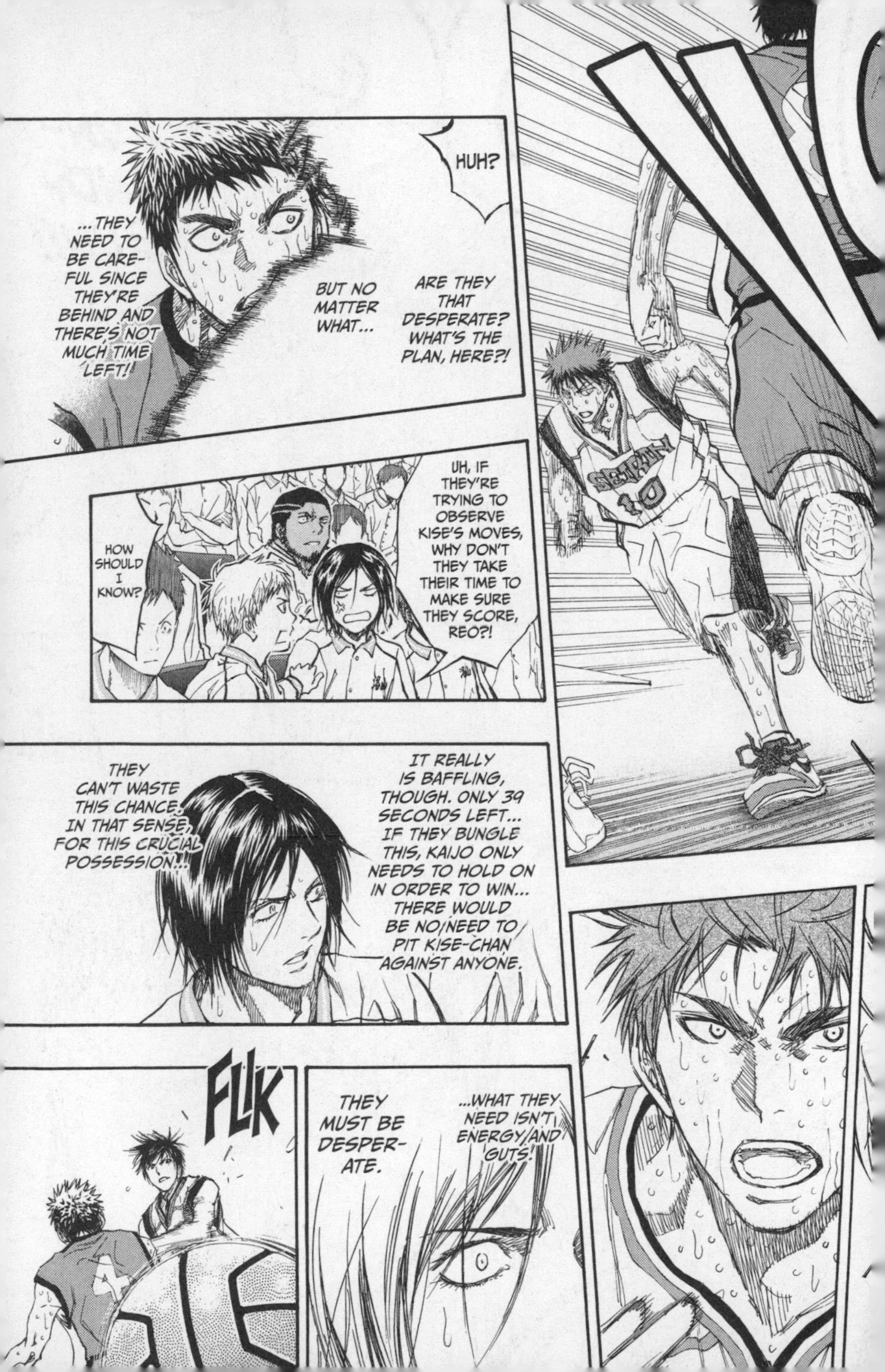
HUH?
ARE THEY THAT DESPERATE? WHAT'S THE PLAN, HERE?!
BUT NO MATTER WHAT...
...THEY NEED TO BE CARE-FUL SINCE THEY'RE BEHIND AND THERE'S NOT MUCH TIME LEFT!
UH, IF THEY'RE TRYING TO OBSERVE KISE'S MOVES, WHY DON'T THEY TAKE THEIR TIME TO MAKE SURE THEY SCORE, REO?!
HOW SHOULD I KNOW?
IT REALLY IS BAFFLING, THOUGH. ONLY 39 SECONDS LEFT... IF THEY BUNGLE THIS, KAIJO ONLY NEEDS TO HOLD ON IN ORDER TO WIN... THERE WOULD BE NO NEED TO PIT KISE-CHAN AGAINST ANYONE.
THEY CAN'T WASTE THIS CHANCE. IN THAT SENSE, FOR THIS CRUCIAL POSSESSION...
...WHAT THEY NEED ISN'T ENERGY AND GUTS!
THEY MUST BE DESPER-ATE.
FLIK

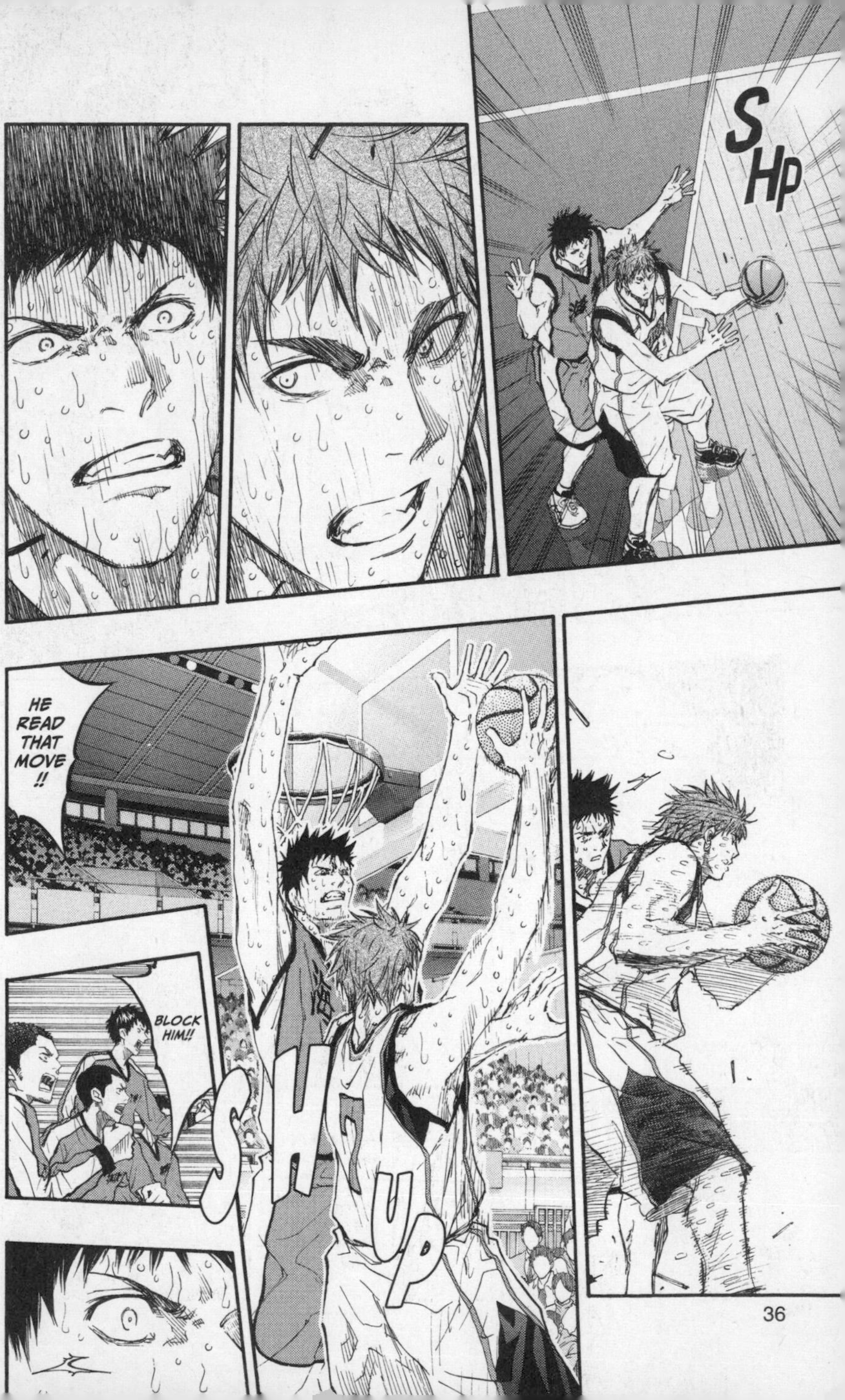
SHP
SHUP
HE READ THAT MOVE !!
BLOCK HIM!!

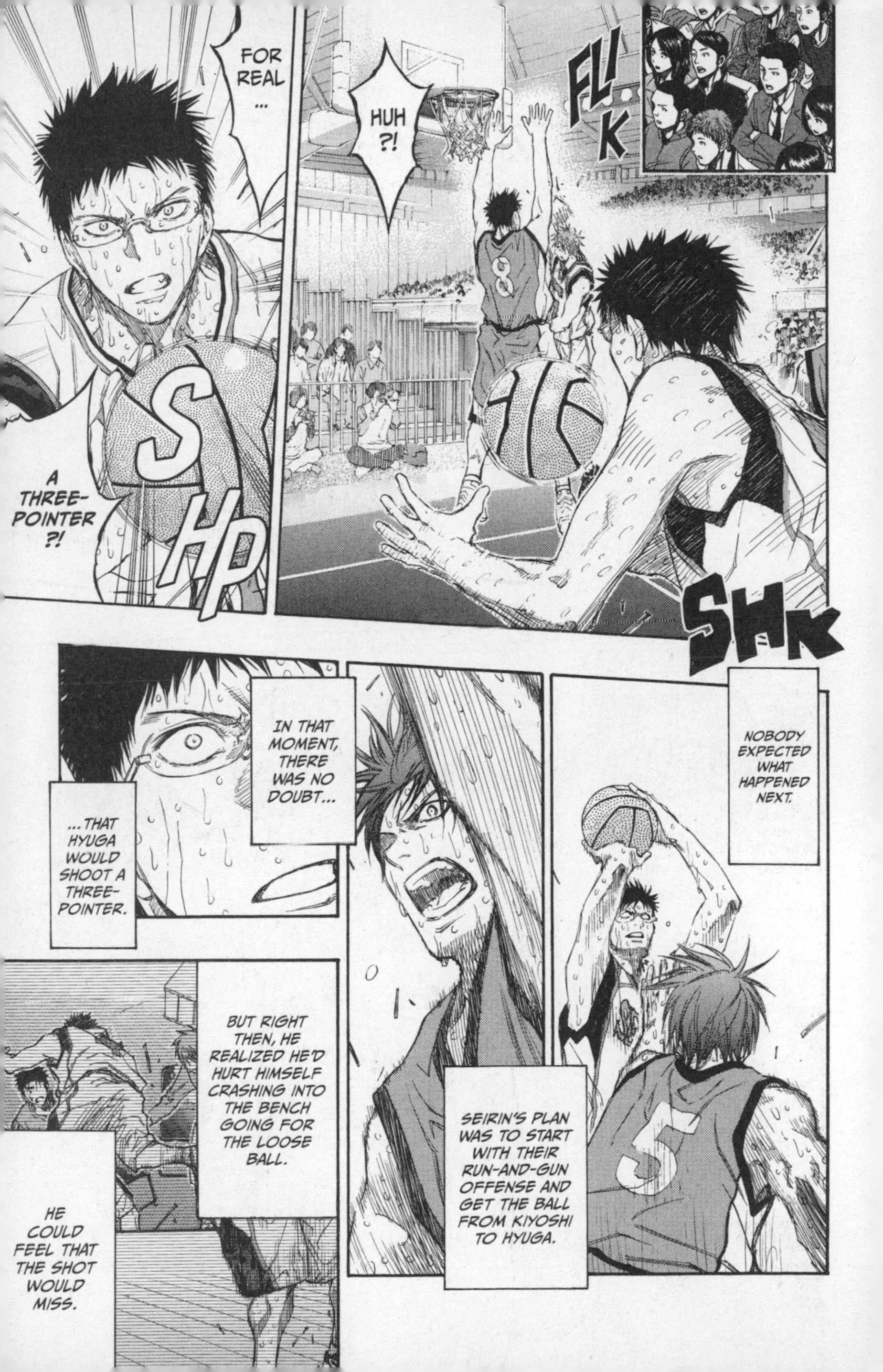
FLIK
HUH ?!
SHK
FOR REAL ...
A THREE-POINTER ?!
SHP
NOBODY EXPECTED WHAT HAPPENED NEXT.
SEIRIN'S PLAN WAS TO START WITH THEIR RUN-AND-GUN OFFENSE AND GET THE BALL FROM KIYOSHI TO HYUGA.
IN THAT MOMENT, THERE WAS NO DOUBT...
...THAT HYUGA WOULD SHOOT A THREE-POINTER.
BUT RIGHT THEN, HE REALIZED HE'D HURT HIMSELF CRASHING INTO THE BENCH GOING FOR THE LOOSE BALL.
HE COULD FEEL THAT THE SHOT WOULD MISS.

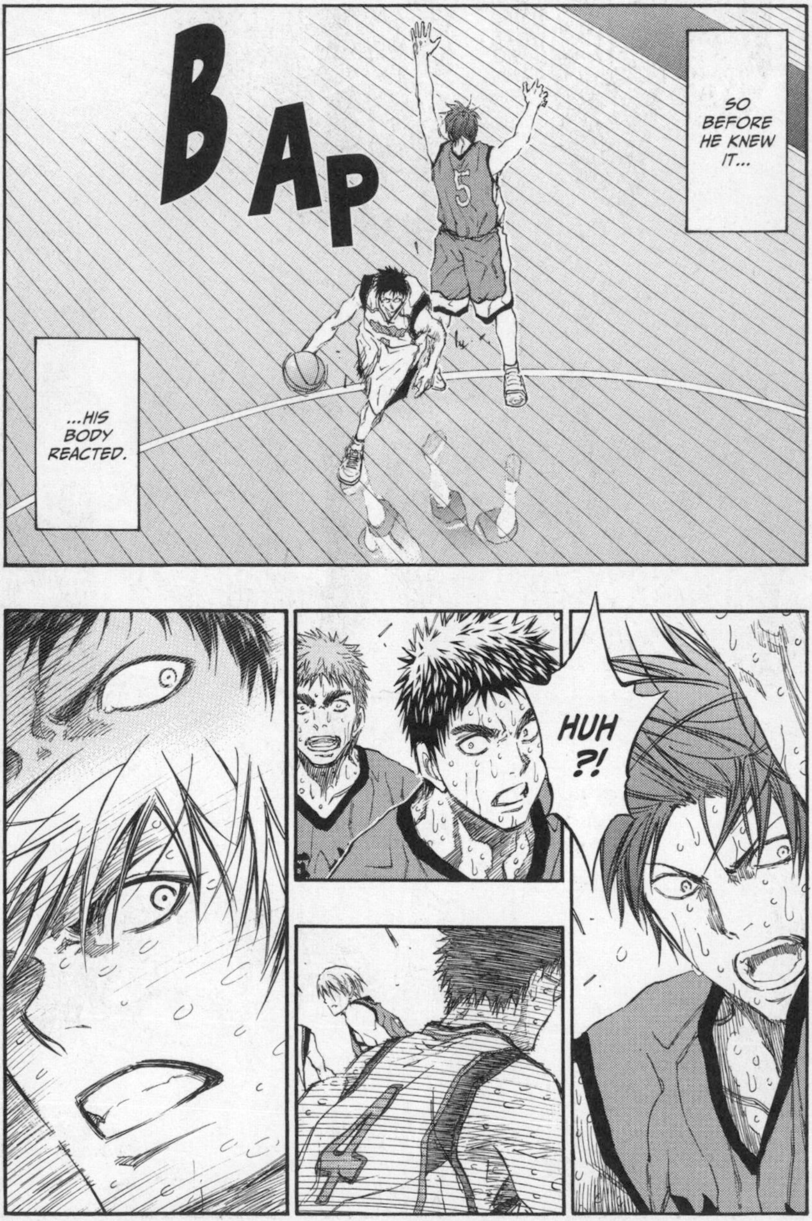
SO BEFORE HE KNEW IT...
BAP
...HIS BODY REACTED.
HUH?!

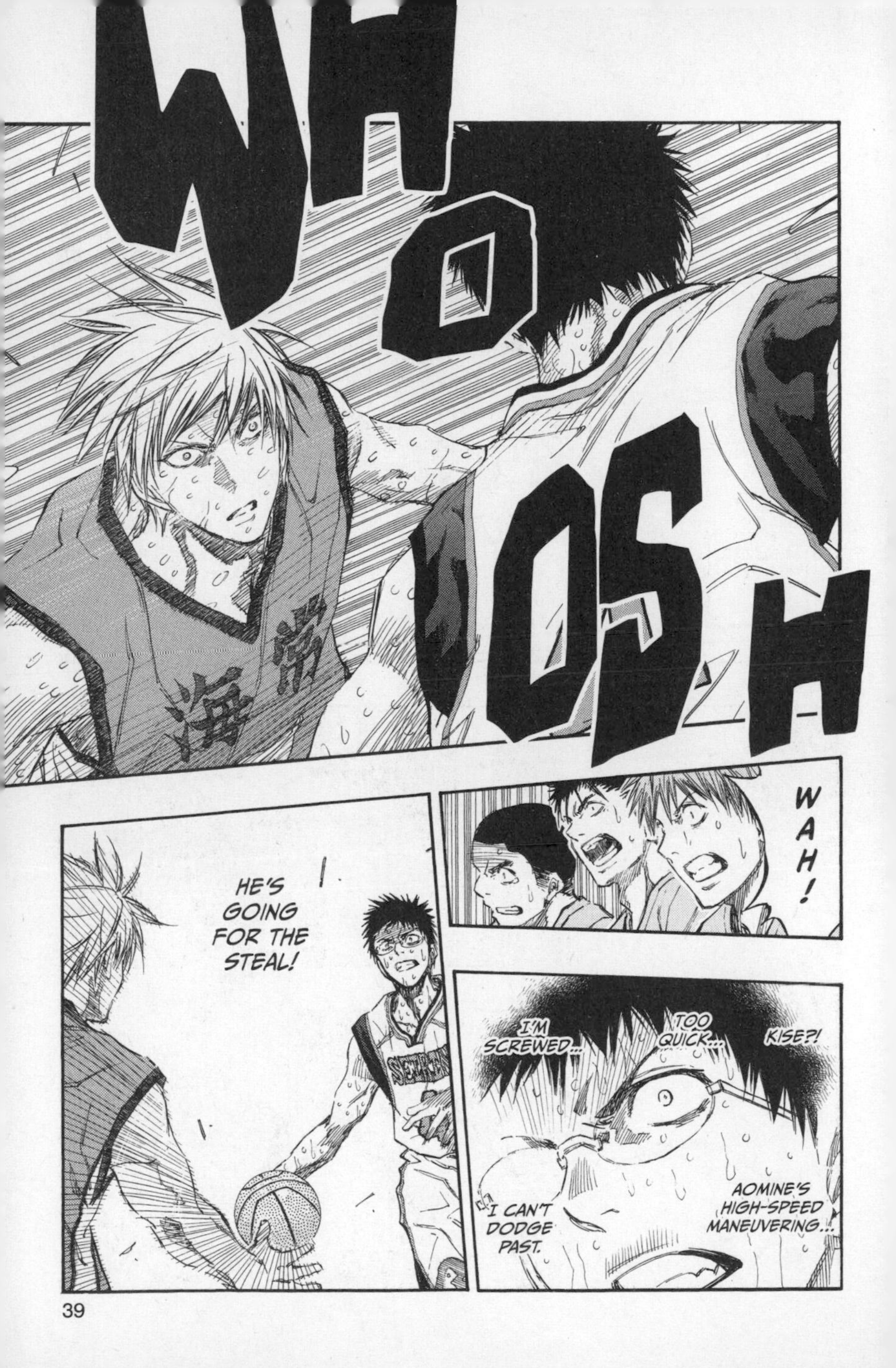
WHOOSH
WAH!
KISE?!
TOO QUICK...
I'M SCREWED...
AOMINE'S HIGH-SPEED MANEUVERING...
I CAN'T DODGE PAST.
HE'S GOING FOR THE STEAL!

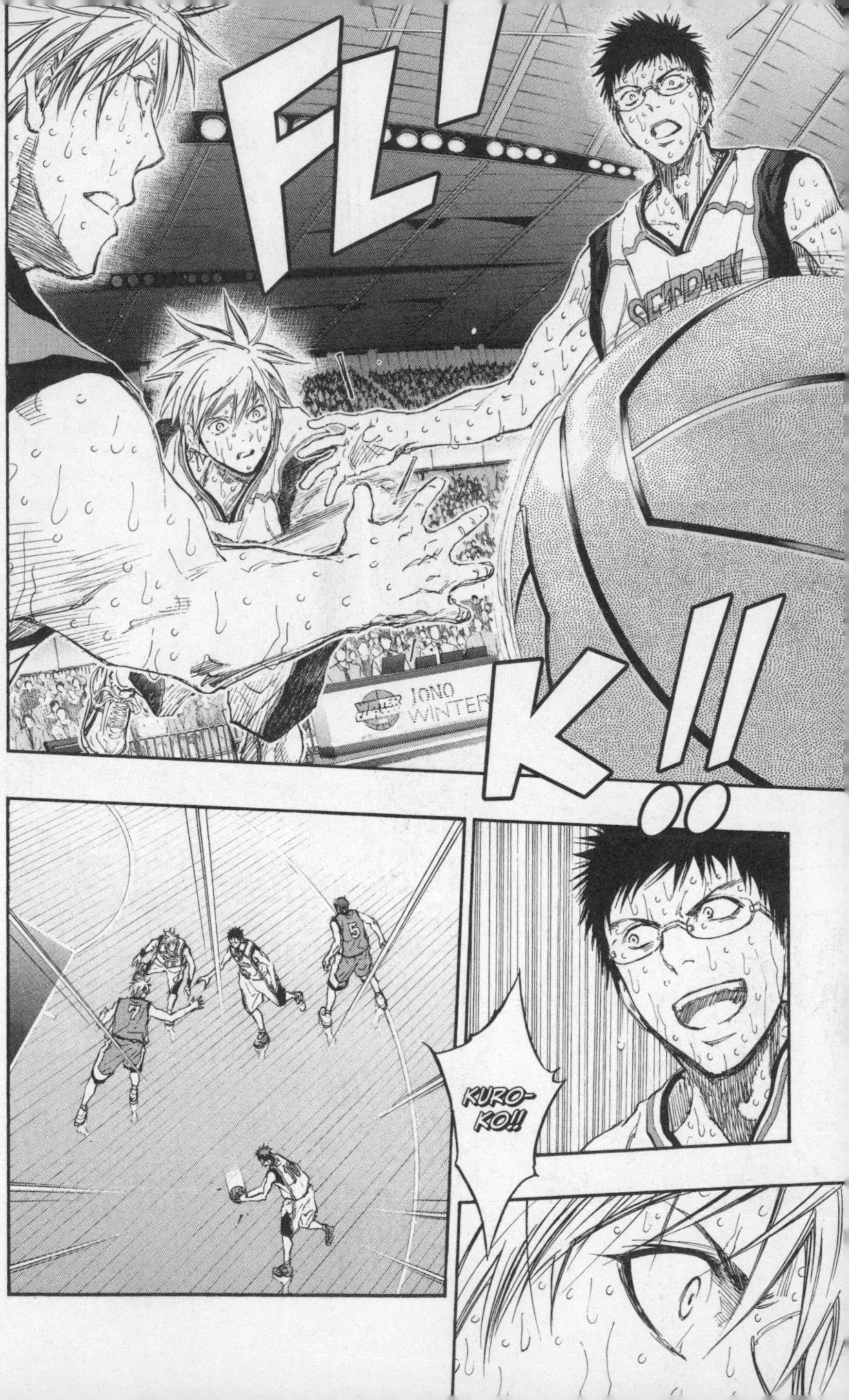
FZ!
K!!
IONO WINTER
KURO-KO!!

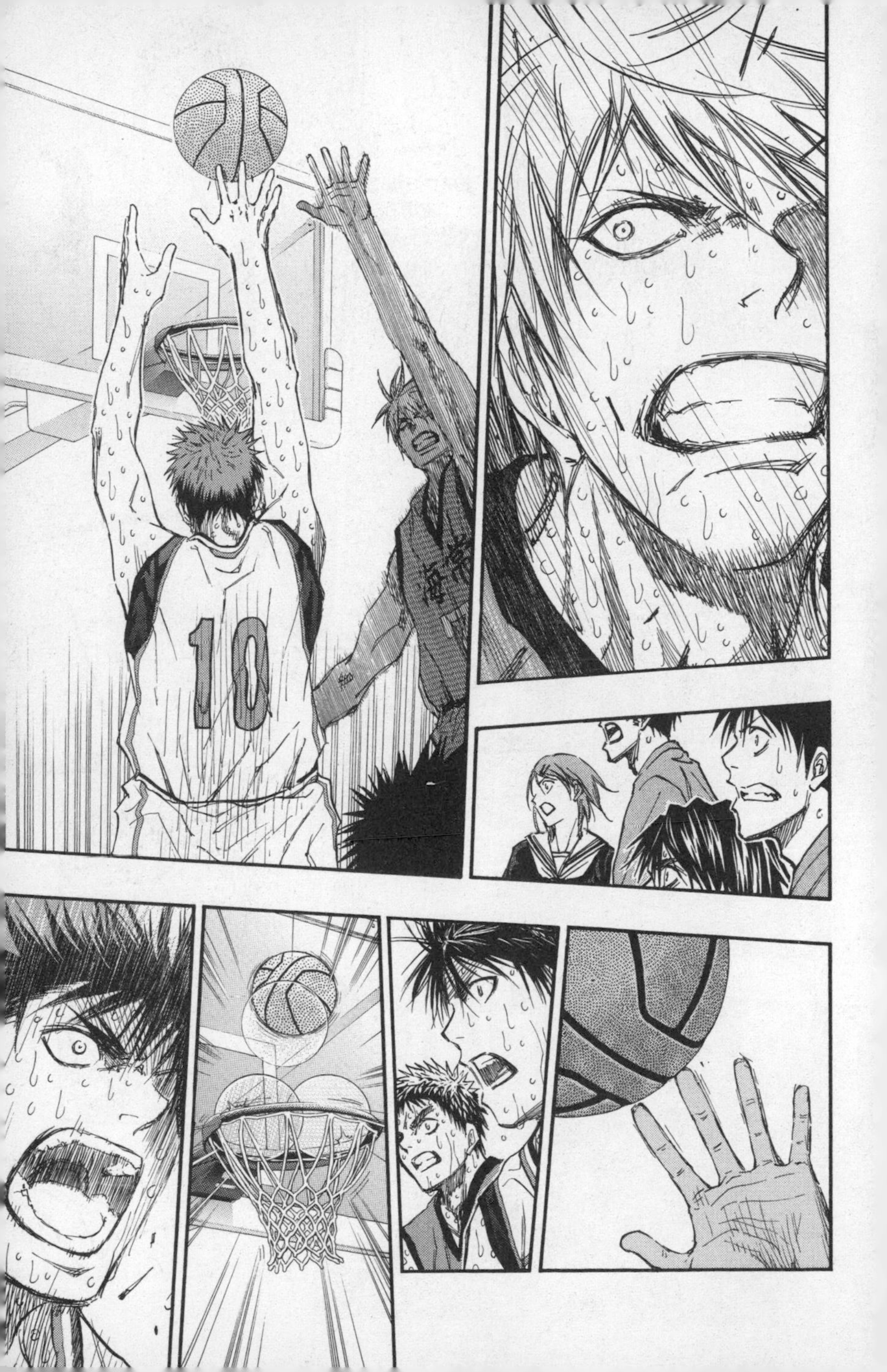

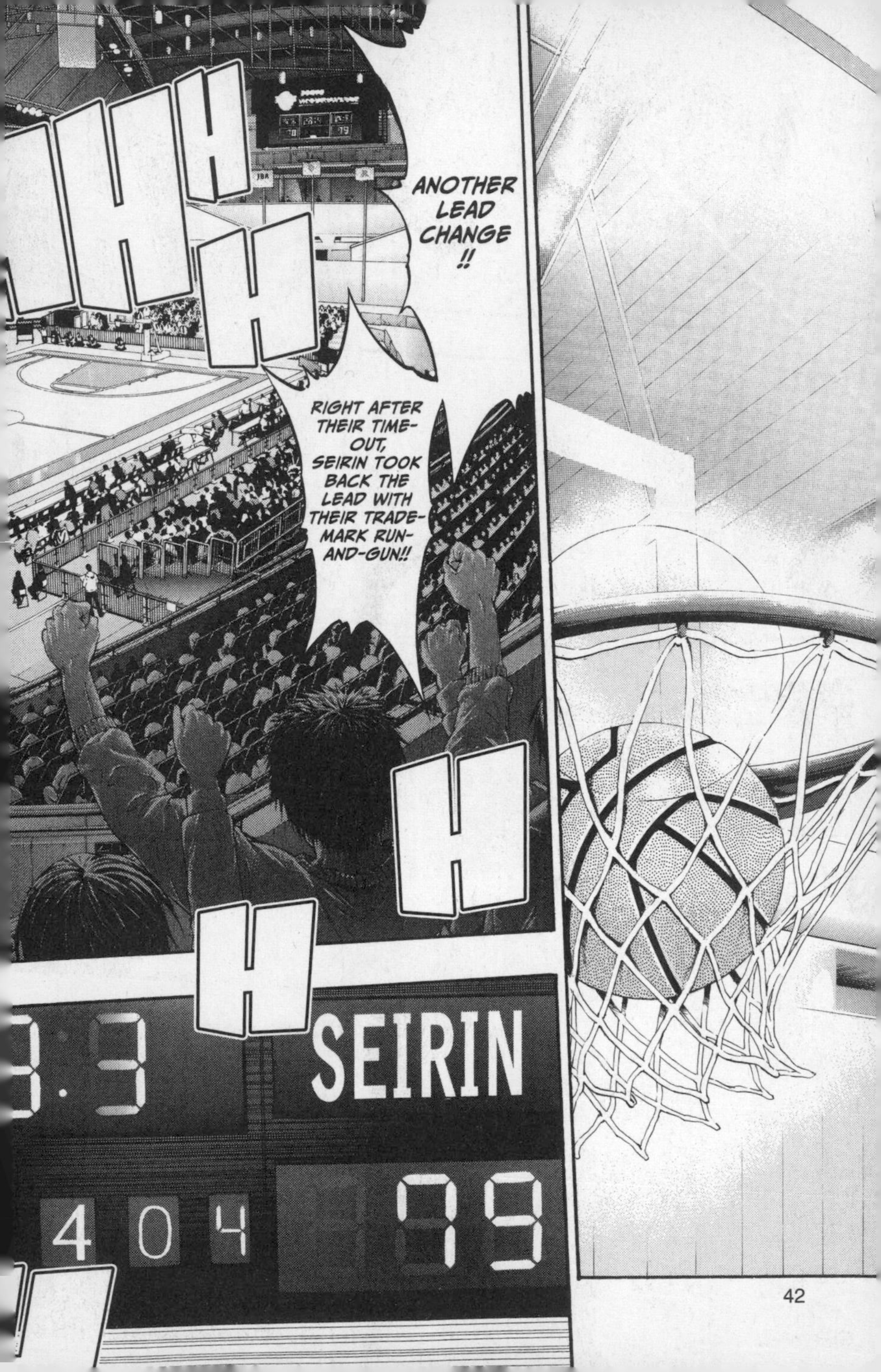
ANOTHER LEAD CHANGE!!
HHHHHH
RIGHT AFTER THEIR TIME-OUT, SEIRIN TOOK BACK THE LEAD WITH THEIR TRADE-MARK RUN-AND-GUN!!
HH
SEIRIN
79

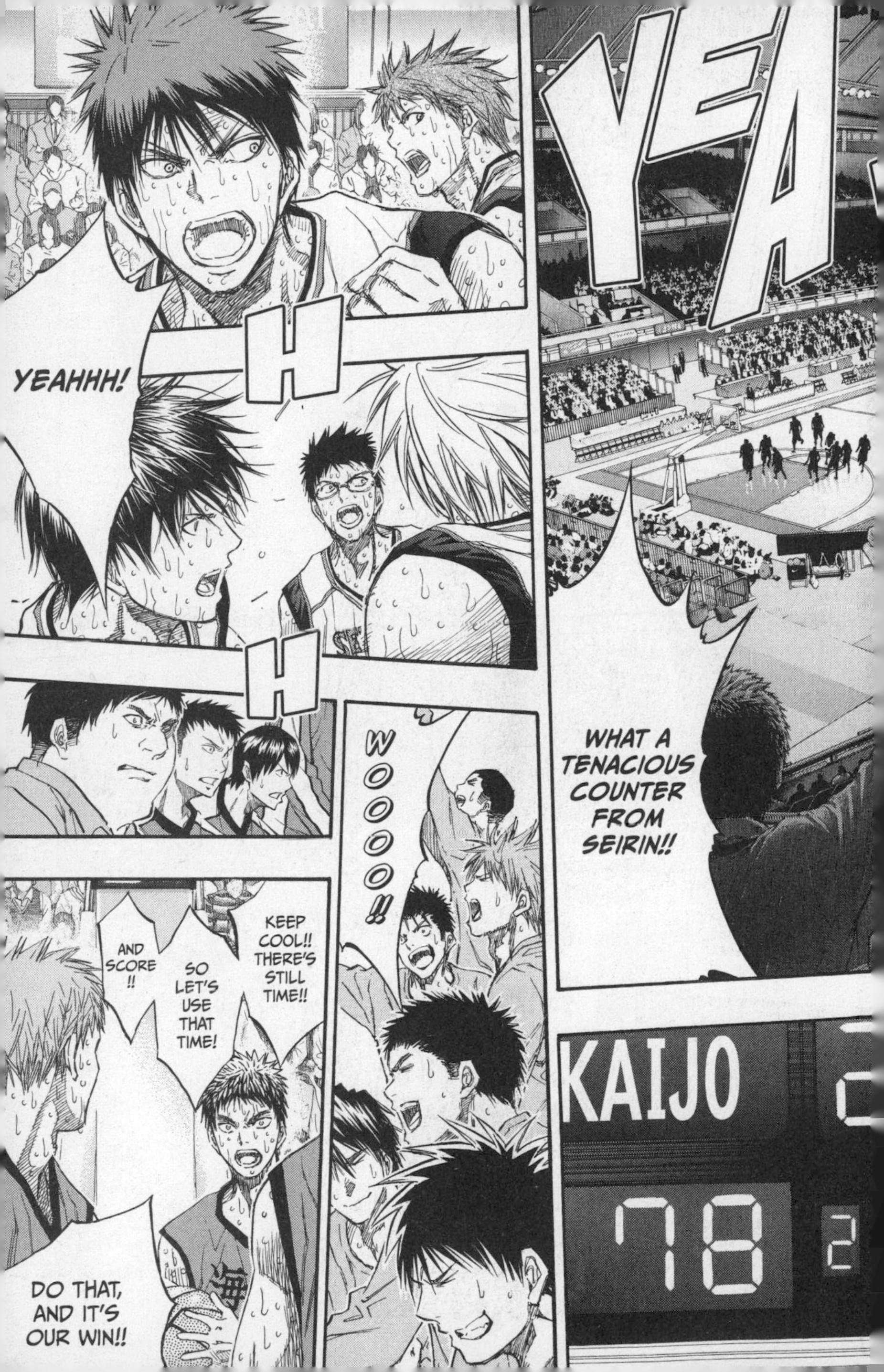
YEA
WHAT A TENACIOUS COUNTER FROM SEIRIN!!
KAIJO
78
2
YEAHHH!
H
H
WOOOOO!!
KEEP COOL!! THERE'S STILL TIME!!
SO LET'S USE THAT TIME!
AND SCORE!!
DO THAT, AND IT'S OUR WIN!!

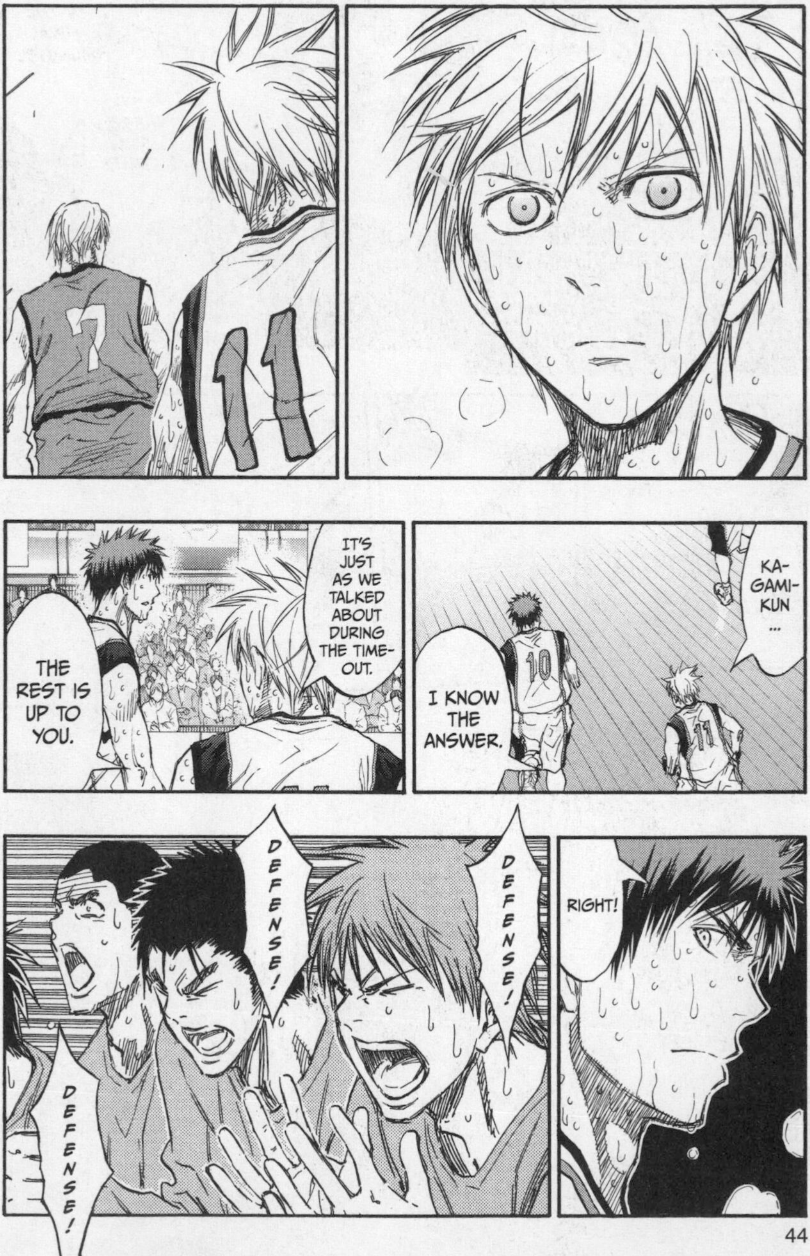
KA-GAMI-KUN ...
I KNOW THE ANSWER.
IT'S JUST AS WE TALKED ABOUT DURING THE TIME-OUT.
THE REST IS UP TO YOU.
RIGHT!
DEFENSE!
DEFENSE!
DEFENSE!

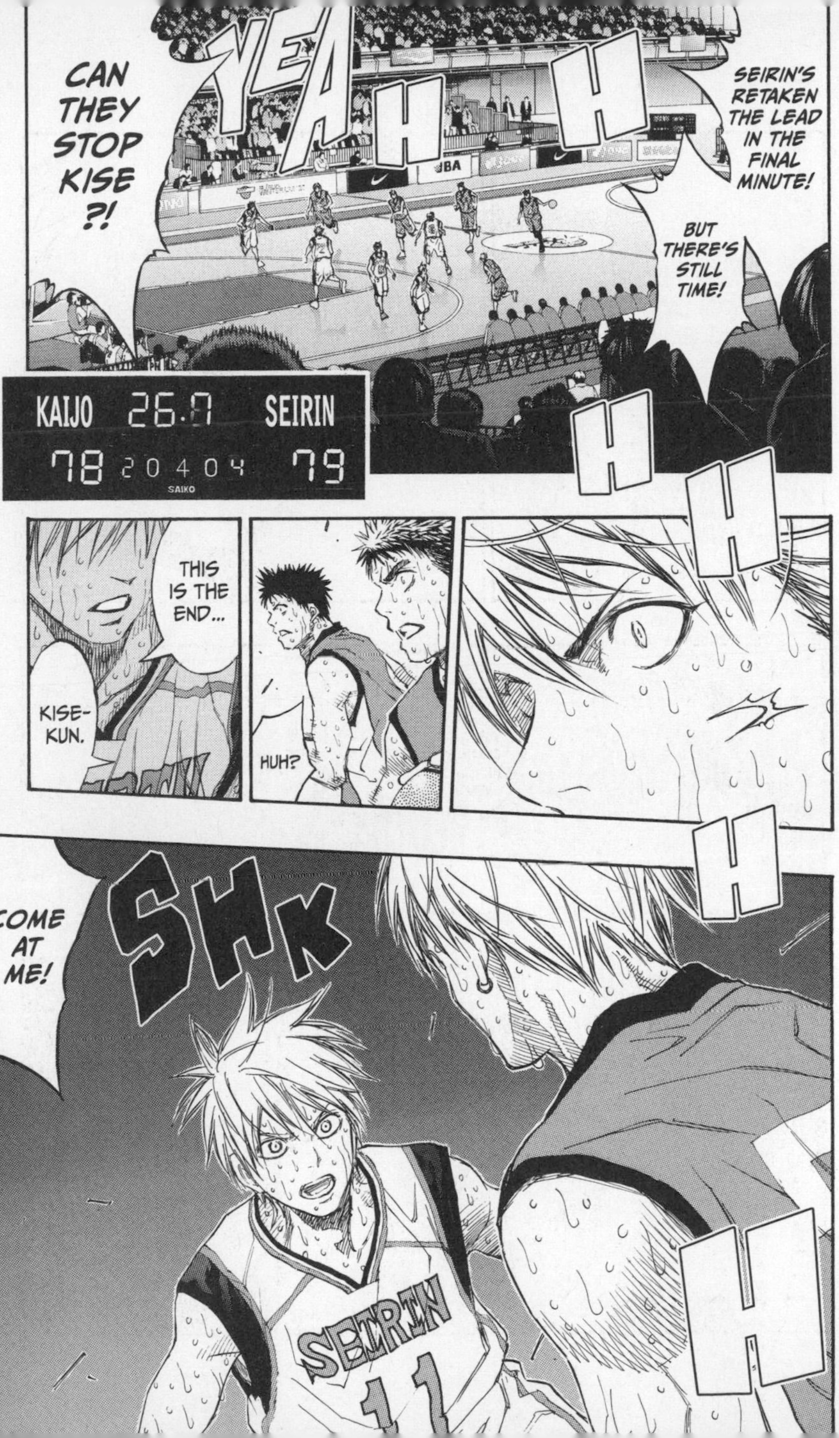
SEIRIN'S RETAKEN THE LEAD IN THE FINAL MINUTE!
BUT THERE'S STILL TIME!
YEAHHHHHHHH
CAN THEY STOP KISE ?!
KAIJO
SEIRIN
78
79
HUH?
THIS IS THE END...
KISE-KUN.
SHK
COME AT ME!

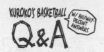

KUROKO'S BASKETBALL

Q&A

W/ HALFWAY-DECENT ANSWERS

Q. **WHY DOES KUROKO-KUN WEAR WRISTBANDS ON BOTH WRISTS BEFORE EACH GAME?**
(KURO NUT from OSAKA)

A. KUROKO'S PASSING PUTS A HEAVY STRAIN ON HIS WRISTS, SO THOSE WRISTBANDS ARE SORT OF LIKE PLACEBOS IN PLACE OF ACTUAL WRAPS. THEY'RE ALSO GOOD-LUCK CHARMS, FOR HIM.

KUROKO'S BASKETBALL BLOOPERS

TAKE 3

SO THEY'RE GONNA LOSE UNLESS THE LITTLE GUY CAN FIGURE OUT KISE'S MOVES ON KAIJO'S NEXT POSSESSION?
YIKES.
IF SEIRIN HOLDS THE BALL ON OFFENSE, THEY'LL ONLY GET TO SEE, WHAT, A MOVE OR TWO OUTTA KISE?
IT'S HOPE-LESS.
SO WE'RE THINKING SEIRIN'S GONNA LOSE?
NOTHING'S DECIDED QUITE YET.
TRY USING YOUR HEAD A LITTLE BIT MORE, PLEASE.
SO DO Y'KNOW WHEN IT'LL BE DECIDED, RED?!
ONCE THE GAME IS OVER, OF COURSE!!
ARE YOU LOOKING TO GET SLAPPED?!
STEAM
STEAM

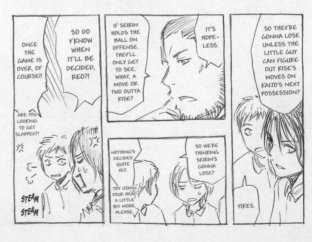

201ST QUARTER:
JUST AS PLANNED!

COME AT ME!!

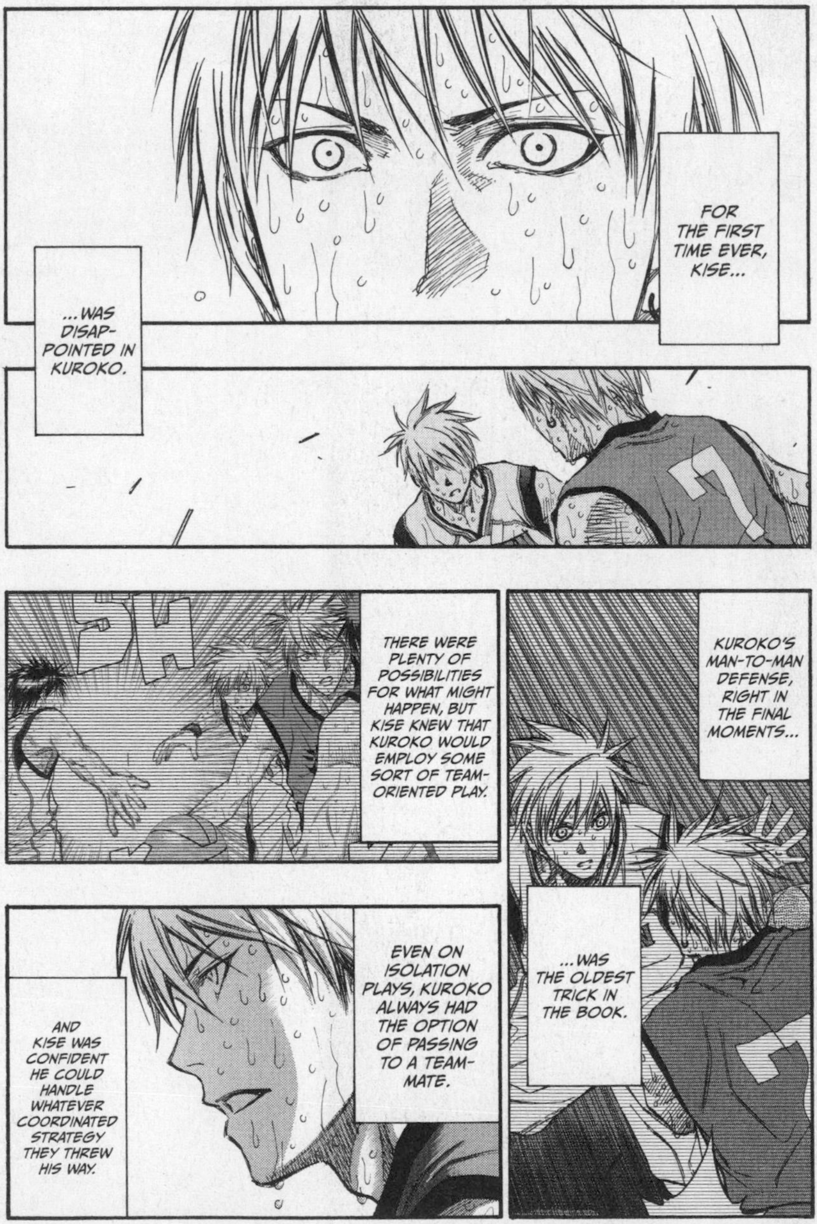

FOR THE FIRST TIME EVER, KISE...
...WAS DISAP-POINTED IN KUROKO.
KUROKO'S MAN-TO-MAN DEFENSE, RIGHT IN THE FINAL MOMENTS...
...WAS THE OLDEST TRICK IN THE BOOK.
SH
THERE WERE PLENTY OF POSSIBILITIES FOR WHAT MIGHT HAPPEN, BUT KISE KNEW THAT KUROKO WOULD EMPLOY SOME SORT OF TEAM-ORIENTED PLAY.
EVEN ON ISOLATION PLAYS, KUROKO ALWAYS HAD THE OPTION OF PASSING TO A TEAM-MATE.
AND KISE WAS CONFIDENT HE COULD HANDLE WHATEVER COORDINATED STRATEGY THEY THREW HIS WAY.

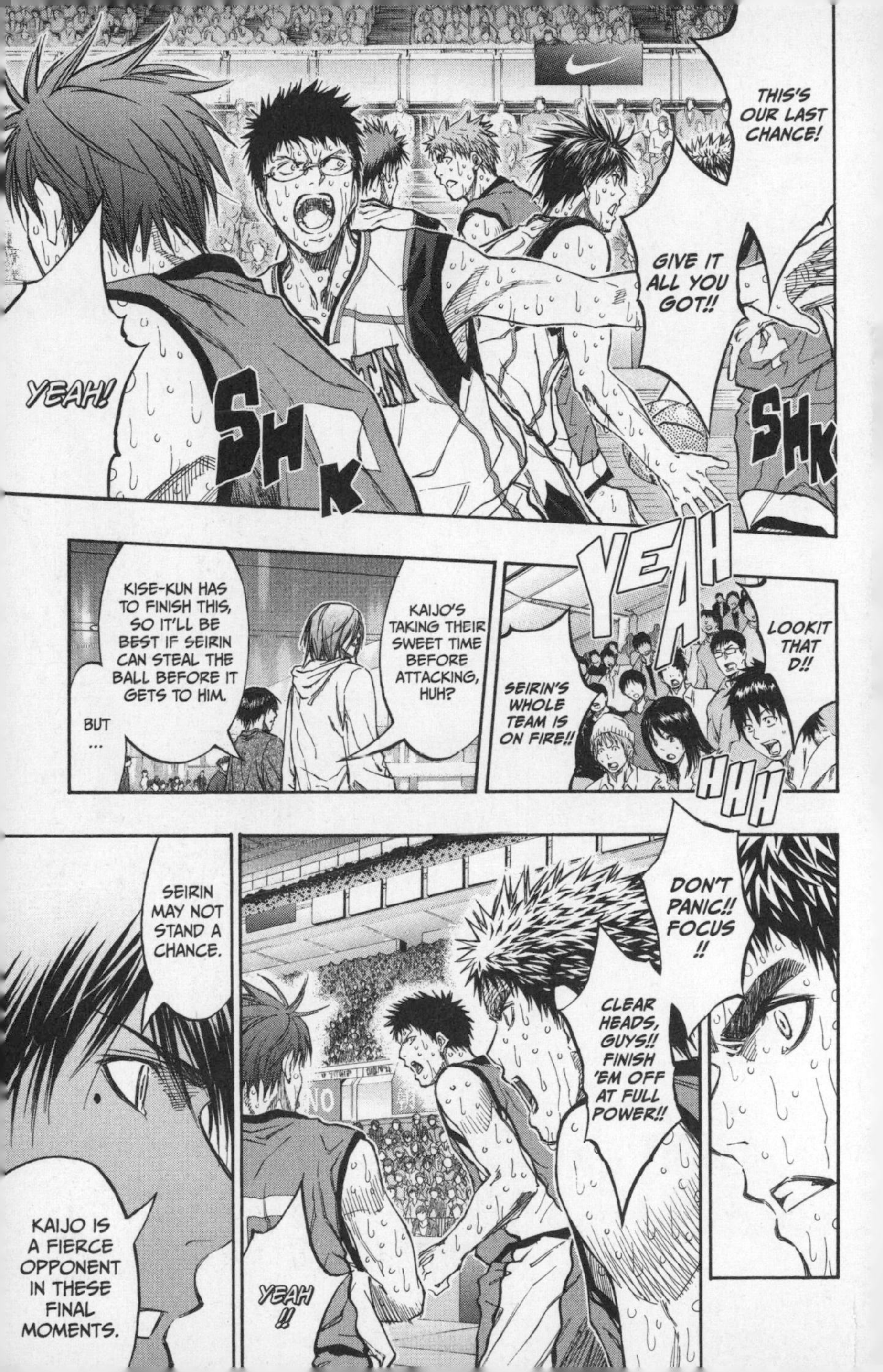
THIS'S OUR LAST CHANCE!
GIVE IT ALL YOU GOT!!
SHK
SHK
YEAH!
YEAH
LOOKIT THAT D!!
SEIRIN'S WHOLE TEAM IS ON FIRE!!
HHH
KAIJO'S TAKING THEIR SWEET TIME BEFORE ATTACKING, HUH?
KISE-KUN HAS TO FINISH THIS, SO IT'LL BE BEST IF SEIRIN CAN STEAL THE BALL BEFORE IT GETS TO HIM.
BUT ...
DON'T PANIC!! FOCUS!!
CLEAR HEADS, GUYS!! FINISH 'EM OFF AT FULL POWER!!
YEAH!!
SEIRIN MAY NOT STAND A CHANCE.
KAIJO IS A FIERCE OPPONENT IN THESE FINAL MOMENTS.

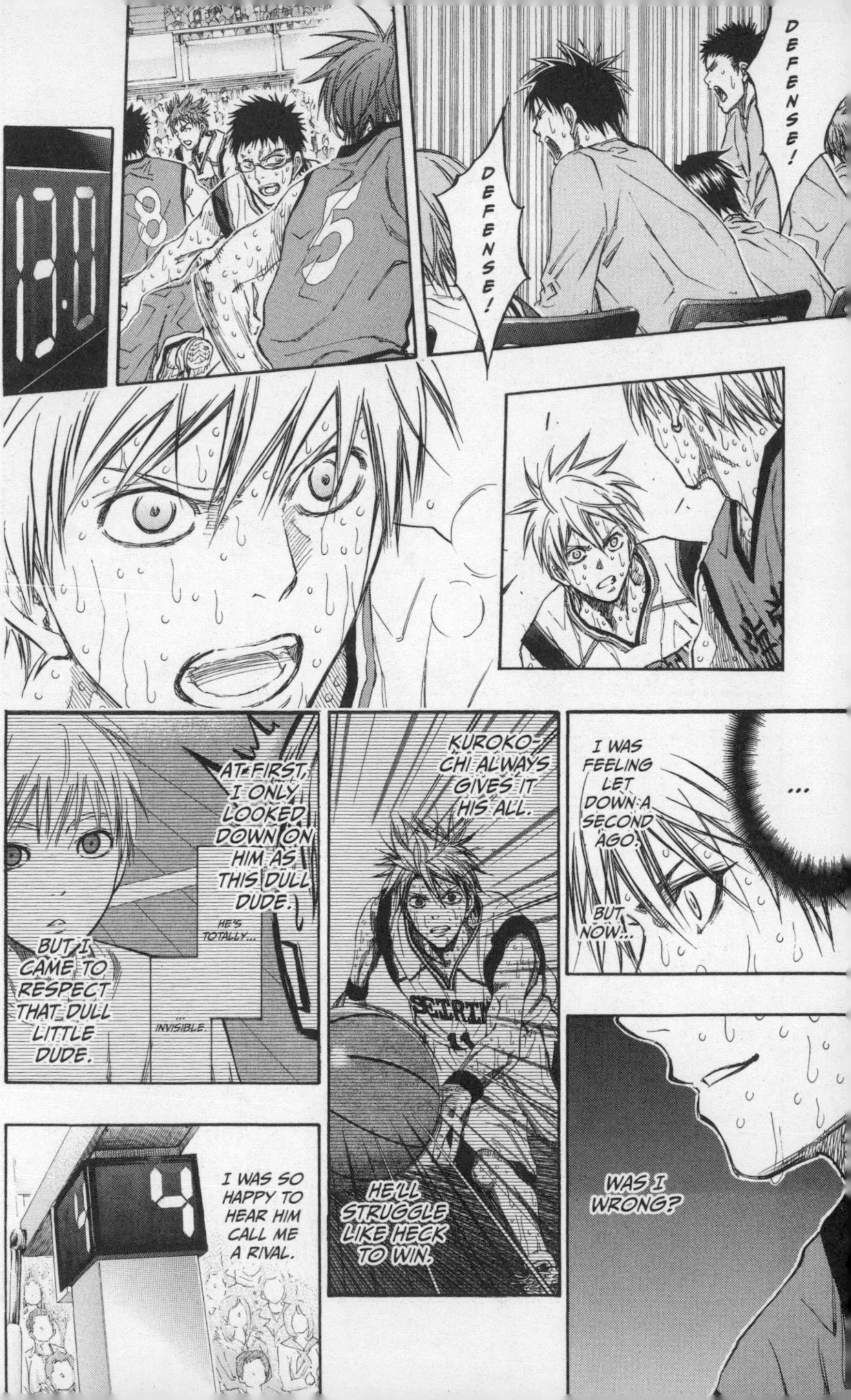
DEFENSE!
DEFENSE!
!
...
I WAS FEELING LET DOWN A SECOND AGO.
BUT NOW...
WAS I WRONG?
KUROKO-CHI ALWAYS GIVES IT HIS ALL.
HE'LL STRUGGLE LIKE HECK TO WIN.
AT FIRST, I ONLY LOOKED DOWN ON HIM AS THIS DULL DUDE.
HE'S TOTALLY...
...INVISIBLE.
BUT I CAME TO RESPECT THAT DULL LITTLE DUDE.
I WAS SO HAPPY TO HEAR HIM CALL ME A RIVAL.

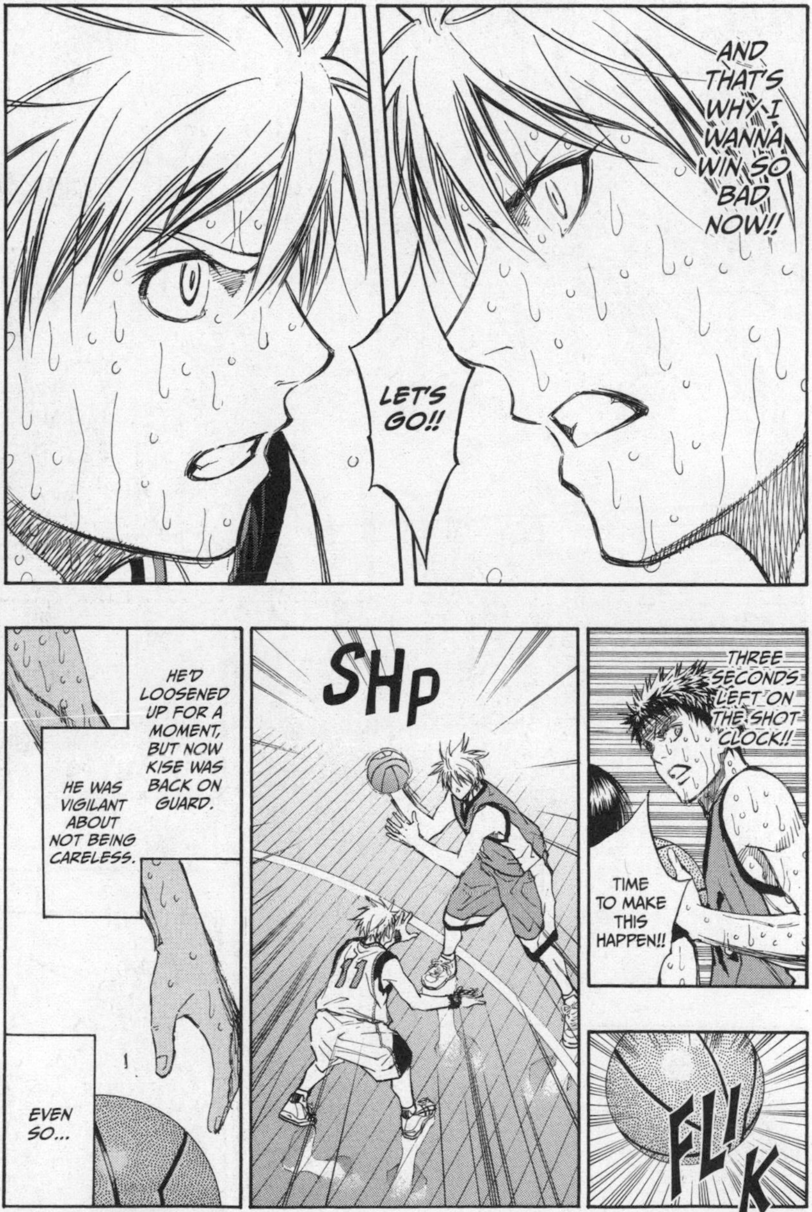
AND THAT'S WHY I WANNA WIN SO BAD NOW!!
LET'S GO!!
THREE SECONDS LEFT ON THE SHOT CLOCK!!
TIME TO MAKE THIS HAPPEN!!
FLIK
SHP
HE'D LOOSENED UP FOR A MOMENT, BUT NOW KISE WAS BACK ON GUARD.
HE WAS VIGILANT ABOUT NOT BEING CARELESS.
EVEN SO...

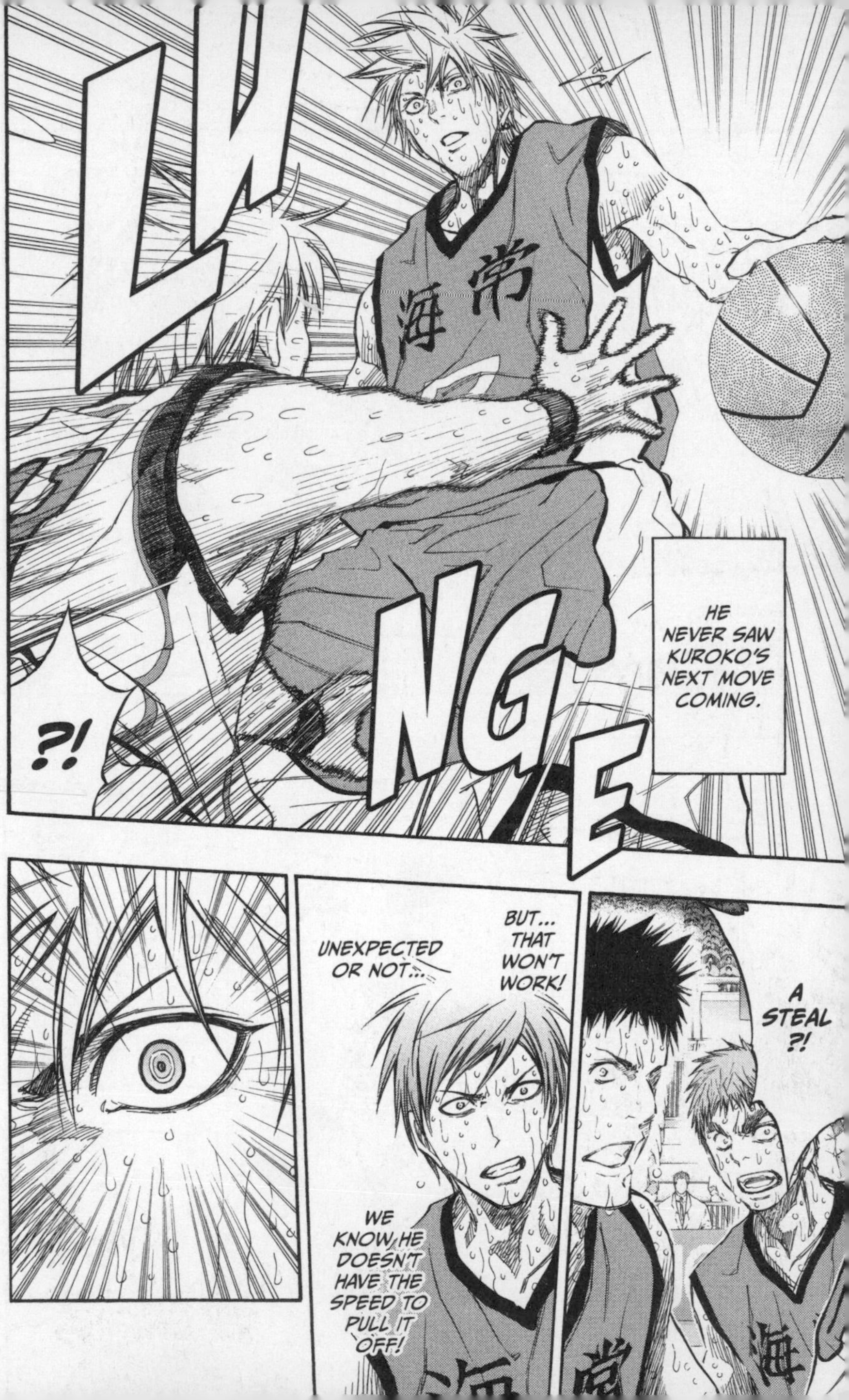
HE NEVER SAW KUROKO'S NEXT MOVE COMING.
?!
A STEAL ?!
UNEXPECTED OR NOT...
BUT... THAT WON'T WORK!
WE KNOW HE DOESN'T HAVE THE SPEED TO PULL IT OFF!

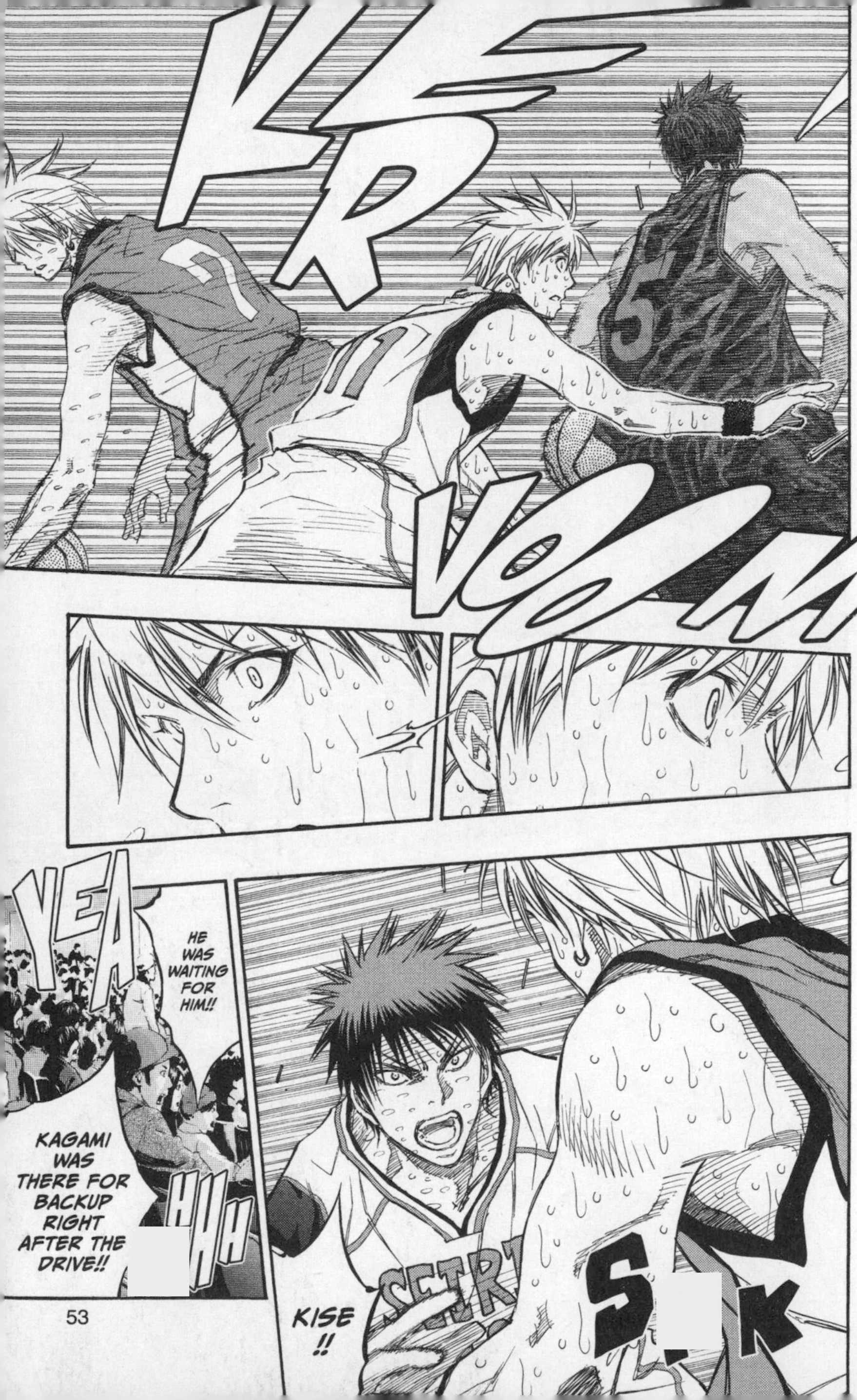
KISE !!
HE WAS WAITING FOR HIM!!
KAGAMI WAS THERE FOR BACKUP RIGHT AFTER THE DRIVE!!
YEAHHH

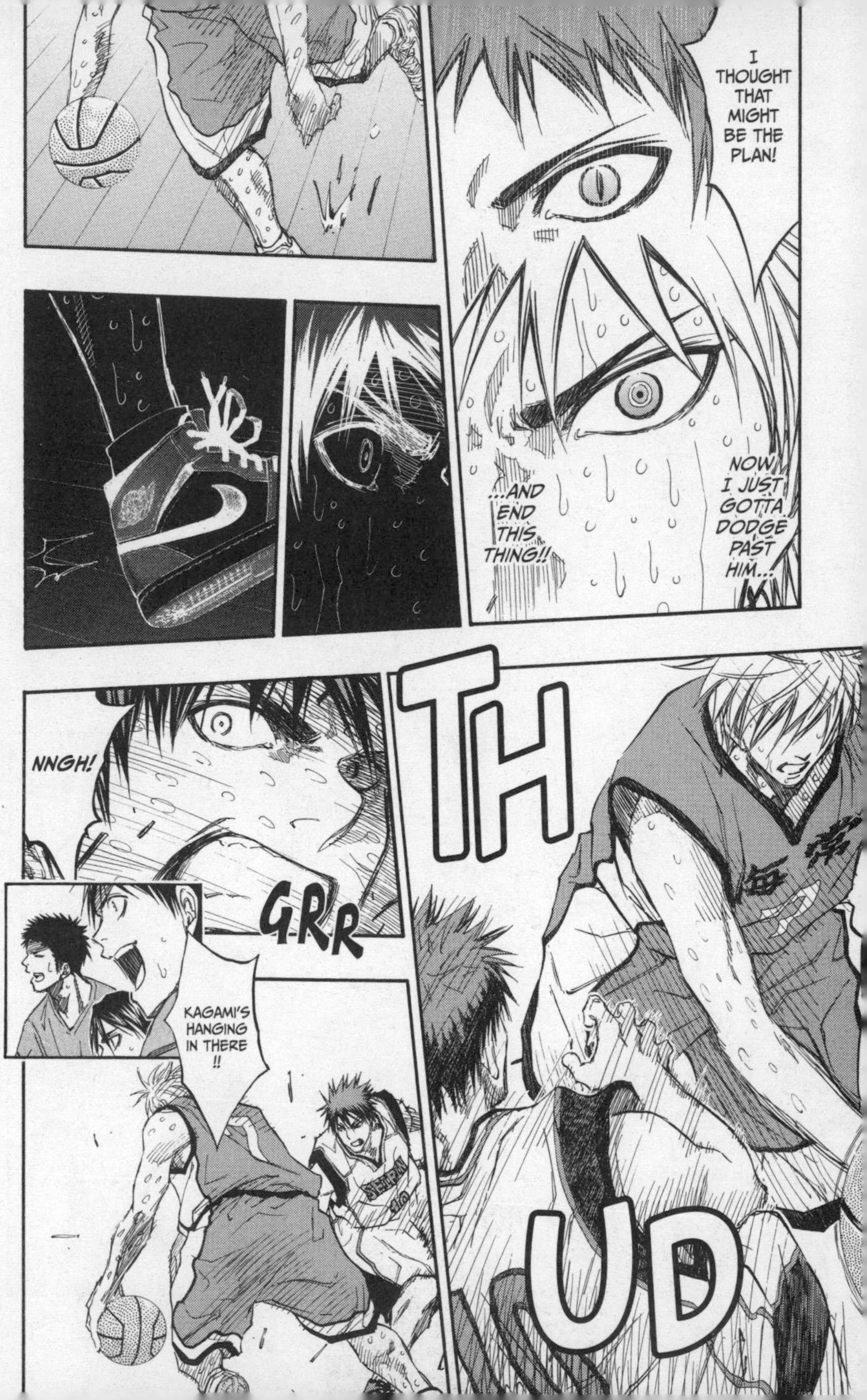
I THOUGHT THAT MIGHT BE THE PLAN!
NOW I JUST GOTTA DODGE PAST HIM...
...AND END THIS THING!!
TH
UD
NNGH!
GRR
KAGAMI'S HANGING IN THERE!!

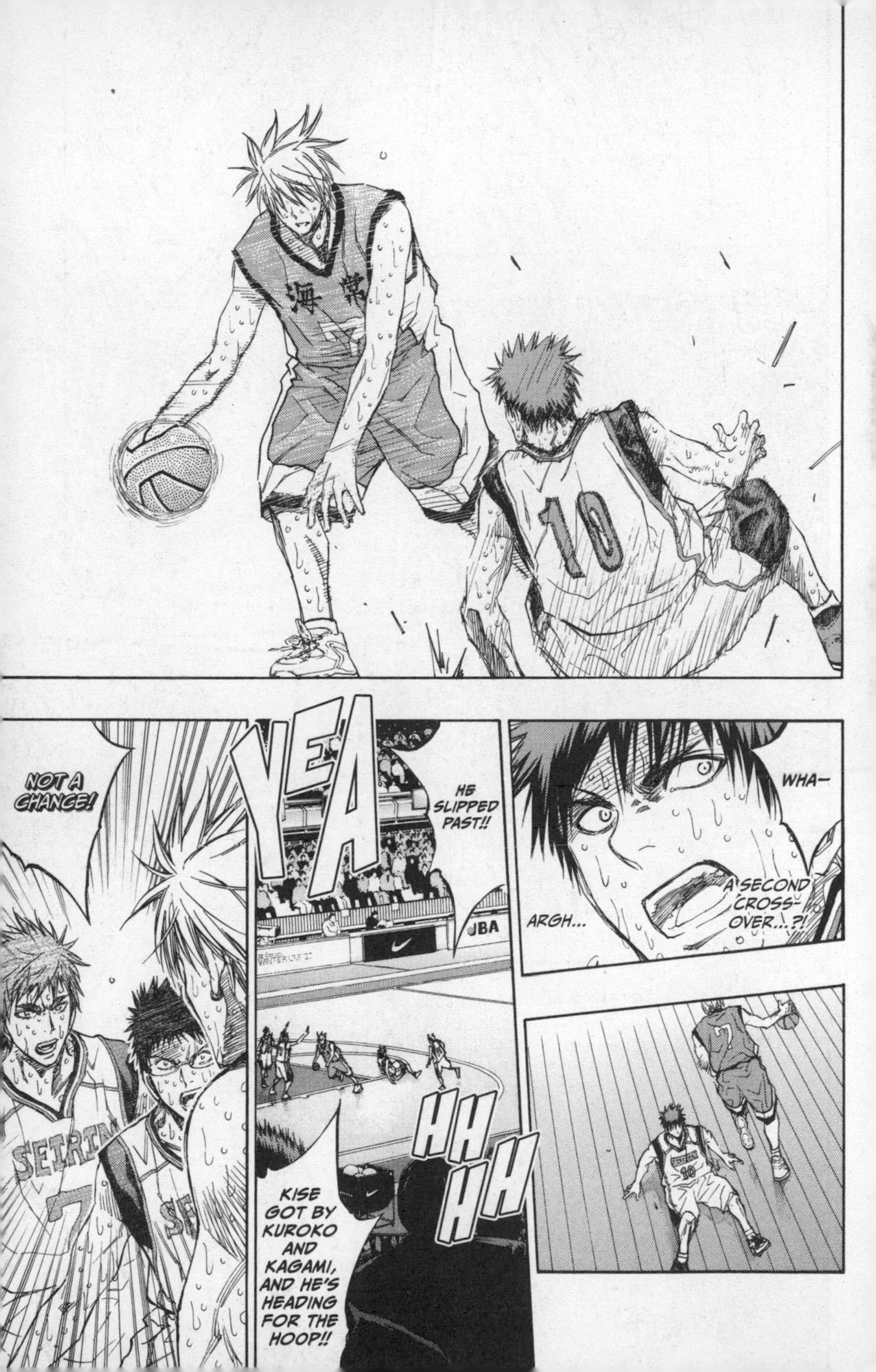

WHA—
A SECOND CROSS-OVER...?!
ARGH...
HE SLIPPED PAST!!
YEA
HHHHH
KISE GOT BY KUROKO AND KAGAMI, AND HE'S HEADING FOR THE HOOP!!
NOT A CHANGE!
JBA

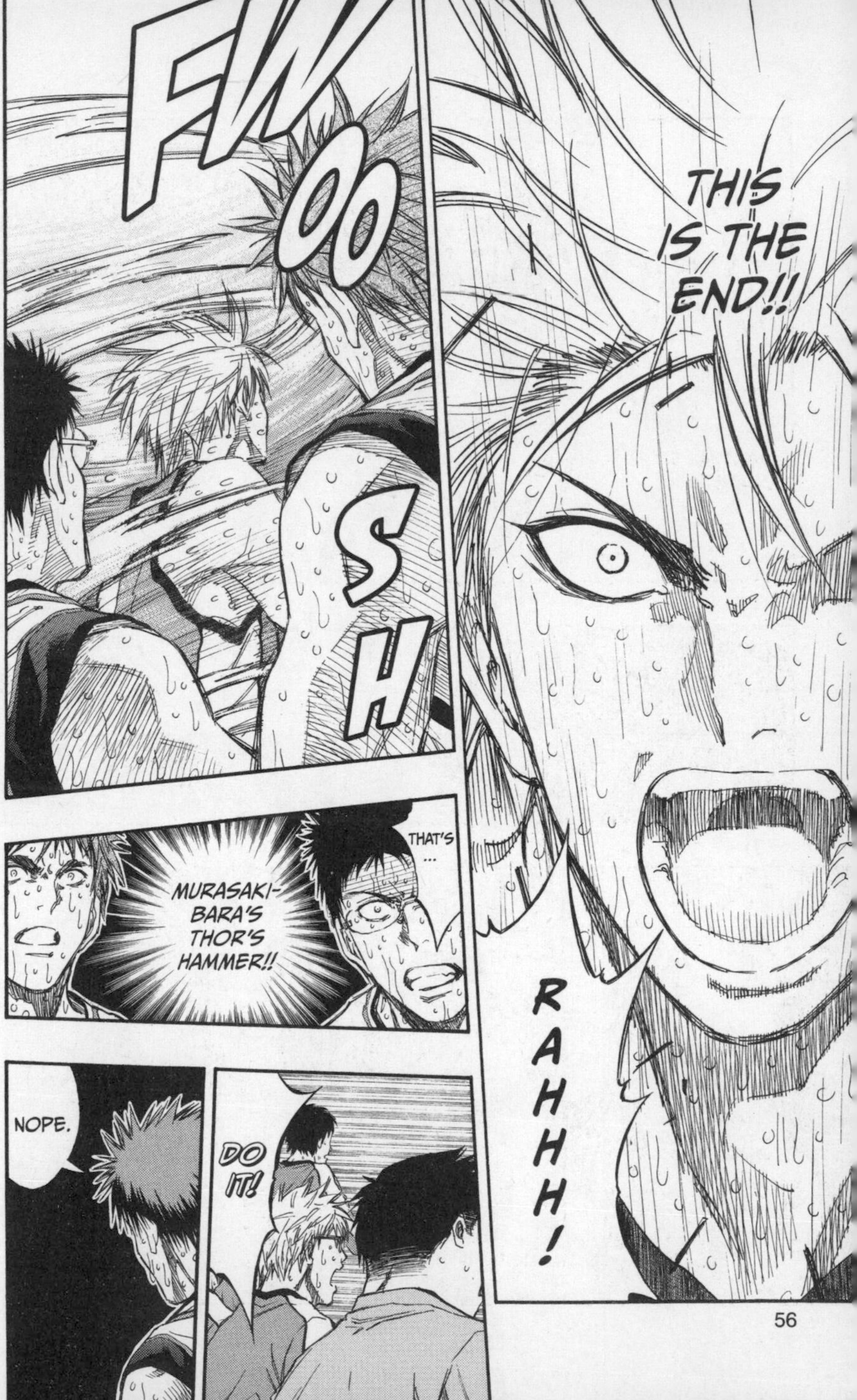
THIS IS THE END!!
RAHHHH!
FWOOSH
THAT'S ...
MURASAKIBARA'S THOR'S HAMMER!!
DO IT!
NOPE.

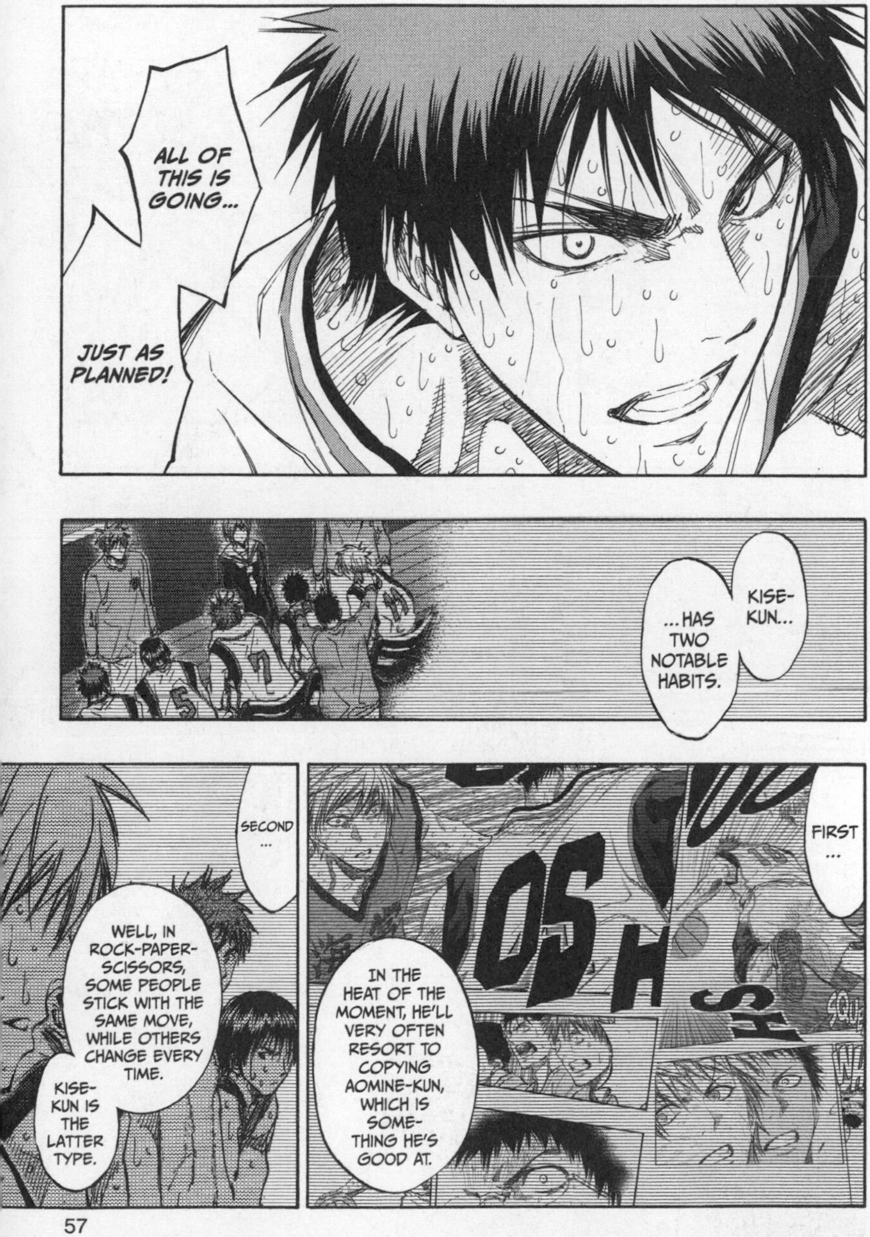
ALL OF THIS IS GOING...
JUST AS PLANNED!
KISE-KUN...
...HAS TWO NOTABLE HABITS.
FIRST ...
IN THE HEAT OF THE MOMENT, HE'LL VERY OFTEN RESORT TO COPYING AOMINE-KUN, WHICH IS SOME-THING HE'S GOOD AT.
SECOND ...
WELL, IN ROCK-PAPER-SCISSORS, SOME PEOPLE STICK WITH THE SAME MOVE, WHILE OTHERS CHANGE EVERY TIME.
KISE-KUN IS THE LATTER TYPE.

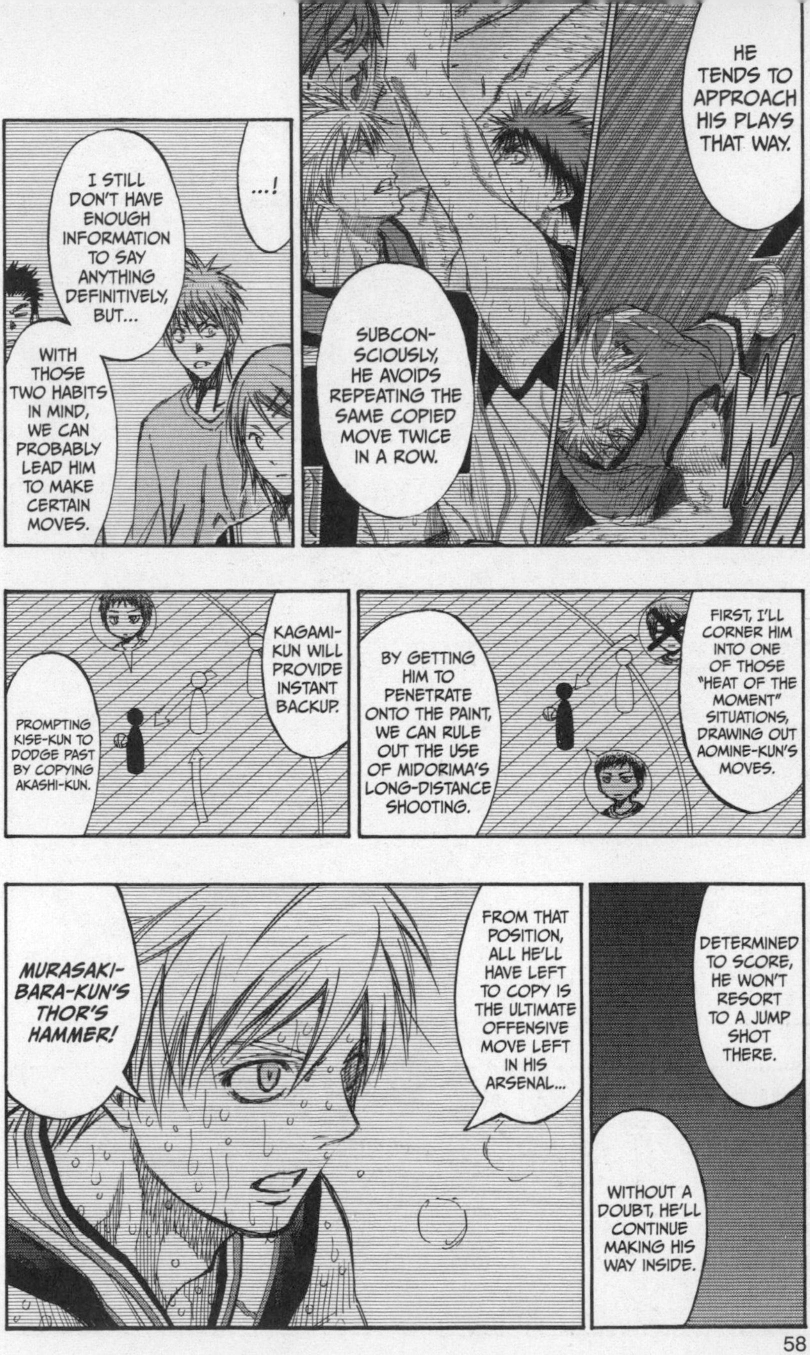

HE TENDS TO APPROACH HIS PLAYS THAT WAY.
SUBCON-SCIOUSLY, HE AVOIDS REPEATING THE SAME COPIED MOVE TWICE IN A ROW.
...!
I STILL DON'T HAVE ENOUGH INFORMATION TO SAY ANYTHING DEFINITIVELY, BUT...
WITH THOSE TWO HABITS IN MIND, WE CAN PROBABLY LEAD HIM TO MAKE CERTAIN MOVES.
FIRST, I'LL CORNER HIM INTO ONE OF THOSE "HEAT OF THE MOMENT" SITUATIONS, DRAWING OUT AOMINE-KUN'S MOVES.
BY GETTING HIM TO PENETRATE ONTO THE PAINT, WE CAN RULE OUT THE USE OF MIDORIMA'S LONG-DISTANCE SHOOTING.
KAGAMI-KUN WILL PROVIDE INSTANT BACKUP.
PROMPTING KISE-KUN TO DODGE PAST BY COPYING AKASHI-KUN.
DETERMINED TO SCORE, HE WON'T RESORT TO A JUMP SHOT THERE.
WITHOUT A DOUBT, HE'LL CONTINUE MAKING HIS WAY INSIDE.
FROM THAT POSITION, ALL HE'LL HAVE LEFT TO COPY IS THE ULTIMATE OFFENSIVE MOVE LEFT IN HIS ARSENAL...
MURASAKI-BARA-KUN'S THOR'S HAMMER!

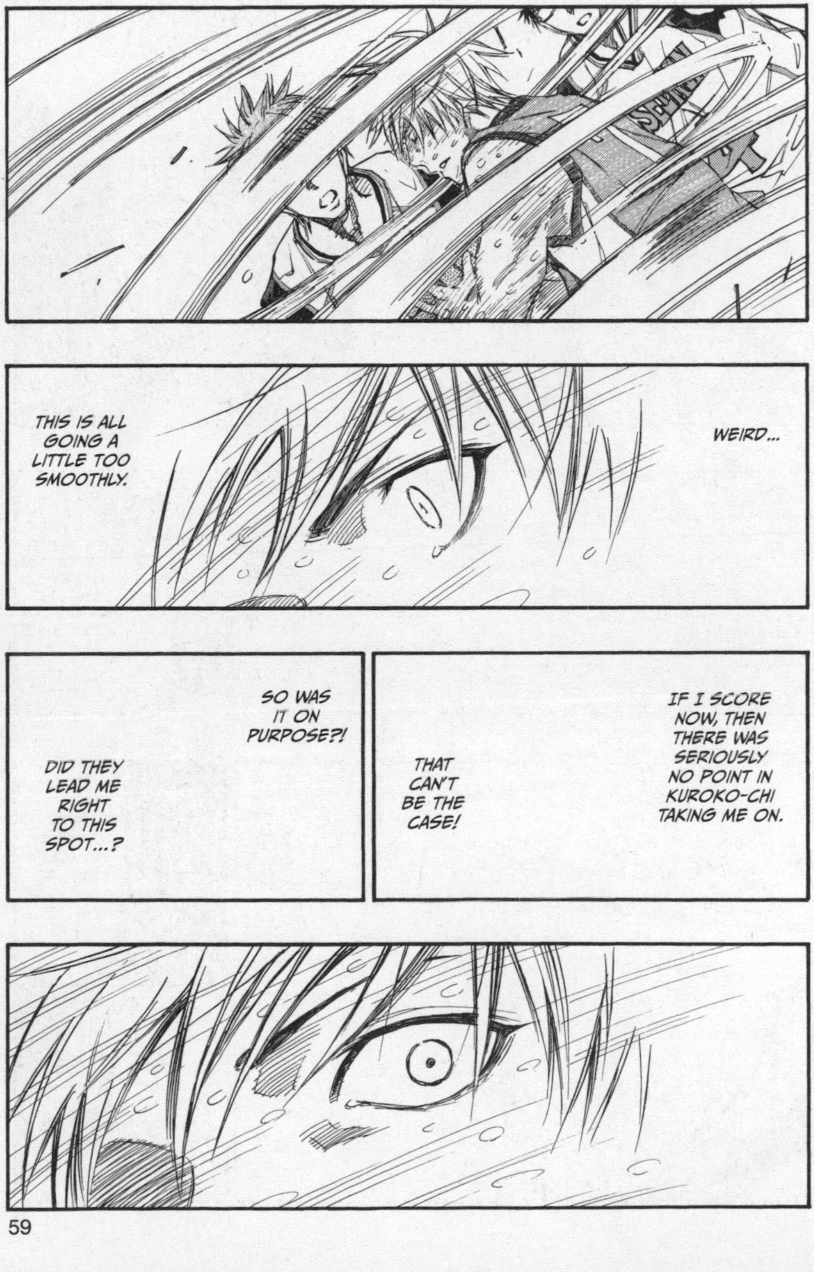
WEIRD...
THIS IS ALL GOING A LITTLE TOO SMOOTHLY.
IF I SCORE NOW, THEN THERE WAS SERIOUSLY NO POINT IN KUROKO-CHI TAKING ME ON.
THAT CAN'T BE THE CASE!
SO WAS IT ON PURPOSE?!
DID THEY LEAD ME RIGHT TO THIS SPOT...?

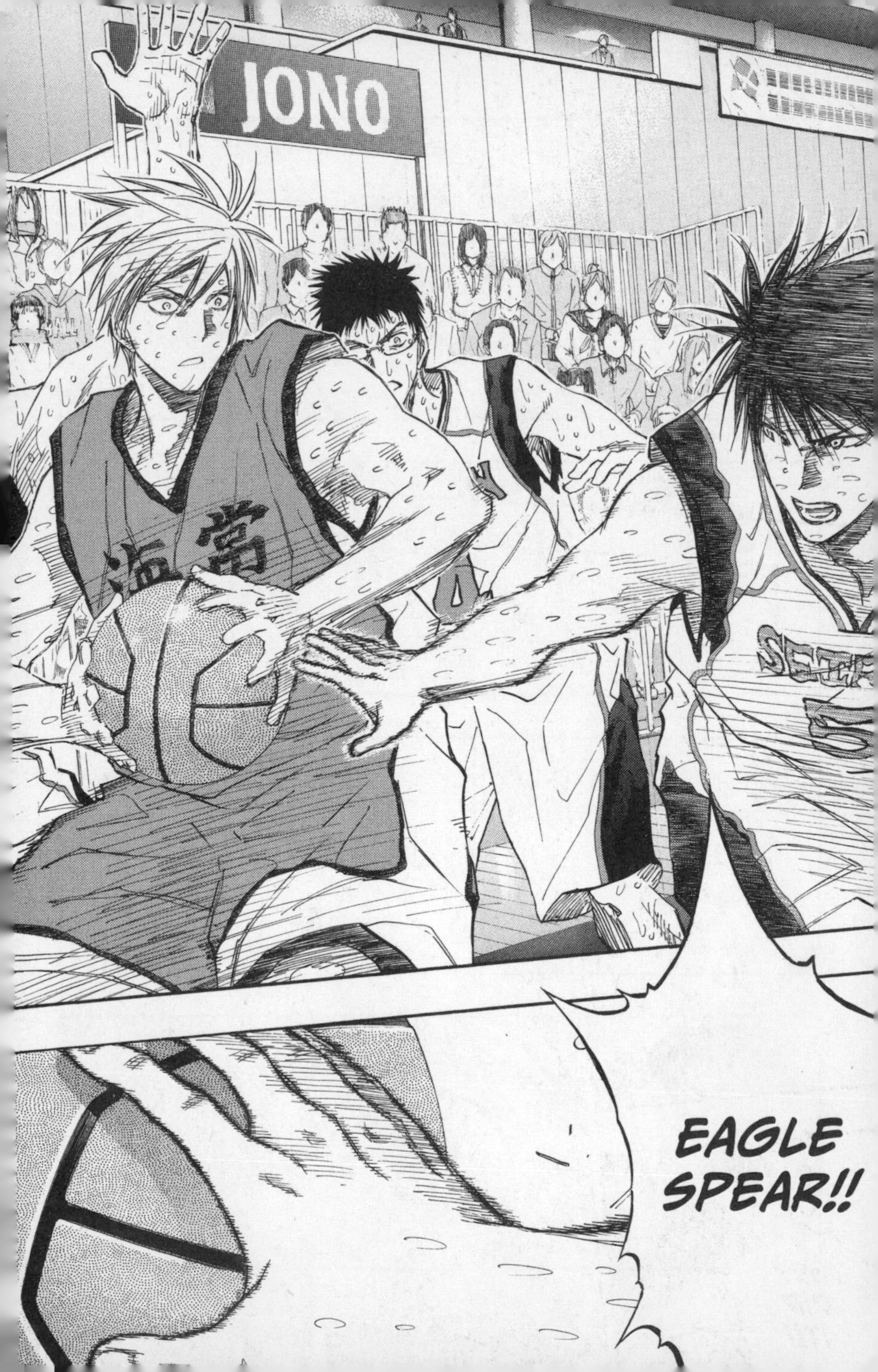
JONO
海常
EAGLE SPEAR!!

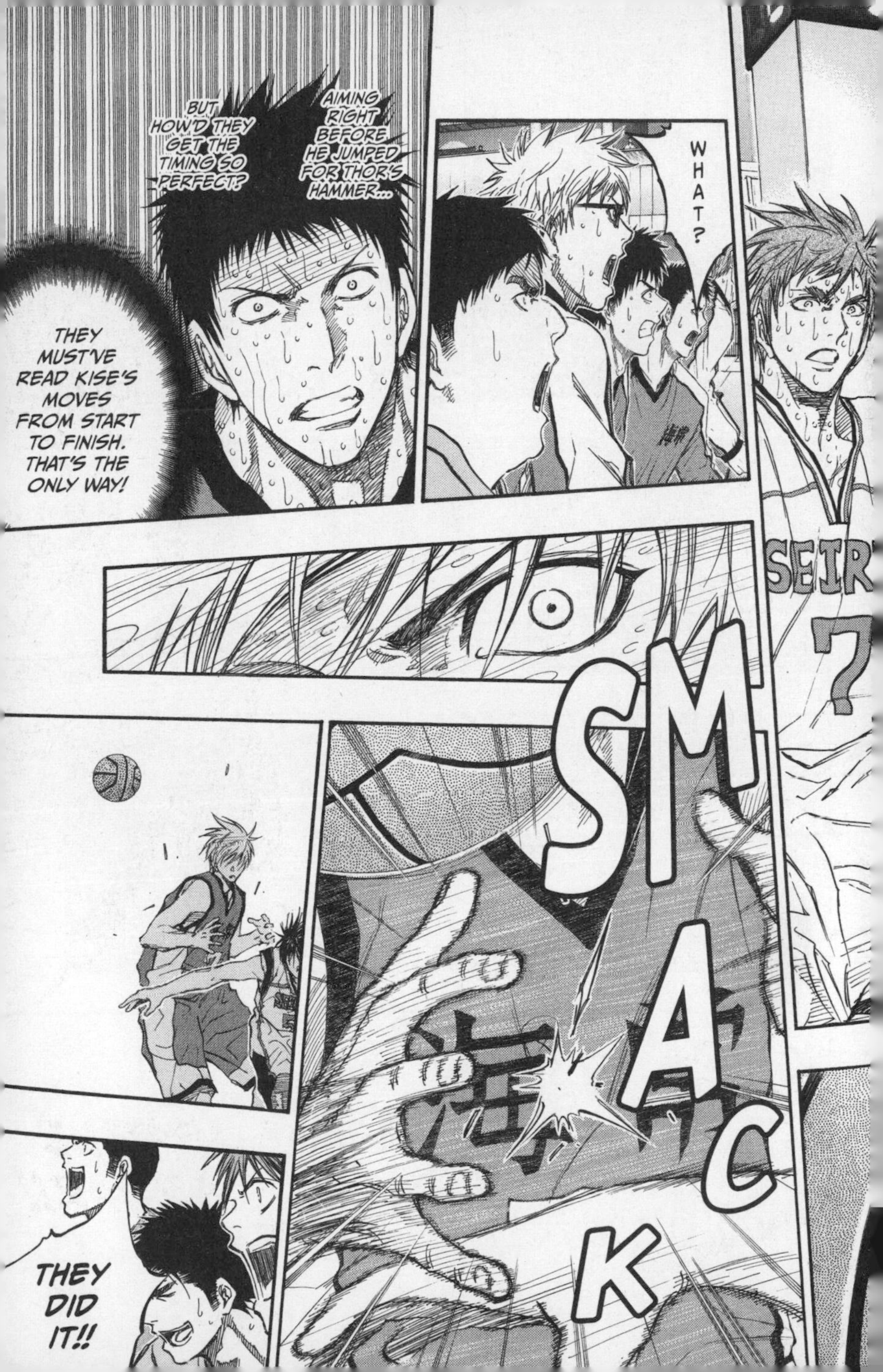
WHAT?
AIMING RIGHT BEFORE HE JUMPED FOR THOR'S HAMMER...
BUT HOW'D THEY GET THE TIMING SO PERFECT?
THEY MUST'VE READ KISE'S MOVES FROM START TO FINISH. THAT'S THE ONLY WAY!
SEIRI
7
SMACK
THEY DID IT!!

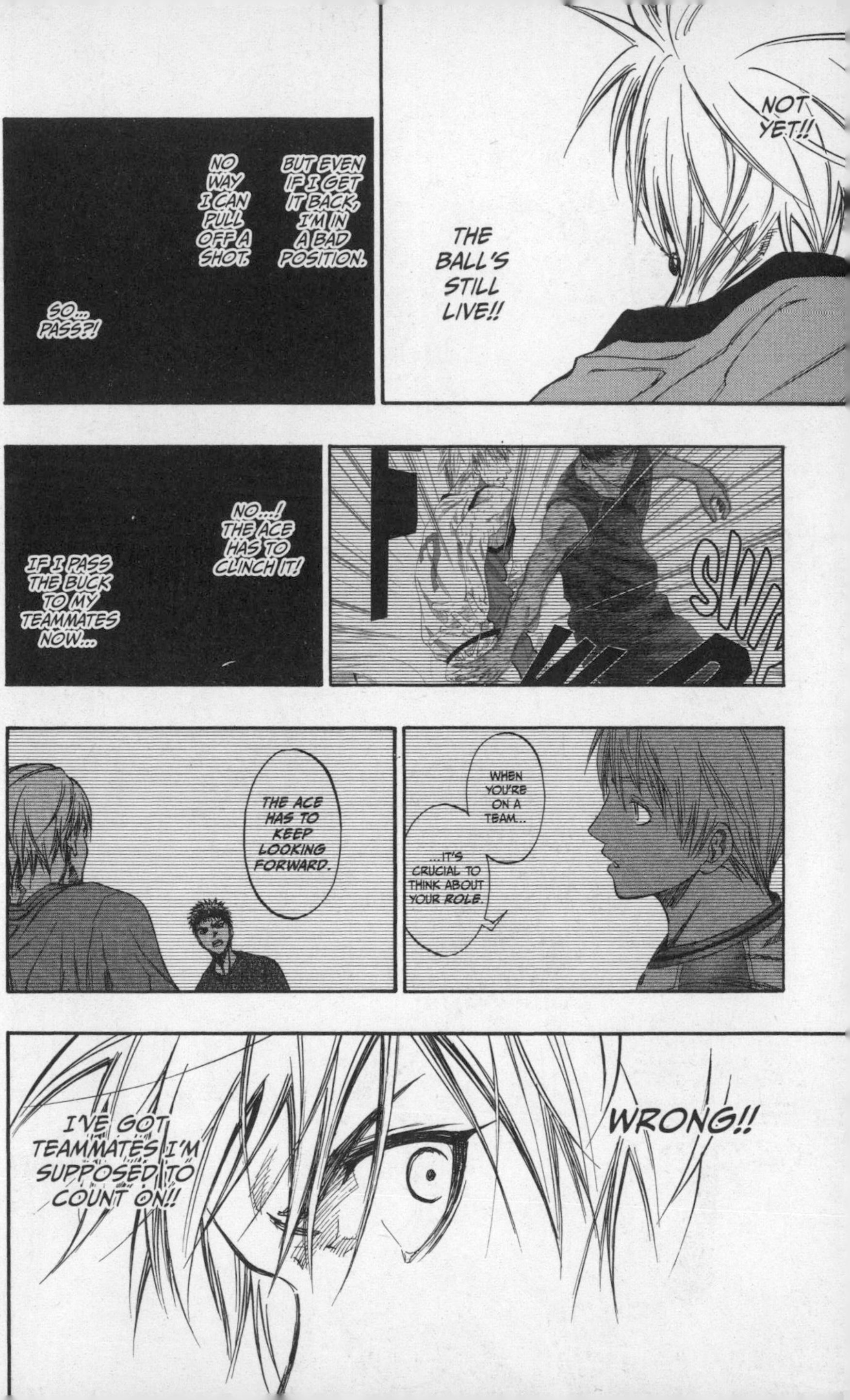
NOT YET!!
THE BALL'S STILL LIVE!!
BUT EVEN IF I GET IT BACK, I'M IN A BAD POSITION.
NO WAY I CAN PULL OFF A SHOT.
SO... PASS?!
SWI
NO...! THE ACE HAS TO CLINCH IT!
IF I PASS THE BUCK TO MY TEAMMATES NOW...
WHEN YOU'RE ON A TEAM...
...IT'S CRUCIAL TO THINK ABOUT YOUR ROLE.
THE ACE HAS TO KEEP LOOKING FORWARD.
WRONG!!
I'VE GOT TEAMMATES I'M SUPPOSED TO COUNT ON!!

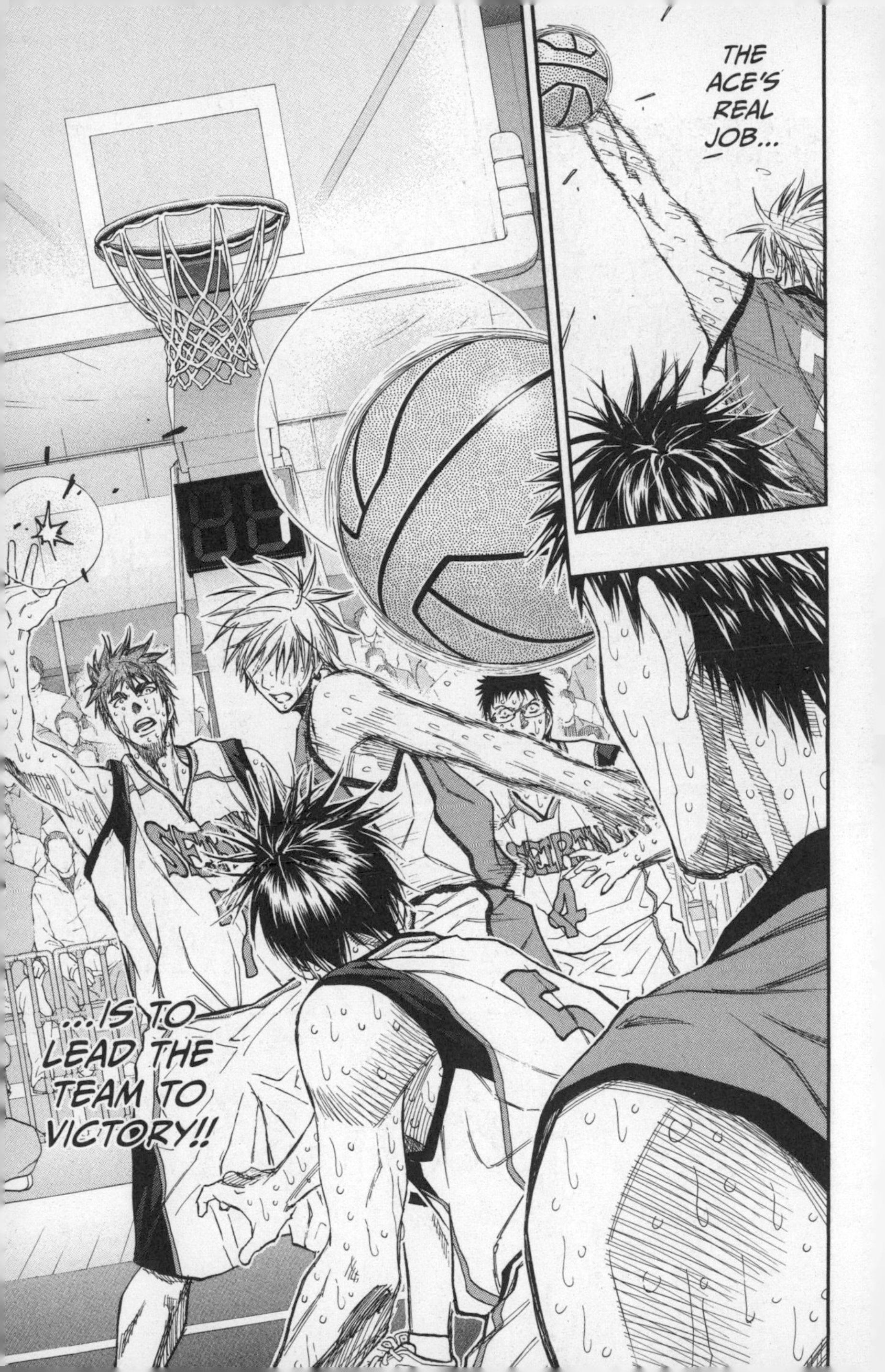
THE ACE'S REAL JOB...
...IS TO LEAD THE TEAM TO VICTORY!!

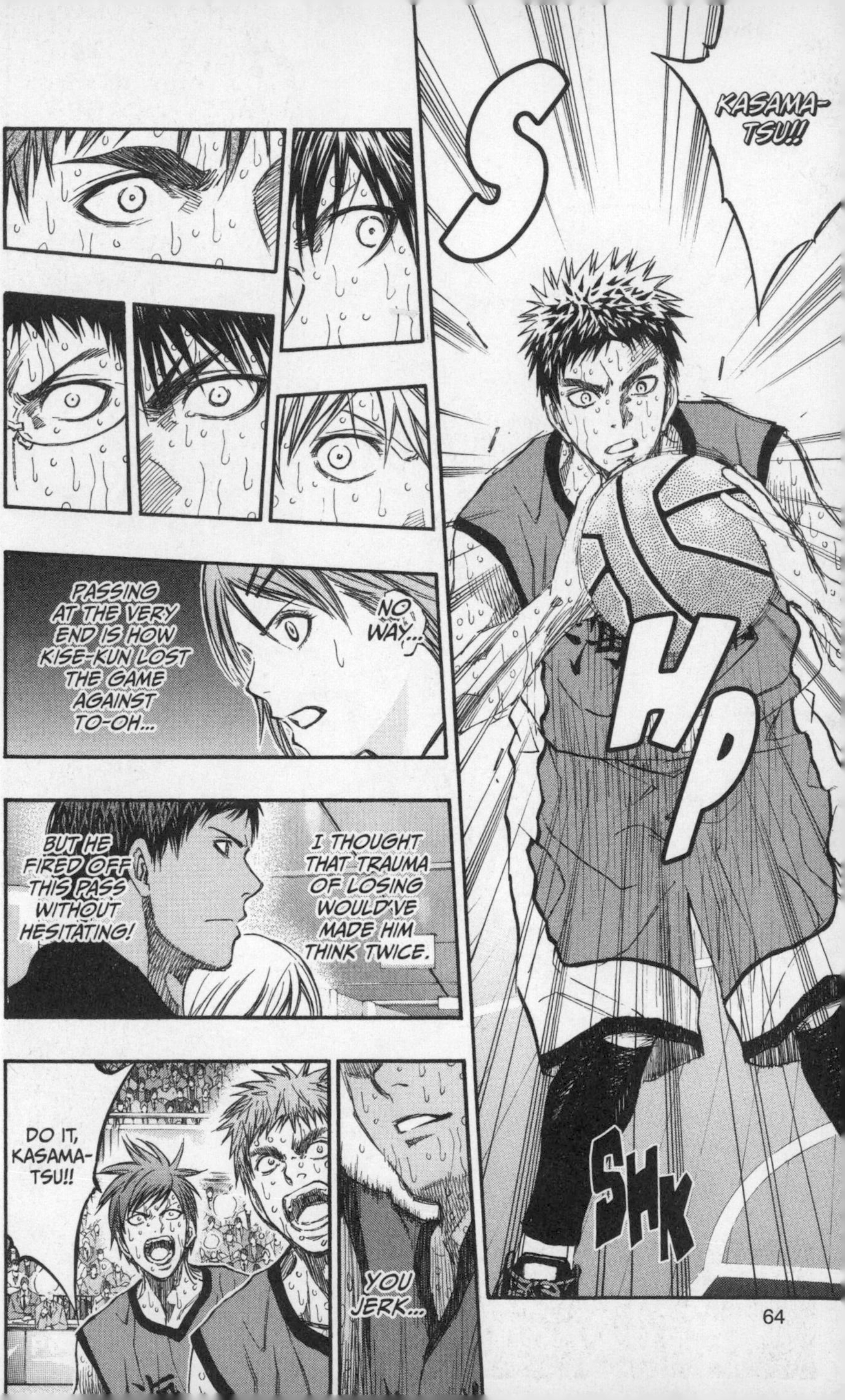
KASAMA-TSU!!
SHP
SHK
NO WAY...
PASSING AT THE VERY END IS HOW KISE-KUN LOST THE GAME AGAINST TO-OH...
I THOUGHT THAT TRAUMA OF LOSING WOULD'VE MADE HIM THINK TWICE.
BUT HE FIRED OFF THIS PASS WITHOUT HESITATING!
YOU JERK...
DO IT, KASAMA-TSU!!

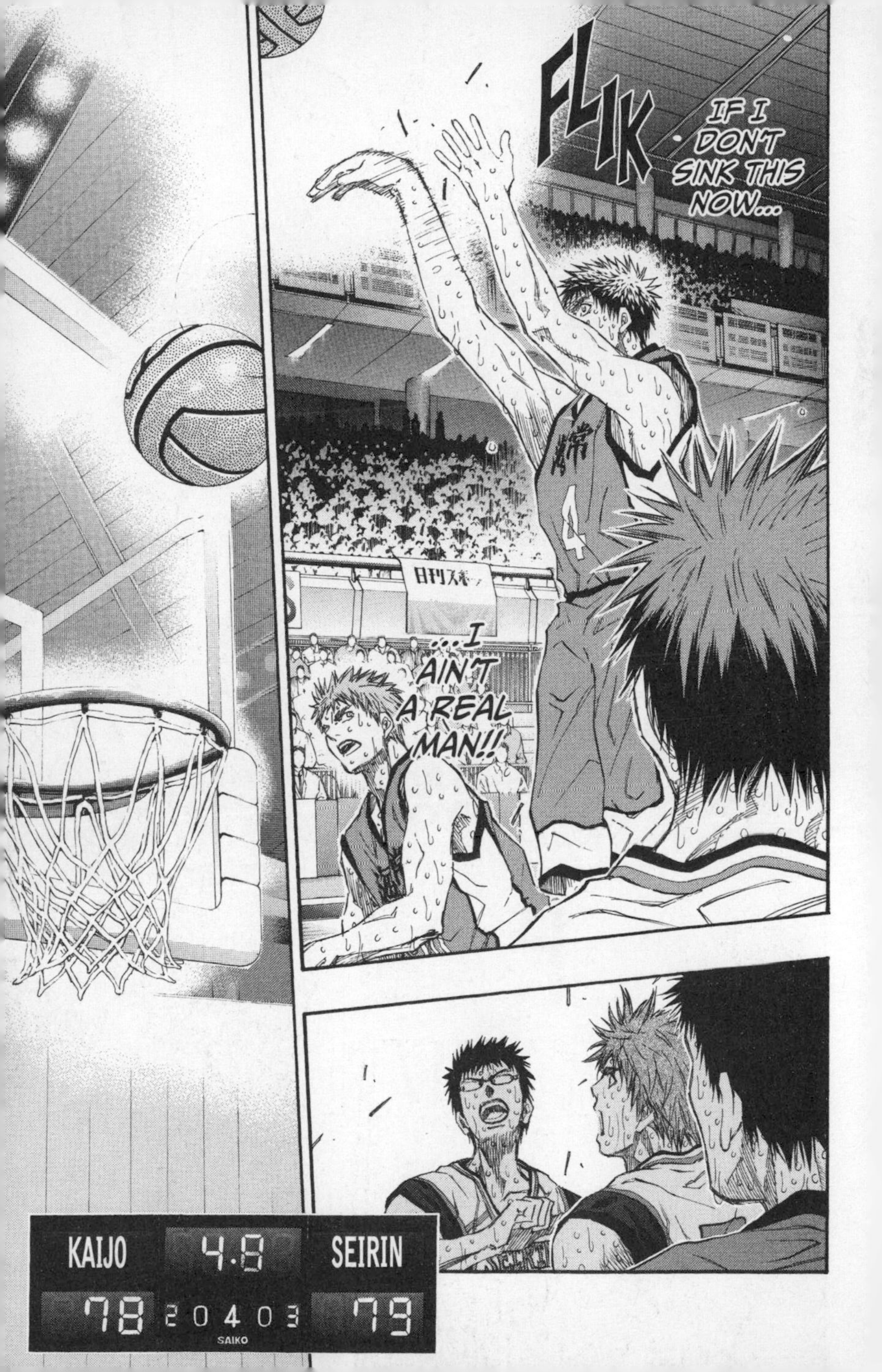
FLIK
IF I DON'T SINK THIS NOW...
...I AIN'T A REAL MAN!!
KAIJO
4.8
SEIRIN
78
20403
79
SAIKO

KUROKO'S BASKETBALL Q&A (W/ HALFWAY-DECENT ANSWERS)

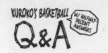

Q. **HOW DID ALEX GET INTO KAGAMI'S APARTMENT?**
(CAN'T HELP BEING CURIOUS ABOUT STUFF UNRELATED TO THE MAIN STORY)

A. SHE SAID "PLEASE <3" TO THE LANDLORD IN THE SEXIEST WAY POSSIBLE.

KUROKO'S BASKETBALL BLOOPERS TAKE 2

EAGLE SPEAR!!
POW
SCREWED UP AGAIN.
YOU GOTTA BE KIDDING ME.

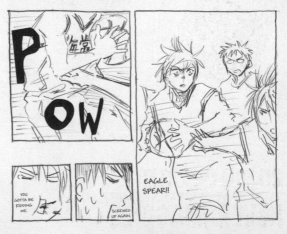

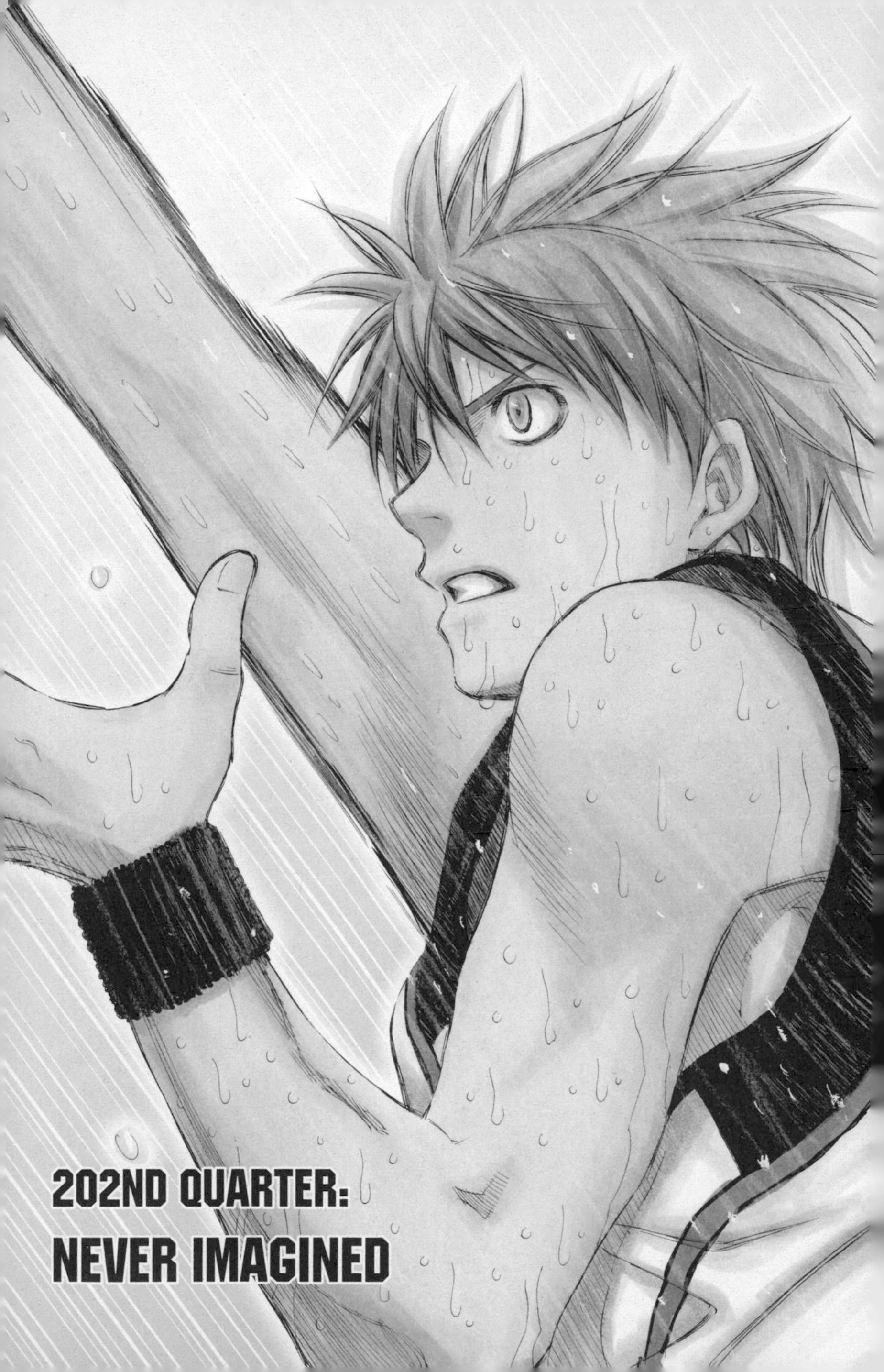
202ND QUARTER:
NEVER IMAGINED

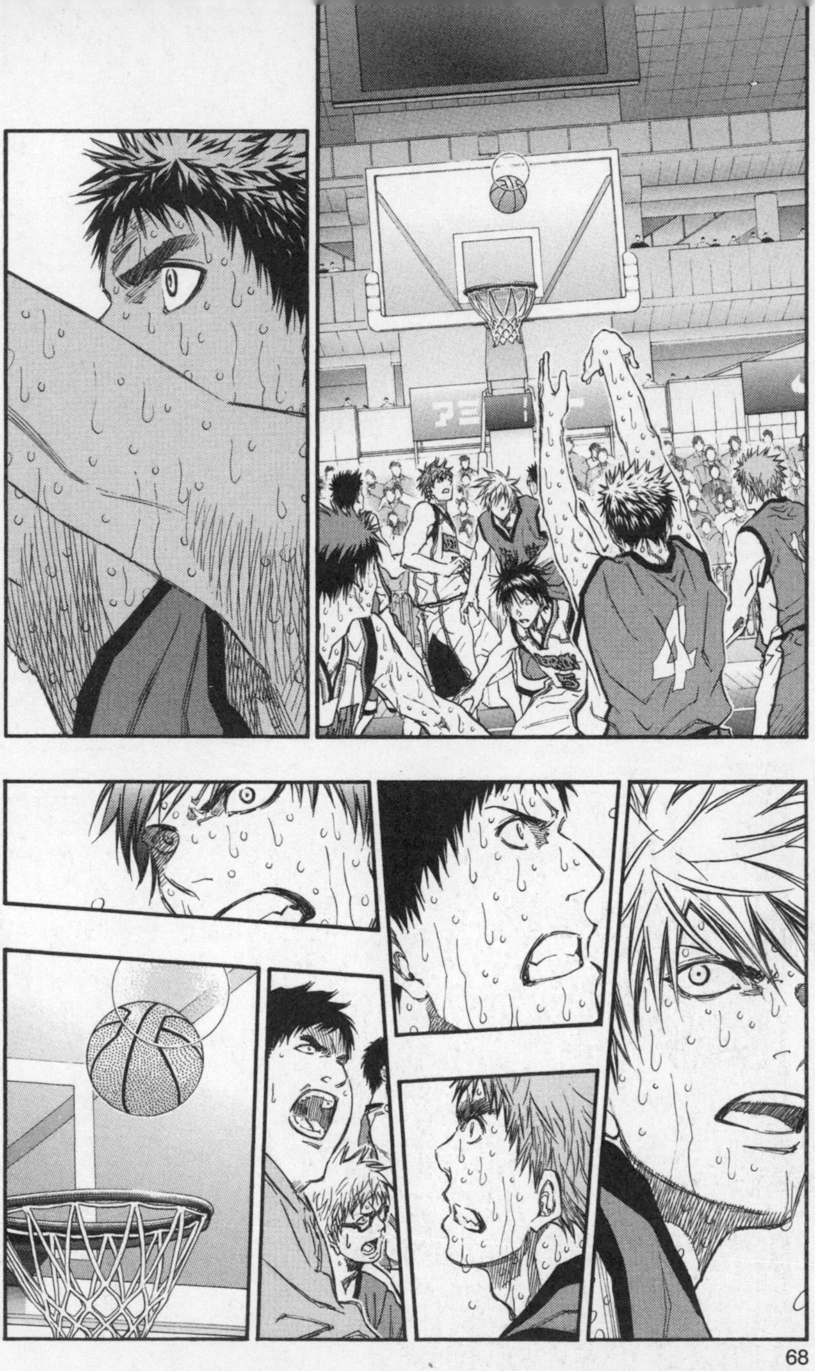

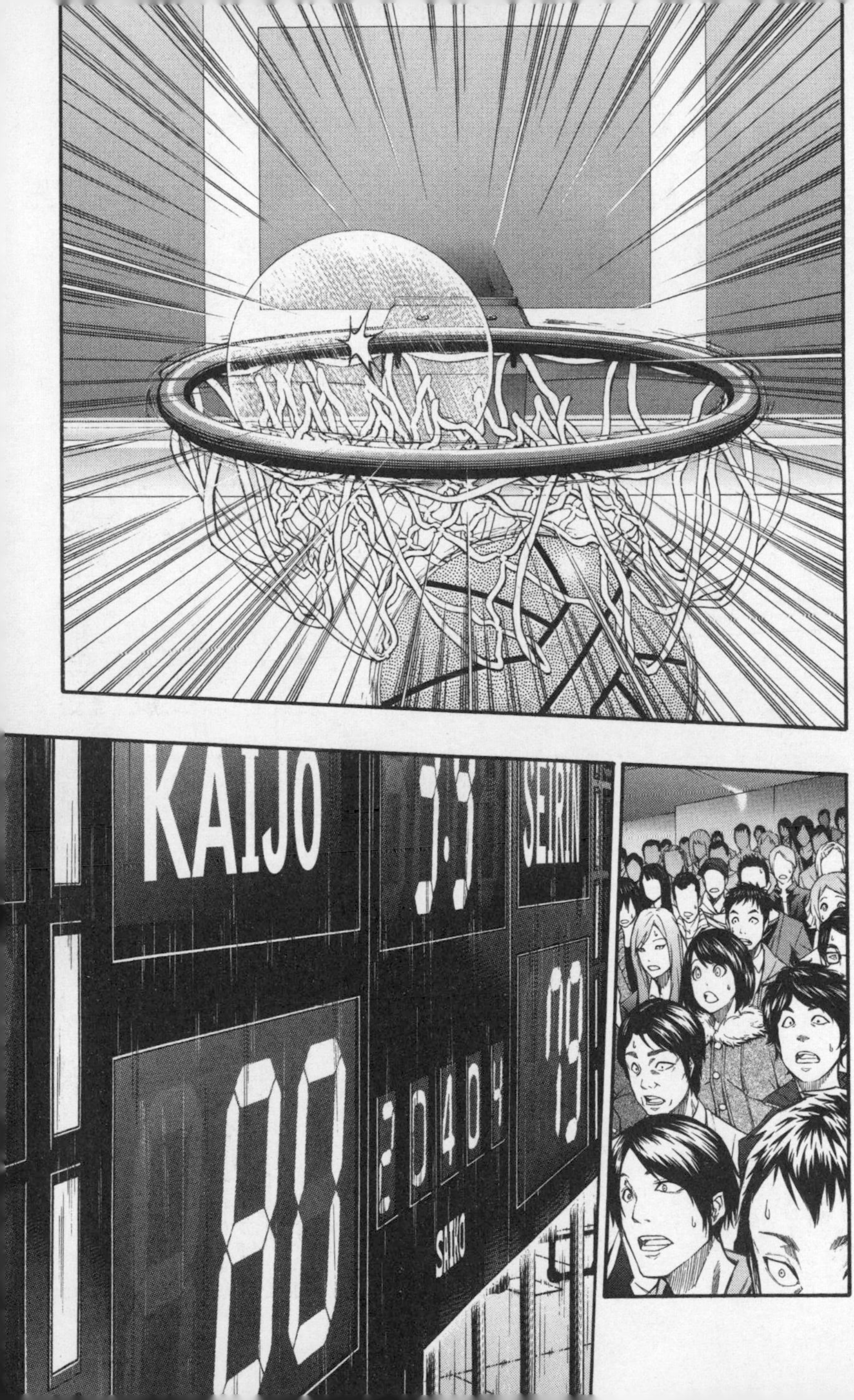
KAIJO
SEIRIN
SAIKO

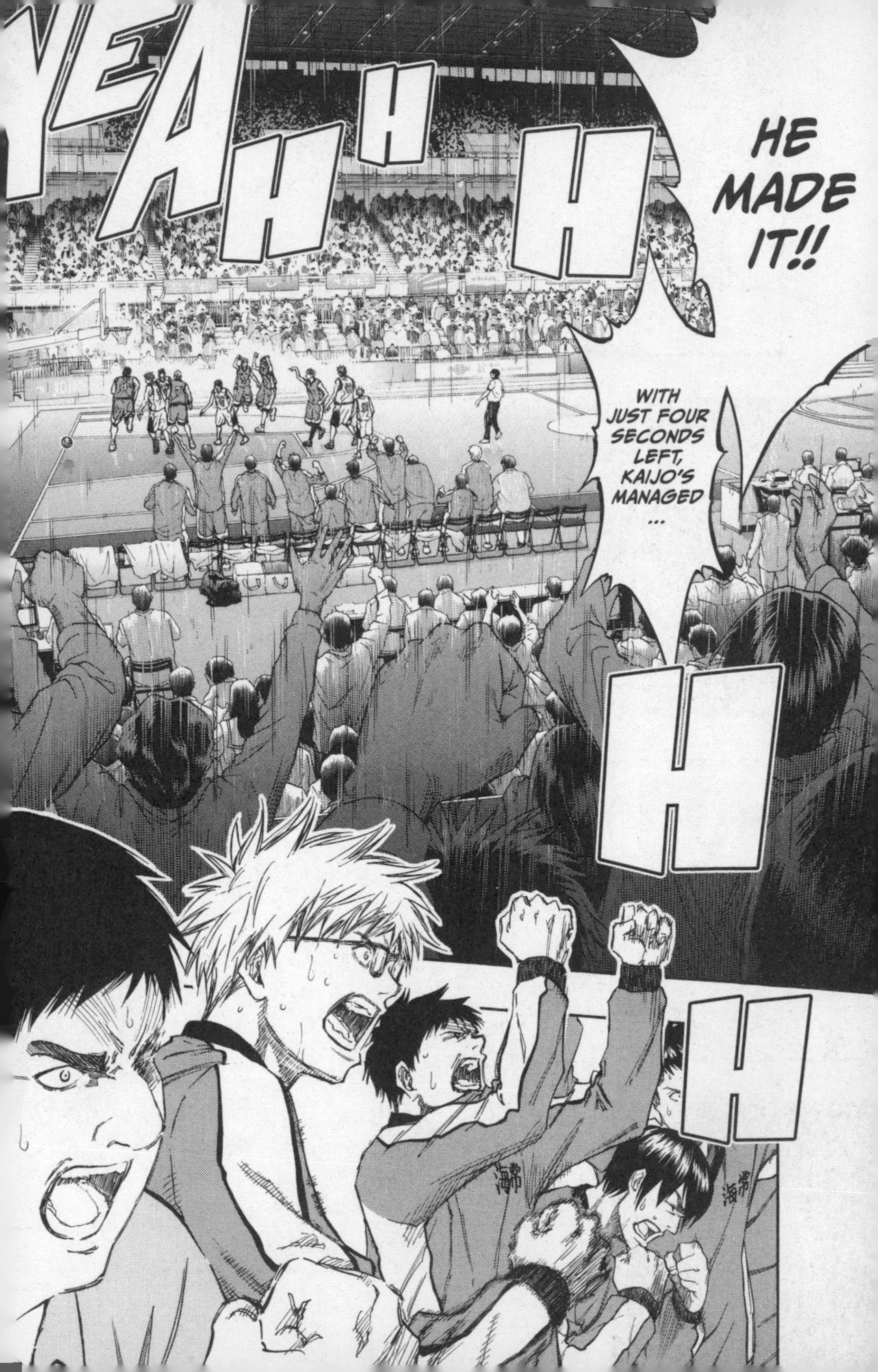
HE MADE IT!!
YEAHHHHHH
WITH JUST FOUR SECONDS LEFT, KAIJO'S MANAGED ...

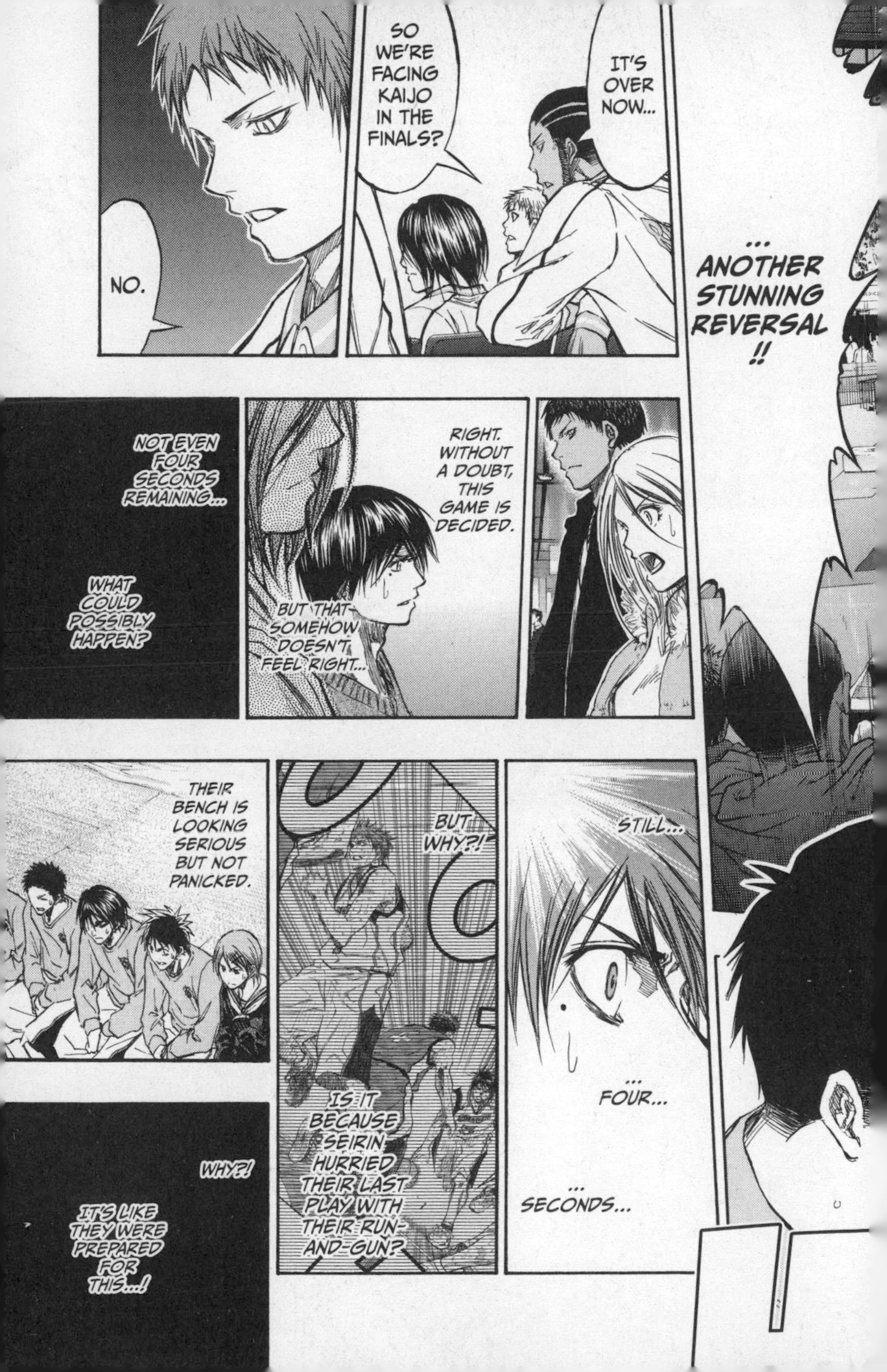
...ANOTHER STUNNING REVERSAL!!
IT'S OVER NOW...
SO WE'RE FACING KAIJO IN THE FINALS?
NO.
RIGHT. WITHOUT A DOUBT, THIS GAME IS DECIDED.
BUT THAT SOMEHOW DOESN'T FEEL RIGHT...
NOT EVEN FOUR SECONDS REMAINING...
WHAT COULD POSSIBLY HAPPEN?
STILL...
...FOUR...
...SECONDS...
BUT WHY?!
IS IT BECAUSE SEIRIN HURRIED THEIR LAST PLAY WITH THEIR RUN-AND-GUN?
THEIR BENCH IS LOOKING SERIOUS BUT NOT PANICKED.
WHY?!
IT'S LIKE THEY WERE PREPARED FOR THIS...!

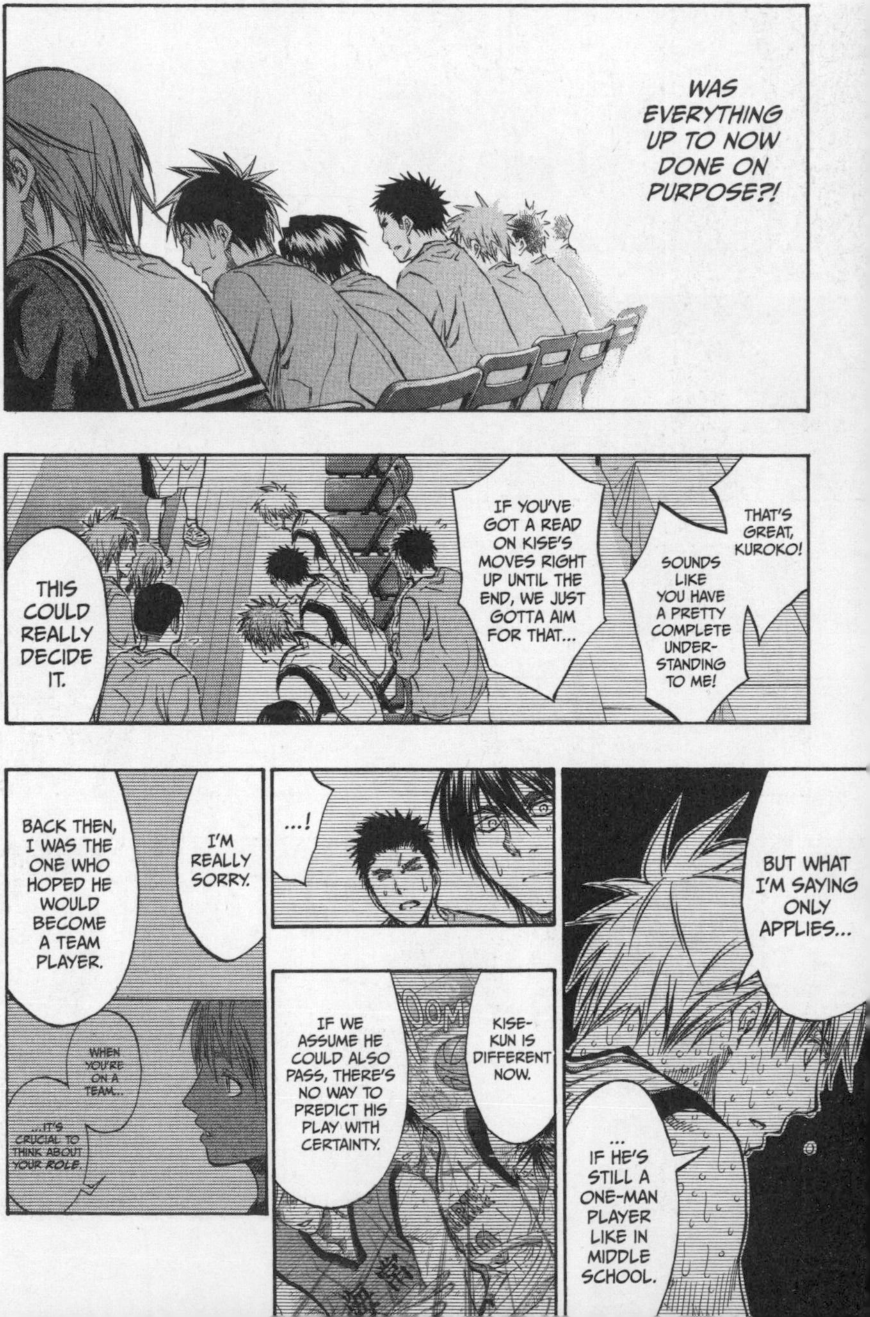
WAS EVERYTHING UP TO NOW DONE ON PURPOSE?!
THAT'S GREAT, KUROKO! SOUNDS LIKE YOU HAVE A PRETTY COMPLETE UNDER-STANDING TO ME!
IF YOU'VE GOT A READ ON KISE'S MOVES RIGHT UP UNTIL THE END, WE JUST GOTTA AIM FOR THAT...
THIS COULD REALLY DECIDE IT.
BUT WHAT I'M SAYING ONLY APPLIES...
... IF HE'S STILL A ONE-MAN PLAYER LIKE IN MIDDLE SCHOOL.
...!
KISE-KUN IS DIFFERENT NOW.
IF WE ASSUME HE COULD ALSO PASS, THERE'S NO WAY TO PREDICT HIS PLAY WITH CERTAINTY.
I'M REALLY SORRY.
BACK THEN, I WAS THE ONE WHO HOPED HE WOULD BECOME A TEAM PLAYER.
WHEN YOU'RE ON A TEAM...
...IT'S CRUCIAL TO THINK ABOUT YOUR *ROLE*.

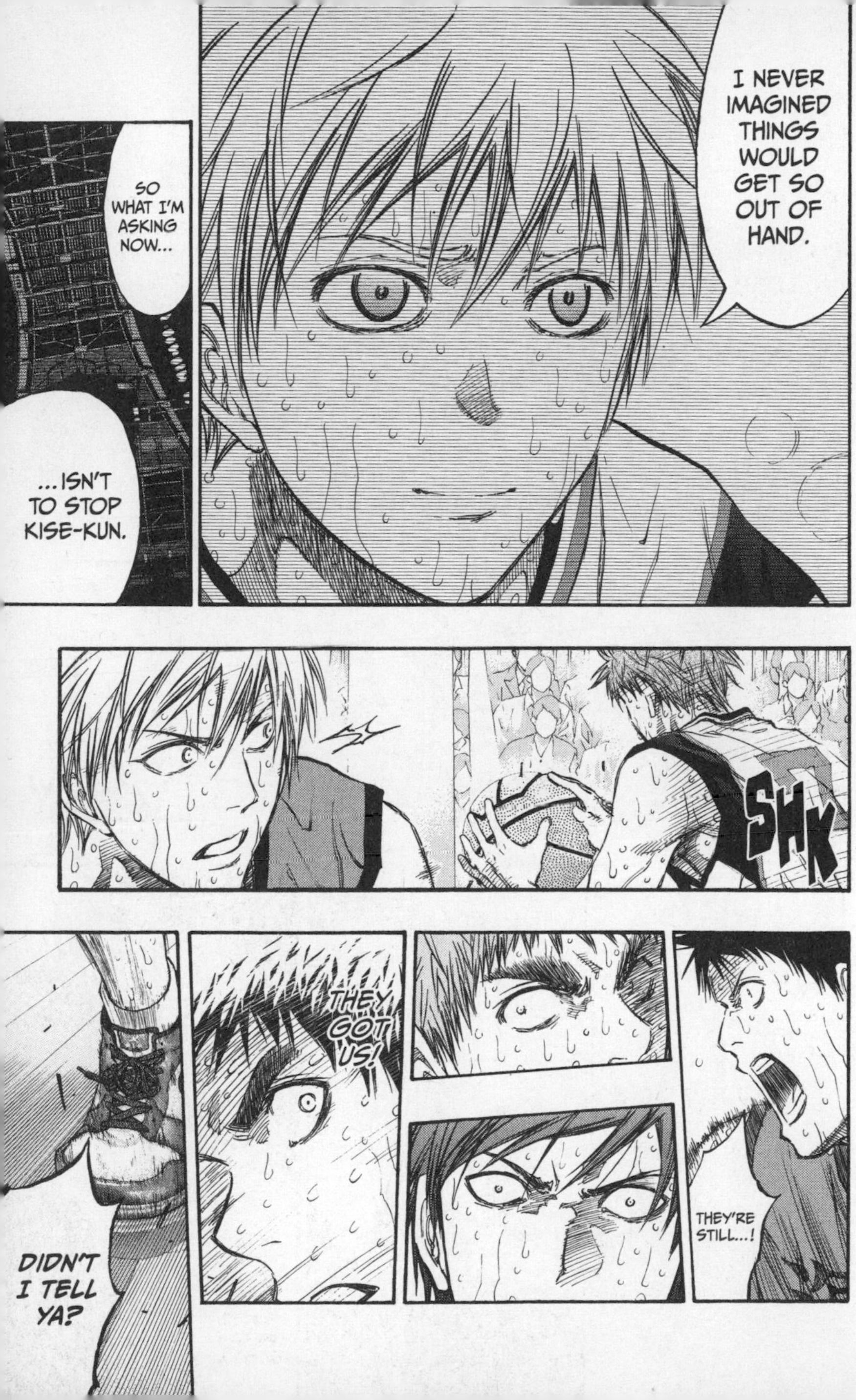
I NEVER IMAGINED THINGS WOULD GET SO OUT OF HAND.
SO WHAT I'M ASKING NOW...
...ISN'T TO STOP KISE-KUN.
SHK
THEY'RE STILL...!
THEY GOT US!
DIDN'T I TELL YA?

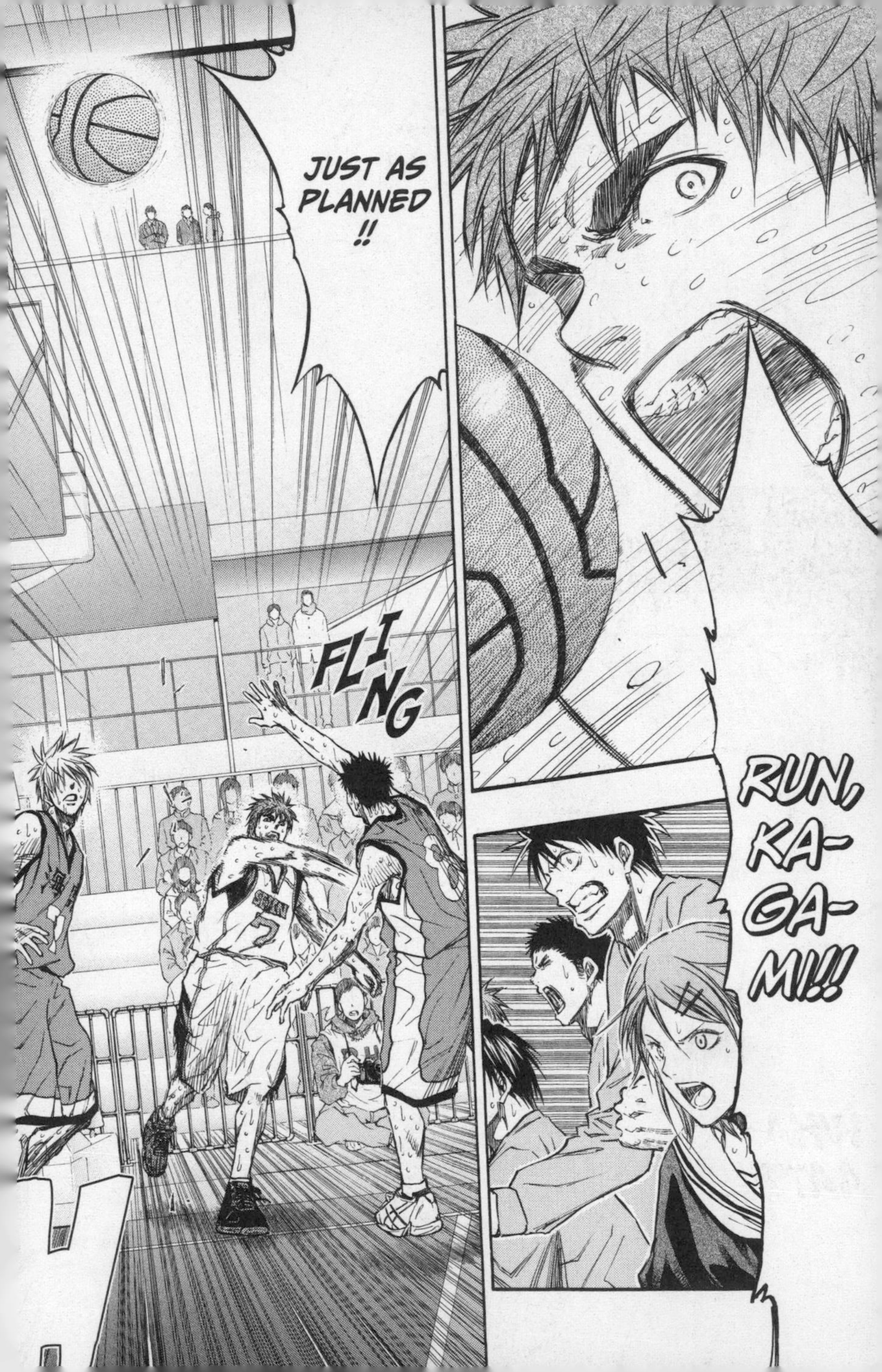
RUN, KA-GA-MI!!
JUST AS PLANNED !!
FLING

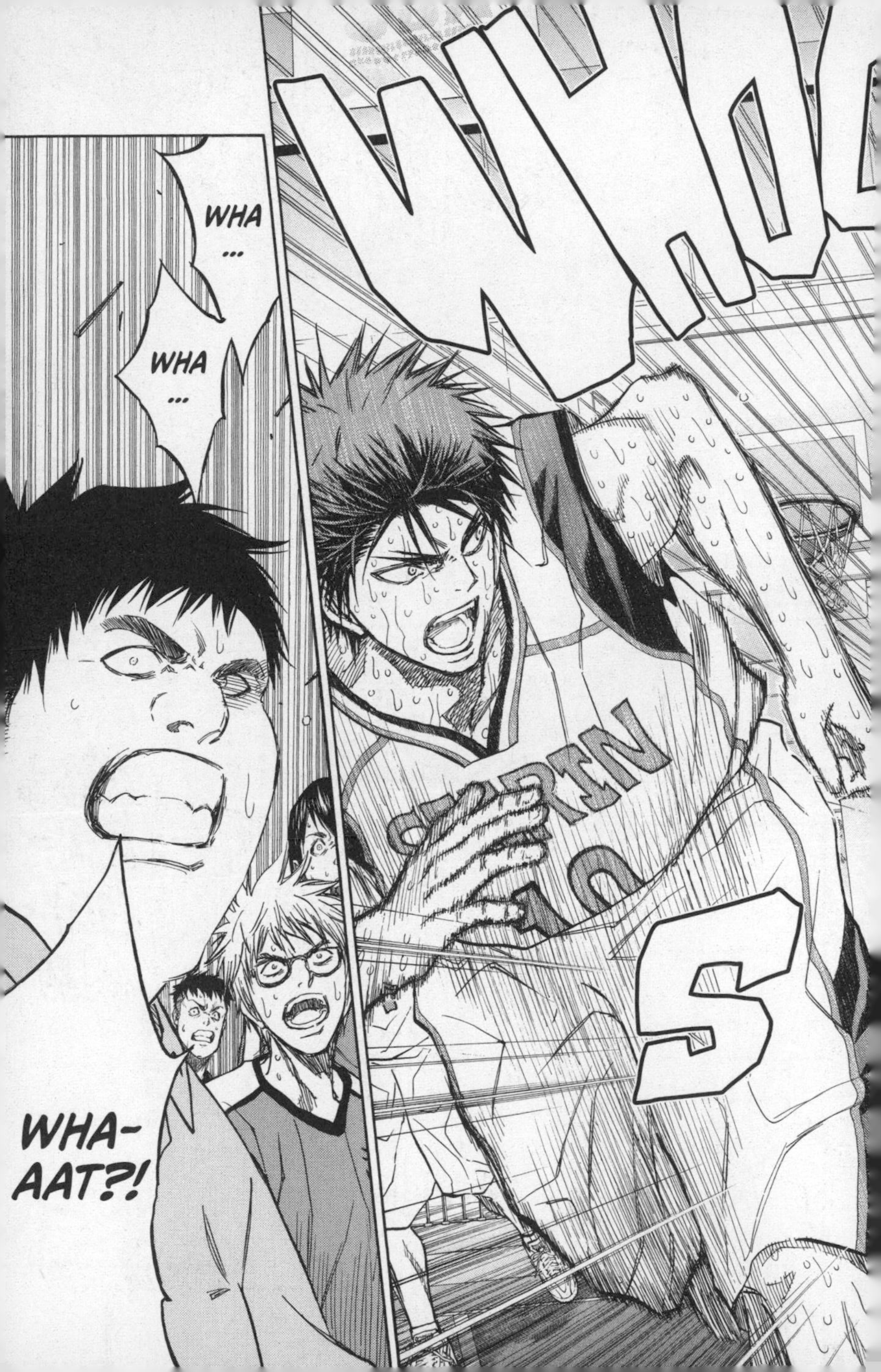
WHO
S
WHA ...
WHA ...
WHA-AAT?!

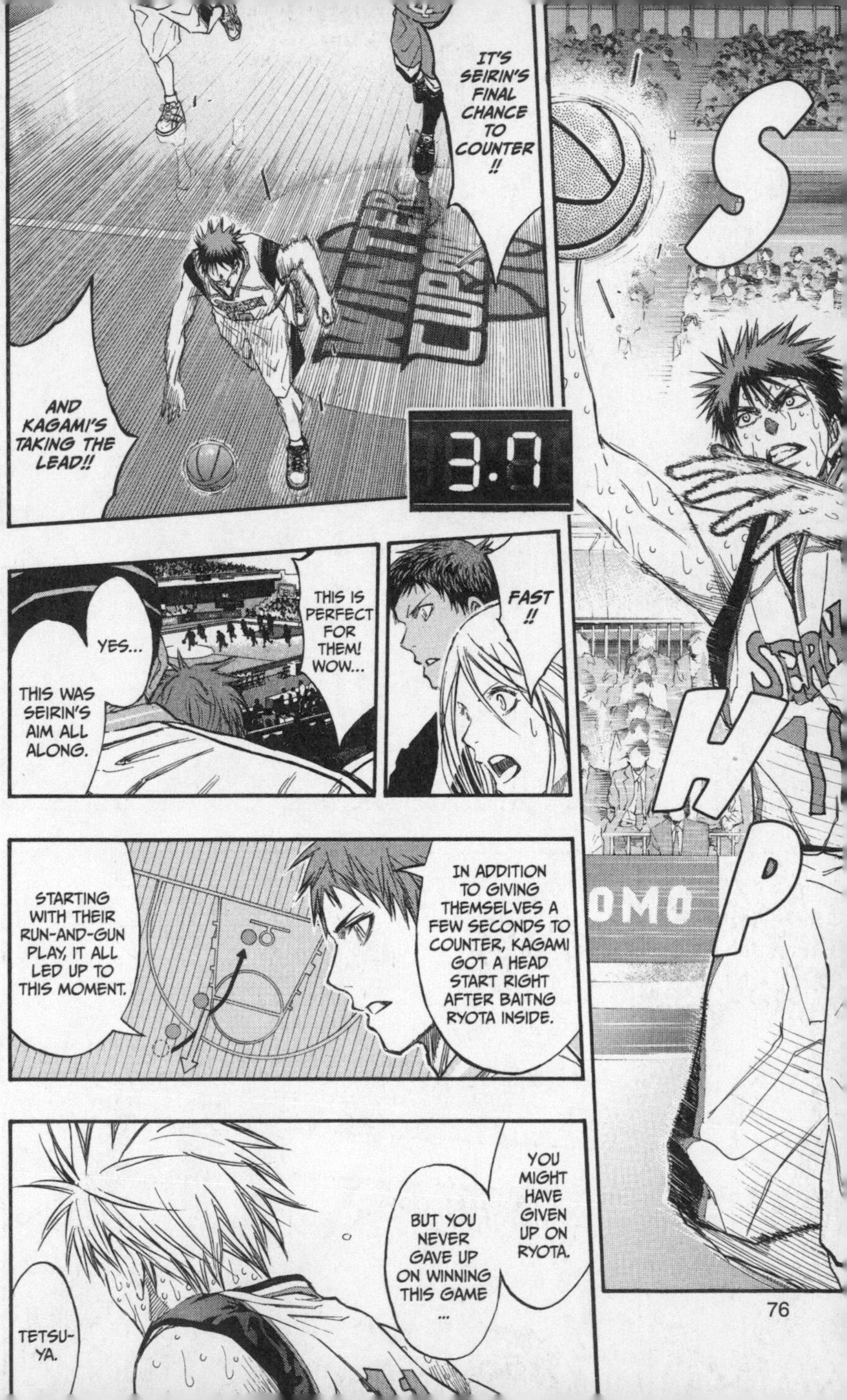
S
H
P
IT'S SEIRIN'S FINAL CHANCE TO COUNTER!!
AND KAGAMI'S TAKING THE LEAD!!
3.7
FAST!!
THIS IS PERFECT FOR THEM! WOW...
YES...
THIS WAS SEIRIN'S AIM ALL ALONG.
IN ADDITION TO GIVING THEMSELVES A FEW SECONDS TO COUNTER, KAGAMI GOT A HEAD START RIGHT AFTER BAITNG RYOTA INSIDE.
STARTING WITH THEIR RUN-AND-GUN PLAY, IT ALL LED UP TO THIS MOMENT.
YOU MIGHT HAVE GIVEN UP ON RYOTA.
BUT YOU NEVER GAVE UP ON WINNING THIS GAME...
TETSU-YA.

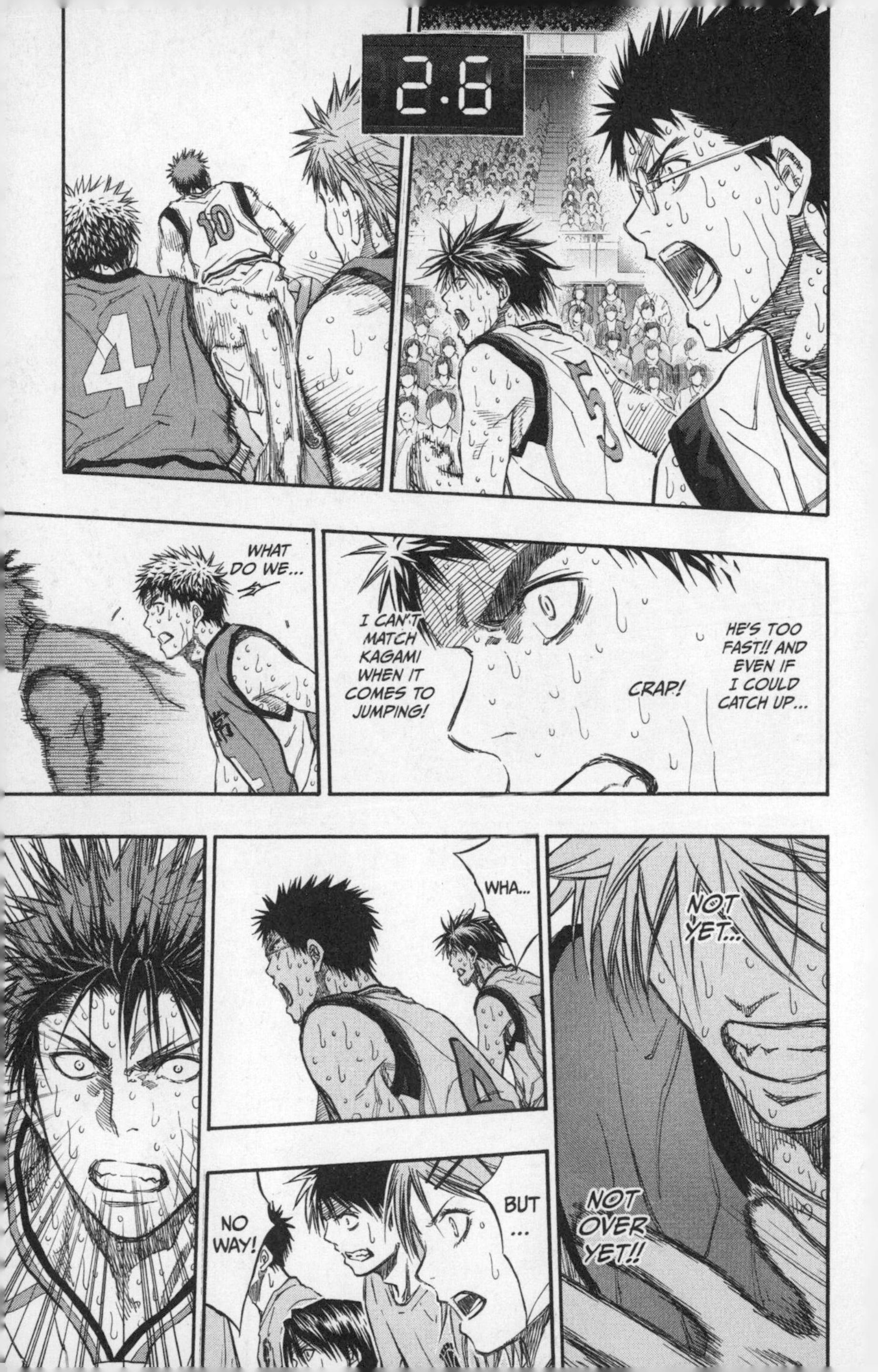
2.6
HE'S TOO FAST!! AND EVEN IF I COULD CATCH UP...
CRAP!
I CAN'T MATCH KAGAMI WHEN IT COMES TO JUMPING!
WHAT DO WE...
NOT YET...
NOT OVER YET!!
WHA...
BUT ...
NO WAY!

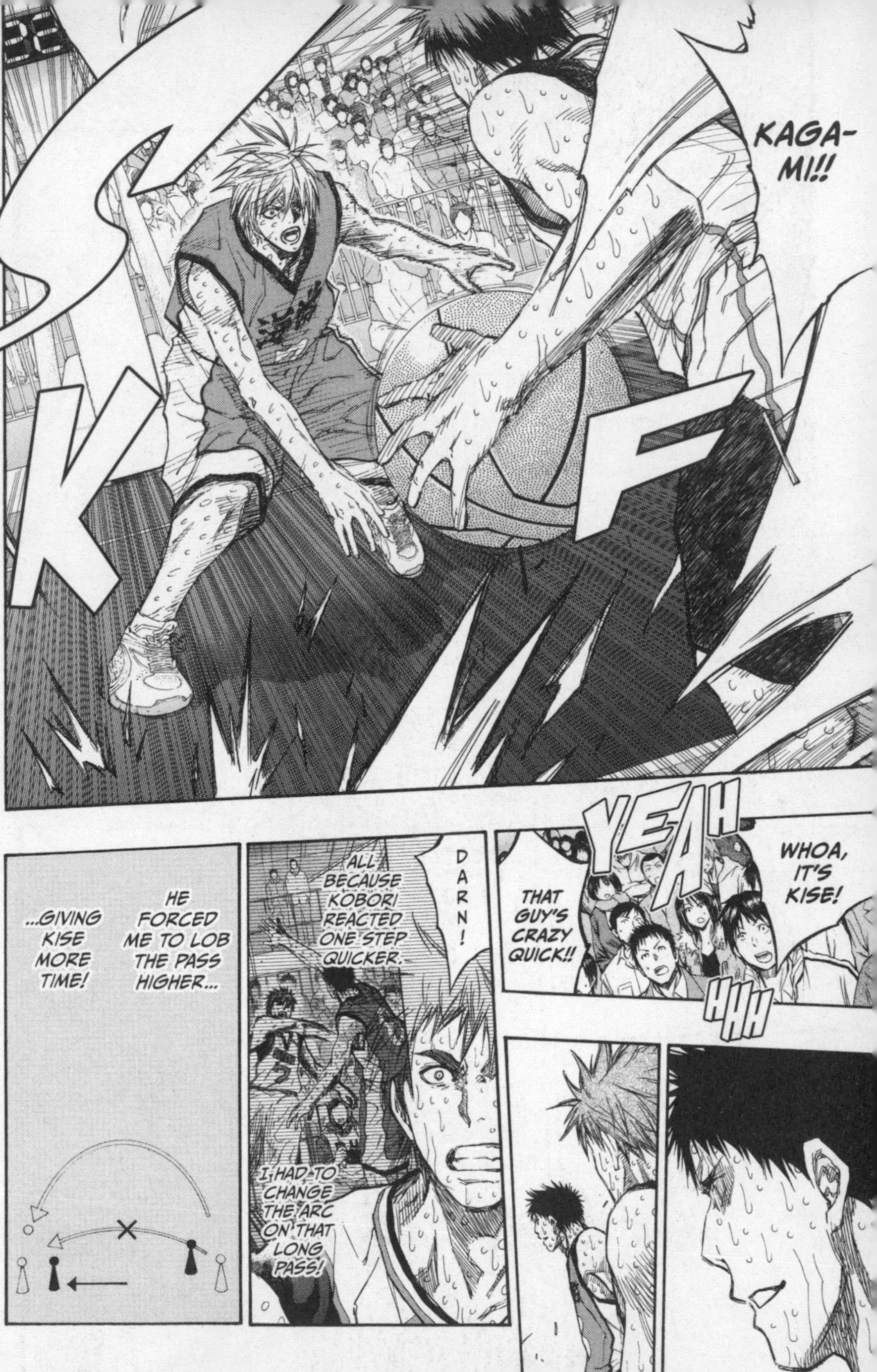
KAGA-MI!!
YEAH
WHOA, IT'S KISE!
THAT GUY'S CRAZY QUICK!!
HHH
DARN!
ALL BECAUSE KOBORI REACTED ONE STEP QUICKER.
I HAD TO CHANGE THE ARC ON THAT LONG PASS!
HE FORCED ME TO LOB THE PASS HIGHER...
...GIVING KISE MORE TIME!

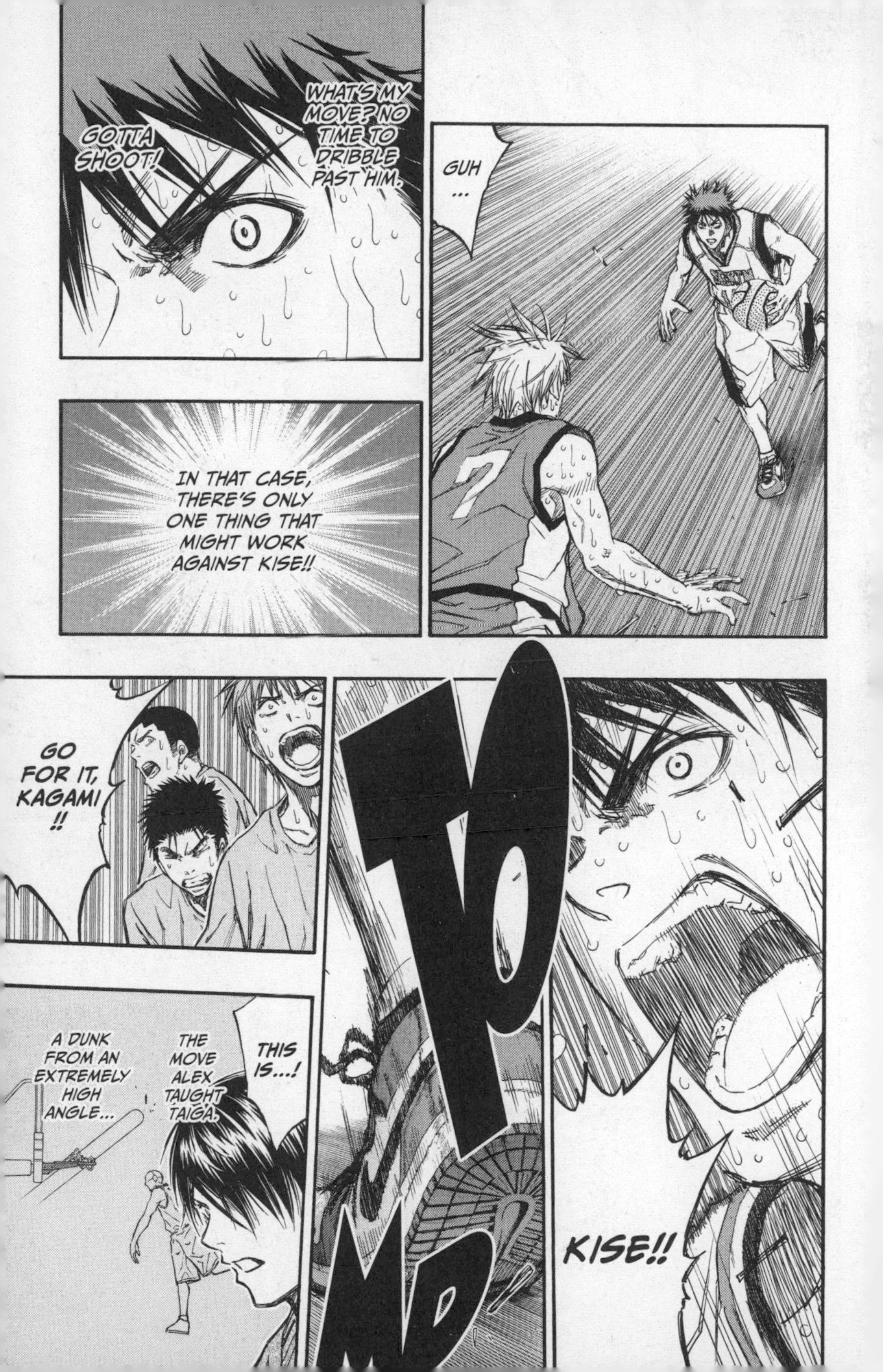
GUH ...
WHAT'S MY MOVE? NO TIME TO DRIBBLE PAST HIM.
GOTTA SHOOT!
IN THAT CASE, THERE'S ONLY ONE THING THAT MIGHT WORK AGAINST KISE!!
KISE!!
TOMP
GO FOR IT, KAGAMI !!
THIS IS...!
THE MOVE ALEX TAUGHT TAIGA.
A DUNK FROM AN EXTREMELY HIGH ANGLE...

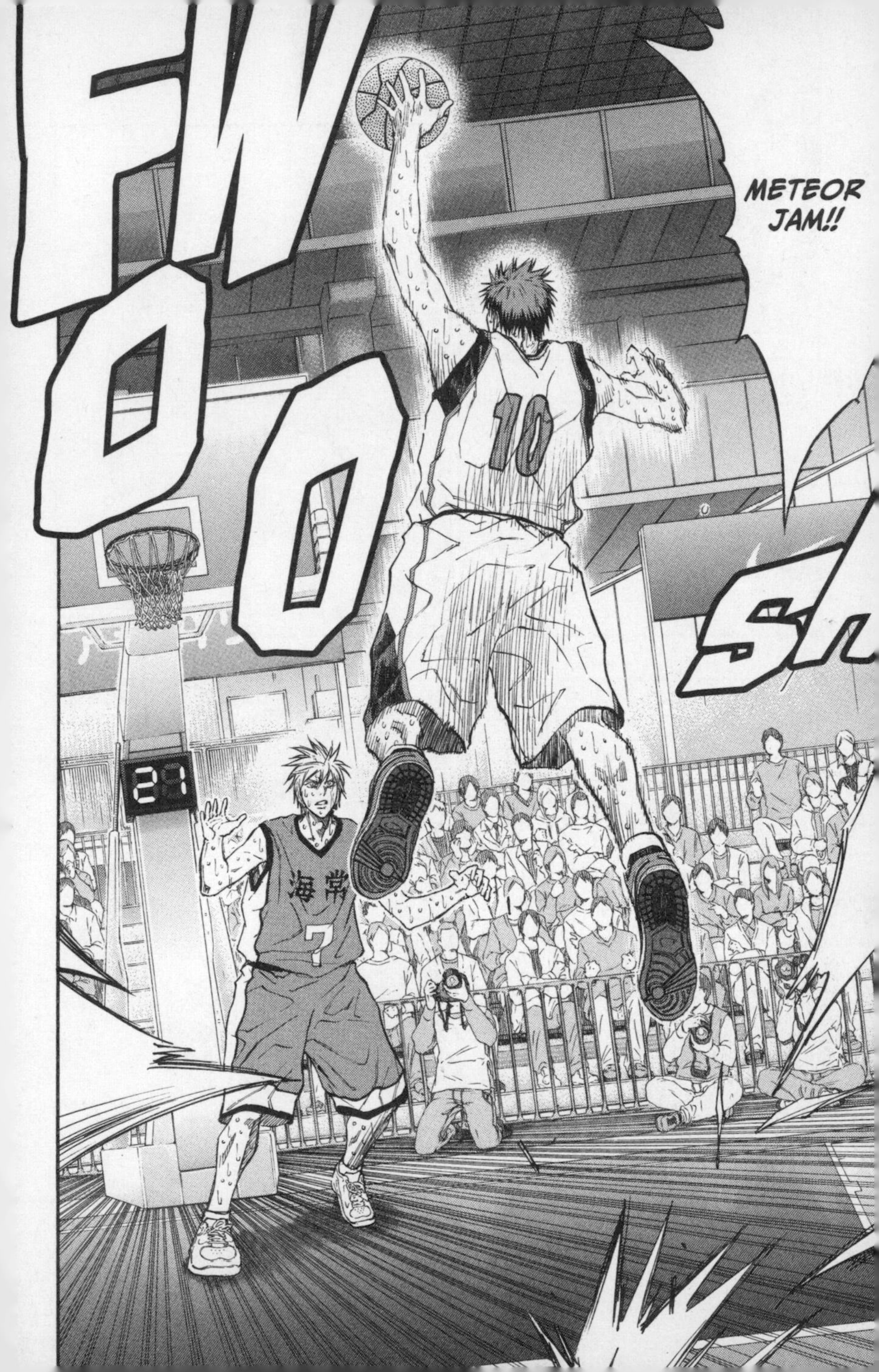
METEOR
JAM!!
FWOO
海常

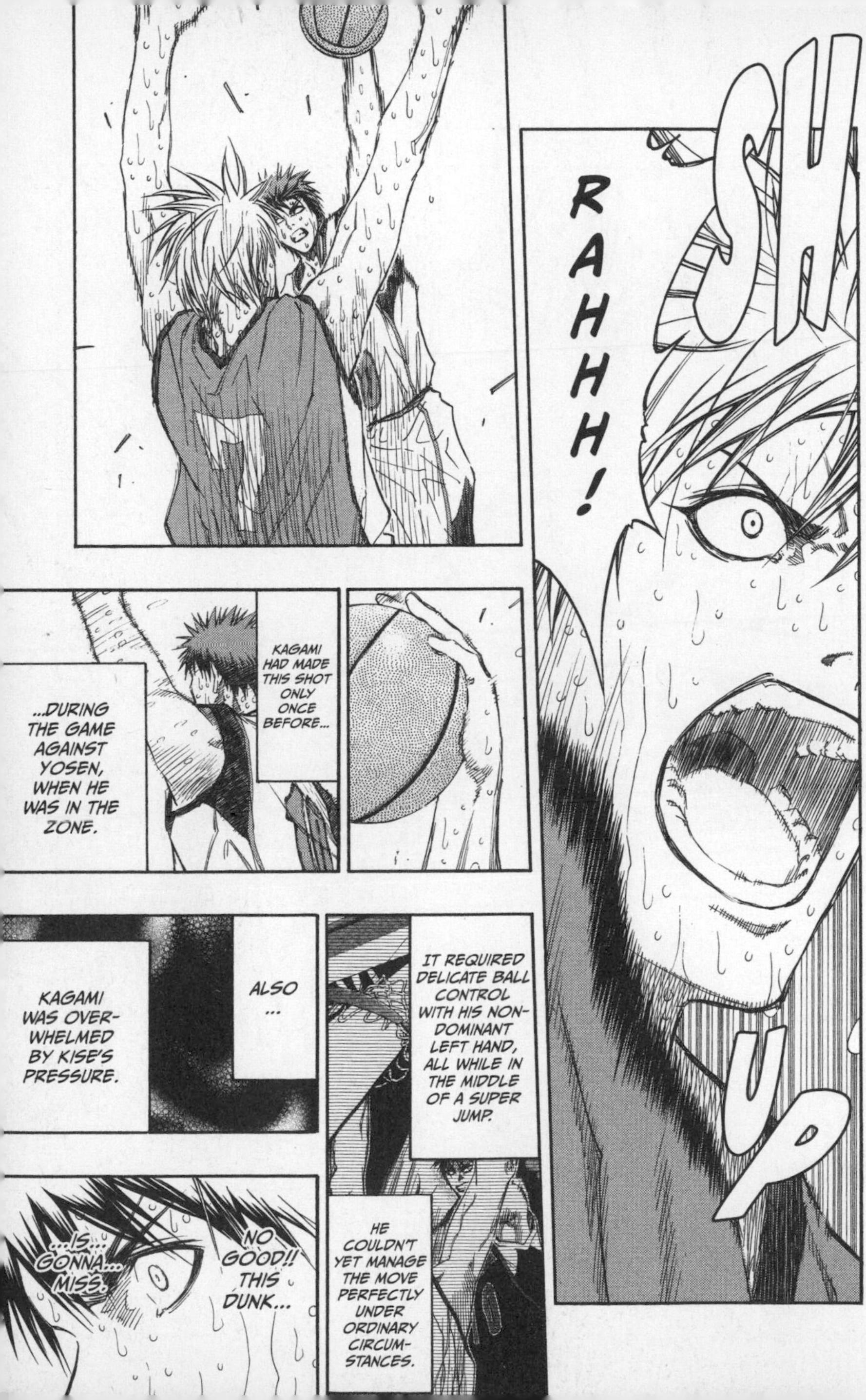
SH
RAHHHH!
UP
KAGAMI HAD MADE THIS SHOT ONLY ONCE BEFORE...
...DURING THE GAME AGAINST YOSEN, WHEN HE WAS IN THE ZONE.
IT REQUIRED DELICATE BALL CONTROL WITH HIS NON-DOMINANT LEFT HAND, ALL WHILE IN THE MIDDLE OF A SUPER JUMP.
HE COULDN'T YET MANAGE THE MOVE PERFECTLY UNDER ORDINARY CIRCUM-STANCES.
ALSO ...
KAGAMI WAS OVER-WHELMED BY KISE'S PRESSURE.
NO GOOD!! THIS DUNK...
...IS... GONNA... MISS.

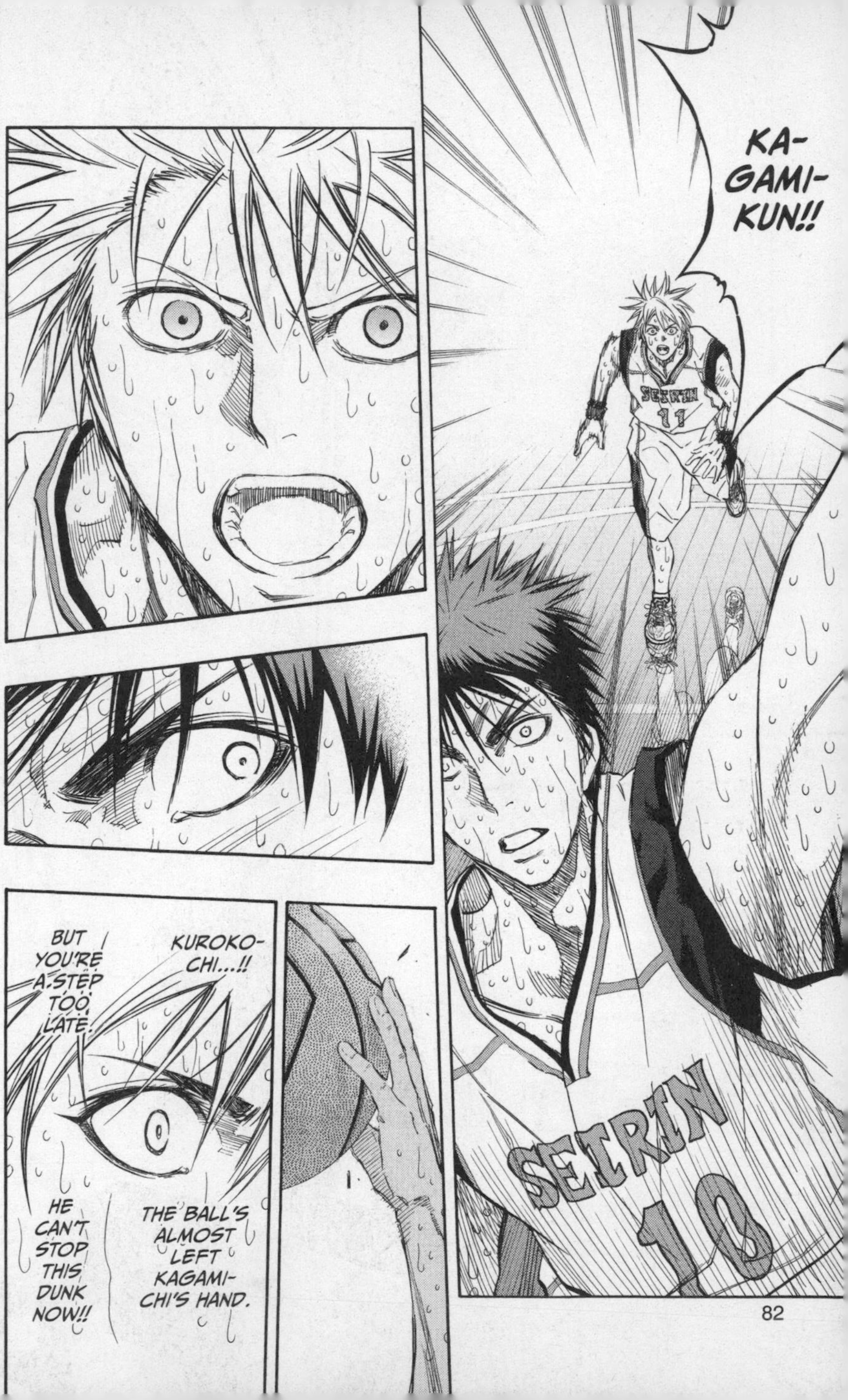
KA-GAMI-KUN!!
KUROKO-CHI...!!
BUT YOU'RE A STEP TOO LATE.
THE BALL'S ALMOST LEFT KAGAMI-CHI'S HAND.
HE CAN'T STOP THIS DUNK NOW!!

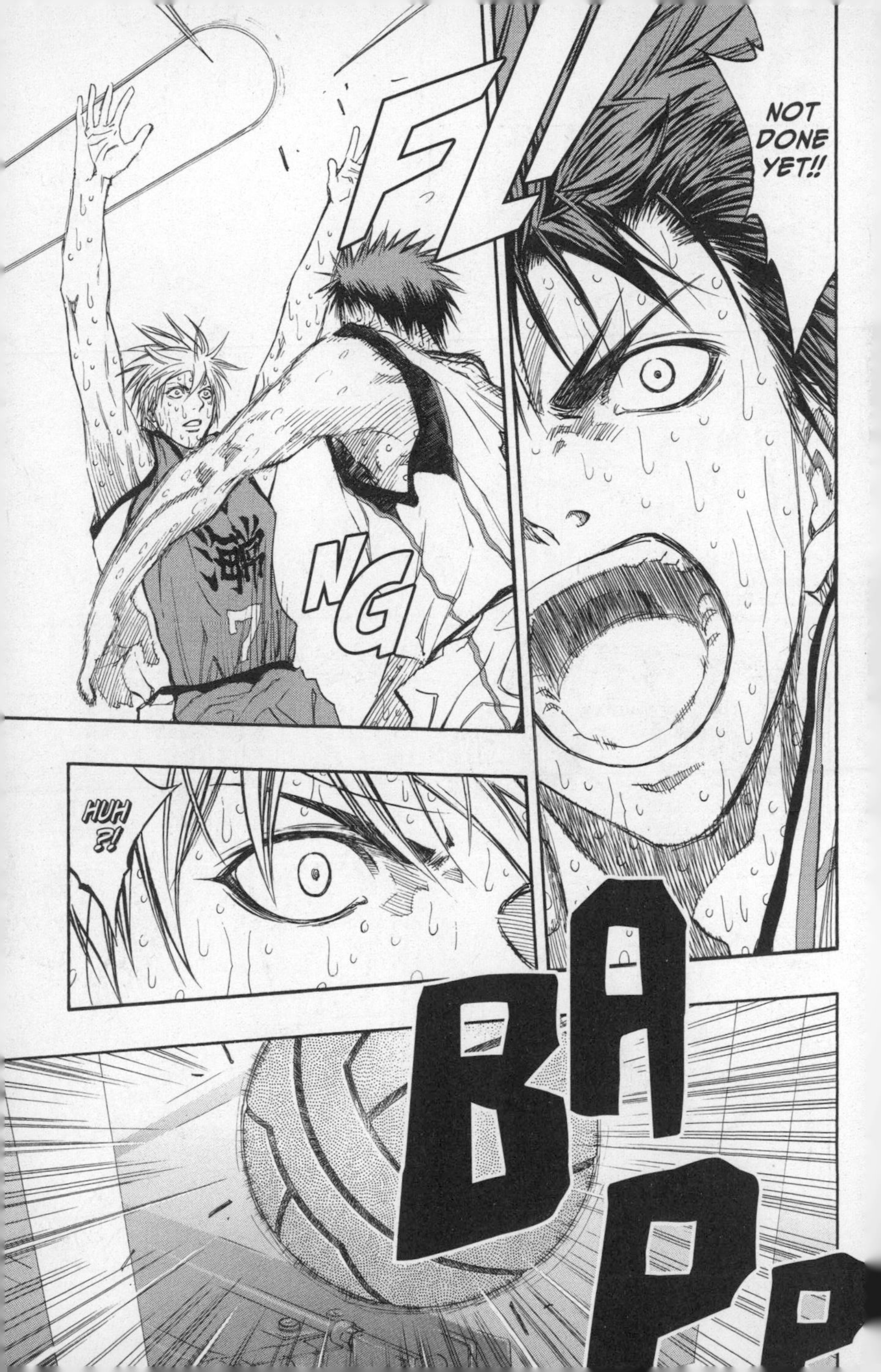
NOT DONE YET!!
NG
HUH ?!
BAPP

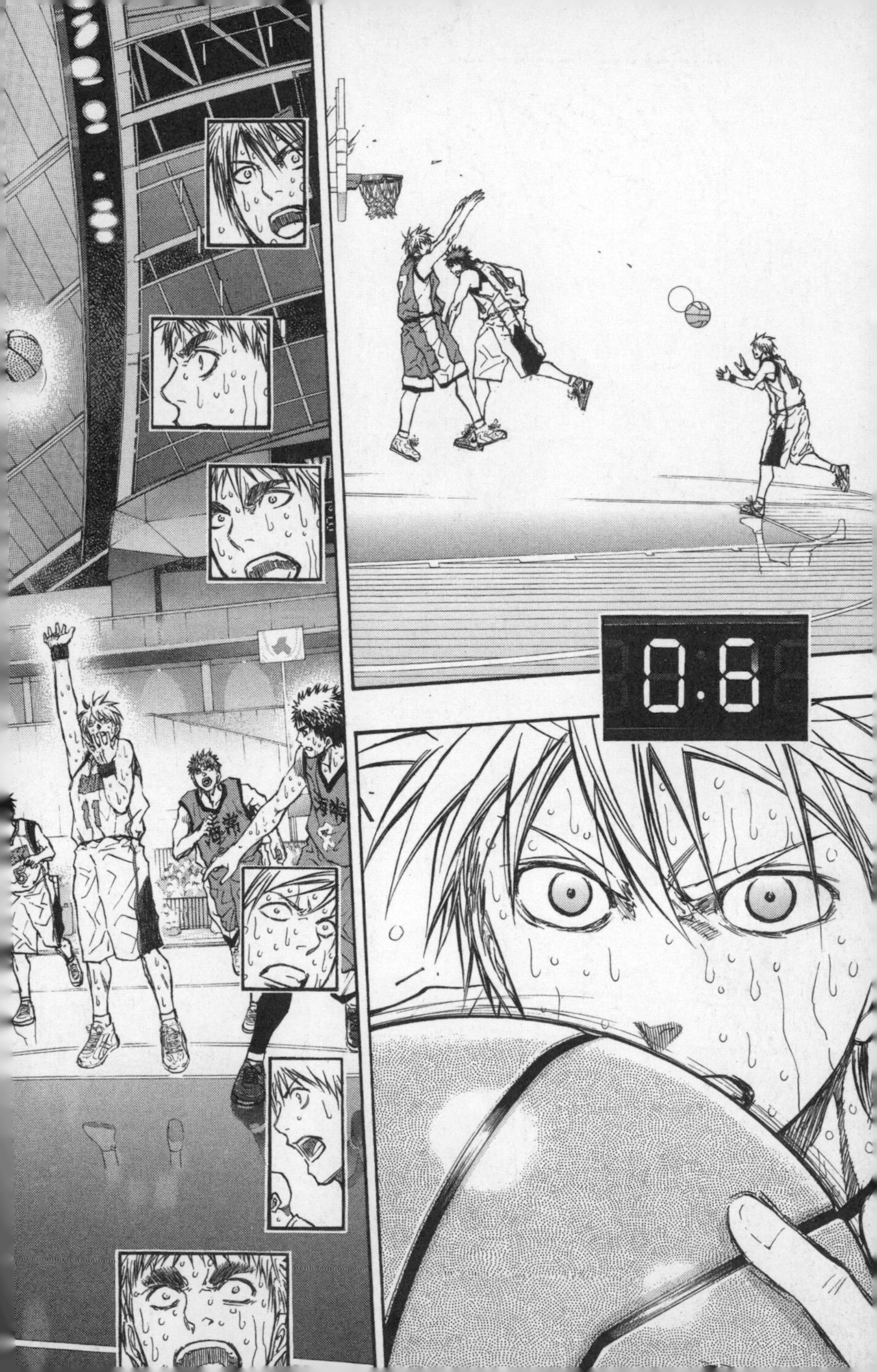
0.6

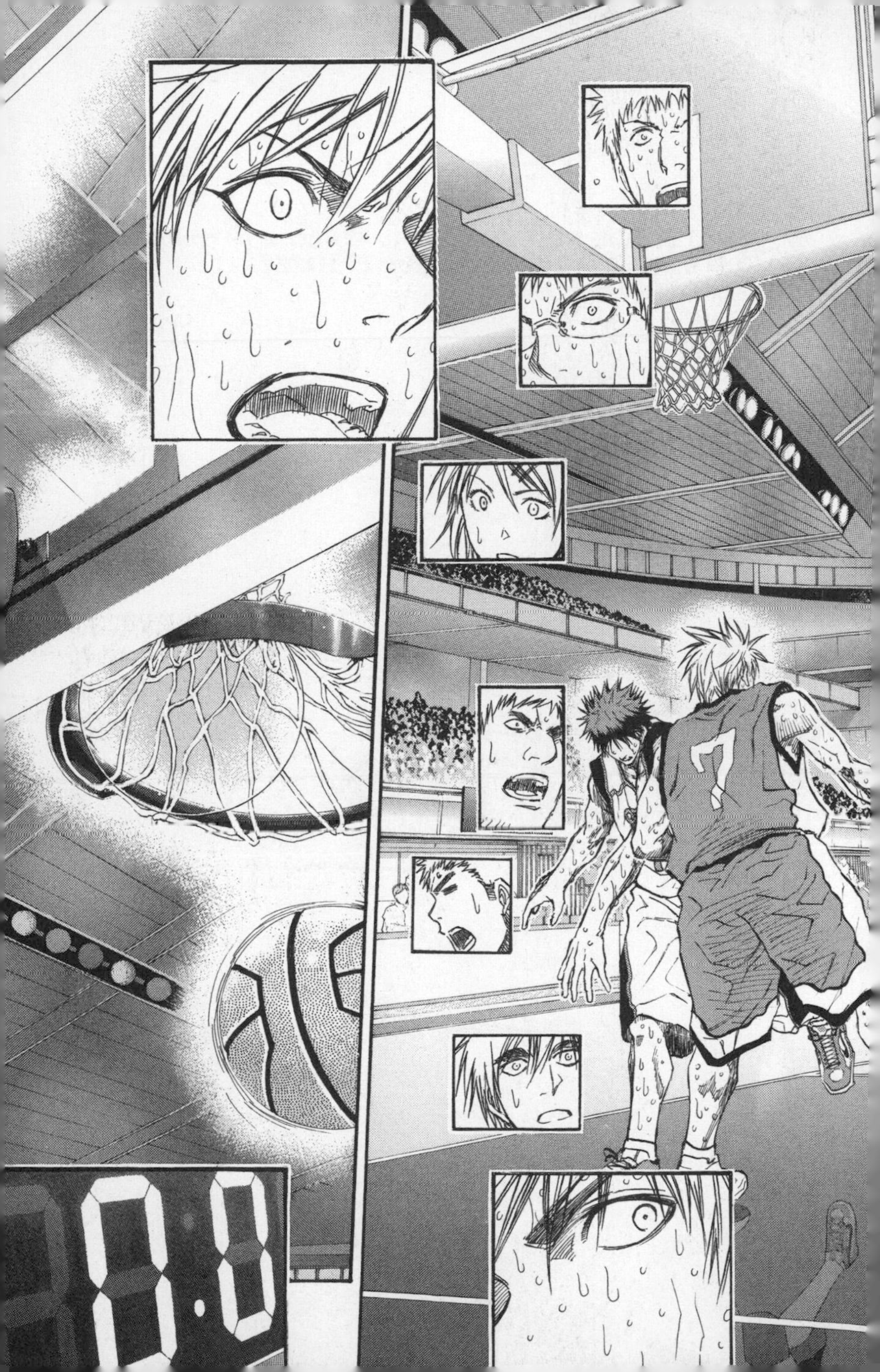
0.0

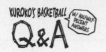

KUROKO'S BASKETBALL Q&A W/ HALFWAY-DECENT ANSWERS

Q. WHAT FOODS DO EACH OF THE MIRACLE GENERATION GUYS (PLUS MOMOI-SAN) REALLY HATE?
(KURO NUT from OSAKA)

A. AKASHI: BROWN SEAWEED (ALL SEAWEED, REALLY)
AOMINE: *GOYA* (TOO BITTER)
KISE: EEL (SWALLOWED A BONE ONCE)
KUROKO: COLA (CAN'T DEAL WITH CARBONATION)
MIDORIMA: *NATTO* (CAN'T STAND THE SMELL)
MURASAKIBARA: CARROTS (JUST DOESN'T LIKE THEM)
MOMOI: KIMCHI (TOO SPICY)

KUROKO'S BASKETBALL BLOOPERS TAKE 7

STILL...
... FOUR...
... SECONDS...
ENOUGH TIME TO EAT SIX TASTY STICKS!
STOP MESSING AROUND, ATSUSHI...
BUT THAT'S REALLY IMPRESSIVE!!
HOW DO YOU DO IT?!

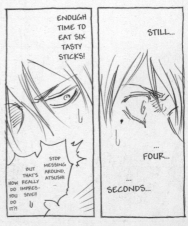

203RD QUARTER: A GREAT PLAYER

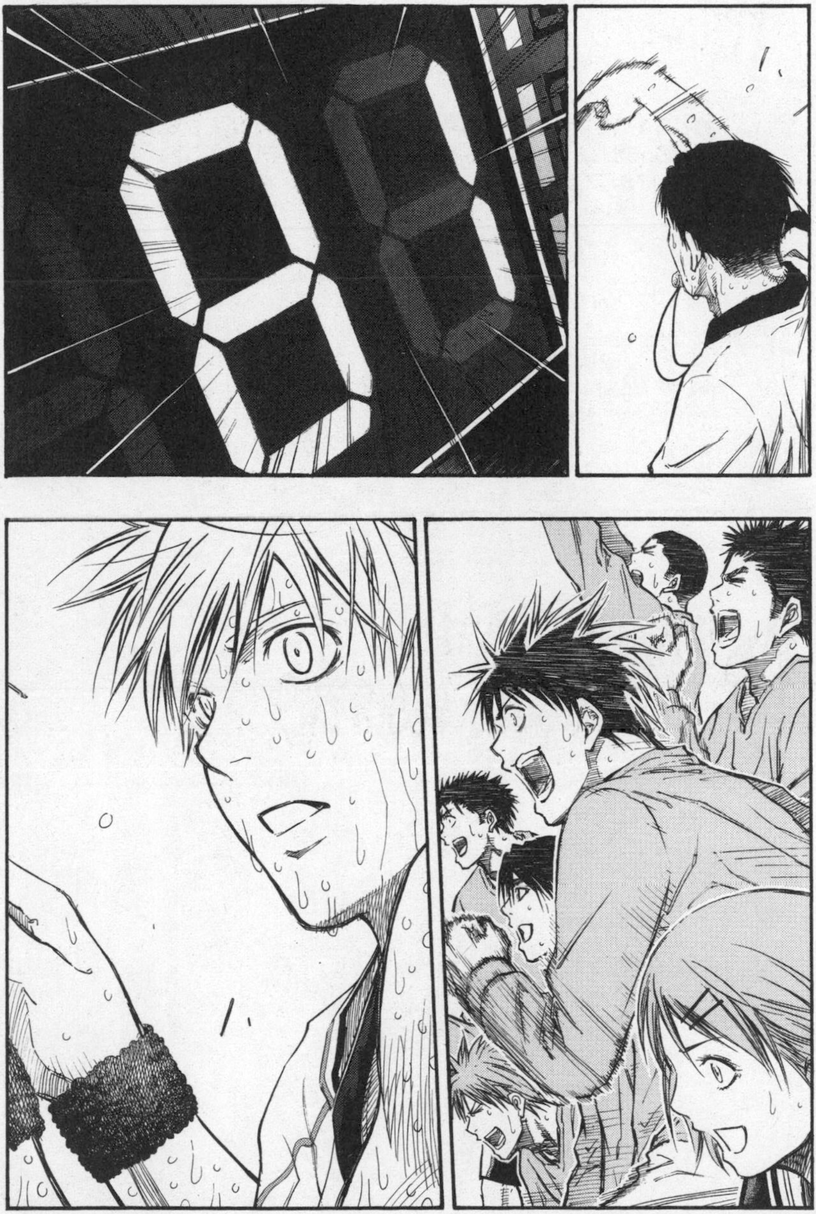

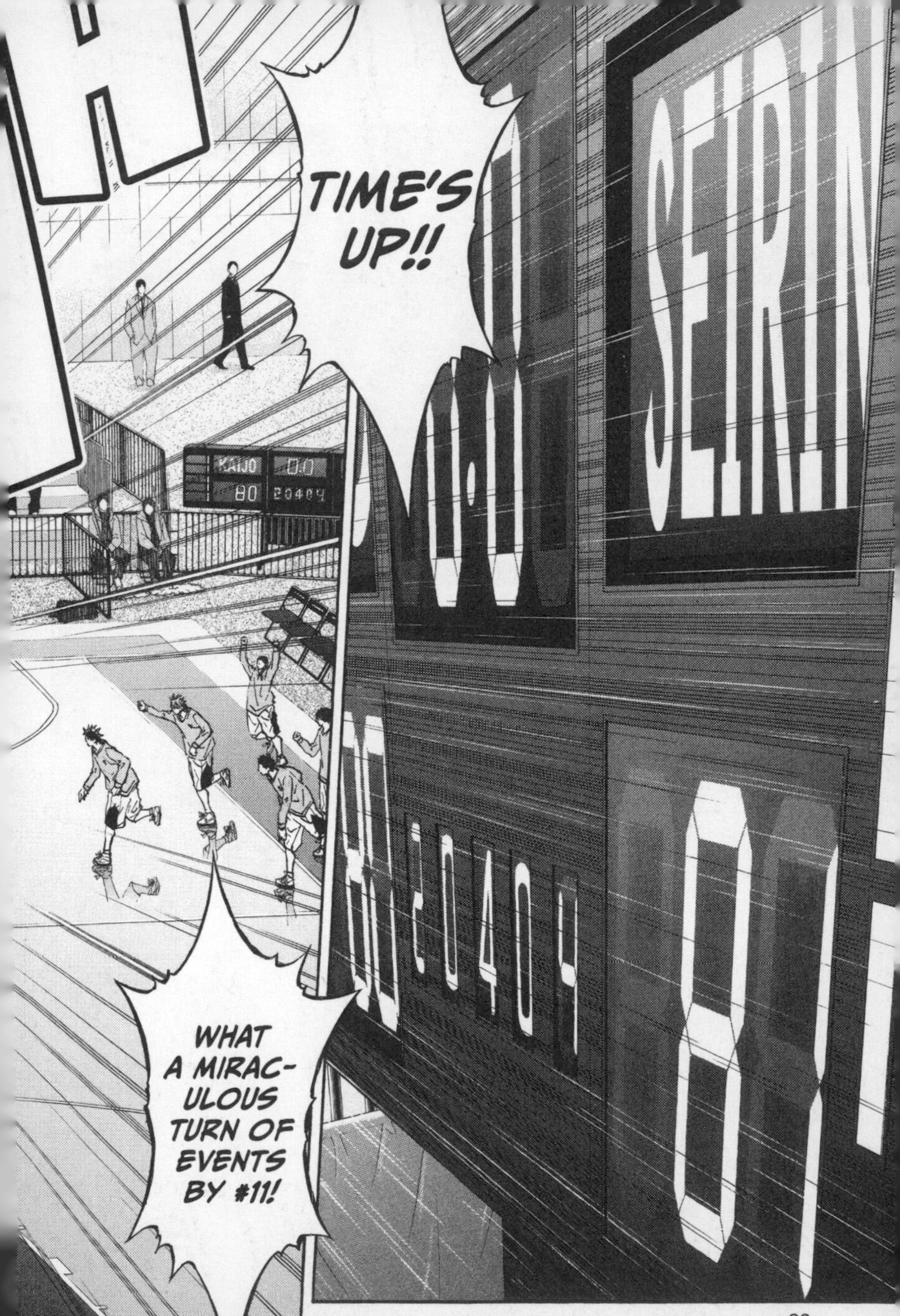
SEIRIN
TIME'S UP!!
KAIJO
WHAT A MIRAC-
ULOUS
TURN OF
EVENTS
BY #11!

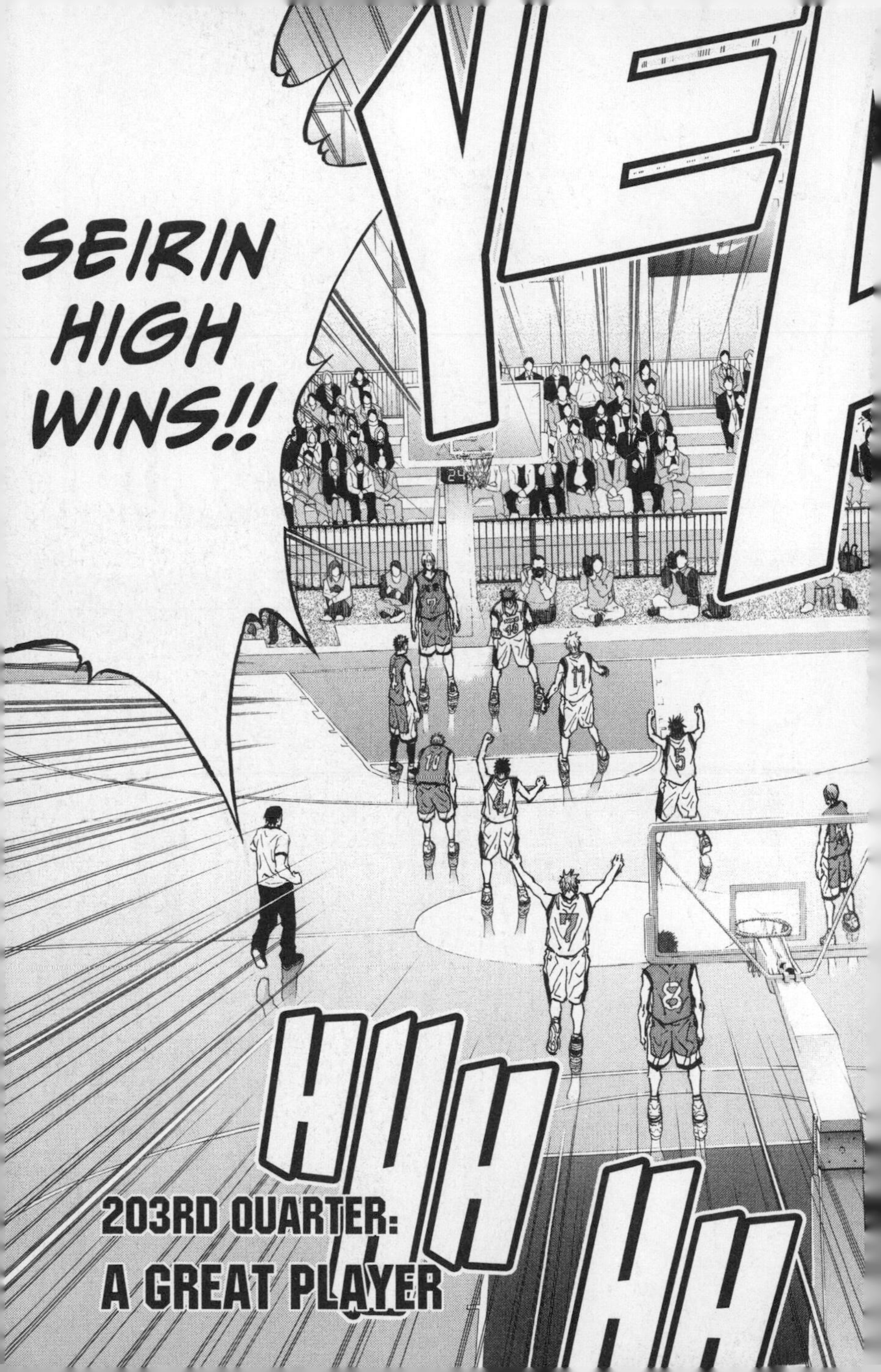
SEIRIN HIGH WINS!!
203RD QUARTER:
A GREAT PLAYER

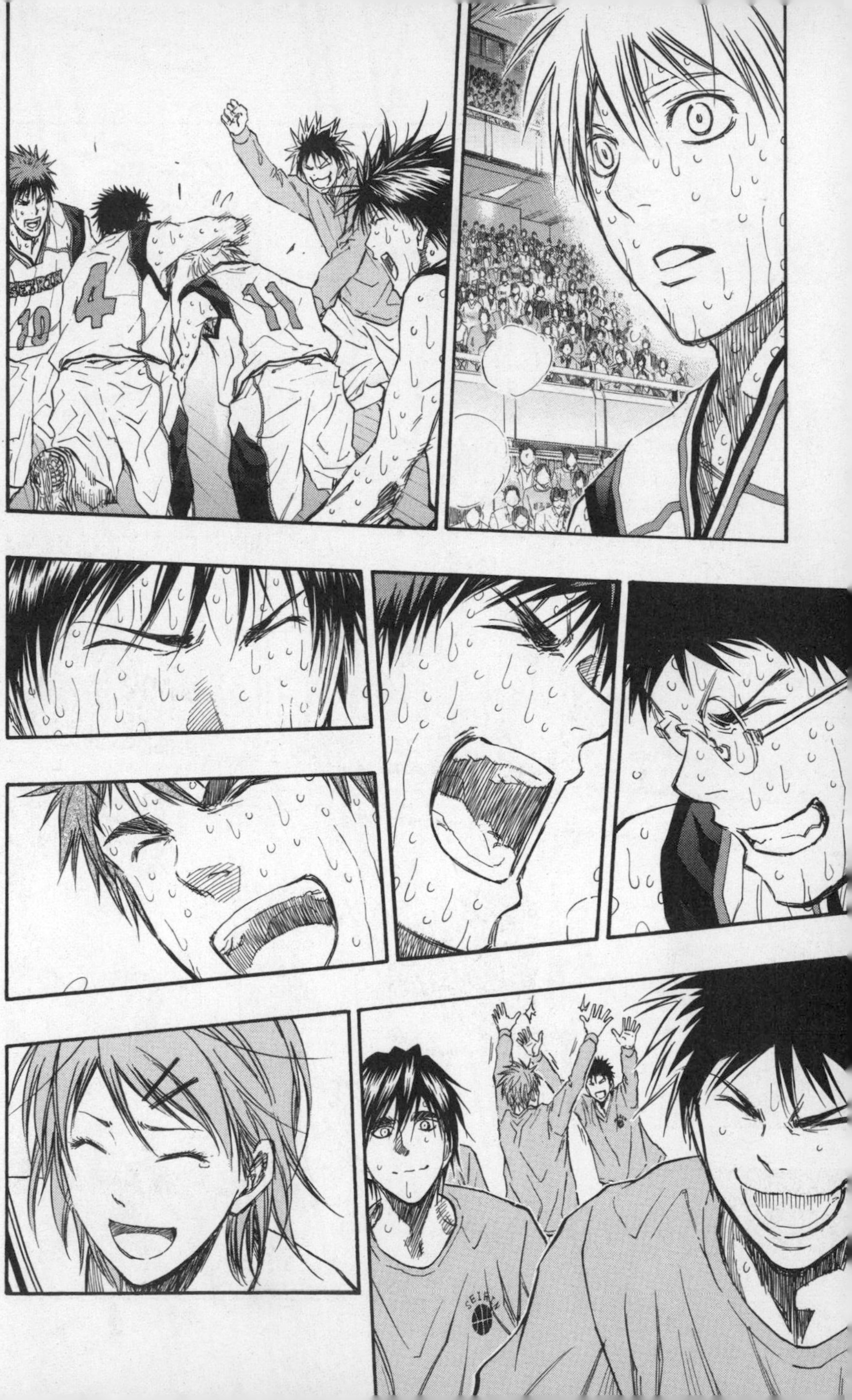

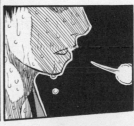

KISE-
KUN...

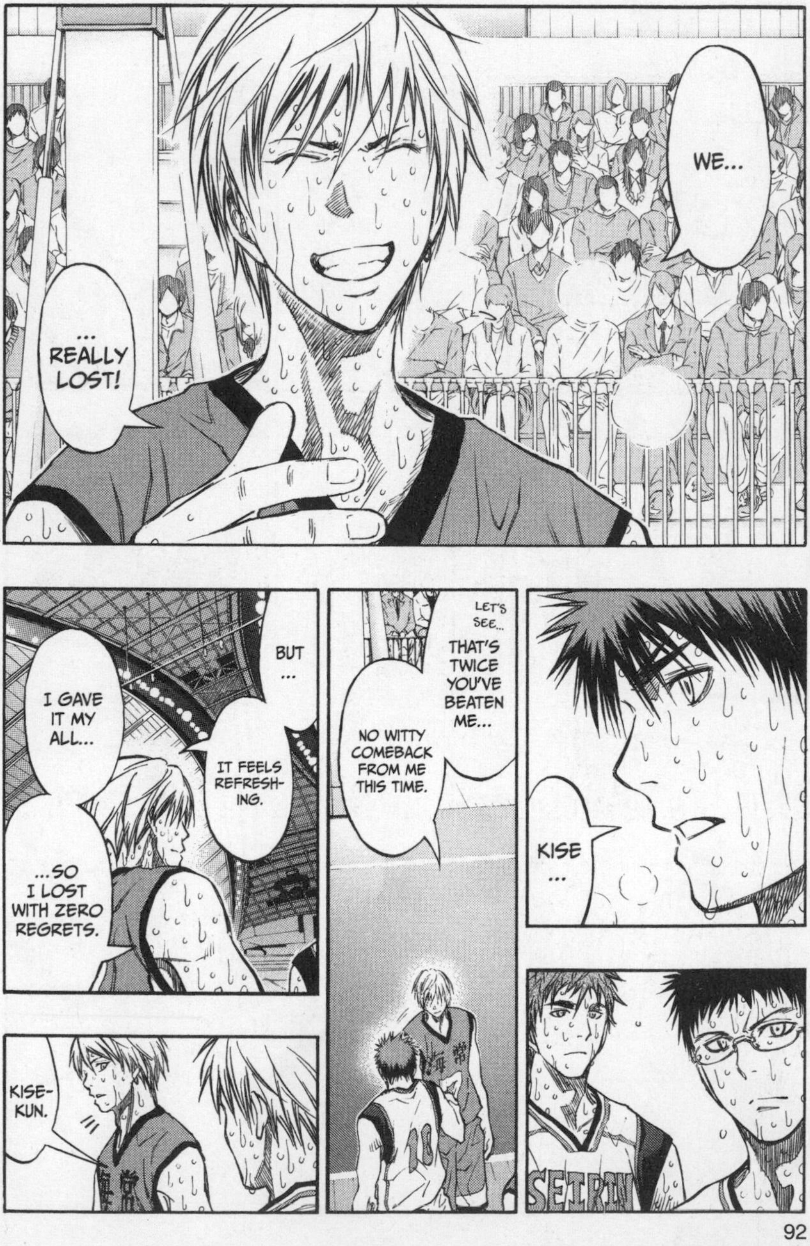
WE...
... REALLY LOST!
KISE ...
LET'S SEE...
THAT'S TWICE YOU'VE BEATEN ME...
NO WITTY COMEBACK FROM ME THIS TIME.
I GAVE IT MY ALL...
...SO I LOST WITH ZERO REGRETS.
BUT ...
IT FEELS REFRESHING.
KISE-KUN.

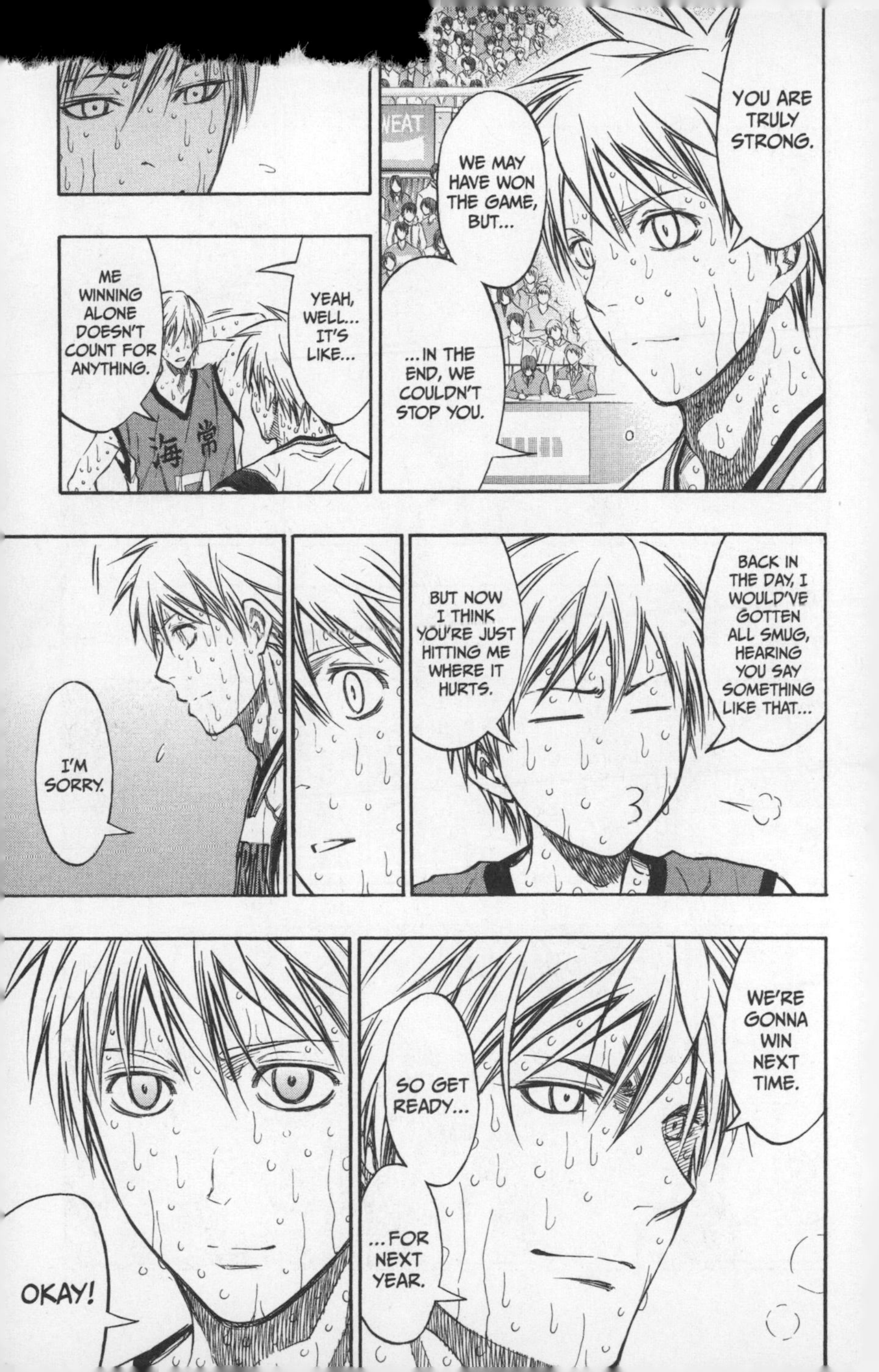
YOU ARE TRULY STRONG.
WE MAY HAVE WON THE GAME, BUT...
...IN THE END, WE COULDN'T STOP YOU.
YEAH, WELL... IT'S LIKE...
ME WINNING ALONE DOESN'T COUNT FOR ANYTHING.
BACK IN THE DAY, I WOULD'VE GOTTEN ALL SMUG, HEARING YOU SAY SOMETHING LIKE THAT...
BUT NOW I THINK YOU'RE JUST HITTING ME WHERE IT HURTS.
I'M SORRY.
WE'RE GONNA WIN NEXT TIME.
SO GET READY...
...FOR NEXT YEAR.
OKAY!

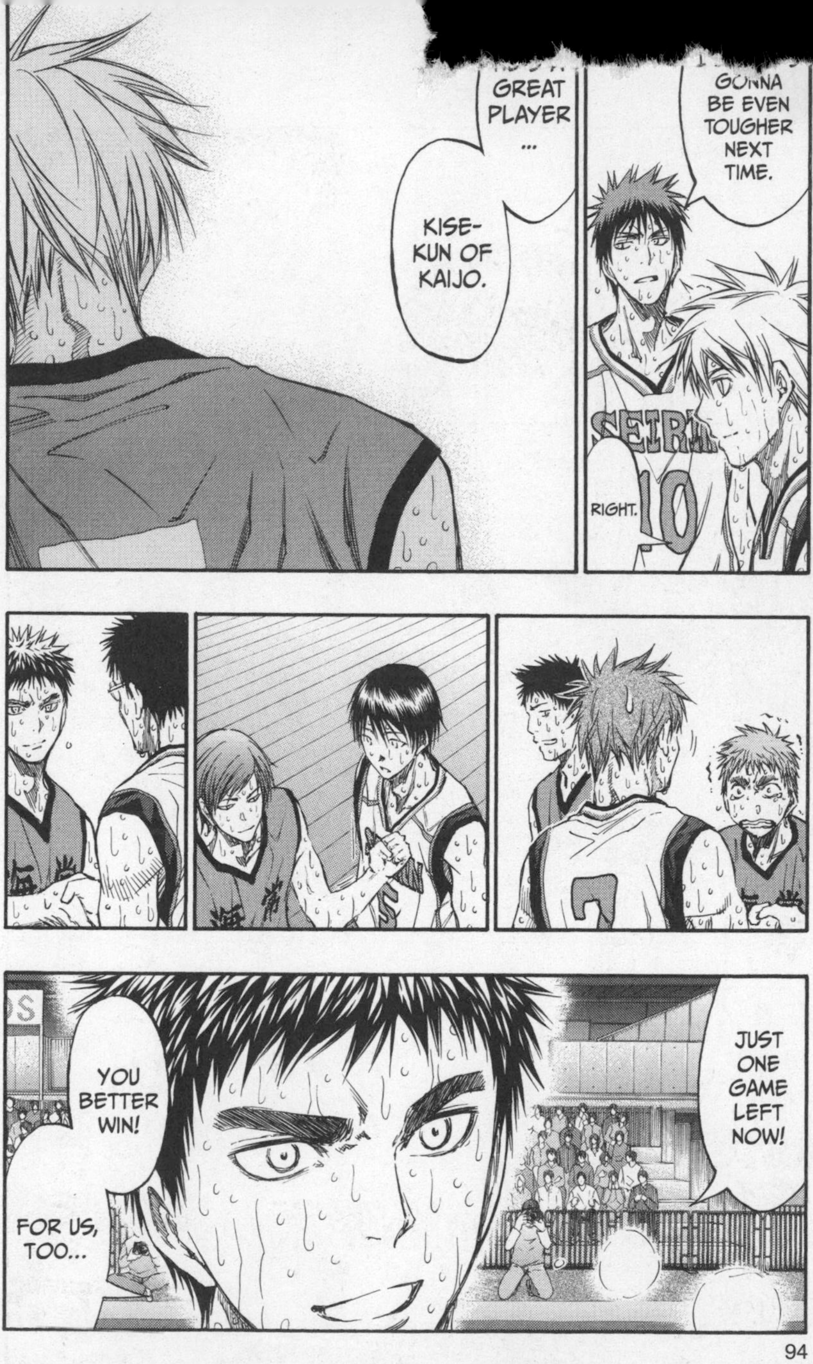
[redacted] GONNA BE EVEN TOUGHER NEXT TIME.
RIGHT.
[redacted] GREAT PLAYER ...
KISE-KUN OF KAIJO.
JUST ONE GAME LEFT NOW!
YOU BETTER WIN!
FOR US, TOO...

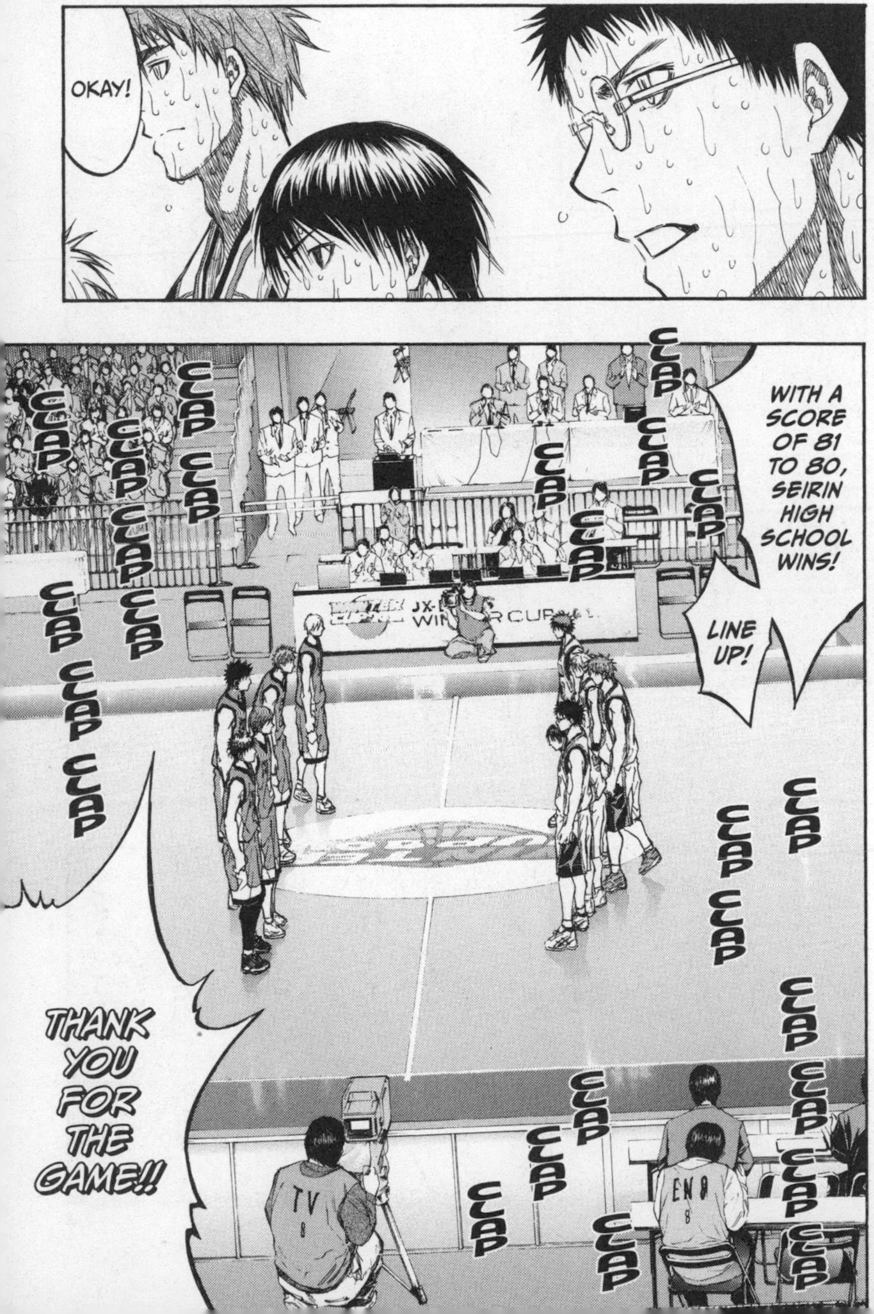
OKAY!
WITH A SCORE OF 81 TO 80, SEIRIN HIGH SCHOOL WINS!
CLAP CLAP CLAP
CLAP CLAP
LINE UP!
CLAP CLAP CLAP
CLAP CLAP
CLAP CLAP CLAP CLAP
CLAP CLAP
CLAP CLAP CLAP CLAP
CLAP CLAP CLAP CLAP CLAP CLAP
CLAP CLAP CLAP
CLAP CLAP
THANK YOU FOR THE GAME!!

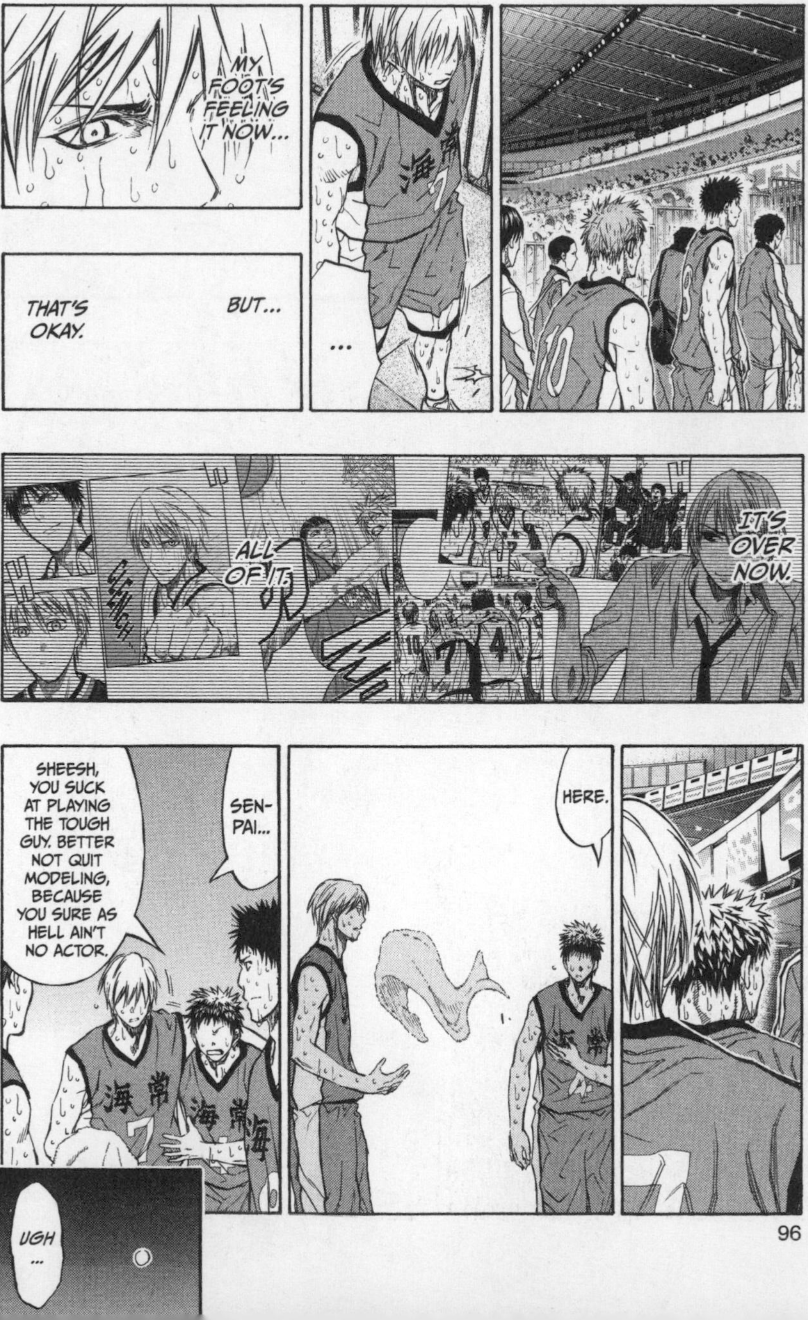
...
MY FOOT'S FEELING IT NOW...
BUT...
THAT'S OKAY.
IT'S OVER NOW.
ALL OF IT.
CLENCH
HERE.
SEN-PAI...
SHEESH, YOU SUCK AT PLAYING THE TOUGH GUY. BETTER NOT QUIT MODELING, BECAUSE YOU SURE AS HELL AIN'T NO ACTOR.
UGH ...

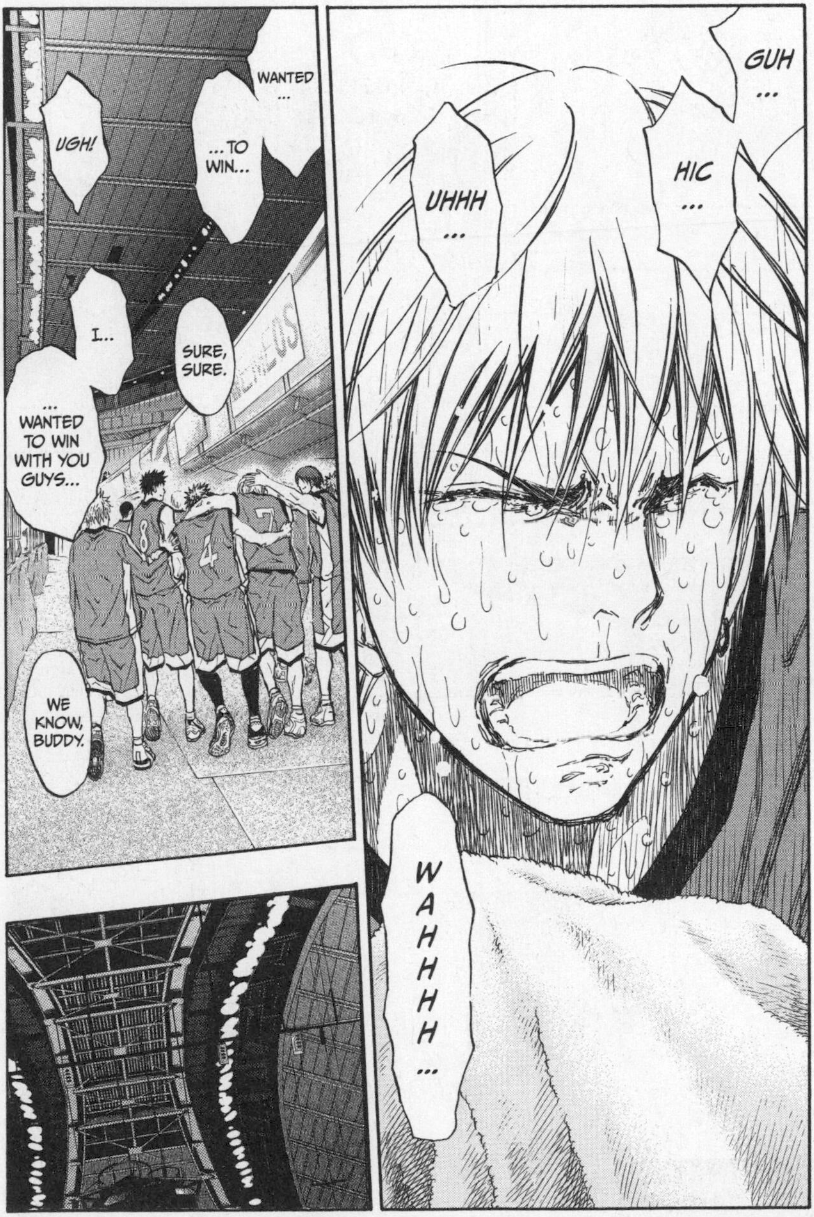
GUH ...
HIC ...
UHHH ...
WAHHHHH ...
WANTED ...
...TO WIN...
UGH!
SURE, SURE.
I...
... WANTED TO WIN WITH YOU GUYS...
WE KNOW, BUDDY.

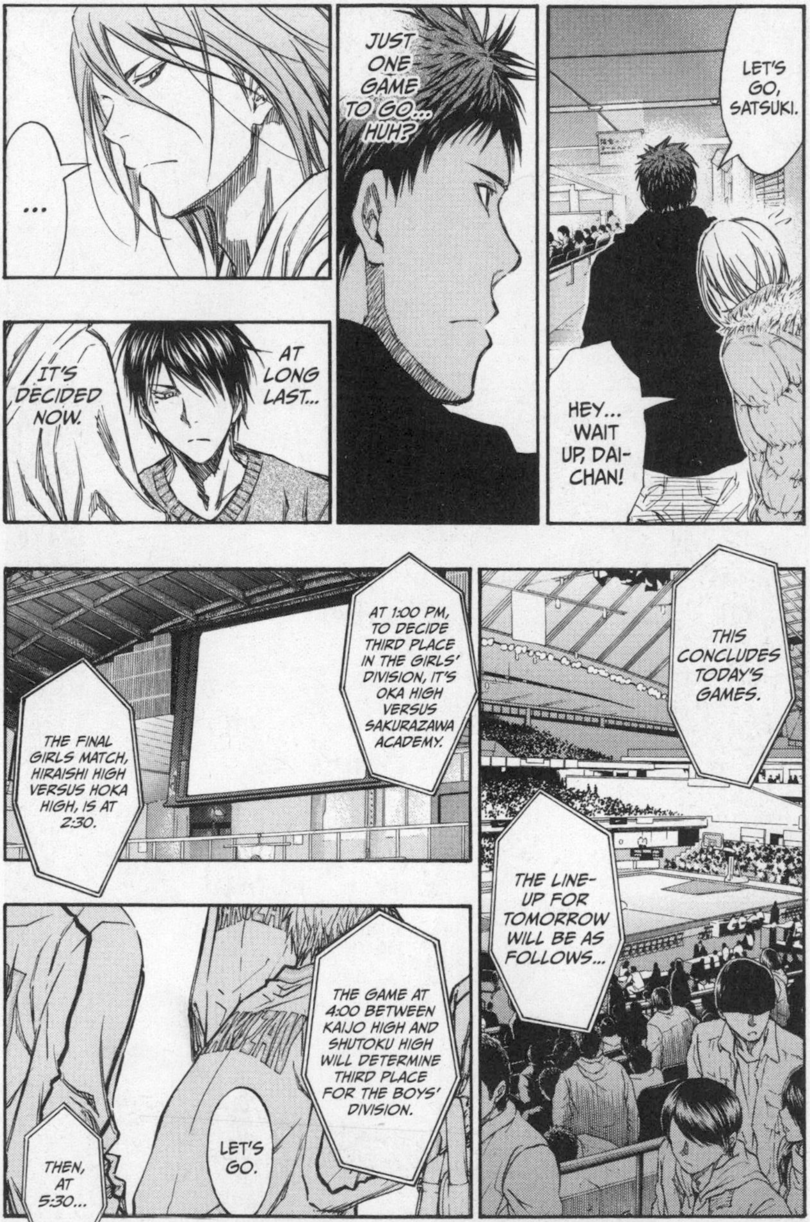
LET'S GO, SATSUKI.
HEY... WAIT UP, DAI-CHAN!
JUST ONE GAME TO GO... HUH?
...
AT LONG LAST...
IT'S DECIDED NOW.
THIS CONCLUDES TODAY'S GAMES.
THE LINE-UP FOR TOMORROW WILL BE AS FOLLOWS...
AT 1:00 PM, TO DECIDE THIRD PLACE IN THE GIRLS' DIVISION, IT'S OKA HIGH VERSUS SAKURAZAWA ACADEMY.
THE FINAL GIRLS MATCH, HIRAISHI HIGH VERSUS HOKA HIGH, IS AT 2:30.
THE GAME AT 4:00 BETWEEN KAIJO HIGH AND SHUTOKU HIGH WILL DETERMINE THIRD PLACE FOR THE BOYS' DIVISION.
LET'S GO.
THEN, AT 5:30...

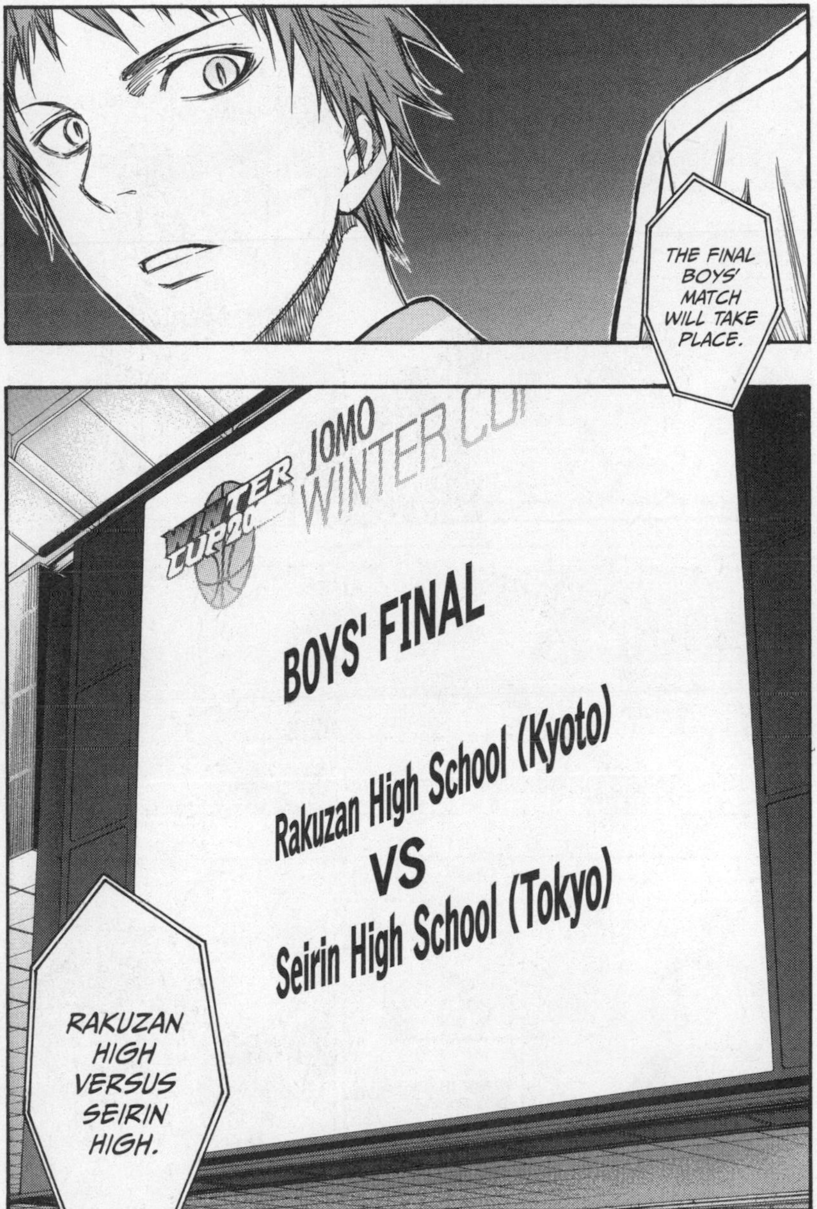
THE FINAL BOYS' MATCH WILL TAKE PLACE.
JOMO
BOYS' FINAL
Rakuzan High School (Kyoto)
VS
Seirin High School (Tokyo)
RAKUZAN HIGH VERSUS SEIRIN HIGH.

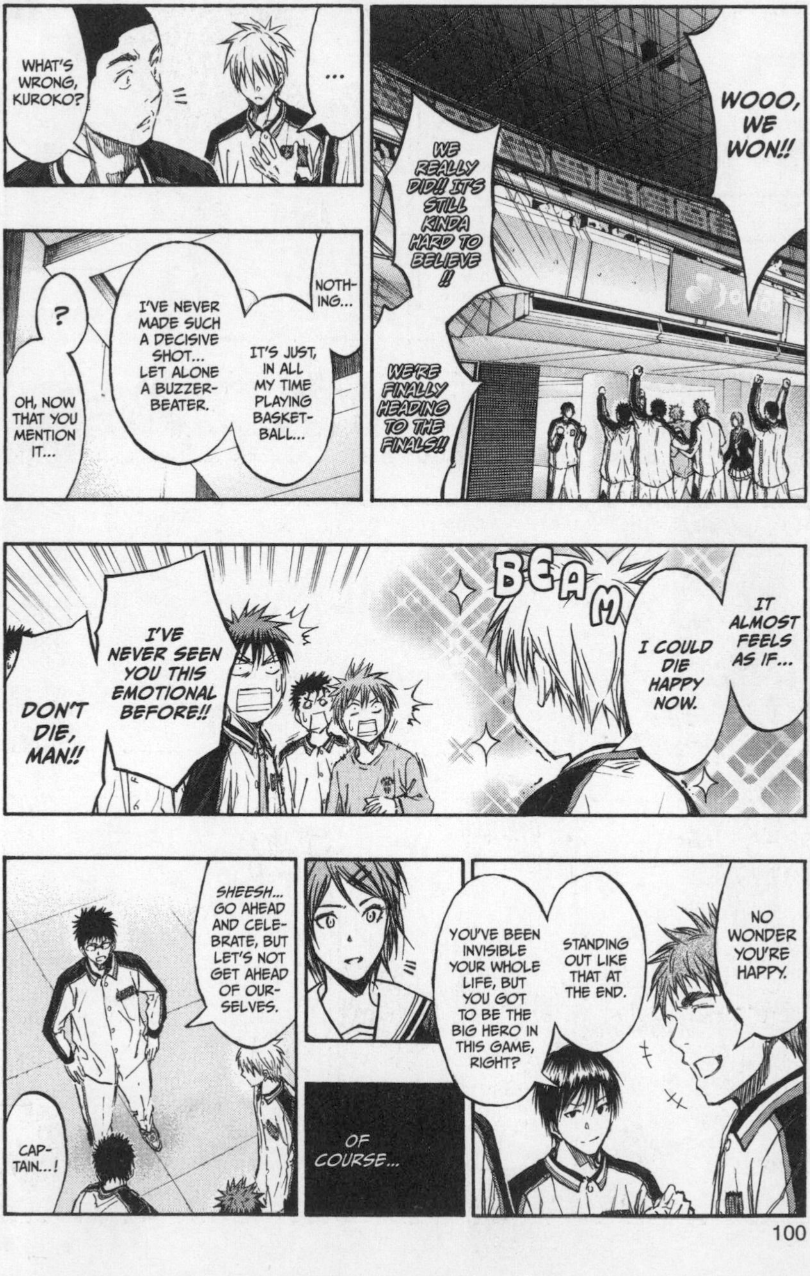
WOOO, WE WON!!
WE REALLY DID!! IT'S STILL KINDA HARD TO BELIEVE!!
WE'RE FINALLY HEADING TO THE FINALS!!
...
WHAT'S WRONG, KUROKO?
NOTH-ING...
IT'S JUST, IN ALL MY TIME PLAYING BASKET-BALL...
I'VE NEVER MADE SUCH A DECISIVE SHOT... LET ALONE A BUZZER-BEATER.
?
OH, NOW THAT YOU MENTION IT...
IT ALMOST FEELS AS IF...
I COULD DIE HAPPY NOW.
BEAM
I'VE NEVER SEEN YOU THIS EMOTIONAL BEFORE!!
DON'T DIE, MAN!!
NO WONDER YOU'RE HAPPY.
STANDING OUT LIKE THAT AT THE END.
YOU'VE BEEN INVISIBLE YOUR WHOLE LIFE, BUT YOU GOT TO BE THE BIG HERO IN THIS GAME, RIGHT?
SHEESH... GO AHEAD AND CELE-BRATE, BUT LET'S NOT GET AHEAD OF OUR-SELVES.
OF COURSE...
CAP-TAIN...!

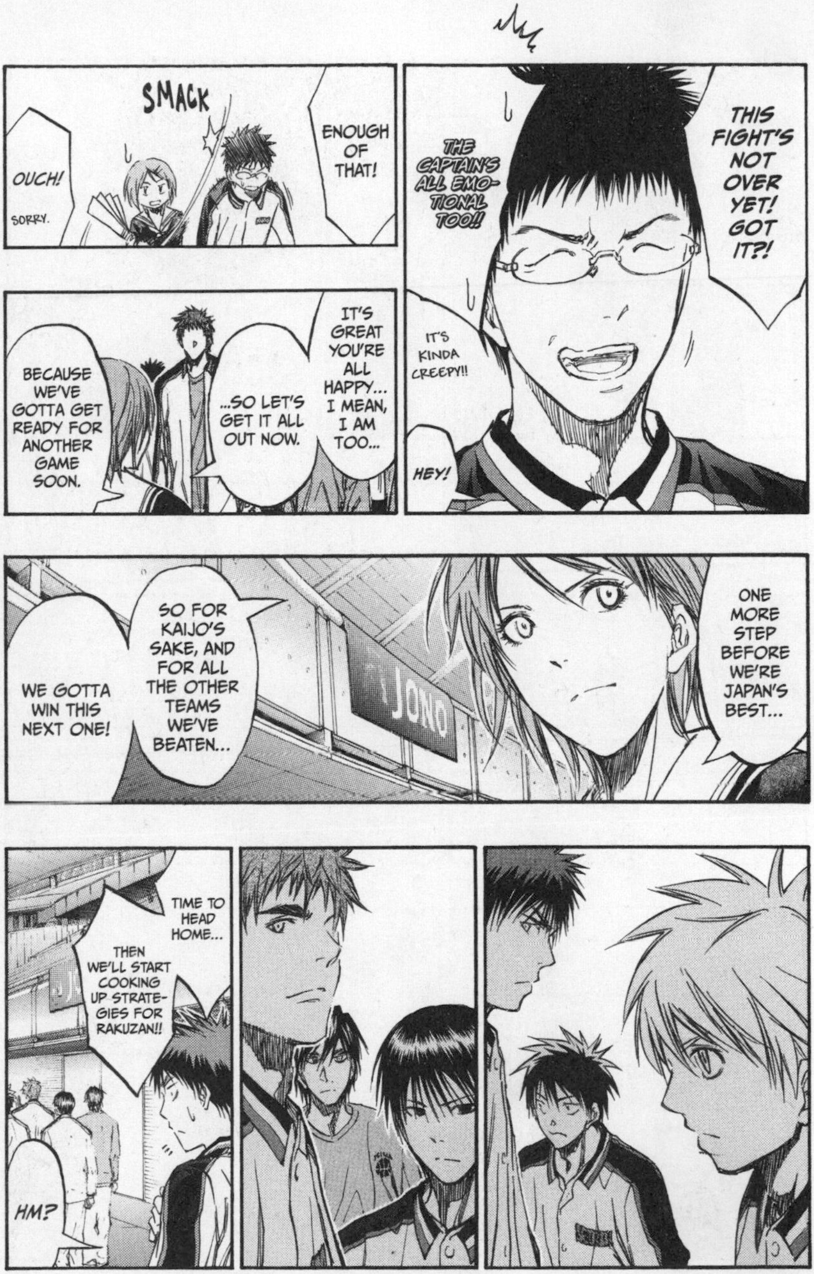
THIS FIGHT'S NOT OVER YET! GOT IT?!
THE CAPTAIN'S ALL EMOTIONAL TOO!!
IT'S KINDA CREEPY!!
HEY!
ENOUGH OF THAT!
SMACK
OUCH!
SORRY.
IT'S GREAT YOU'RE ALL HAPPY... I MEAN, I AM TOO...
...SO LET'S GET IT ALL OUT NOW.
BECAUSE WE'VE GOTTA GET READY FOR ANOTHER GAME SOON.
ONE MORE STEP BEFORE WE'RE JAPAN'S BEST...
SO FOR KAIJO'S SAKE, AND FOR ALL THE OTHER TEAMS WE'VE BEATEN...
WE GOTTA WIN THIS NEXT ONE!
TIME TO HEAD HOME...
THEN WE'LL START COOKING UP STRATEGIES FOR RAKUZAN!!
HM?

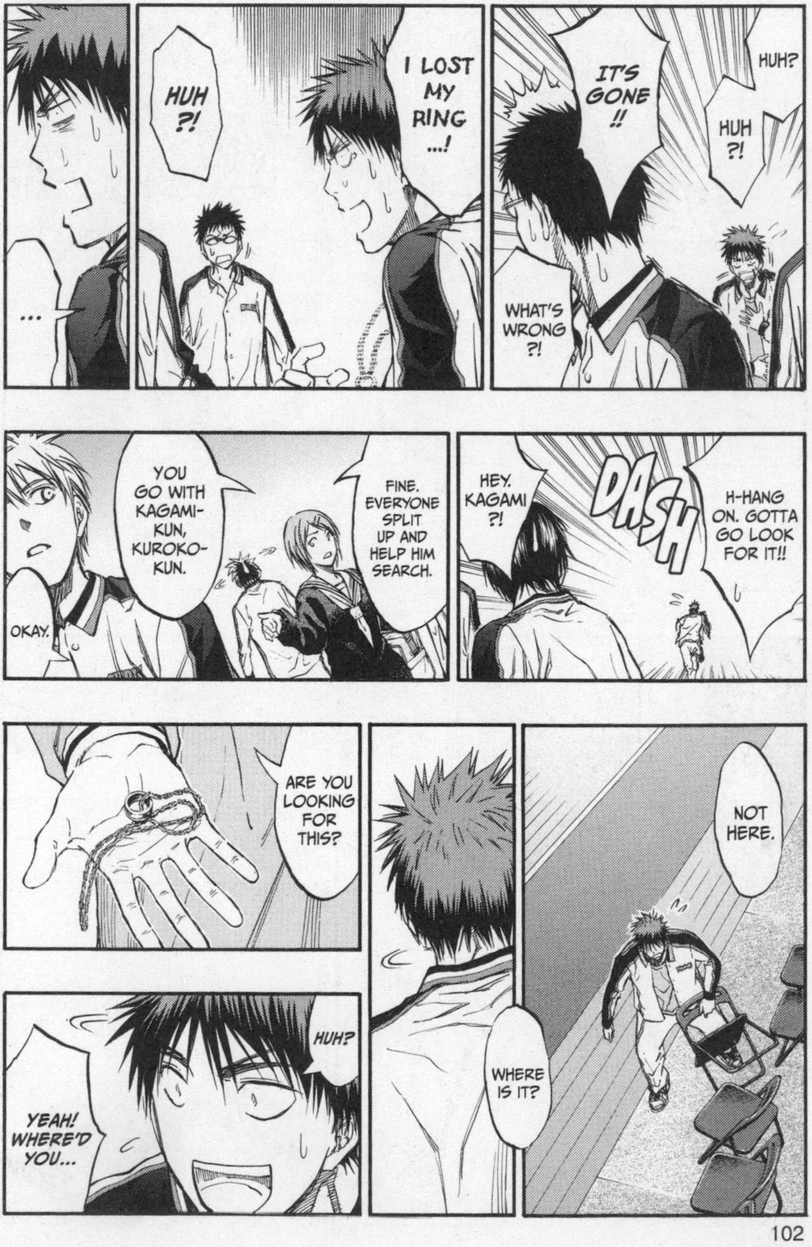
HUH?
IT'S GONE!!
HUH?!
WHAT'S WRONG?!
I LOST MY RING...!
HUH?!
...
H-HANG ON. GOTTA GO LOOK FOR IT!!
DASH
HEY. KAGAMI?!
FINE. EVERYONE SPLIT UP AND HELP HIM SEARCH.
YOU GO WITH KAGAMI-KUN, KUROKO-KUN.
OKAY.
NOT HERE.
WHERE IS IT?
ARE YOU LOOKING FOR THIS?
HUH?
YEAH! WHERE'D YOU...

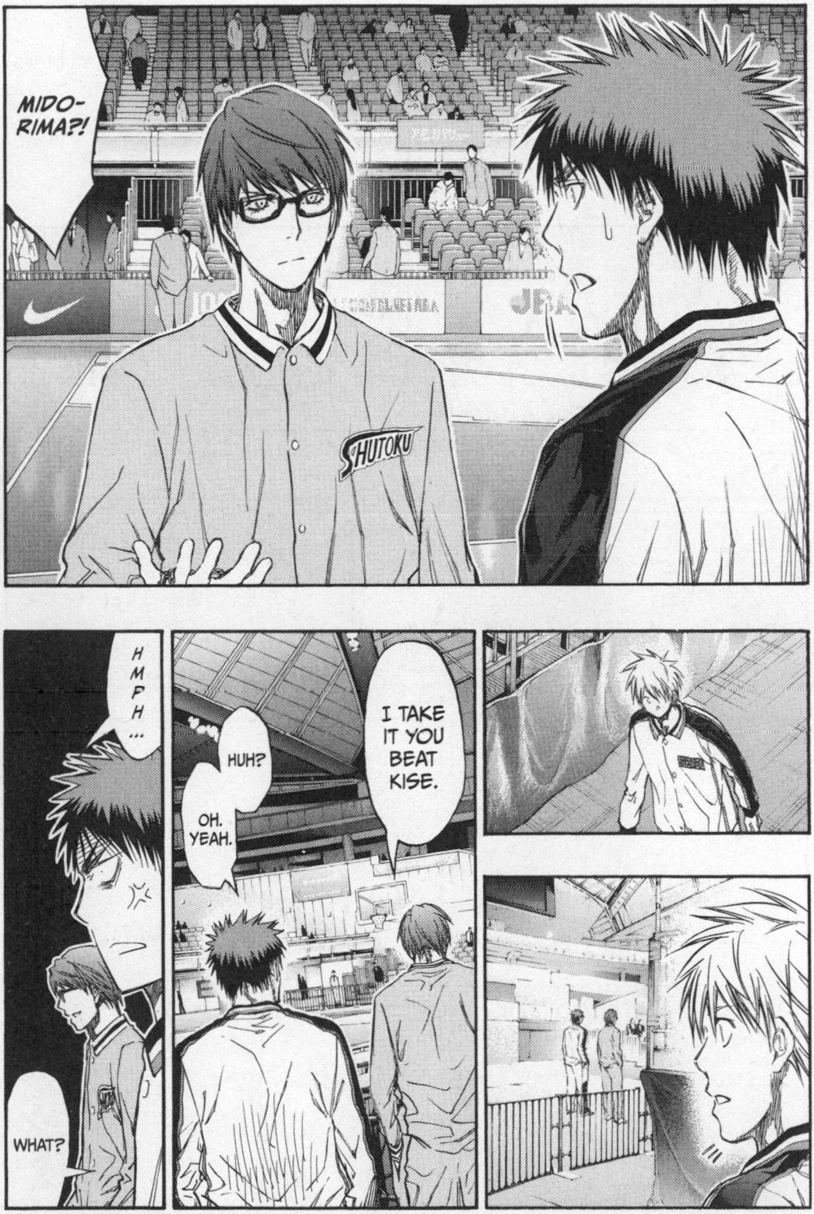
MIDO-RIMA?!
I TAKE IT YOU BEAT KISE.
HUH?
OH. YEAH.
HMPH...
WHAT?

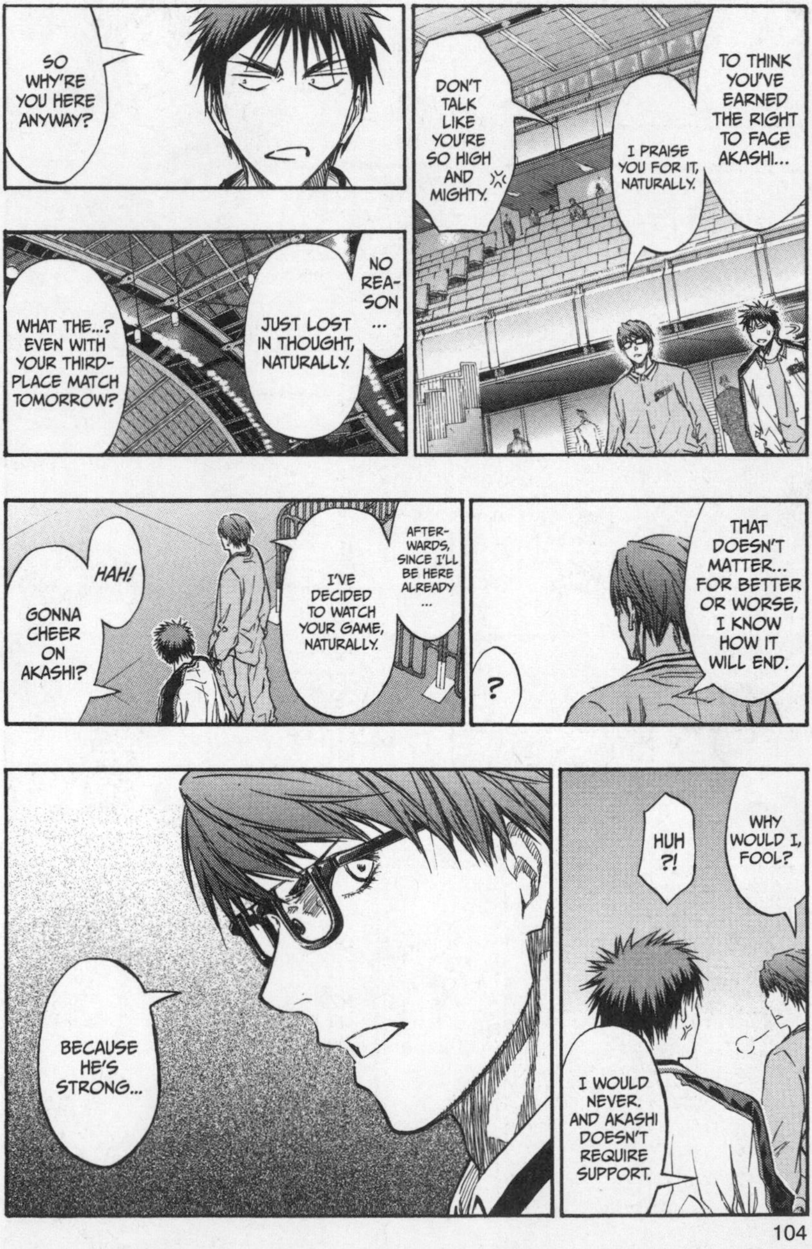
TO THINK YOU'VE EARNED THE RIGHT TO FACE AKASHI...
I PRAISE YOU FOR IT, NATURALLY.
DON'T TALK LIKE YOU'RE SO HIGH AND MIGHTY.
SO WHY'RE YOU HERE ANYWAY?
NO REA-SON...
JUST LOST IN THOUGHT, NATURALLY.
WHAT THE...? EVEN WITH YOUR THIRD-PLACE MATCH TOMORROW?
THAT DOESN'T MATTER... FOR BETTER OR WORSE, I KNOW HOW IT WILL END.
?
AFTER-WARDS, SINCE I'LL BE HERE ALREADY...
I'VE DECIDED TO WATCH YOUR GAME, NATURALLY.
HAH!
GONNA CHEER ON AKASHI?
WHY WOULD I, FOOL?
HUH?!
I WOULD NEVER. AND AKASHI DOESN'T REQUIRE SUPPORT.
BECAUSE HE'S STRONG...

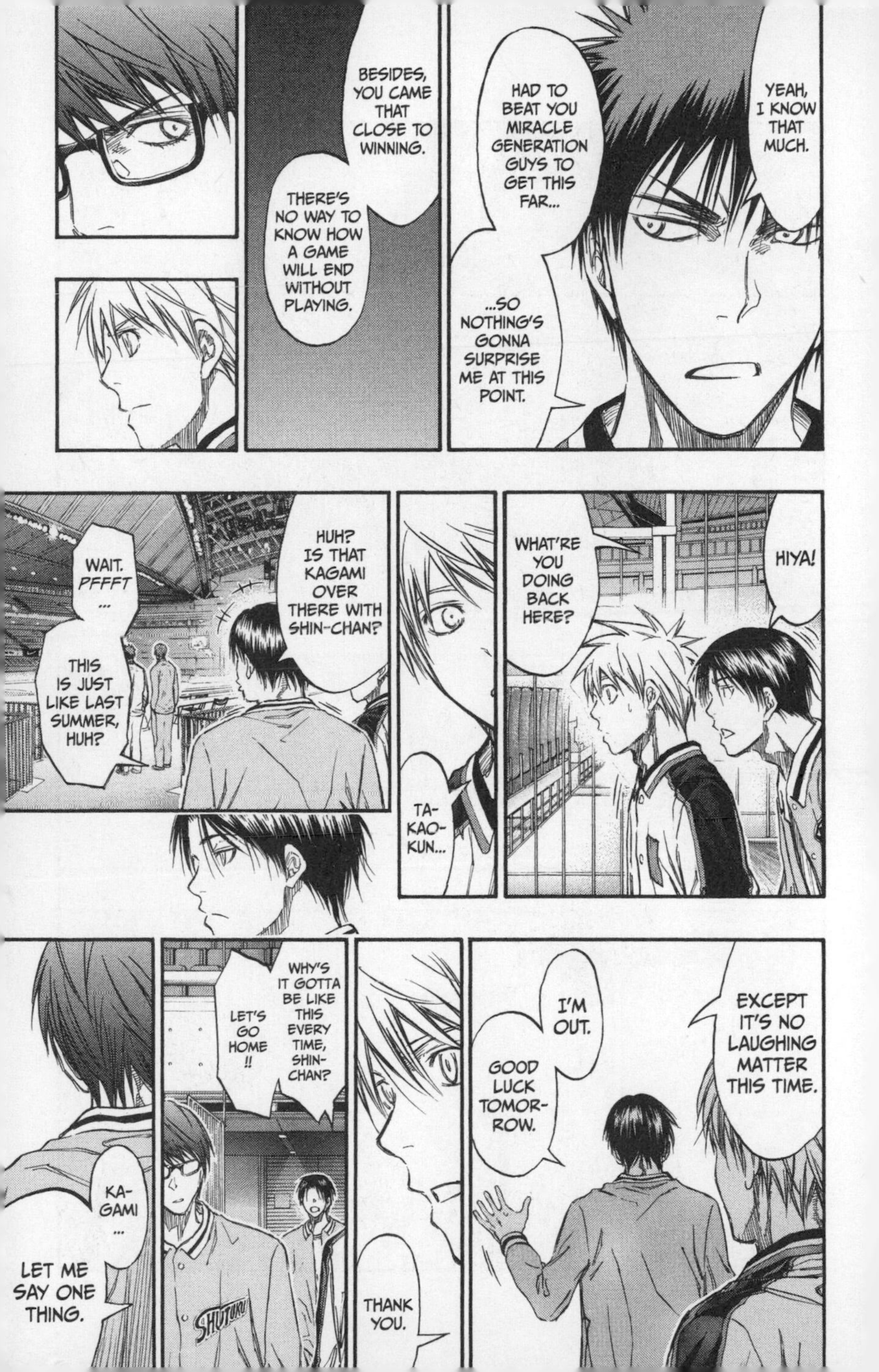
YEAH, I KNOW THAT MUCH.
HAD TO BEAT YOU MIRACLE GENERATION GUYS TO GET THIS FAR...
...SO NOTHING'S GONNA SURPRISE ME AT THIS POINT.
BESIDES, YOU CAME THAT CLOSE TO WINNING.
THERE'S NO WAY TO KNOW HOW A GAME WILL END WITHOUT PLAYING.
HIYA!
WHAT'RE YOU DOING BACK HERE?
HUH? IS THAT KAGAMI OVER THERE WITH SHIN-CHAN?
TA-KAO-KUN...
WAIT. PFFFT ...
THIS IS JUST LIKE LAST SUMMER, HUH?
EXCEPT IT'S NO LAUGHING MATTER THIS TIME.
I'M OUT.
GOOD LUCK TOMOR-ROW.
THANK YOU.
WHY'S IT GOTTA BE LIKE THIS EVERY TIME, SHIN-CHAN?
LET'S GO HOME !!
SHUTOKU
KA-GAMI ...
LET ME SAY ONE THING.

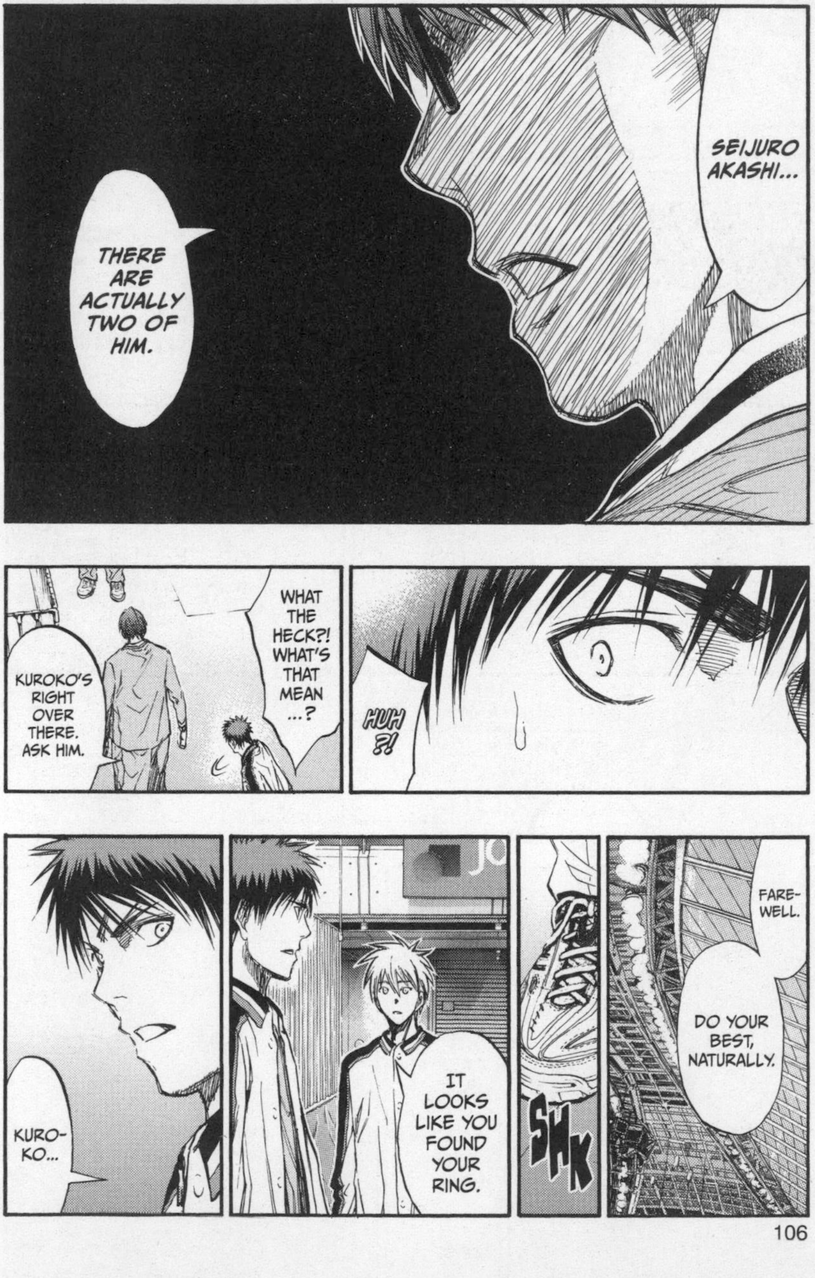
SEIJURO AKASHI...
THERE ARE ACTUALLY TWO OF HIM.
HUH ?!
WHAT THE HECK?! WHAT'S THAT MEAN ...?
KUROKO'S RIGHT OVER THERE. ASK HIM.
FARE-WELL.
DO YOUR BEST, NATURALLY.
SHK
IT LOOKS LIKE YOU FOUND YOUR RING.
KURO-KO...

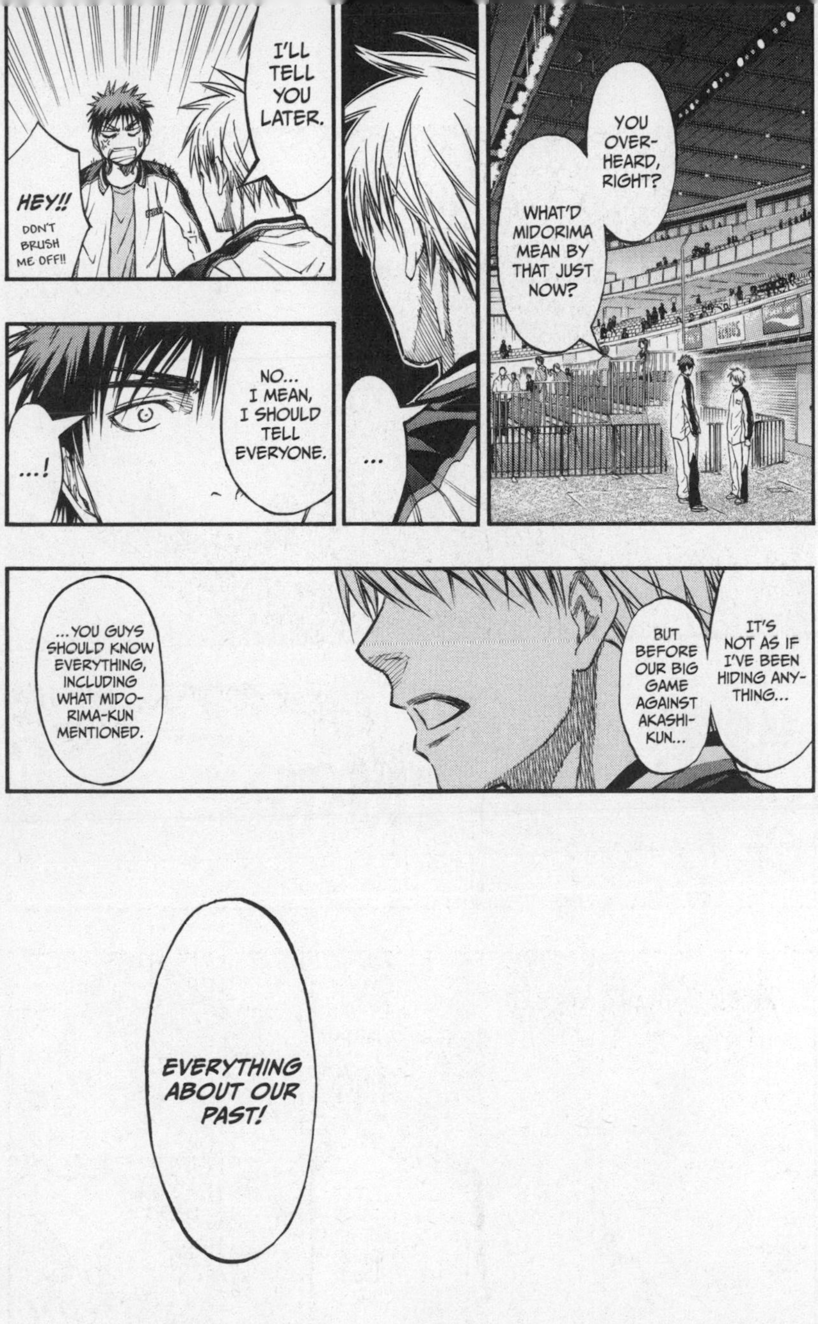
YOU OVER-HEARD, RIGHT?
WHAT'D MIDORIMA MEAN BY THAT JUST NOW?
...
I'LL TELL YOU LATER.
HEY!!
DON'T BRUSH ME OFF!!
NO... I MEAN, I SHOULD TELL EVERYONE.
...!
IT'S NOT AS IF I'VE BEEN HIDING ANY-THING...
BUT BEFORE OUR BIG GAME AGAINST AKASHI-KUN...
...YOU GUYS SHOULD KNOW EVERYTHING, INCLUDING WHAT MIDO-RIMA-KUN MENTIONED.
EVERYTHING ABOUT OUR PAST!

KUROKO'S BASKETBALL Q&A
W/ HALFWAY-DECENT ANSWERS

Q. WHAT EXACTLY IS RIKO'S SPECIAL DISH WITH ALL THE SUPPLEMENTS IN IT?!
(KAKIA from OITA PREFECTURE)

A. SUPPLEMENT PILAF.

KUROKO'S BASKETBALL BLOOPERS
TAKE 9

ARE YOU LOOKING FOR THIS?
DOOM
IT'S THAT SPOOKY RING AGAIN!!
EEK

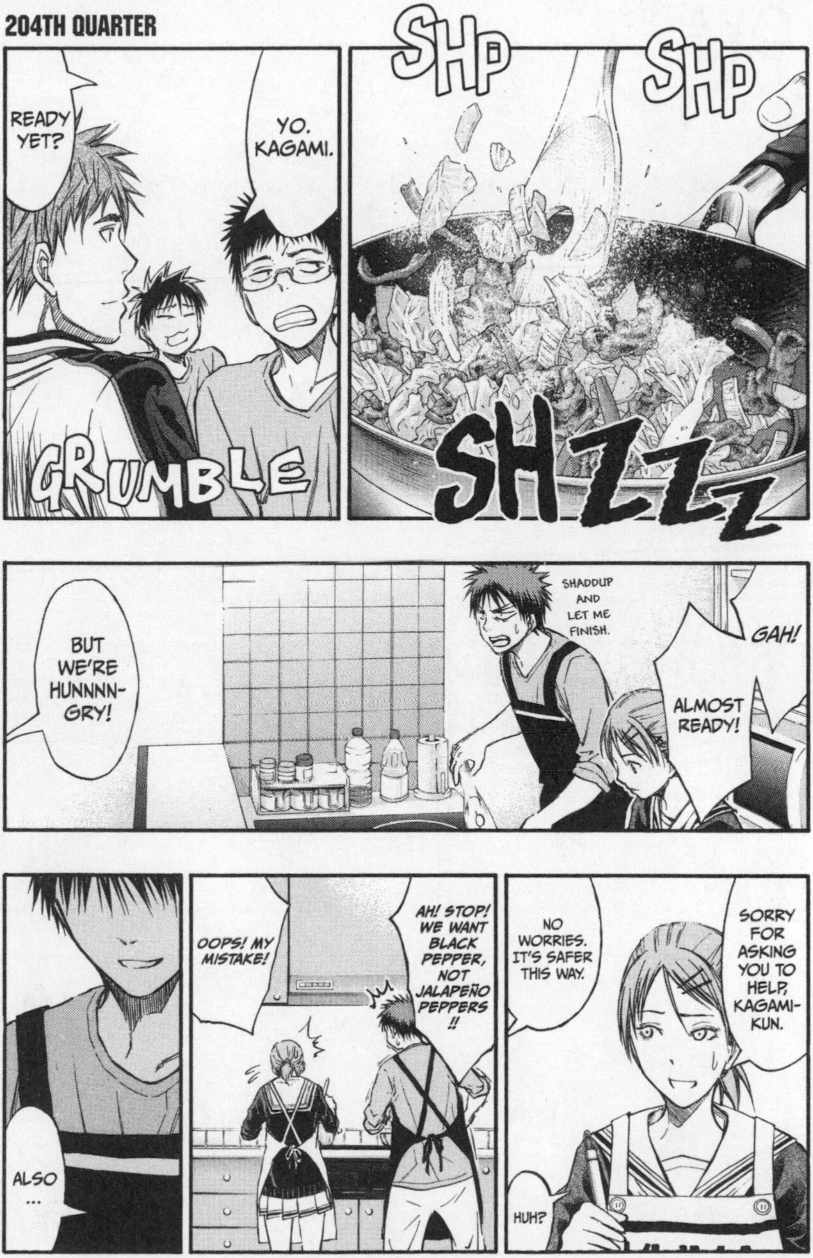
SHP
SHP
SHZZZ
YO. KAGAMI.
READY YET?
GRUMBLE
GAH!
ALMOST READY!
SHADDUP AND LET ME FINISH.
BUT WE'RE HUNNNN-GRY!
SORRY FOR ASKING YOU TO HELP, KAGAMI-KUN.
NO WORRIES. IT'S SAFER THIS WAY.
HUH?
AH! STOP! WE WANT BLACK PEPPER, NOT JALAPEÑO PEPPERS !!
OOPS! MY MISTAKE!
ALSO ...

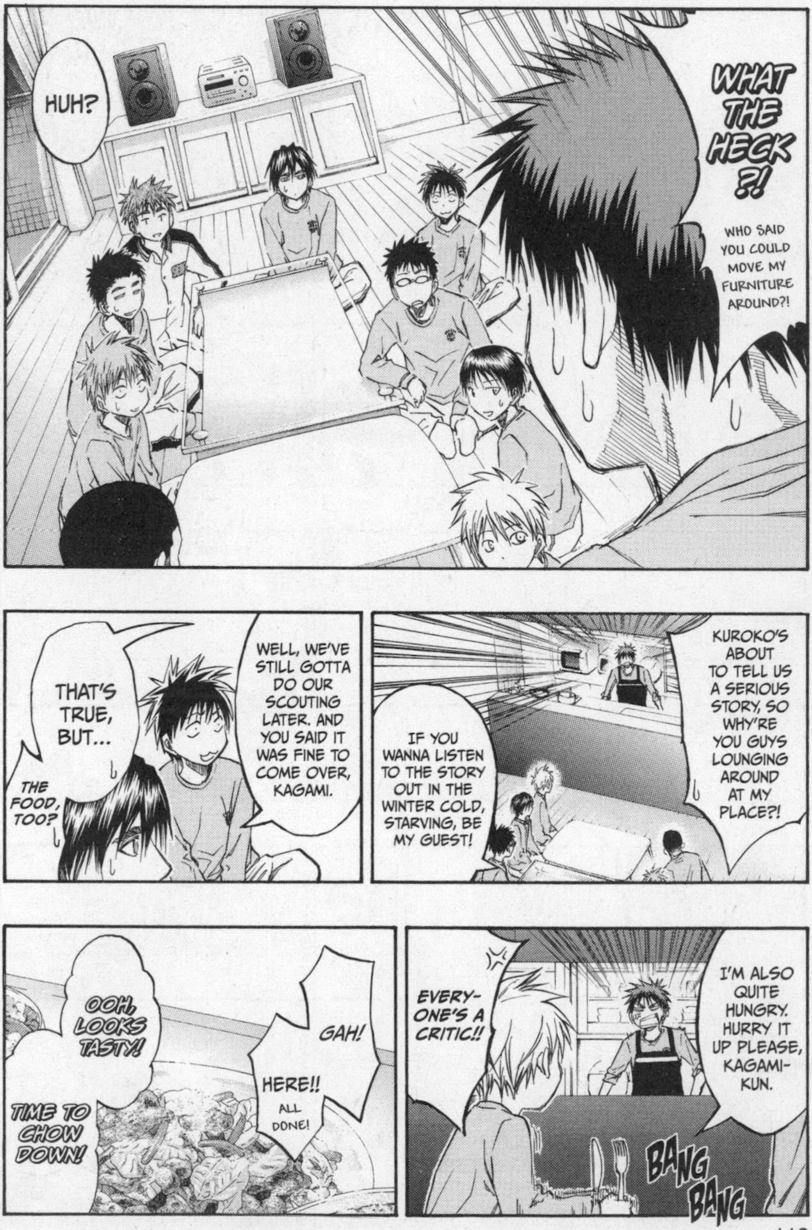
WHAT THE HECK ?!
WHO SAID YOU COULD MOVE MY FURNITURE AROUND?!
HUH?
KUROKO'S ABOUT TO TELL US A SERIOUS STORY, SO WHY'RE YOU GUYS LOUNGING AROUND AT MY PLACE?!
IF YOU WANNA LISTEN TO THE STORY OUT IN THE WINTER COLD, STARVING, BE MY GUEST!
WELL, WE'VE STILL GOTTA DO OUR SCOUTING LATER. AND YOU SAID IT WAS FINE TO COME OVER, KAGAMI.
THAT'S TRUE, BUT...
THE FOOD, TOO?
I'M ALSO QUITE HUNGRY. HURRY IT UP PLEASE, KAGAMI-KUN.
BANG BANG
EVERY-ONE'S A CRITIC!!
GAH!
HERE!!
ALL DONE!
OOH, LOOKS TASTY!
TIME TO CHOW DOWN!

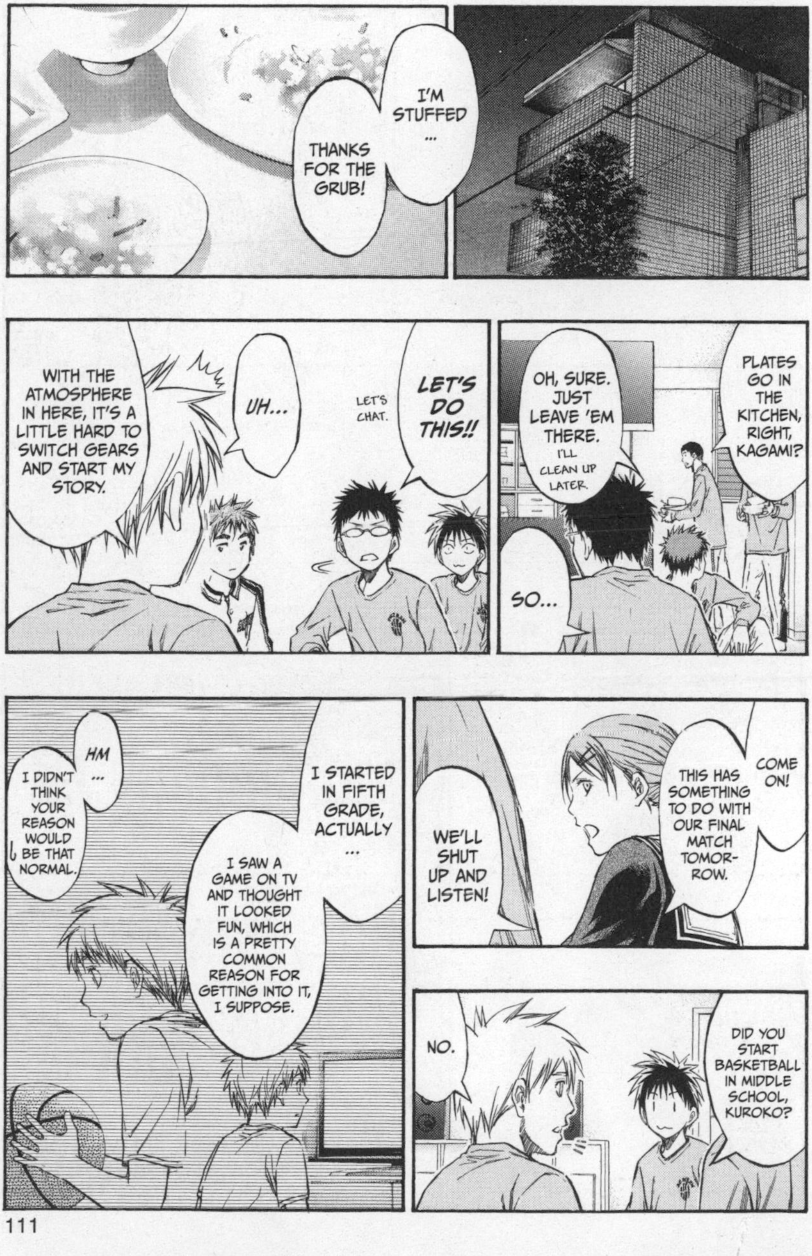
I'M STUFFED ...
THANKS FOR THE GRUB!
PLATES GO IN THE KITCHEN, RIGHT, KAGAMI?
OH, SURE. JUST LEAVE 'EM THERE. I'LL CLEAN UP LATER.
SO...
LET'S DO THIS!!
LET'S CHAT.
UH...
WITH THE ATMOSPHERE IN HERE, IT'S A LITTLE HARD TO SWITCH GEARS AND START MY STORY.
COME ON!
THIS HAS SOMETHING TO DO WITH OUR FINAL MATCH TOMOR-ROW.
WE'LL SHUT UP AND LISTEN!
DID YOU START BASKETBALL IN MIDDLE SCHOOL, KUROKO?
NO.
I STARTED IN FIFTH GRADE, ACTUALLY ...
I SAW A GAME ON TV AND THOUGHT IT LOOKED FUN, WHICH IS A PRETTY COMMON REASON FOR GETTING INTO IT, I SUPPOSE.
HM ...
I DIDN'T THINK YOUR REASON WOULD BE THAT NORMAL.

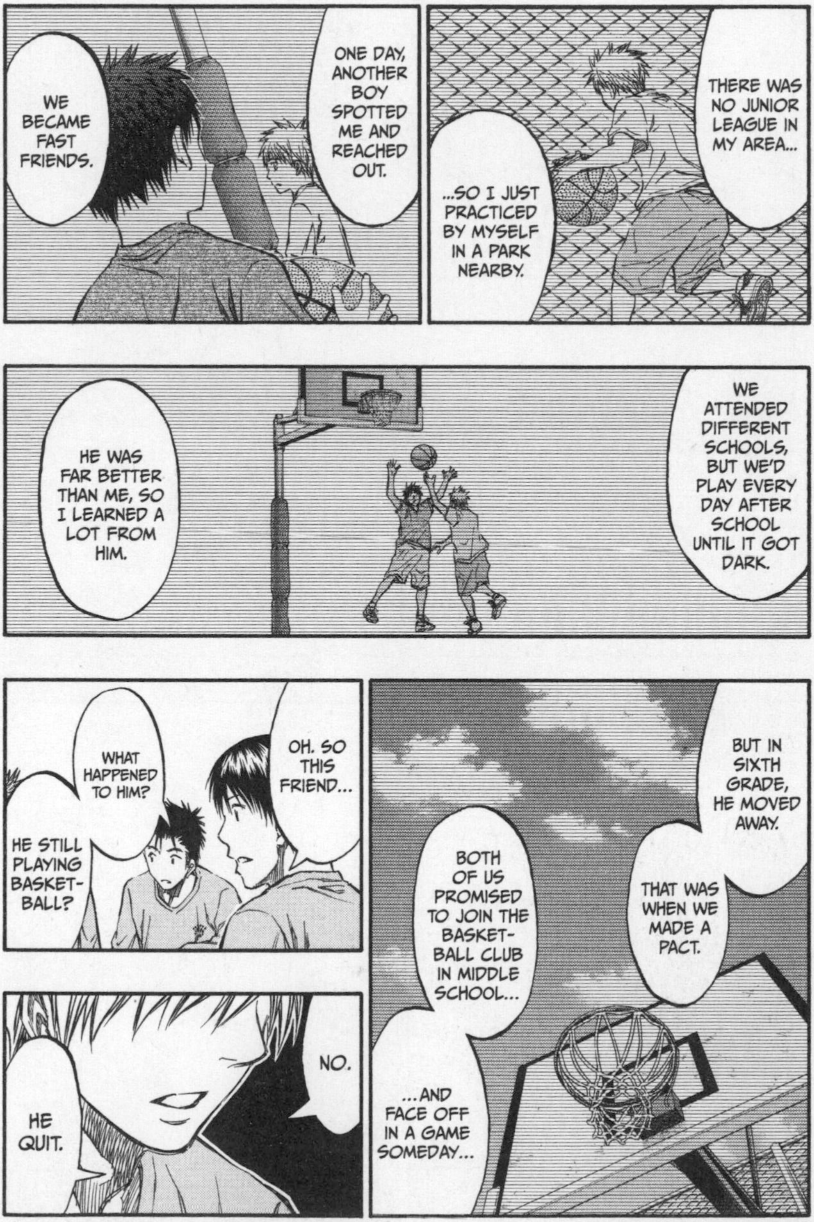
THERE WAS NO JUNIOR LEAGUE IN MY AREA...
...SO I JUST PRACTICED BY MYSELF IN A PARK NEARBY.
ONE DAY, ANOTHER BOY SPOTTED ME AND REACHED OUT.
WE BECAME FAST FRIENDS.
WE ATTENDED DIFFERENT SCHOOLS, BUT WE'D PLAY EVERY DAY AFTER SCHOOL UNTIL IT GOT DARK.
HE WAS FAR BETTER THAN ME, SO I LEARNED A LOT FROM HIM.
BUT IN SIXTH GRADE, HE MOVED AWAY.
THAT WAS WHEN WE MADE A PACT.
BOTH OF US PROMISED TO JOIN THE BASKET-BALL CLUB IN MIDDLE SCHOOL...
...AND FACE OFF IN A GAME SOMEDAY...
OH. SO THIS FRIEND...
WHAT HAPPENED TO HIM?
HE STILL PLAYING BASKET-BALL?
NO.
HE QUIT.

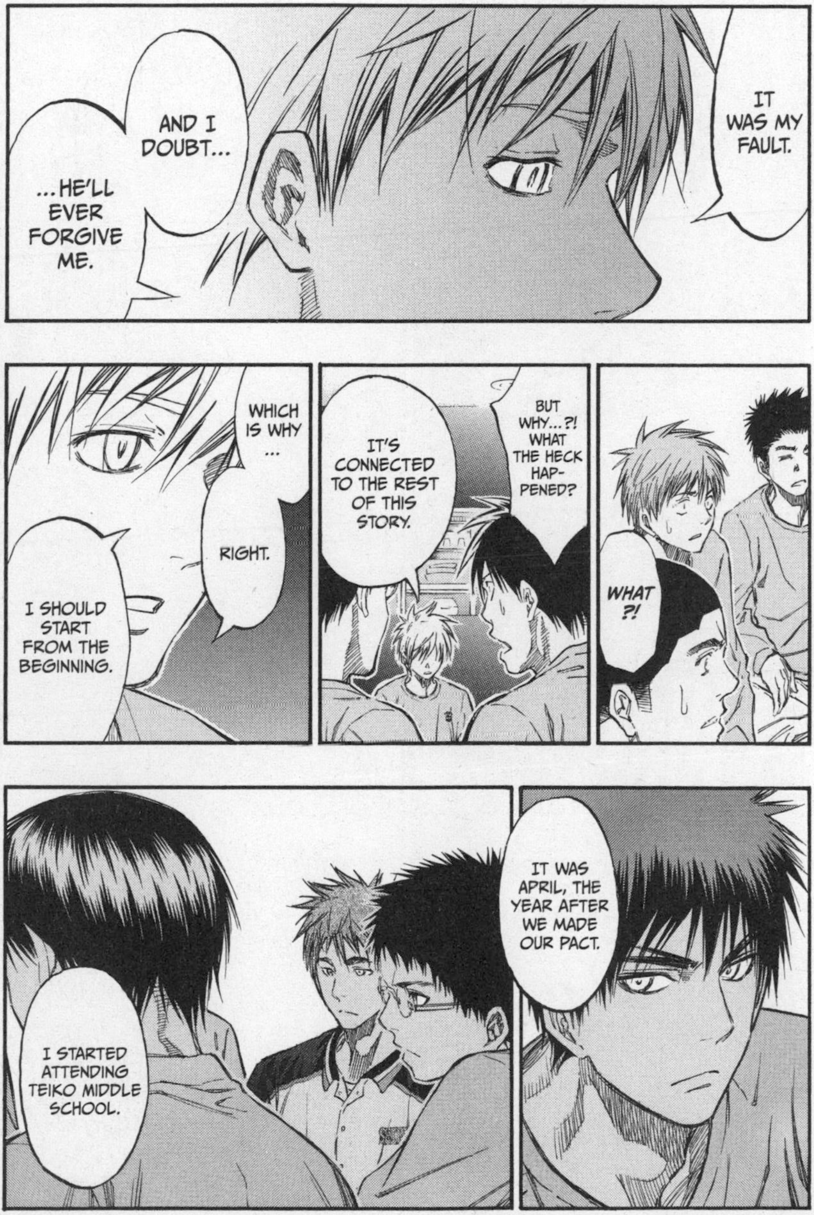
IT WAS MY FAULT.
AND I DOUBT...
...HE'LL EVER FORGIVE ME.
WHAT?!
BUT WHY...?! WHAT THE HECK HAPPENED?
IT'S CONNECTED TO THE REST OF THIS STORY.
WHICH IS WHY ...
RIGHT.
I SHOULD START FROM THE BEGINNING.
IT WAS APRIL, THE YEAR AFTER WE MADE OUR PACT.
I STARTED ATTENDING TEIKO MIDDLE SCHOOL.

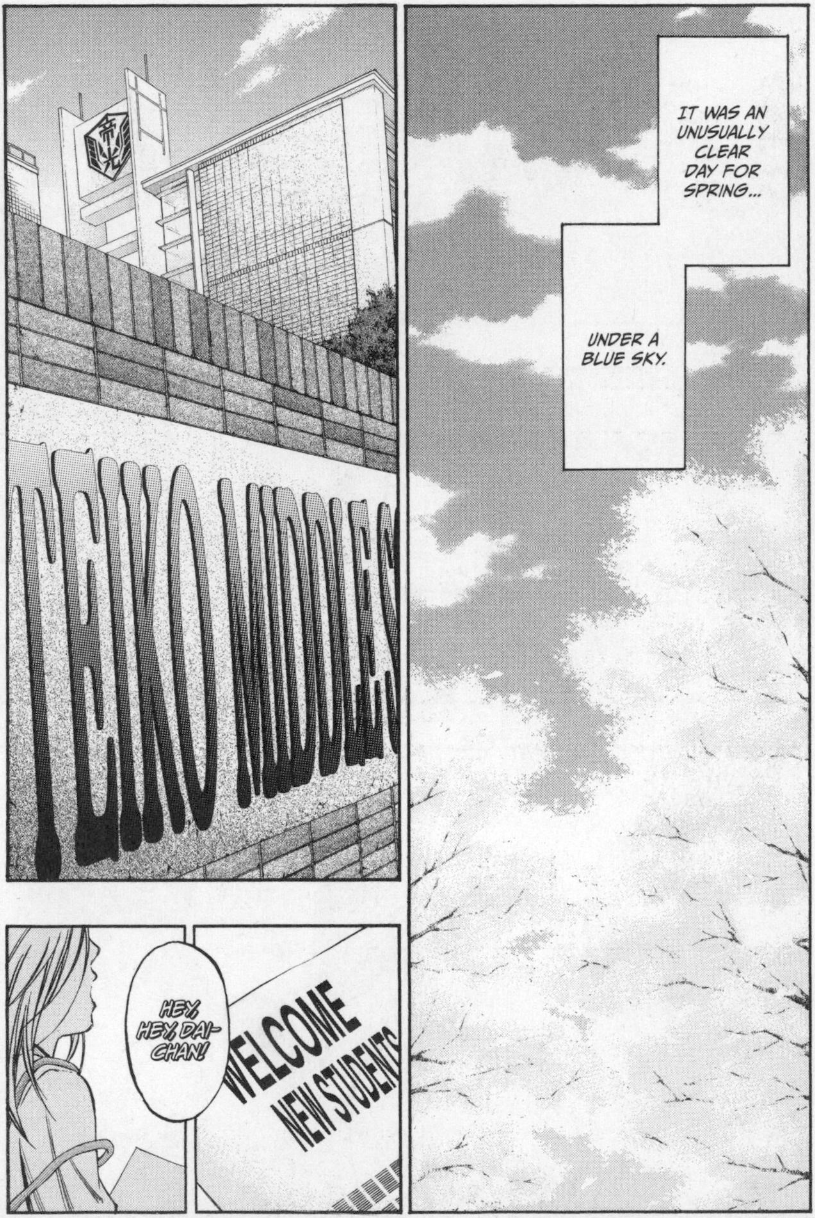
IT WAS AN UNUSUALLY CLEAR DAY FOR SPRING...
UNDER A BLUE SKY.
TEIKO MIDDLE
WELCOME NEW STUDENTS
HEY, HEY, DAI-CHAN!

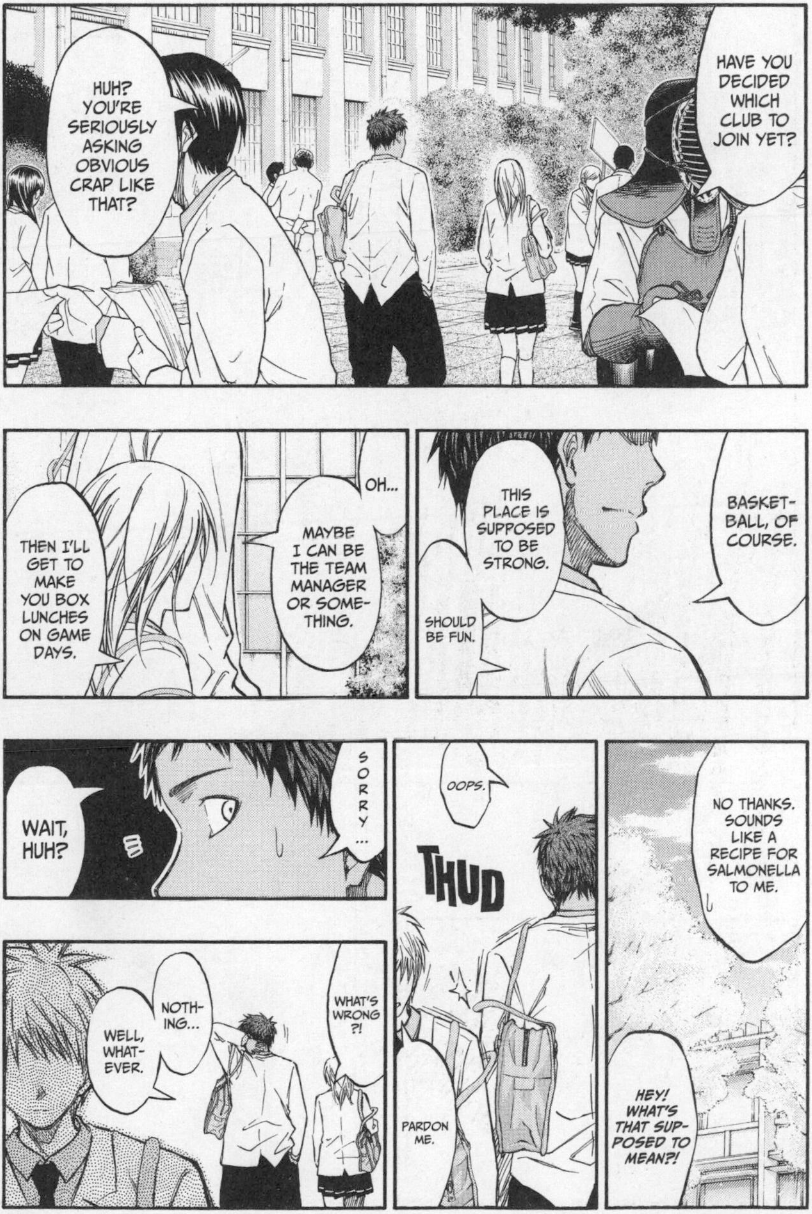
HAVE YOU DECIDED WHICH CLUB TO JOIN YET?
HUH? YOU'RE SERIOUSLY ASKING OBVIOUS CRAP LIKE THAT?
BASKETBALL, OF COURSE.
THIS PLACE IS SUPPOSED TO BE STRONG.
SHOULD BE FUN.
OH...
MAYBE I CAN BE THE TEAM MANAGER OR SOMETHING.
THEN I'LL GET TO MAKE YOU BOX LUNCHES ON GAME DAYS.
NO THANKS. SOUNDS LIKE A RECIPE FOR SALMONELLA TO ME.
HEY! WHAT'S THAT SUPPOSED TO MEAN?!
OOPS.
THUD
PARDON ME.
SORRY...
WAIT, HUH?
WHAT'S WRONG?!
NOTHING...
WELL, WHATEVER.

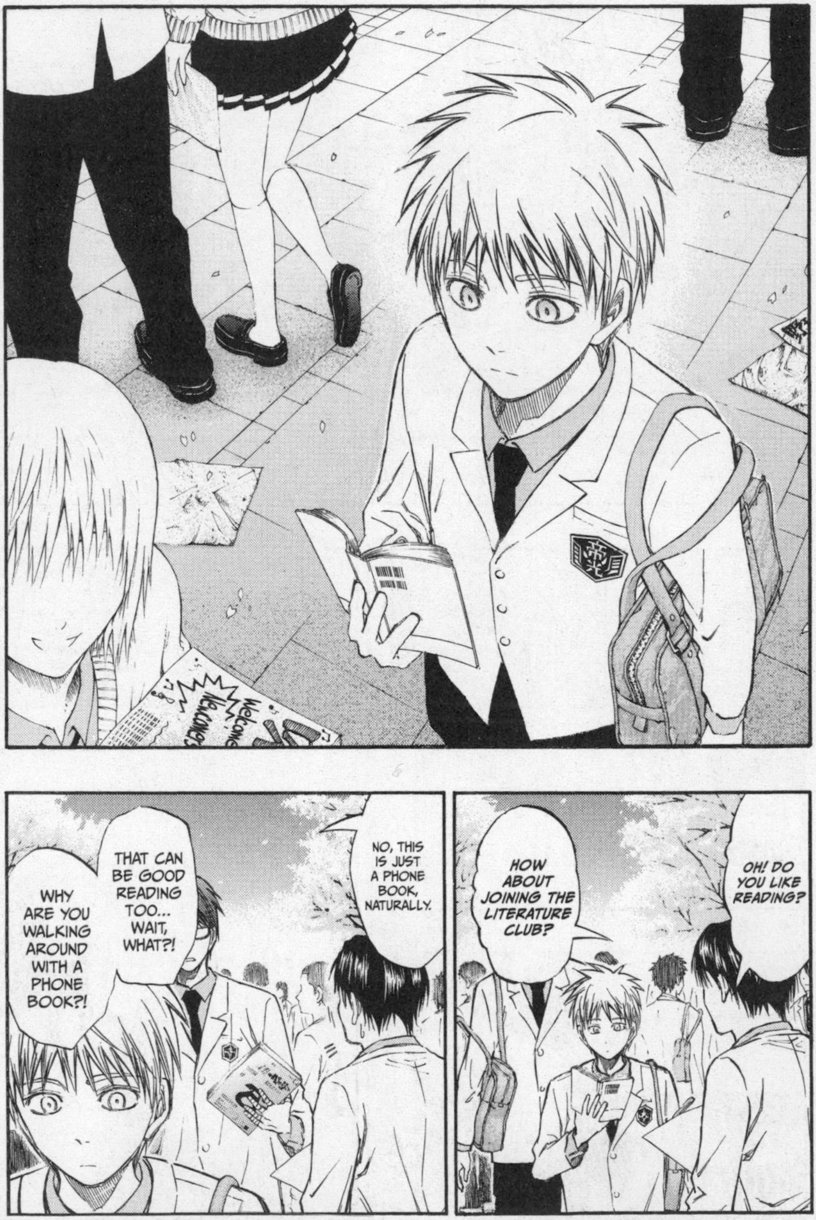
Welcome Newcomers
OH! DO YOU LIKE READING?
HOW ABOUT JOINING THE LITERATURE CLUB?
NO, THIS IS JUST A PHONE BOOK, NATURALLY.
THAT CAN BE GOOD READING TOO... WAIT, WHAT?!
WHY ARE YOU WALKING AROUND WITH A PHONE BOOK?!

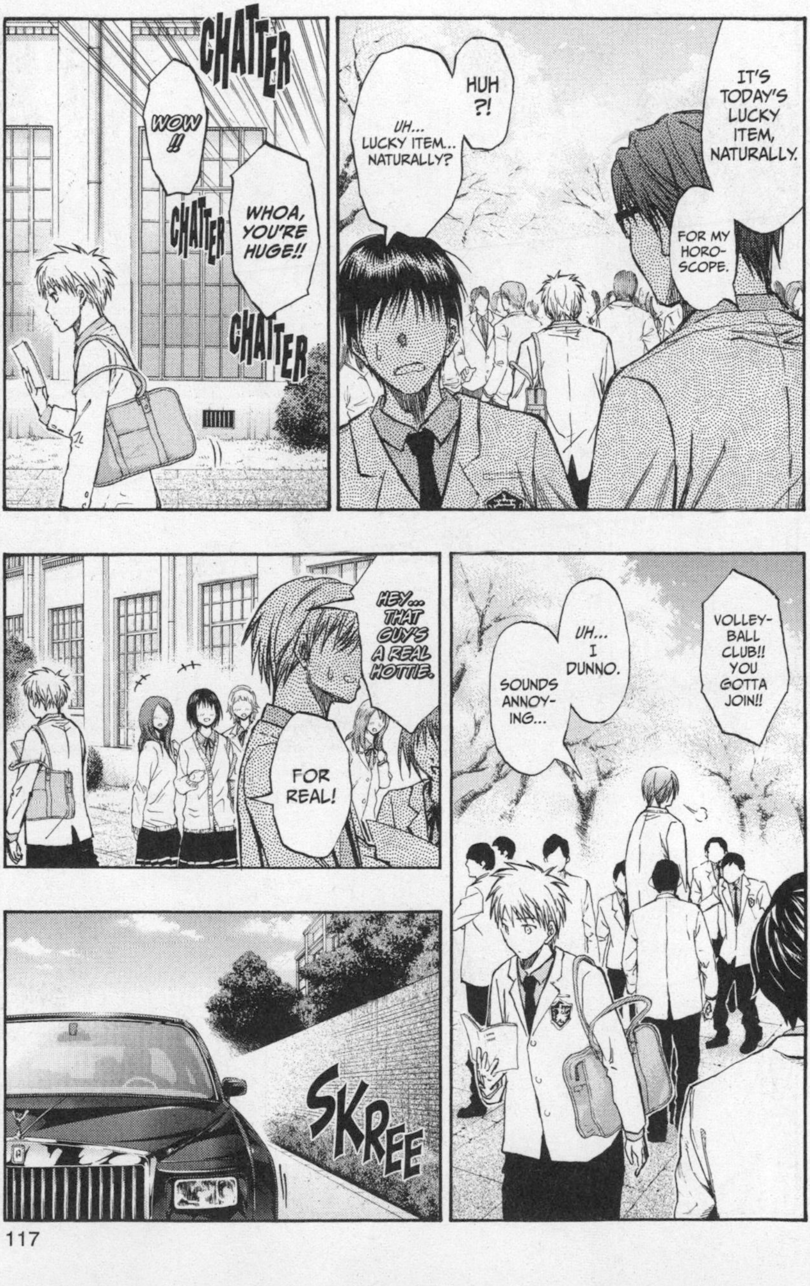
IT'S TODAY'S LUCKY ITEM, NATURALLY.
FOR MY HOROSCOPE.
HUH ?!
UH... LUCKY ITEM... NATURALLY?
CHATTER
WOW !!
WHOA, YOU'RE HUGE!!
CHATTER
CHATTER
VOLLEY-BALL CLUB!! YOU GOTTA JOIN!!
UH... I DUNNO.
SOUNDS ANNOY-ING...
HEY... THAT GUY'S A REAL HOTTIE.
FOR REAL!
SKREE

SHOULD I REALLY DROP YOU OFF HERE, SIR?
YES.
AND I WON'T NEED YOU TO DRIVE ME AT ALL, STARTING TOMOR-ROW.
BUT I'M AFRAID... YOUR FATHER ASKED ME TO DRIVE YOU TO THE FRONT GATE...
NEVER MIND MY FATHER.
GETTING DRIVEN EVERY MORNING WOULD ONLY MAKE ME A LAUGHING-STOCK.
I OUGHT TO BE FREE AT SCHOOL, IF NOWHERE ELSE.
SLIP
DID YOU JOIN A CLUB YET?
I'M IN THE THE B-BALL CLUB
OF COURSE!!
LET'S BOTH GIVE IT OUR ALL SO
WE CAN PLAY IN REAL GAMES AND KEEP
THAT PROMISE TO EACH OTHER!

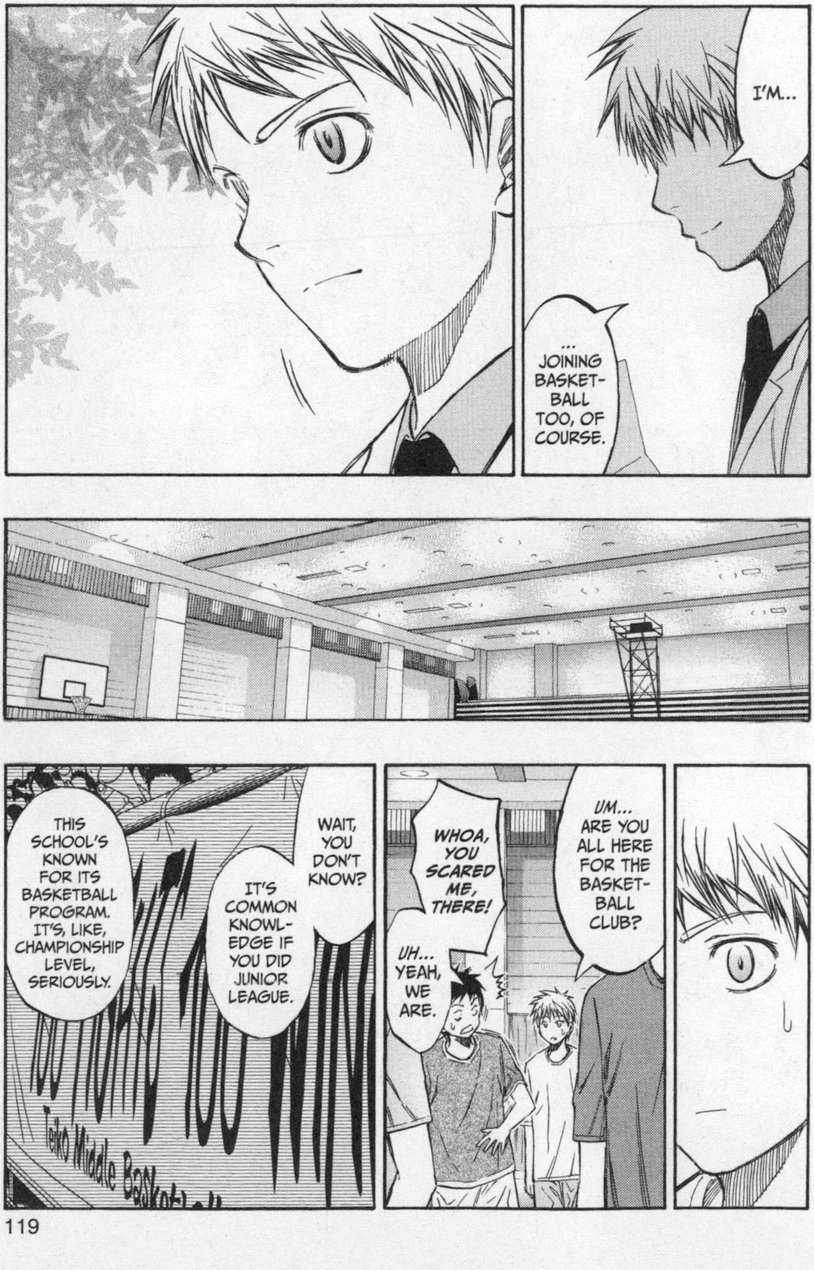

I'M...
... JOINING BASKET-BALL TOO, OF COURSE.
UM... ARE YOU ALL HERE FOR THE BASKET-BALL CLUB?
WHOA, YOU SCARED ME, THERE!
UH... YEAH, WE ARE.
WAIT, YOU DON'T KNOW?
IT'S COMMON KNOWL-EDGE IF YOU DID JUNIOR LEAGUE.
THIS SCHOOL'S KNOWN FOR ITS BASKETBALL PROGRAM. IT'S, LIKE, CHAMPIONSHIP LEVEL, SERIOUSLY.
Teiko Middle

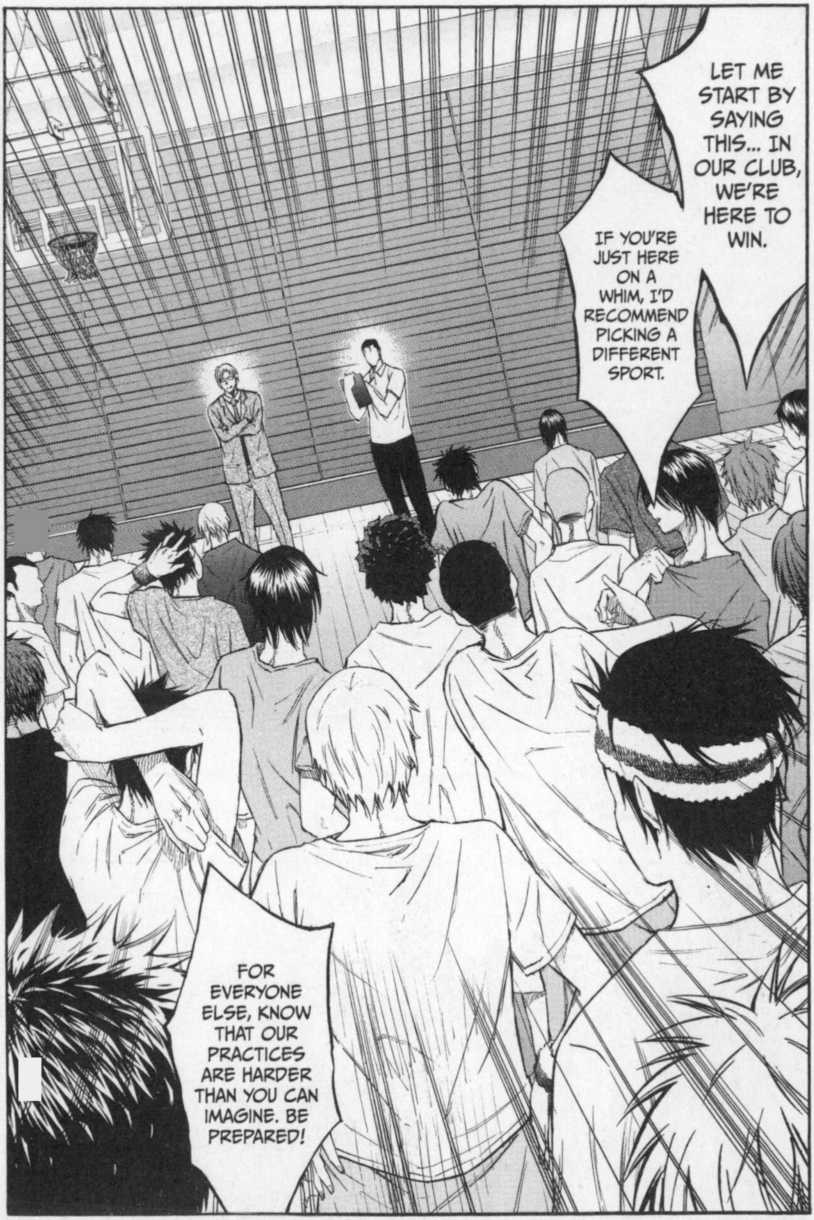
LET ME START BY SAYING THIS... IN OUR CLUB, WE'RE HERE TO WIN.
IF YOU'RE JUST HERE ON A WHIM, I'D RECOMMEND PICKING A DIFFERENT SPORT.
FOR EVERYONE ELSE, KNOW THAT OUR PRACTICES ARE HARDER THAN YOU CAN IMAGINE. BE PREPARED!

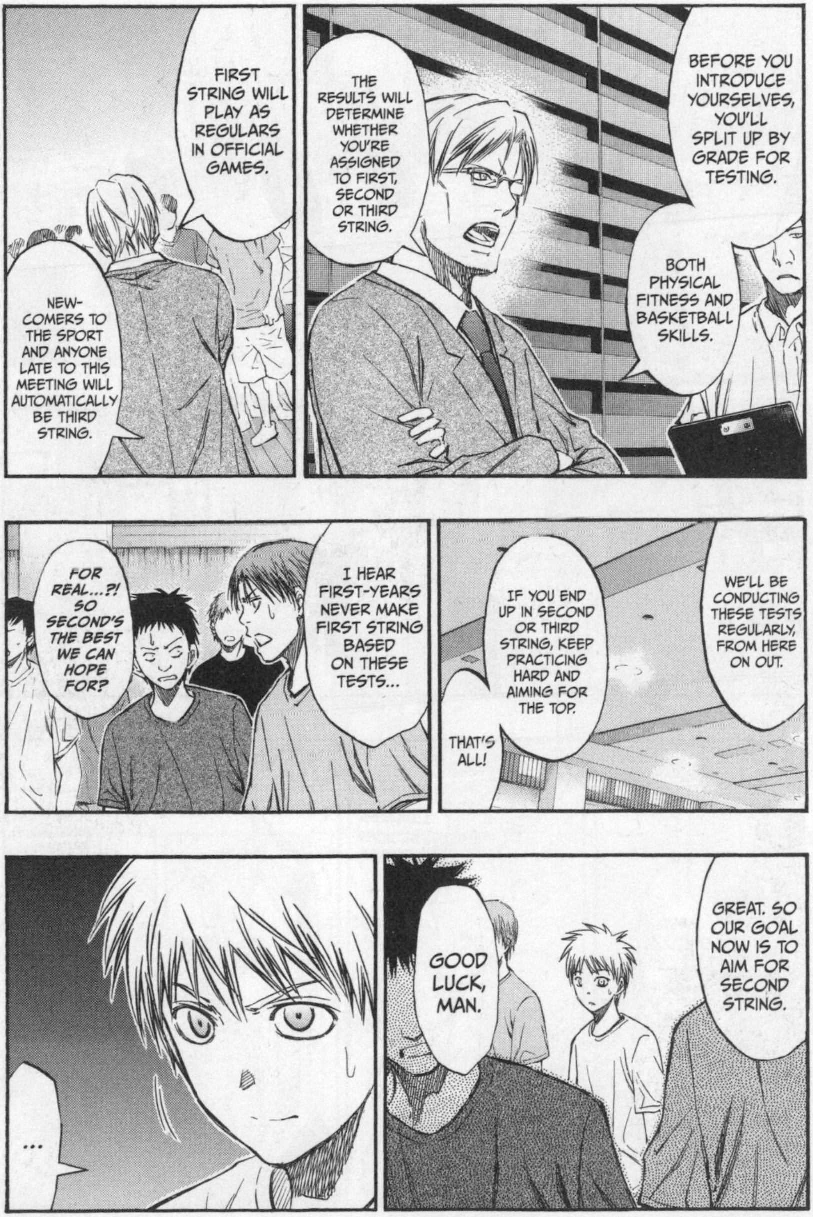
BEFORE YOU INTRODUCE YOURSELVES, YOU'LL SPLIT UP BY GRADE FOR TESTING.
BOTH PHYSICAL FITNESS AND BASKETBALL SKILLS.
THE RESULTS WILL DETERMINE WHETHER YOU'RE ASSIGNED TO FIRST, SECOND OR THIRD STRING.
FIRST STRING WILL PLAY AS REGULARS IN OFFICIAL GAMES.
NEW-COMERS TO THE SPORT AND ANYONE LATE TO THIS MEETING WILL AUTOMATICALLY BE THIRD STRING.
WE'LL BE CONDUCTING THESE TESTS REGULARLY, FROM HERE ON OUT.
IF YOU END UP IN SECOND OR THIRD STRING, KEEP PRACTICING HARD AND AIMING FOR THE TOP.
THAT'S ALL!
I HEAR FIRST-YEARS NEVER MAKE FIRST STRING BASED ON THESE TESTS...
FOR REAL...?! SO SECOND'S THE BEST WE CAN HOPE FOR?
GREAT. SO OUR GOAL NOW IS TO AIM FOR SECOND STRING.
GOOD LUCK, MAN.
...

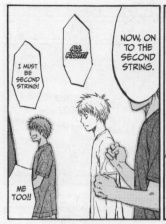

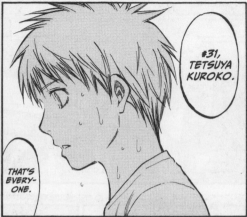

#31, TETSUYA KUROKO.
THAT'S EVERY-ONE.
NOW, ON TO THE SECOND STRING.
ALL RIGHT!
I MUST BE SECOND STRING!
ME TOO!!
OU JOIN A CLUB YET?
IN THE THE B-BALL
F COURSE!!
LET'S BOTH GIVE IT
WE CAN PLAY IN REA
THAT PROMISE TO
OSAMU TAKEDA.
THAT'S ALL.
FINALLY, FIRST STRING.
HUH?
CHATTER

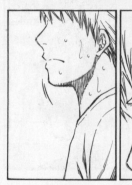

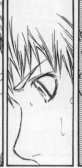

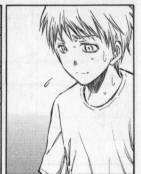

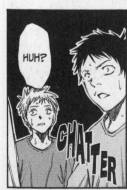

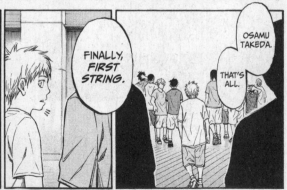

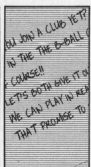

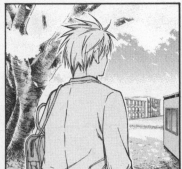

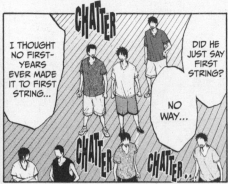

DID HE JUST SAY FIRST STRING?
CHATTER
I THOUGHT NO FIRST-YEARS EVER MADE IT TO FIRST STRING...
NO WAY...
CHATTER...
CHATTER
#8, DAIKI AOMINE.
#11, SHINTARO MIDORIMA.
#23, ATSUSHI MURASAKI-BARA.
#29, SEIJURO AKASHI.

KUROKO'S BASKETBALL

TEIKO ARC

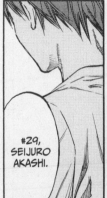

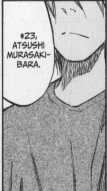

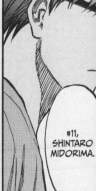

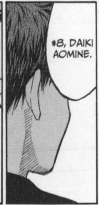

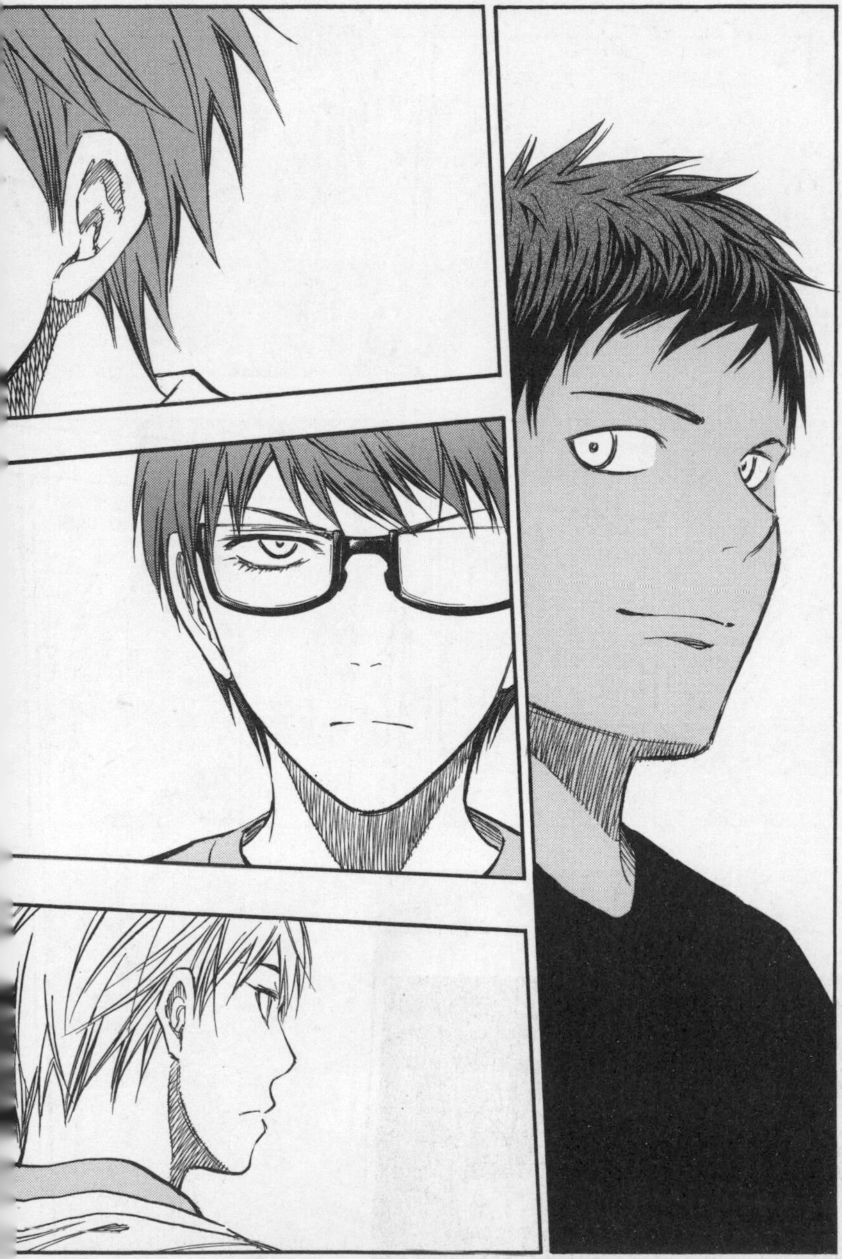

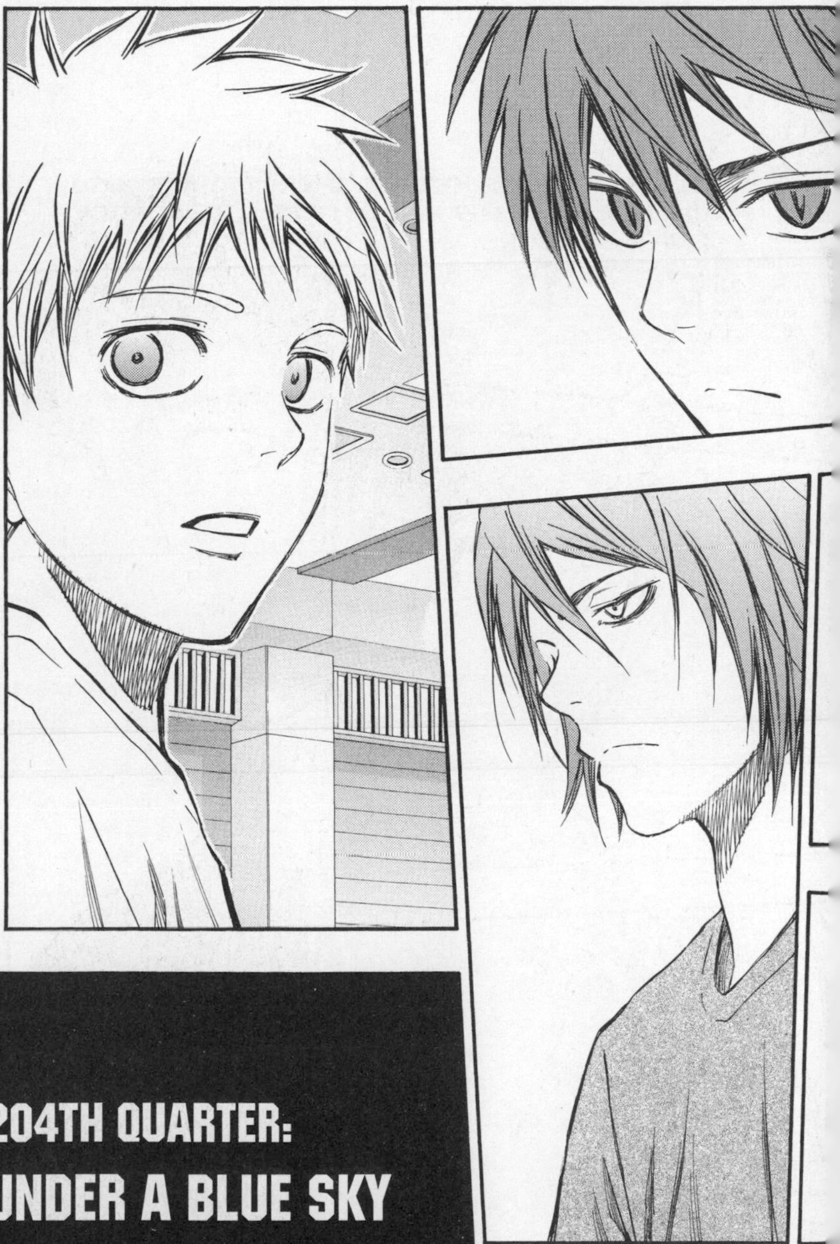

204TH QUARTER:
UNDER A BLUE SKY

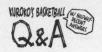

KUROKO'S BASKETBALL

Q&A

W/ HALFWAY-DECENT ANSWERS

Q. AKASHI-KUN SAYS HE'S NEVER LOST AT ANYTHING, BUT DOES THAT MEAN HE'S NEVER LOST AT ROCK-PAPER-SCISSORS?
(MOJA from HYOGO PREFECTURE)

A. HE HASN'T. BUT HE SEES WINNING AT SILLY GAMES LIKE THAT AS JUST AS BAD AS LOSING, SO HE AVOIDS THEM.

TEIKO ... ... ARC?!
SO WE WON'T BE IN THE STORY FOR A WHILE!
Kuroko's BASKETBALL volume 23
BUT I'M THE "LIGHT"...
WHOAAAA!!
YUP.

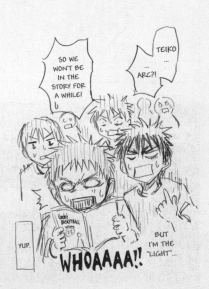

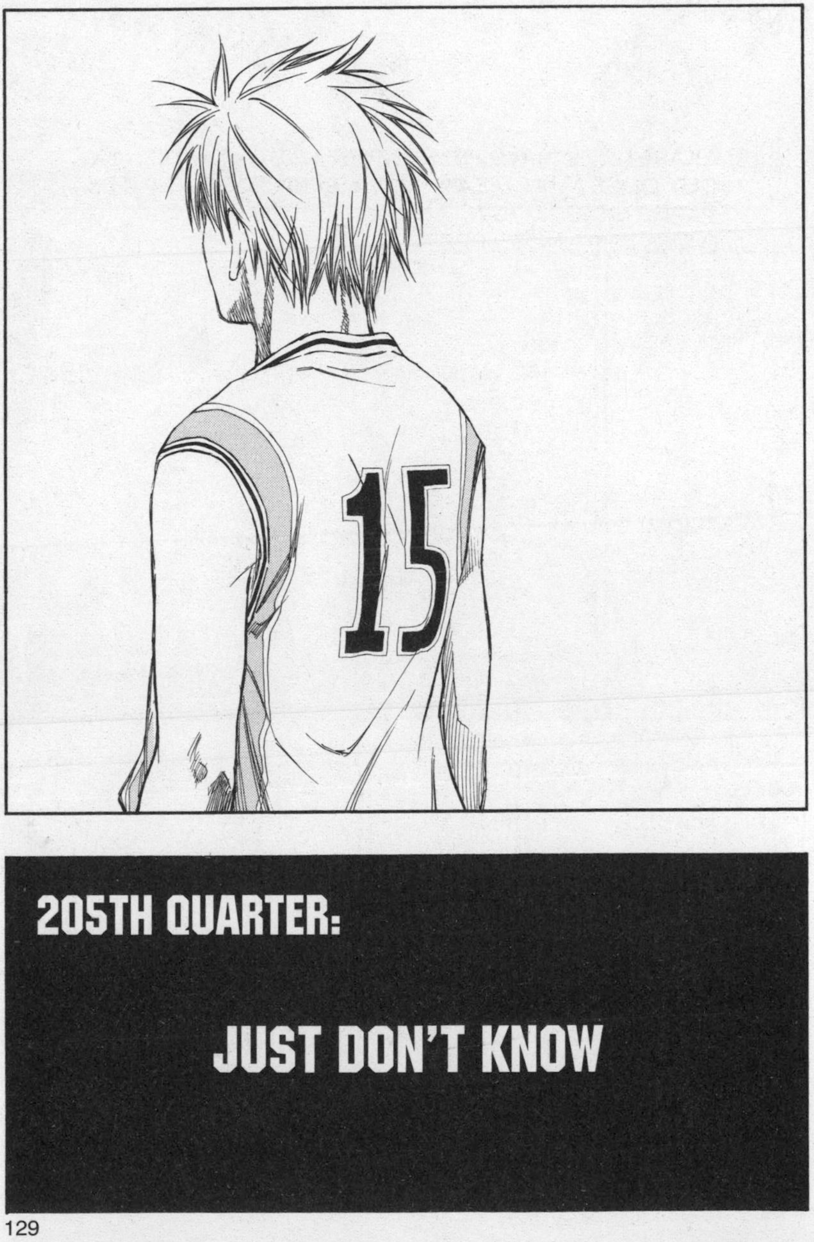
15

205TH QUARTER:

JUST DON'T KNOW

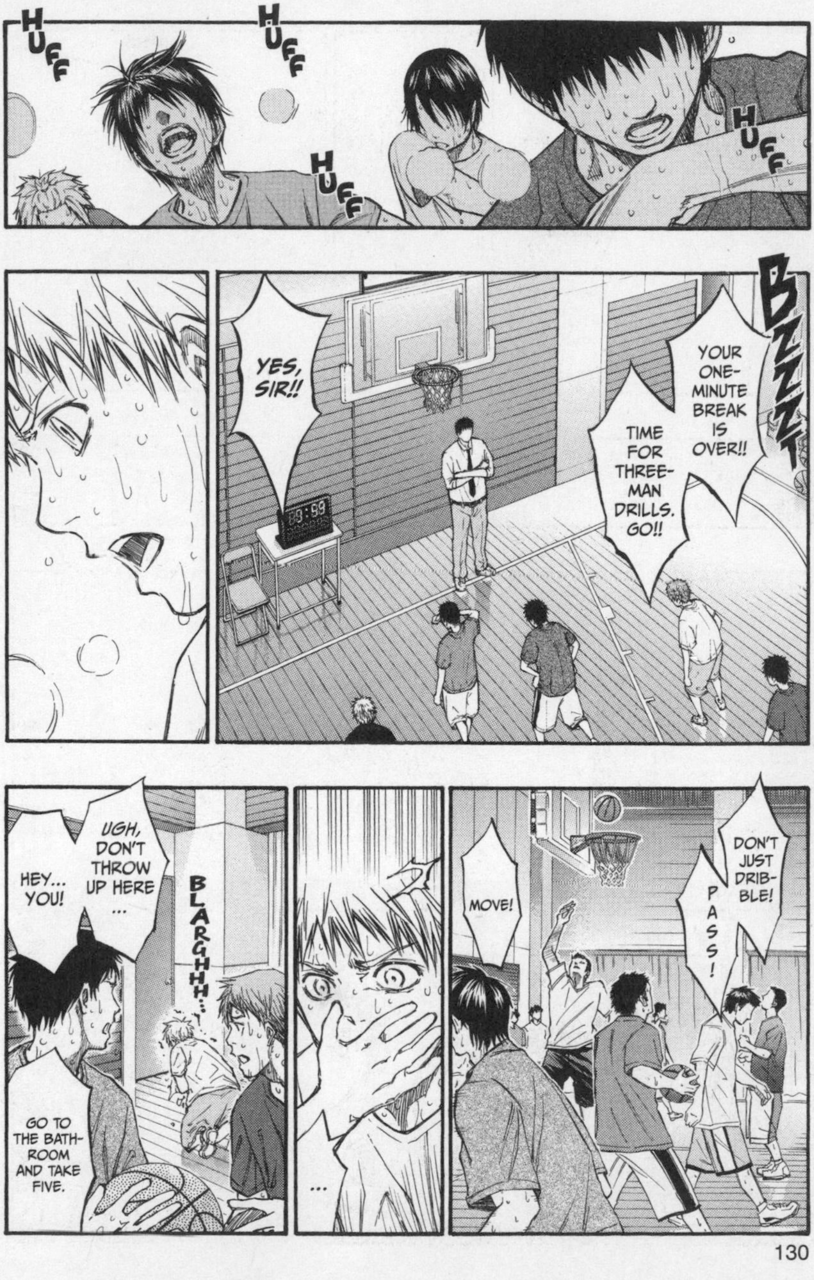
HUFF
HUFF
HUFF
HUFF
BZZZT
YOUR ONE-MINUTE BREAK IS OVER!!
TIME FOR THREE-MAN DRILLS. GO!!
YES, SIR!!
DON'T JUST DRIBBLE!
PASS!
MOVE!
...
UGH, DON'T THROW UP HERE ...
BLARGHHH...
HEY... YOU!
GO TO THE BATHROOM AND TAKE FIVE.

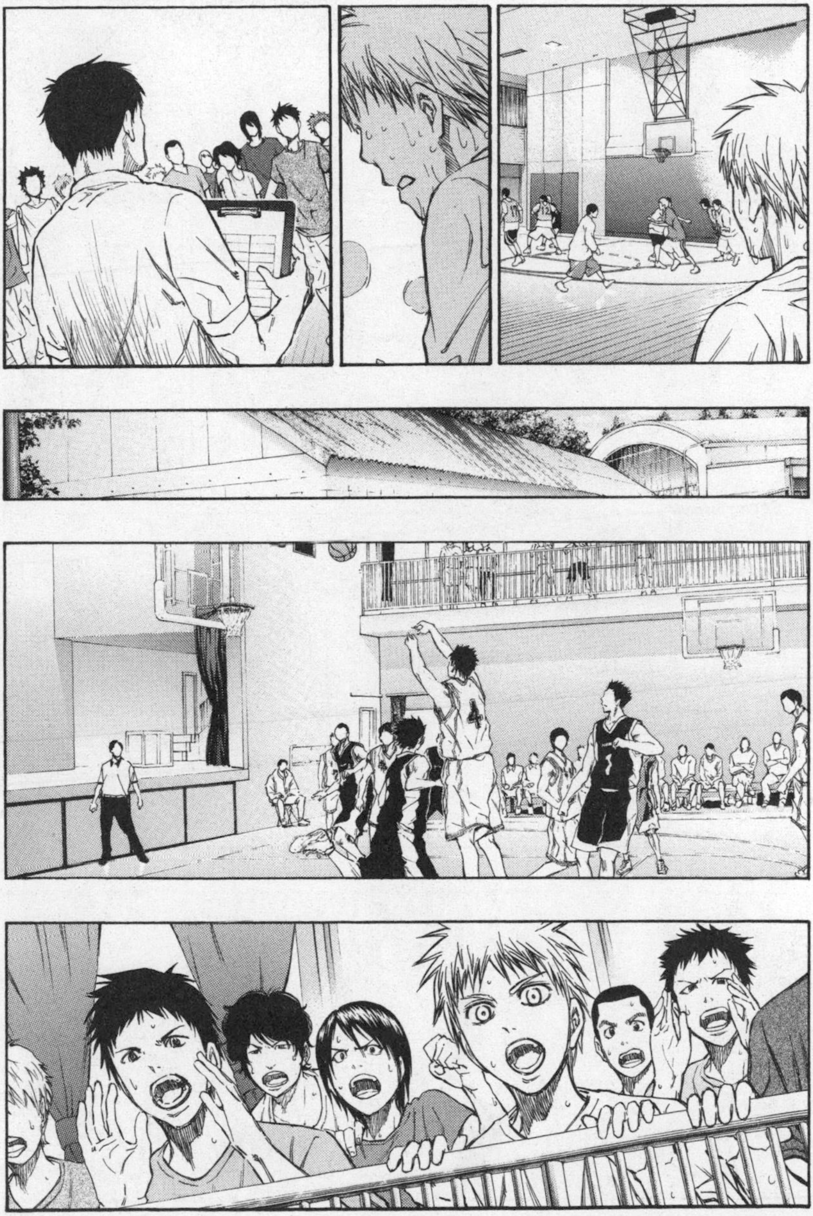

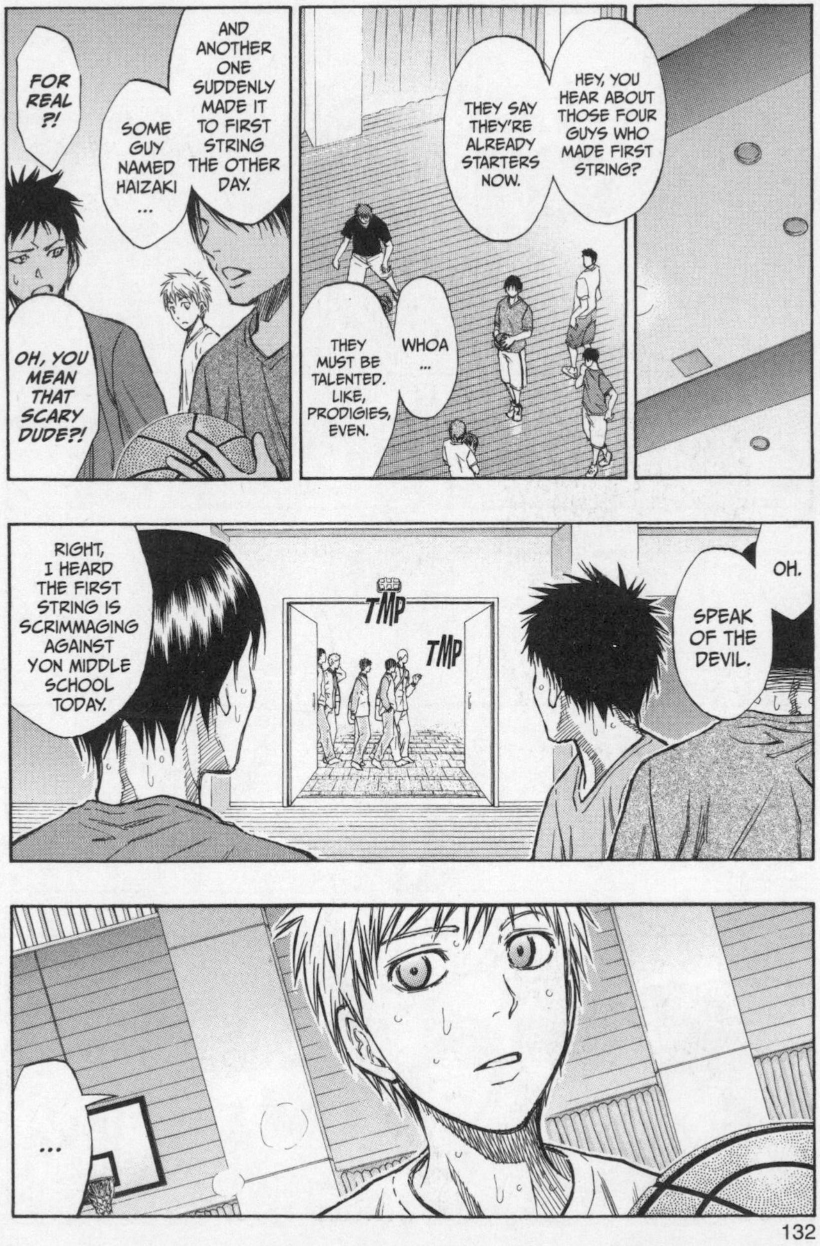
HEY, YOU HEAR ABOUT THOSE FOUR GUYS WHO MADE FIRST STRING?
THEY SAY THEY'RE ALREADY STARTERS NOW.
WHOA ...
THEY MUST BE TALENTED. LIKE, PRODIGIES, EVEN.
AND ANOTHER ONE SUDDENLY MADE IT TO FIRST STRING THE OTHER DAY.
SOME GUY NAMED HAIZAKI ...
FOR REAL?!
OH, YOU MEAN THAT SCARY DUDE?!
OH.
SPEAK OF THE DEVIL.
TMP
TMP
RIGHT, I HEARD THE FIRST STRING IS SCRIMMAGING AGAINST YON MIDDLE SCHOOL TODAY.
...

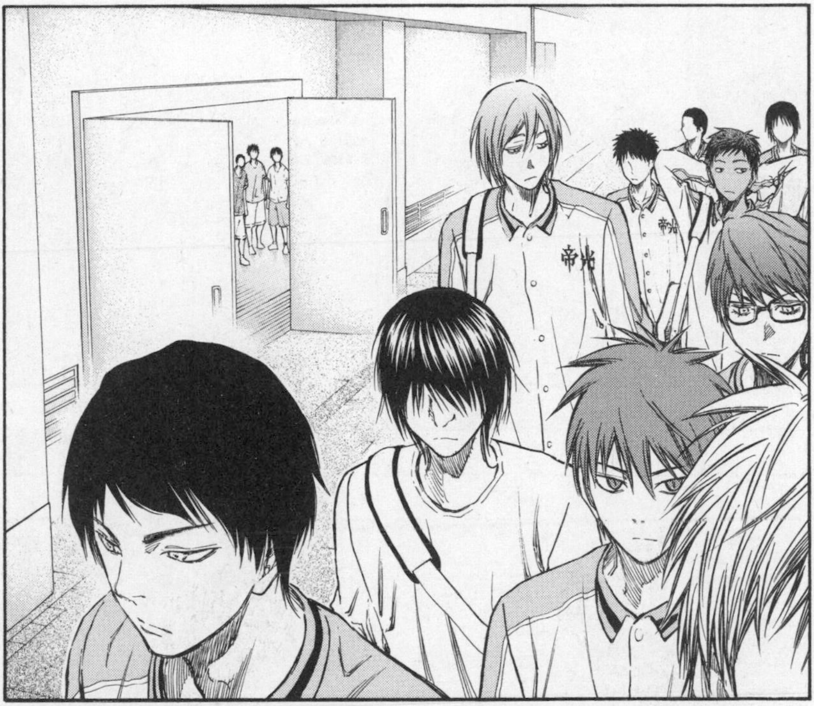

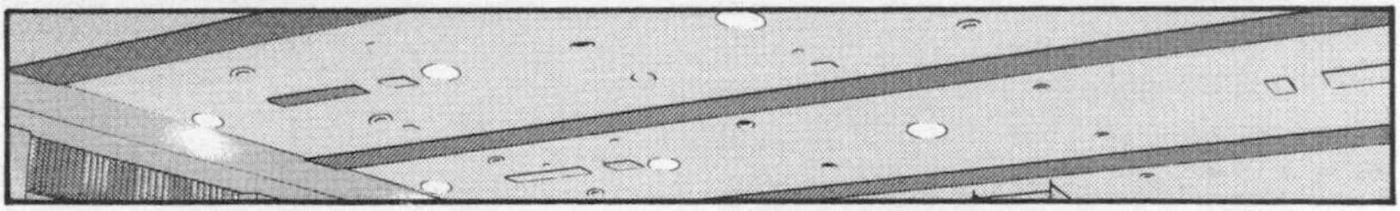

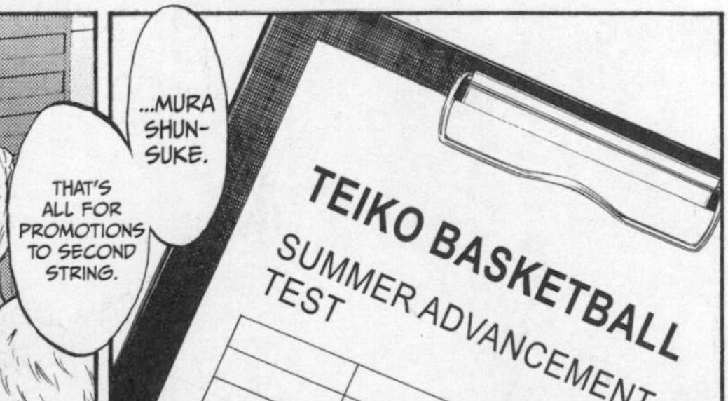
...MURA SHUN-SUKE.
THAT'S ALL FOR PROMOTIONS TO SECOND STRING.
TEIKO BASKETBALL
SUMMER ADVANCEMENT TEST

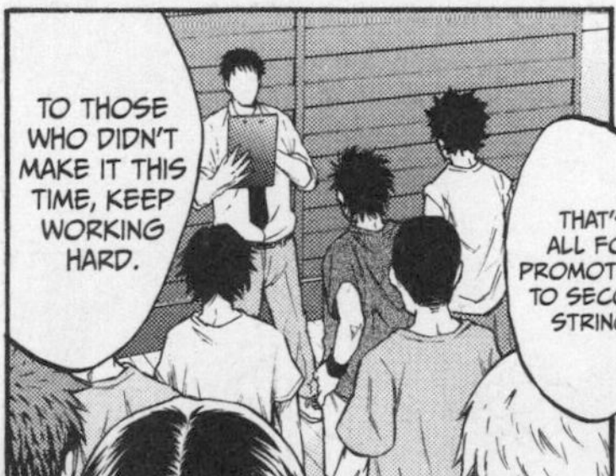
TO THOSE WHO DIDN'T MAKE IT THIS TIME, KEEP WORKING HARD.

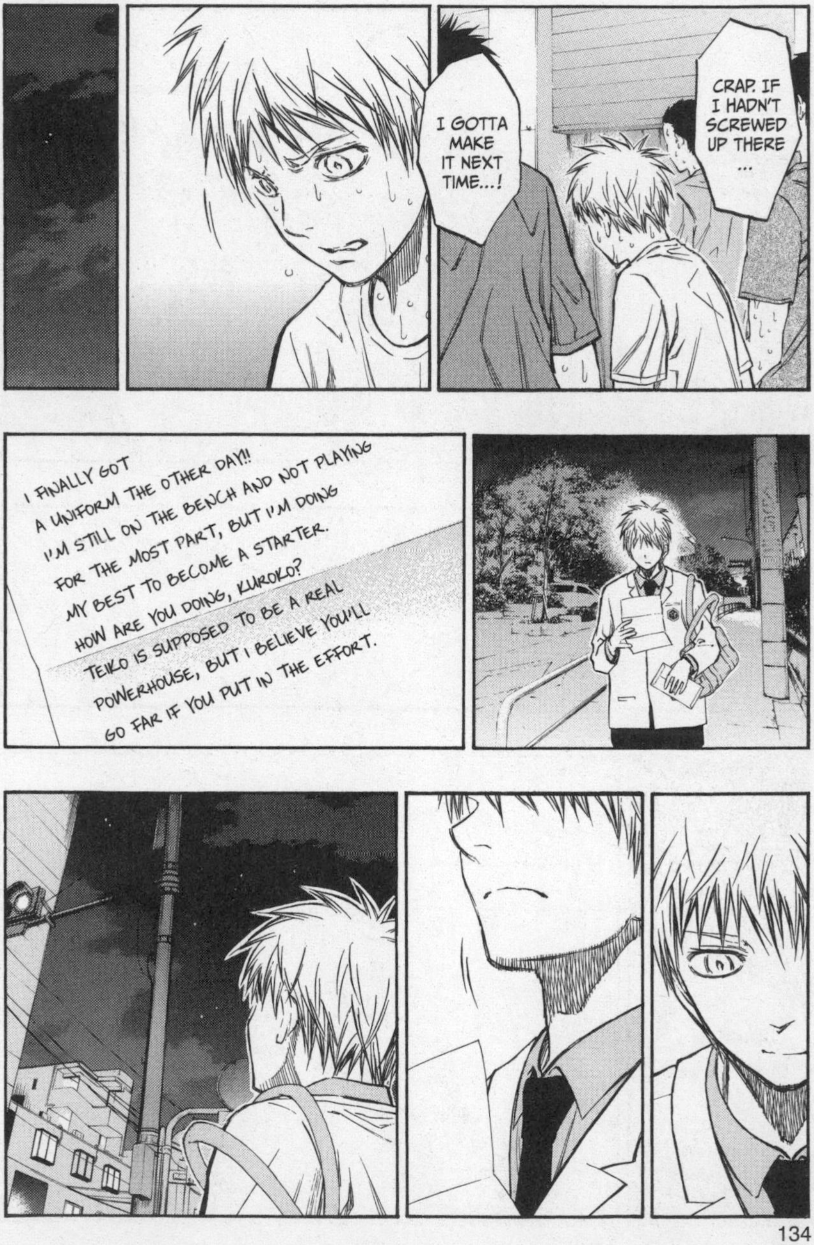
CRAP. IF I HADN'T SCREWED UP THERE ...
I GOTTA MAKE IT NEXT TIME...!
I FINALLY GOT A UNIFORM THE OTHER DAY!! I'M STILL ON THE BENCH AND NOT PLAYING FOR THE MOST PART, BUT I'M DOING MY BEST TO BECOME A STARTER. HOW ARE YOU DOING, KUROKO? TEIKO IS SUPPOSED TO BE A REAL POWERHOUSE, BUT I BELIEVE YOU'LL GO FAR IF YOU PUT IN THE EFFORT.

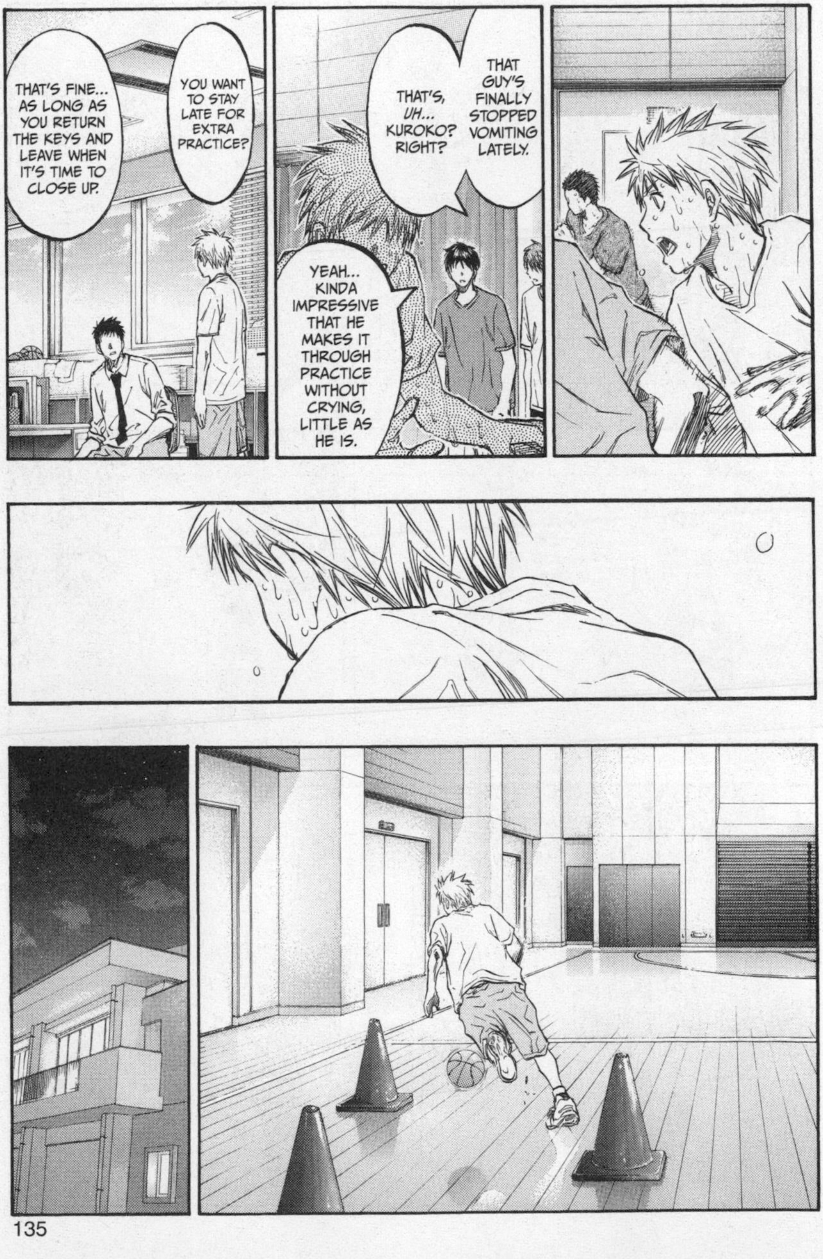
THAT GUY'S FINALLY STOPPED VOMITING LATELY.
THAT'S, *UH*... KUROKO? RIGHT?
YEAH... KINDA IMPRESSIVE THAT HE MAKES IT THROUGH PRACTICE WITHOUT CRYING, LITTLE AS HE IS.
YOU WANT TO STAY LATE FOR EXTRA PRACTICE?
THAT'S FINE... AS LONG AS YOU RETURN THE KEYS AND LEAVE WHEN IT'S TIME TO CLOSE UP.

RECENTLY, THEY'RE SAYING...
...THERE'S A GHOST IN THERE.
GULP
HUH?
WHAT'RE YOU BABBLING ABOUT, SATSUKI?
YOU HIT YOUR HEAD?
I'M BEING SERIOUS, HERE!!
LATE AT NIGHT, PEOPLE ARE HEARING THE SOUNDS OF SHOES SQUEAKING AND BALLS BOUNCING IN THE THIRD-STRING GYM...
YOU DUMB OR WHAT? NO WAY THAT'S TRUE!
TMP
TMP
HEY ...
DAI-CHA... AOMINE-KUN!
HEY, SATSUKI-CHAN!
HM?
YOU'RE CHILDHOOD FRIENDS WITH AOMINE-KUN? SWEET!
C'MON! DIDN'T YOU SEE HIM PLAY AT ALL-MIDDLE? HE WAS SO COOL.
DOES HE HAVE A GIRLFRIEND OR NOT?
HUH?
UH... YEAH... I GUESS ...
THAT WAS COOL ...?!
SHLUMP
AH!

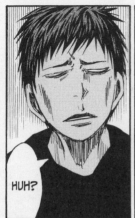

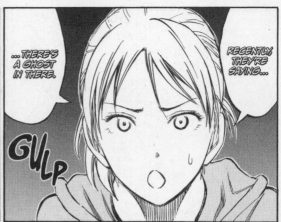

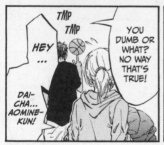

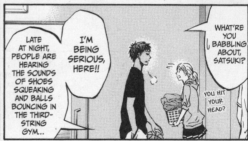

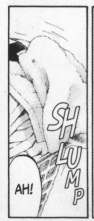

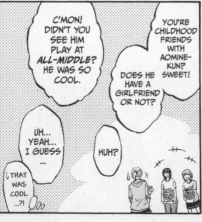

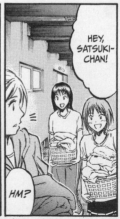

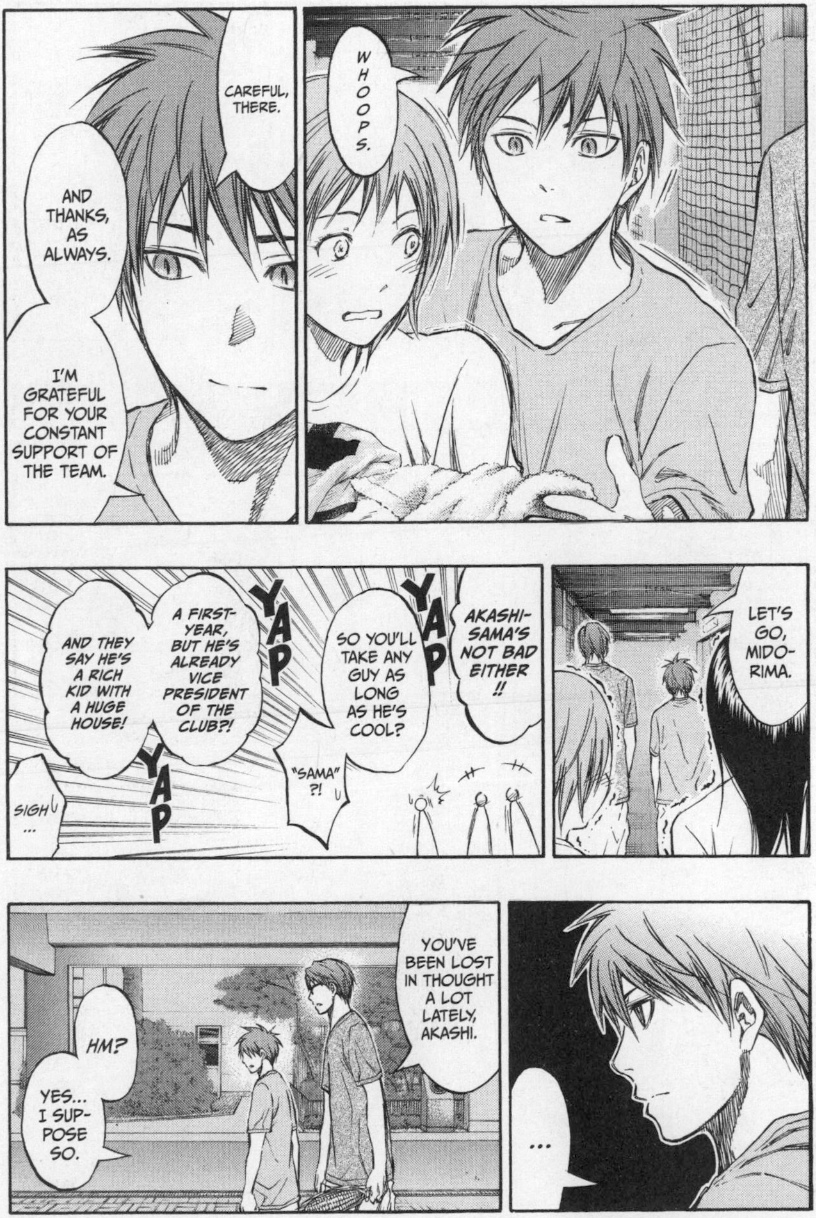
WHOOPS.
CAREFUL, THERE.
AND THANKS, AS ALWAYS.
I'M GRATEFUL FOR YOUR CONSTANT SUPPORT OF THE TEAM.
LET'S GO, MIDORIMA.
AKASHI-SAMA'S NOT BAD EITHER!!
YAP
"SAMA"?!
SO YOU'LL TAKE ANY GUY AS LONG AS HE'S COOL?
YAP
A FIRST-YEAR, BUT HE'S ALREADY VICE PRESIDENT OF THE CLUB?!
AND THEY SAY HE'S A RICH KID WITH A HUGE HOUSE!
YAP
SIGH...
...
YOU'VE BEEN LOST IN THOUGHT A LOT LATELY, AKASHI.
HM?
YES... I SUPPOSE SO.

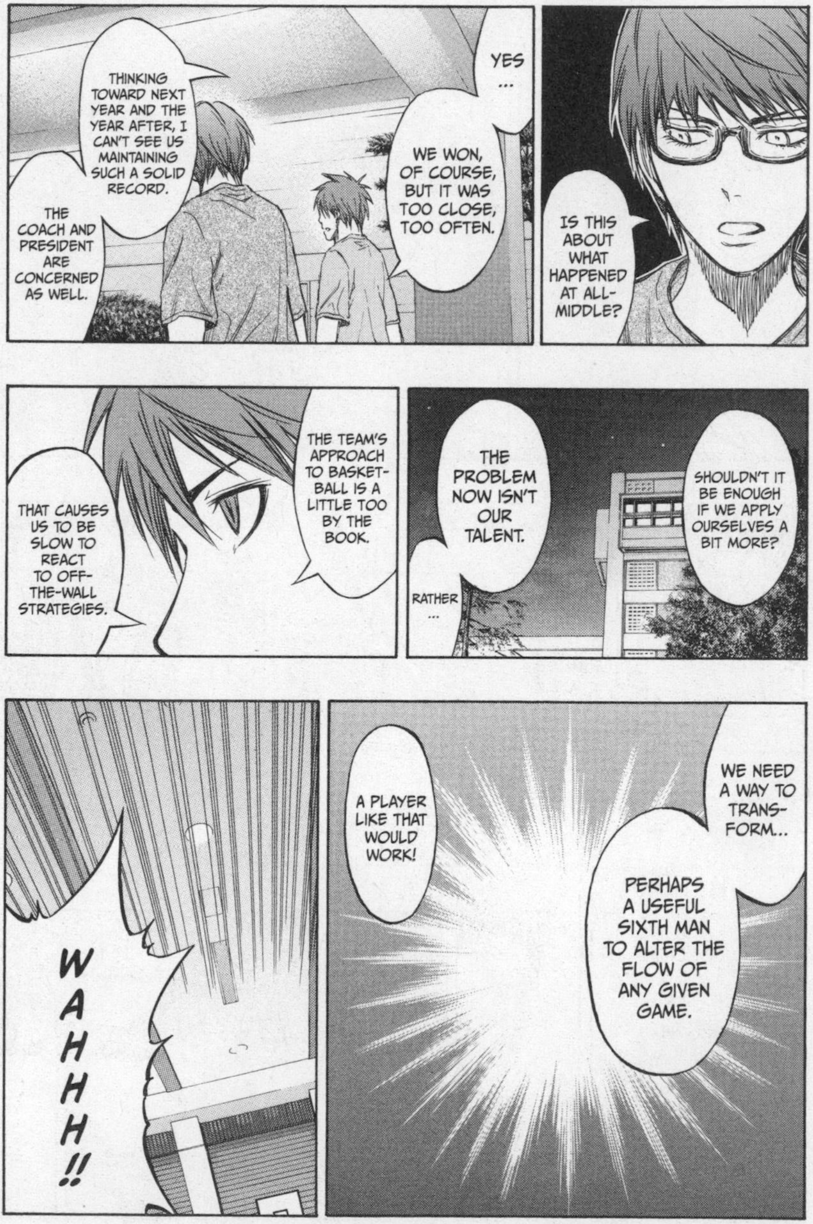
IS THIS ABOUT WHAT HAPPENED AT ALL-MIDDLE?
YES ...
WE WON, OF COURSE, BUT IT WAS TOO CLOSE, TOO OFTEN.
THINKING TOWARD NEXT YEAR AND THE YEAR AFTER, I CAN'T SEE US MAINTAINING SUCH A SOLID RECORD.
THE COACH AND PRESIDENT ARE CONCERNED AS WELL.
SHOULDN'T IT BE ENOUGH IF WE APPLY OURSELVES A BIT MORE?
THE PROBLEM NOW ISN'T OUR TALENT.
RATHER ...
THE TEAM'S APPROACH TO BASKET-BALL IS A LITTLE TOO BY THE BOOK.
THAT CAUSES US TO BE SLOW TO REACT TO OFF-THE-WALL STRATEGIES.
WE NEED A WAY TO TRANS-FORM...
PERHAPS A USEFUL SIXTH MAN TO ALTER THE FLOW OF ANY GIVEN GAME.
A PLAYER LIKE THAT WOULD WORK!
WAHHHH!!

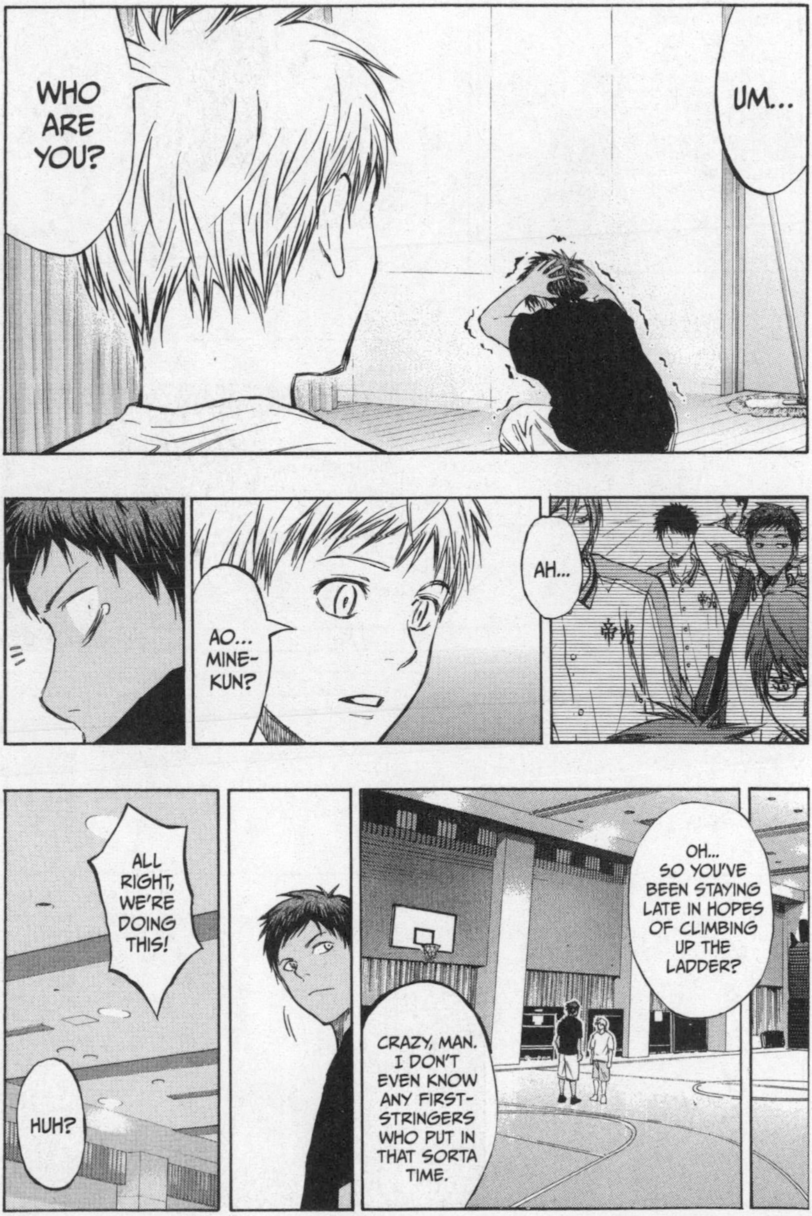
UM...
WHO ARE YOU?
AH...
AO... MINE-KUN?
OH... SO YOU'VE BEEN STAYING LATE IN HOPES OF CLIMBING UP THE LADDER?
CRAZY, MAN. I DON'T EVEN KNOW ANY FIRST-STRINGERS WHO PUT IN THAT SORTA TIME.
ALL RIGHT, WE'RE DOING THIS!
HUH?

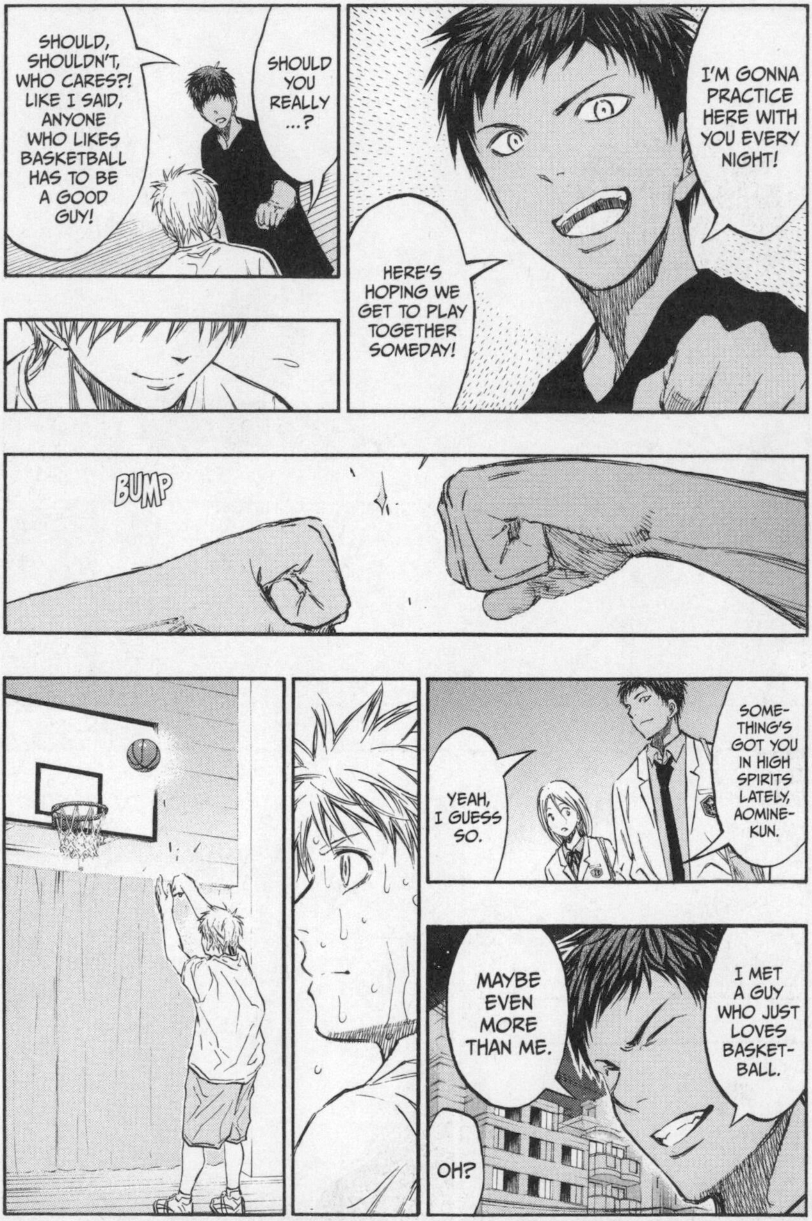
I'M GONNA PRACTICE HERE WITH YOU EVERY NIGHT!
HERE'S HOPING WE GET TO PLAY TOGETHER SOMEDAY!
SHOULD YOU REALLY ...?
SHOULD, SHOULDN'T, WHO CARES?! LIKE I SAID, ANYONE WHO LIKES BASKETBALL HAS TO BE A GOOD GUY!
BUMP
SOME-THING'S GOT YOU IN HIGH SPIRITS LATELY, AOMINE-KUN.
YEAH, I GUESS SO.
I MET A GUY WHO JUST LOVES BASKET-BALL.
MAYBE EVEN MORE THAN ME.
OH?

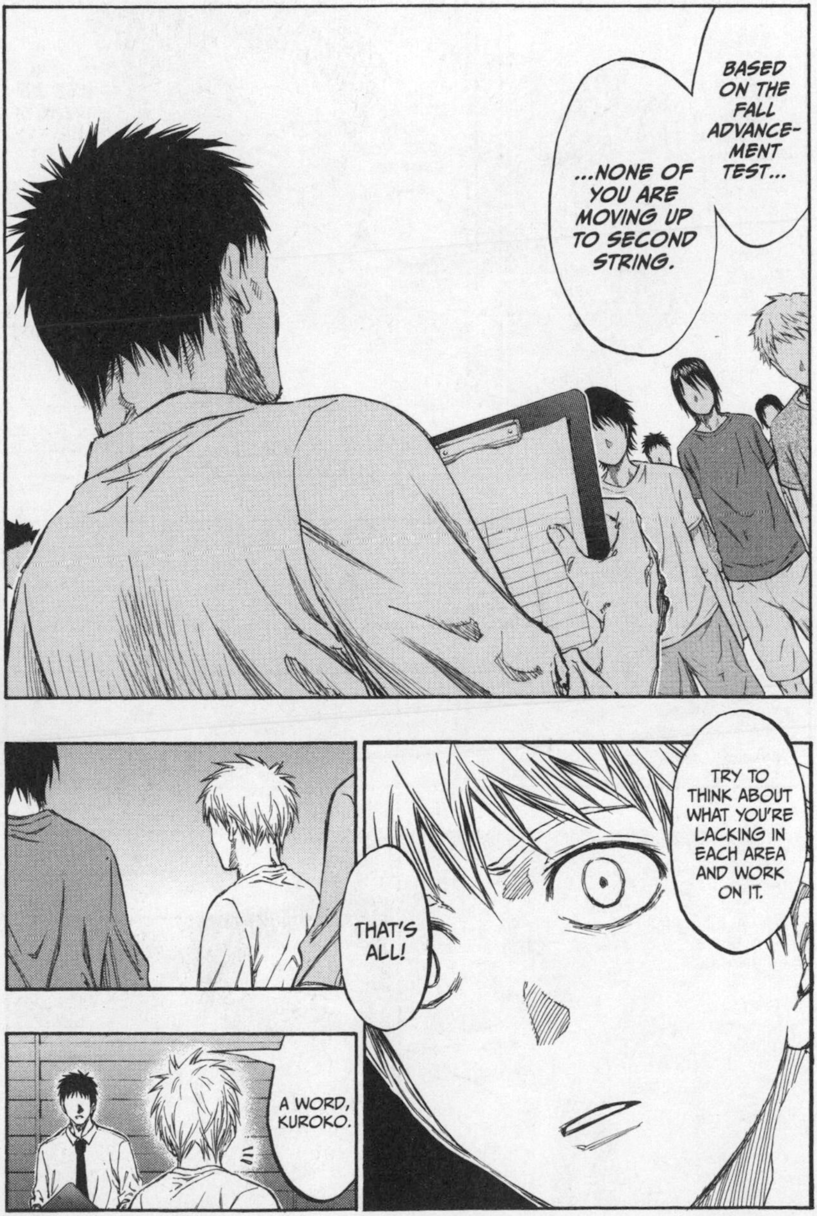
BASED ON THE FALL ADVANCEMENT TEST...
...NONE OF YOU ARE MOVING UP TO SECOND STRING.
TRY TO THINK ABOUT WHAT YOU'RE LACKING IN EACH AREA AND WORK ON IT.
THAT'S ALL!
A WORD, KUROKO.

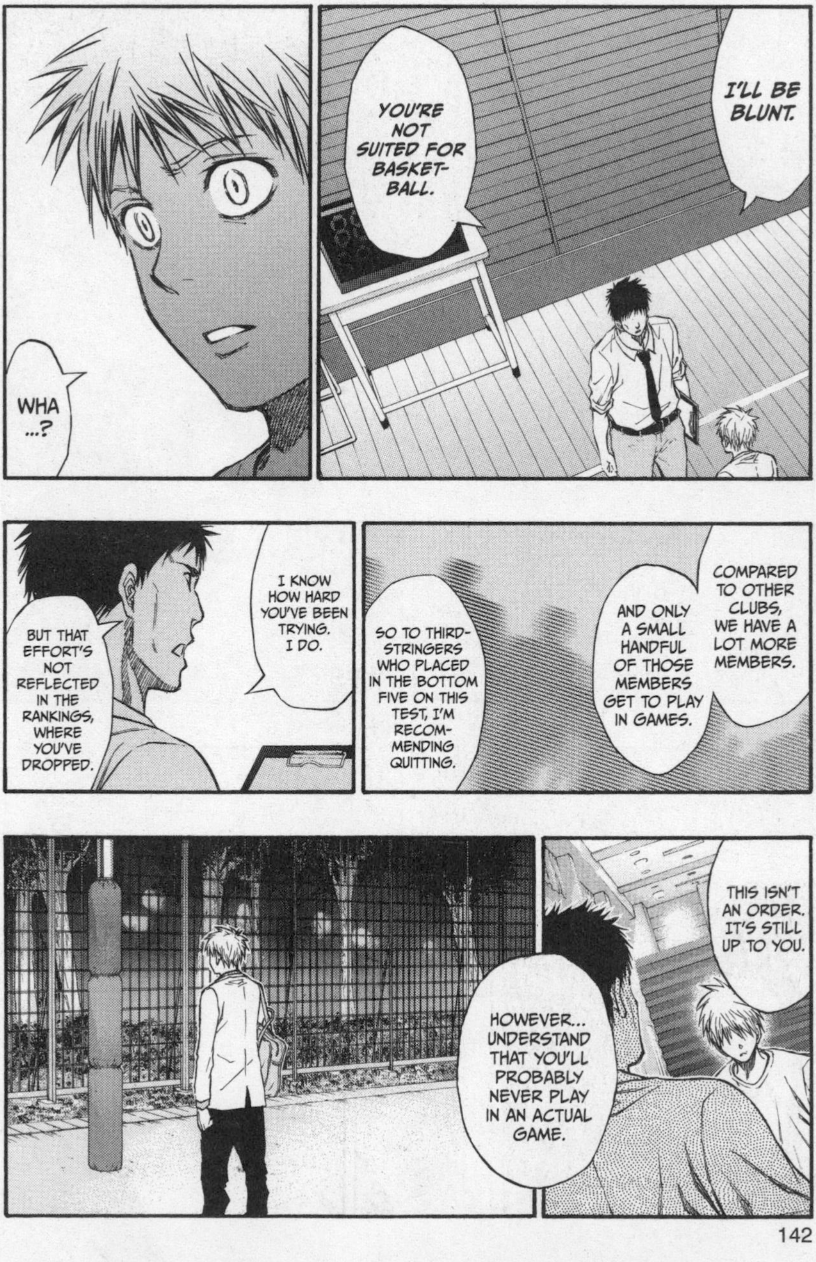
I'LL BE BLUNT.
YOU'RE NOT SUITED FOR BASKET-BALL.
WHA ...?
COMPARED TO OTHER CLUBS, WE HAVE A LOT MORE MEMBERS.
AND ONLY A SMALL HANDFUL OF THOSE MEMBERS GET TO PLAY IN GAMES.
SO TO THIRD-STRINGERS WHO PLACED IN THE BOTTOM FIVE ON THIS TEST, I'M RECOM-MENDING QUITTING.
I KNOW HOW HARD YOU'VE BEEN TRYING. I DO.
BUT THAT EFFORT'S NOT REFLECTED IN THE RANKINGS, WHERE YOU'VE DROPPED.
THIS ISN'T AN ORDER. IT'S STILL UP TO YOU.
HOWEVER... UNDERSTAND THAT YOU'LL PROBABLY NEVER PLAY IN AN ACTUAL GAME.

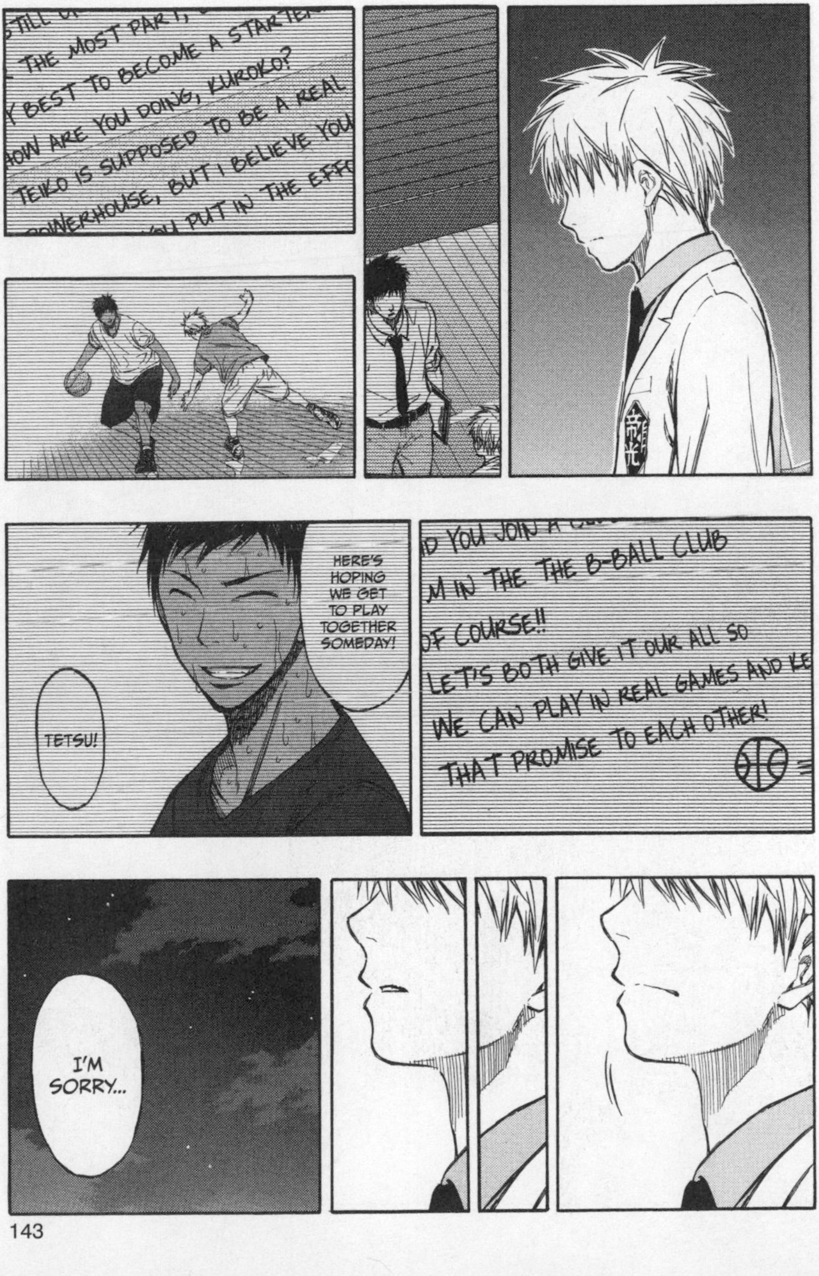
THE MOST PART,
BEST TO BECOME A START
HOW ARE YOU DOING, KUROKO?
TEIKO IS SUPPOSED TO BE A REAL
POWERHOUSE, BUT I BELIEVE YOU
YOU PUT IN THE EFF
D YOU JOIN A
M IN THE THE B-BALL CLUB
OF COURSE!!
LET'S BOTH GIVE IT OUR ALL SO
WE CAN PLAY IN REAL GAMES AND KE
THAT PROMISE TO EACH OTHER!
HERE'S HOPING WE GET TO PLAY TOGETHER SOMEDAY!
TETSU!
I'M SORRY...

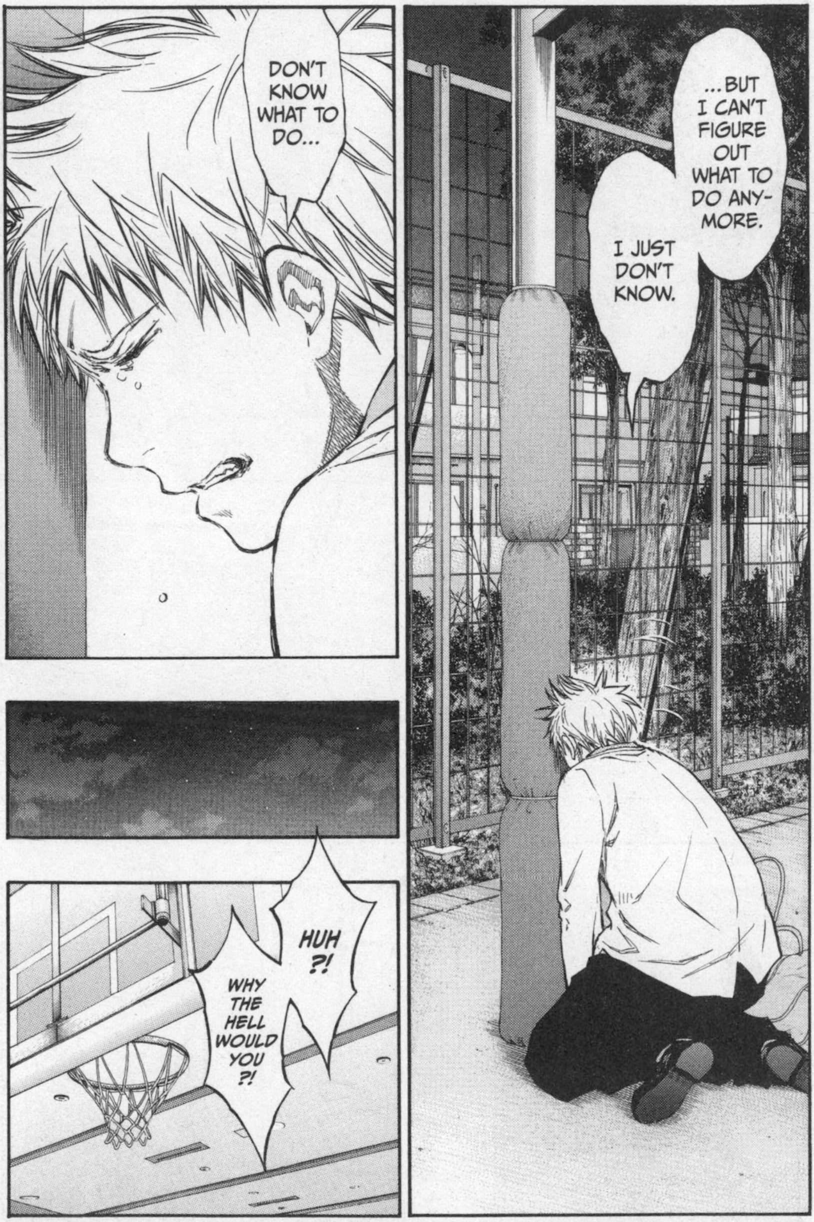
...BUT I CAN'T FIGURE OUT WHAT TO DO ANY-MORE.
I JUST DON'T KNOW.
DON'T KNOW WHAT TO DO...
HUH?!
WHY THE HELL WOULD YOU?!

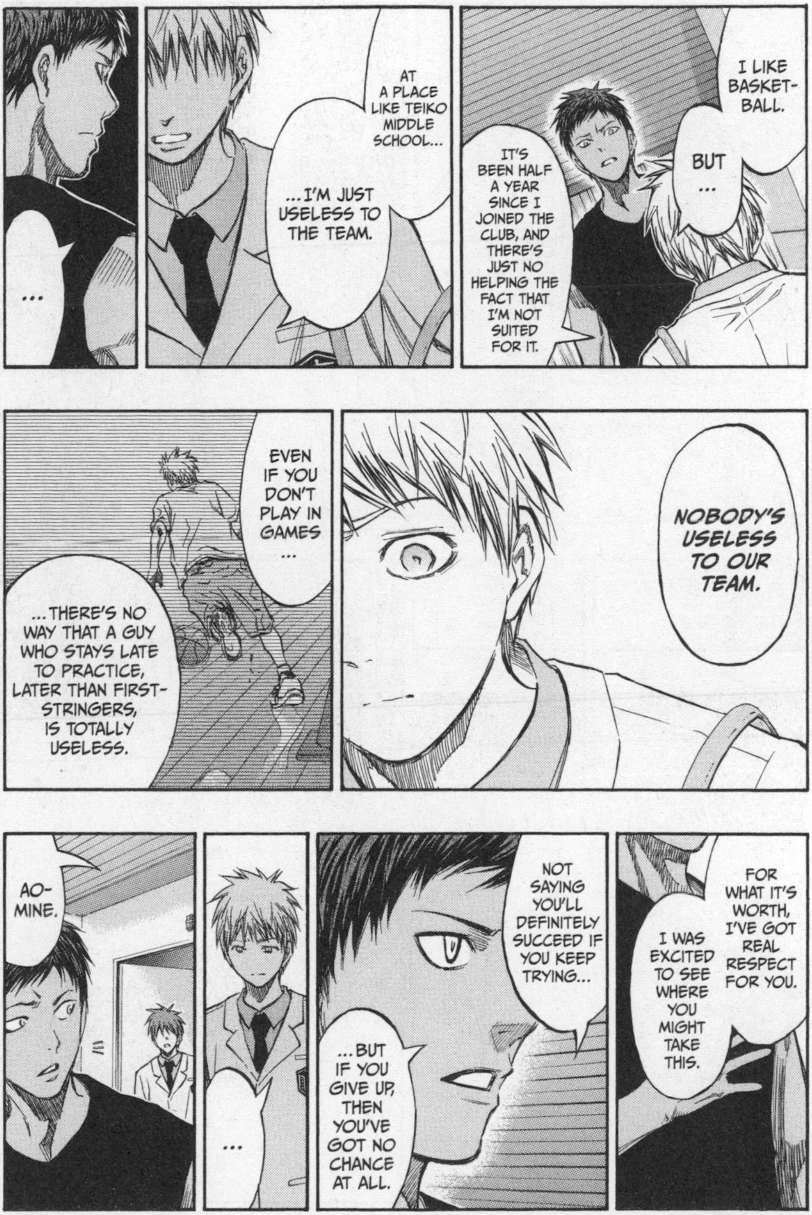
I LIKE BASKETBALL.
BUT...
IT'S BEEN HALF A YEAR SINCE I JOINED THE CLUB, AND THERE'S JUST NO HELPING THE FACT THAT I'M NOT SUITED FOR IT.
AT A PLACE LIKE TEIKO MIDDLE SCHOOL...
...I'M JUST USELESS TO THE TEAM.
...
NOBODY'S USELESS TO OUR TEAM.
EVEN IF YOU DON'T PLAY IN GAMES...
...THERE'S NO WAY THAT A GUY WHO STAYS LATE TO PRACTICE, LATER THAN FIRST-STRINGERS, IS TOTALLY USELESS.
FOR WHAT IT'S WORTH, I'VE GOT REAL RESPECT FOR YOU.
I WAS EXCITED TO SEE WHERE YOU MIGHT TAKE THIS.
NOT SAYING YOU'LL DEFINITELY SUCCEED IF YOU KEEP TRYING...
...BUT IF YOU GIVE UP, THEN YOU'VE GOT NO CHANCE AT ALL.
...
AO-MINE.

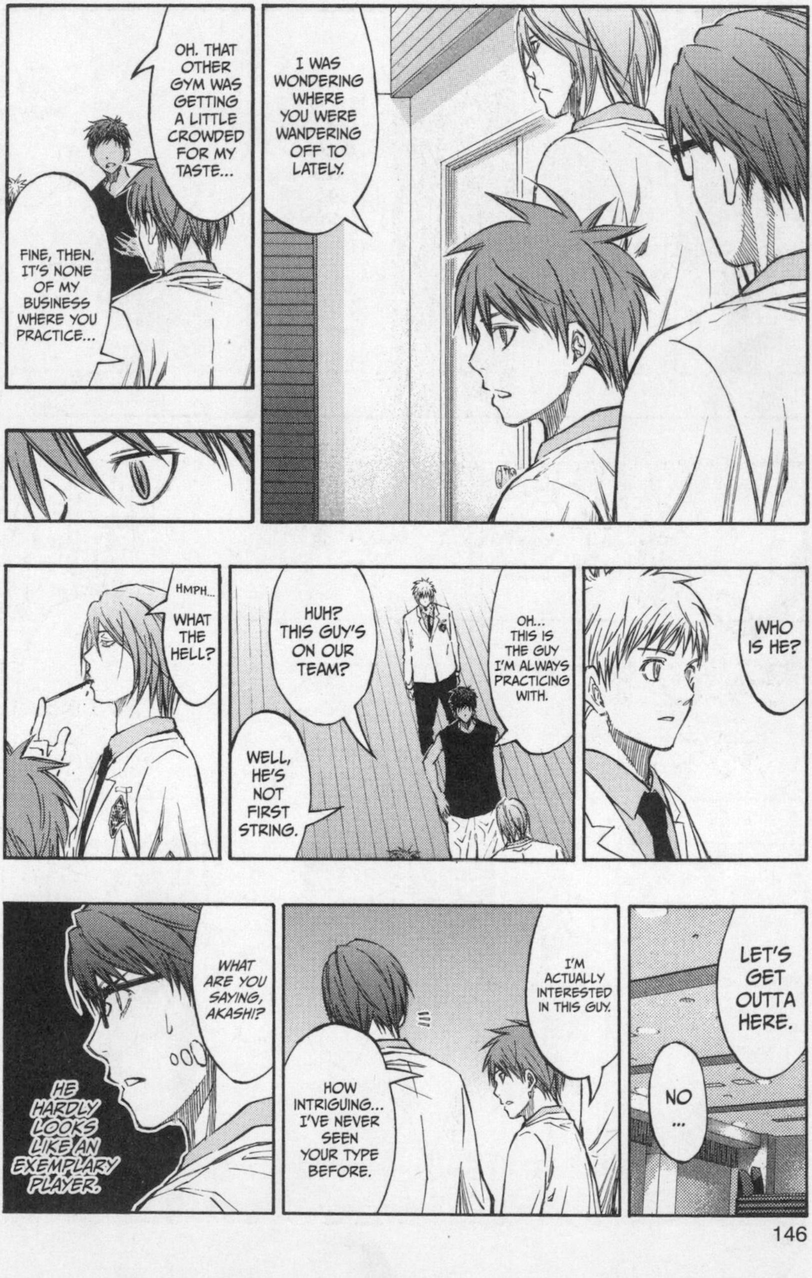
I WAS WONDERING WHERE YOU WERE WANDERING OFF TO LATELY.
OH. THAT OTHER GYM WAS GETTING A LITTLE CROWDED FOR MY TASTE...
FINE, THEN. IT'S NONE OF MY BUSINESS WHERE YOU PRACTICE...
WHO IS HE?
OH... THIS IS THE GUY I'M ALWAYS PRACTICING WITH.
HUH? THIS GUY'S ON OUR TEAM?
WELL, HE'S NOT FIRST STRING.
HMPH...
WHAT THE HELL?
LET'S GET OUTTA HERE.
NO ...
I'M ACTUALLY INTERESTED IN THIS GUY.
HOW INTRIGUING... I'VE NEVER SEEN YOUR TYPE BEFORE.
WHAT ARE YOU SAYING, AKASHI?
HE HARDLY LOOKS LIKE AN EXEMPLARY PLAYER.

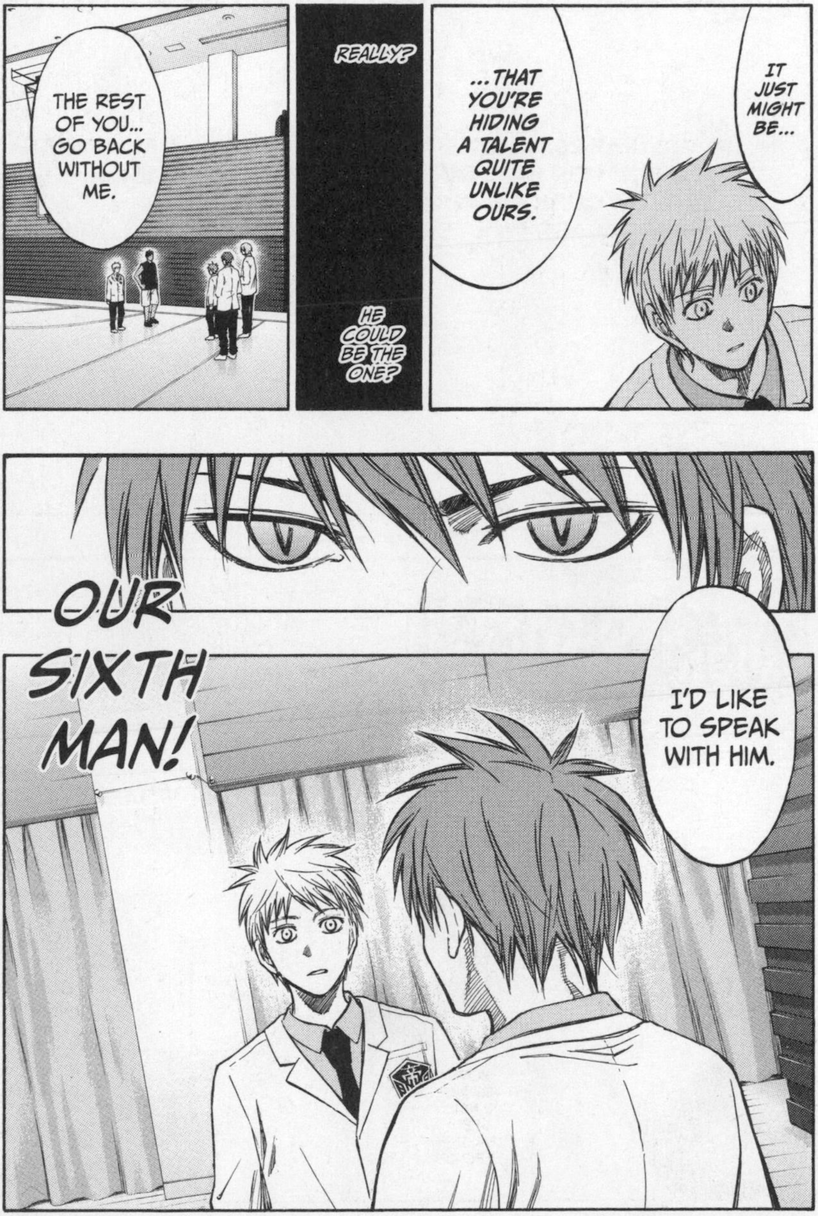
IT JUST MIGHT BE...
...THAT YOU'RE HIDING A TALENT QUITE UNLIKE OURS.
REALLY?
HE COULD BE THE ONE?
THE REST OF YOU... GO BACK WITHOUT ME.
I'D LIKE TO SPEAK WITH HIM.
OUR SIXTH MAN!

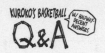

KUROKO'S BASKETBALL Q&A (W/ HALFWAY-DECENT ANSWERS)

Q. **IN VOLUME 20, WHAT'S THE NAME OF MIYAJI SENPAI'S FAVORITE POP IDOL GIRL? AND HER NICKNAME? ALSO, I'M CURIOUS WHAT GROUP SHE'S IN?**
(MARIMO ASANO from TOKYO)

A. MIYAMIYA.

KUROKO'S BASKETBALL BLOOPERS TAKE 12

YOU'RE CHILDHOOD FRIENDS WITH ADMINE-KUN? SWEET!
DOES HE HAVE A GIRLFRIEND OR NOT?
C'MON! DIDN'T YOU SEE HIM PLAY AT ALL-MIDDLE? HE WAS SO COOL.
HUH?
UH... YEAH... I GUESS...
THAT WAS COOL...?!
ROLL
?
DID YOU LADIES HAPPEN TO SEE A BALL ROLL THIS WAY?
HA HA HA...
DON'T COME OVER HERE WITH THAT OBVIOUS ULTERIOR MOTIVE!
THAT WAS TOTALLY ON PURPOSE.
GET OUTTA HERE, YOU!!

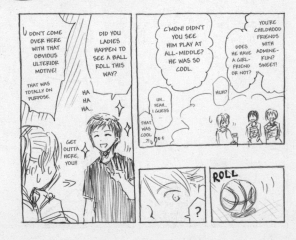

206TH QUARTER: DEPENDS ON HIM

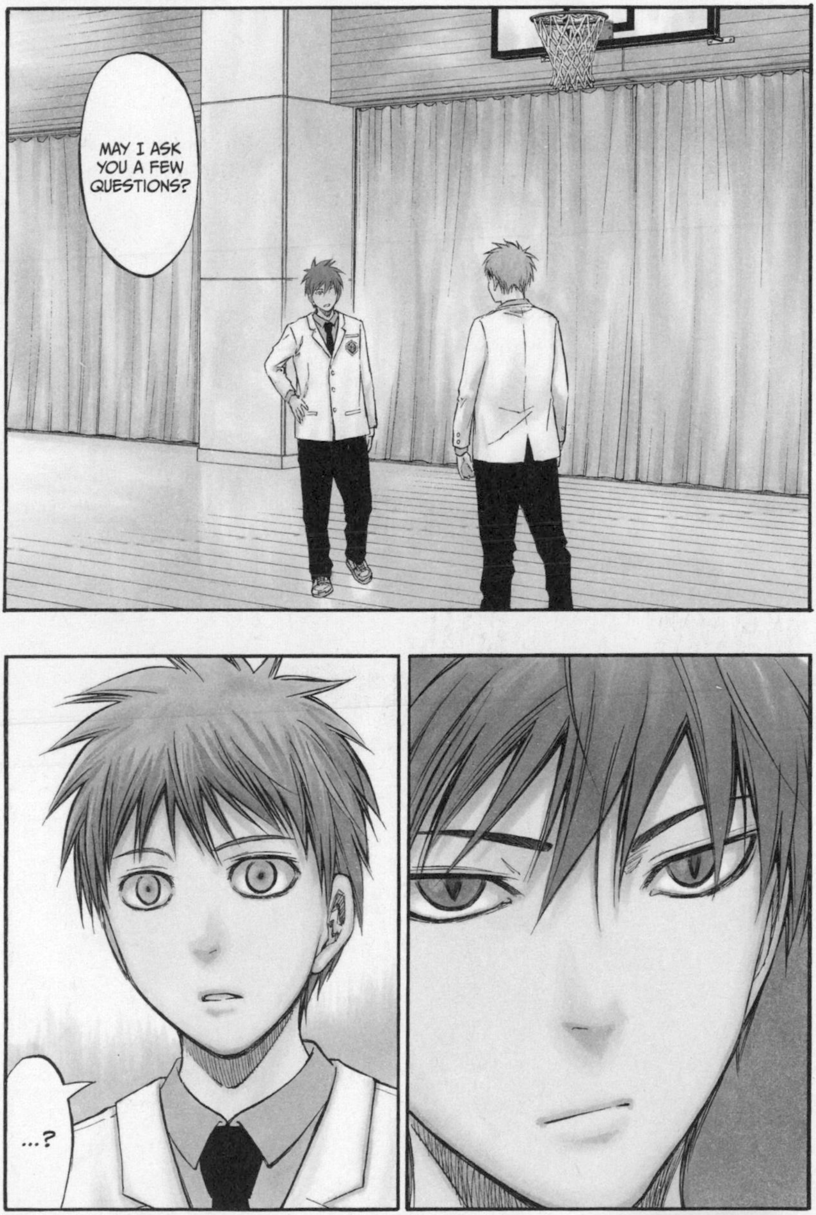
MAY I ASK YOU A FEW QUESTIONS?
...?

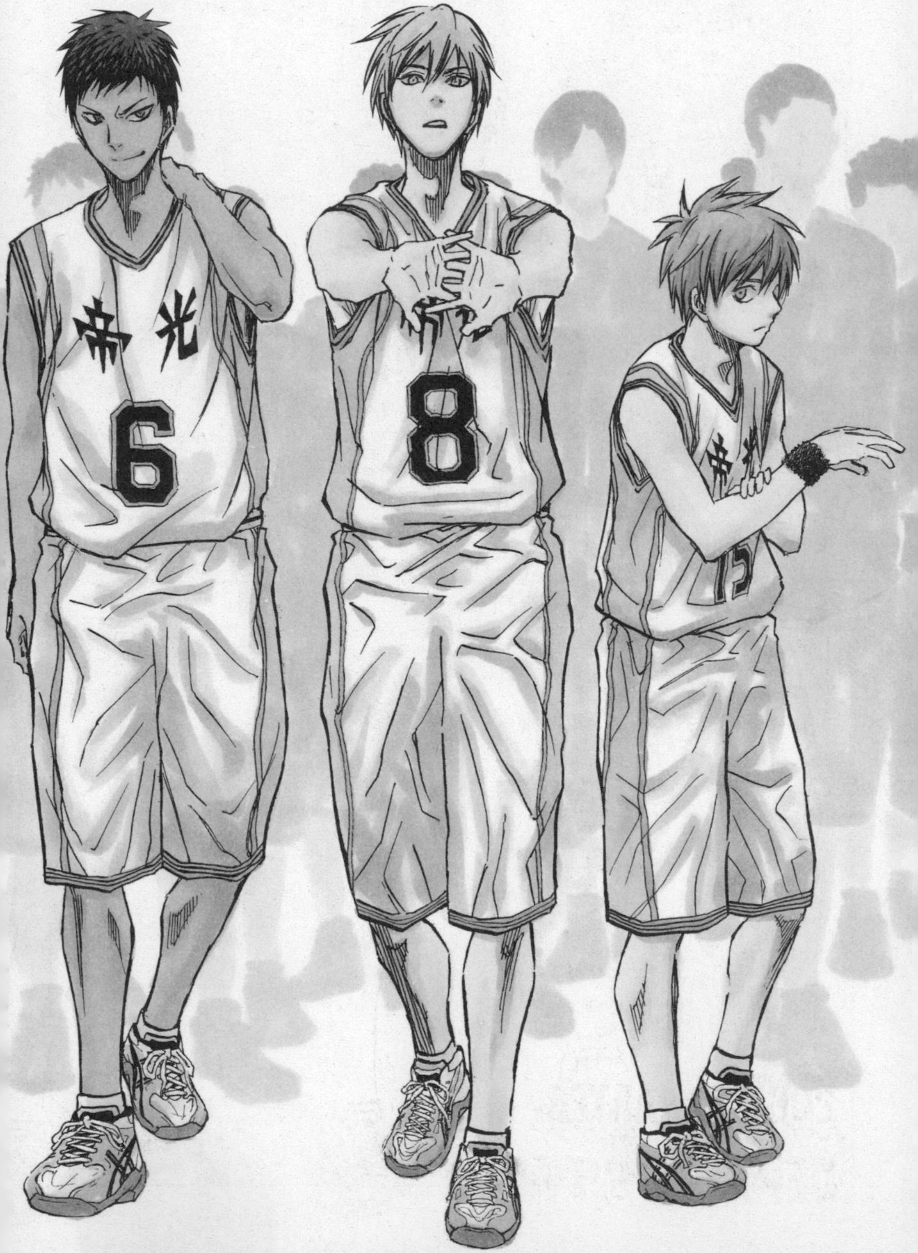
帝光
6
8

206TH QUARTER: DEPENDS ON HIM

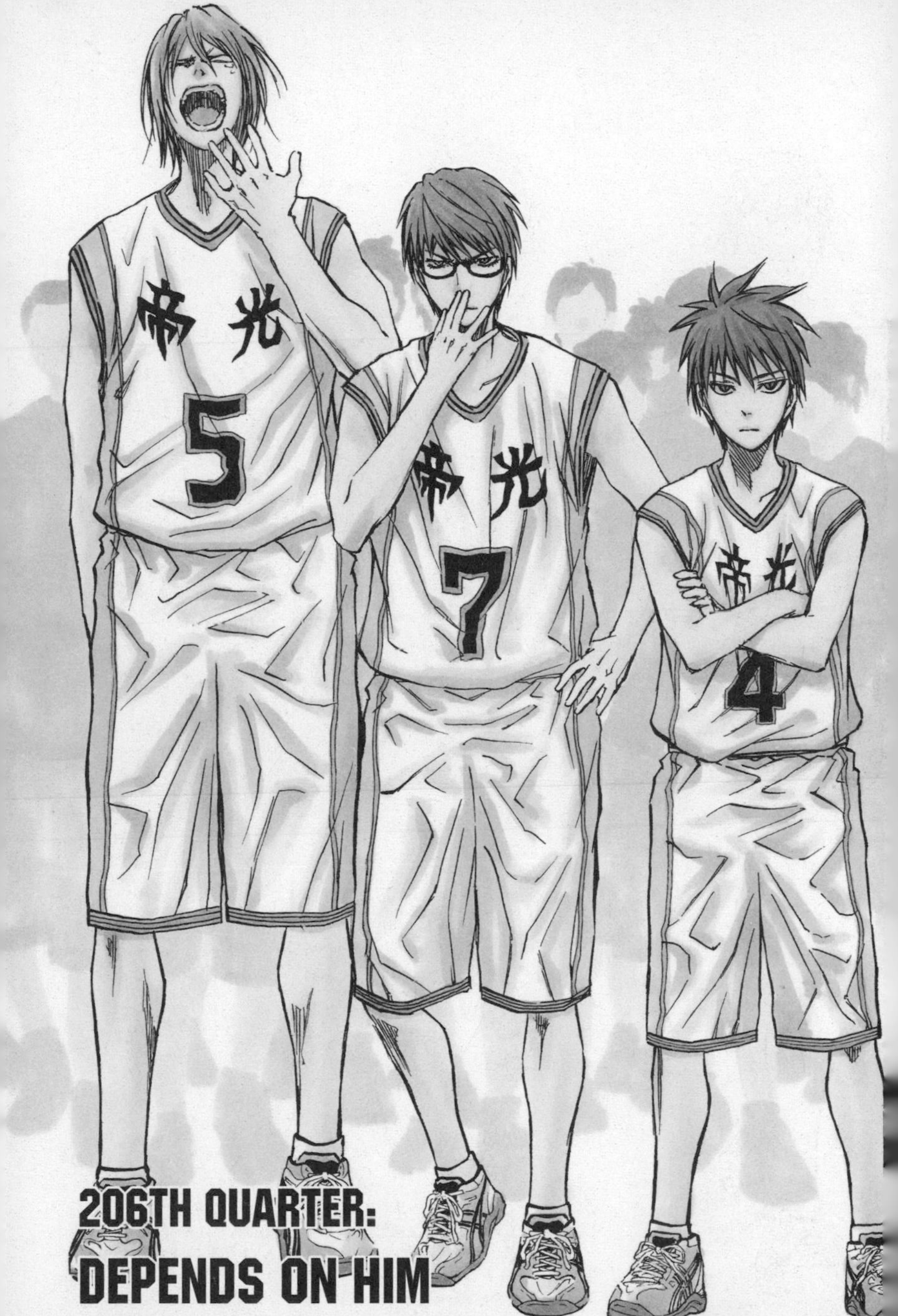
帝光
5
帝光
7
帝光
4

Kuroko's BASKETBALL

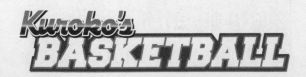

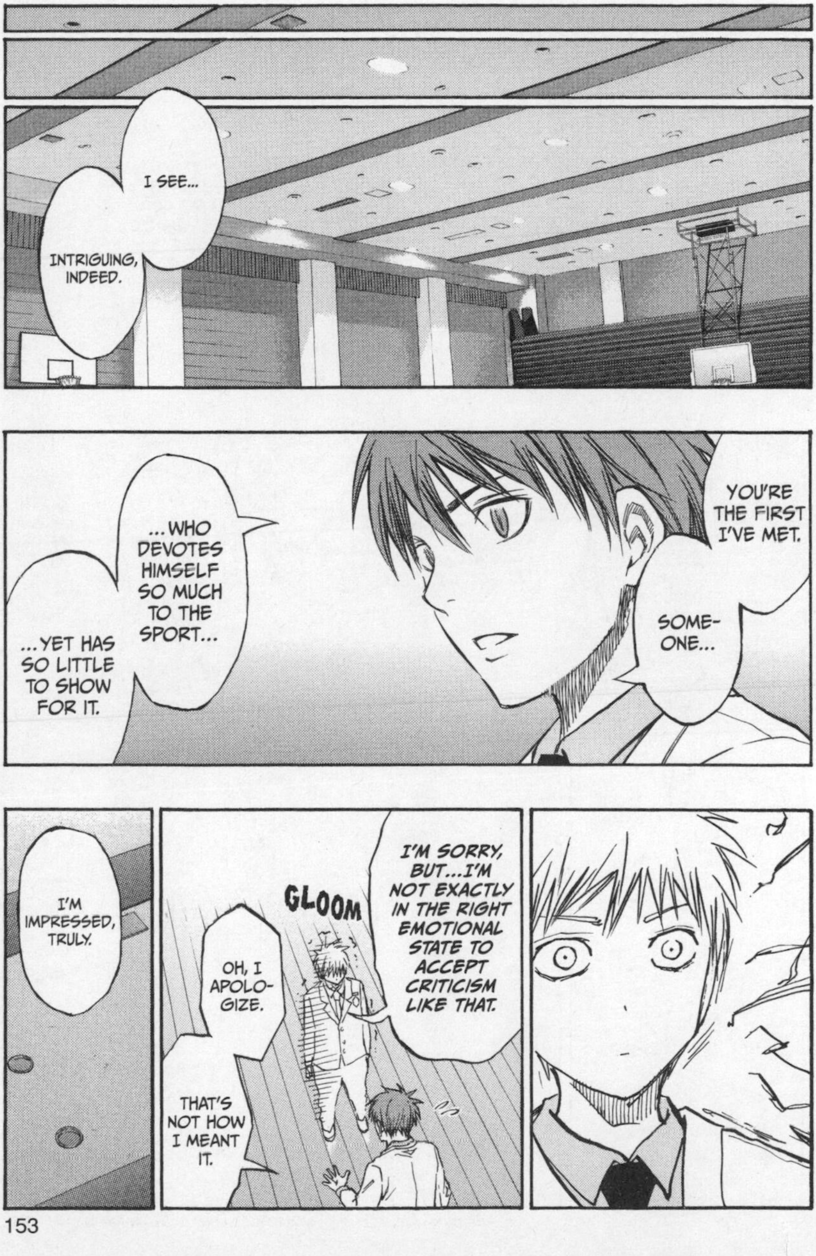
I SEE...
INTRIGUING, INDEED.
YOU'RE THE FIRST I'VE MET.
SOME-ONE...
...WHO DEVOTES HIMSELF SO MUCH TO THE SPORT...
...YET HAS SO LITTLE TO SHOW FOR IT.
I'M SORRY, BUT...I'M NOT EXACTLY IN THE RIGHT EMOTIONAL STATE TO ACCEPT CRITICISM LIKE THAT.
GLOOM
OH, I APOLO-GIZE.
THAT'S NOT HOW I MEANT IT.
I'M IMPRESSED, TRULY.

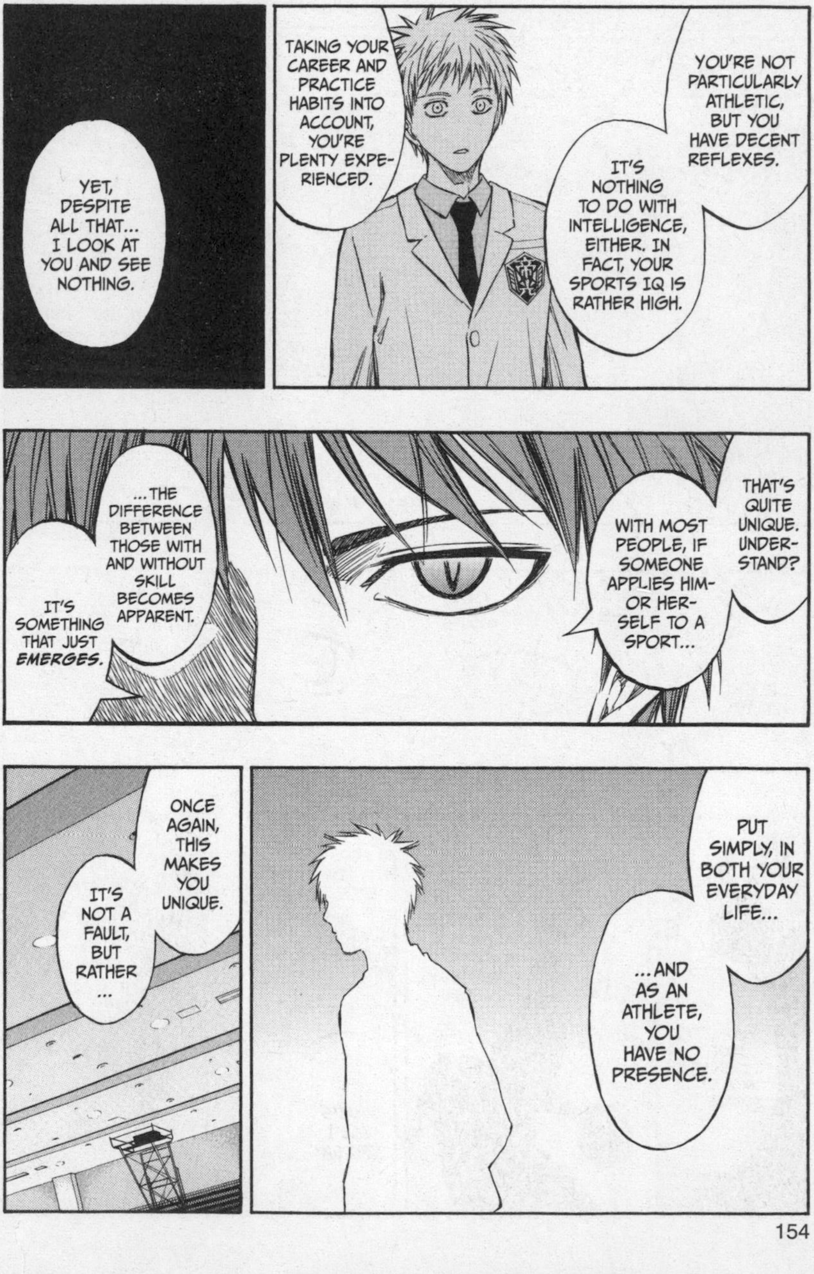
YOU'RE NOT PARTICULARLY ATHLETIC, BUT YOU HAVE DECENT REFLEXES.
IT'S NOTHING TO DO WITH INTELLIGENCE, EITHER. IN FACT, YOUR SPORTS IQ IS RATHER HIGH.
TAKING YOUR CAREER AND PRACTICE HABITS INTO ACCOUNT, YOU'RE PLENTY EXPE-RIENCED.
YET, DESPITE ALL THAT... I LOOK AT YOU AND SEE NOTHING.
THAT'S QUITE UNIQUE. UNDER-STAND?
WITH MOST PEOPLE, IF SOMEONE APPLIES HIM- OR HER-SELF TO A SPORT...
...THE DIFFERENCE BETWEEN THOSE WITH AND WITHOUT SKILL BECOMES APPARENT.
IT'S SOMETHING THAT JUST *EMERGES*.
PUT SIMPLY, IN BOTH YOUR EVERYDAY LIFE...
...AND AS AN ATHLETE, YOU HAVE NO PRESENCE.
ONCE AGAIN, THIS MAKES YOU UNIQUE.
IT'S NOT A FAULT, BUT RATHER ...

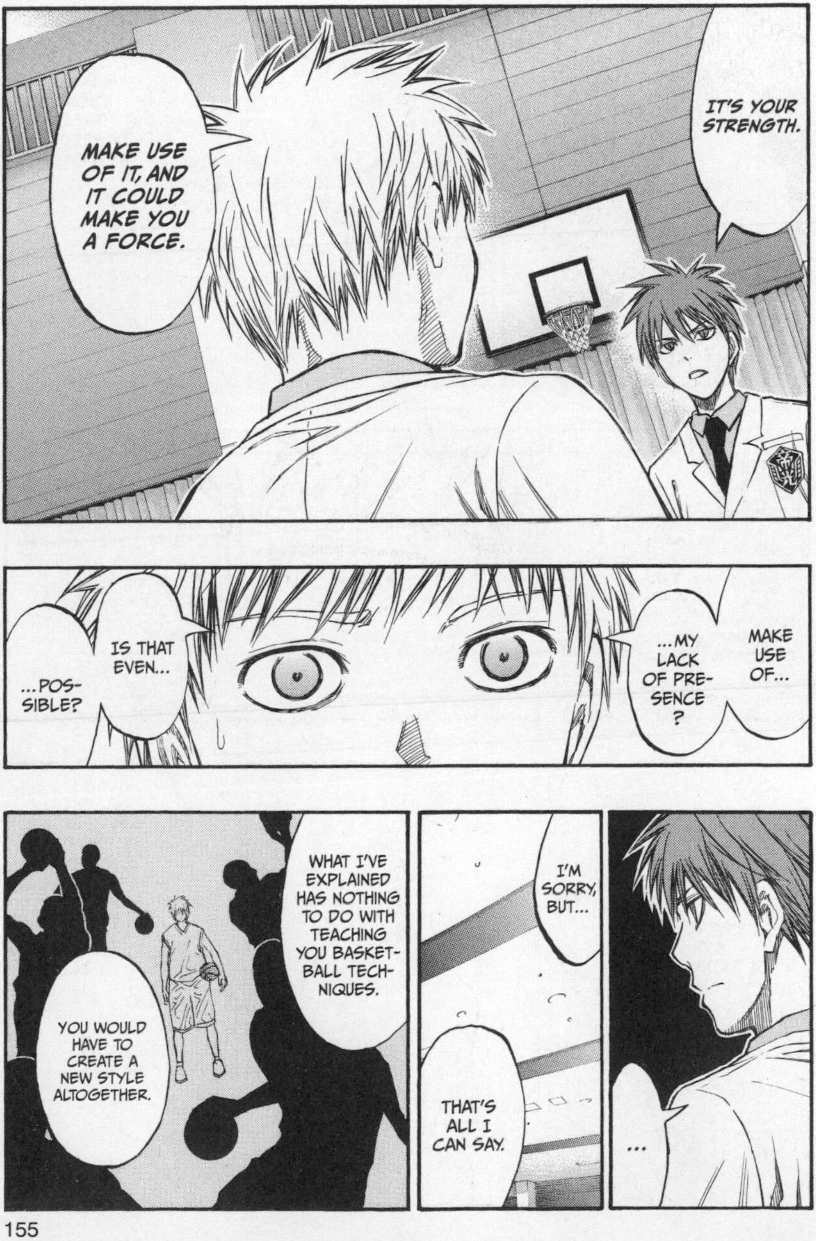

IT'S YOUR STRENGTH.
MAKE USE OF IT, AND IT COULD MAKE YOU A FORCE.
MAKE USE OF...
...MY LACK OF PRE-SENCE ?
IS THAT EVEN...
...POS-SIBLE?
...
I'M SORRY, BUT...
THAT'S ALL I CAN SAY.
WHAT I'VE EXPLAINED HAS NOTHING TO DO WITH TEACHING YOU BASKET-BALL TECH-NIQUES.
YOU WOULD HAVE TO CREATE A NEW STYLE ALTOGETHER.

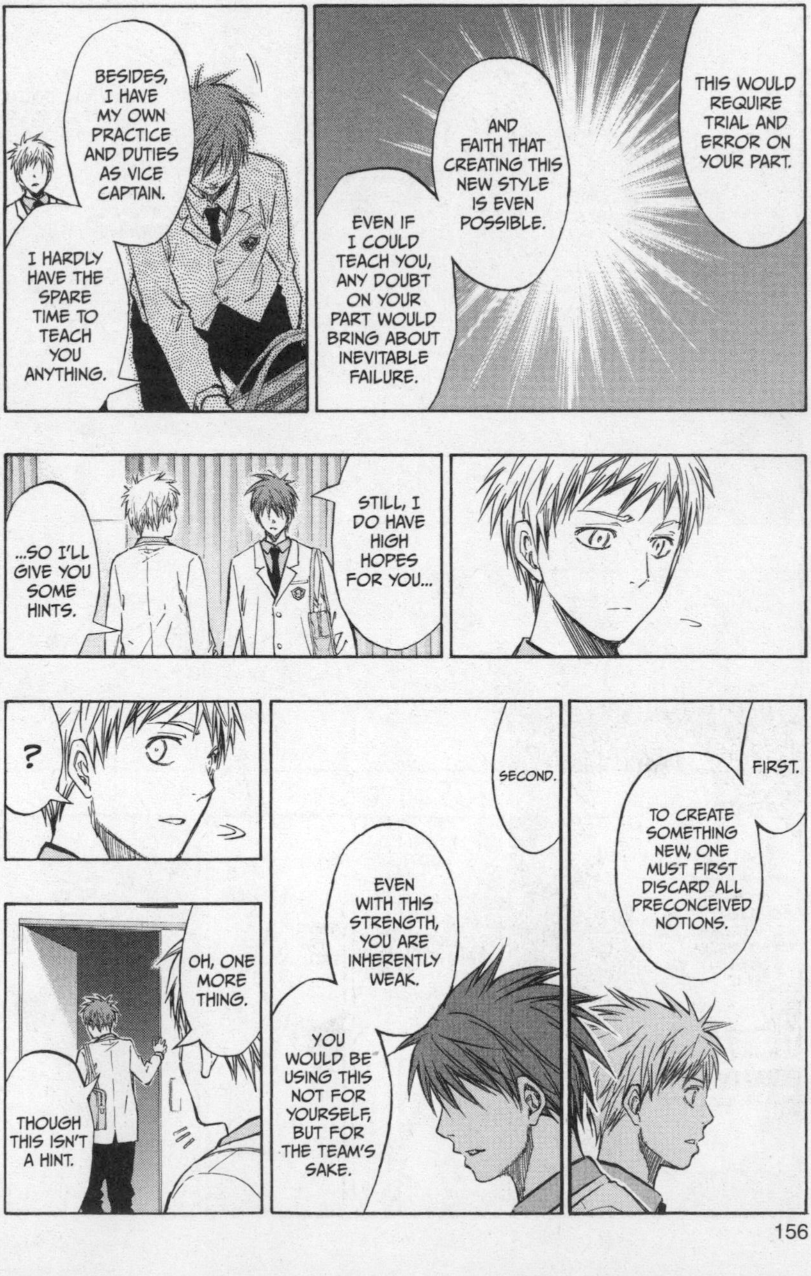
THIS WOULD REQUIRE TRIAL AND ERROR ON YOUR PART.
AND FAITH THAT CREATING THIS NEW STYLE IS EVEN POSSIBLE.
EVEN IF I COULD TEACH YOU, ANY DOUBT ON YOUR PART WOULD BRING ABOUT INEVITABLE FAILURE.
BESIDES, I HAVE MY OWN PRACTICE AND DUTIES AS VICE CAPTAIN.
I HARDLY HAVE THE SPARE TIME TO TEACH YOU ANYTHING.
STILL, I DO HAVE HIGH HOPES FOR YOU...
...SO I'LL GIVE YOU SOME HINTS.
FIRST.
TO CREATE SOMETHING NEW, ONE MUST FIRST DISCARD ALL PRECONCEIVED NOTIONS.
SECOND.
EVEN WITH THIS STRENGTH, YOU ARE INHERENTLY WEAK.
YOU WOULD BE USING THIS NOT FOR YOURSELF, BUT FOR THE TEAM'S SAKE.
?
OH, ONE MORE THING.
THOUGH THIS ISN'T A HINT.

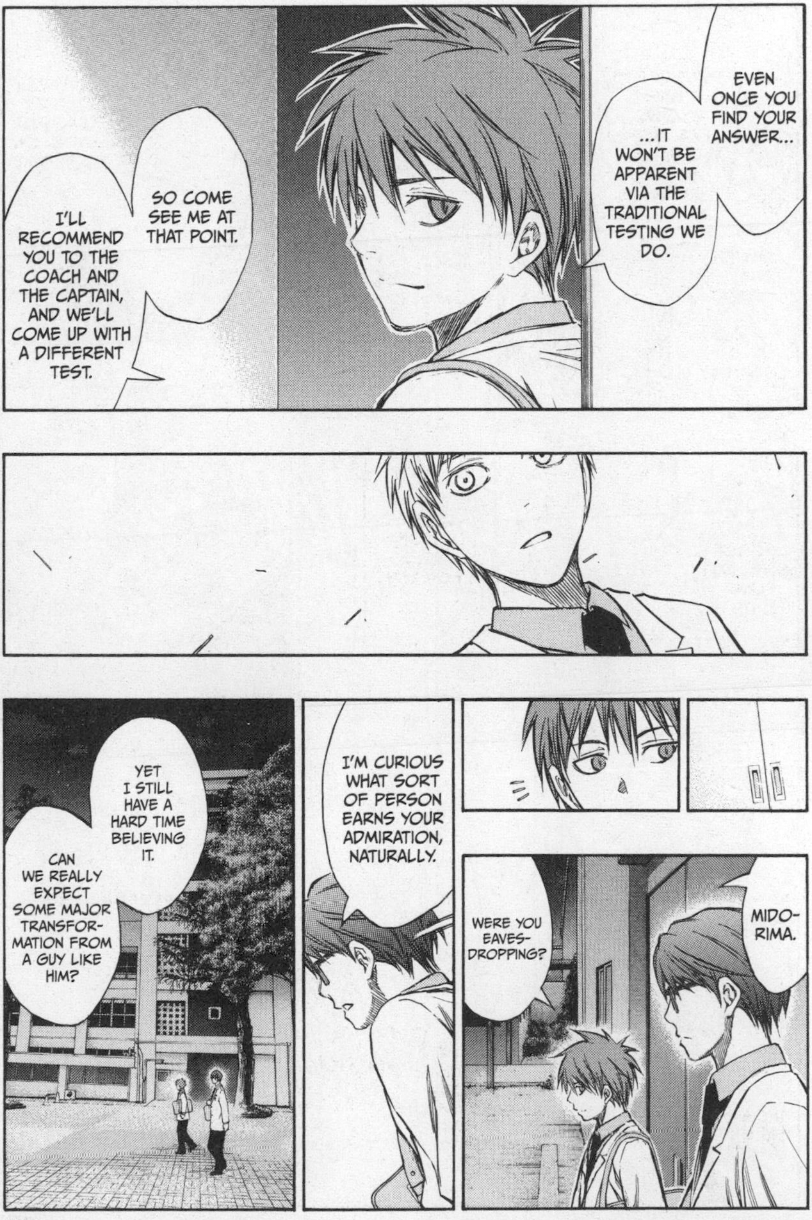
EVEN ONCE YOU FIND YOUR ANSWER...
...IT WON'T BE APPARENT VIA THE TRADITIONAL TESTING WE DO.
SO COME SEE ME AT THAT POINT.
I'LL RECOMMEND YOU TO THE COACH AND THE CAPTAIN, AND WE'LL COME UP WITH A DIFFERENT TEST.
MIDO-RIMA.
WERE YOU EAVES-DROPPING?
I'M CURIOUS WHAT SORT OF PERSON EARNS YOUR ADMIRATION, NATURALLY.
YET I STILL HAVE A HARD TIME BELIEVING IT.
CAN WE REALLY EXPECT SOME MAJOR TRANSFOR-MATION FROM A GUY LIKE HIM?

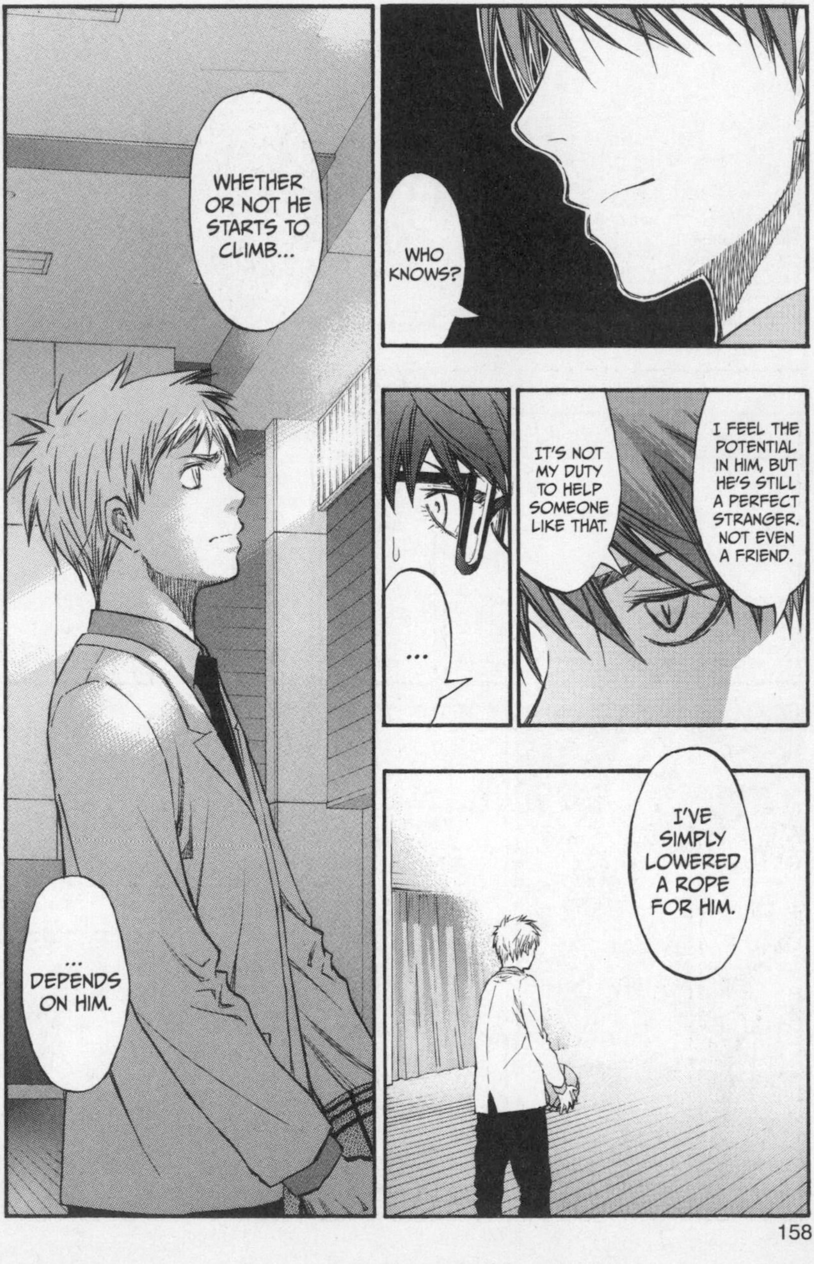
WHO KNOWS?
I FEEL THE POTENTIAL IN HIM, BUT HE'S STILL A PERFECT STRANGER. NOT EVEN A FRIEND.
IT'S NOT MY DUTY TO HELP SOMEONE LIKE THAT.
...
I'VE SIMPLY LOWERED A ROPE FOR HIM.
WHETHER OR NOT HE STARTS TO CLIMB...
... DEPENDS ON HIM.

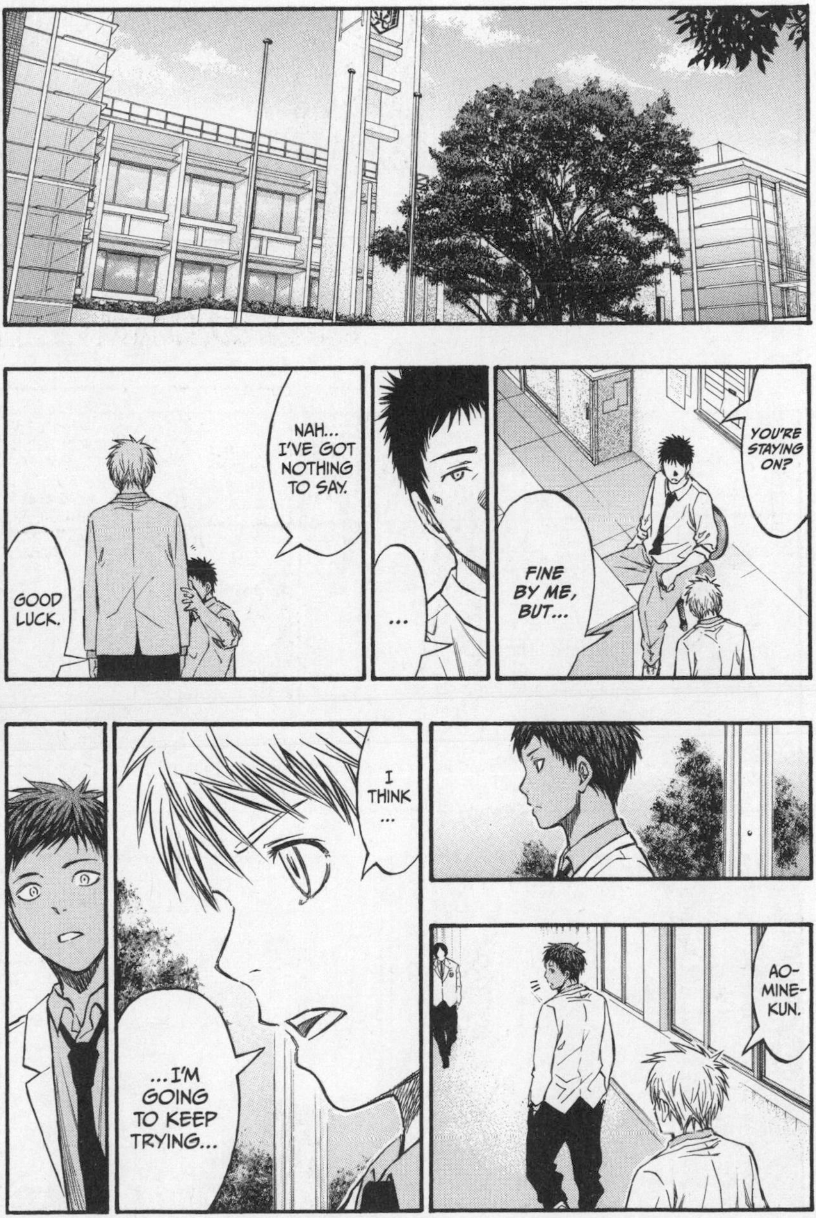
YOU'RE STAYING ON?
FINE BY ME, BUT...
...
NAH... I'VE GOT NOTHING TO SAY.
GOOD LUCK.
AO-MINE-KUN.
I THINK ...
...I'M GOING TO KEEP TRYING...

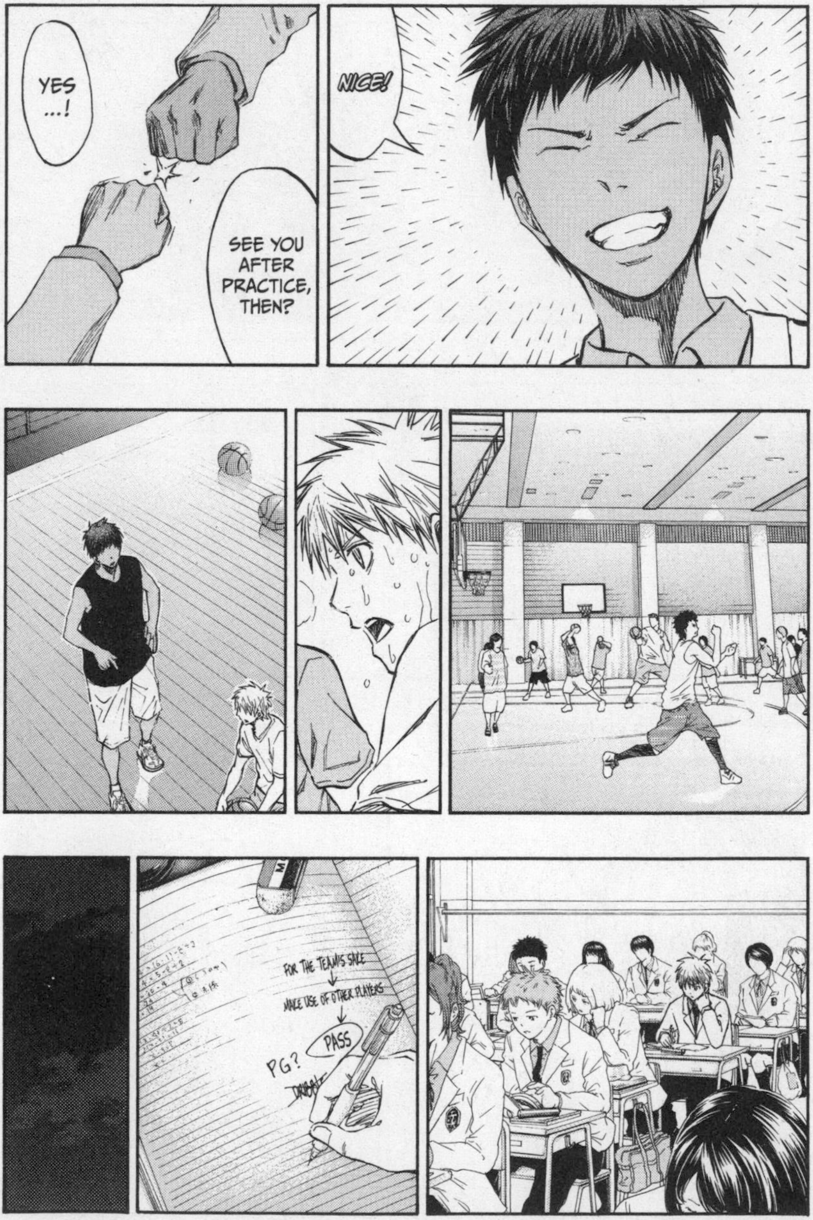
NICE!
SEE YOU AFTER PRACTICE, THEN?
YES ...!
FOR THE TEAM'S SAKE
MAKE USE OF OTHER PLAYERS
PASS
PG?

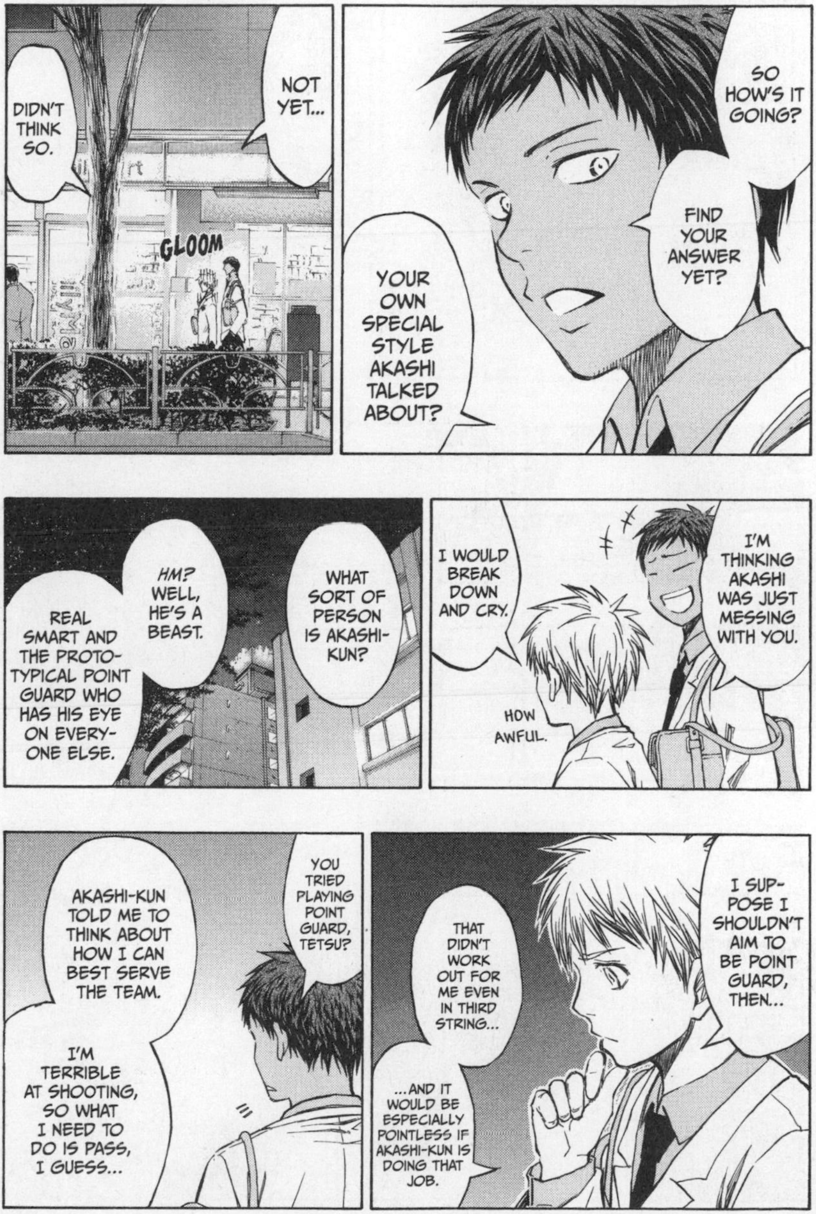
SO HOW'S IT GOING?
FIND YOUR ANSWER YET?
YOUR OWN SPECIAL STYLE AKASHI TALKED ABOUT?
NOT YET...
GLOOM
DIDN'T THINK SO.
I'M THINKING AKASHI WAS JUST MESSING WITH YOU.
I WOULD BREAK DOWN AND CRY.
HOW AWFUL.
WHAT SORT OF PERSON IS AKASHI-KUN?
HM? WELL, HE'S A BEAST.
REAL SMART AND THE PROTO-TYPICAL POINT GUARD WHO HAS HIS EYE ON EVERY-ONE ELSE.
I SUP-POSE I SHOULDN'T AIM TO BE POINT GUARD, THEN...
THAT DIDN'T WORK OUT FOR ME EVEN IN THIRD STRING...
...AND IT WOULD BE ESPECIALLY POINTLESS IF AKASHI-KUN IS DOING THAT JOB.
YOU TRIED PLAYING POINT GUARD, TETSU?
AKASHI-KUN TOLD ME TO THINK ABOUT HOW I CAN BEST SERVE THE TEAM.
I'M TERRIBLE AT SHOOTING, SO WHAT I NEED TO DO IS PASS, I GUESS...

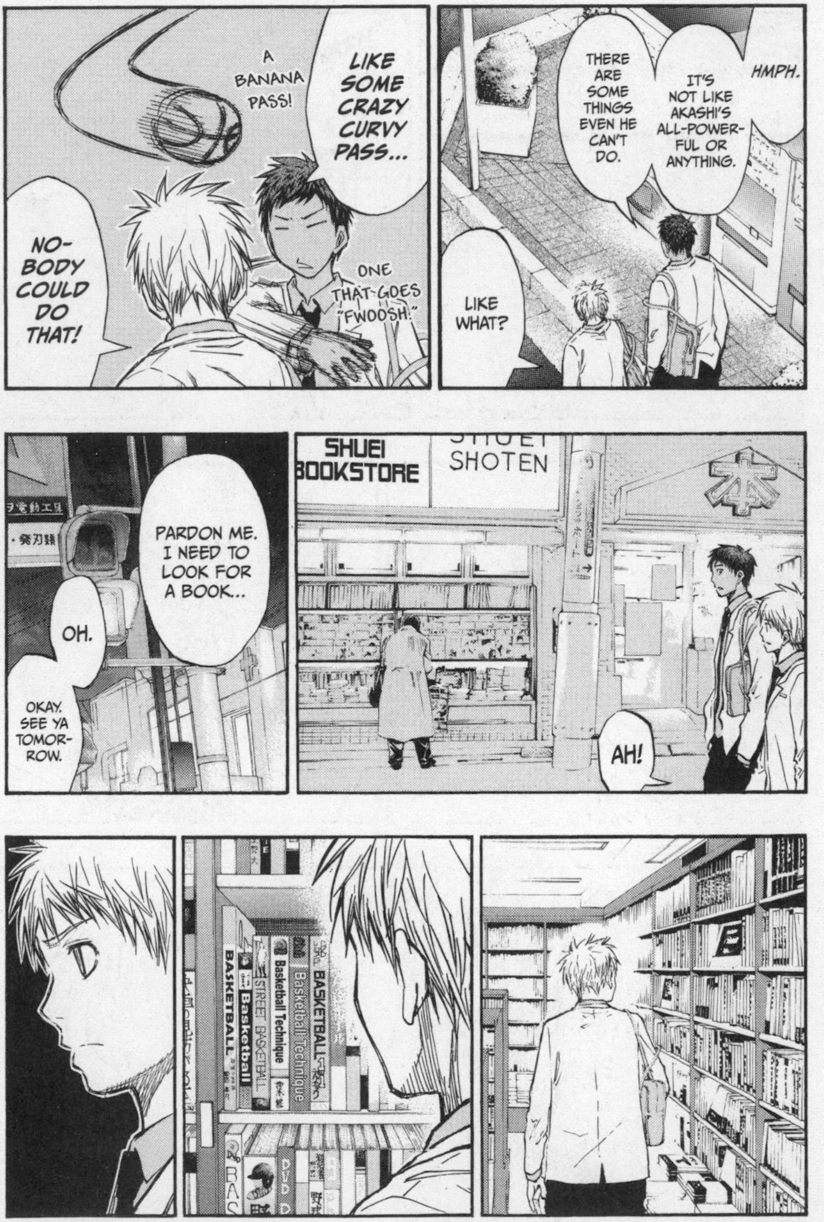
HMPH.
IT'S NOT LIKE AKASHI'S ALL-POWER-FUL OR ANYTHING.
THERE ARE SOME THINGS EVEN HE CAN'T DO.
LIKE WHAT?
LIKE SOME CRAZY CURVY PASS...
A BANANA PASS!
ONE THAT GOES "FWOOSH."
NO-BODY COULD DO THAT!
SHUEI BOOKSTORE
SHOTEN
AH!
PARDON ME. I NEED TO LOOK FOR A BOOK...
OH.
OKAY. SEE YA TOMOR-ROW.
BASKETBALL
Basketball Technique
Basketball Technique
STREET BASKETBALL
Basketball
BASKETBALL

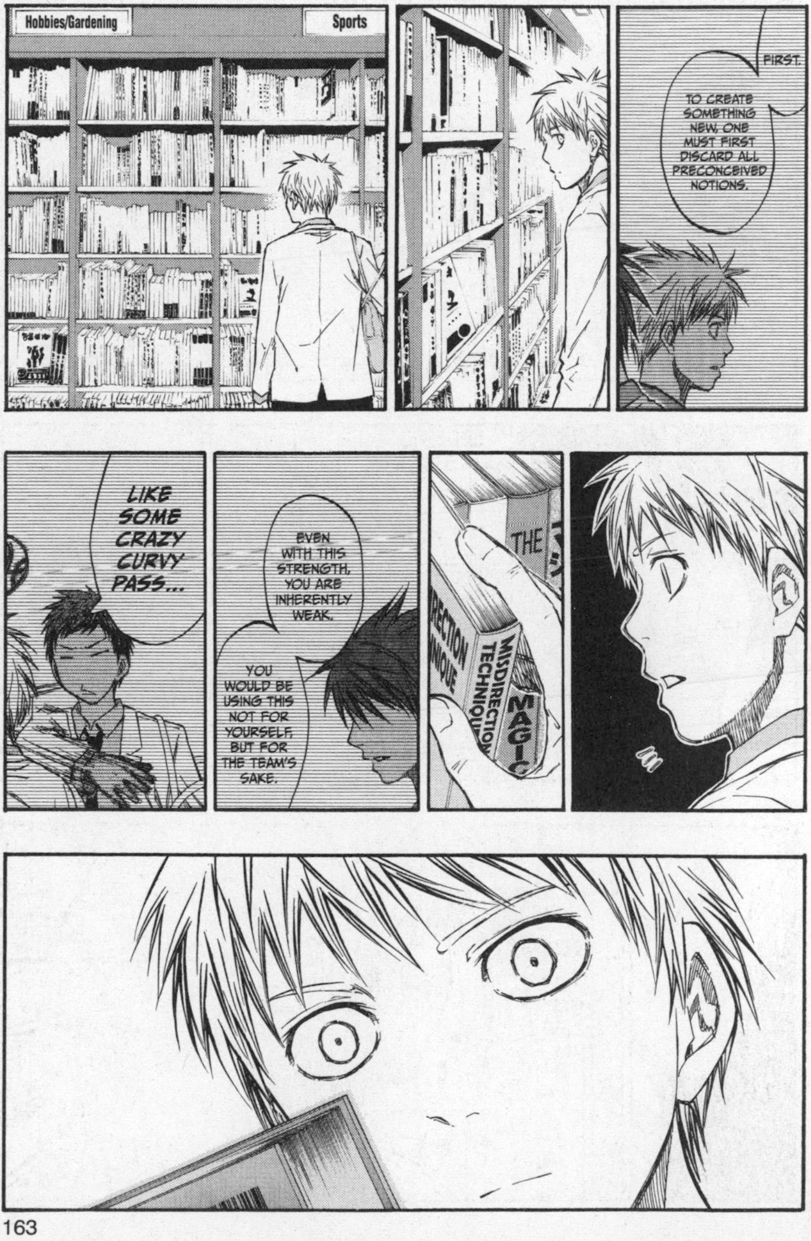
FIRST.
TO CREATE SOMETHING NEW, ONE MUST FIRST DISCARD ALL PRECONCEIVED NOTIONS.
Hobbies/Gardening
Sports
THE
MISDIRECTION TECHNIQUE
MAGIC
EVEN WITH THIS STRENGTH, YOU ARE INHERENTLY WEAK.
YOU WOULD BE USING THIS NOT FOR YOURSELF, BUT FOR THE TEAM'S SAKE.
LIKE SOME CRAZY CURVY PASS...

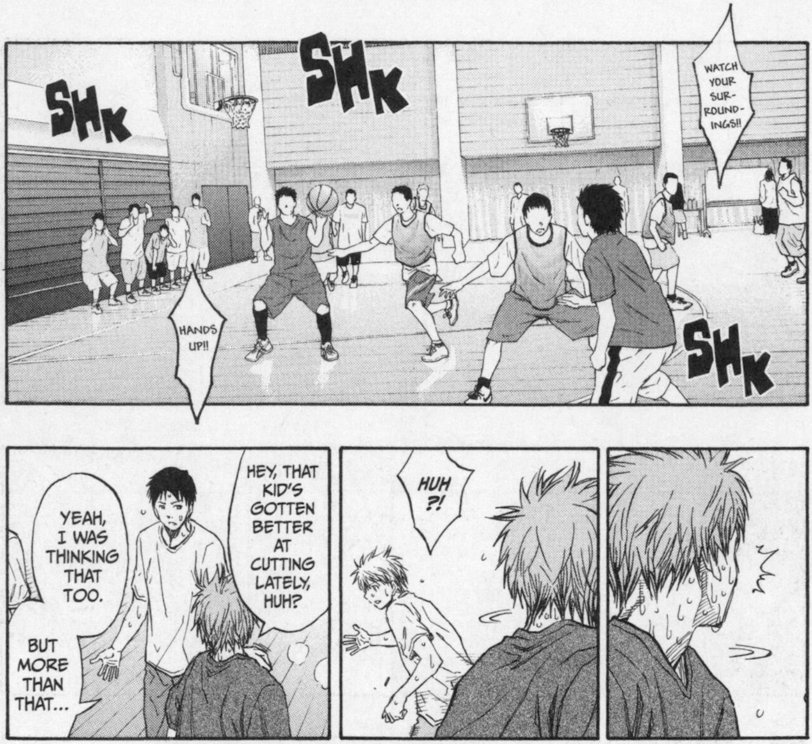
WATCH YOUR SUR-ROUNDINGS!!
SHK
SHK
SHK
SHK
HANDS UP!!
HUH?!
HEY, THAT KID'S GOTTEN BETTER AT CUTTING LATELY, HUH?
YEAH, I WAS THINKING THAT TOO.
BUT MORE THAN THAT...

*Cutting is a quick move to the basket to evade a defender.

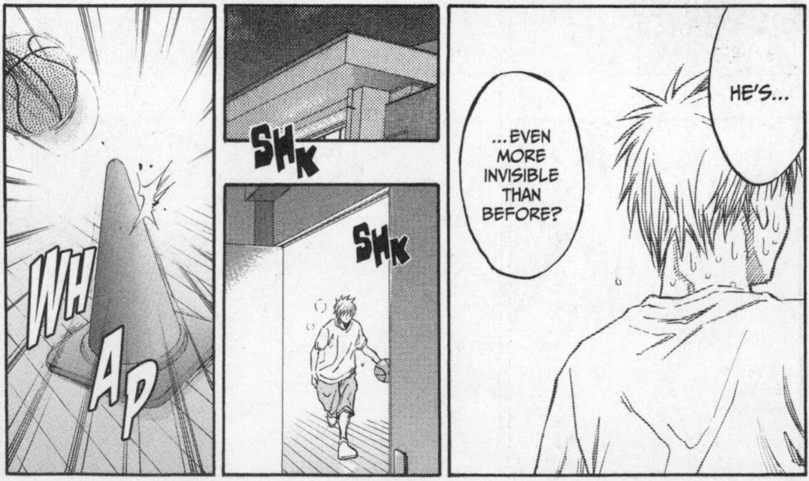
HE'S...
...EVEN MORE INVISIBLE THAN BEFORE?
SHK
SHK
WHAP

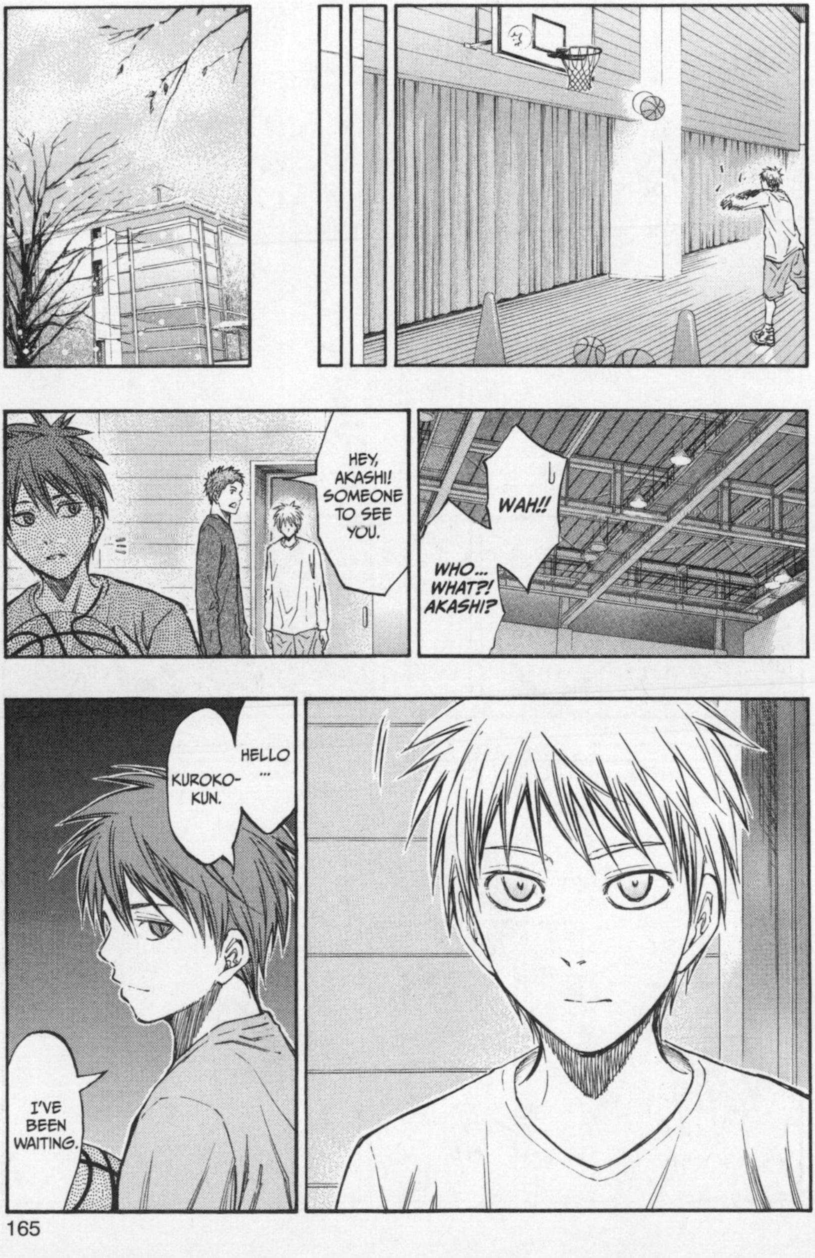
WAH!!
WHO... WHAT?! AKASHI?
HEY, AKASHI! SOMEONE TO SEE YOU.
HELLO... KUROKO-KUN.
I'VE BEEN WAITING.

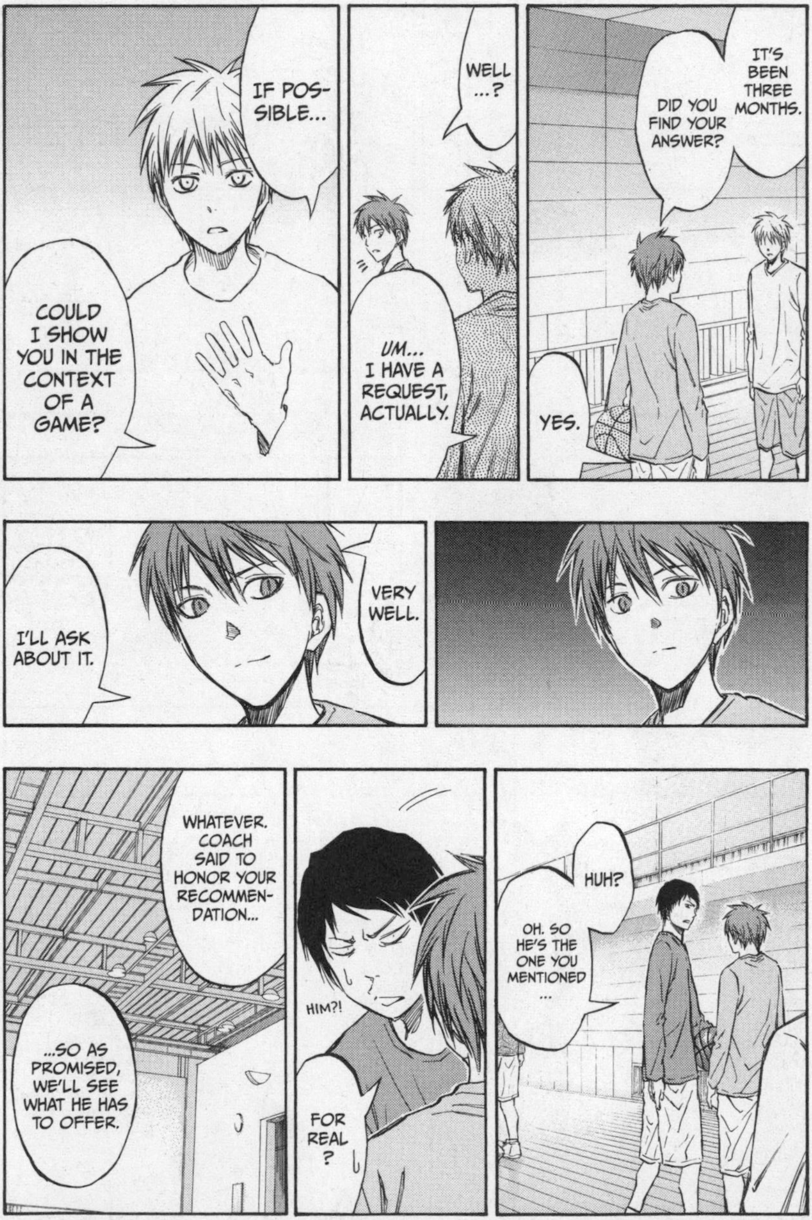
IT'S BEEN THREE MONTHS.
DID YOU FIND YOUR ANSWER?
YES.
WELL ...?
UM... I HAVE A REQUEST, ACTUALLY.
IF POSSIBLE...
COULD I SHOW YOU IN THE CONTEXT OF A GAME?
VERY WELL.
I'LL ASK ABOUT IT.
HUH?
OH. SO HE'S THE ONE YOU MENTIONED ...
HIM?!
FOR REAL ?
WHATEVER. COACH SAID TO HONOR YOUR RECOMMENDATION...
...SO AS PROMISED, WE'LL SEE WHAT HE HAS TO OFFER.

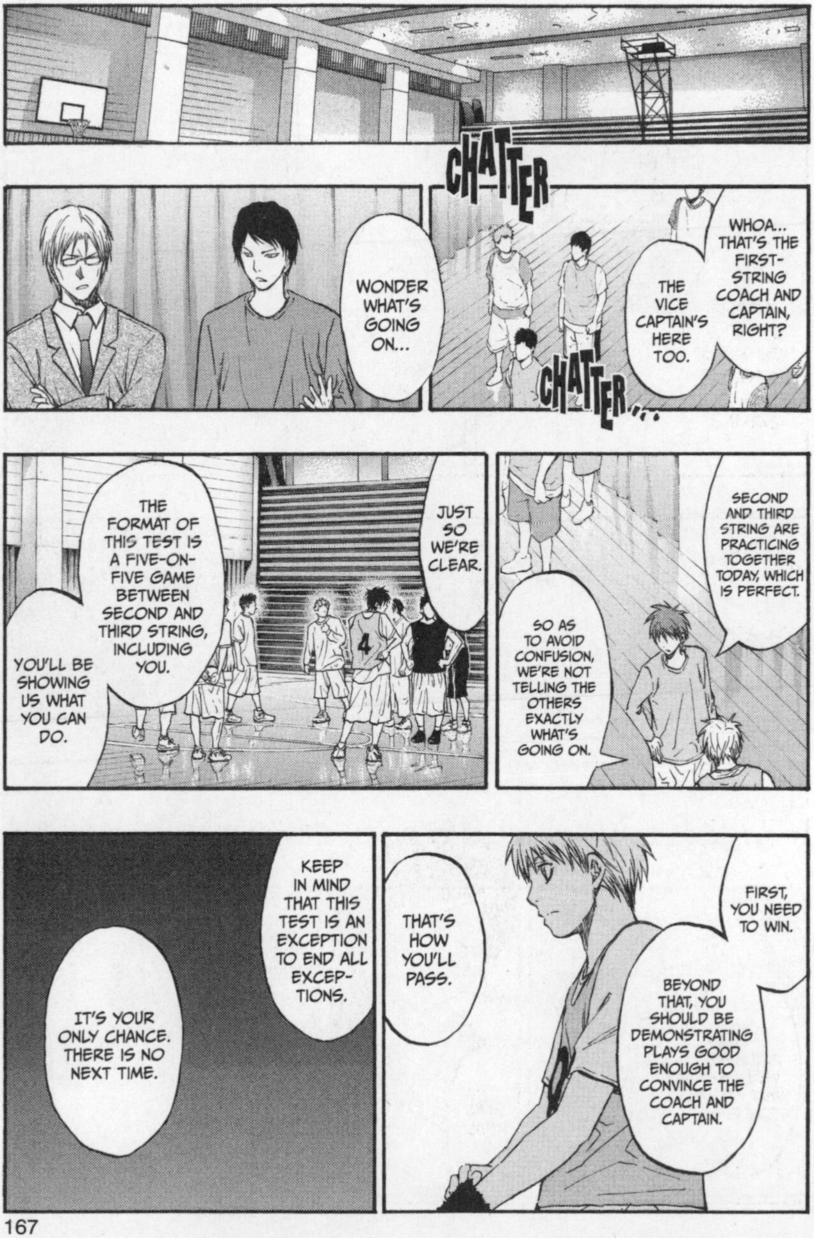
CHATTER
WHOA... THAT'S THE FIRST-STRING COACH AND CAPTAIN, RIGHT?
THE VICE CAPTAIN'S HERE TOO.
CHATTER...
WONDER WHAT'S GOING ON...
SECOND AND THIRD STRING ARE PRACTICING TOGETHER TODAY, WHICH IS PERFECT.
SO AS TO AVOID CONFUSION, WE'RE NOT TELLING THE OTHERS EXACTLY WHAT'S GOING ON.
JUST SO WE'RE CLEAR.
THE FORMAT OF THIS TEST IS A FIVE-ON-FIVE GAME BETWEEN SECOND AND THIRD STRING, INCLUDING YOU.
YOU'LL BE SHOWING US WHAT YOU CAN DO.
FIRST, YOU NEED TO WIN.
BEYOND THAT, YOU SHOULD BE DEMONSTRATING PLAYS GOOD ENOUGH TO CONVINCE THE COACH AND CAPTAIN.
THAT'S HOW YOU'LL PASS.
KEEP IN MIND THAT THIS TEST IS AN EXCEPTION TO END ALL EXCEPTIONS.
IT'S YOUR ONLY CHANCE. THERE IS NO NEXT TIME.

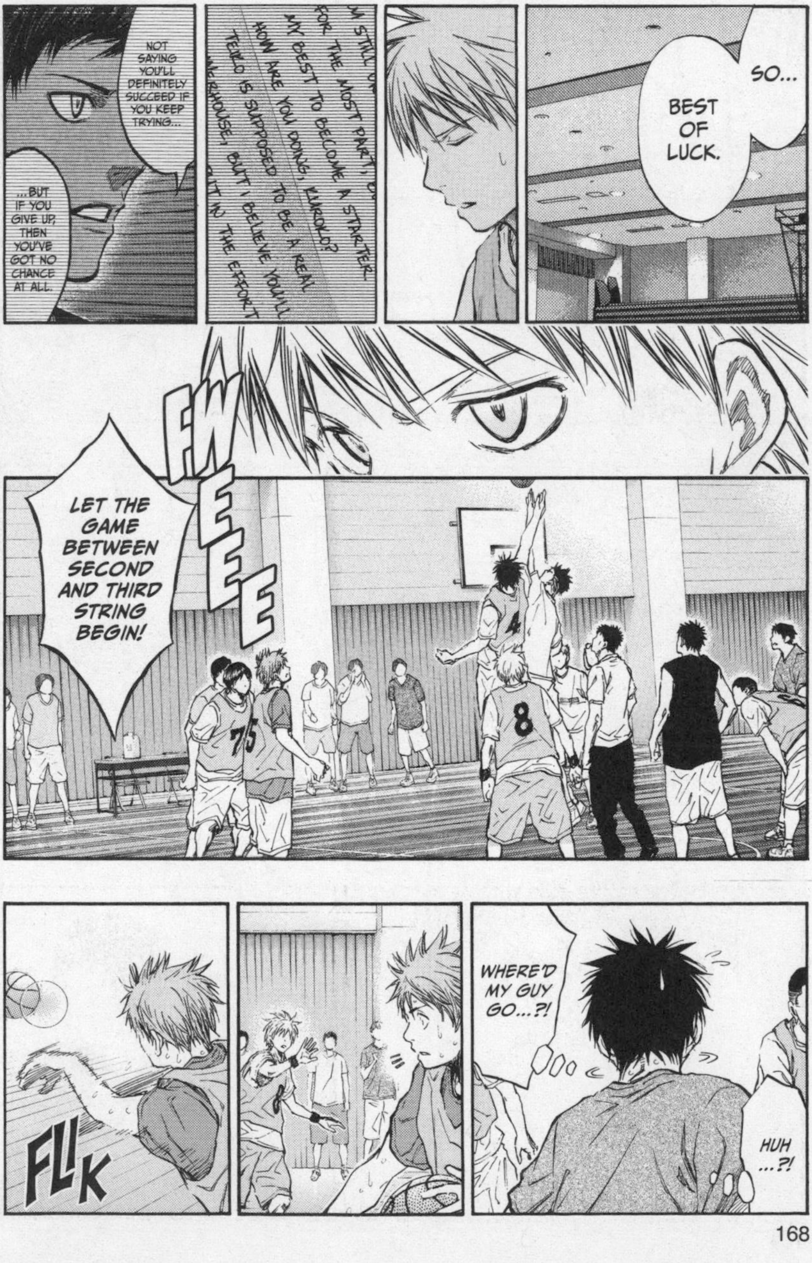
SO... BEST OF LUCK.
FOR THE MOST PART,
MY BEST TO BECOME A STARTER.
HOW ARE YOU DOING, KUROKO?
TEIKO IS SUPPOSED TO BE A REAL
BUT I BELIEVE YOU'LL
IN THE EFFORT
NOT SAYING YOU'LL DEFINITELY SUCCEED IF YOU KEEP TRYING...
...BUT IF YOU GIVE UP, THEN YOU'VE GOT NO CHANCE AT ALL.
FWEEE
LET THE GAME BETWEEN SECOND AND THIRD STRING BEGIN!
WHERE'D MY GUY GO...?!
HUH ...?!
FLIK

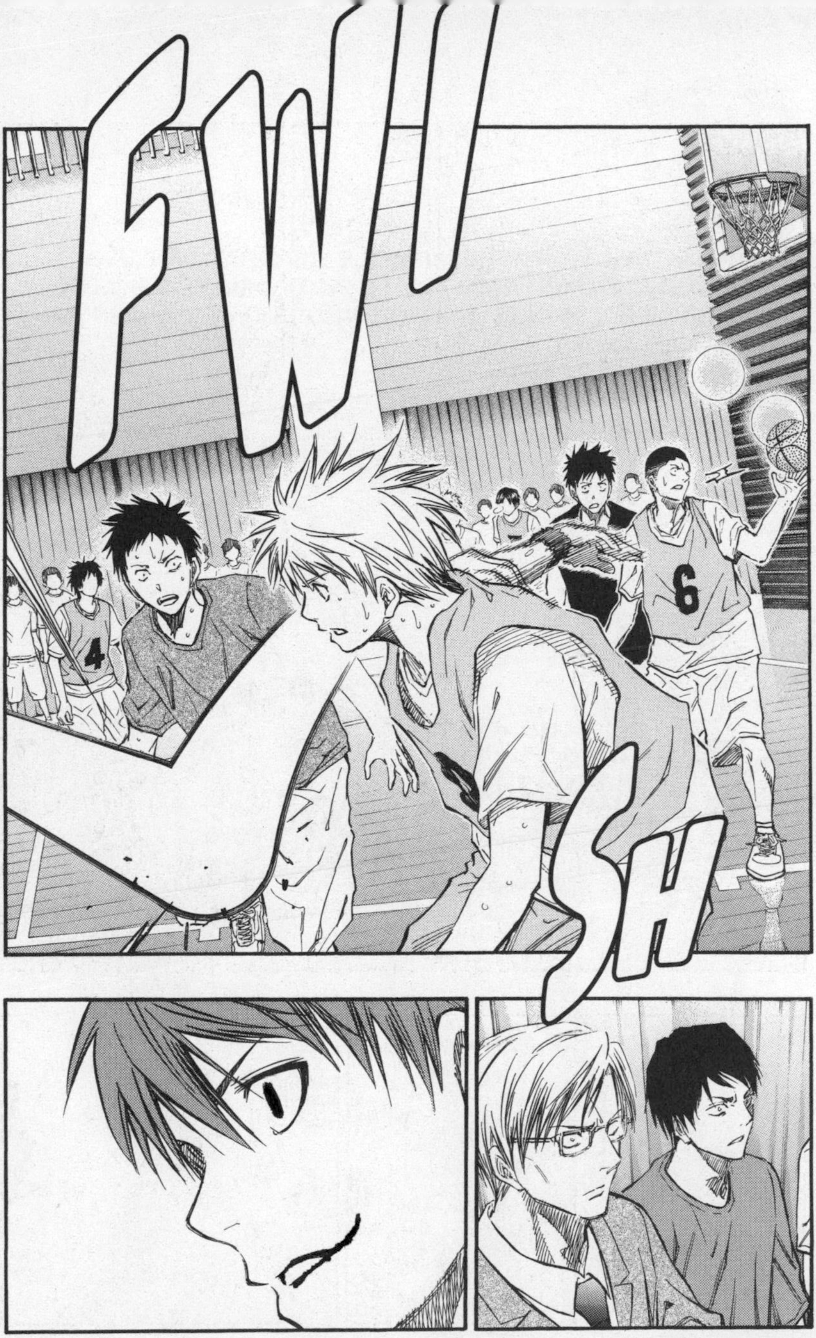
FWUSH

KUROKO'S BASKETBALL

Q&A

W/ HALFWAY-DECENT ANSWERS

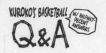

Q. HOW TALL WERE THE MIRACLE GENERATION GUYS PLUS KUROKO WHEN THEY STARTED MIDDLE SCHOOL?
(TONIGHT'S DINNER IS COACH'S CURRY from KAGOSHIMA PREFECTURE)

A. AKASHI: 5'2"
AOMINE: 5'9"
KISE: 5'7"
MIDORIMA: 5'8"
MURASAKIBARA: 6'1"
KUROKO: 5'1"

KUROKO'S BASKETBALL BLOOPERS

TAKE 10

Adults Only
DARN! WHY DO THEY GOTTA WRAP THESE IN PLASTIC?
JUST A LITTLE MORE... CAN ALMOST SEE THROUGH THIS GAP...
WHAT ARE YOU DOING, AOMINE-KUN?
HUH ?!
I WAS JUST, UH... THINKING ABOUT PICKING UP A BOOK MYSELF...
I DON'T BELIEVE YOU'RE ALLOWED TO BUY THAT.
EROTIC

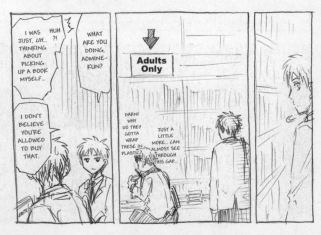

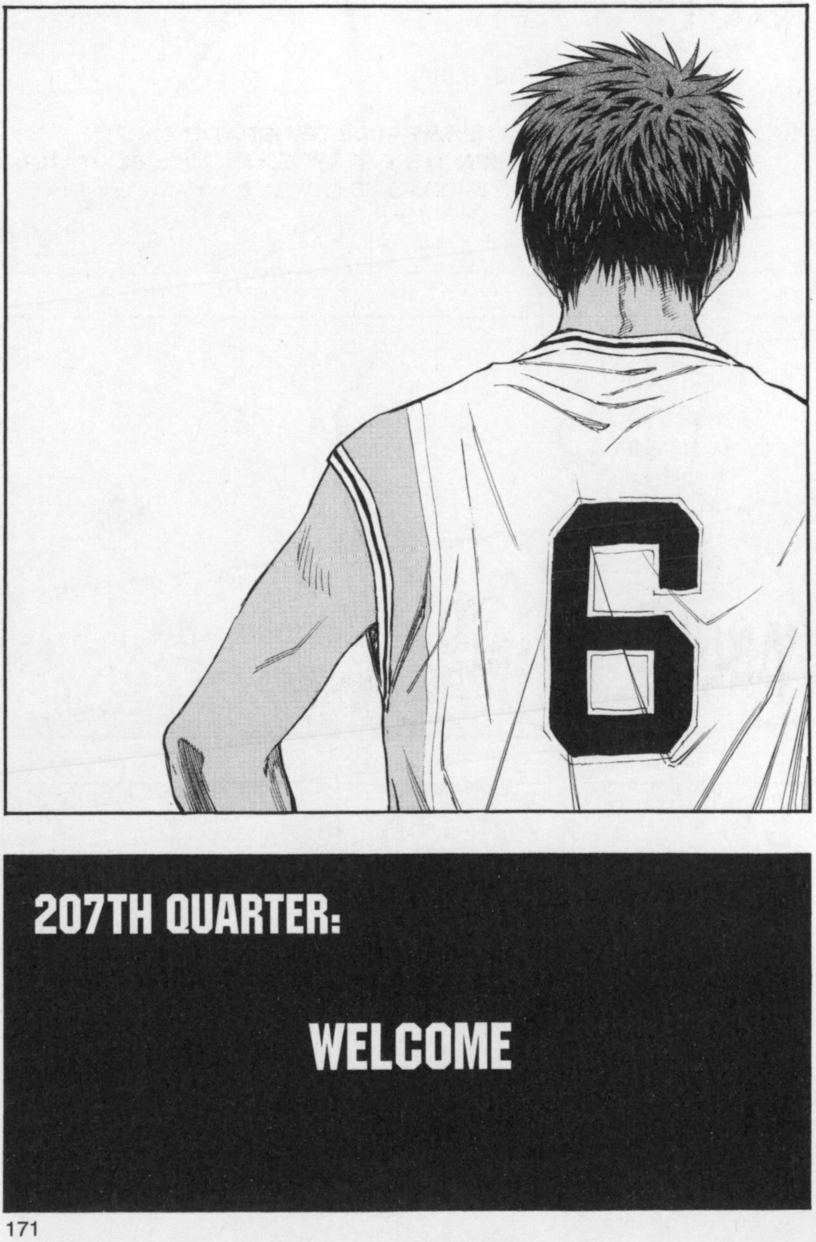

207TH QUARTER:

WELCOME

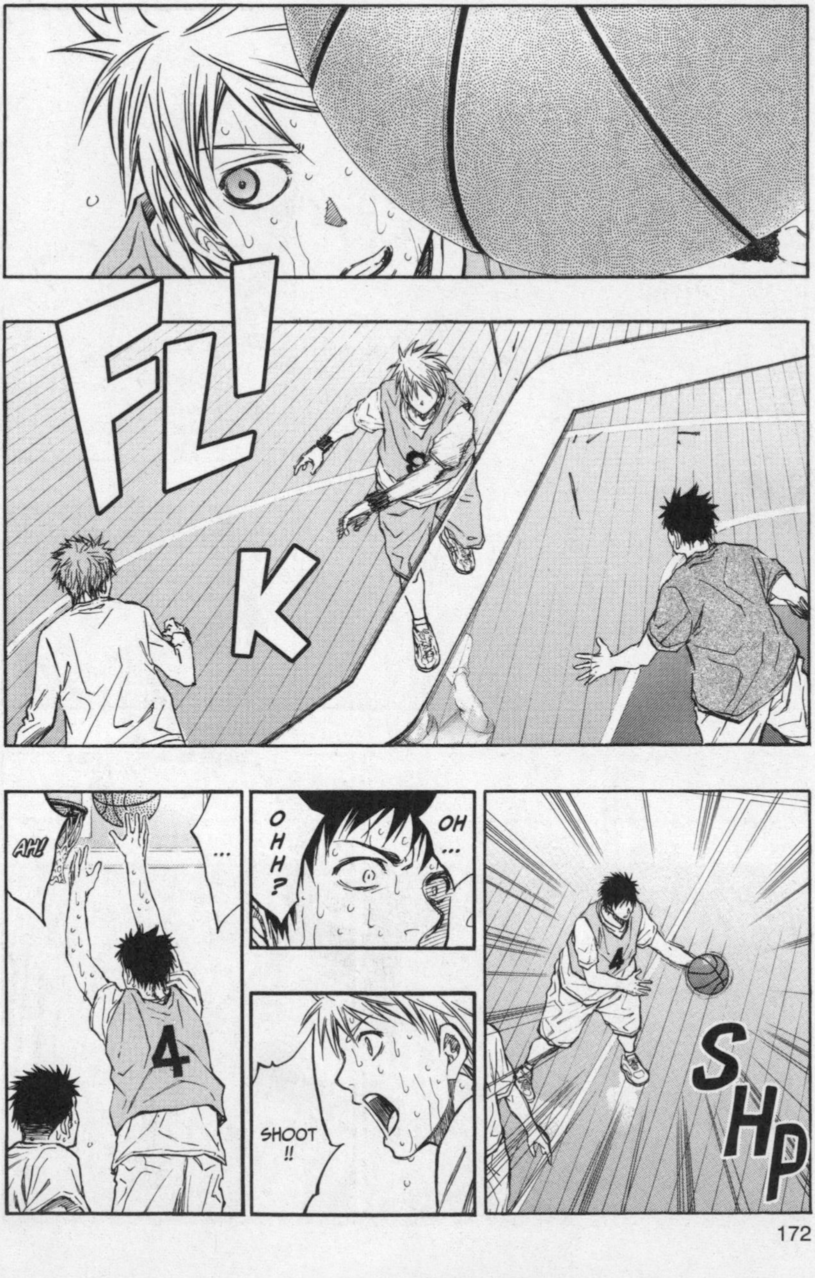
FLI
K
SHP
OH ...
OHHH?
SHOOT !!
...
AH!

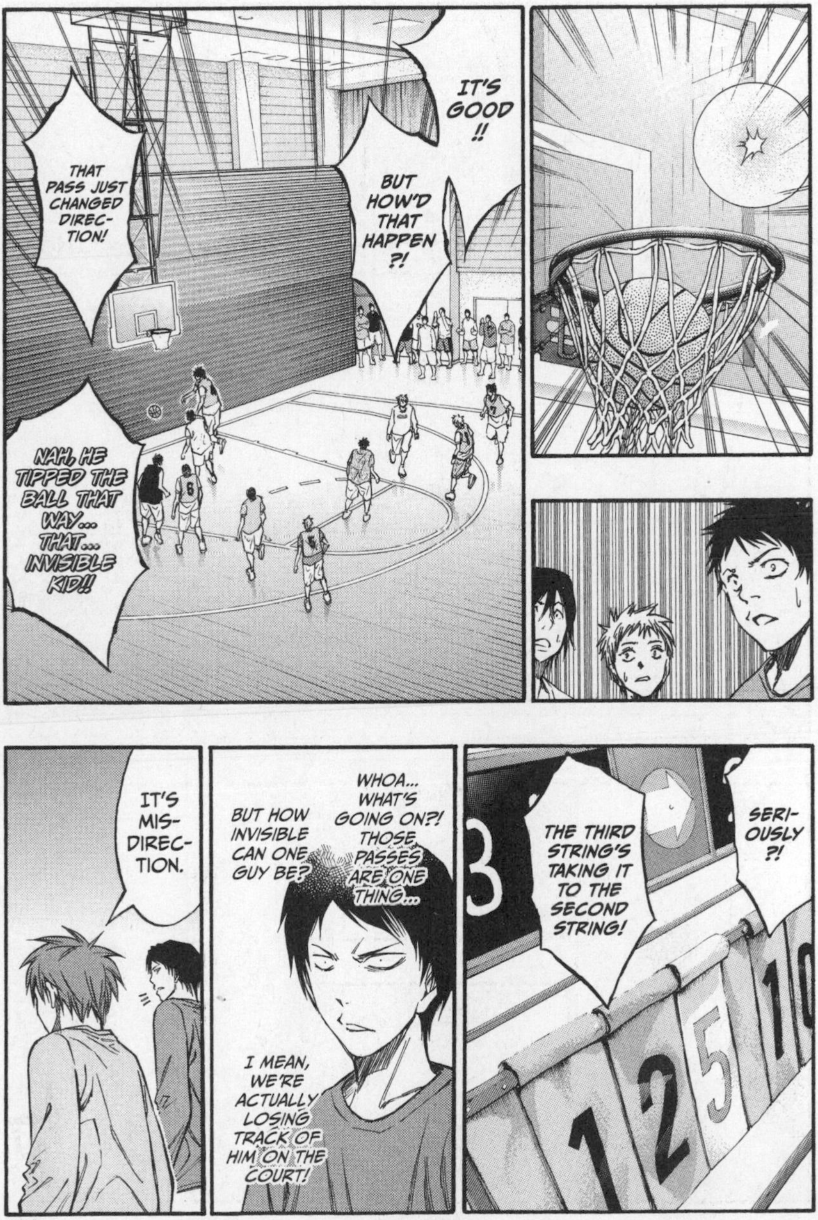
IT'S GOOD!!
BUT HOW'D THAT HAPPEN?!
THAT PASS JUST CHANGED DIRECTION!
NAH, HE TIPPED THE BALL THAT WAY... THAT... INVISIBLE KID!!
SERIOUSLY?!
THE THIRD STRING'S TAKING IT TO THE SECOND STRING!
WHOA... WHAT'S GOING ON?! THOSE PASSES ARE ONE THING...
BUT HOW INVISIBLE CAN ONE GUY BE?
I MEAN, WE'RE ACTUALLY LOSING TRACK OF HIM ON THE COURT!
IT'S MISDIRECTION.

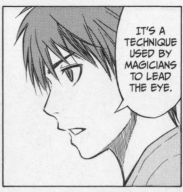

IT'S A TECHNIQUE USED BY MAGICIANS TO LEAD THE EYE.
MAGICIANS?!
THEY MIGHT DO SOMETHING FLASHY WITH THEIR RIGHT HAND TO DRAW ATTENTION, WHILE SETTING UP THE NEXT MOVE WITH THEIR LEFT.
IT'S THAT SORT OF TRICK.
BUT SUCH TECHNIQUES AREN'T LIMITED TO JUST MAGIC.
OUR EYES EXHIBIT CERTAIN INNATE TENDENCIES.
IF A FAST OBJECT AND A SLOWER ONE APPEAR BEFORE US, OUR EYES TEND TO FOLLOW THE FAST ONE.
IF THE PERSON WE'RE FACING TURNS TO LOOK AT SOMETHING, WE TEND TO DO THE SAME.
IN OTHER WORDS...
MISDIRECTION IS THE ART OF MANIPULATING LINES OF SIGHT.
NOW HE'S MAKING USE OF IT IN BASKETBALL.
FOR INSTANCE, JUST BEFORE HE CUTS...
HE'LL USE HIS OWN EYES AND ACTIONS TO LURE HIS MARK INTO LOOKING AWAY, AT THE BALL OR ANOTHER PLAYER.

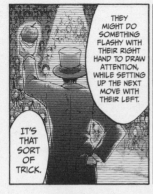

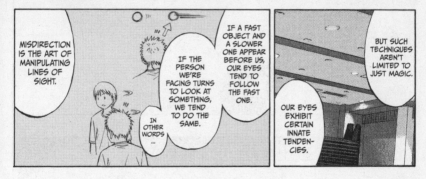

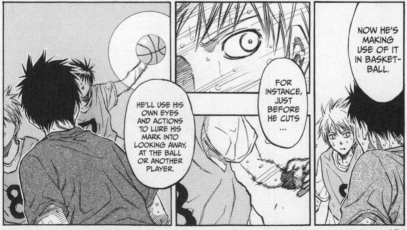

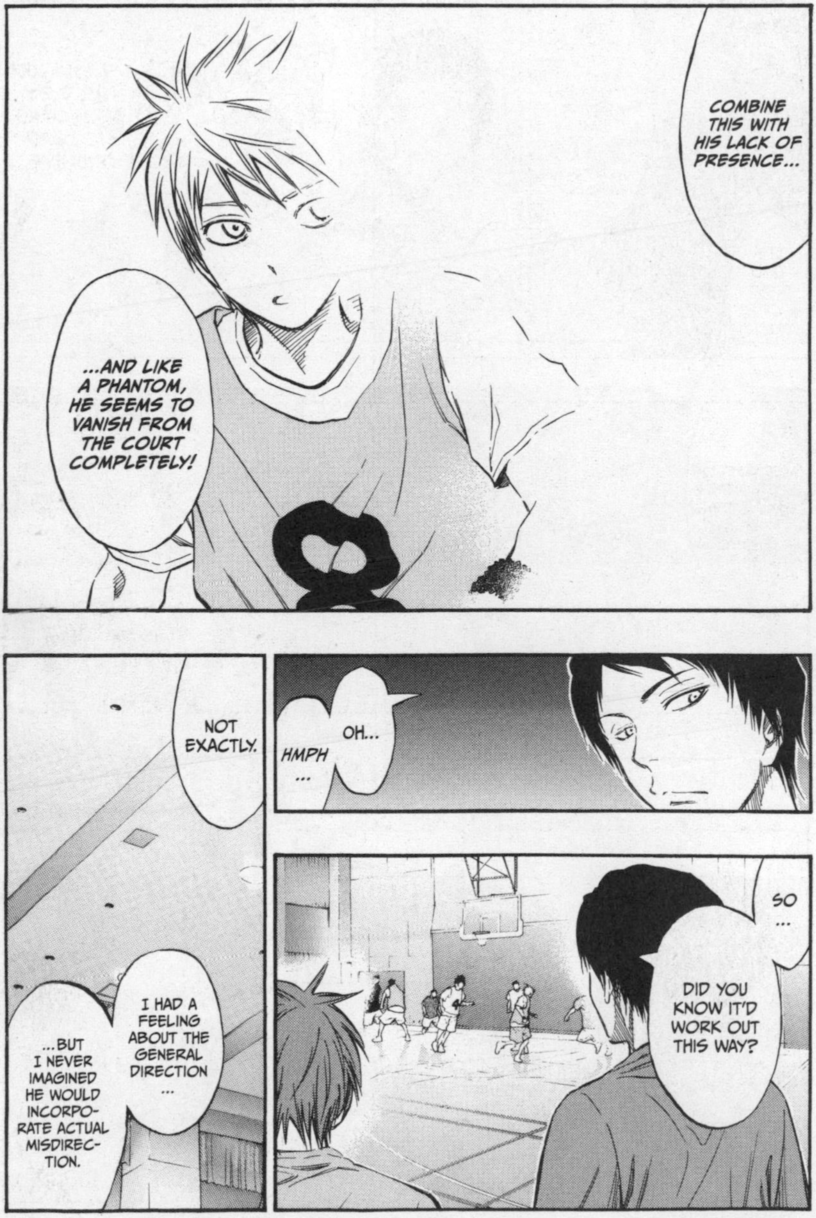
COMBINE THIS WITH HIS LACK OF PRESENCE...
...AND LIKE A PHANTOM, HE SEEMS TO VANISH FROM THE COURT COMPLETELY!
OH...
HMPH ...
SO ...
DID YOU KNOW IT'D WORK OUT THIS WAY?
NOT EXACTLY.
I HAD A FEELING ABOUT THE GENERAL DIRECTION ...
...BUT I NEVER IMAGINED HE WOULD INCORPORATE ACTUAL MISDIRECTION.

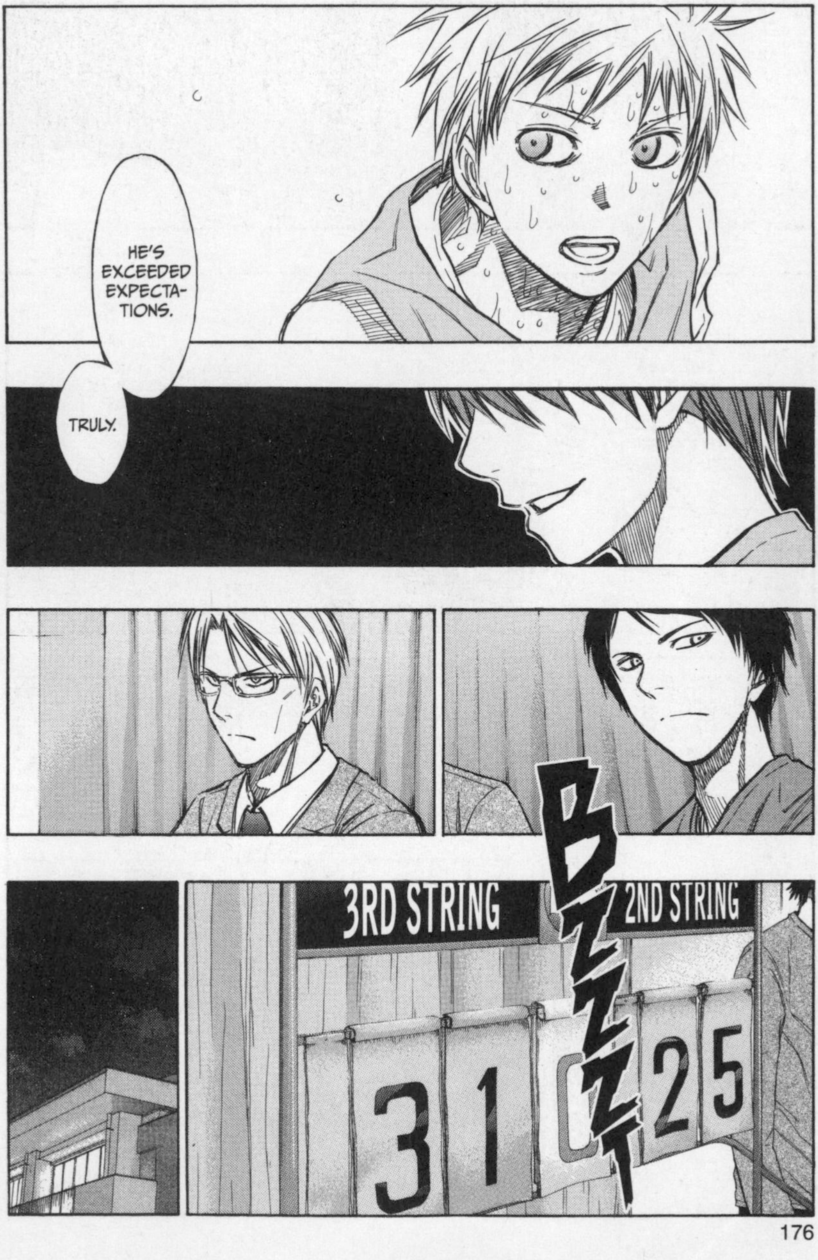

HE'S EXCEEDED EXPECTATIONS.
TRULY.
BZZZT
2ND STRING
3RD STRING
25
31

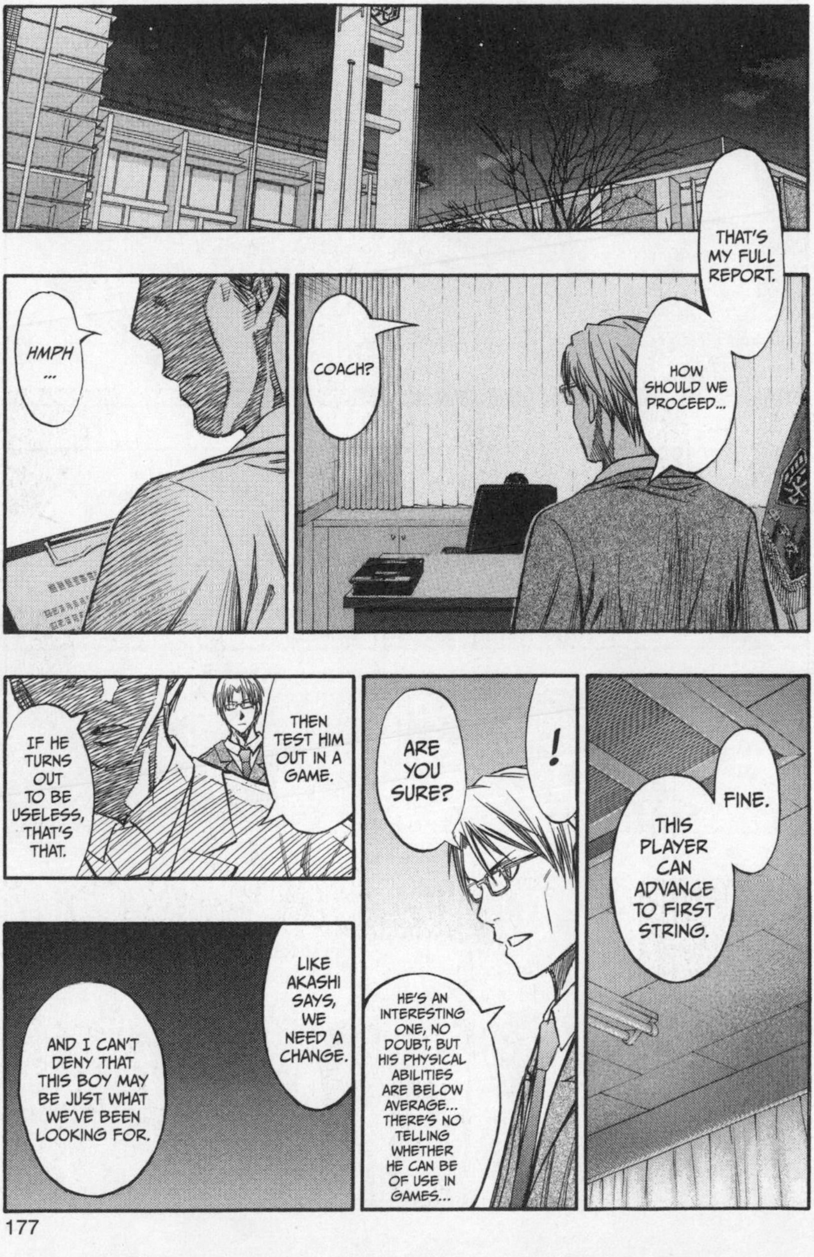
THAT'S MY FULL REPORT.
HOW SHOULD WE PROCEED...
COACH?
HMPH ...
FINE.
THIS PLAYER CAN ADVANCE TO FIRST STRING.
!
ARE YOU SURE?
HE'S AN INTERESTING ONE, NO DOUBT, BUT HIS PHYSICAL ABILITIES ARE BELOW AVERAGE... THERE'S NO TELLING WHETHER HE CAN BE OF USE IN GAMES...
THEN TEST HIM OUT IN A GAME.
IF HE TURNS OUT TO BE USELESS, THAT'S THAT.
LIKE AKASHI SAYS, WE NEED A CHANGE.
AND I CAN'T DENY THAT THIS BOY MAY BE JUST WHAT WE'VE BEEN LOOKING FOR.

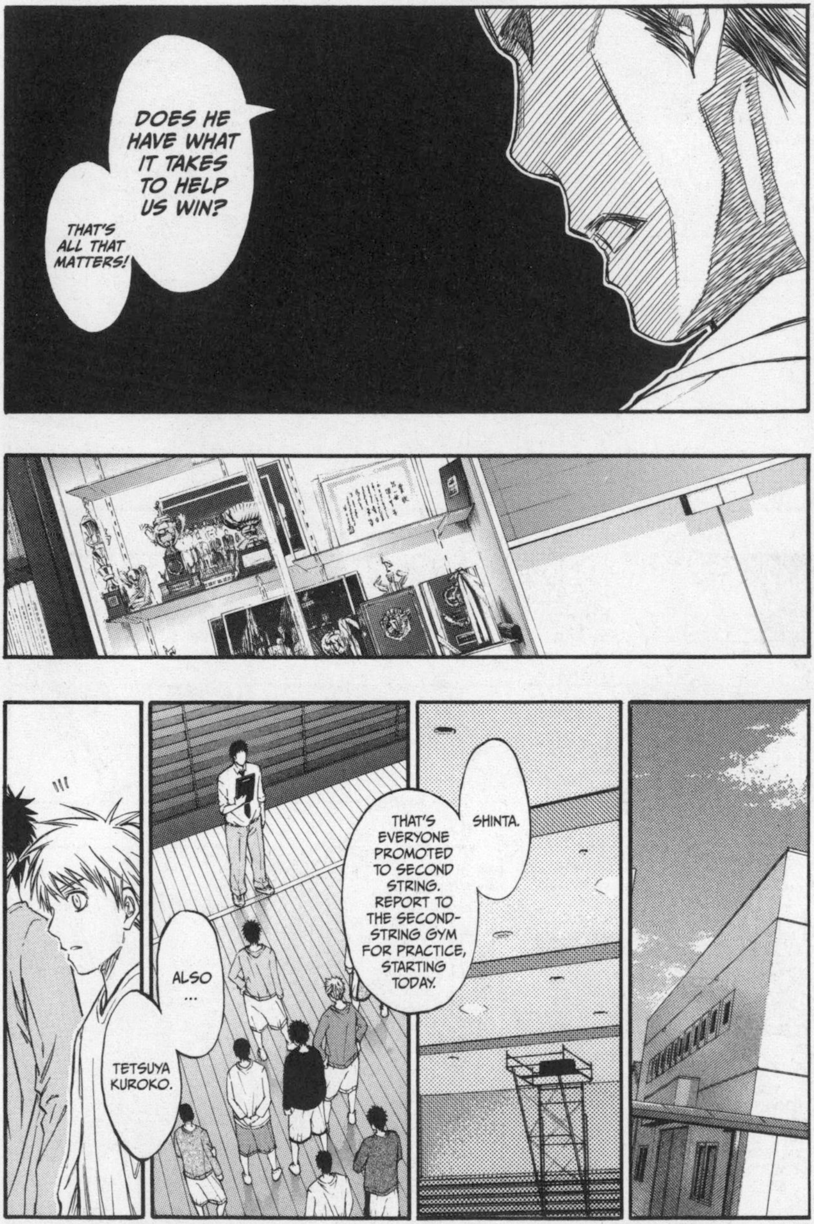
DOES HE HAVE WHAT IT TAKES TO HELP US WIN?
THAT'S ALL THAT MATTERS!
SHINTA.
THAT'S EVERYONE PROMOTED TO SECOND STRING. REPORT TO THE SECOND-STRING GYM FOR PRACTICE, STARTING TODAY.
ALSO ...
TETSUYA KUROKO.

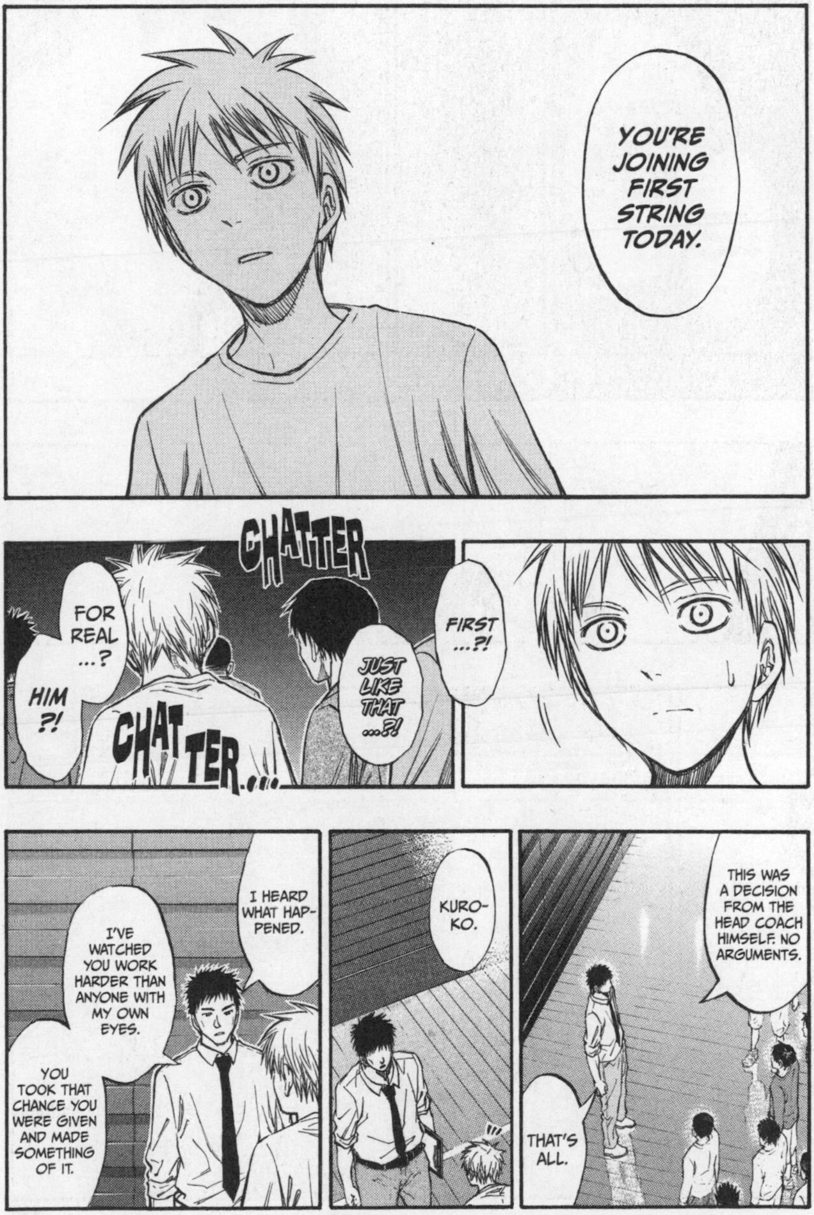
YOU'RE JOINING FIRST STRING TODAY.
FIRST ...?!
CHATTER
JUST LIKE THAT ...?!
FOR REAL ...?
HIM ?!
CHATTER...
THIS WAS A DECISION FROM THE HEAD COACH HIMSELF. NO ARGUMENTS.
THAT'S ALL.
KURO-KO.
I HEARD WHAT HAP-PENED.
I'VE WATCHED YOU WORK HARDER THAN ANYONE WITH MY OWN EYES.
YOU TOOK THAT CHANCE YOU WERE GIVEN AND MADE SOMETHING OF IT.

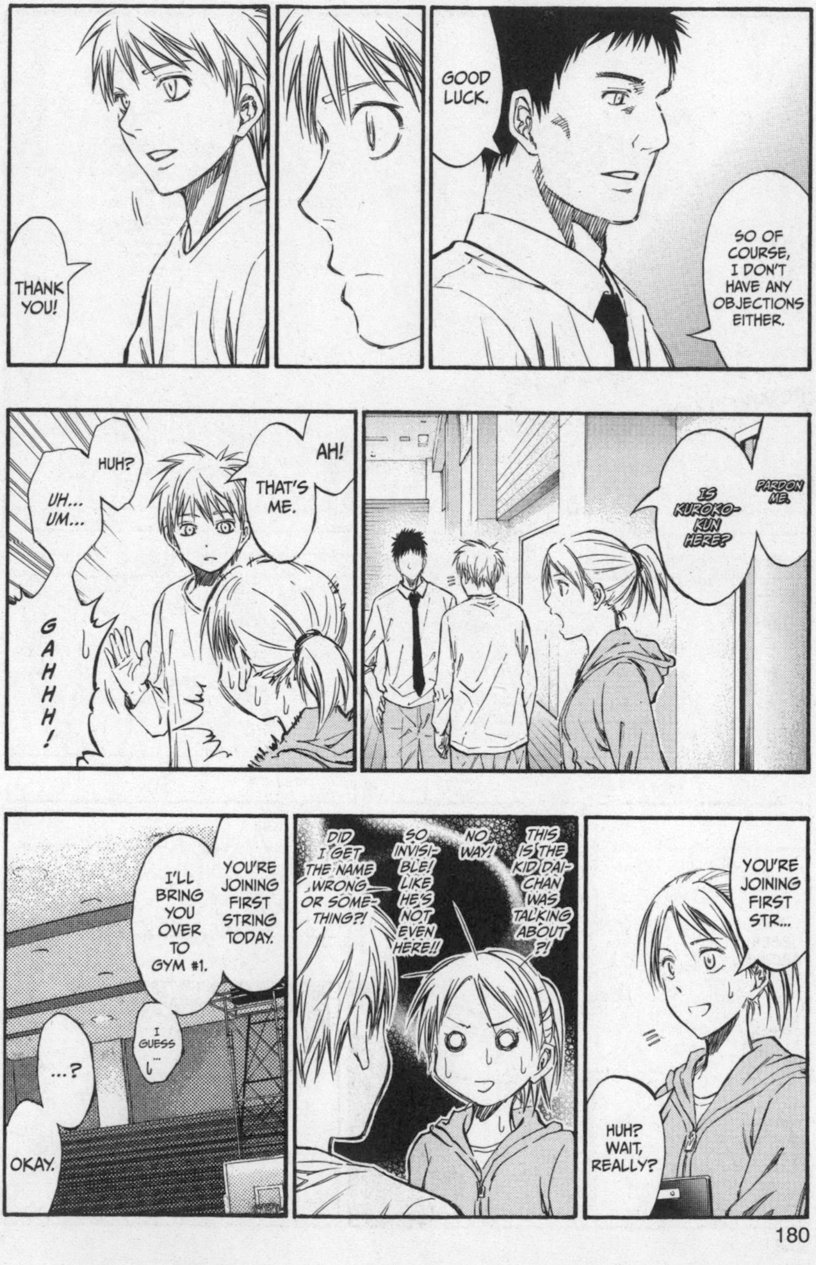
SO OF COURSE, I DON'T HAVE ANY OBJECTIONS EITHER.
GOOD LUCK.
THANK YOU!
PARDON ME.
IS KUROKO-KUN HERE?
AH!
THAT'S ME.
HUH?
UH... UM...
GAHHHH!
YOU'RE JOINING FIRST STR...
HUH? WAIT, REALLY?
THIS IS THE KID DAI-CHAN WAS TALKING ABOUT?!
NO WAY!
SO INVISIBLE! LIKE HE'S NOT EVEN HERE!!
DID I GET THE NAME WRONG OR SOMETHING?!
YOU'RE JOINING FIRST STRING TODAY.
I'LL BRING YOU OVER TO GYM #1.
I GUESS...
...?
OKAY.

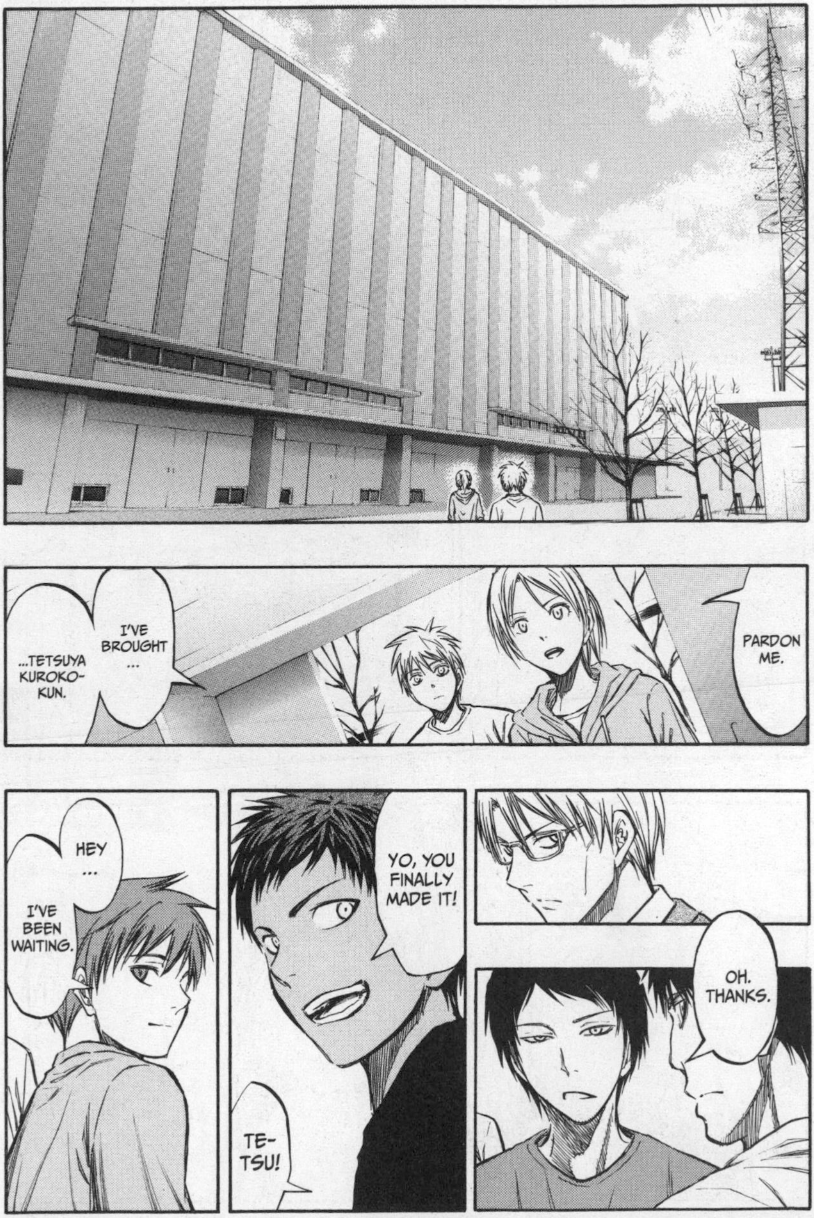
PARDON ME.
I'VE BROUGHT ...
...TETSUYA KUROKO-KUN.
OH. THANKS.
YO, YOU FINALLY MADE IT!
TE-TSU!
HEY ...
I'VE BEEN WAITING.

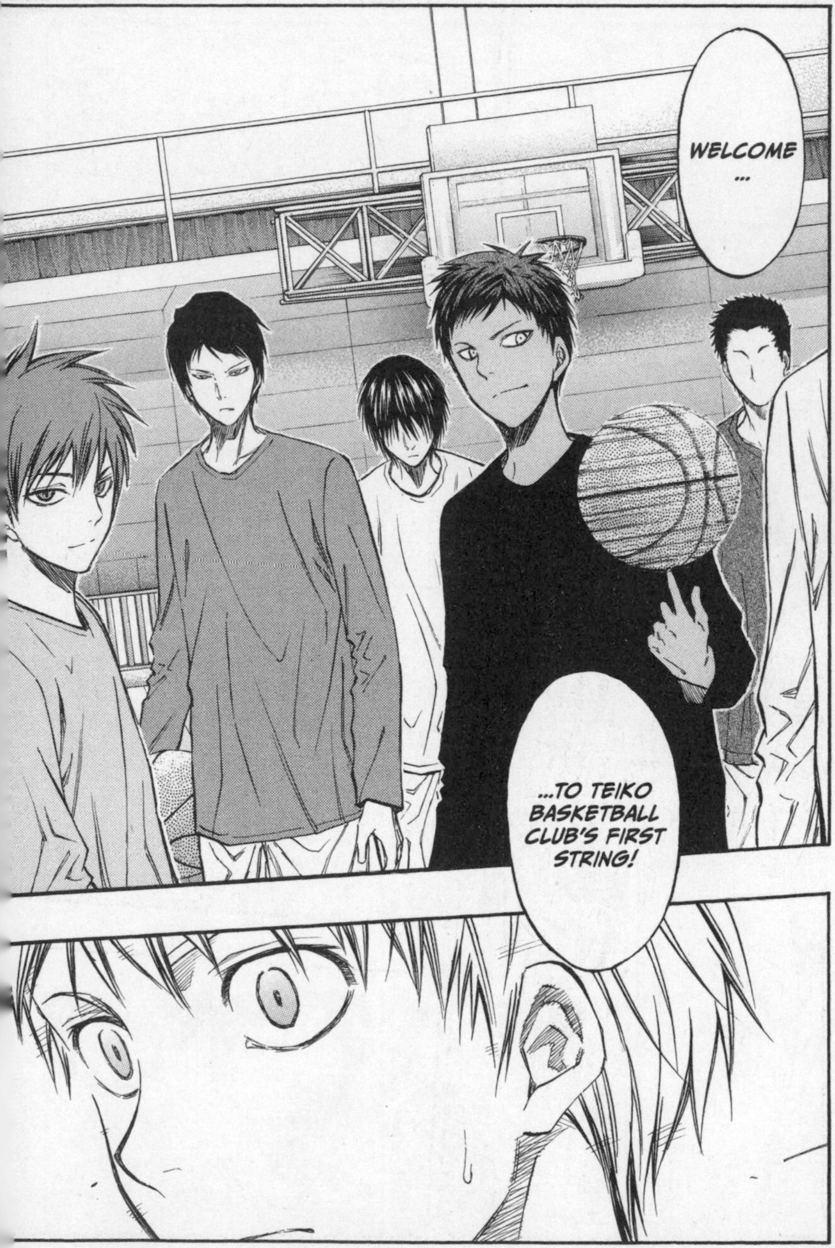
WELCOME ...
...TO TEIKO BASKETBALL CLUB'S FIRST STRING!

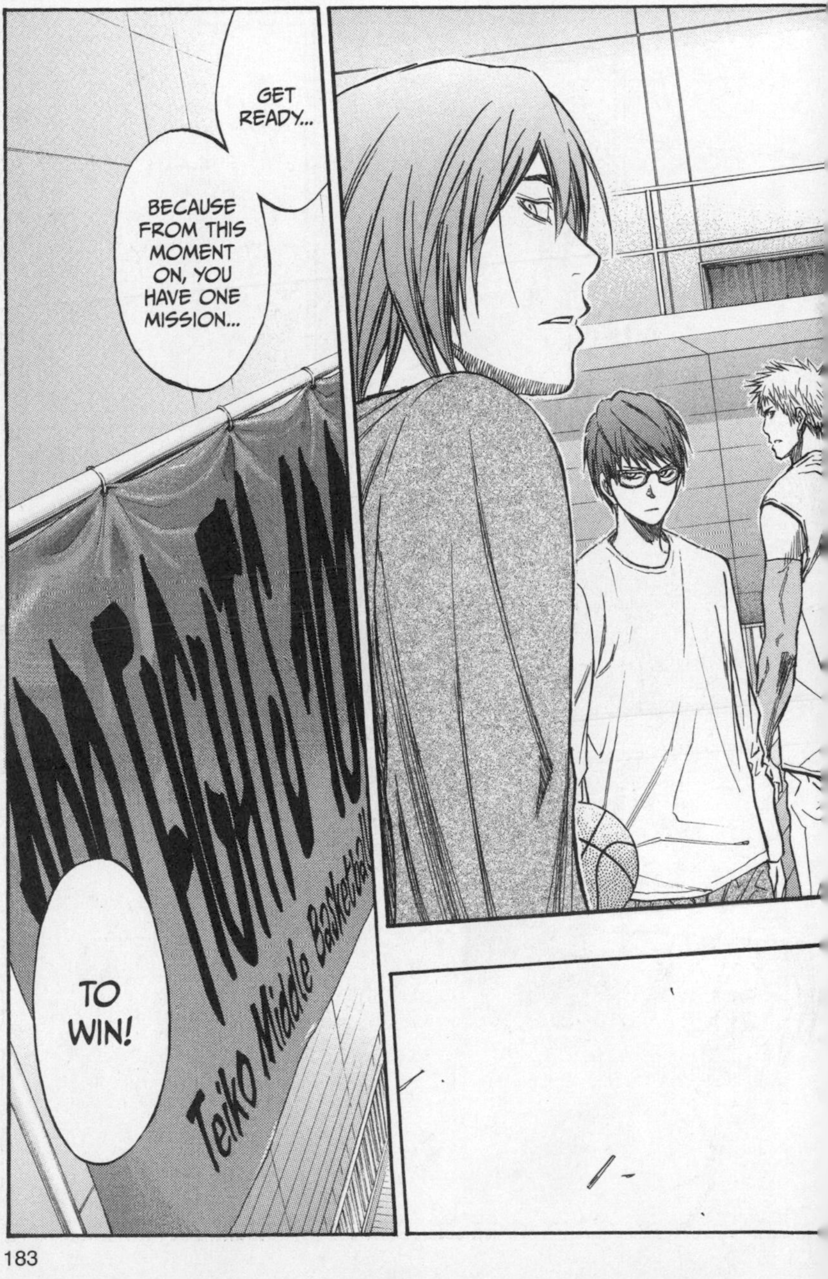
GET READY...
BECAUSE FROM THIS MOMENT ON, YOU HAVE ONE MISSION...
Teiko Middle Basketbal
TO WIN!

HUH?
HE REALLY MADE IT?
I HEAR HE PASSED A SPECIAL TEST AND WAS APPROVED BY THE HEAD COACH HIMSELF, BUT...
I STILL HAVE A HARD TIME BELIEVING IT, NATURALLY.
WAS-SUP?
YOU'RE LATE, HAIZAKI.
HEH HEH... IT WON'T HAPPEN AGAIN, PROMISE.
YOWCH!
AH.
EXCUSE ME.
WAHHHH!
WHO THE HECK'RE YOU?!
I'M TETSUYA KUROKO.
I'VE JUST JOINED FIRST STRING.
NICE TO MEET YOU.
HUH ?!
FOR REAL ?!
THIS SHRIMP ...?!
TIME TO START!
STRETCH AND THEN PRACTICE YOUR FOOTWORK.

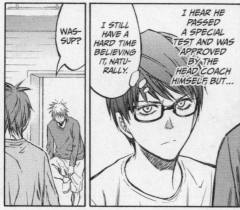

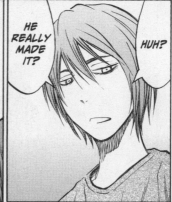

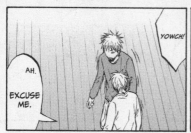

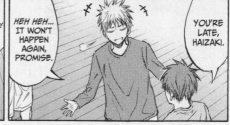

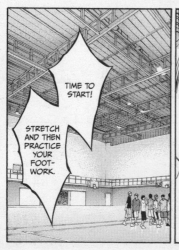

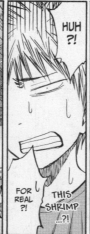

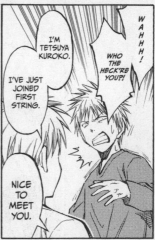

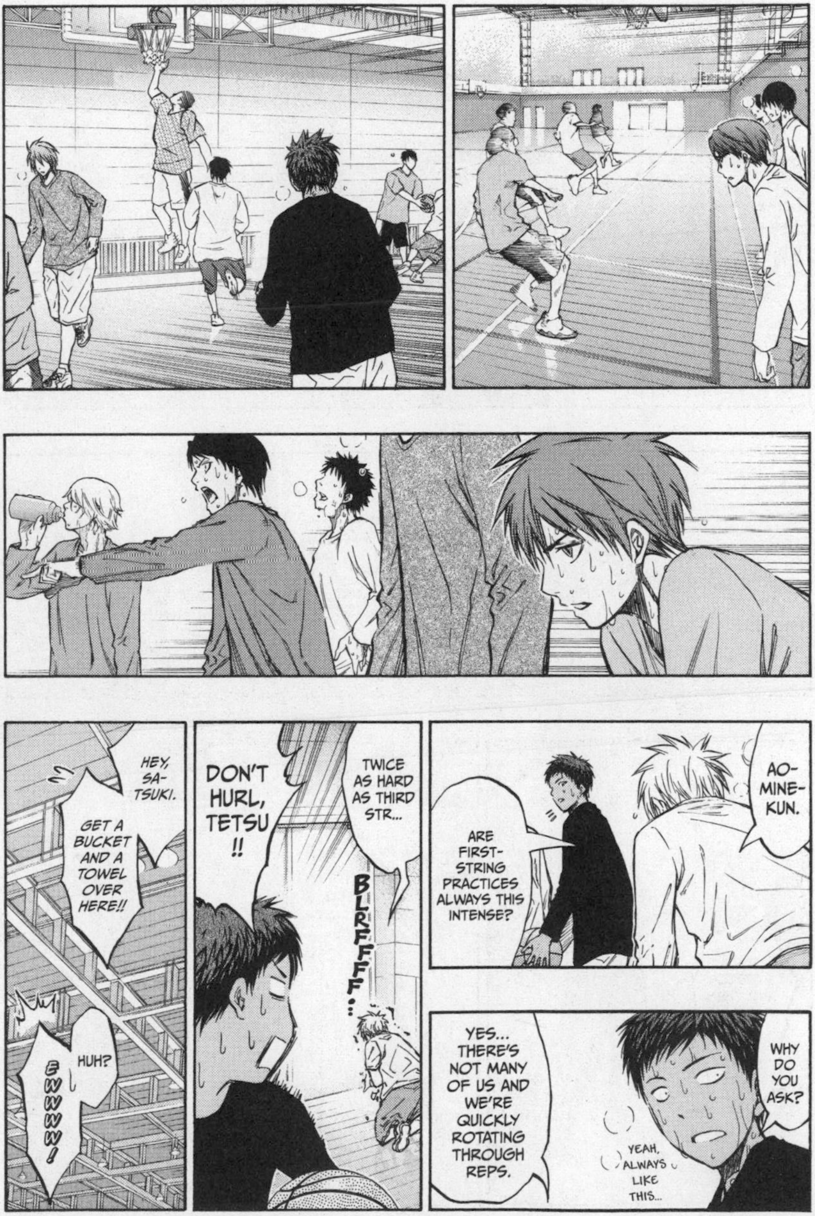
AO-MINE-KUN.
ARE FIRST-STRING PRACTICES ALWAYS THIS INTENSE?
WHY DO YOU ASK?
YES... THERE'S NOT MANY OF US AND WE'RE QUICKLY ROTATING THROUGH REPS.
YEAH, ALWAYS LIKE THIS...
TWICE AS HARD AS THIRD STR...
DON'T HURL, TETSU!!
BLRFFFF...
HEY, SA-TSUKI.
GET A BUCKET AND A TOWEL OVER HERE!!
HUH?
EWWWWW!

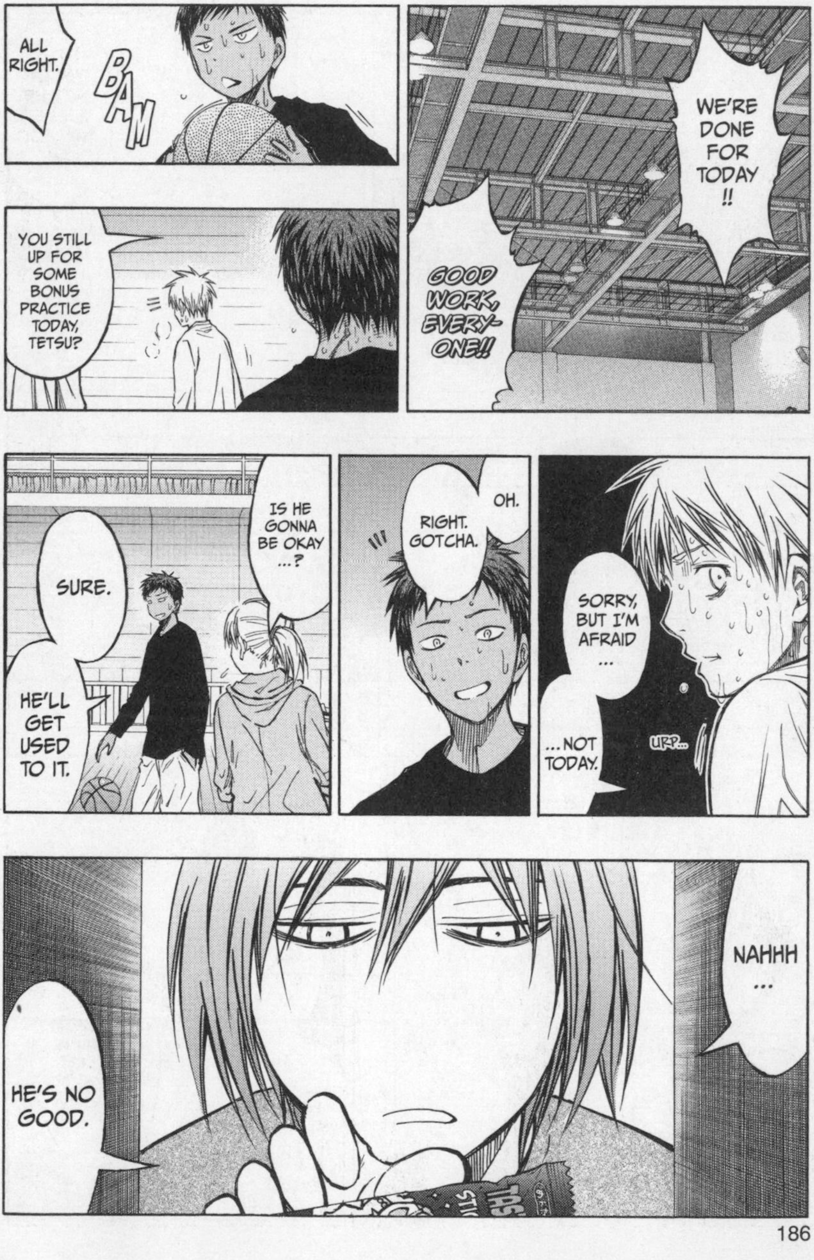
WE'RE DONE FOR TODAY !!
GOOD WORK, EVERY-ONE!!
ALL RIGHT.
BAM
YOU STILL UP FOR SOME BONUS PRACTICE TODAY, TETSU?
SORRY, BUT I'M AFRAID ...
URP...
...NOT TODAY.
OH.
RIGHT. GOTCHA.
IS HE GONNA BE OKAY ...?
SURE.
HE'LL GET USED TO IT.
NAHHH ...
HE'S NO GOOD.

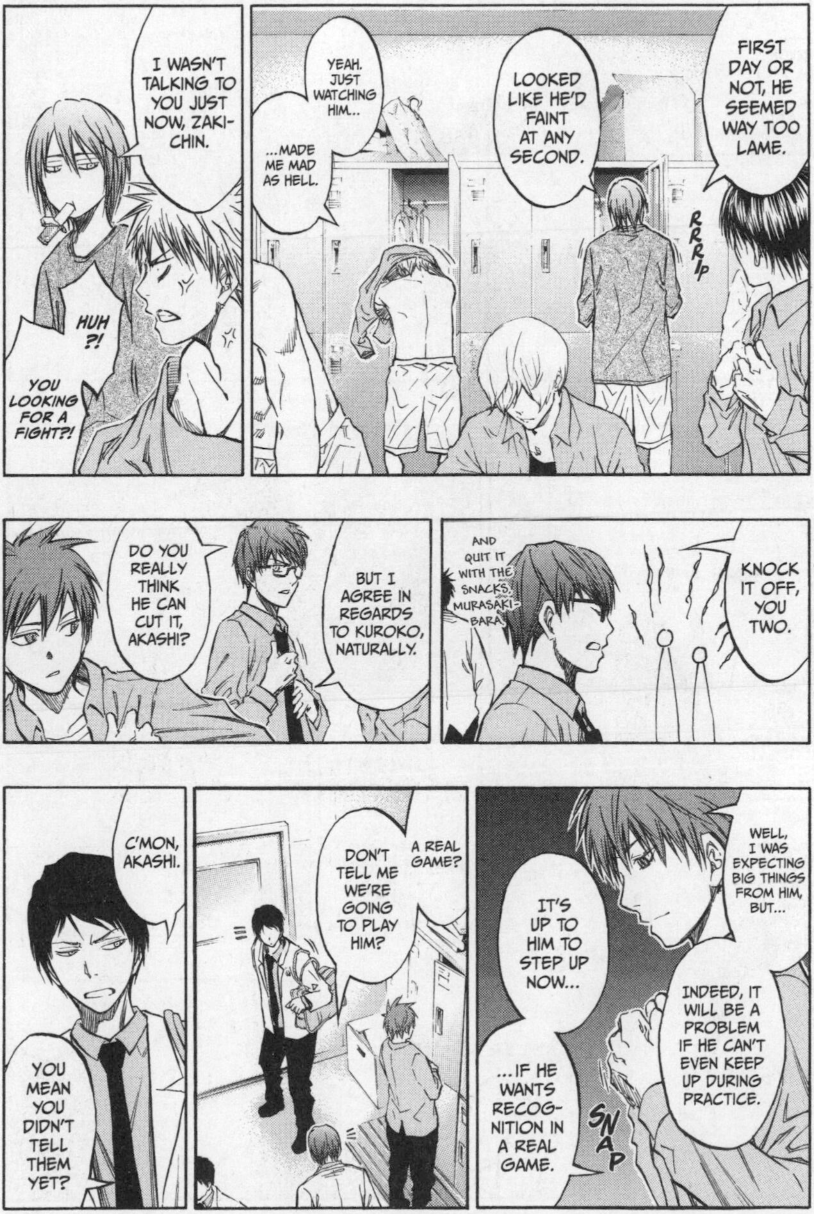
FIRST DAY OR NOT, HE SEEMED WAY TOO LAME.
RRRIP
LOOKED LIKE HE'D FAINT AT ANY SECOND.
YEAH. JUST WATCHING HIM...
...MADE ME MAD AS HELL.
I WASN'T TALKING TO YOU JUST NOW, ZAKI-CHIN.
HUH?!
YOU LOOKING FOR A FIGHT?!
KNOCK IT OFF, YOU TWO.
AND QUIT IT WITH THE SNACKS, MURASAKIBARA.
BUT I AGREE IN REGARDS TO KUROKO, NATURALLY.
DO YOU REALLY THINK HE CAN CUT IT, AKASHI?
WELL, I WAS EXPECTING BIG THINGS FROM HIM, BUT...
INDEED, IT WILL BE A PROBLEM IF HE CAN'T EVEN KEEP UP DURING PRACTICE.
IT'S UP TO HIM TO STEP UP NOW...
SNAP
...IF HE WANTS RECOGNITION IN A REAL GAME.
A REAL GAME?
DON'T TELL ME WE'RE GOING TO PLAY HIM?
C'MON, AKASHI.
YOU MEAN YOU DIDN'T TELL THEM YET?

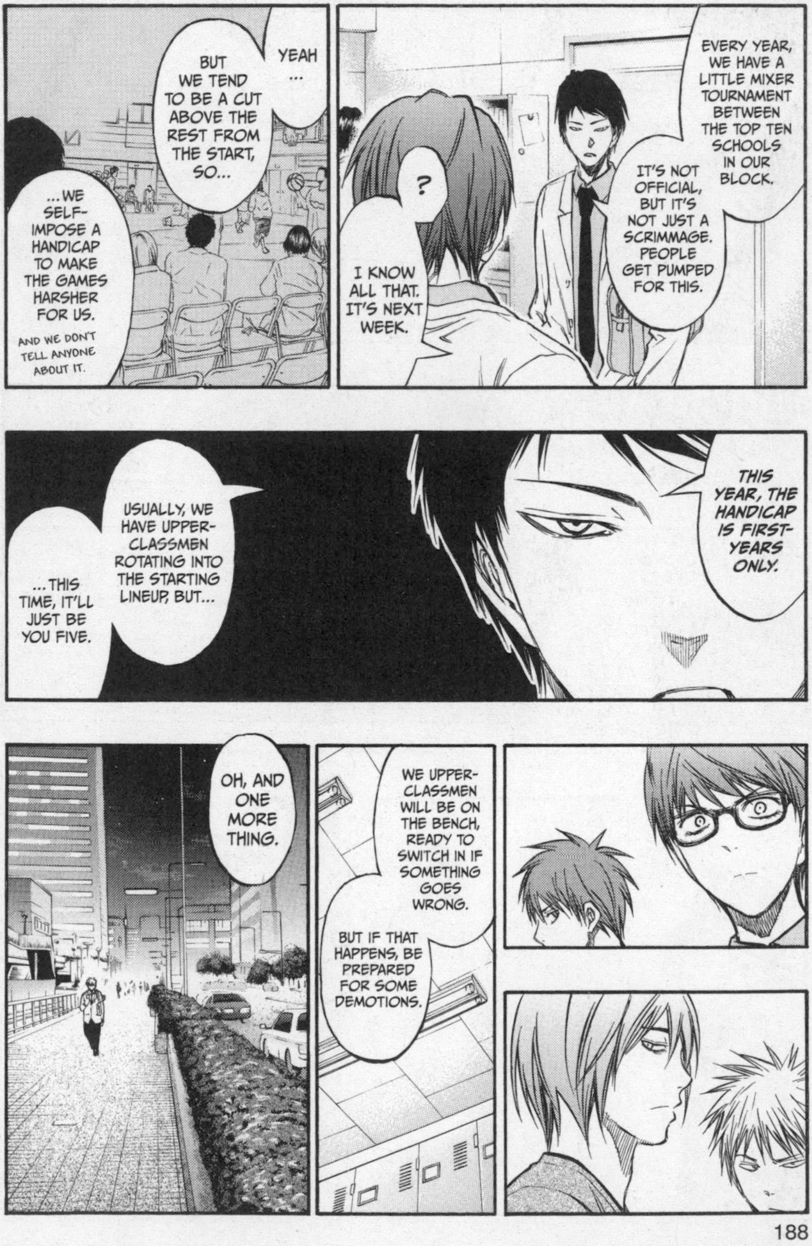
EVERY YEAR, WE HAVE A LITTLE MIXER TOURNAMENT BETWEEN THE TOP TEN SCHOOLS IN OUR BLOCK.
IT'S NOT OFFICIAL, BUT IT'S NOT JUST A SCRIMMAGE. PEOPLE GET PUMPED FOR THIS.
?
I KNOW ALL THAT. IT'S NEXT WEEK.
YEAH ...
BUT WE TEND TO BE A CUT ABOVE THE REST FROM THE START, SO...
...WE SELF-IMPOSE A HANDICAP TO MAKE THE GAMES HARSHER FOR US.
AND WE DON'T TELL ANYONE ABOUT IT.
THIS YEAR, THE HANDICAP IS FIRST-YEARS ONLY.
USUALLY, WE HAVE UPPER-CLASSMEN ROTATING INTO THE STARTING LINEUP, BUT...
...THIS TIME, IT'LL JUST BE YOU FIVE.
WE UPPER-CLASSMEN WILL BE ON THE BENCH, READY TO SWITCH IN IF SOMETHING GOES WRONG.
BUT IF THAT HAPPENS, BE PREPARED FOR SOME DEMOTIONS.
OH, AND ONE MORE THING.

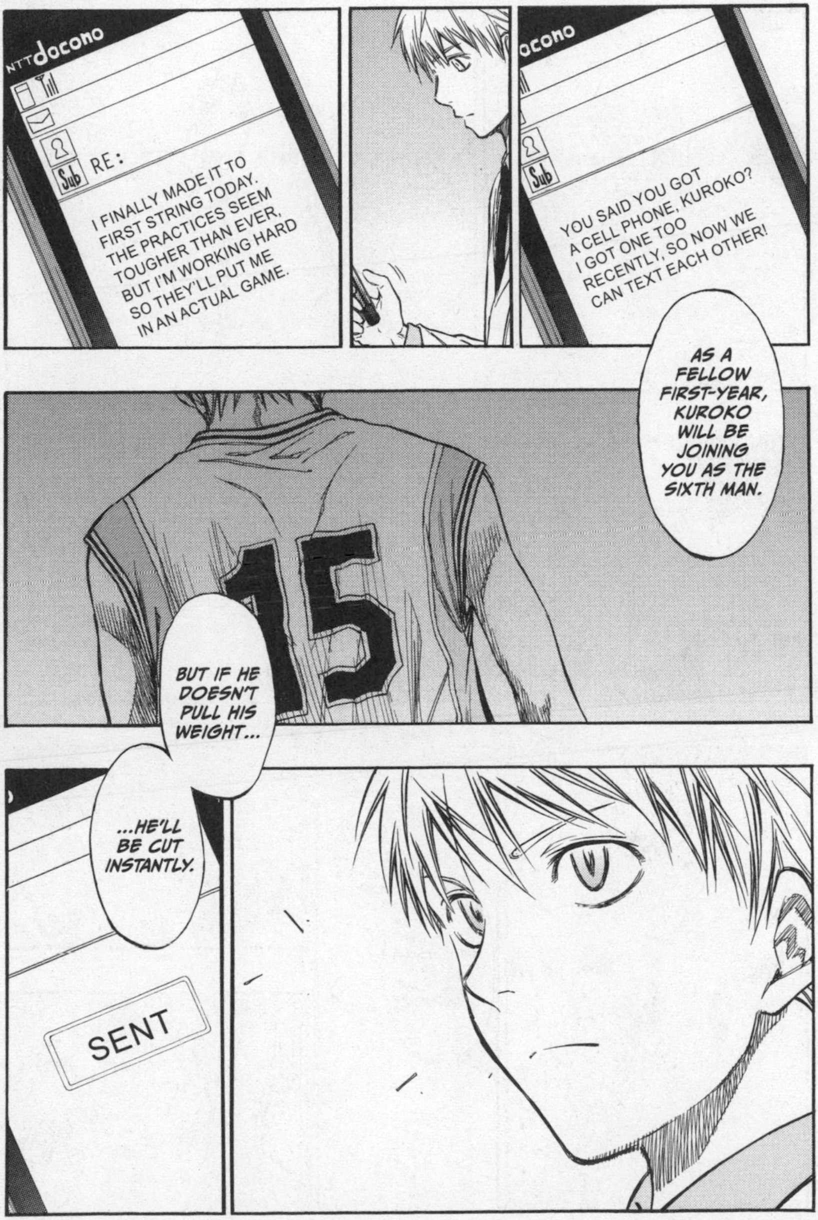
docomo
YOU SAID YOU GOT A CELL PHONE, KUROKO? I GOT ONE TOO RECENTLY, SO NOW WE CAN TEXT EACH OTHER!
NTT docomo
RE:
I FINALLY MADE IT TO FIRST STRING TODAY. THE PRACTICES SEEM TOUGHER THAN EVER, BUT I'M WORKING HARD SO THEY'LL PUT ME IN AN ACTUAL GAME.
AS A FELLOW FIRST-YEAR, KUROKO WILL BE JOINING YOU AS THE SIXTH MAN.
15
BUT IF HE DOESN'T PULL HIS WEIGHT...
...HE'LL BE CUT INSTANTLY.
SENT

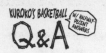

KUROKO'S BASKETBALL Q&A
W/ HALFWAY-DECENT ANSWERS

Q. **WHICH IS HARDER TO THINK UP—THE MAIN STORY OR THE BLOOPERS?**
(DROP OF LIGHT from YAMAGATA PREFECTURE)

A. THE BLOOPERS, IN A SENSE.

KUROKO'S BASKETBALL BLOOPERS
TAKE 4

NAHHH...
HE'S NO GOOD.
TASTY STICK
Chips
W/PORK PUNCH
Yummy Crackers
Choco Ponpon
CHIPPIES
SNACKS
PRETZEL
HOW DO YOU EAT ALL THAT CRAP?!
TOO MANY SNACKS, MAN!! AND WHAT'S WITH THE BLANK STARE?!
?

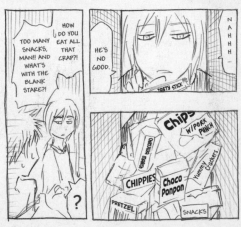

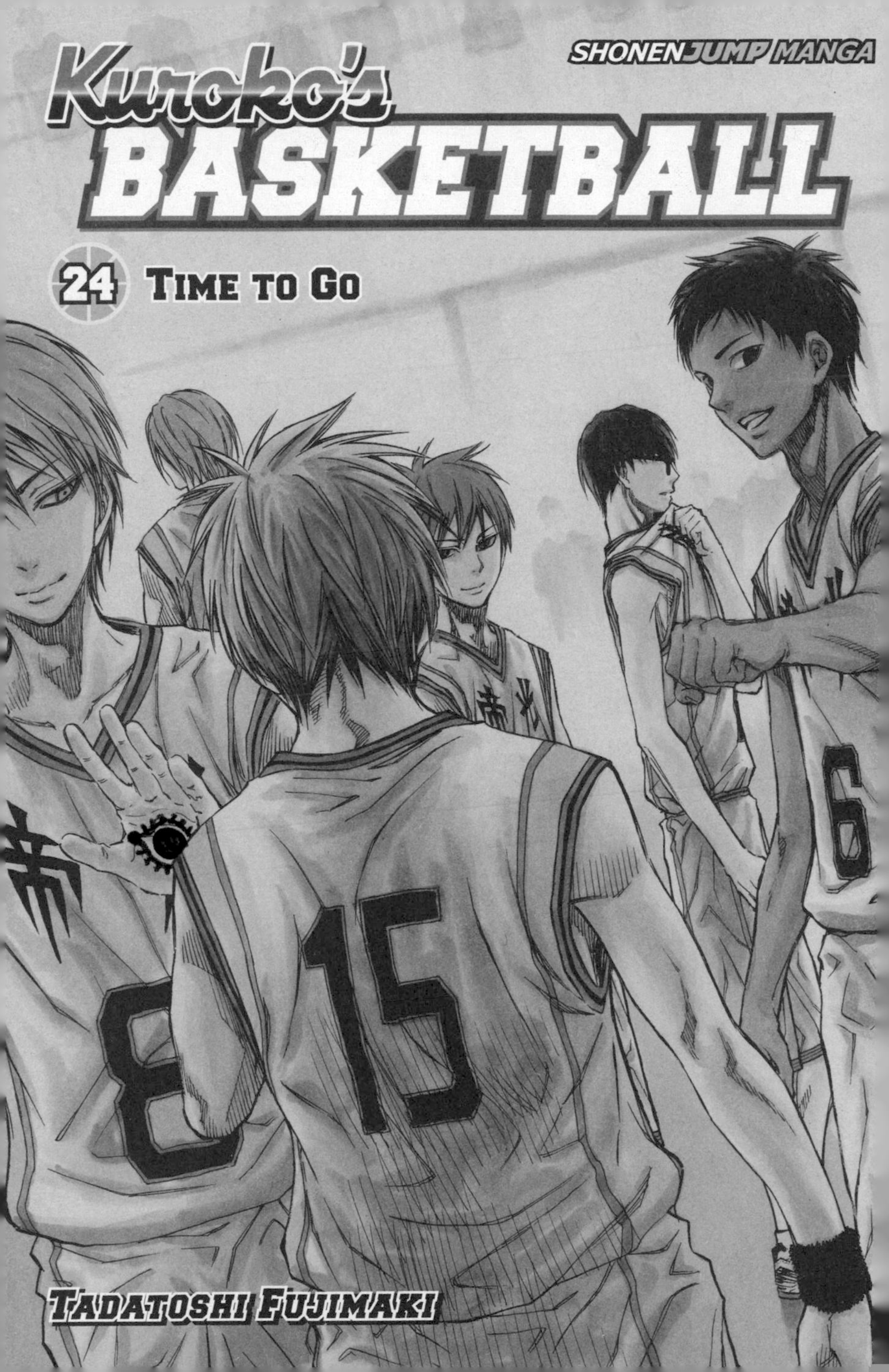
SHONEN JUMP MANGA
Kuroko's
BASKETBALL
24 TIME TO GO
15
8
6
TADATOSHI FUJIMAKI

TADATOSHI FUJIMAKI

I received the following letter from a fan:

"Fujimaki Sensei,

To even be able to write such charming characters, you must be as smooth as Kuroko, as hot-blooded as Kagami, as cool as Kise, as wild as Aomine, as quirky as Midorima, as tall as Murasakibara and as smart as Akashi."

Someone like that wouldn't need to draw manga for a living...

—2013

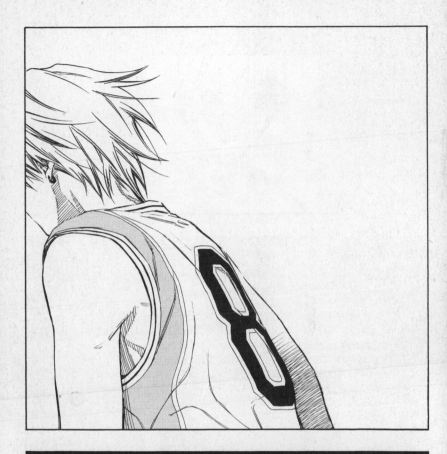

208TH QUARTER:

I'M FINE

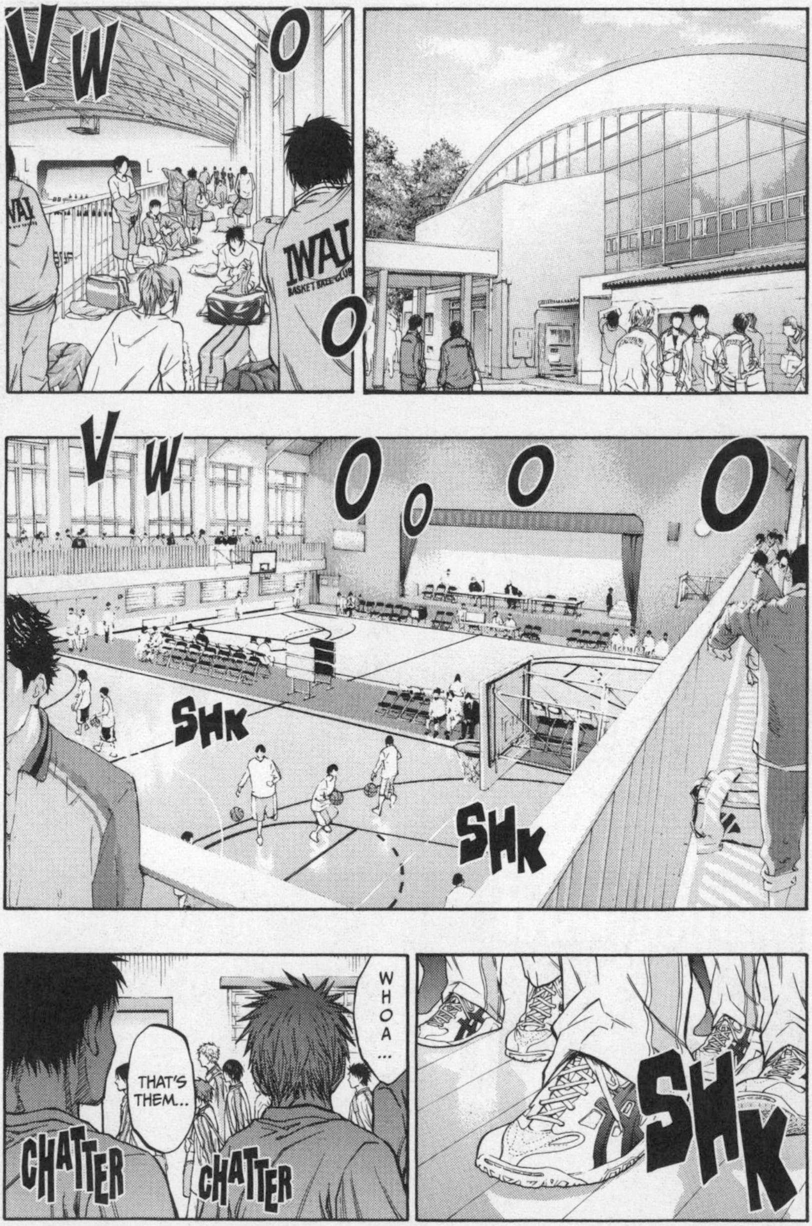
VWO
O
IWAI
BASKET BALL CLUB
IWAI
VWOOOO
SHK
SHK
SHK
WHOA...
THAT'S THEM...
CHATTER
CHATTER

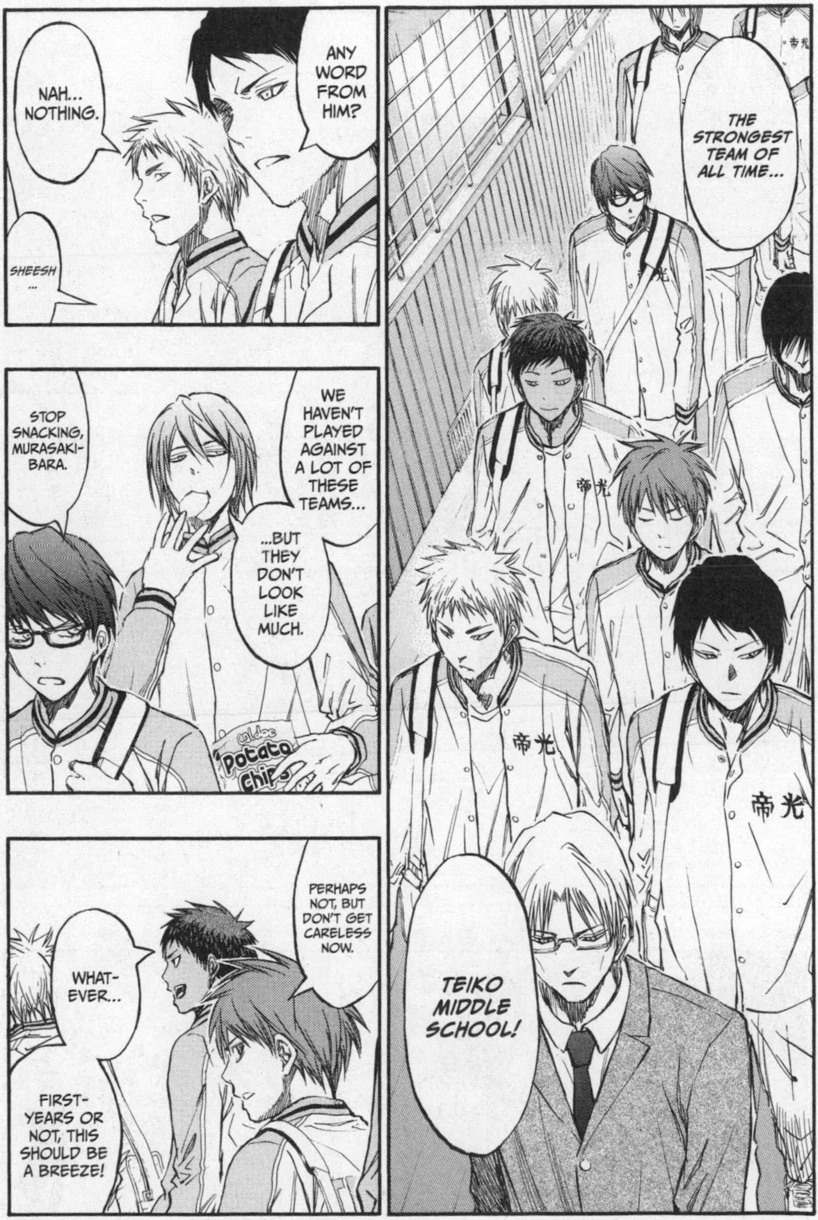
THE STRONGEST TEAM OF ALL TIME...
帝光
TEIKO MIDDLE SCHOOL!
ANY WORD FROM HIM?
NAH... NOTHING.
SHEESH ...
WE HAVEN'T PLAYED AGAINST A LOT OF THESE TEAMS...
...BUT THEY DON'T LOOK LIKE MUCH.
STOP SNACKING, MURASAKI-BARA.
Potato Chips
PERHAPS NOT, BUT DON'T GET CARELESS NOW.
WHAT-EVER...
FIRST-YEARS OR NOT, THIS SHOULD BE A BREEZE!

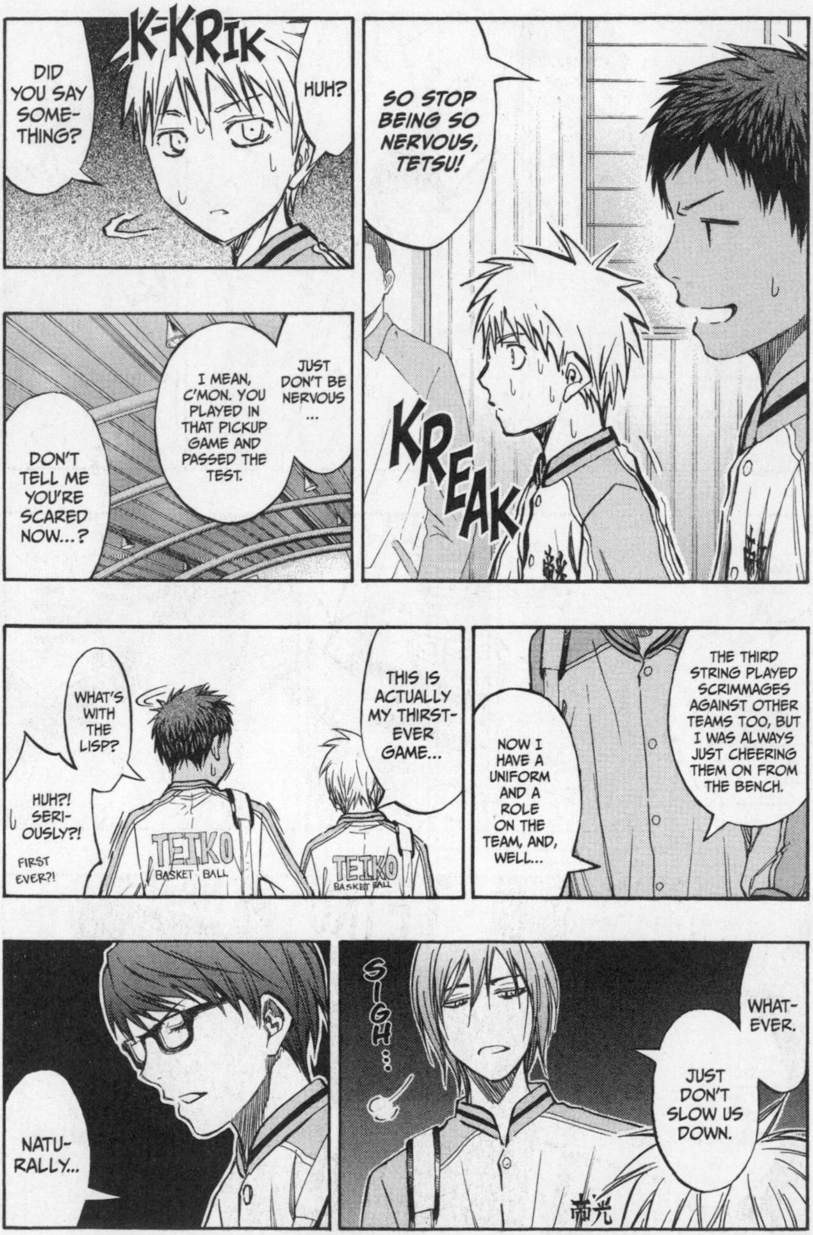
SO STOP BEING SO NERVOUS, TETSU!
KREAK
HUH?
DID YOU SAY SOME-THING?
K-KRIK
JUST DON'T BE NERVOUS ...
I MEAN, C'MON. YOU PLAYED IN THAT PICKUP GAME AND PASSED THE TEST.
DON'T TELL ME YOU'RE SCARED NOW...?
THE THIRD STRING PLAYED SCRIMMAGES AGAINST OTHER TEAMS TOO, BUT I WAS ALWAYS JUST CHEERING THEM ON FROM THE BENCH.
NOW I HAVE A UNIFORM AND A ROLE ON THE TEAM, AND, WELL...
THIS IS ACTUALLY MY THIRST-EVER GAME...
WHAT'S WITH THE LISP?
HUH?! SERI-OUSLY?!
FIRST EVER?!
TEIKO BASKET BALL
TEIKO BASKET BALL
SIGH...
WHAT-EVER.
JUST DON'T SLOW US DOWN.
NATU-RALLY...

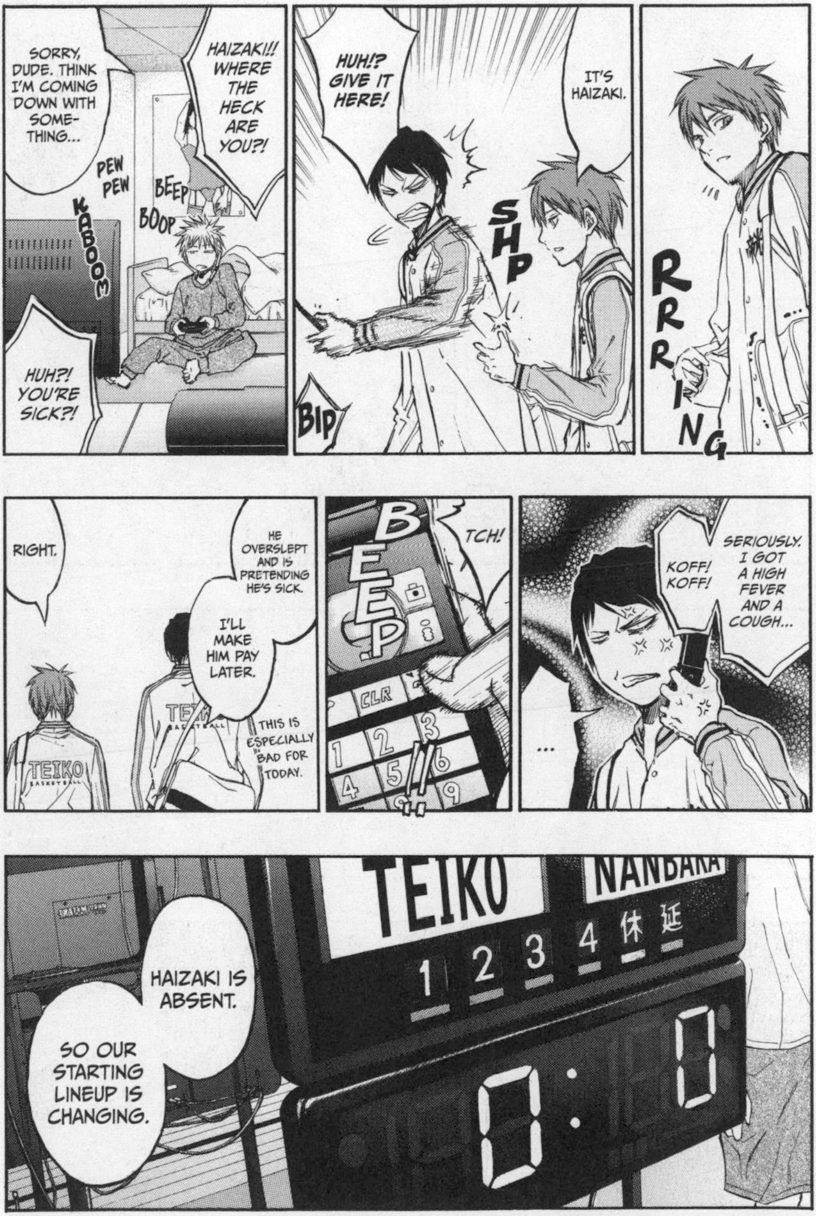
RRRING
IT'S HAIZAKI.
HUH!? GIVE IT HERE!
SHP
BIP
HAIZAKI!! WHERE THE HECK ARE YOU?!
SORRY, DUDE. THINK I'M COMING DOWN WITH SOME-THING...
PEW PEW
BEEP
BOOP
KABOOM
HUH?! YOU'RE SICK?!
SERIOUSLY. I GOT A HIGH FEVER AND A COUGH...
KOFF! KOFF!
...
TCH!
BEEP
CLR
HE OVERSLEPT AND IS PRETENDING HE'S SICK.
I'LL MAKE HIM PAY LATER.
THIS IS ESPECIALLY BAD FOR TODAY.
RIGHT.
TEIKO
TEIKO
NANBARA
1 2 3 4 休 延
HAIZAKI IS ABSENT.
SO OUR STARTING LINEUP IS CHANGING.

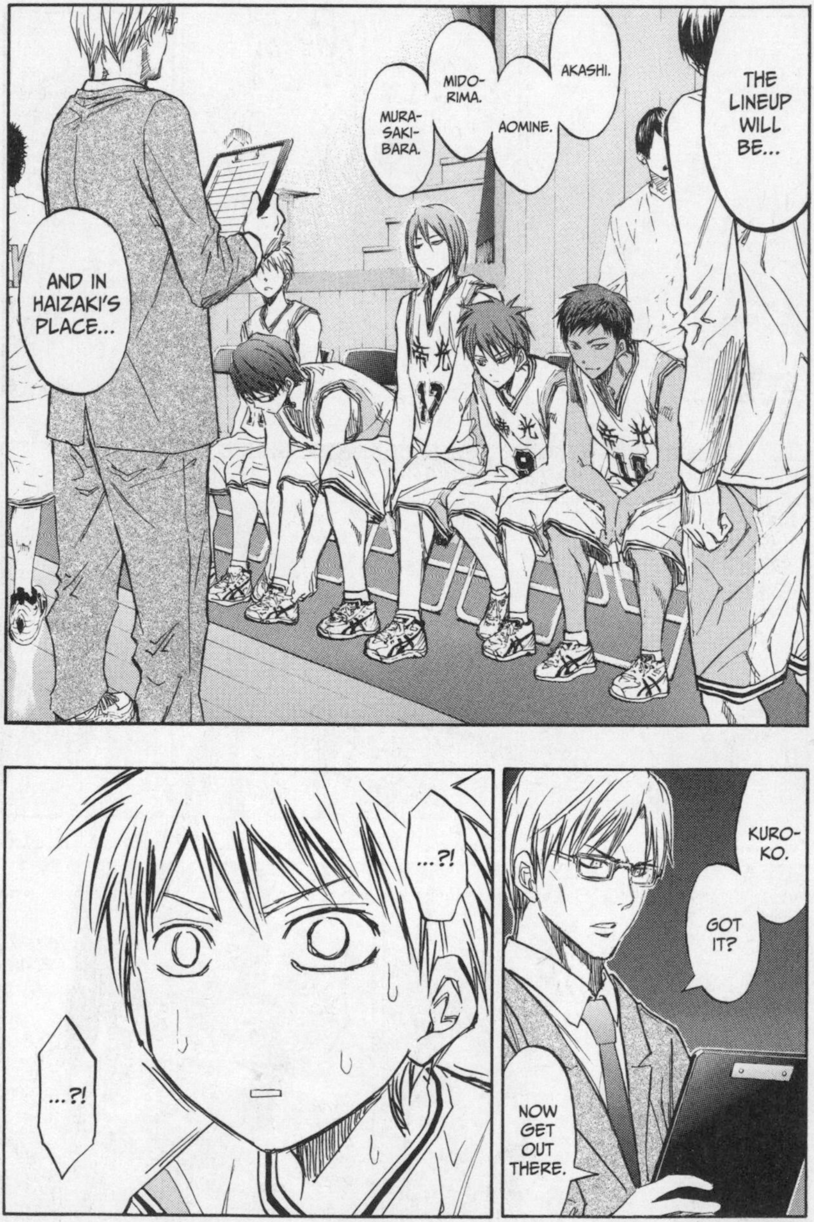
THE LINEUP WILL BE...
AKASHI.
AOMINE.
MIDO-RIMA.
MURA-SAKI-BARA.
AND IN HAIZAKI'S PLACE...
KURO-KO.
GOT IT?
NOW GET OUT THERE.
...?!
...?!

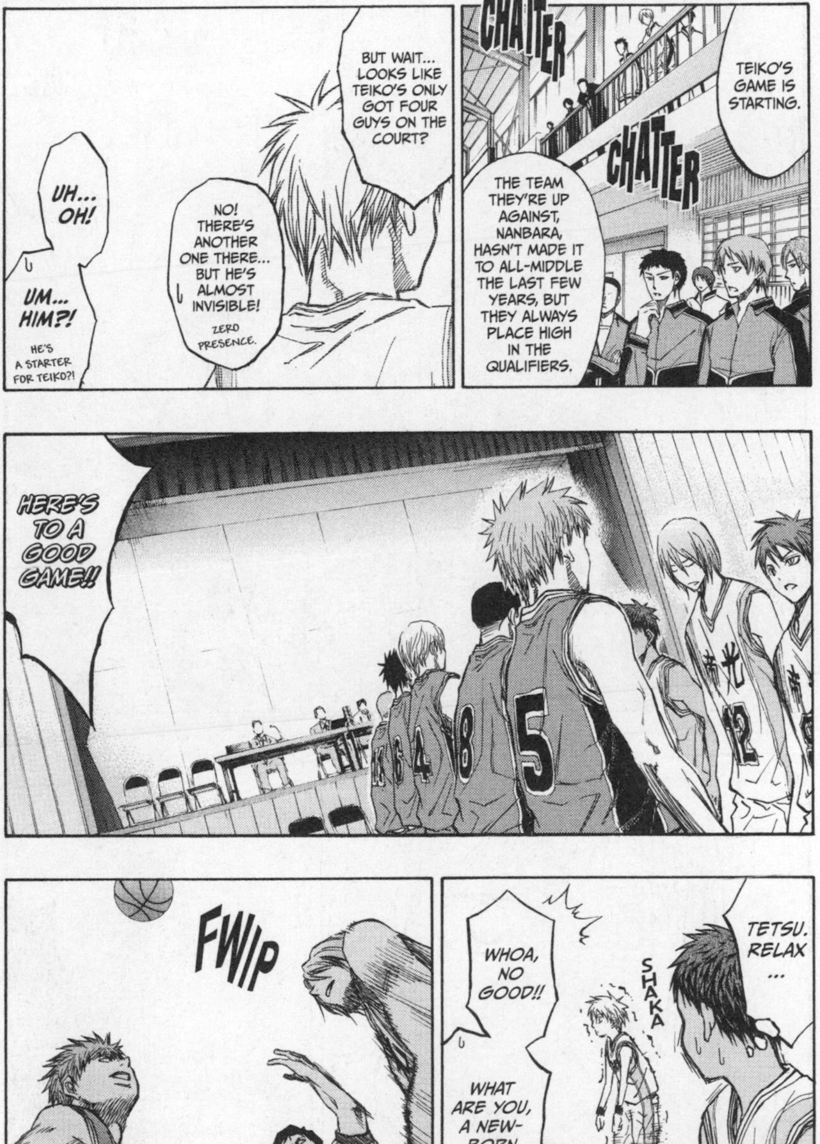
CHATTER
TEIKO'S GAME IS STARTING.
CHATTER
THE TEAM THEY'RE UP AGAINST, NANBARA, HASN'T MADE IT TO ALL-MIDDLE THE LAST FEW YEARS, BUT THEY ALWAYS PLACE HIGH IN THE QUALIFIERS.
BUT WAIT... LOOKS LIKE TEIKO'S ONLY GOT FOUR GUYS ON THE COURT?
NO! THERE'S ANOTHER ONE THERE... BUT HE'S ALMOST INVISIBLE!
ZERO PRESENCE.
UH... OH!
UM... HIM?!
HE'S A STARTER FOR TEIKO?!
HERE'S TO A GOOD GAME!!
TETSU. RELAX...
SHAKA
WHOA, NO GOOD!!
WHAT ARE YOU, A NEW-BORN DEER?!
FWIP

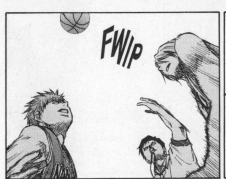

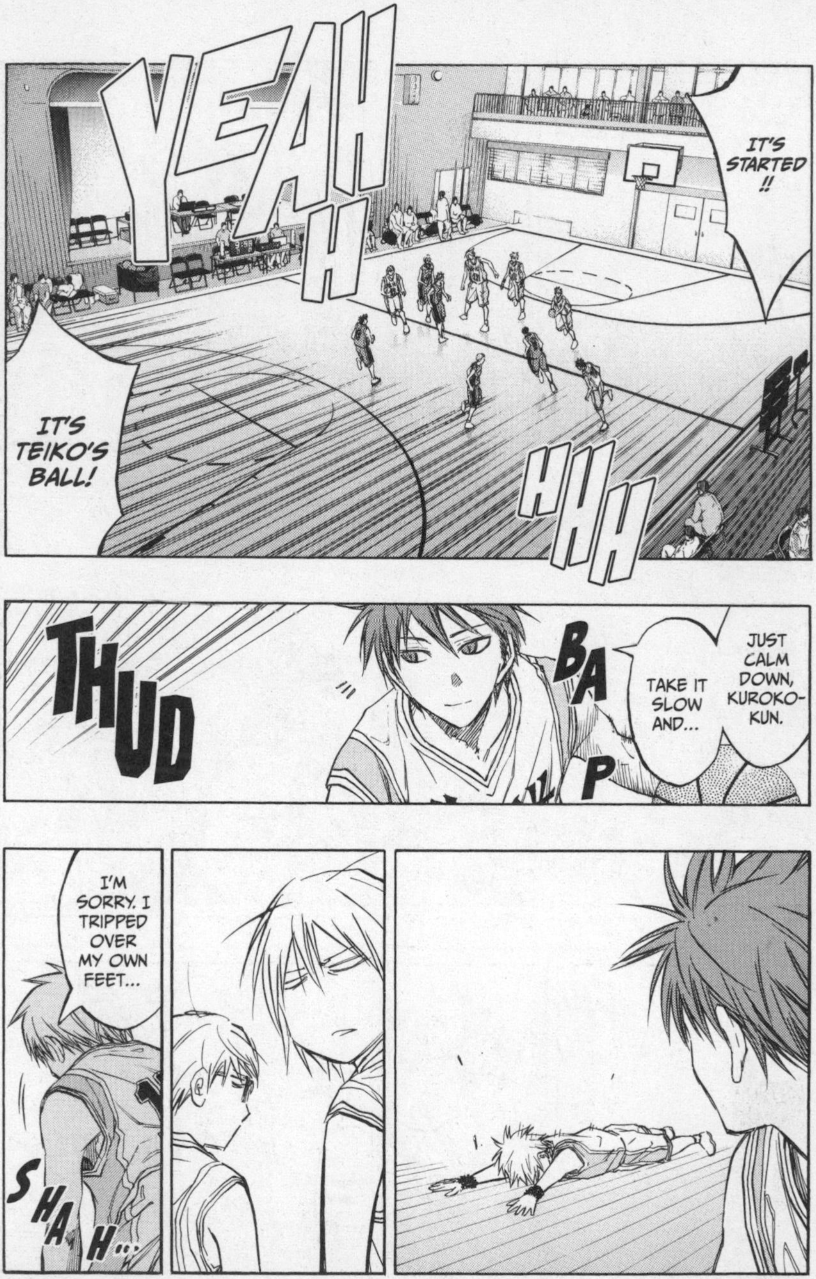
IT'S STARTED!!
YEAHH
HHHH
IT'S TEIKO'S BALL!
JUST CALM DOWN, KUROKO-KUN.
TAKE IT SLOW AND...
BAP
THUD
I'M SORRY. I TRIPPED OVER MY OWN FEET...
SHAH...

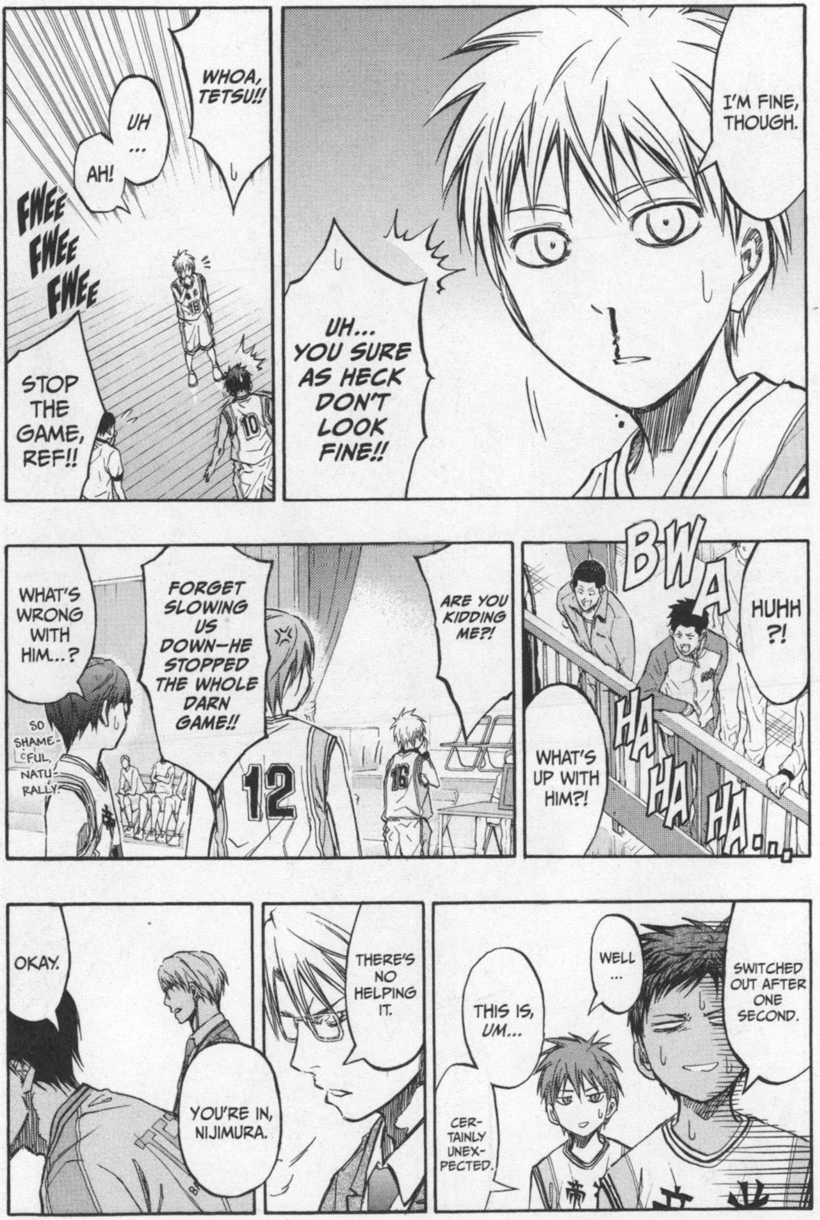
I'M FINE, THOUGH.
UH... YOU SURE AS HECK DON'T LOOK FINE!!
WHOA, TETSU!!
UH ...
AH!
FWEE FWEE FWEE
STOP THE GAME, REF!!
BWA HA HA HA...
HUHH ?!
WHAT'S UP WITH HIM?!
ARE YOU KIDDING ME?!
FORGET SLOWING US DOWN—HE STOPPED THE WHOLE DARN GAME!!
WHAT'S WRONG WITH HIM...?
SO SHAME-FUL, NATU-RALLY.
SWITCHED OUT AFTER ONE SECOND.
WELL ...
THIS IS, UM...
CER-TAINLY UNEX-PECTED.
THERE'S NO HELPING IT.
YOU'RE IN, NIJIMURA.
OKAY.

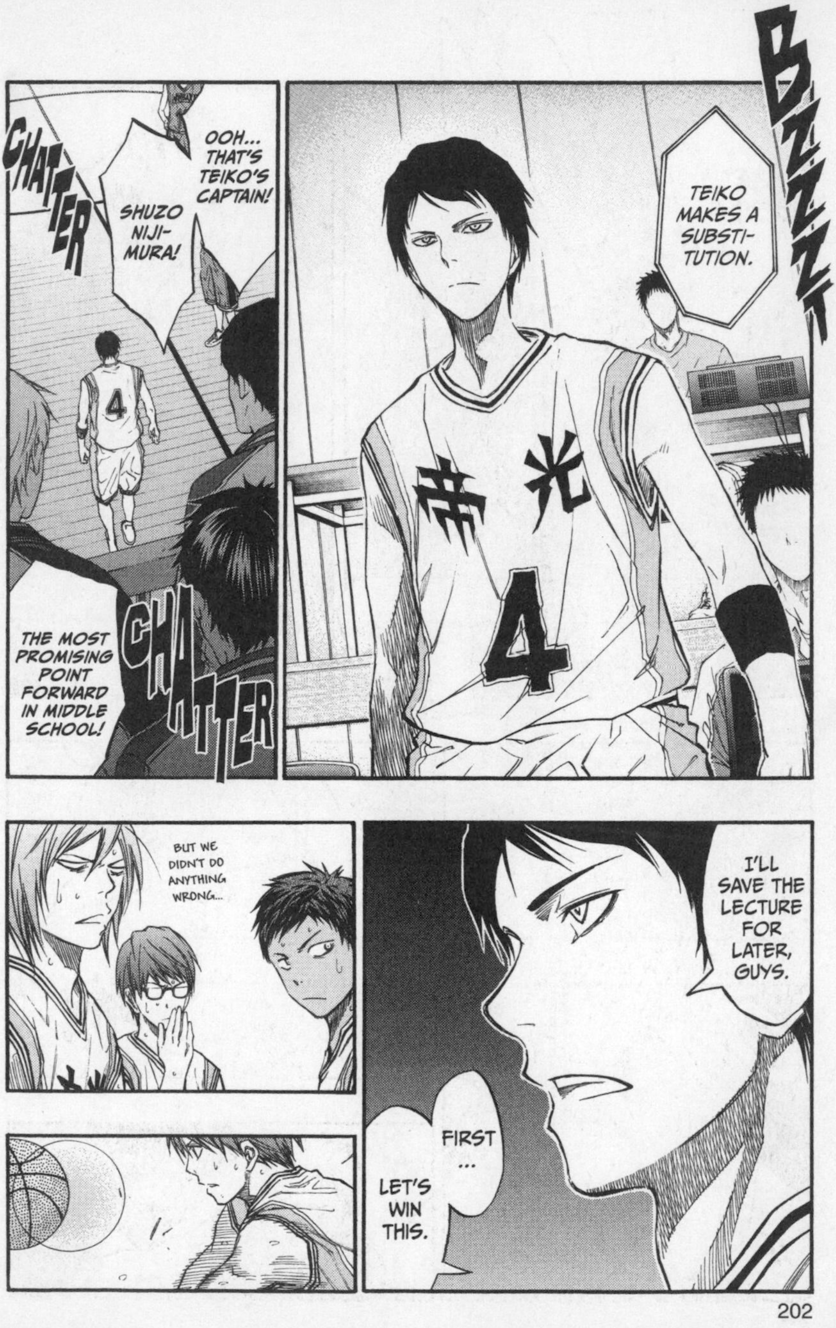
BZZZT
TEIKO MAKES A SUBSTI-TUTION.
OOH... THAT'S TEIKO'S CAPTAIN!
SHUZO NIJI-MURA!
CHATTER
THE MOST PROMISING POINT FORWARD IN MIDDLE SCHOOL!
CHATTER
I'LL SAVE THE LECTURE FOR LATER, GUYS.
FIRST...
LET'S WIN THIS.
BUT WE DIDN'T DO ANYTHING WRONG...

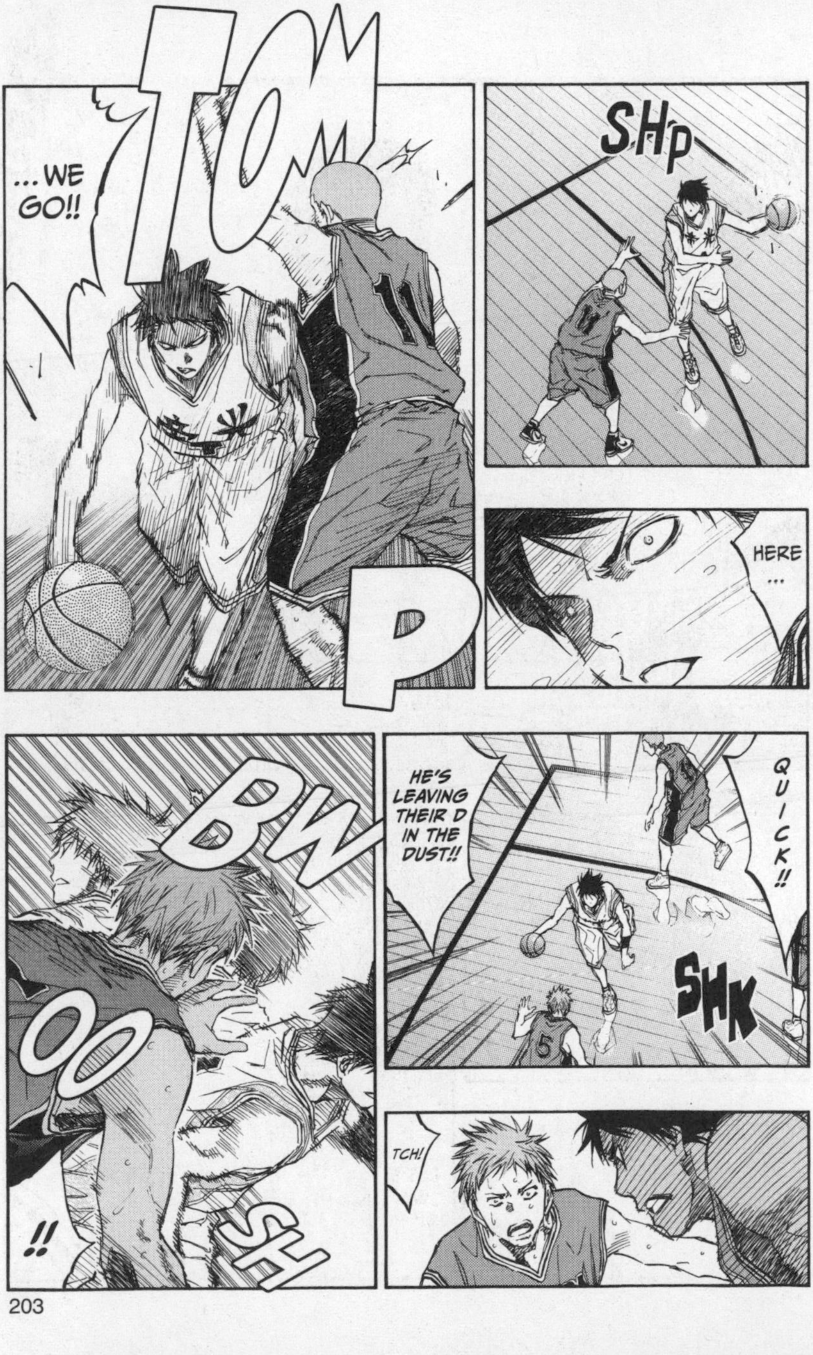

SHp
HERE ...
TOM
...WE GO!!
P
QUICK!!
HE'S LEAVING THEIR D IN THE DUST!!
SHK
TCH!
BW
OO
SH
!!

AH!
SHP
FLIK
SWISH

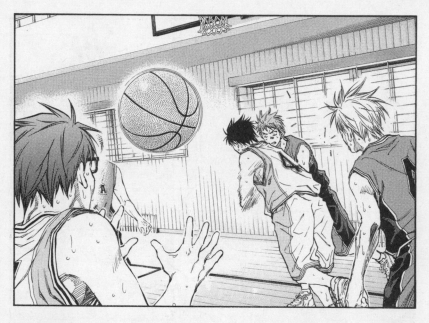

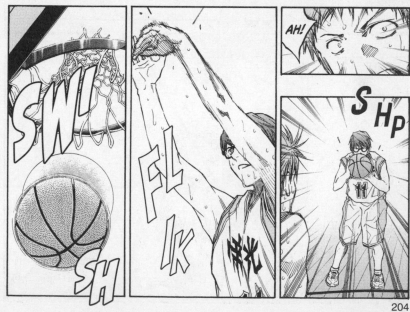

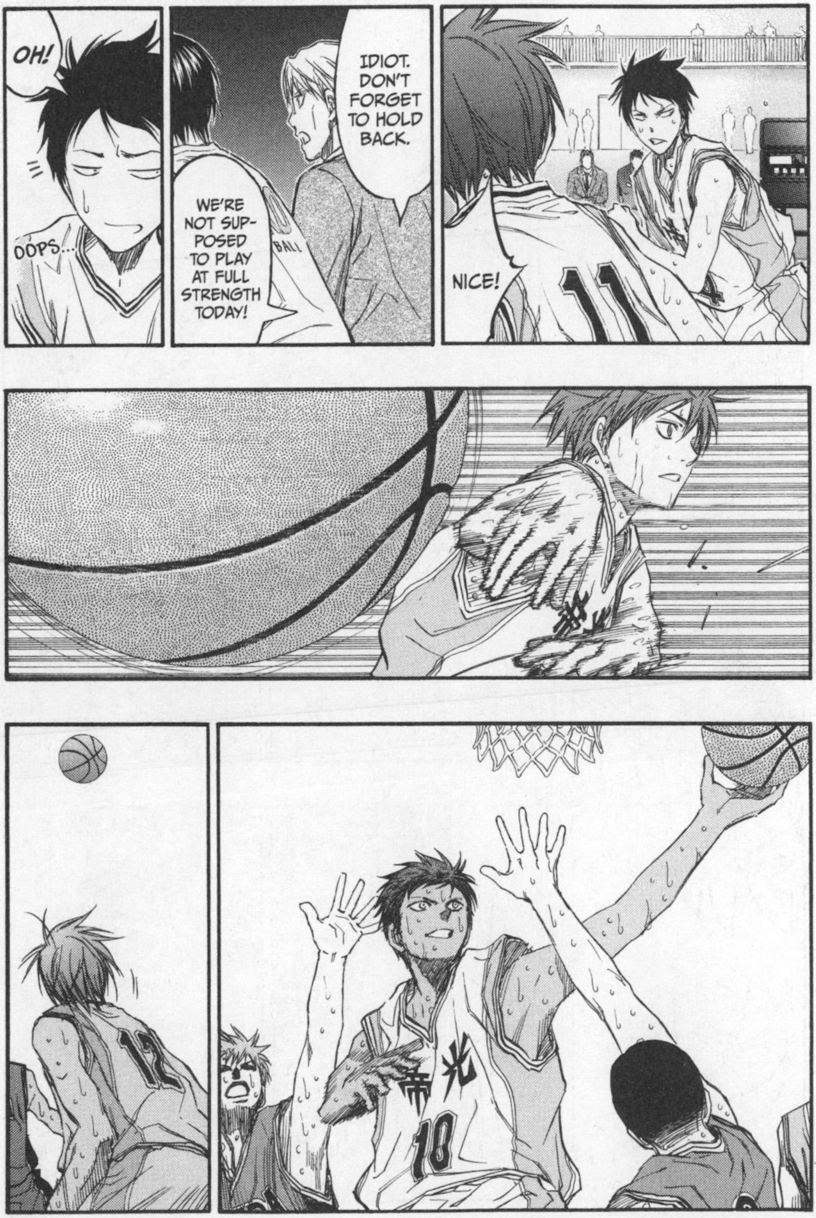
NICE!
IDIOT. DON'T FORGET TO HOLD BACK.
WE'RE NOT SUP-POSED TO PLAY AT FULL STRENGTH TODAY!
OH!
OOPS...

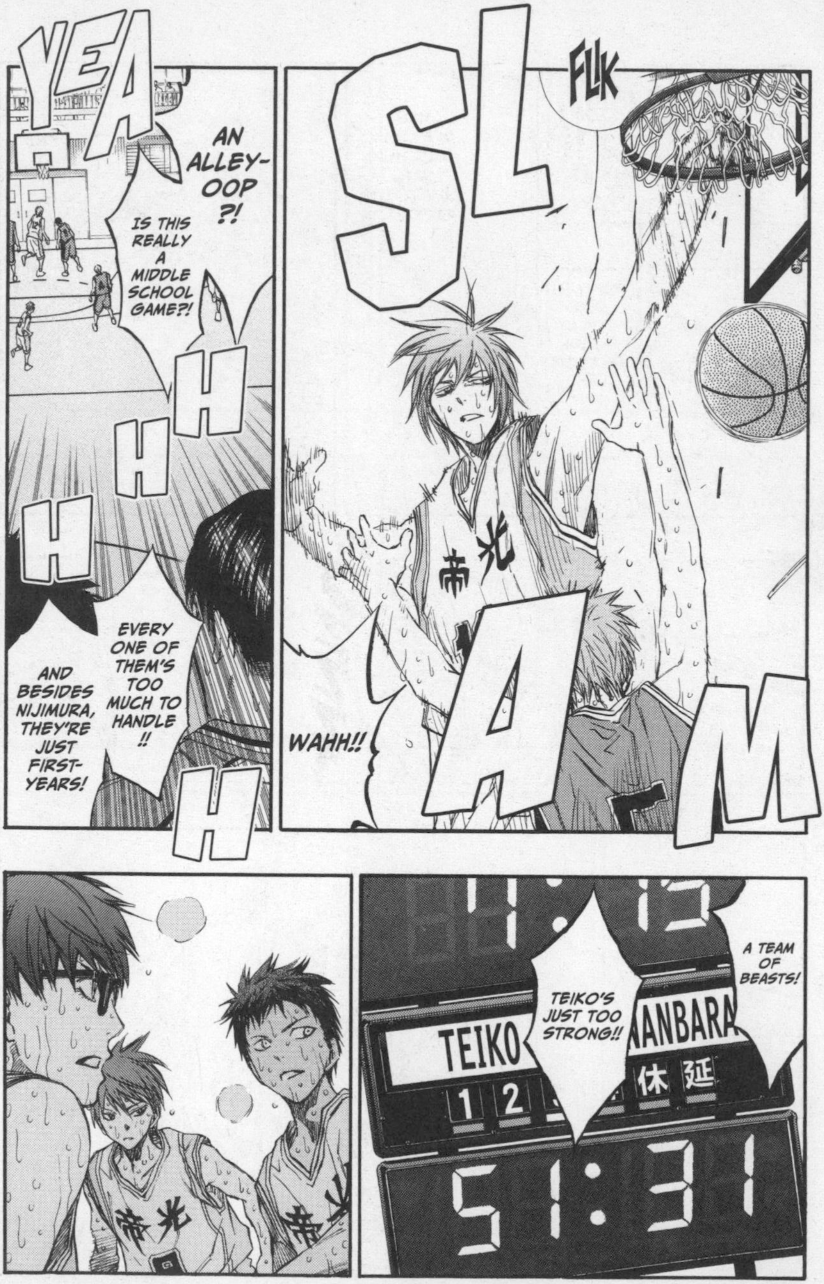
FLIK
SLAM
WAHH!!
YEA
AN ALLEY-OOP?!
IS THIS REALLY A MIDDLE SCHOOL GAME?!
HHHH
EVERY ONE OF THEM'S TOO MUCH TO HANDLE!!
AND BESIDES NIJIMURA, THEY'RE JUST FIRST-YEARS!
A TEAM OF BEASTS!
TEIKO'S JUST TOO STRONG!!
TEIKO
ANBARA
1 2
休 延
51:31

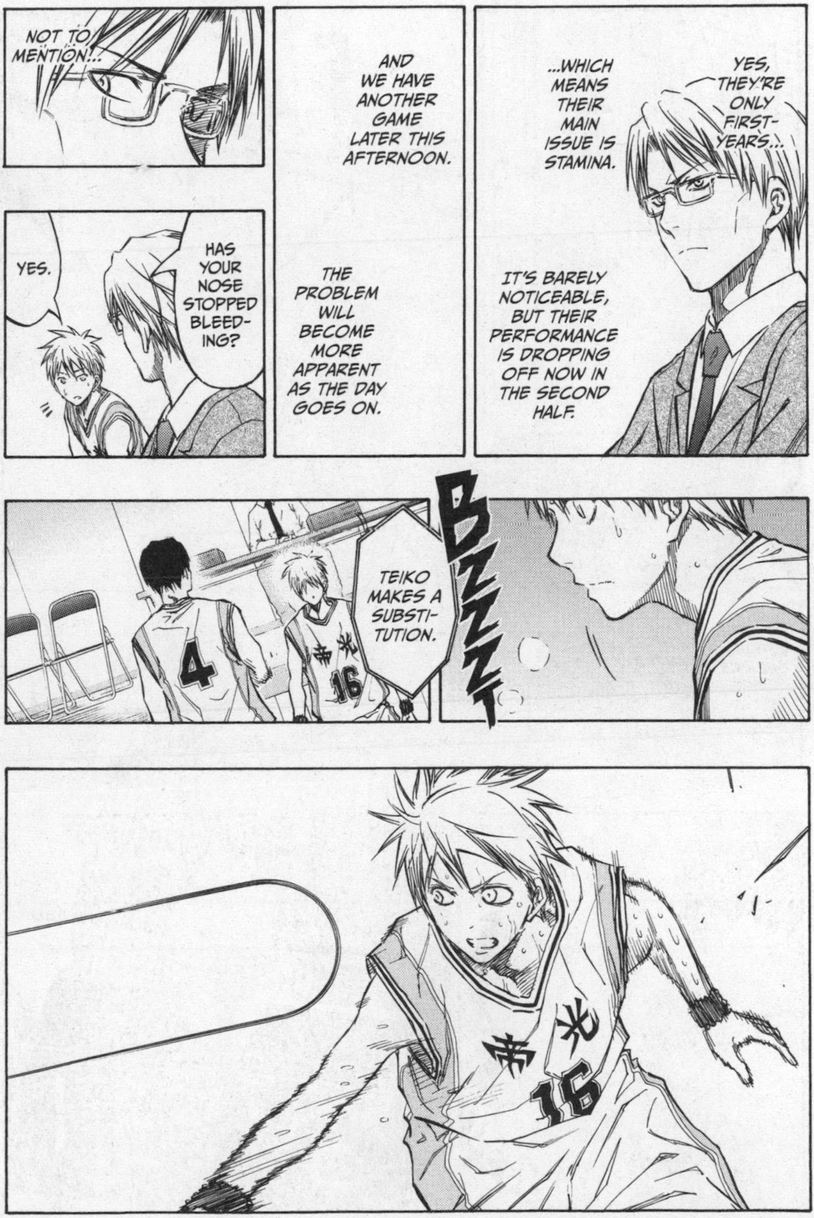
YES, THEY'RE ONLY FIRST-YEARS...
...WHICH MEANS THEIR MAIN ISSUE IS STAMINA.
IT'S BARELY NOTICEABLE, BUT THEIR PERFORMANCE IS DROPPING OFF NOW IN THE SECOND HALF.
AND WE HAVE ANOTHER GAME LATER THIS AFTERNOON.
THE PROBLEM WILL BECOME MORE APPARENT AS THE DAY GOES ON.
NOT TO MENTION...
HAS YOUR NOSE STOPPED BLEEDING?
YES.
BZZZT
TEIKO MAKES A SUBSTITUTION.

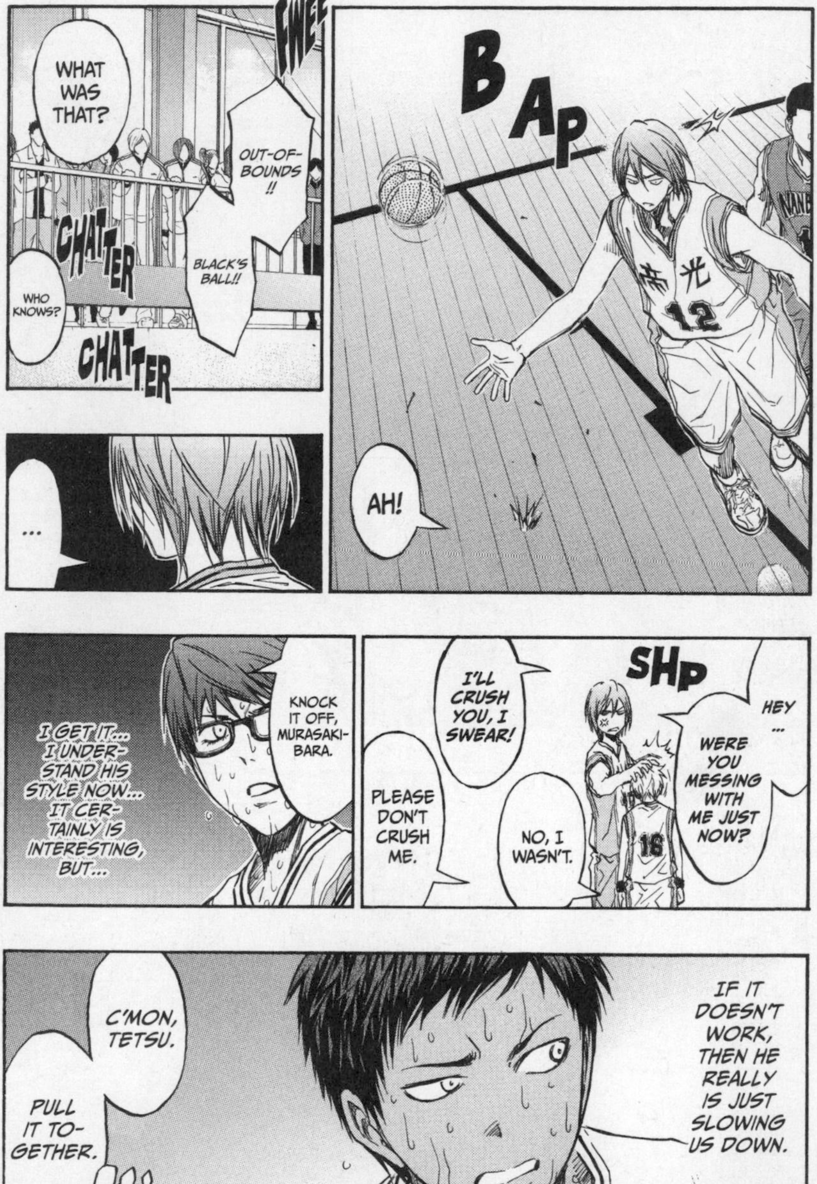
BAP
AH!
FWEE
OUT-OF-BOUNDS!!
BLACK'S BALL!!
WHAT WAS THAT?
CHATTER
WHO KNOWS?
CHATTER
...
SHP
HEY... WERE YOU MESSING WITH ME JUST NOW?
NO, I WASN'T.
I'LL CRUSH YOU, I SWEAR!
PLEASE DON'T CRUSH ME.
KNOCK IT OFF, MURASAKIBARA.
I GET IT... I UNDERSTAND HIS STYLE NOW... IT CERTAINLY IS INTERESTING, BUT...
IF IT DOESN'T WORK, THEN HE REALLY IS JUST SLOWING US DOWN.
C'MON, TETSU.
PULL IT TOGETHER.

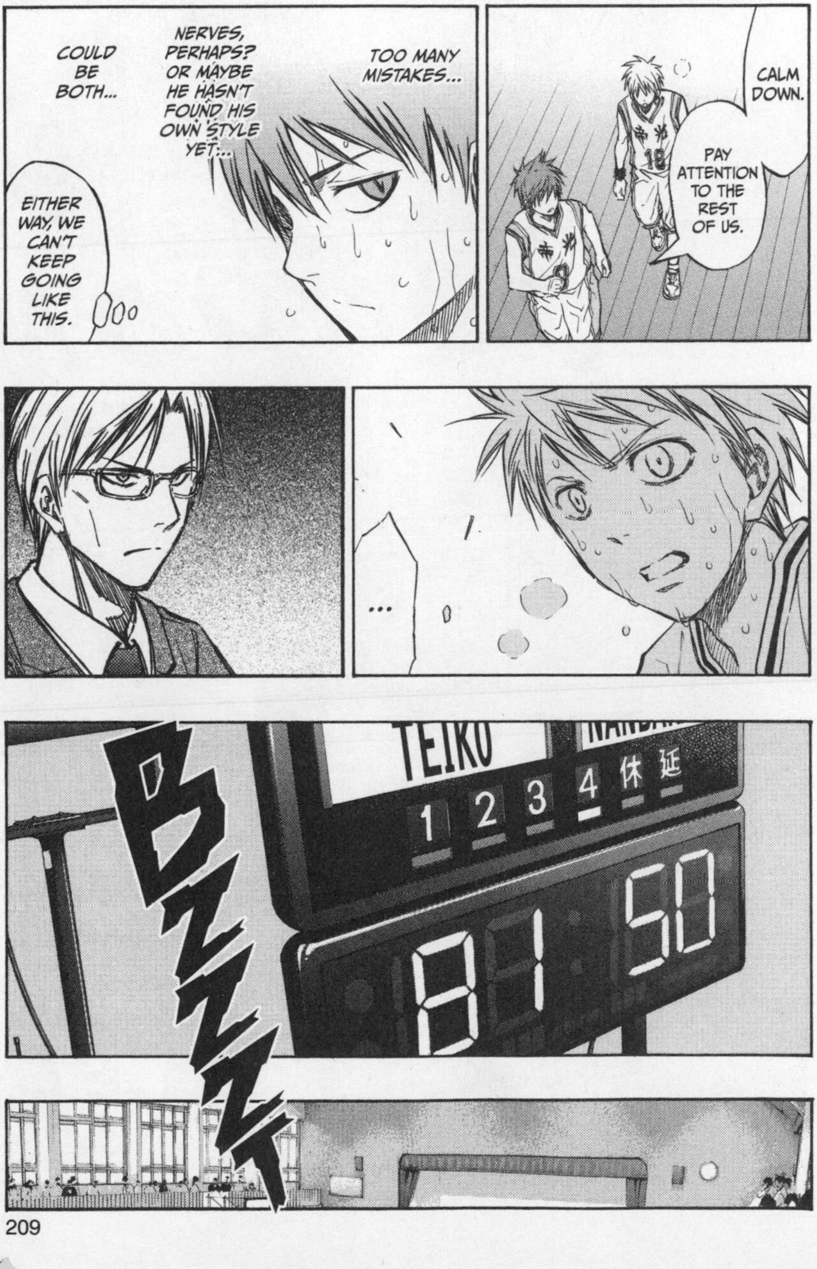
CALM DOWN.
PAY ATTENTION TO THE REST OF US.
TOO MANY MISTAKES...
NERVES, PERHAPS? OR MAYBE HE HASN'T FOUND HIS OWN STYLE YET...
COULD BE BOTH...
EITHER WAY, WE CAN'T KEEP GOING LIKE THIS.
...
TEIKO
1 2 3 4 休 延
81
50
BZZZZT

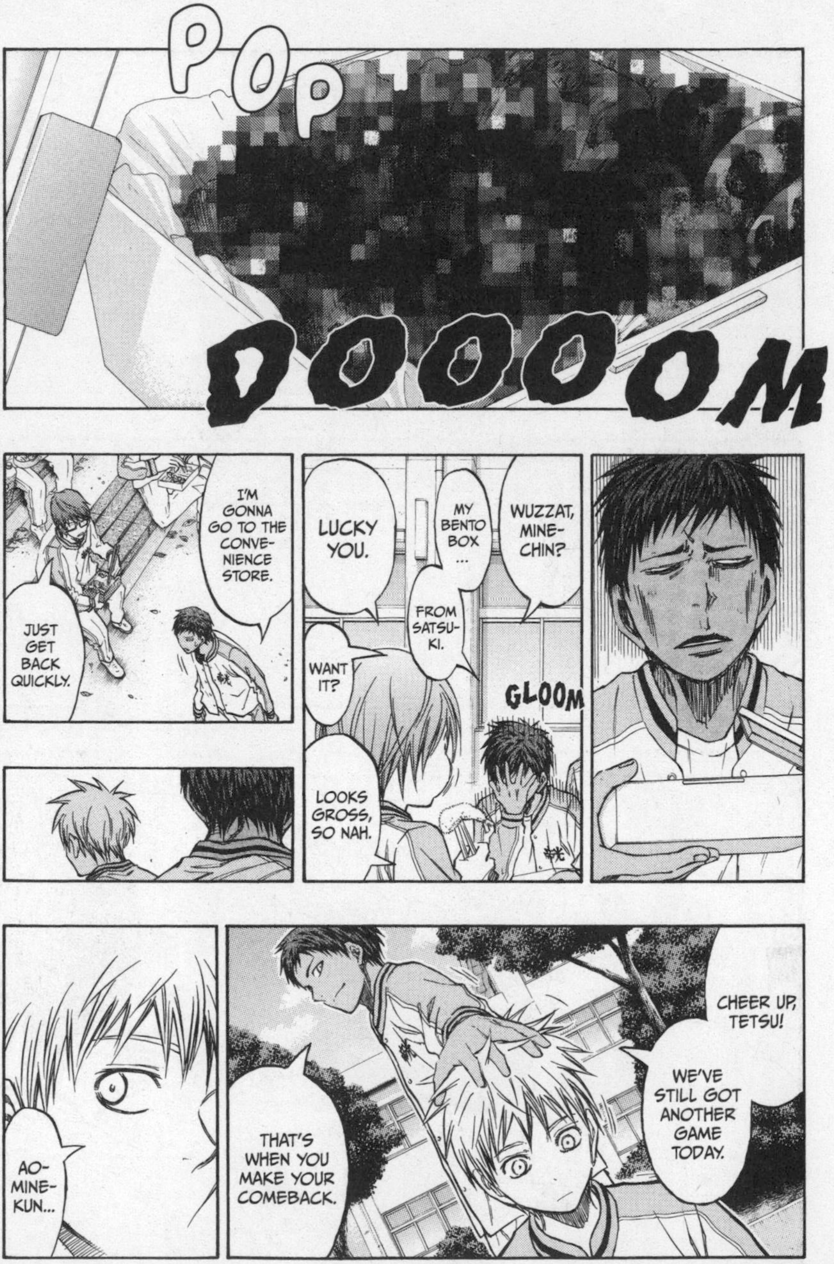
POP
DOOOOM
WUZZAT, MINE-CHIN?
MY BENTO BOX ...
FROM SATSU-KI.
LUCKY YOU.
WANT IT?
GLOOM
LOOKS GROSS, SO NAH.
I'M GONNA GO TO THE CONVE-NIENCE STORE.
JUST GET BACK QUICKLY.
CHEER UP, TETSU!
WE'VE STILL GOT ANOTHER GAME TODAY.
THAT'S WHEN YOU MAKE YOUR COMEBACK.
AO-MINE-KUN...

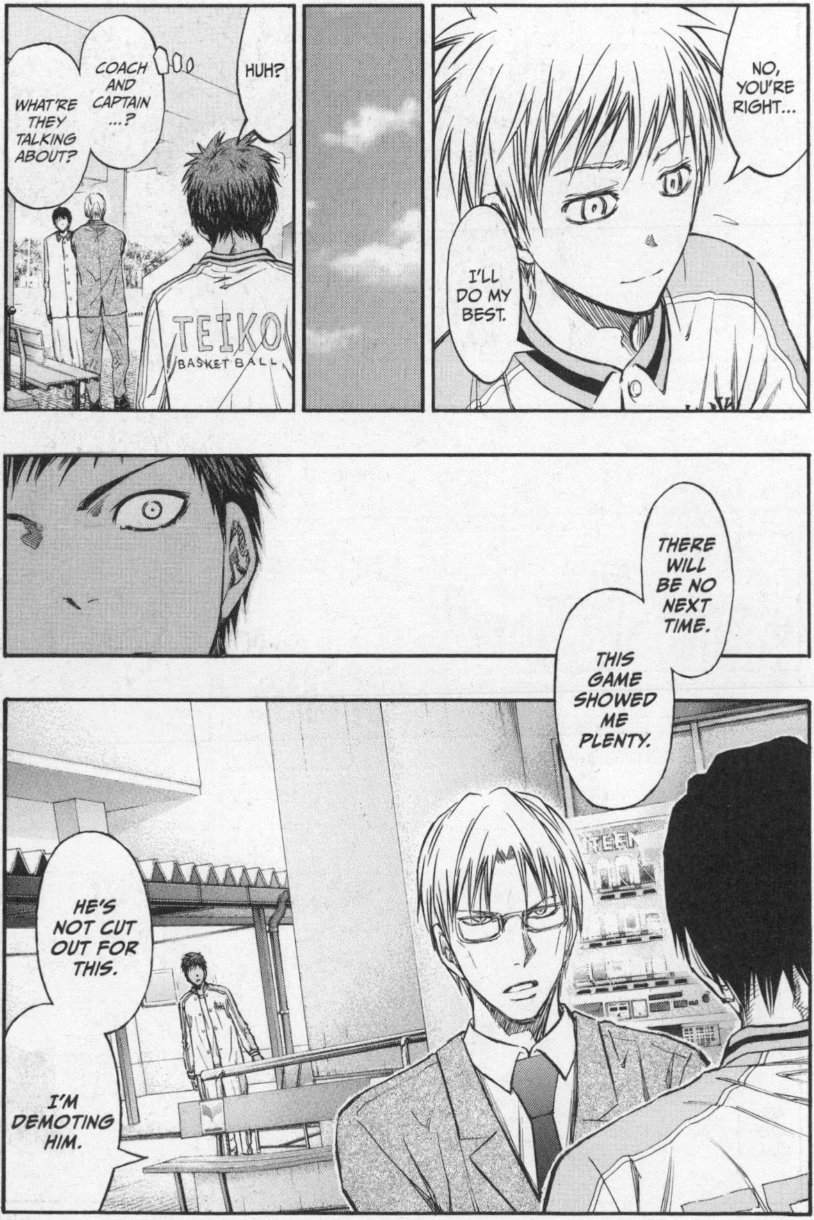
NO, YOU'RE RIGHT...
I'LL DO MY BEST.
HUH?
COACH AND CAPTAIN ...?
WHAT'RE THEY TALKING ABOUT?
TEIKO BASKETBALL
THERE WILL BE NO NEXT TIME.
THIS GAME SHOWED ME PLENTY.
HE'S NOT CUT OUT FOR THIS.
I'M DEMOTING HIM.

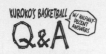

KUROKO'S BASKETBALL Q&A (W/ HALFWAY-DECENT ANSWERS)

Q. **WE'VE GOT EAGLE EYE, HAWK EYE, EMPEROR EYE... SO WHAT'S THE NAME OF RIKO'S EYE-BASED TECHNIQUE?**
(ORANGEPEKO from AOMORI PREFECTURE)

A. ANALYZER EYE.

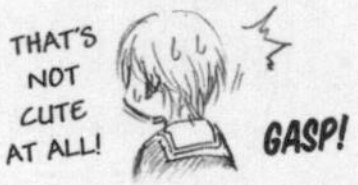

GASP!
THAT'S NOT CUTE AT ALL!

KUROKO'S BASKETBALL BLOOPERS
TAKE 1

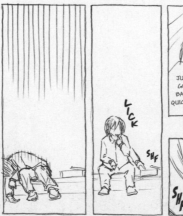

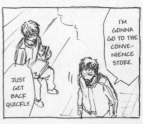

I'M GONNA GO TO THE CONVENIENCE STORE.
JUST GET BACK QUICKLY.
SATSUKI'S BENTO
CURIOUS
SHF
SHF
LICK

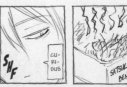

209TH QUARTER:
YOU CAN DO IT!

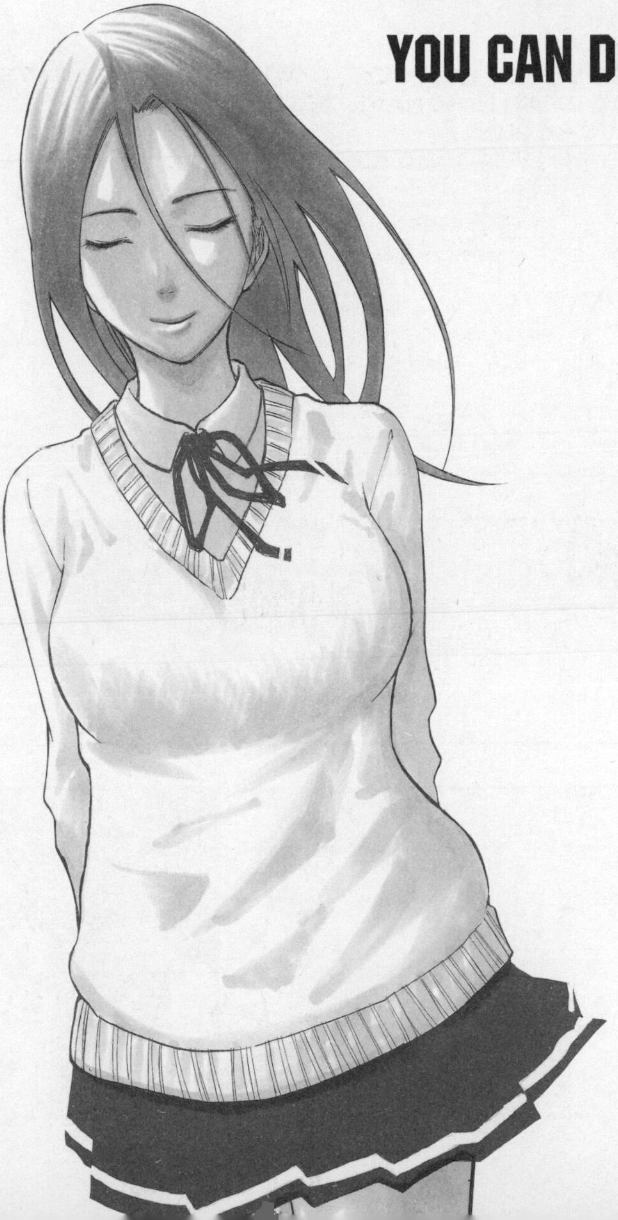

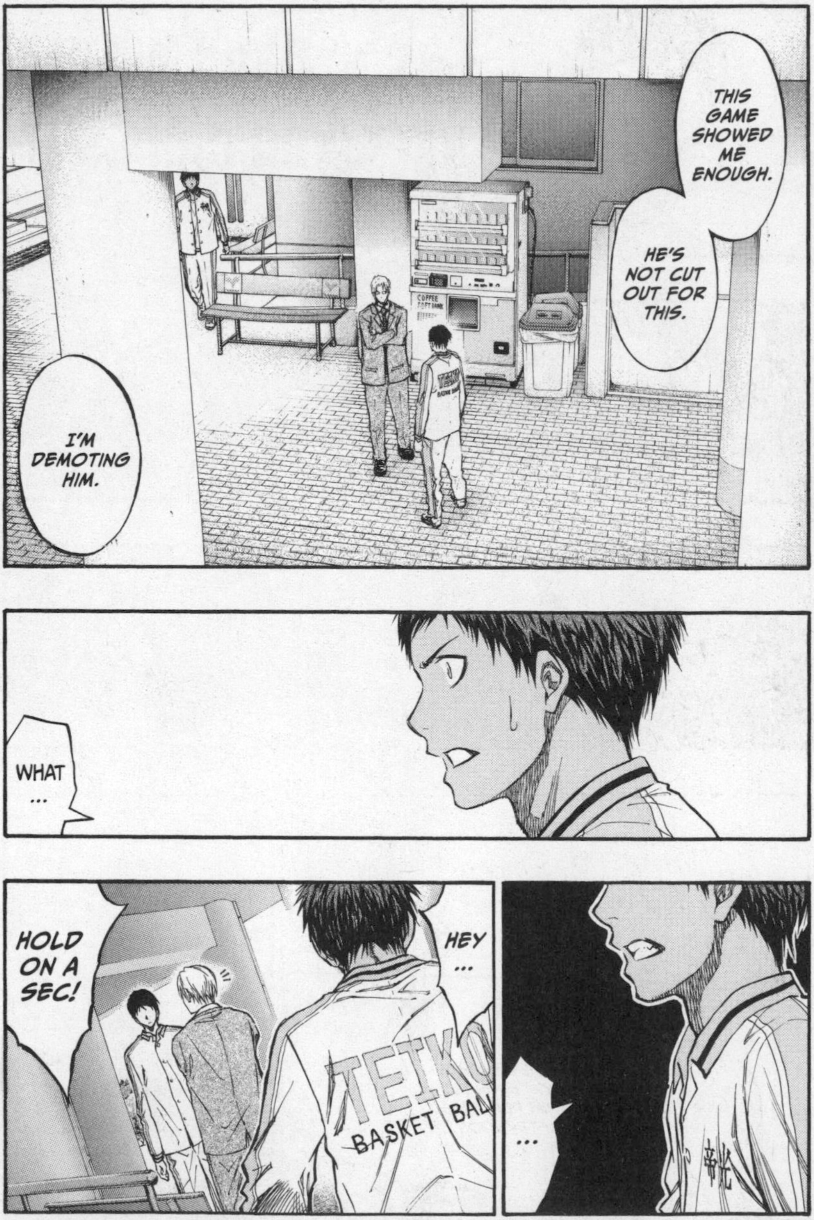
THIS GAME SHOWED ME ENOUGH.
HE'S NOT CUT OUT FOR THIS.
I'M DEMOTING HIM.
WHAT ...
...
HEY ...
HOLD ON A SEC!

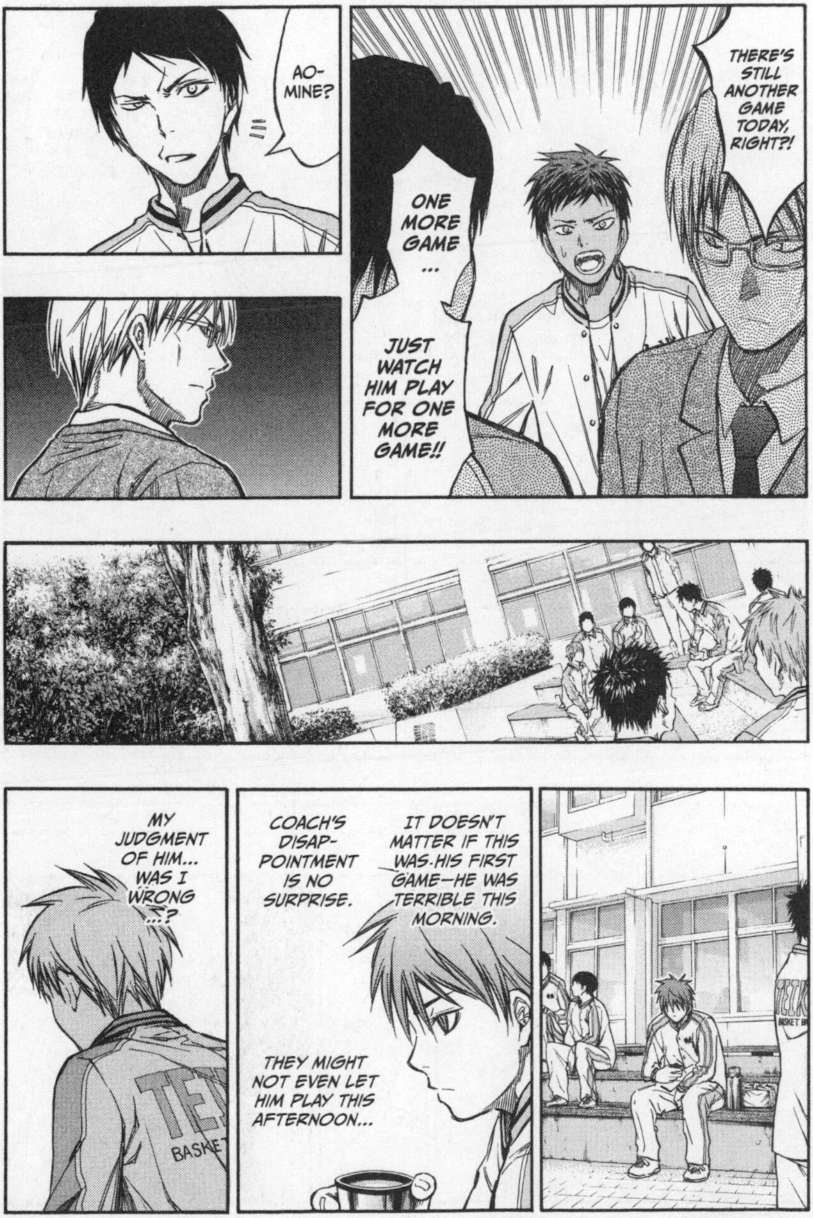
THERE'S STILL ANOTHER GAME TODAY, RIGHT?!
ONE MORE GAME ...
JUST WATCH HIM PLAY FOR ONE MORE GAME!!
AO-MINE?
IT DOESN'T MATTER IF THIS WAS HIS FIRST GAME—HE WAS TERRIBLE THIS MORNING.
COACH'S DISAP-POINTMENT IS NO SURPRISE.
THEY MIGHT NOT EVEN LET HIM PLAY THIS AFTERNOON...
MY JUDGMENT OF HIM... WAS I WRONG ...?

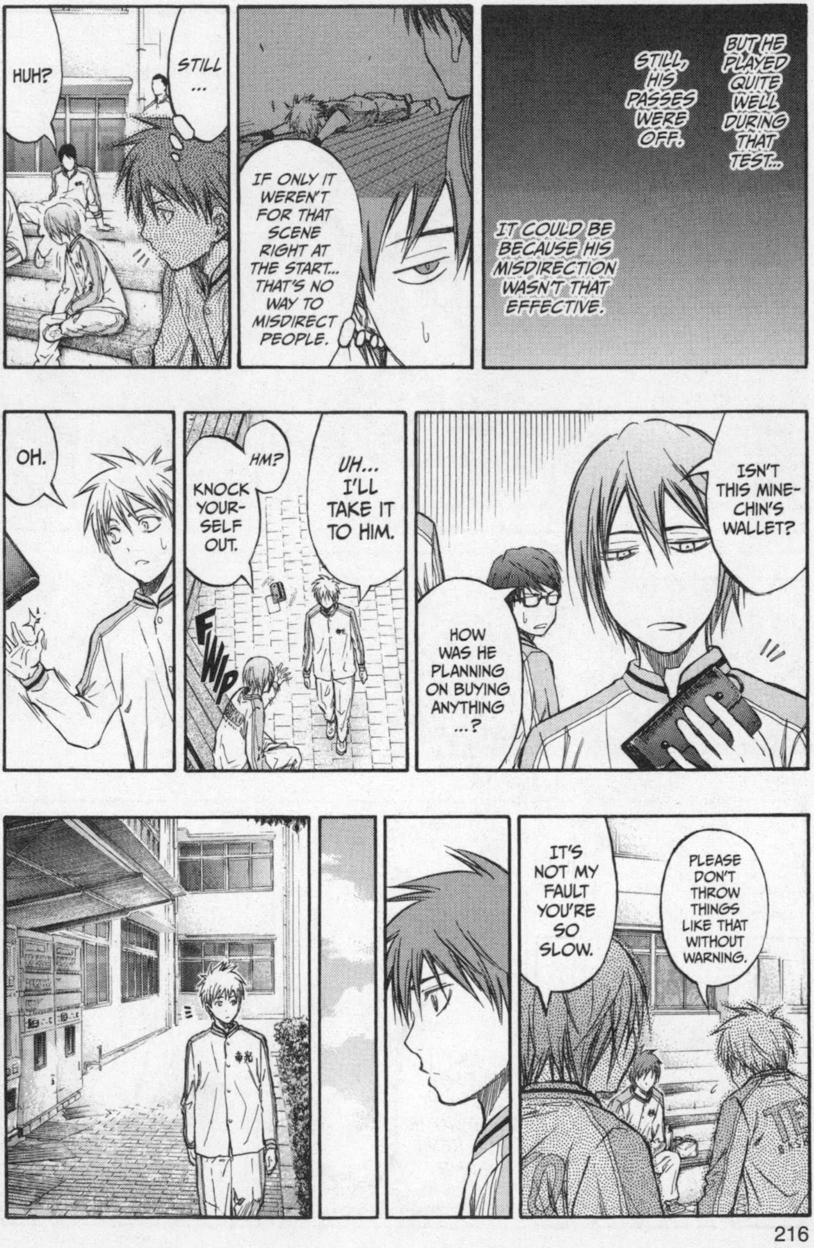
BUT HE PLAYED QUITE WELL DURING THAT TEST...
STILL, HIS PASSES WERE OFF.
IT COULD BE BECAUSE HIS MISDIRECTION WASN'T THAT EFFECTIVE.
IF ONLY IT WEREN'T FOR THAT SCENE RIGHT AT THE START... THAT'S NO WAY TO MISDIRECT PEOPLE.
STILL ...
HUH?
ISN'T THIS MINE-CHIN'S WALLET?
HOW WAS HE PLANNING ON BUYING ANYTHING ...?
UH... I'LL TAKE IT TO HIM.
HM?
KNOCK YOURSELF OUT.
FWIP
OH.
PLEASE DON'T THROW THINGS LIKE THAT WITHOUT WARNING.
IT'S NOT MY FAULT YOU'RE SO SLOW.

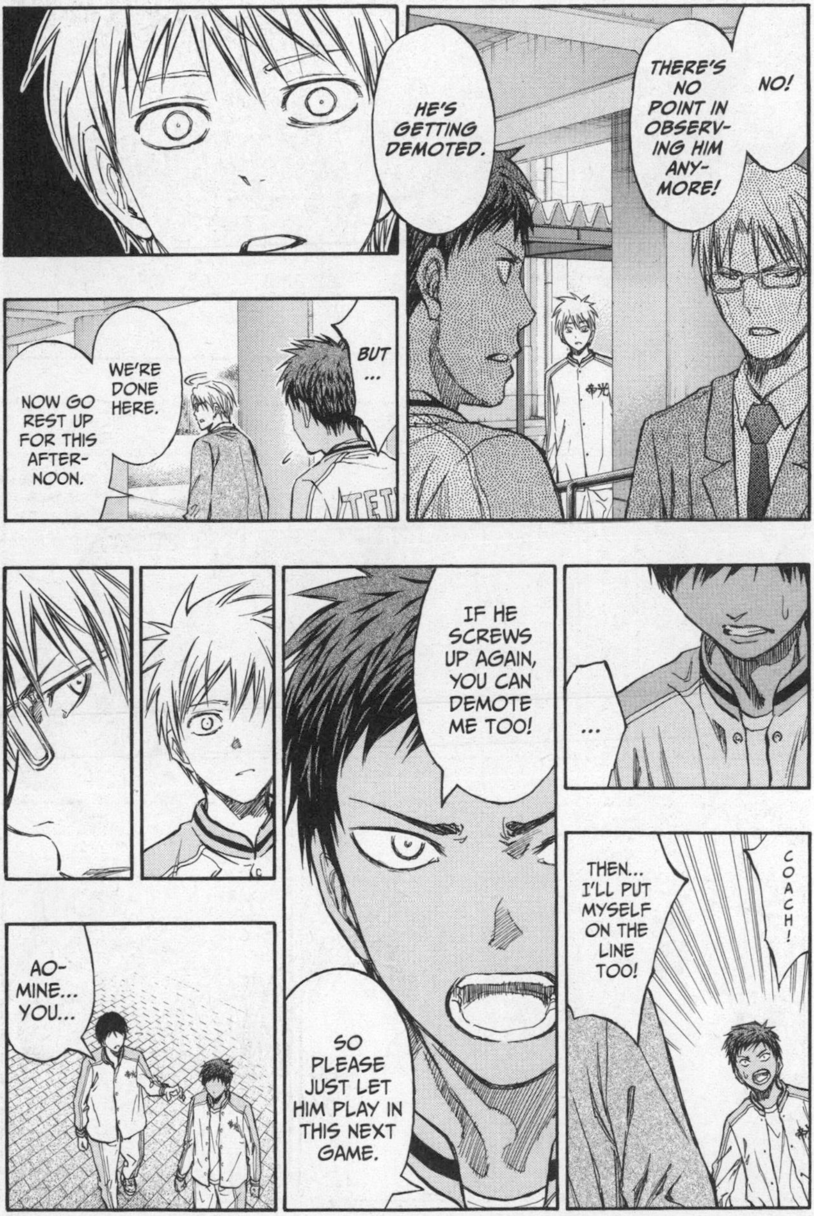
NO!
THERE'S NO POINT IN OBSERVING HIM ANYMORE!
HE'S GETTING DEMOTED.
BUT ...
WE'RE DONE HERE.
NOW GO REST UP FOR THIS AFTERNOON.
...
COACH!
THEN... I'LL PUT MYSELF ON THE LINE TOO!
IF HE SCREWS UP AGAIN, YOU CAN DEMOTE ME TOO!
SO PLEASE JUST LET HIM PLAY IN THIS NEXT GAME.
AO-MINE... YOU...

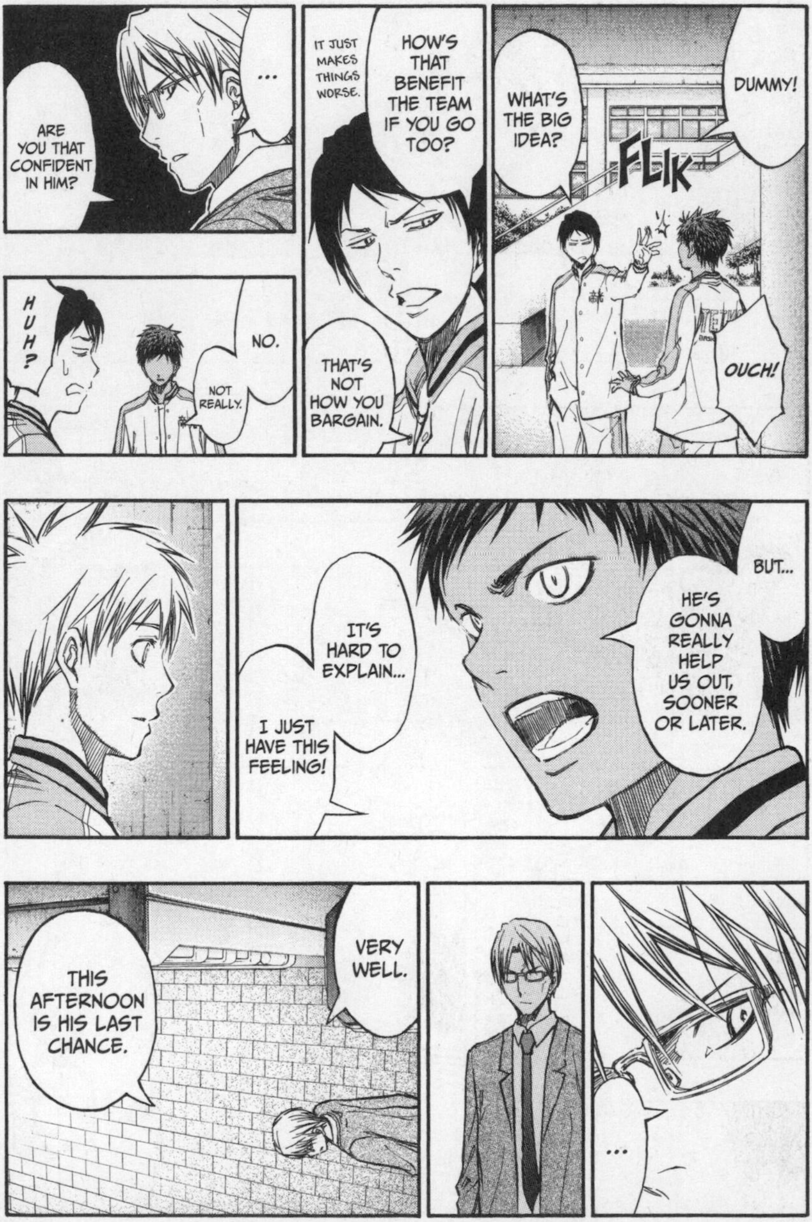
DUMMY!
WHAT'S THE BIG IDEA?
FLIK
OUCH!
HOW'S THAT BENEFIT THE TEAM IF YOU GO TOO?
IT JUST MAKES THINGS WORSE.
THAT'S NOT HOW YOU BARGAIN.
...
ARE YOU THAT CONFIDENT IN HIM?
NO.
NOT REALLY.
HUH?
BUT...
HE'S GONNA REALLY HELP US OUT, SOONER OR LATER.
IT'S HARD TO EXPLAIN...
I JUST HAVE THIS FEELING!
...
VERY WELL.
THIS AFTERNOON IS HIS LAST CHANCE.

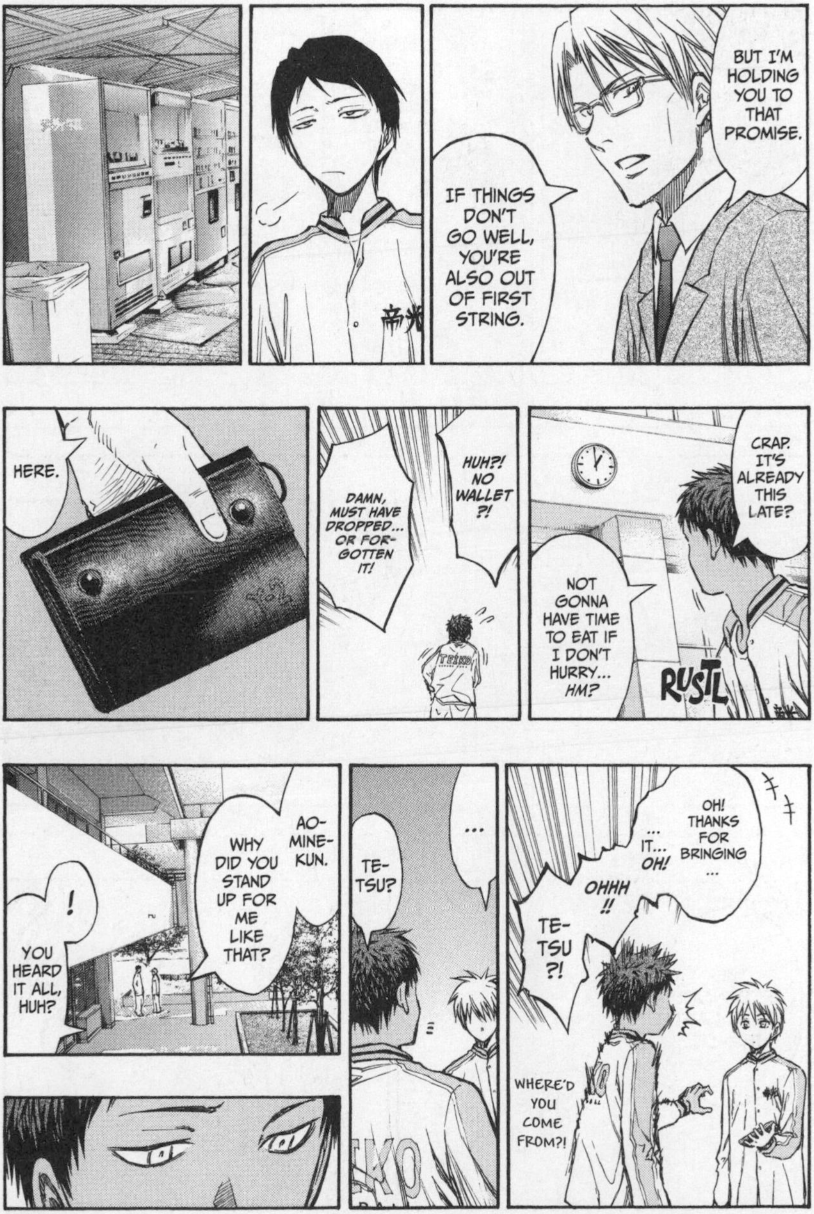
BUT I'M HOLDING YOU TO THAT PROMISE.
IF THINGS DON'T GO WELL, YOU'RE ALSO OUT OF FIRST STRING.
CRAP. IT'S ALREADY THIS LATE?
NOT GONNA HAVE TIME TO EAT IF I DON'T HURRY... HM?
RUSTL
HUH?! NO WALLET ?!
DAMN, MUST HAVE DROPPED... OR FORGOTTEN IT!
HERE.
OH! THANKS FOR BRINGING ...
... IT... OH!
OHHH !!
TE-TSU ?!
WHERE'D YOU COME FROM?!
...
TE-TSU?
AO-MINE-KUN.
WHY DID YOU STAND UP FOR ME LIKE THAT?
!
YOU HEARD IT ALL, HUH?

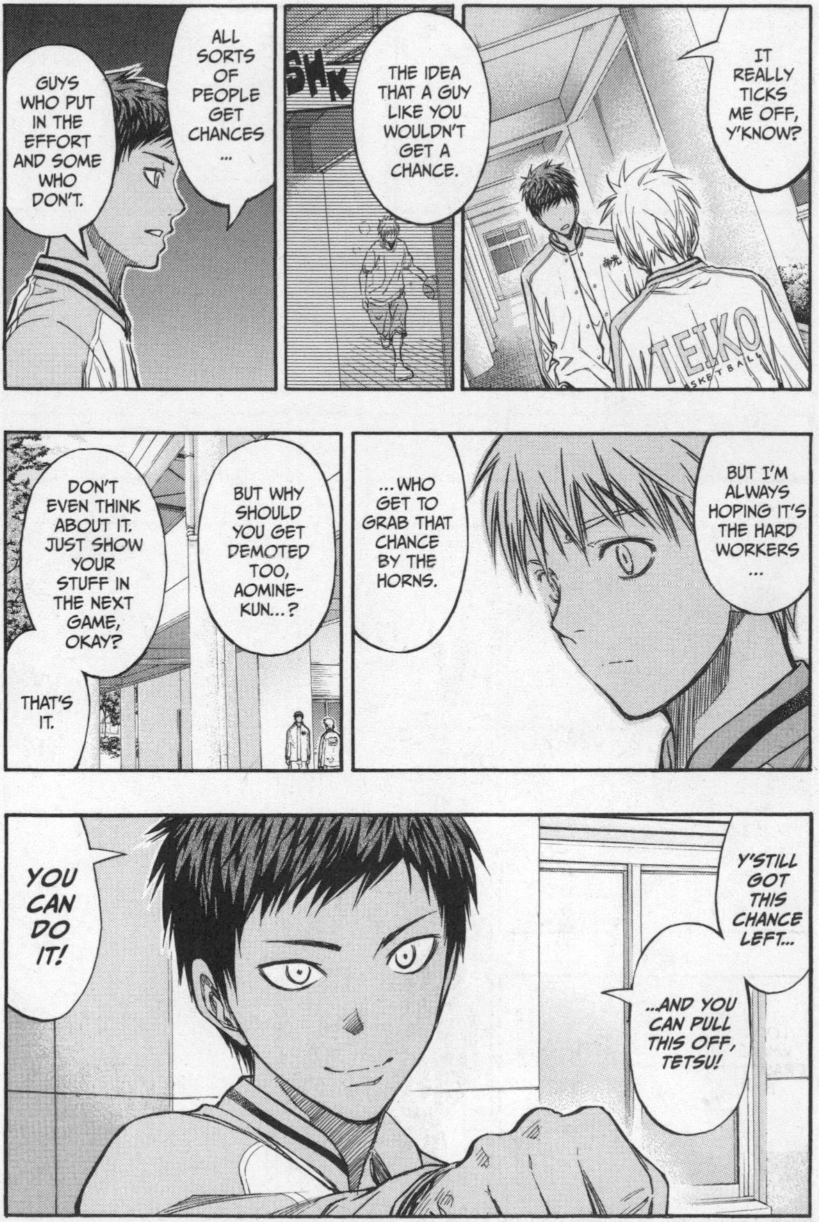
IT REALLY TICKS ME OFF, Y'KNOW?
SHK
THE IDEA THAT A GUY LIKE YOU WOULDN'T GET A CHANCE.
ALL SORTS OF PEOPLE GET CHANCES...
GUYS WHO PUT IN THE EFFORT AND SOME WHO DON'T.
BUT I'M ALWAYS HOPING IT'S THE HARD WORKERS...
...WHO GET TO GRAB THAT CHANCE BY THE HORNS.
BUT WHY SHOULD YOU GET DEMOTED TOO, AOMINE-KUN...?
DON'T EVEN THINK ABOUT IT. JUST SHOW YOUR STUFF IN THE NEXT GAME, OKAY?
THAT'S IT.
Y'STILL GOT THIS CHANCE LEFT...
...AND YOU CAN PULL THIS OFF, TETSU!
YOU CAN DO IT!

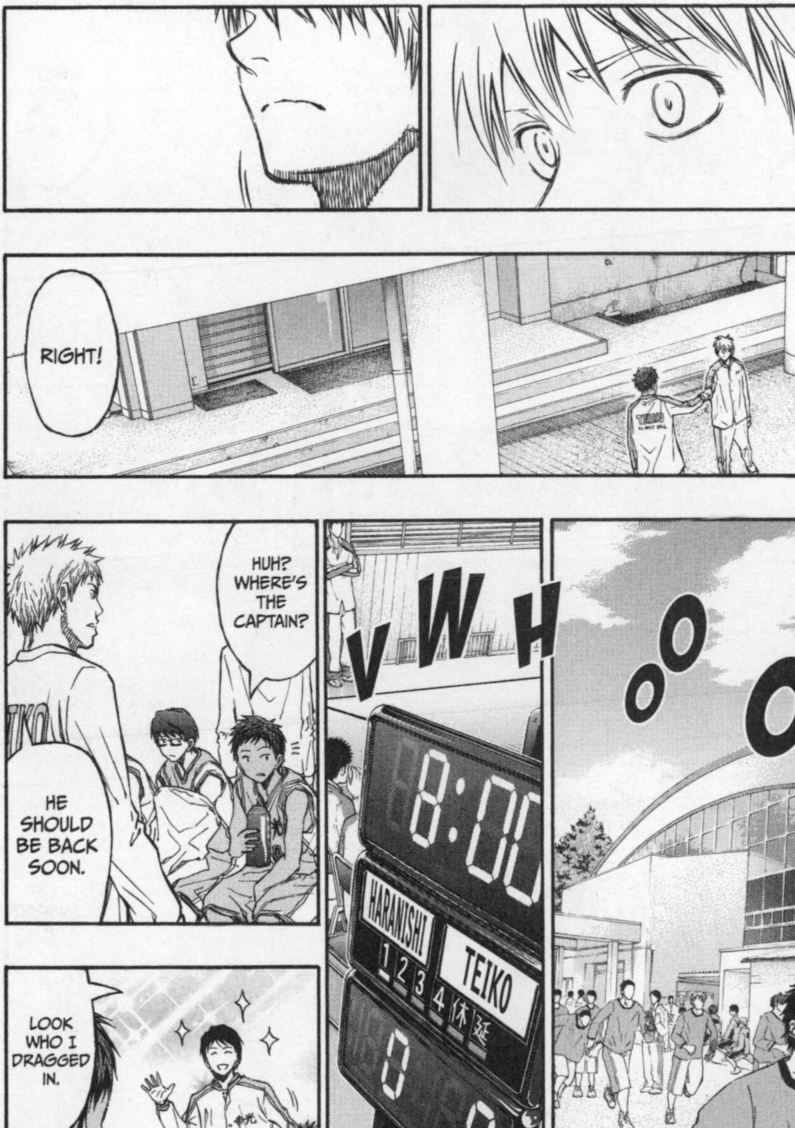
RIGHT!
VWHOOO
8:00
HARANISHI
TEIKO
1 2 3 4 休 延
0
0
HUH? WHERE'S THE CAPTAIN?
HE SHOULD BE BACK SOON.
LOOK WHO I DRAGGED IN.

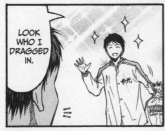

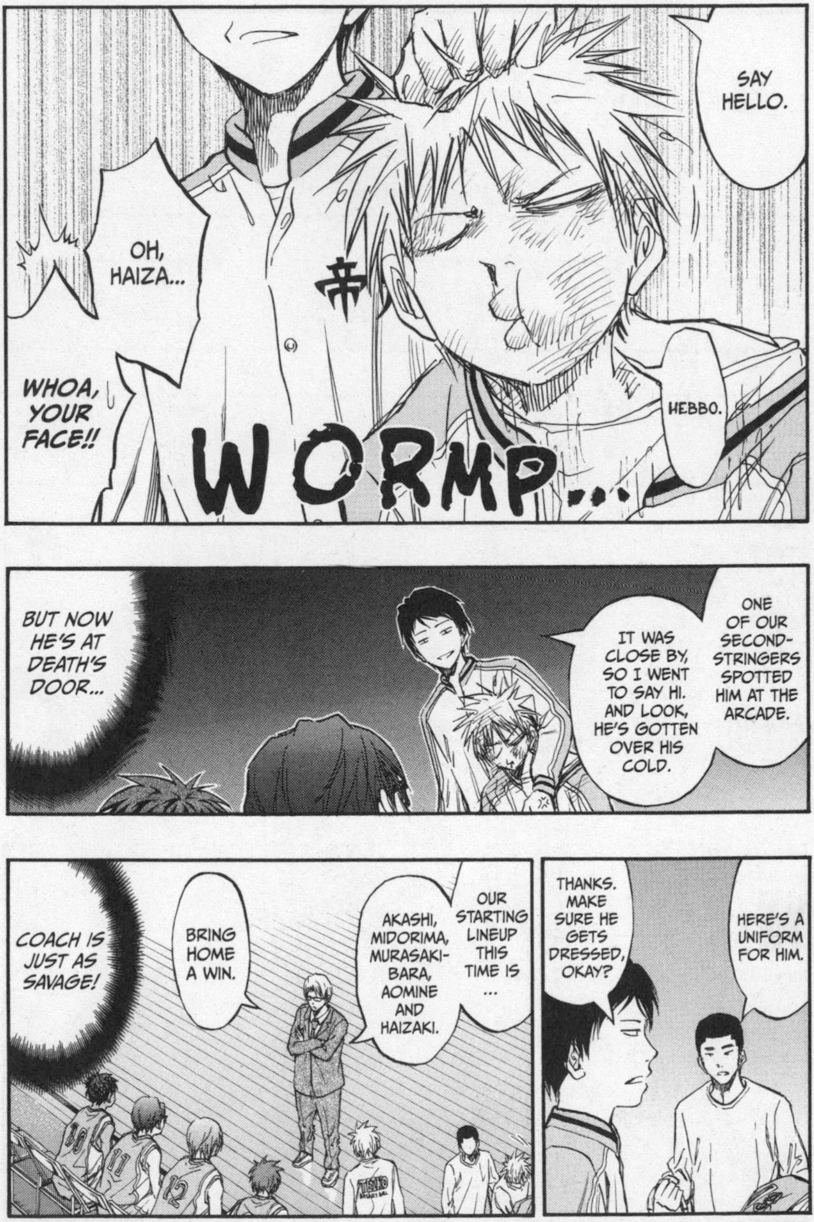
SAY HELLO.
HEBBO.
WORMP...
OH, HAIZA...
WHOA, YOUR FACE!!
ONE OF OUR SECOND-STRINGERS SPOTTED HIM AT THE ARCADE.
IT WAS CLOSE BY, SO I WENT TO SAY HI. AND LOOK, HE'S GOTTEN OVER HIS COLD.
BUT NOW HE'S AT DEATH'S DOOR...
HERE'S A UNIFORM FOR HIM.
THANKS. MAKE SURE HE GETS DRESSED, OKAY?
OUR STARTING LINEUP THIS TIME IS ...
AKASHI, MIDORIMA, MURASAKI-BARA, AOMINE AND HAIZAKI.
BRING HOME A WIN.
COACH IS JUST AS SAVAGE!

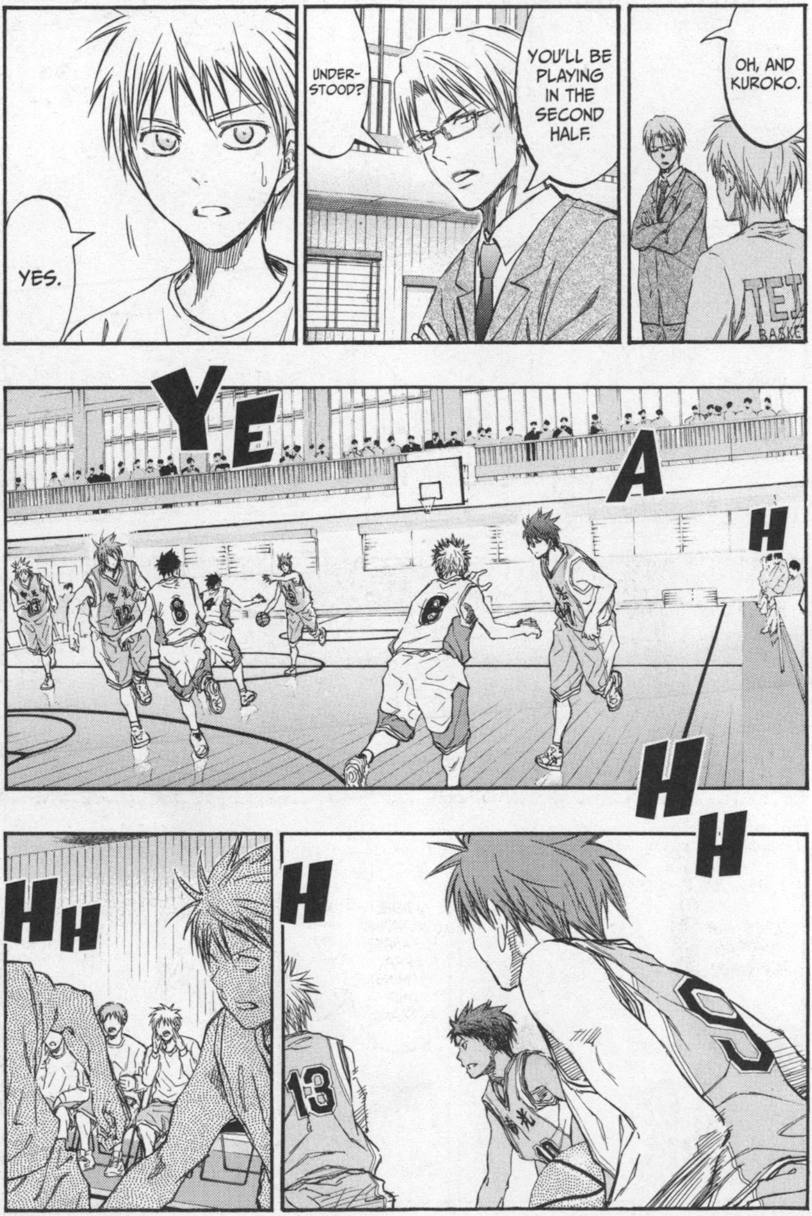
OH, AND KUROKO.
YOU'LL BE PLAYING IN THE SECOND HALF.
UNDER-STOOD?
YES.
YEAHHHHHH

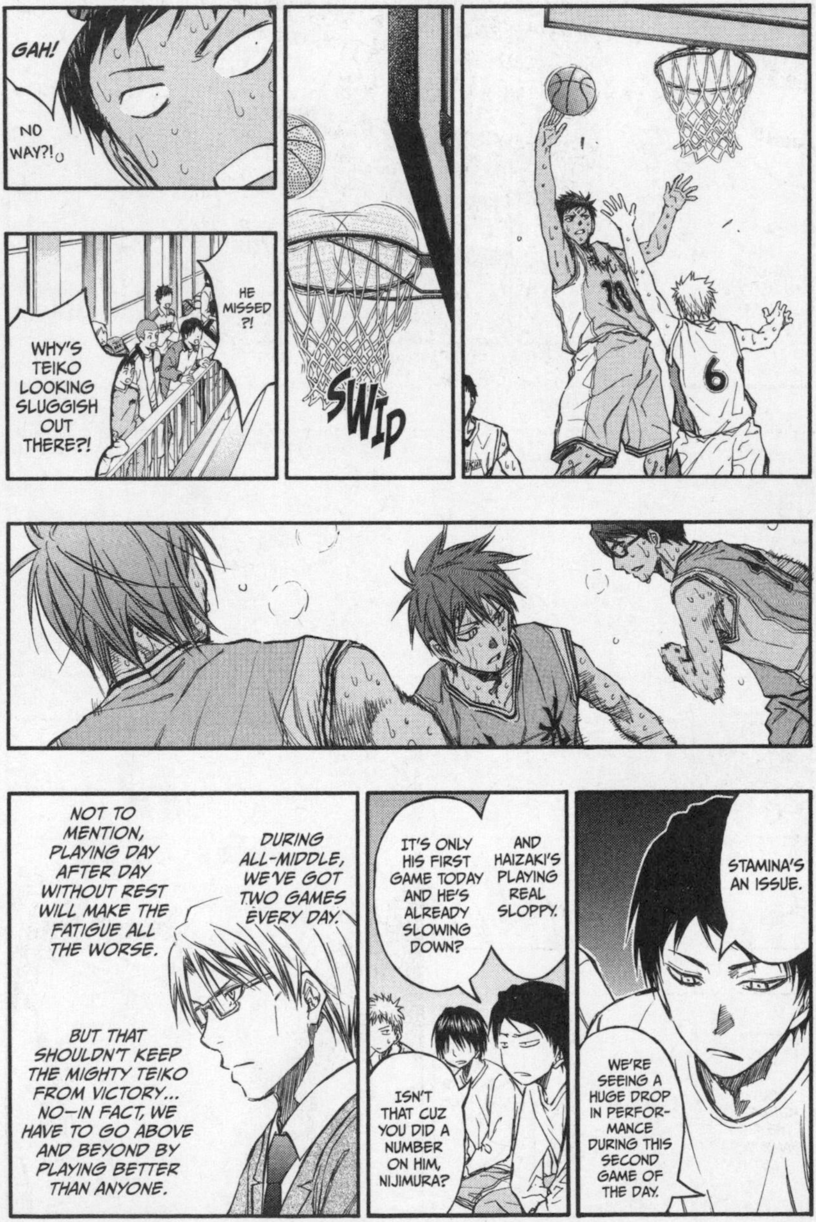
!
SWIP
GAH!
NO WAY?!
HE MISSED ?!
WHY'S TEIKO LOOKING SLUGGISH OUT THERE?!
STAMINA'S AN ISSUE.
WE'RE SEEING A HUGE DROP IN PERFORMANCE DURING THIS SECOND GAME OF THE DAY.
AND HAIZAKI'S PLAYING REAL SLOPPY.
IT'S ONLY HIS FIRST GAME TODAY AND HE'S ALREADY SLOWING DOWN?
ISN'T THAT CUZ YOU DID A NUMBER ON HIM, NIJIMURA?
DURING ALL-MIDDLE, WE'VE GOT TWO GAMES EVERY DAY.
NOT TO MENTION, PLAYING DAY AFTER DAY WITHOUT REST WILL MAKE THE FATIGUE ALL THE WORSE.
BUT THAT SHOULDN'T KEEP THE MIGHTY TEIKO FROM VICTORY... NO—IN FACT, WE HAVE TO GO ABOVE AND BEYOND BY PLAYING BETTER THAN ANYONE.

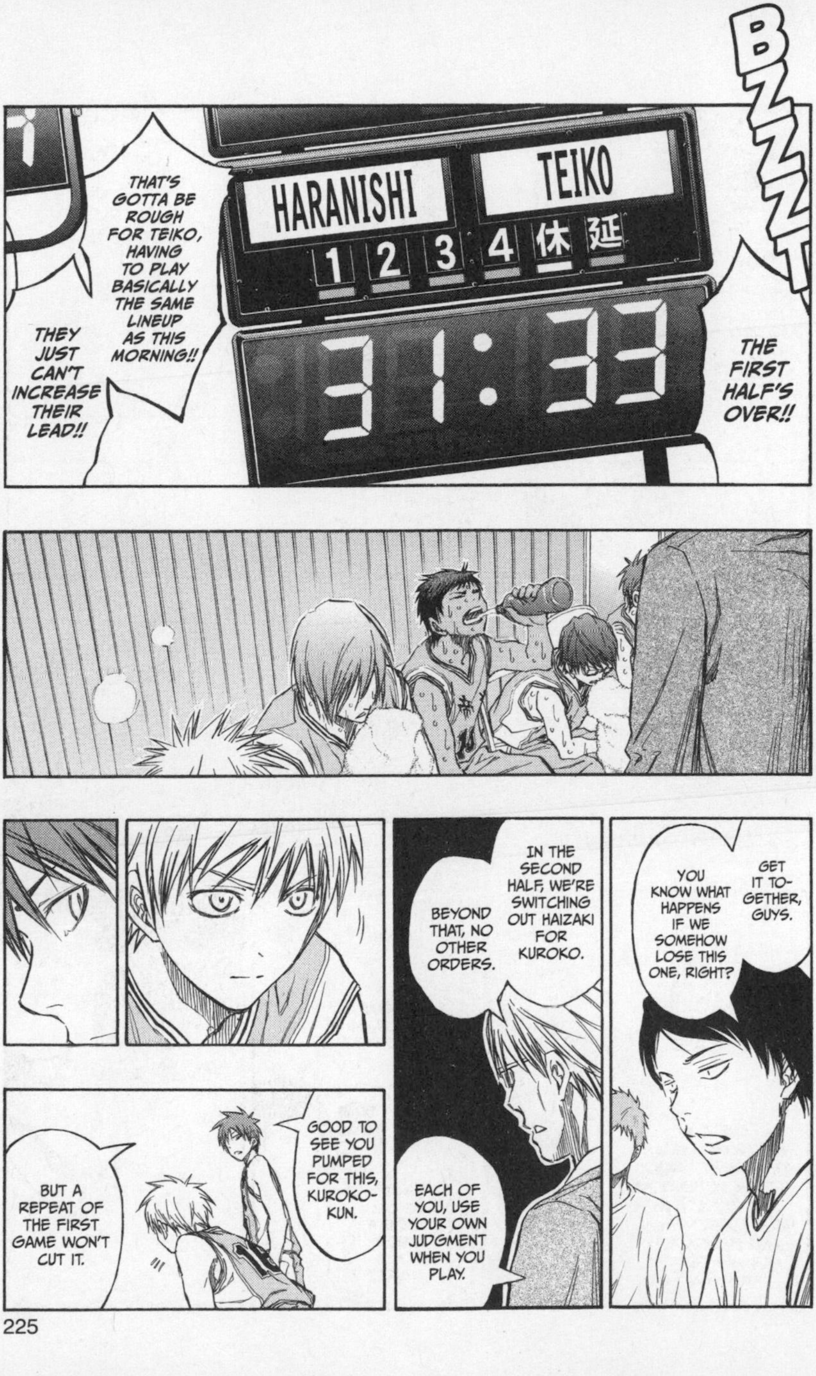
BZZZT
HARANISHI
TEIKO
1 2 3 4 休 延
31:33
THE FIRST HALF'S OVER!!
THAT'S GOTTA BE ROUGH FOR TEIKO, HAVING TO PLAY BASICALLY THE SAME LINEUP AS THIS MORNING!!
THEY JUST CAN'T INCREASE THEIR LEAD!!
GET IT TO-GETHER, GUYS.
YOU KNOW WHAT HAPPENS IF WE SOMEHOW LOSE THIS ONE, RIGHT?
IN THE SECOND HALF, WE'RE SWITCHING OUT HAIZAKI FOR KUROKO.
BEYOND THAT, NO OTHER ORDERS.
EACH OF YOU, USE YOUR OWN JUDGMENT WHEN YOU PLAY.
GOOD TO SEE YOU PUMPED FOR THIS, KUROKO-KUN.
BUT A REPEAT OF THE FIRST GAME WON'T CUT IT.

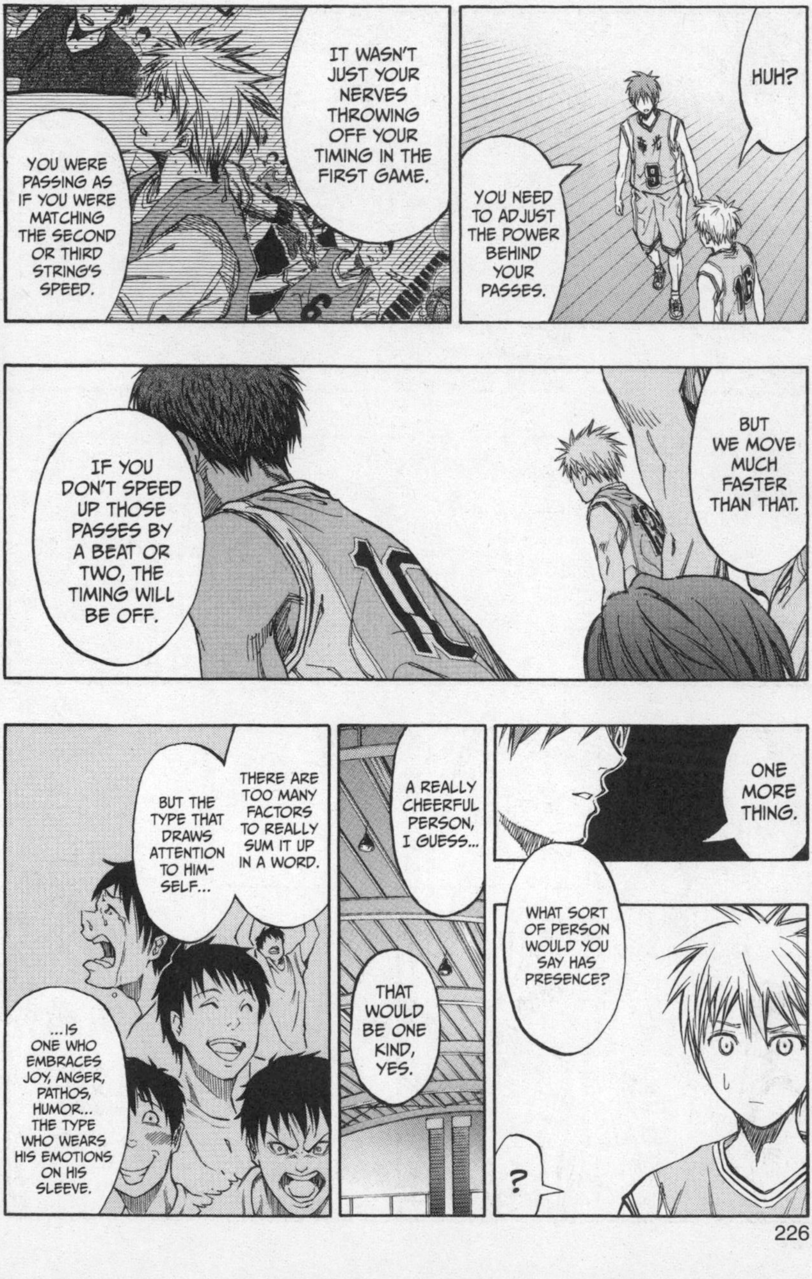
HUH?
YOU NEED TO ADJUST THE POWER BEHIND YOUR PASSES.
IT WASN'T JUST YOUR NERVES THROWING OFF YOUR TIMING IN THE FIRST GAME.
YOU WERE PASSING AS IF YOU WERE MATCHING THE SECOND OR THIRD STRING'S SPEED.
BUT WE MOVE MUCH FASTER THAN THAT.
IF YOU DON'T SPEED UP THOSE PASSES BY A BEAT OR TWO, THE TIMING WILL BE OFF.
ONE MORE THING.
WHAT SORT OF PERSON WOULD YOU SAY HAS PRESENCE?
?
A REALLY CHEERFUL PERSON, I GUESS...
THAT WOULD BE ONE KIND, YES.
THERE ARE TOO MANY FACTORS TO REALLY SUM IT UP IN A WORD.
BUT THE TYPE THAT DRAWS ATTENTION TO HIM-SELF...
...IS ONE WHO EMBRACES JOY, ANGER, PATHOS, HUMOR... THE TYPE WHO WEARS HIS EMOTIONS ON HIS SLEEVE.

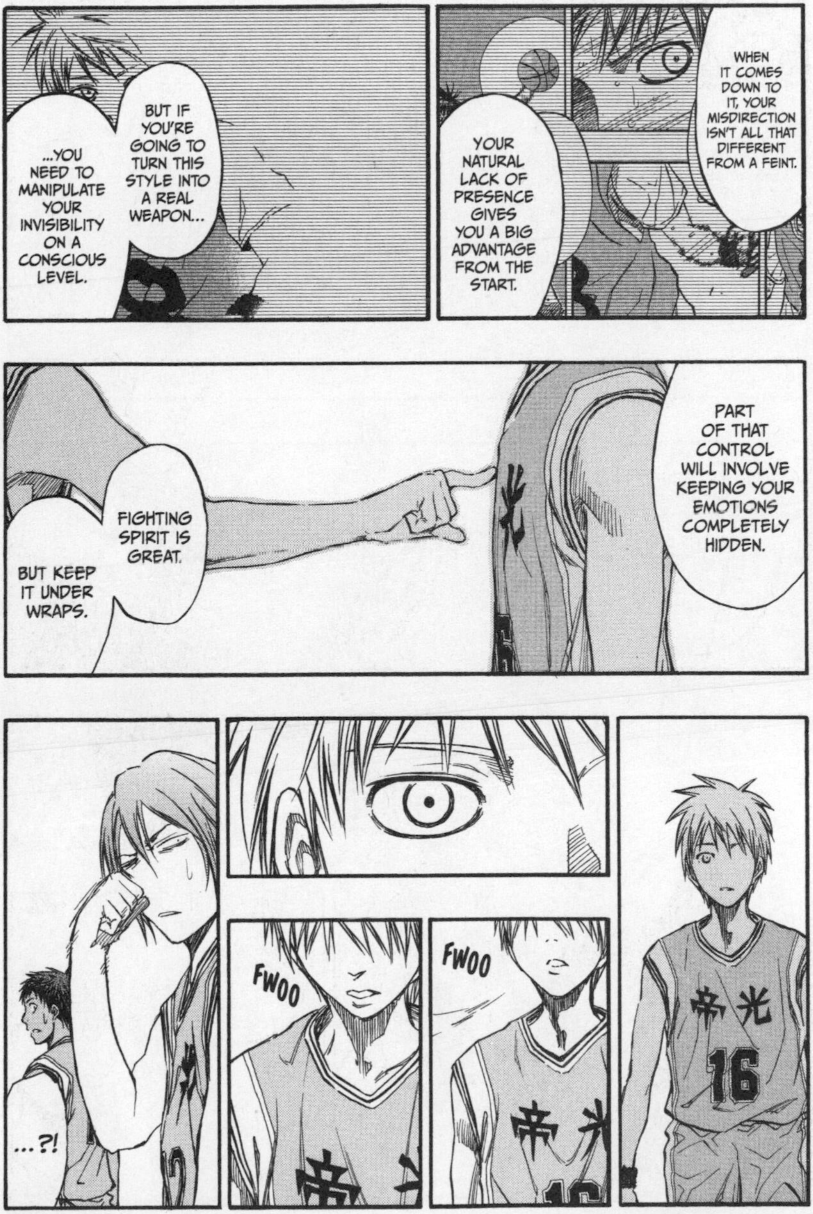
WHEN IT COMES DOWN TO IT, YOUR MISDIRECTION ISN'T ALL THAT DIFFERENT FROM A FEINT.
YOUR NATURAL LACK OF PRESENCE GIVES YOU A BIG ADVANTAGE FROM THE START.
BUT IF YOU'RE GOING TO TURN THIS STYLE INTO A REAL WEAPON...
...YOU NEED TO MANIPULATE YOUR INVISIBILITY ON A CONSCIOUS LEVEL.
PART OF THAT CONTROL WILL INVOLVE KEEPING YOUR EMOTIONS COMPLETELY HIDDEN.
FIGHTING SPIRIT IS GREAT.
BUT KEEP IT UNDER WRAPS.
FWOO
FWOO
...?!

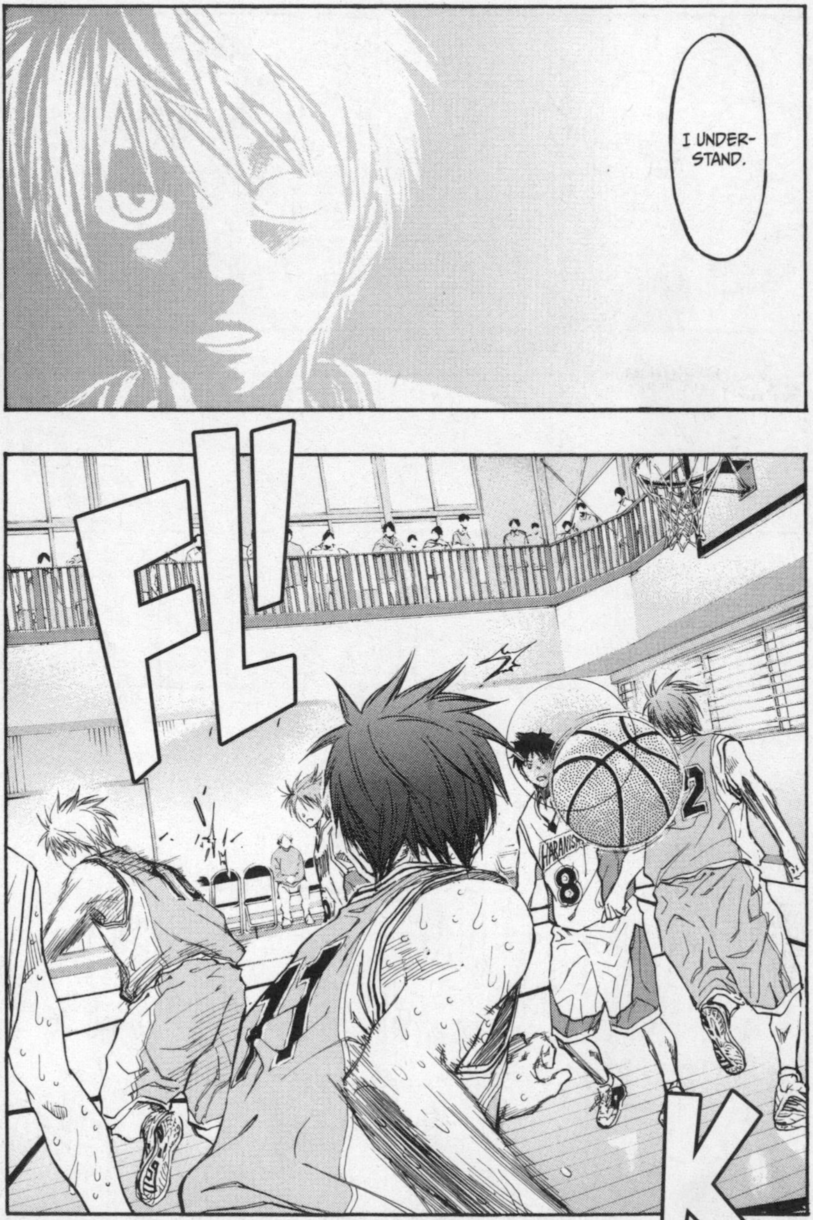
I UNDER-
STAND.
FLI
K

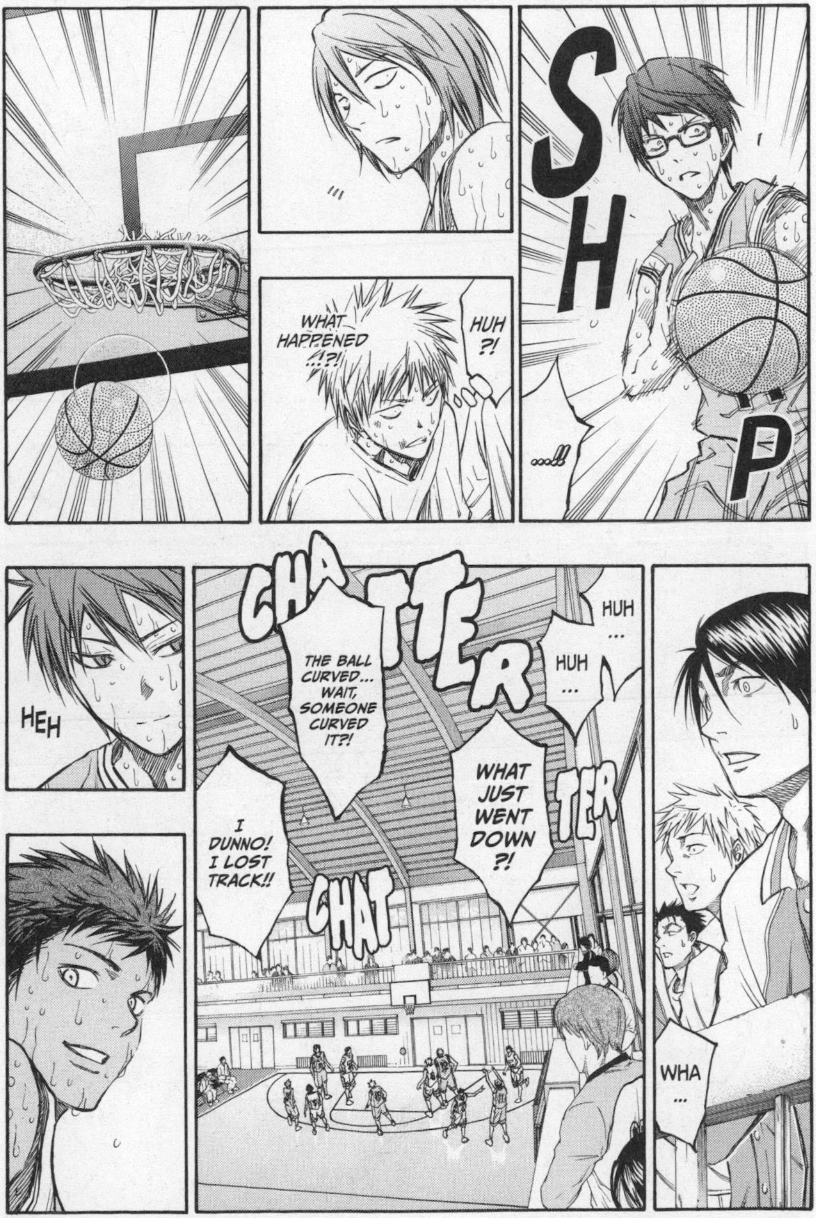
SH
P
...!!
HUH ?!
WHAT HAPPENED ...!?!
HUH ...
HUH ...
WHA ...
CHATTER
THE BALL CURVED... WAIT, SOMEONE CURVED IT?!
WHAT JUST WENT DOWN ?!
TER
I DUNNO! I LOST TRACK!!
CHAT
HEH

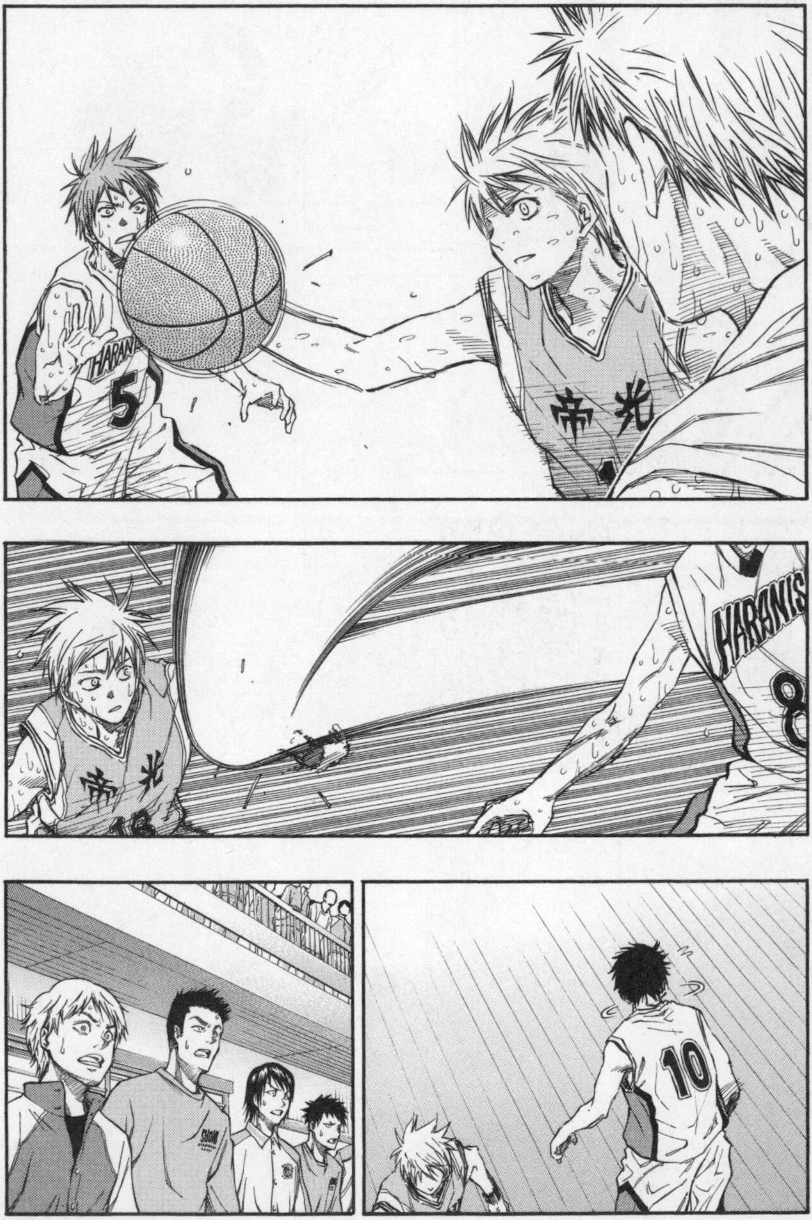

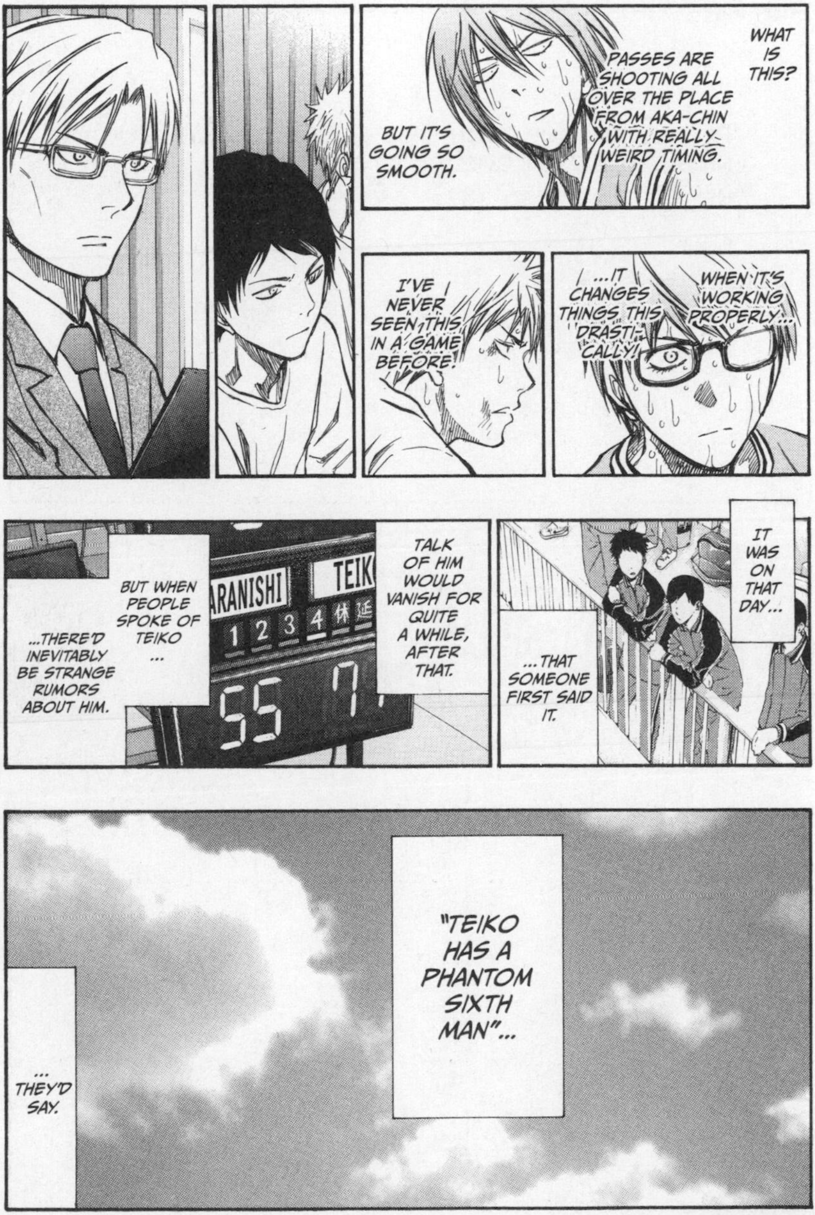
WHAT IS THIS?
PASSES ARE SHOOTING ALL OVER THE PLACE FROM AKA-CHIN WITH REALLY WEIRD TIMING.
BUT IT'S GOING SO SMOOTH.
WHEN IT'S WORKING PROPERLY...
...IT CHANGES THINGS THIS DRASTICALLY!
I'VE NEVER SEEN THIS IN A GAME BEFORE.
IT WAS ON THAT DAY...
...THAT SOMEONE FIRST SAID IT.
TALK OF HIM WOULD VANISH FOR QUITE A WHILE, AFTER THAT.
BUT WHEN PEOPLE SPOKE OF TEIKO ...
...THERE'D INEVITABLY BE STRANGE RUMORS ABOUT HIM.
"TEIKO HAS A PHANTOM SIXTH MAN"...
... THEY'D SAY.

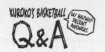

KUROKO'S BASKETBALL
Q&A
W/ HALFWAY-DECENT ANSWERS

Q. **PLEASE TELL ME EACH OF THE MIRACLE GENERATION MEMBER'S BEST SUBJECTS IN SCHOOL.**
(AKATSUKI from IWATE PREFECTURE)

A. KUROKO -> MODERN JAPANESE/CLASSICAL LITERATURE
AOMINE -> JAPANESE HISTORY (IF SERIOUSLY FORCED TO SAY)
MURASAKIBARA -> PHYSICS
KISE -> ENGLISH (IF FORCED TO SAY)
MIDORIMA -> BIOLOGY/CHEMISTRY
AKASHI -> ALL SUBJECTS

KUROKO'S BASKETBALL BLOOPERS
TAKE 4

IT DOESN'T MATTER IF THIS WAS HIS FIRST GAME—HE WAS TERRIBLE THIS MORNING.
COACH'S DISAP-POINTMENT IS NO SURPRISE.
THEY MIGHT NOT EVEN LET HIM PLAY THIS AFTERNOON...
SIP
OWW ... ...
CAN'T HANDLE HOT THINGS, HUH?

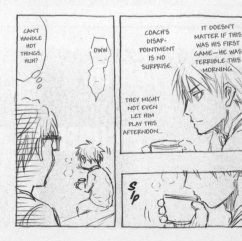

210TH QUARTER:

FIGURED AS MUCH

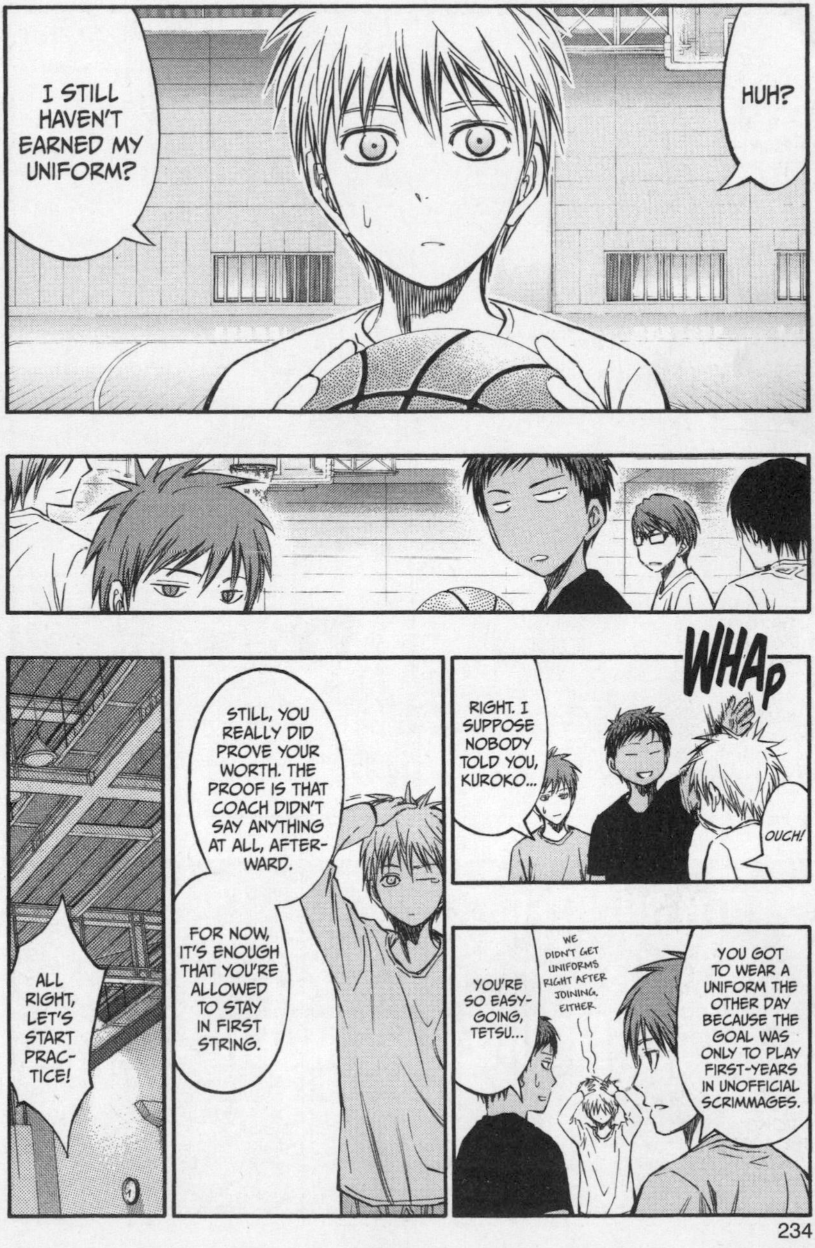
HUH?
I STILL HAVEN'T EARNED MY UNIFORM?
WHAP
OUCH!
RIGHT. I SUPPOSE NOBODY TOLD YOU, KUROKO...
YOU GOT TO WEAR A UNIFORM THE OTHER DAY BECAUSE THE GOAL WAS ONLY TO PLAY FIRST-YEARS IN UNOFFICIAL SCRIMMAGES.
WE DIDN'T GET UNIFORMS RIGHT AFTER JOINING, EITHER
YOU'RE SO EASY-GOING, TETSU...
STILL, YOU REALLY DID PROVE YOUR WORTH. THE PROOF IS THAT COACH DIDN'T SAY ANYTHING AT ALL, AFTER-WARD.
FOR NOW, IT'S ENOUGH THAT YOU'RE ALLOWED TO STAY IN FIRST STRING.
ALL RIGHT, LET'S START PRAC-TICE!

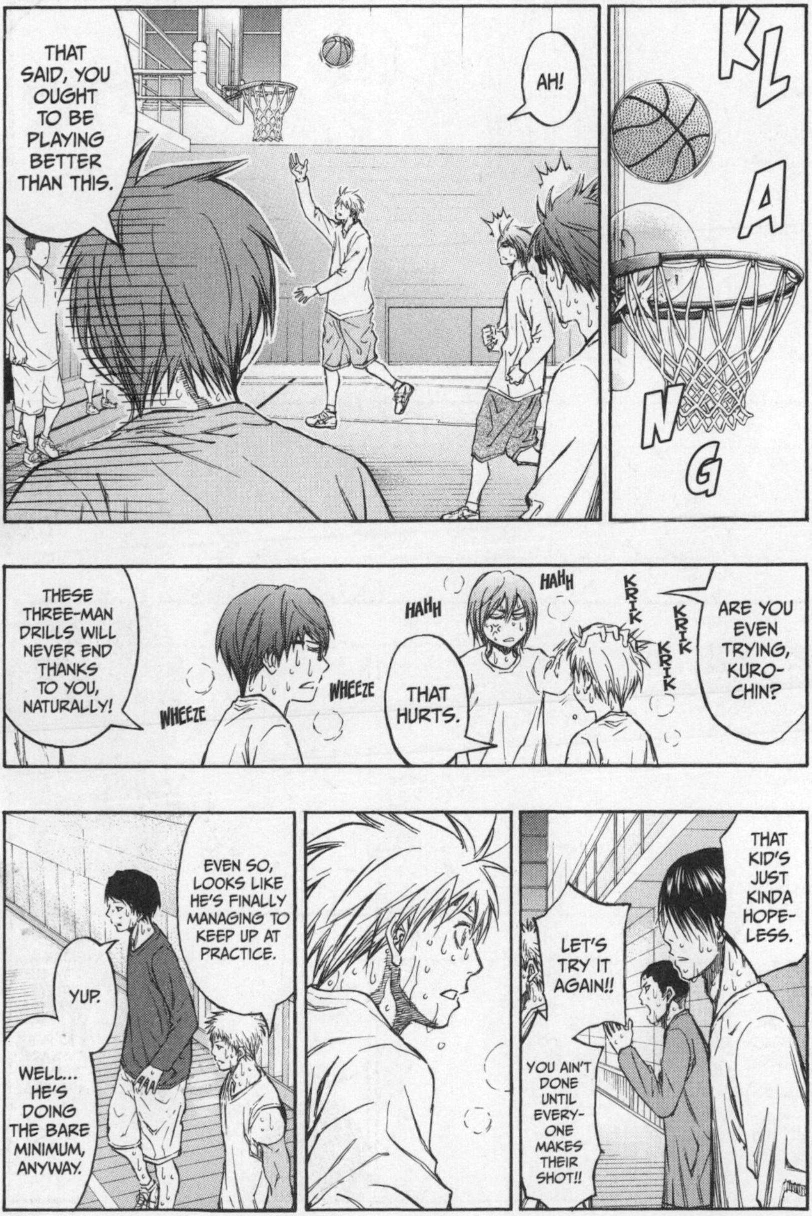
KLANG
AH!
THAT SAID, YOU OUGHT TO BE PLAYING BETTER THAN THIS.
ARE YOU EVEN TRYING, KURO-CHIN?
KRIK KRIK KRIK
HAHH
THAT HURTS.
HAHH
WHEEZE
THESE THREE-MAN DRILLS WILL NEVER END THANKS TO YOU, NATURALLY!
WHEEZE
THAT KID'S JUST KINDA HOPE-LESS.
LET'S TRY IT AGAIN!!
YOU AIN'T DONE UNTIL EVERY-ONE MAKES THEIR SHOT!!
EVEN SO, LOOKS LIKE HE'S FINALLY MANAGING TO KEEP UP AT PRACTICE.
YUP.
WELL... HE'S DOING THE BARE MINIMUM, ANYWAY.

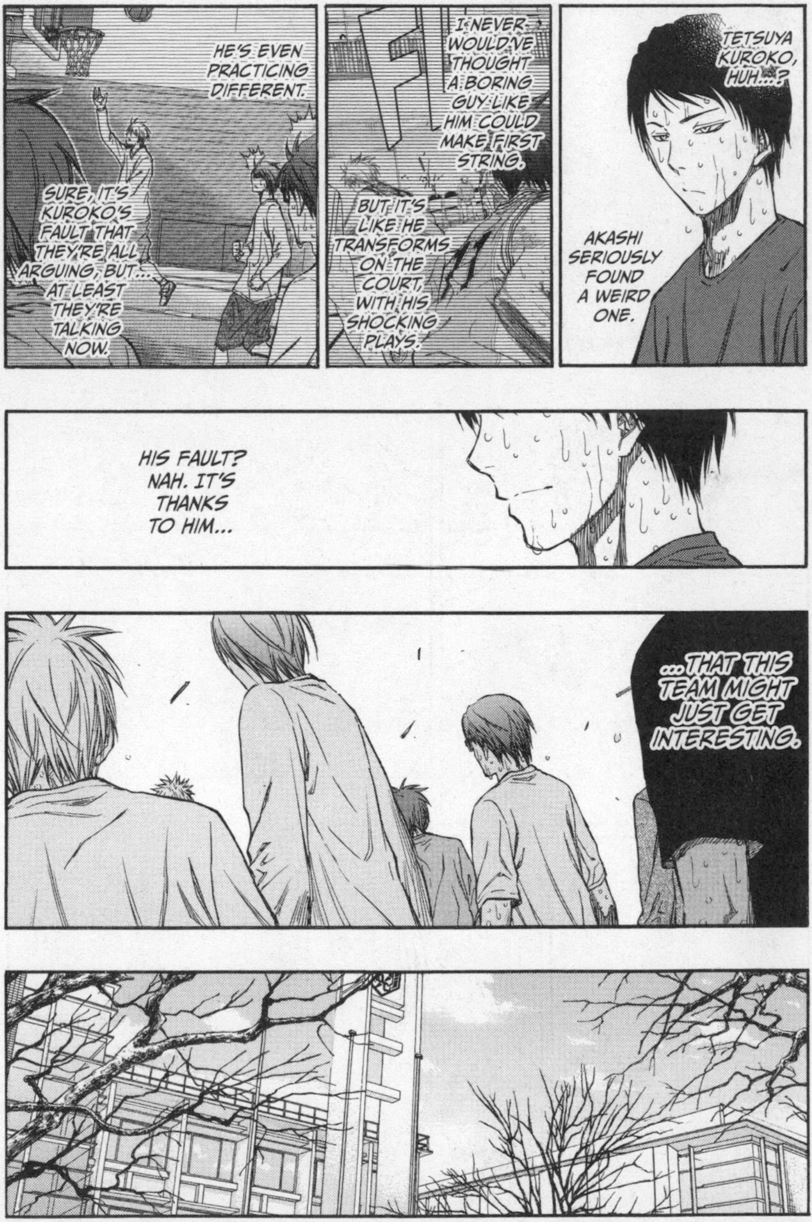
TETSUYA KUROKO, HUH...?
AKASHI SERIOUSLY FOUND A WEIRD ONE.
I NEVER WOULD'VE THOUGHT A BORING GUY LIKE HIM COULD MAKE FIRST STRING.
BUT IT'S LIKE HE TRANSFORMS ON THE COURT, WITH HIS SHOCKING PLAYS.
HE'S EVEN PRACTICING DIFFERENT.
SURE, IT'S KUROKO'S FAULT THAT THEY'RE ALL ARGUING, BUT... AT LEAST THEY'RE TALKING NOW.
HIS FAULT? NAH. IT'S THANKS TO HIM...
...THAT THIS TEAM MIGHT JUST GET INTERESTING.

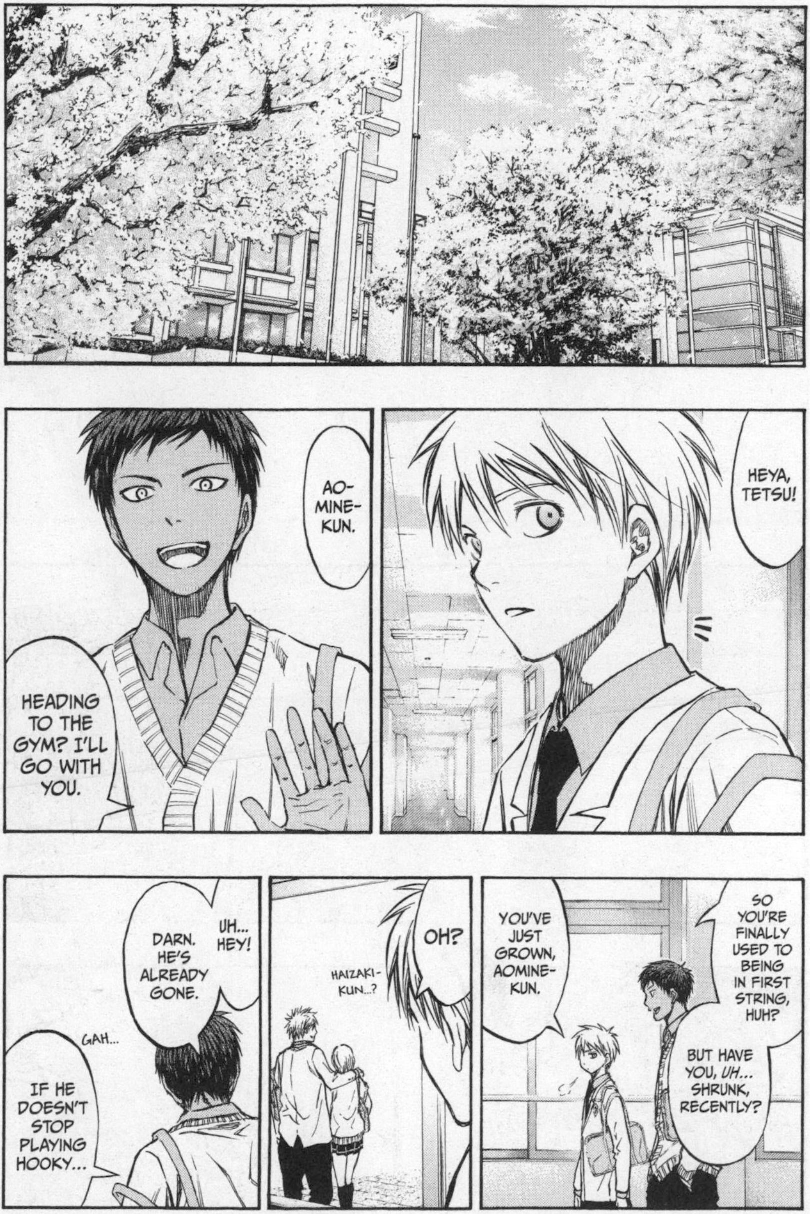
HEYA, TETSU!
AO-MINE-KUN.
HEADING TO THE GYM? I'LL GO WITH YOU.
SO YOU'RE FINALLY USED TO BEING IN FIRST STRING, HUH?
YOU'VE JUST GROWN, AOMINE-KUN.
BUT HAVE YOU, UH... SHRUNK, RECENTLY?
OH?
HAIZAKI-KUN...?
UH... HEY!
DARN. HE'S ALREADY GONE.
GAH...
IF HE DOESN'T STOP PLAYING HOOKY...

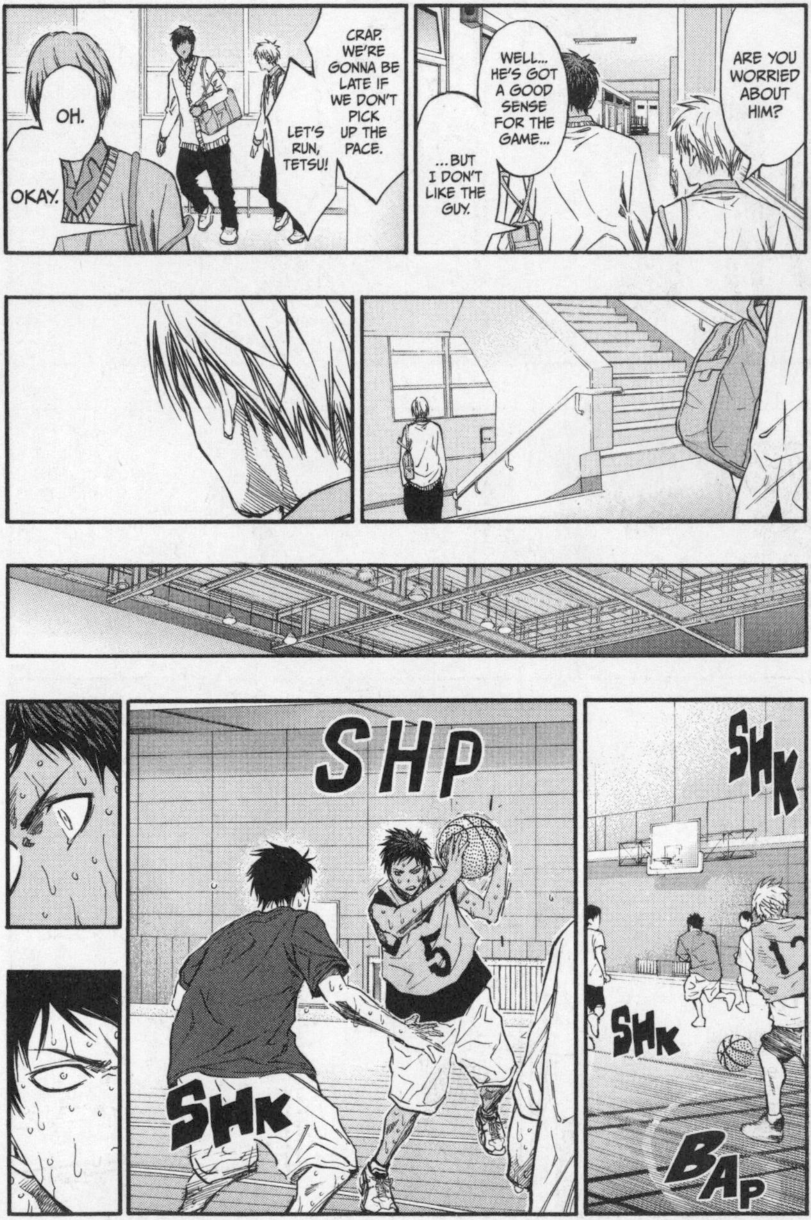
ARE YOU WORRIED ABOUT HIM?
WELL... HE'S GOT A GOOD SENSE FOR THE GAME...
...BUT I DON'T LIKE THE GUY.
CRAP. WE'RE GONNA BE LATE IF WE DON'T PICK UP THE PACE.
LET'S RUN, TETSU!
OH.
OKAY.
SHK
SHK
BAP
SHP
SHK

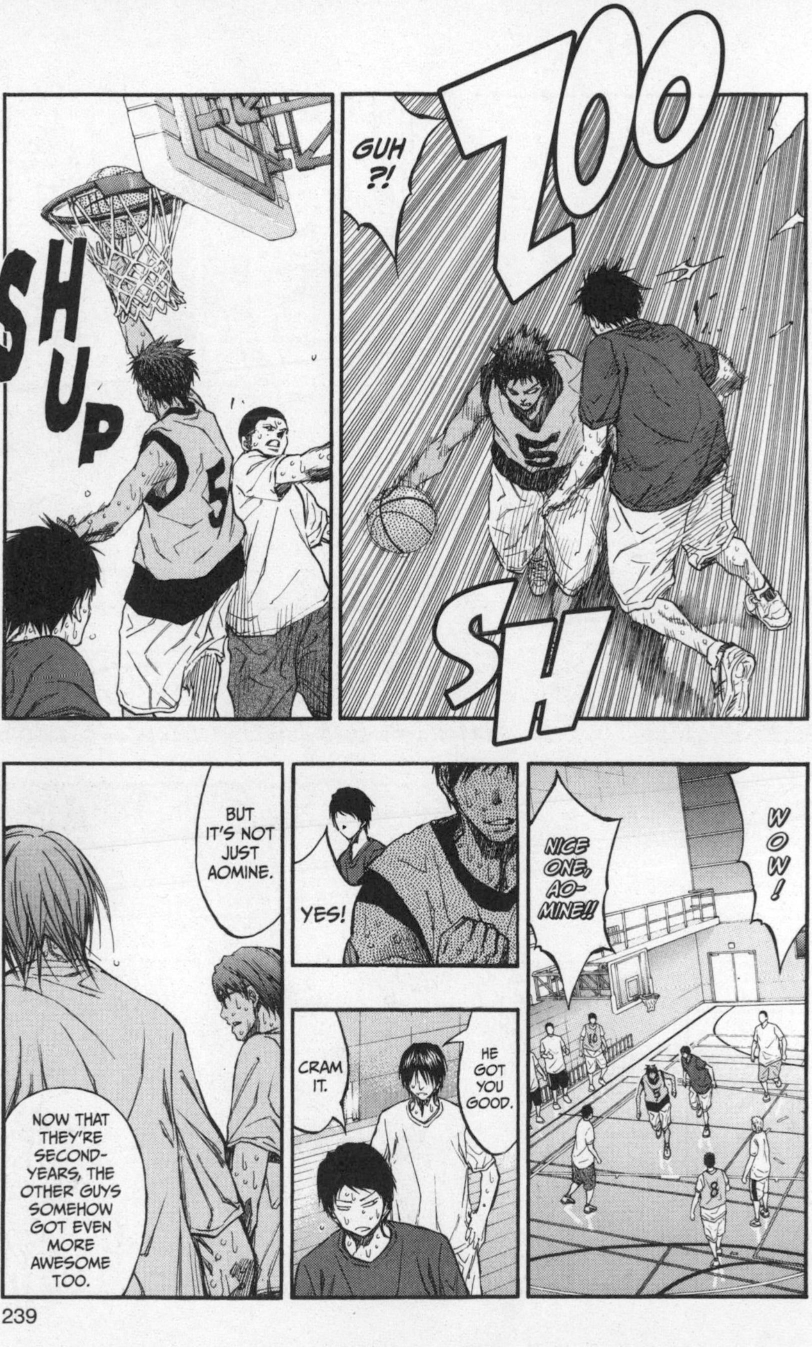
ZOO
GUH ?!
SH
SHUP
WOW!
NICE ONE, AOMINE!!
YES!
HE GOT YOU GOOD.
CRAM IT.
BUT IT'S NOT JUST AOMINE.
NOW THAT THEY'RE SECOND-YEARS, THE OTHER GUYS SOMEHOW GOT EVEN MORE AWESOME TOO.

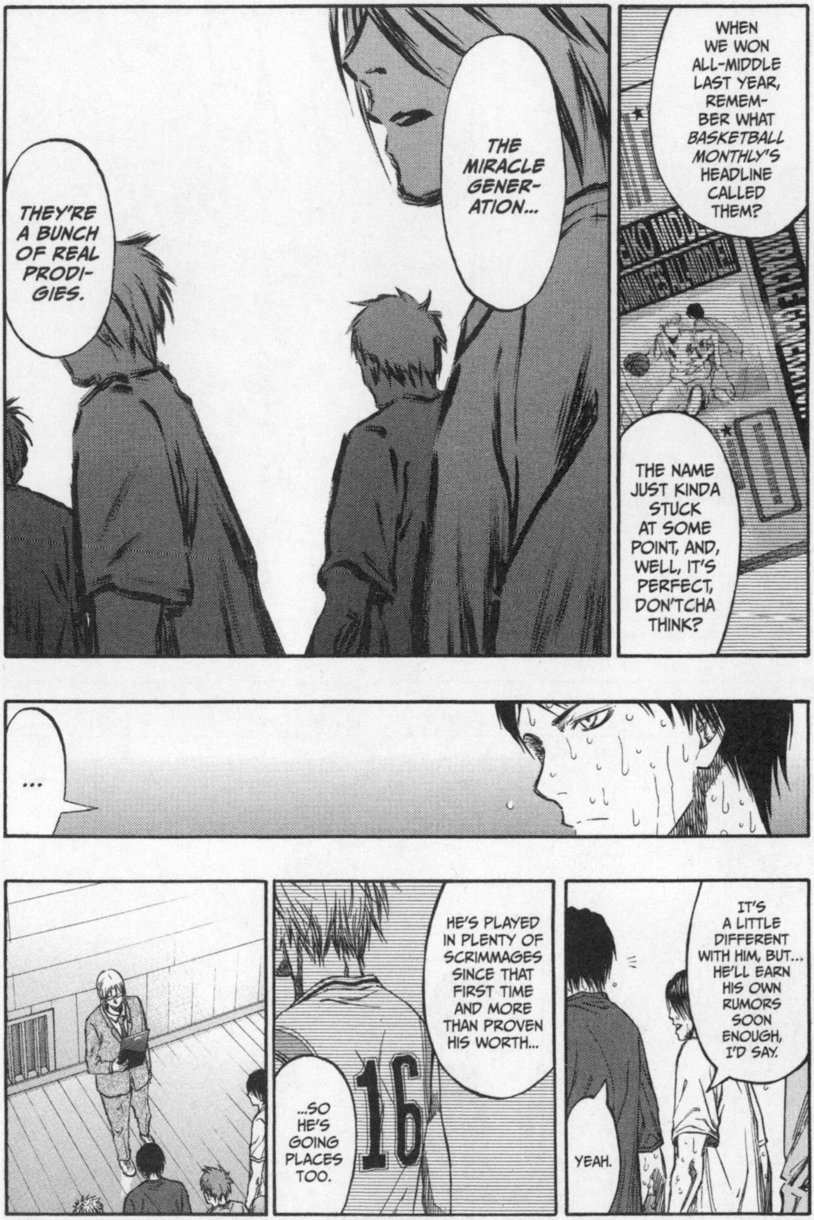
WHEN WE WON ALL-MIDDLE LAST YEAR, REMEMBER WHAT *BASKETBALL MONTHLY*'S HEADLINE CALLED THEM?
THE NAME JUST KINDA STUCK AT SOME POINT, AND, WELL, IT'S PERFECT, DON'TCHA THINK?
THE MIRACLE GENERATION...
THEY'RE A BUNCH OF REAL PRODIGIES.
...
IT'S A LITTLE DIFFERENT WITH HIM, BUT... HE'LL EARN HIS OWN RUMORS SOON ENOUGH, I'D SAY.
YEAH.
HE'S PLAYED IN PLENTY OF SCRIMMAGES SINCE THAT FIRST TIME AND MORE THAN PROVEN HIS WORTH...
...SO HE'S GOING PLACES TOO.
16

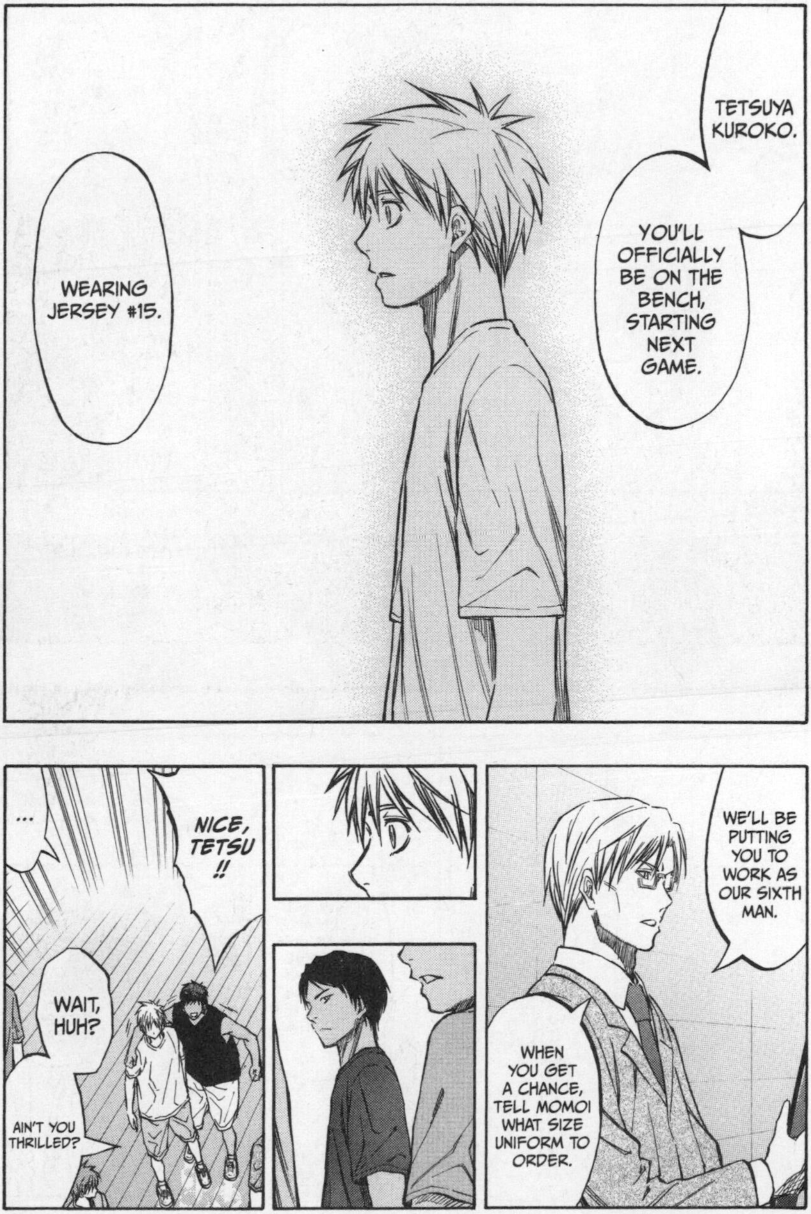
TETSUYA KUROKO.
YOU'LL OFFICIALLY BE ON THE BENCH, STARTING NEXT GAME.
WEARING JERSEY #15.
WE'LL BE PUTTING YOU TO WORK AS OUR SIXTH MAN.
WHEN YOU GET A CHANCE, TELL MOMOI WHAT SIZE UNIFORM TO ORDER.
NICE, TETSU!!
...
WAIT, HUH?
AIN'T YOU THRILLED?

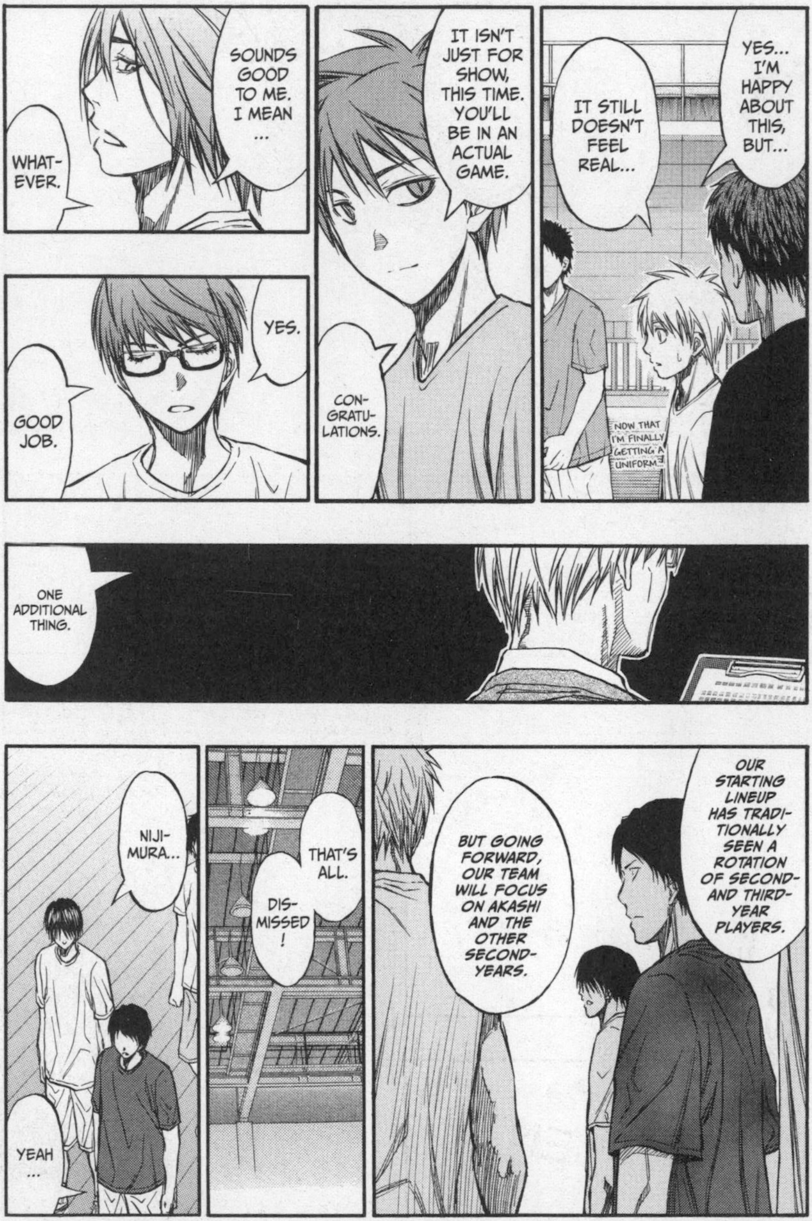
YES... I'M HAPPY ABOUT THIS, BUT...
IT STILL DOESN'T FEEL REAL...
NOW THAT I'M FINALLY GETTING A UNIFORM.
IT ISN'T JUST FOR SHOW, THIS TIME. YOU'LL BE IN AN ACTUAL GAME.
CON-GRATU-LATIONS.
SOUNDS GOOD TO ME. I MEAN ...
WHAT-EVER.
YES.
GOOD JOB.
ONE ADDITIONAL THING.
OUR STARTING LINEUP HAS TRADI-TIONALLY SEEN A ROTATION OF SECOND- AND THIRD-YEAR PLAYERS.
BUT GOING FORWARD, OUR TEAM WILL FOCUS ON AKASHI AND THE OTHER SECOND-YEARS.
THAT'S ALL.
DIS-MISSED!
NIJI-MURA...
YEAH ...

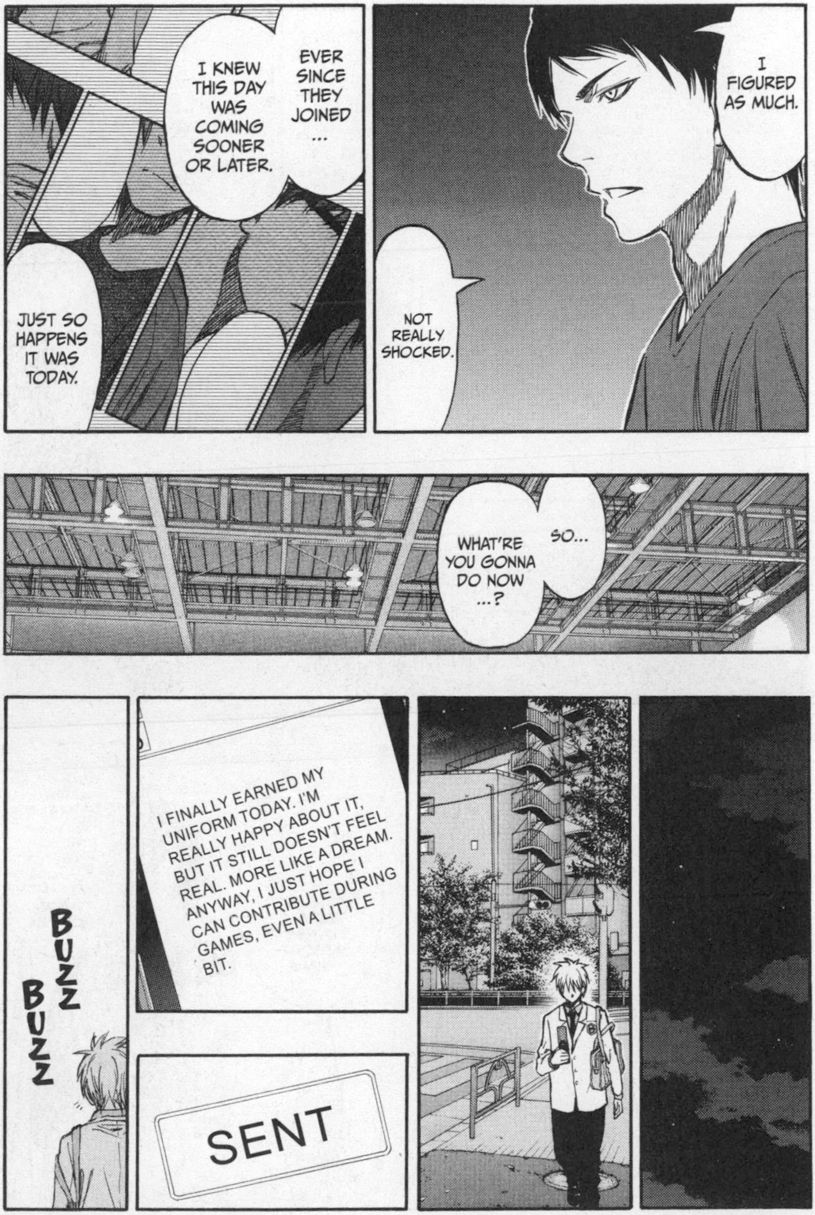
I FIGURED AS MUCH.
NOT REALLY SHOCKED.
EVER SINCE THEY JOINED...
I KNEW THIS DAY WAS COMING SOONER OR LATER.
JUST SO HAPPENS IT WAS TODAY.
SO...
WHAT'RE YOU GONNA DO NOW...?
I FINALLY EARNED MY UNIFORM TODAY. I'M REALLY HAPPY ABOUT IT, BUT IT STILL DOESN'T FEEL REAL. MORE LIKE A DREAM. ANYWAY, I JUST HOPE I CAN CONTRIBUTE DURING GAMES, EVEN A LITTLE BIT.
SENT
BUZZ
BUZZ

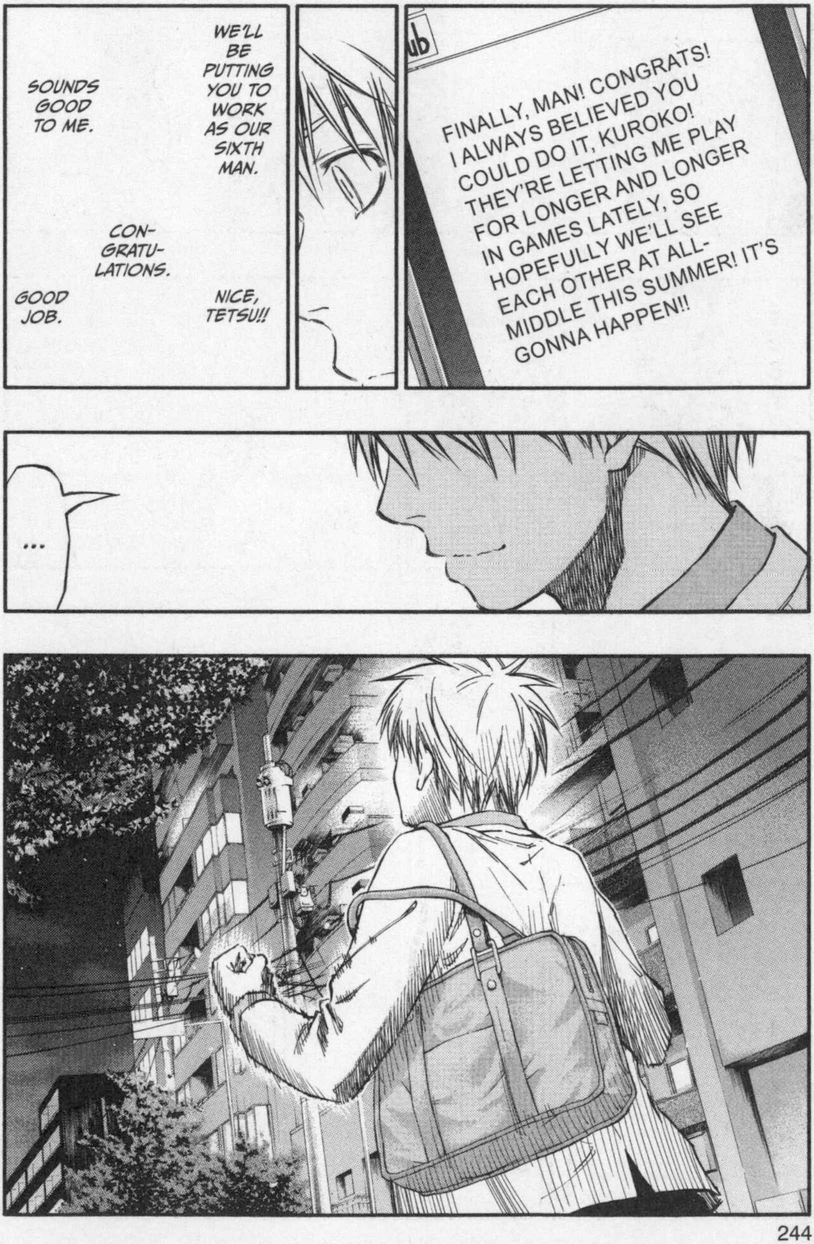
FINALLY, MAN! CONGRATS! I ALWAYS BELIEVED YOU COULD DO IT, KUROKO! THEY'RE LETTING ME PLAY FOR LONGER AND LONGER IN GAMES LATELY, SO HOPEFULLY WE'LL SEE EACH OTHER AT ALL-MIDDLE THIS SUMMER! IT'S GONNA HAPPEN!!
WE'LL BE PUTTING YOU TO WORK AS OUR SIXTH MAN.
SOUNDS GOOD TO ME.
CON-GRATU-LATIONS.
NICE, TETSU!!
GOOD JOB.
...

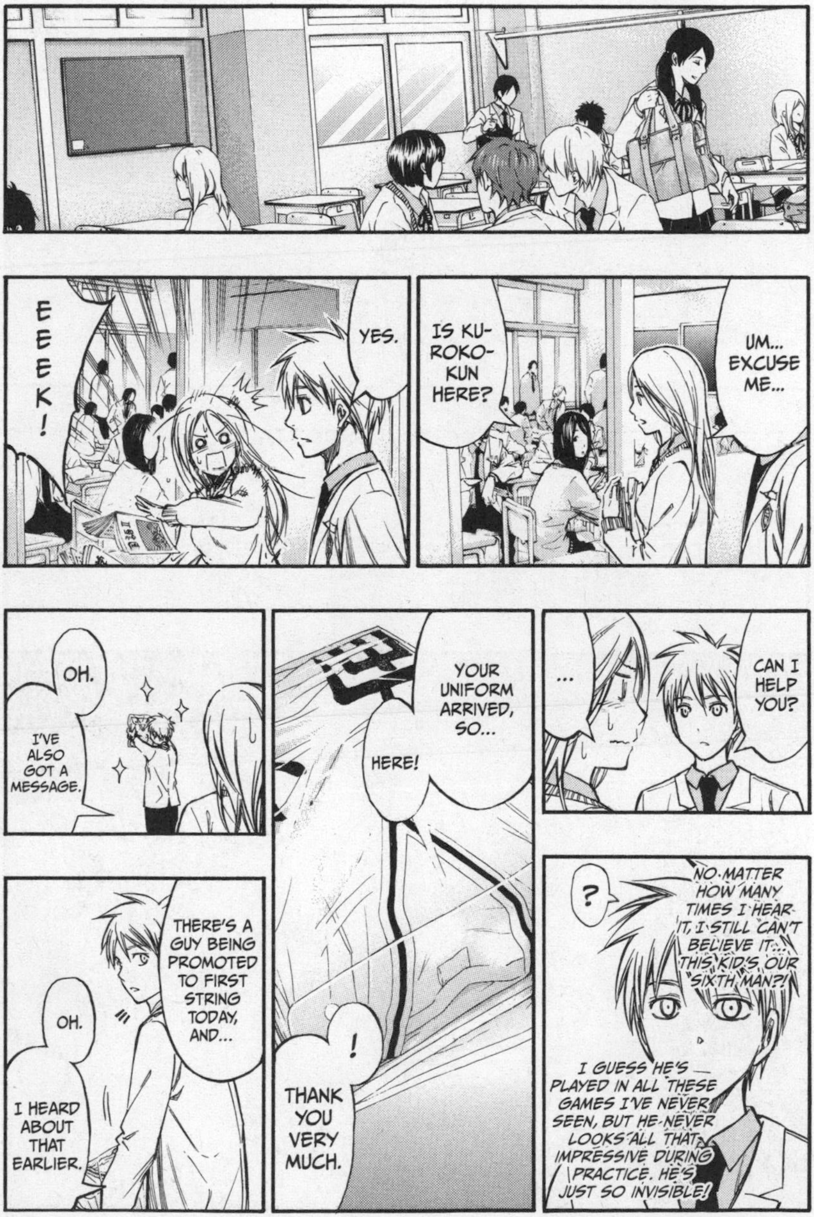
UM... EXCUSE ME...
IS KUROKO-KUN HERE?
YES.
EEEEK!
CAN I HELP YOU?
...
?
NO MATTER HOW MANY TIMES I HEAR IT, I STILL CAN'T BELIEVE IT... THIS KID'S OUR SIXTH MAN?!
I GUESS HE'S PLAYED IN ALL THESE GAMES I'VE NEVER SEEN, BUT HE NEVER LOOKS ALL THAT IMPRESSIVE DURING PRACTICE. HE'S JUST SO INVISIBLE!
YOUR UNIFORM ARRIVED, SO...
HERE!
!
THANK YOU VERY MUCH.
OH.
I'VE ALSO GOT A MESSAGE.
THERE'S A GUY BEING PROMOTED TO FIRST STRING TODAY, AND...
OH.
I HEARD ABOUT THAT EARLIER.

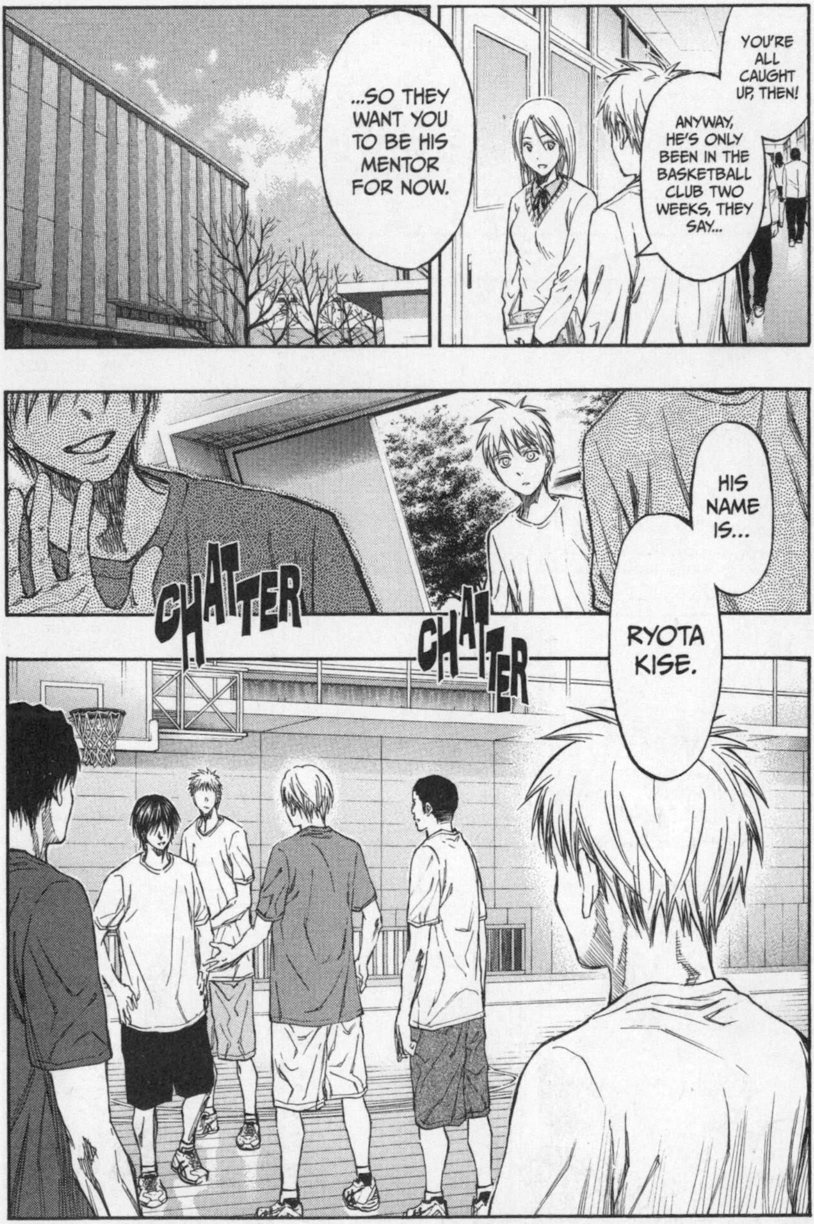
YOU'RE ALL CAUGHT UP, THEN!
ANYWAY, HE'S ONLY BEEN IN THE BASKETBALL CLUB TWO WEEKS, THEY SAY...
...SO THEY WANT YOU TO BE HIS MENTOR FOR NOW.
HIS NAME IS...
CHATTER
CHATTER
RYOTA KISE.

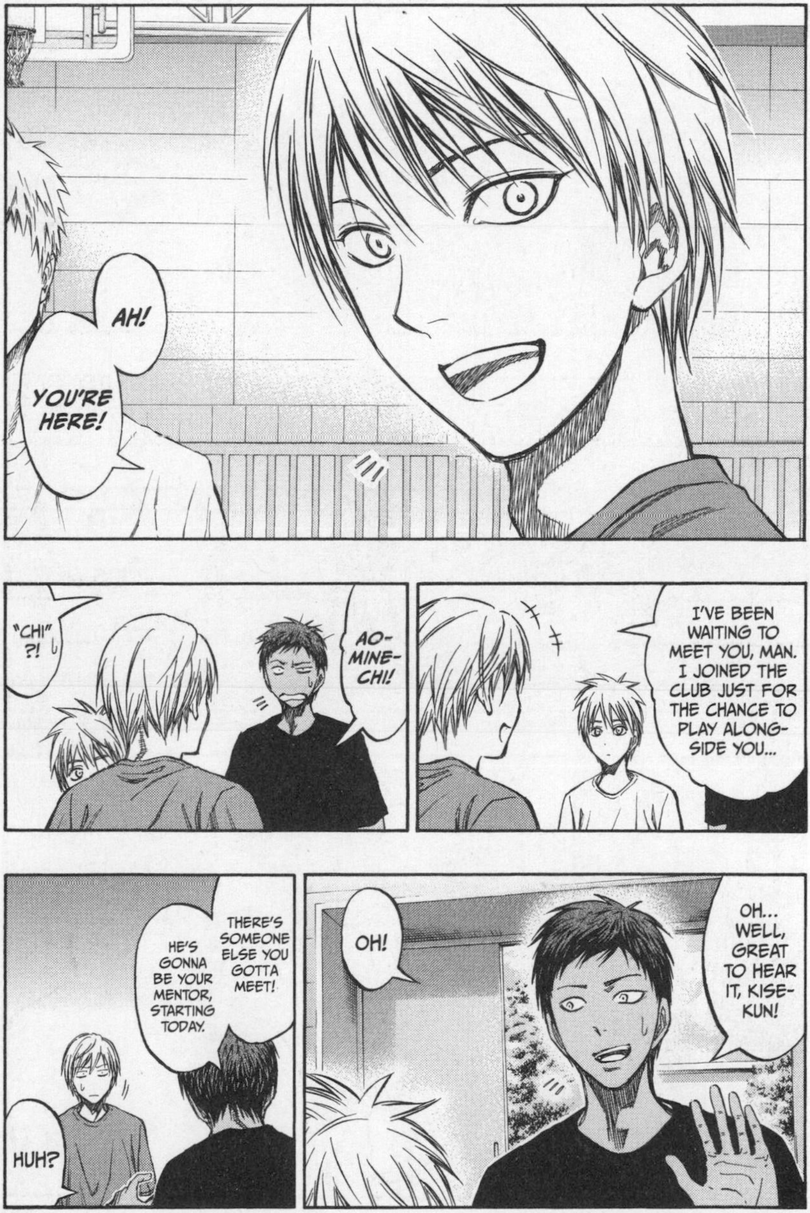
AH!
YOU'RE HERE!
I'VE BEEN WAITING TO MEET YOU, MAN. I JOINED THE CLUB JUST FOR THE CHANCE TO PLAY ALONG-SIDE YOU...
AO-MINE-CHI!
"CHI" ?!
OH... WELL, GREAT TO HEAR IT, KISE-KUN!
OH!
THERE'S SOMEONE ELSE YOU GOTTA MEET!
HE'S GONNA BE YOUR MENTOR, STARTING TODAY.
HUH?

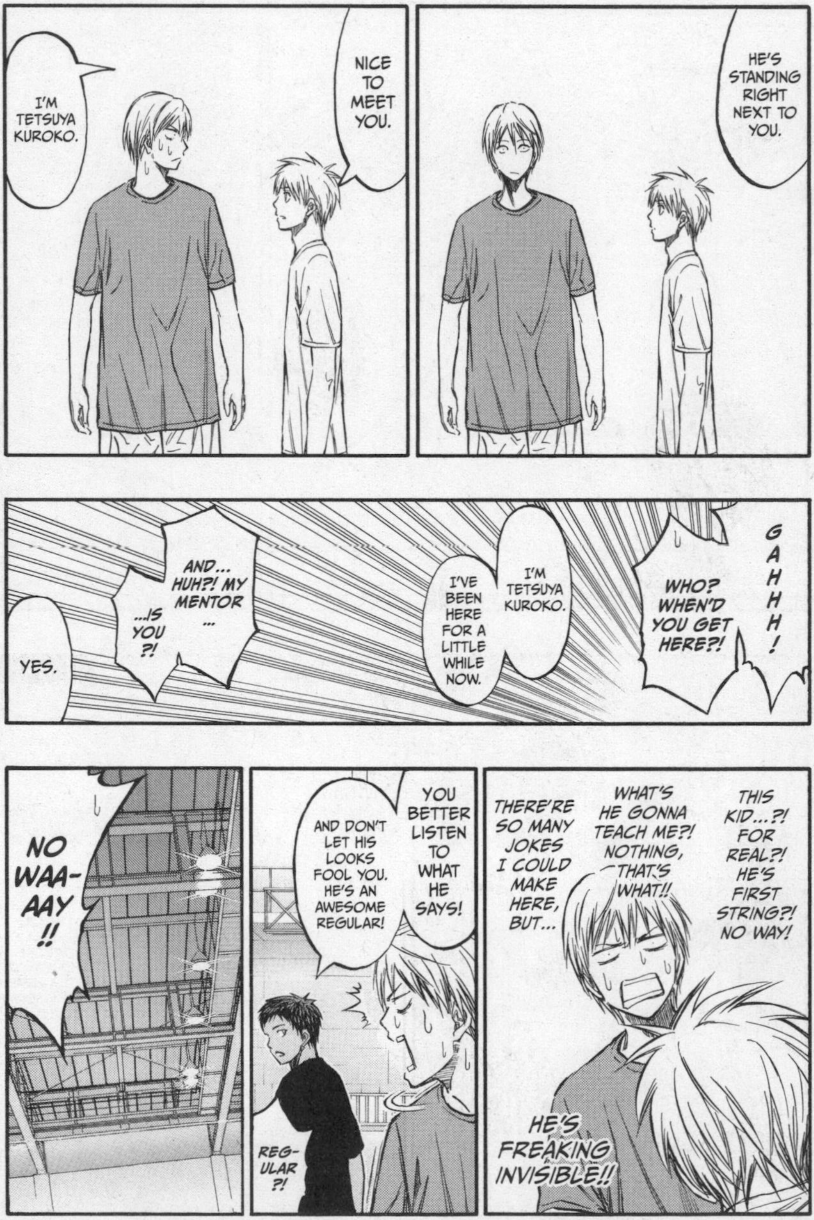
HE'S STANDING RIGHT NEXT TO YOU.
NICE TO MEET YOU.
I'M TETSUYA KUROKO.
GAHHH!
WHO? WHEN'D YOU GET HERE?!
I'M TETSUYA KUROKO.
I'VE BEEN HERE FOR A LITTLE WHILE NOW.
AND... HUH?! MY MENTOR ...
...IS YOU ?!
YES.
THIS KID...?! FOR REAL?! HE'S FIRST STRING?! NO WAY!
WHAT'S HE GONNA TEACH ME?! NOTHING, THAT'S WHAT!!
THERE'RE SO MANY JOKES I COULD MAKE HERE, BUT...
HE'S FREAKING INVISIBLE!!
YOU BETTER LISTEN TO WHAT HE SAYS!
AND DON'T LET HIS LOOKS FOOL YOU. HE'S AN AWESOME REGULAR!
REG-ULAR ?!
NO WAA-AAY !!

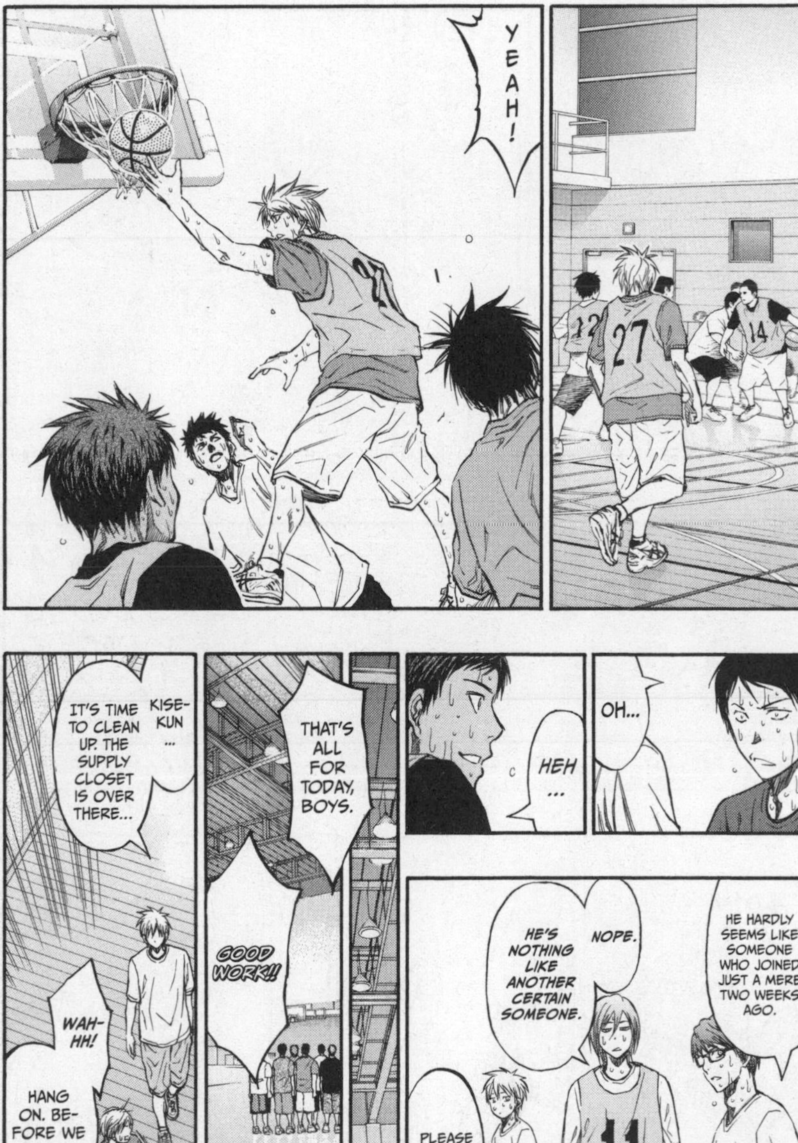
YEAH!
OH...
HEH...
HE HARDLY SEEMS LIKE SOMEONE WHO JOINED JUST A MERE TWO WEEKS AGO.
NOPE.
HE'S NOTHING LIKE ANOTHER CERTAIN SOMEONE.
PLEASE BE NICE.
THAT'S ALL FOR TODAY, BOYS.
GOOD WORK!!
KISE-KUN...
IT'S TIME TO CLEAN UP. THE SUPPLY CLOSET IS OVER THERE...
WAH-HH!
HANG ON. BE-FORE WE GET TO THAT...

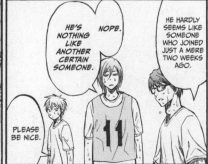

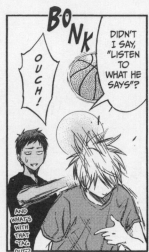

I WANT A DIFFERENT MENTOR.
HUH?
TAG OUT.
B-O-N-K
DIDN'T I SAY, "LISTEN TO WHAT HE SAYS"?
OUCH!
AND WHAT'S WITH THAT "TAG OUT"?
NO THANKS! HOW'M I S'POSED TO LEARN ANYTHING FROM A DULL GUY LIKE HIM?!
HEY, TETSU'S NOT DULL!
DIDN'T I PROVE HOW GREAT I AM DURING PRACTICE TODAY?!
WELL, YOU... NO, YOU DIDN'T!!
YAP YAP
AKA-SHI...
GOOD GRIEF.
HE'LL NEVER BE CONVINCED BY ANY MERE EXPLA-NATION.
SEE YA LATER...
SHOULD WE GIVE HIM A DIFFERENT MENTOR?
NO... I'LL THINK OF SOME-THING.
ALSO, WHERE'D THE CAPTAIN GO?
IT SEEMS HE NEEDED TO TALK TO THE COACH ABOUT SOME-THING.
I SEE...

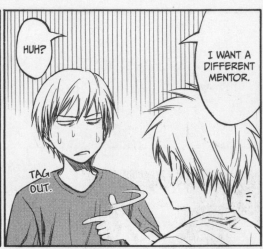

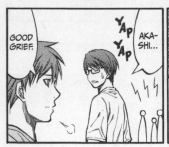

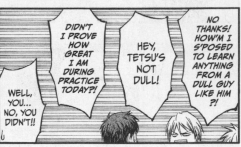

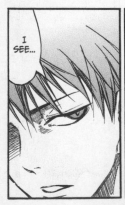

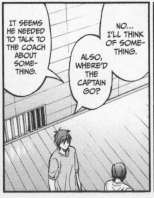

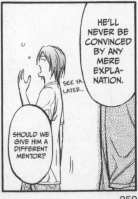

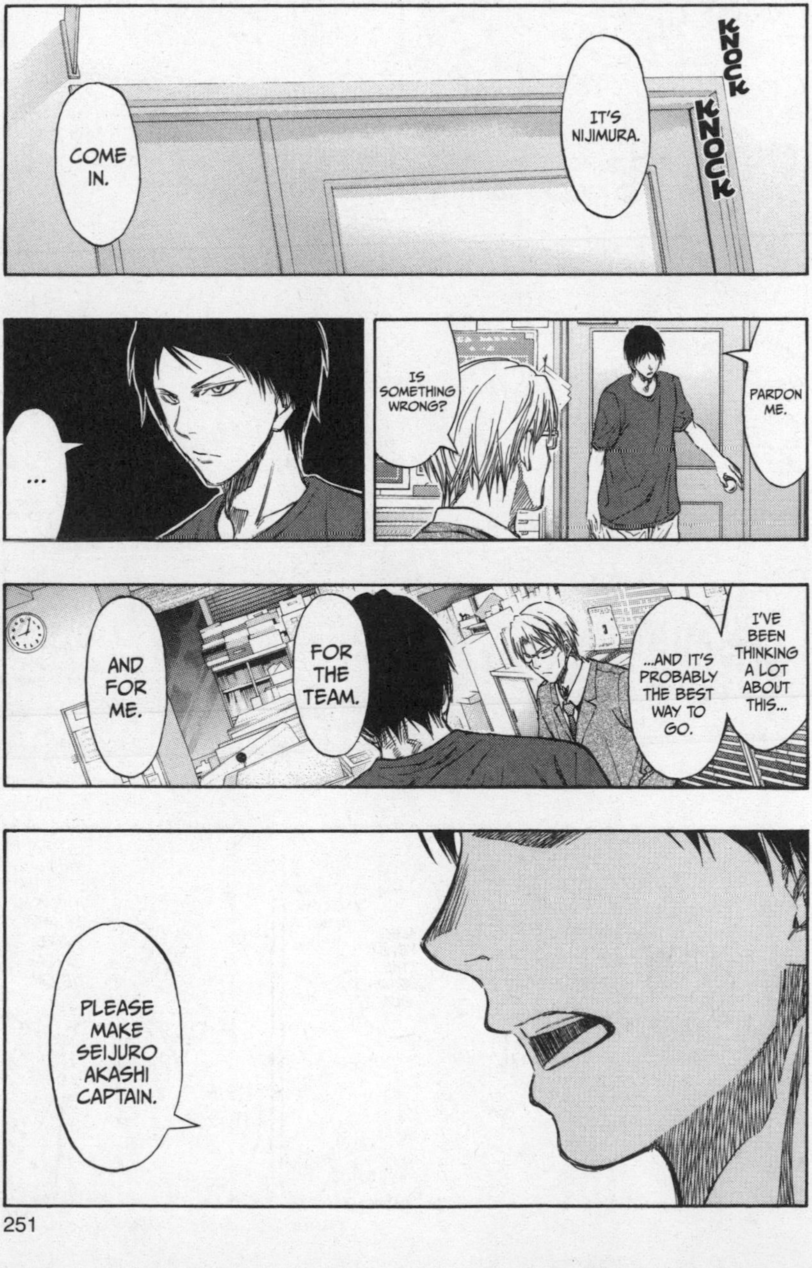
KNOCK KNOCK
IT'S NIJIMURA.
COME IN.
PARDON ME.
IS SOMETHING WRONG?
...
I'VE BEEN THINKING A LOT ABOUT THIS...
...AND IT'S PROBABLY THE BEST WAY TO GO.
FOR THE TEAM.
AND FOR ME.
PLEASE MAKE SEIJURO AKASHI CAPTAIN.

KUROKO'S BASKETBALL Q&A (W/ HALFWAY-DECENT ANSWERS)

Q. **IS RIKO'S PAPA ABOUT TO GET A DIVORCE?**
(ANKORO MOCHI from YAMANASHI PREFECTURE)

A. KNOCK IT OFF, YOU.

KUROKO'S BASKETBALL BLOOPERS TAKE 3

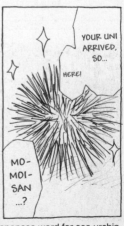

YOUR UNI ARRIVED, SO...

HERE!

MO-MOI-SAN ...?

*Uni is the Japanese word for sea urchin.

211TH QUARTER:

SEE YA

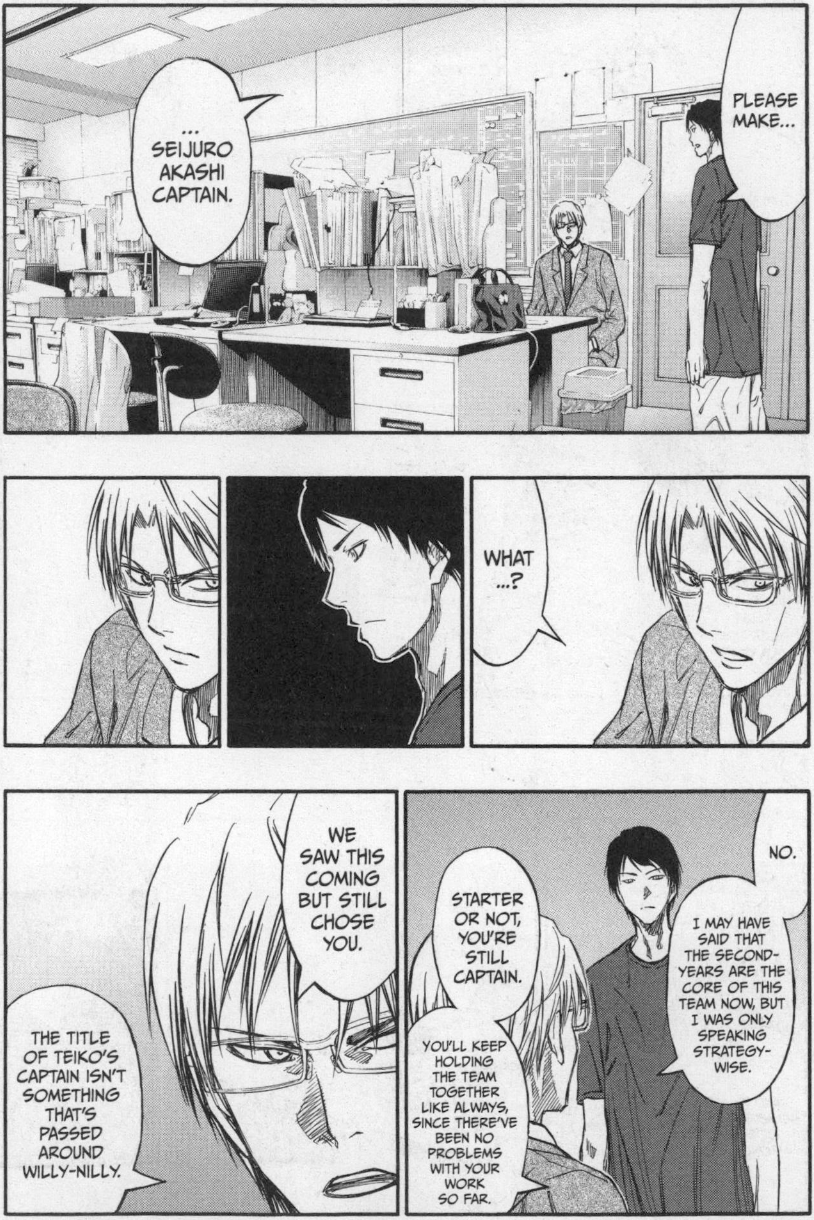
PLEASE MAKE...
... SEIJURO AKASHI CAPTAIN.
WHAT ...?
NO.
I MAY HAVE SAID THAT THE SECOND-YEARS ARE THE CORE OF THIS TEAM NOW, BUT I WAS ONLY SPEAKING STRATEGY-WISE.
STARTER OR NOT, YOU'RE STILL CAPTAIN.
YOU'LL KEEP HOLDING THE TEAM TOGETHER LIKE ALWAYS, SINCE THERE'VE BEEN NO PROBLEMS WITH YOUR WORK SO FAR.
WE SAW THIS COMING BUT STILL CHOSE YOU.
THE TITLE OF TEIKO'S CAPTAIN ISN'T SOMETHING THAT'S PASSED AROUND WILLY-NILLY.

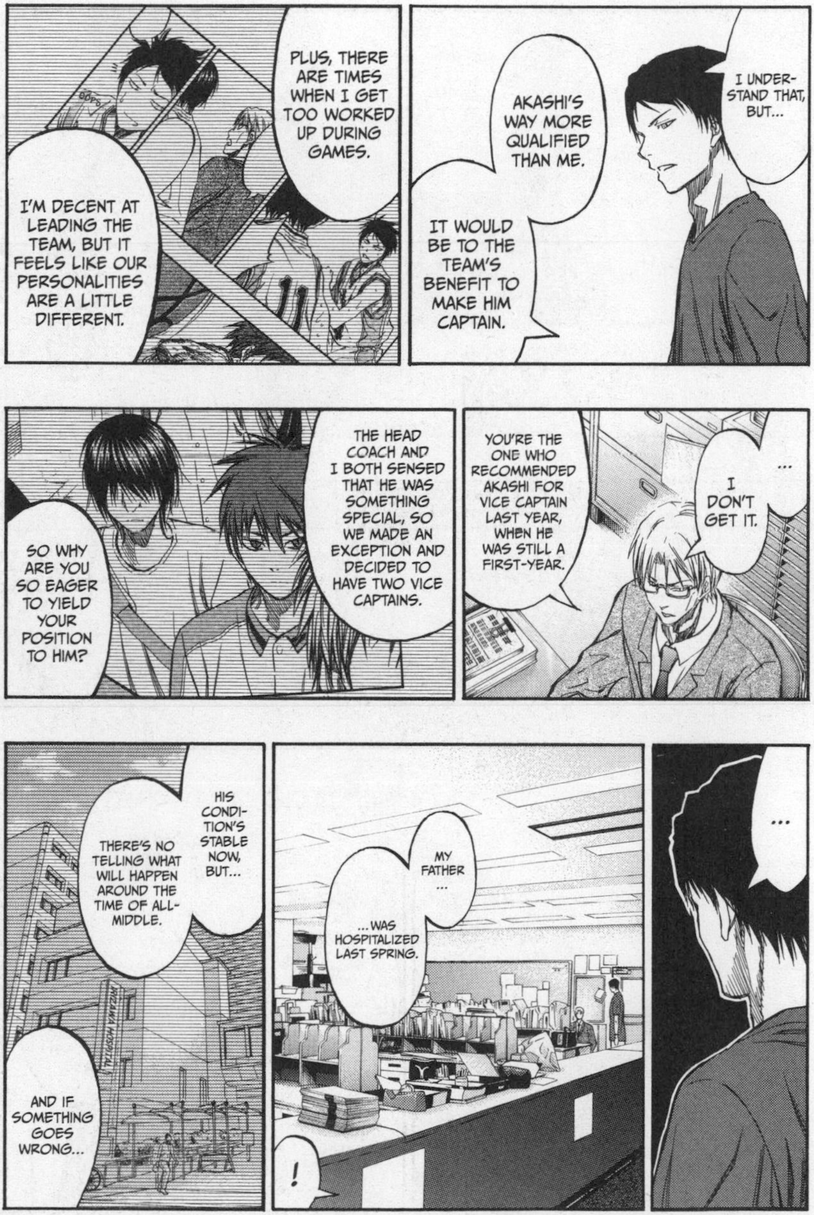
I UNDER-STAND THAT, BUT...
AKASHI'S WAY MORE QUALIFIED THAN ME.
IT WOULD BE TO THE TEAM'S BENEFIT TO MAKE HIM CAPTAIN.
I'M DECENT AT LEADING THE TEAM, BUT IT FEELS LIKE OUR PERSONALITIES ARE A LITTLE DIFFERENT.
PLUS, THERE ARE TIMES WHEN I GET TOO WORKED UP DURING GAMES.
...
I DON'T GET IT.
YOU'RE THE ONE WHO RECOMMENDED AKASHI FOR VICE CAPTAIN LAST YEAR, WHEN HE WAS STILL A FIRST-YEAR.
THE HEAD COACH AND I BOTH SENSED THAT HE WAS SOMETHING SPECIAL, SO WE MADE AN EXCEPTION AND DECIDED TO HAVE TWO VICE CAPTAINS.
SO WHY ARE YOU SO EAGER TO YIELD YOUR POSITION TO HIM?
...
MY FATHER...
...WAS HOSPITALIZED LAST SPRING.
!
HIS CONDITION'S STABLE NOW, BUT...
THERE'S NO TELLING WHAT WILL HAPPEN AROUND THE TIME OF ALL-MIDDLE.
AND IF SOMETHING GOES WRONG...

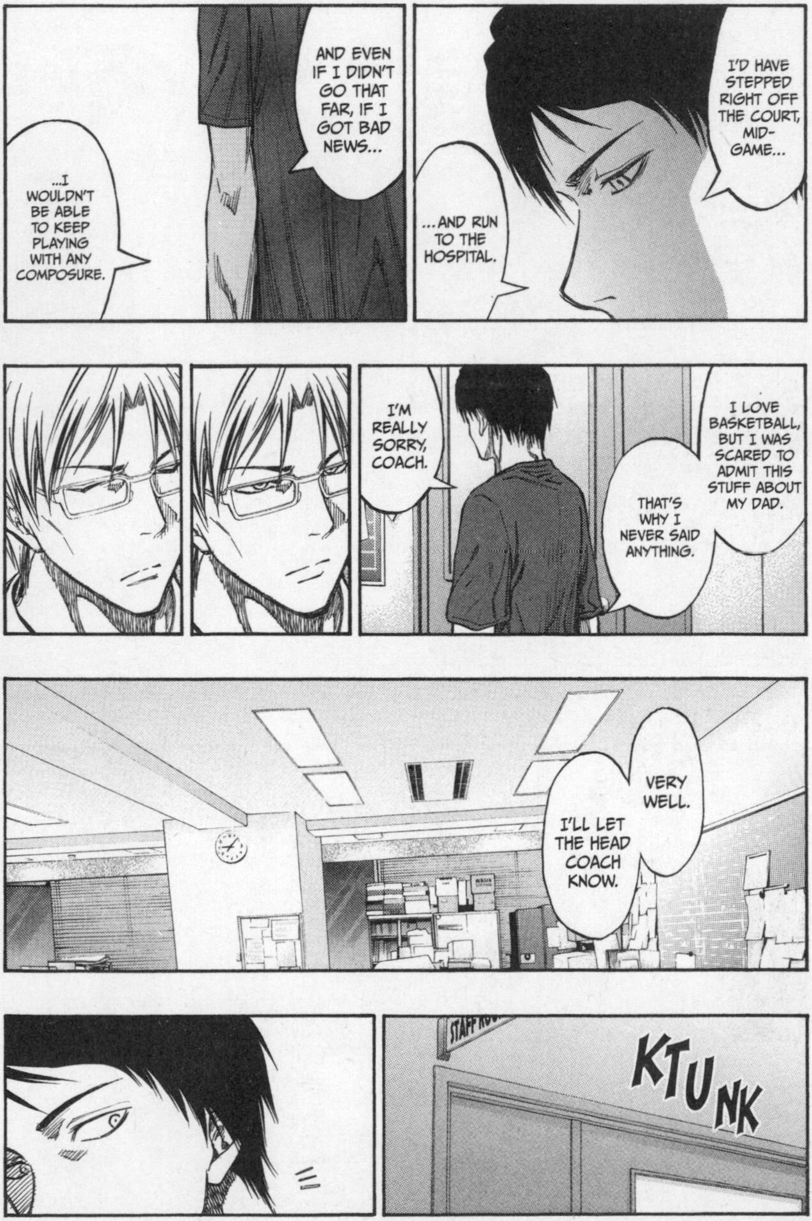
I'D HAVE STEPPED RIGHT OFF THE COURT, MID-GAME...
...AND RUN TO THE HOSPITAL.
AND EVEN IF I DIDN'T GO THAT FAR, IF I GOT BAD NEWS...
...I WOULDN'T BE ABLE TO KEEP PLAYING WITH ANY COMPOSURE.
I LOVE BASKETBALL, BUT I WAS SCARED TO ADMIT THIS STUFF ABOUT MY DAD.
THAT'S WHY I NEVER SAID ANYTHING.
I'M REALLY SORRY, COACH.
VERY WELL.
I'LL LET THE HEAD COACH KNOW.
KTUNK

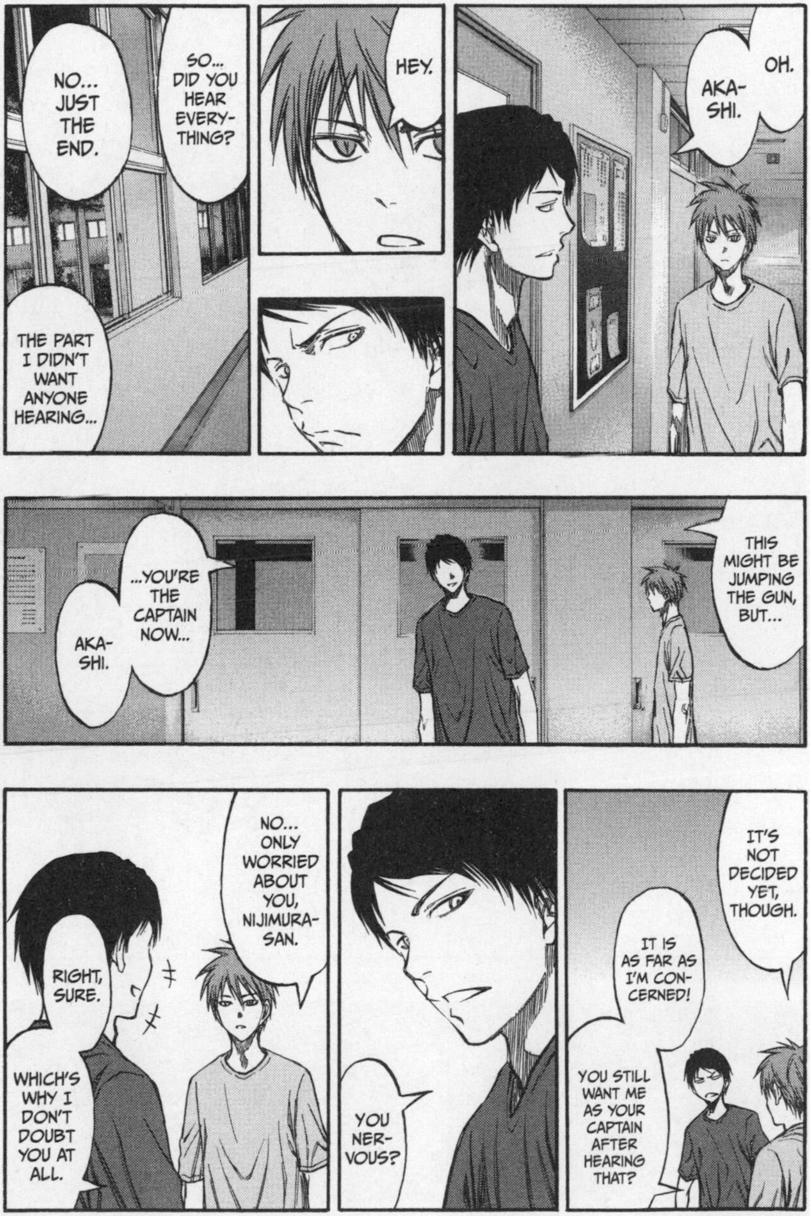
OH. AKA-SHI.
HEY.
SO... DID YOU HEAR EVERY-THING?
NO... JUST THE END.
THE PART I DIDN'T WANT ANYONE HEARING...
THIS MIGHT BE JUMPING THE GUN, BUT...
...YOU'RE THE CAPTAIN NOW...
AKA-SHI.
IT'S NOT DECIDED YET, THOUGH.
IT IS AS FAR AS I'M CON-CERNED!
YOU STILL WANT ME AS YOUR CAPTAIN AFTER HEARING THAT?
YOU NER-VOUS?
NO... ONLY WORRIED ABOUT YOU, NIJIMURA-SAN.
RIGHT, SURE.
WHICH'S WHY I DON'T DOUBT YOU AT ALL.

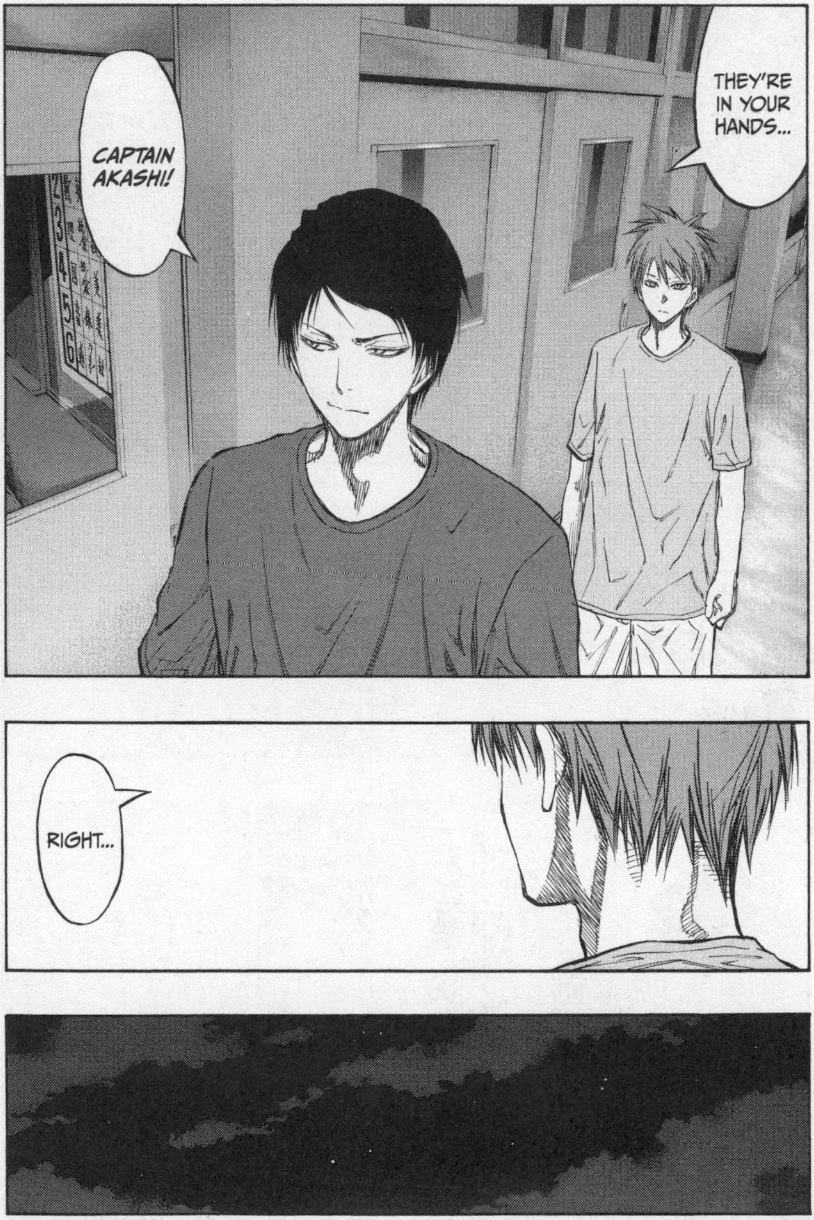
THEY'RE IN YOUR HANDS...
CAPTAIN AKASHI!
RIGHT...

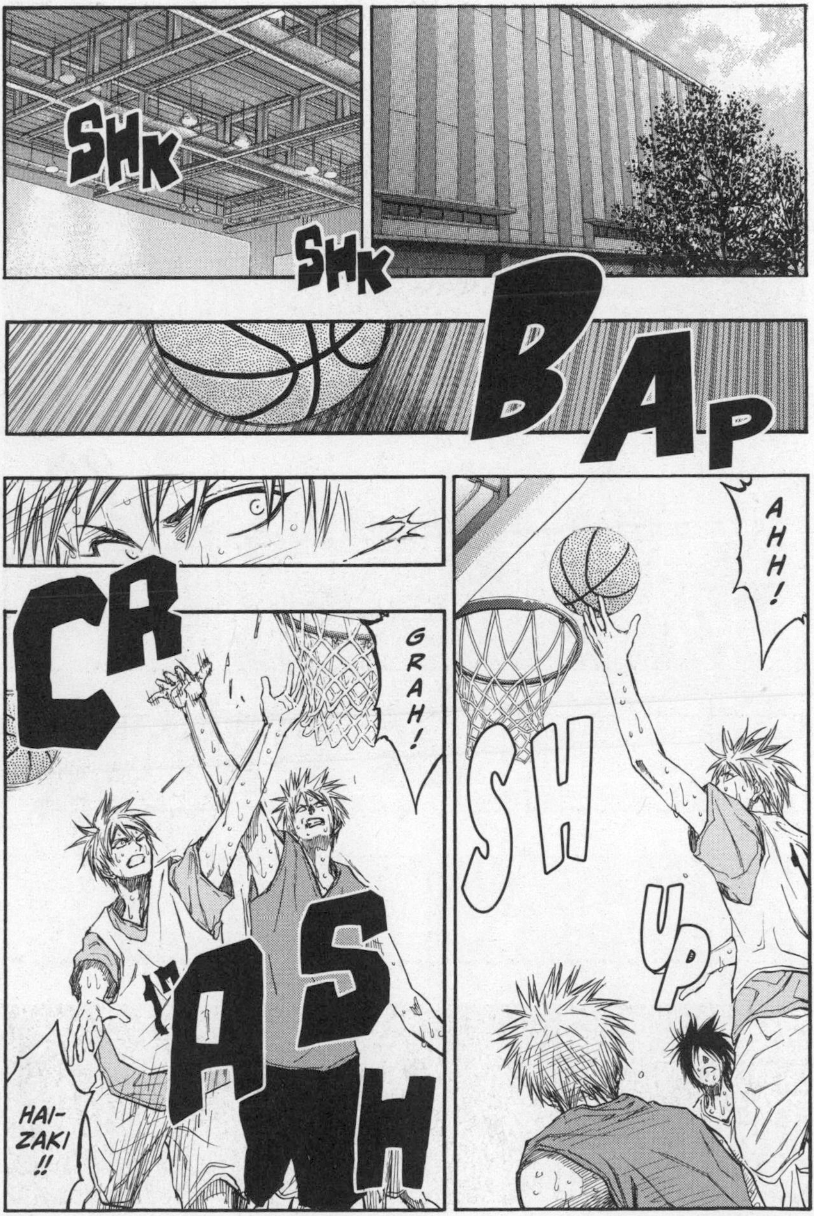
SHK
SHK
BAP
AHH!
SHUP
CRASH
GRAH!
HAI-ZAKI!!

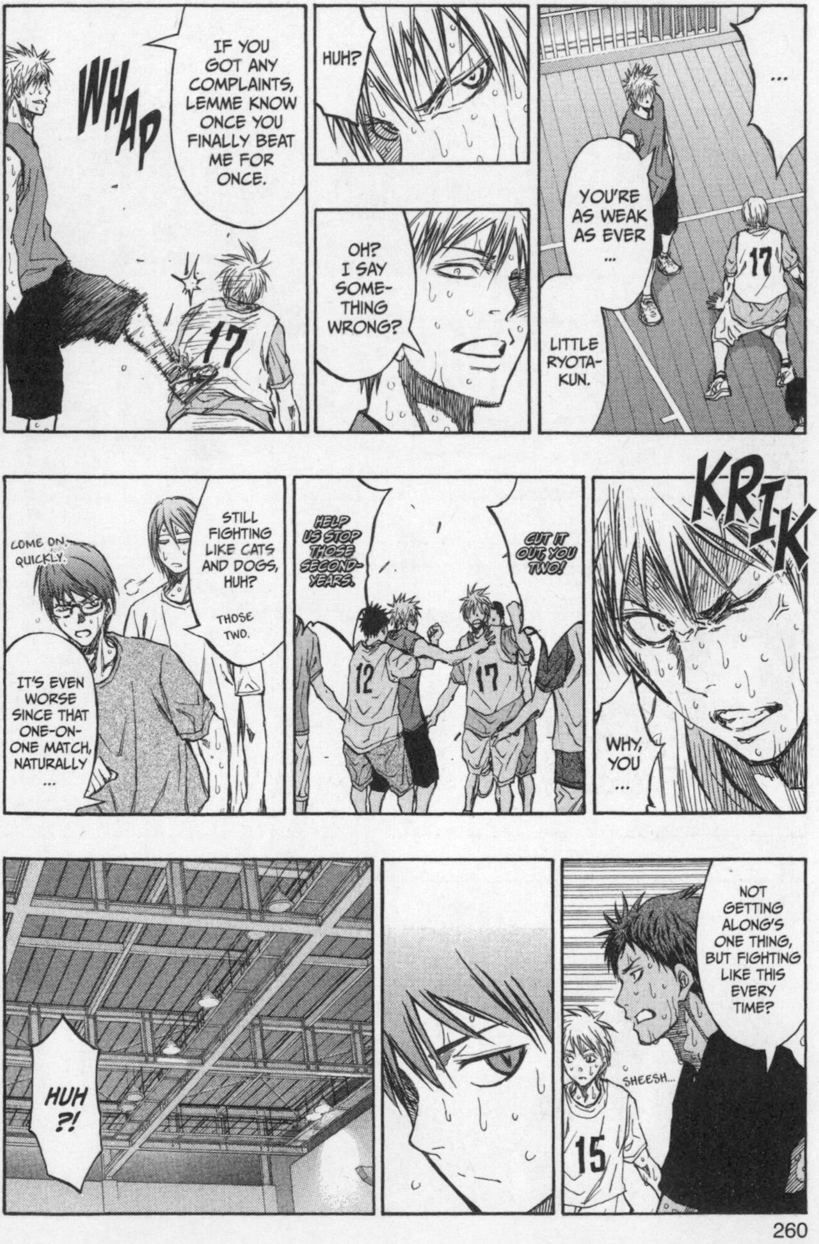
...
YOU'RE AS WEAK AS EVER ...
LITTLE RYOTA-KUN.
HUH?
OH? I SAY SOME-THING WRONG?
WHAP
IF YOU GOT ANY COMPLAINTS, LEMME KNOW ONCE YOU FINALLY BEAT ME FOR ONCE.
KRIK
WHY, YOU ...
CUT IT OUT, YOU TWO!
HELP US STOP THOSE SECOND-YEARS.
STILL FIGHTING LIKE CATS AND DOGS, HUH?
THOSE TWO.
COME ON. QUICKLY.
IT'S EVEN WORSE SINCE THAT ONE-ON-ONE MATCH, NATURALLY ...
NOT GETTING ALONG'S ONE THING, BUT FIGHTING LIKE THIS EVERY TIME?
SHEESH...
HUH ?!

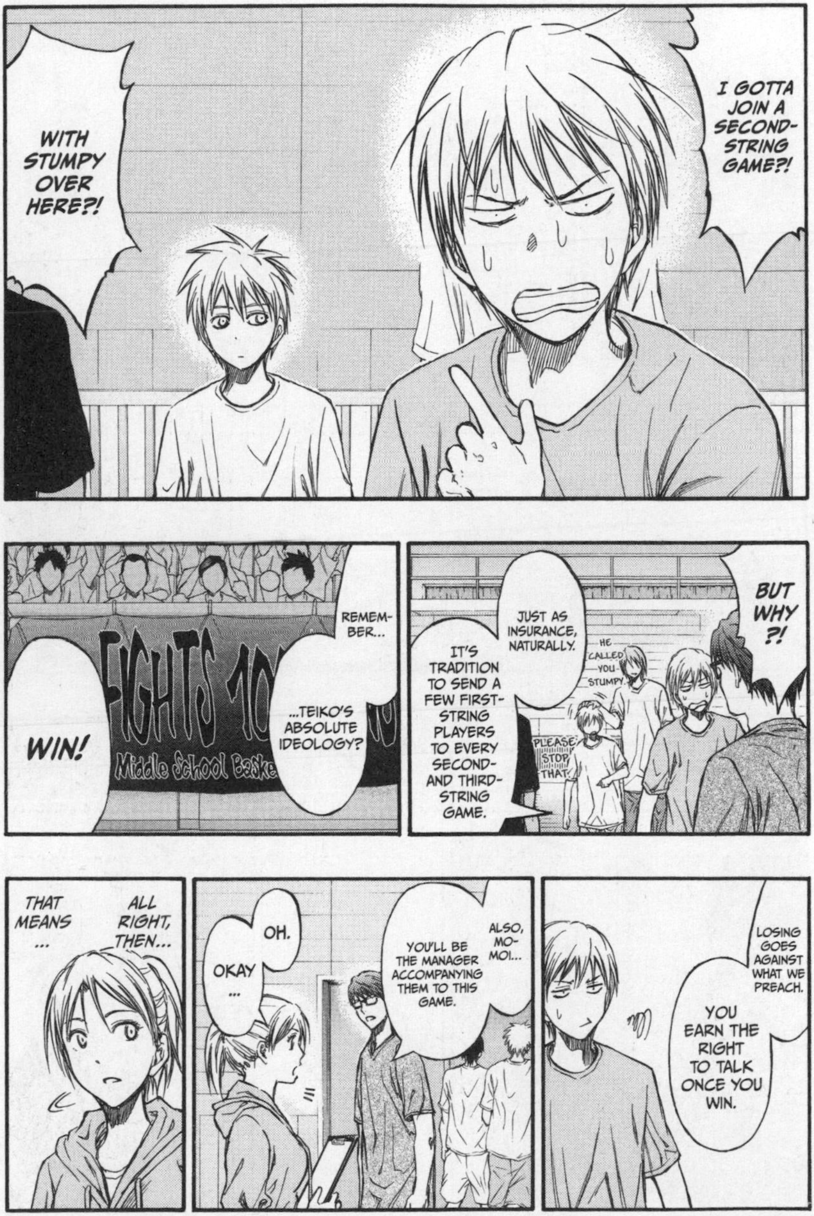
I GOTTA JOIN A SECOND-STRING GAME?!
WITH STUMPY OVER HERE?!
BUT WHY?!
JUST AS INSURANCE, NATURALLY.
IT'S TRADITION TO SEND A FEW FIRST-STRING PLAYERS TO EVERY SECOND- AND THIRD-STRING GAME.
HE CALLED YOU STUMPY.
PLEASE STOP THAT.
REMEMBER...
...TEIKO'S ABSOLUTE IDEOLOGY?
WIN!
LOSING GOES AGAINST WHAT WE PREACH.
YOU EARN THE RIGHT TO TALK ONCE YOU WIN.
ALSO, MOMOI...
YOU'LL BE THE MANAGER ACCOMPANYING THEM TO THIS GAME.
OH.
OKAY...
ALL RIGHT, THEN...
THAT MEANS...

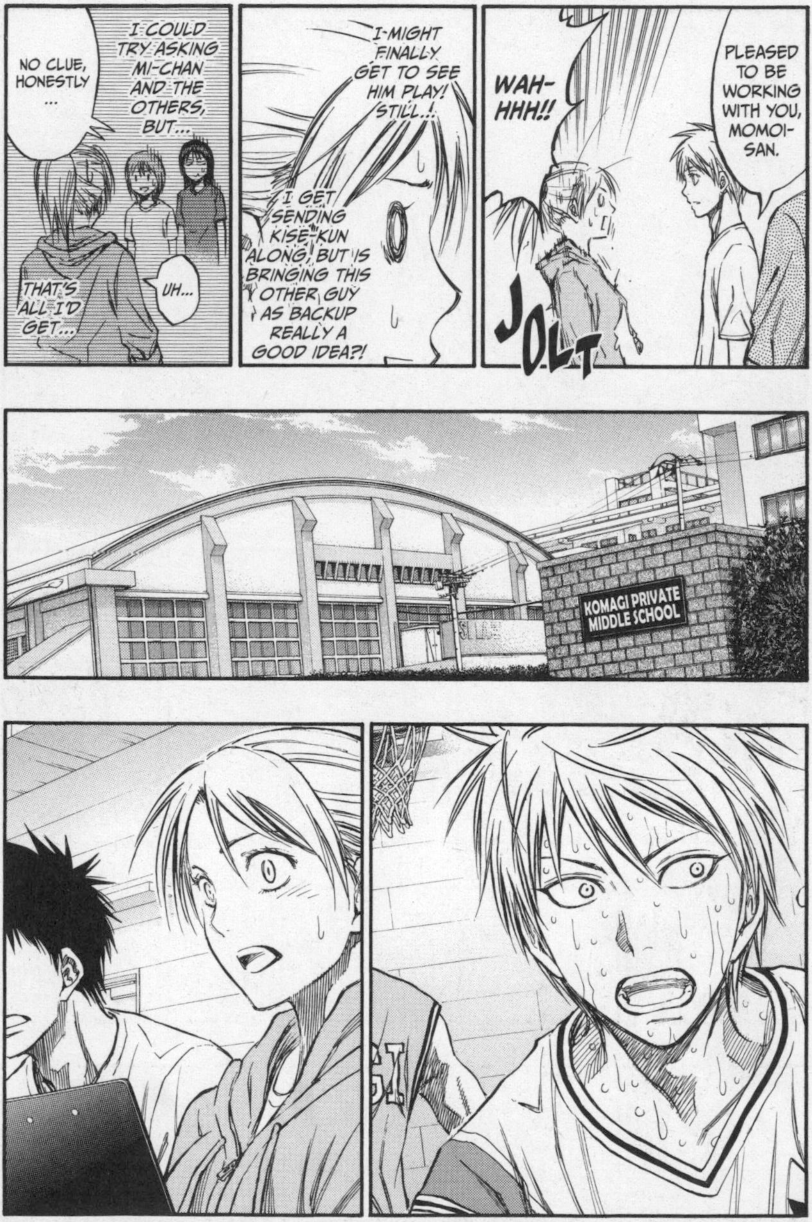
PLEASED TO BE WORKING WITH YOU, MOMOI-SAN.
WAH-HHH!!
JOLT
I-MIGHT FINALLY GET TO SEE HIM PLAY! STILL..!
I GET SENDING KISE-KUN ALONG, BUT IS BRINGING THIS OTHER GUY AS BACKUP REALLY A GOOD IDEA?!
I COULD TRY ASKING MI-CHAN AND THE OTHERS, BUT...
NO CLUE, HONESTLY ...
UH...
THAT'S ALL I'D GET...
KOMAGI PRIVATE MIDDLE SCHOOL

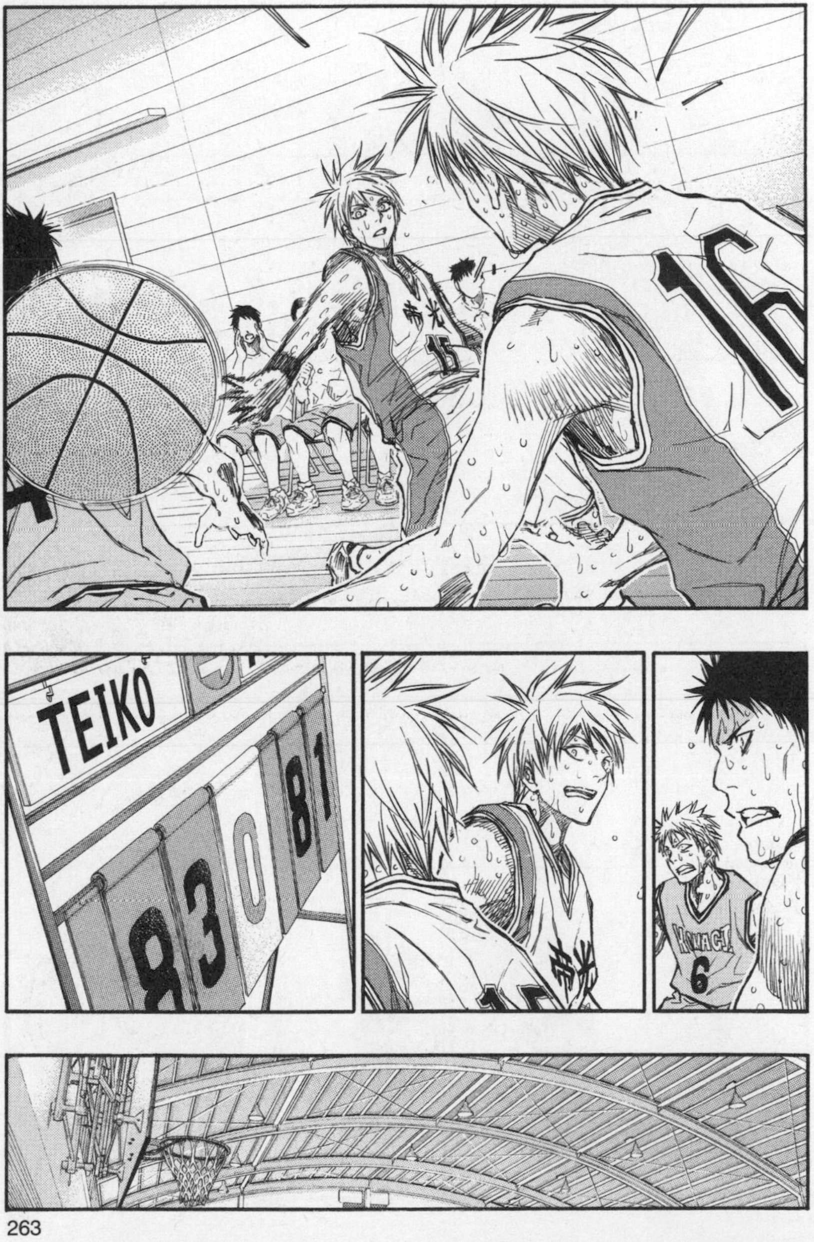
TEIKO
83
81

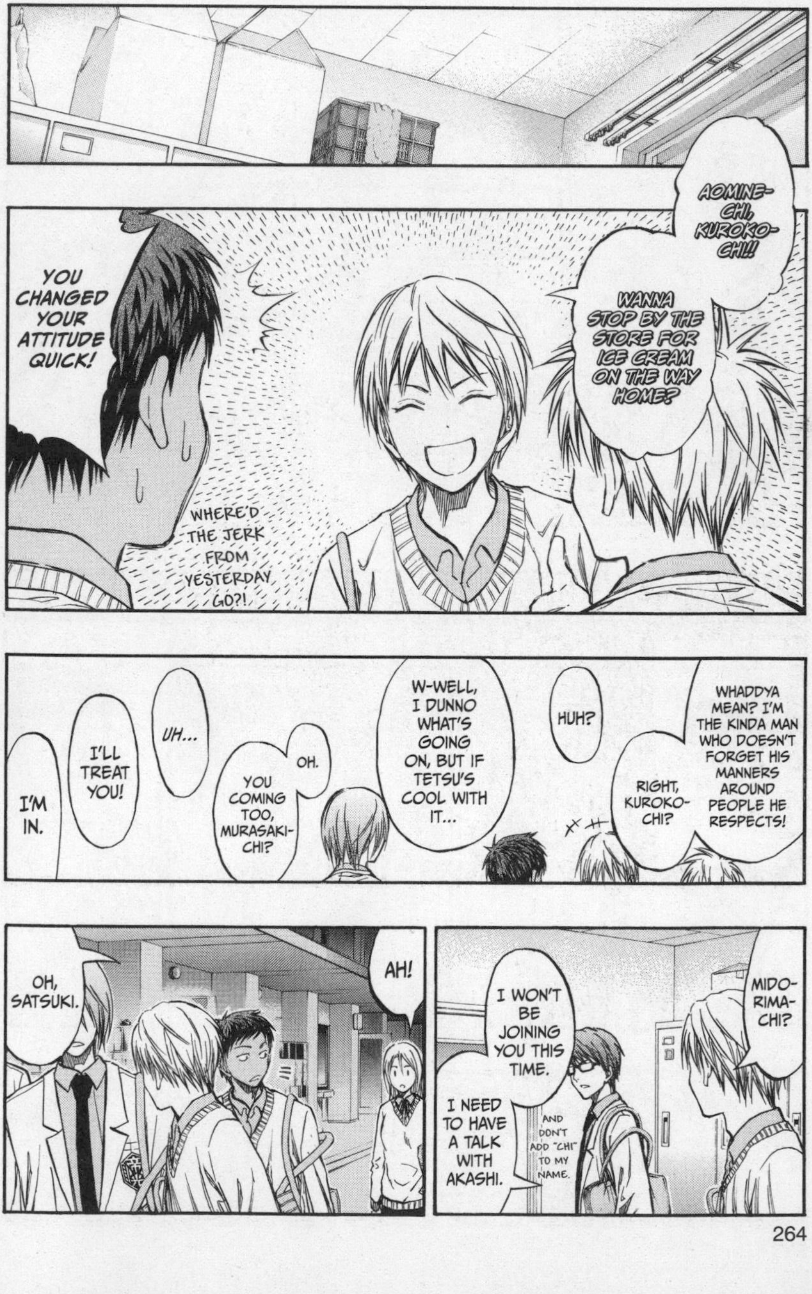
AOMINE-CHI, KUROKO-CHI!!
WANNA STOP BY THE STORE FOR ICE CREAM ON THE WAY HOME?
YOU CHANGED YOUR ATTITUDE QUICK!
WHERE'D THE JERK FROM YESTERDAY GO?!
WHADDYA MEAN? I'M THE KINDA MAN WHO DOESN'T FORGET HIS MANNERS AROUND PEOPLE HE RESPECTS!
RIGHT, KUROKO-CHI?
HUH?
W-WELL, I DUNNO WHAT'S GOING ON, BUT IF TETSU'S COOL WITH IT...
OH.
YOU COMING TOO, MURASAKI-CHI?
UH...
I'LL TREAT YOU!
I'M IN.
MIDO-RIMA-CHI?
I WON'T BE JOINING YOU THIS TIME.
AND DON'T ADD "CHI" TO MY NAME.
I NEED TO HAVE A TALK WITH AKASHI.
AH!
OH, SATSUKI.

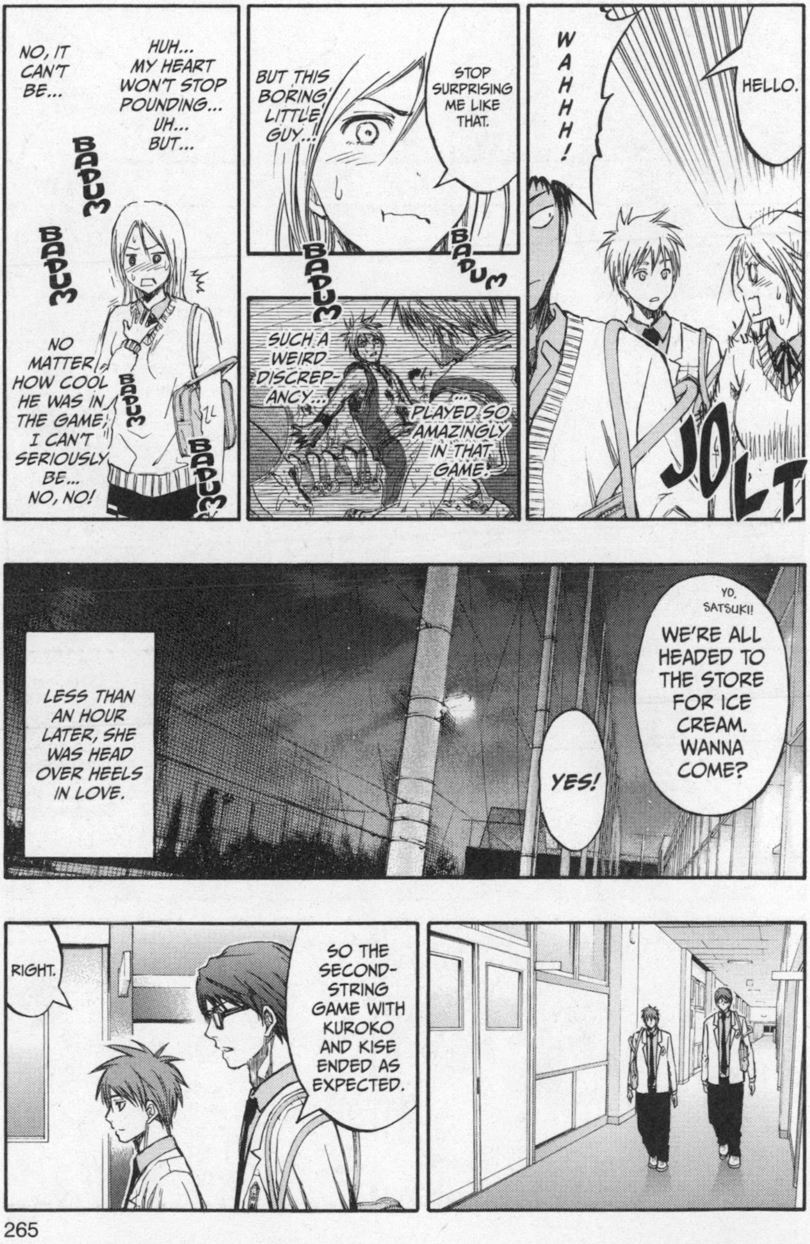
HELLO.
WAHHH!
JOLT
STOP SURPRISING ME LIKE THAT.
BUT THIS BORING LITTLE GUY...
BADUM
BADUM
...PLAYED SO AMAZINGLY IN THAT GAME.
SUCH A WEIRD DISCREPANCY...
HUH... MY HEART WON'T STOP POUNDING... UH... BUT...
NO, IT CAN'T BE...
BADUM
BADUM
BADUM
BADUM
NO MATTER HOW COOL HE WAS IN THE GAME, I CAN'T SERIOUSLY BE... NO, NO!
YO, SATSUKI!
WE'RE ALL HEADED TO THE STORE FOR ICE CREAM. WANNA COME?
YES!
LESS THAN AN HOUR LATER, SHE WAS HEAD OVER HEELS IN LOVE.
SO THE SECOND-STRING GAME WITH KUROKO AND KISE ENDED AS EXPECTED.
RIGHT.

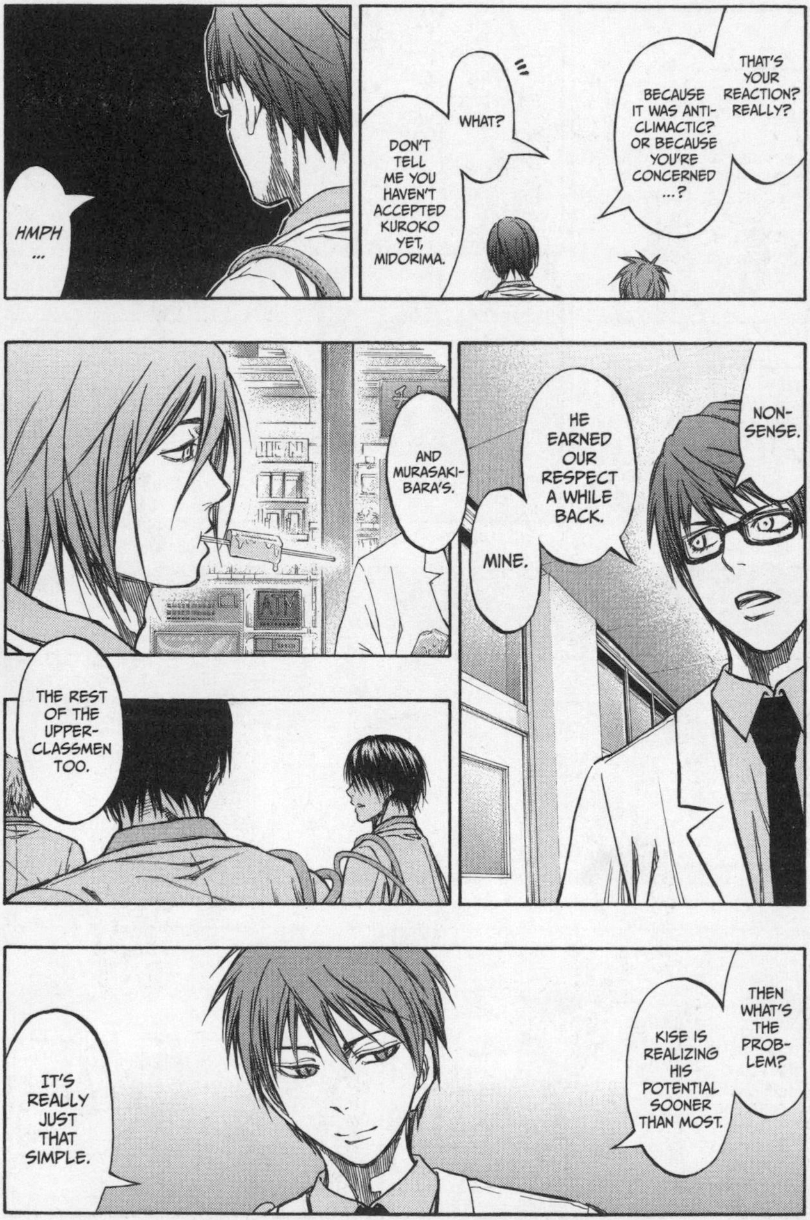
THAT'S YOUR REACTION? REALLY?
BECAUSE IT WAS ANTI-CLIMACTIC? OR BECAUSE YOU'RE CONCERNED ...?
WHAT?
DON'T TELL ME YOU HAVEN'T ACCEPTED KUROKO YET, MIDORIMA.
HMPH ...
NON-SENSE.
HE EARNED OUR RESPECT A WHILE BACK.
MINE.
AND MURASAKI-BARA'S.
THE REST OF THE UPPER-CLASSMEN TOO.
THEN WHAT'S THE PROB-LEM?
KISE IS REALIZING HIS POTENTIAL SOONER THAN MOST.
IT'S REALLY JUST THAT SIMPLE.

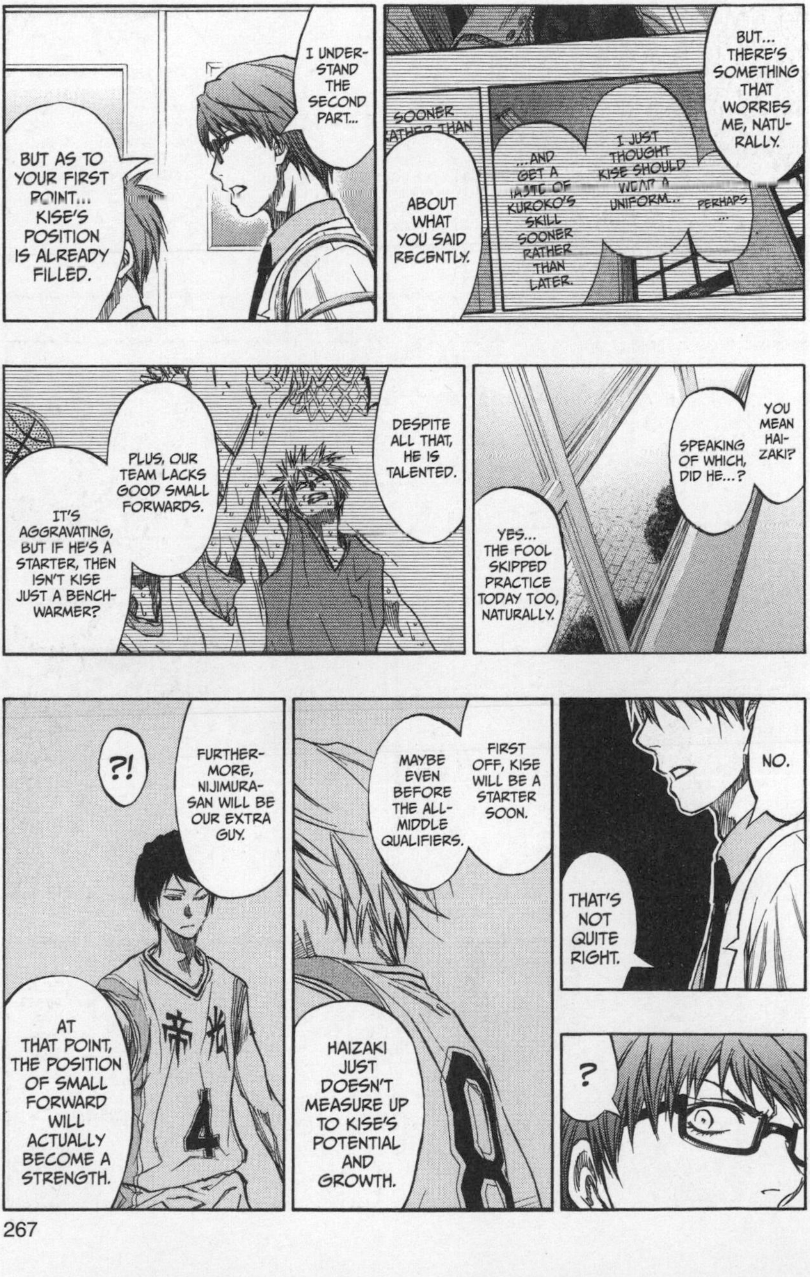
BUT... THERE'S SOMETHING THAT WORRIES ME, NATURALLY.
PERHAPS...
I JUST THOUGHT KISE SHOULD WEAR A UNIFORM...
...AND GET A TASTE OF KUROKO'S SKILL SOONER RATHER THAN LATER.
SOONER
ABOUT WHAT YOU SAID RECENTLY.
I UNDERSTAND THE SECOND PART...
BUT AS TO YOUR FIRST POINT... KISE'S POSITION IS ALREADY FILLED.
YOU MEAN HAIZAKI?
SPEAKING OF WHICH, DID HE...?
YES... THE FOOL SKIPPED PRACTICE TODAY TOO, NATURALLY.
DESPITE ALL THAT, HE IS TALENTED.
PLUS, OUR TEAM LACKS GOOD SMALL FORWARDS.
IT'S AGGRAVATING, BUT IF HE'S A STARTER, THEN ISN'T KISE JUST A BENCHWARMER?
NO.
THAT'S NOT QUITE RIGHT.
?
FIRST OFF, KISE WILL BE A STARTER SOON.
MAYBE EVEN BEFORE THE ALL-MIDDLE QUALIFIERS.
HAIZAKI JUST DOESN'T MEASURE UP TO KISE'S POTENTIAL AND GROWTH.
FURTHERMORE, NIJIMURA-SAN WILL BE OUR EXTRA GUY.
?!
AT THAT POINT, THE POSITION OF SMALL FORWARD WILL ACTUALLY BECOME A STRENGTH.

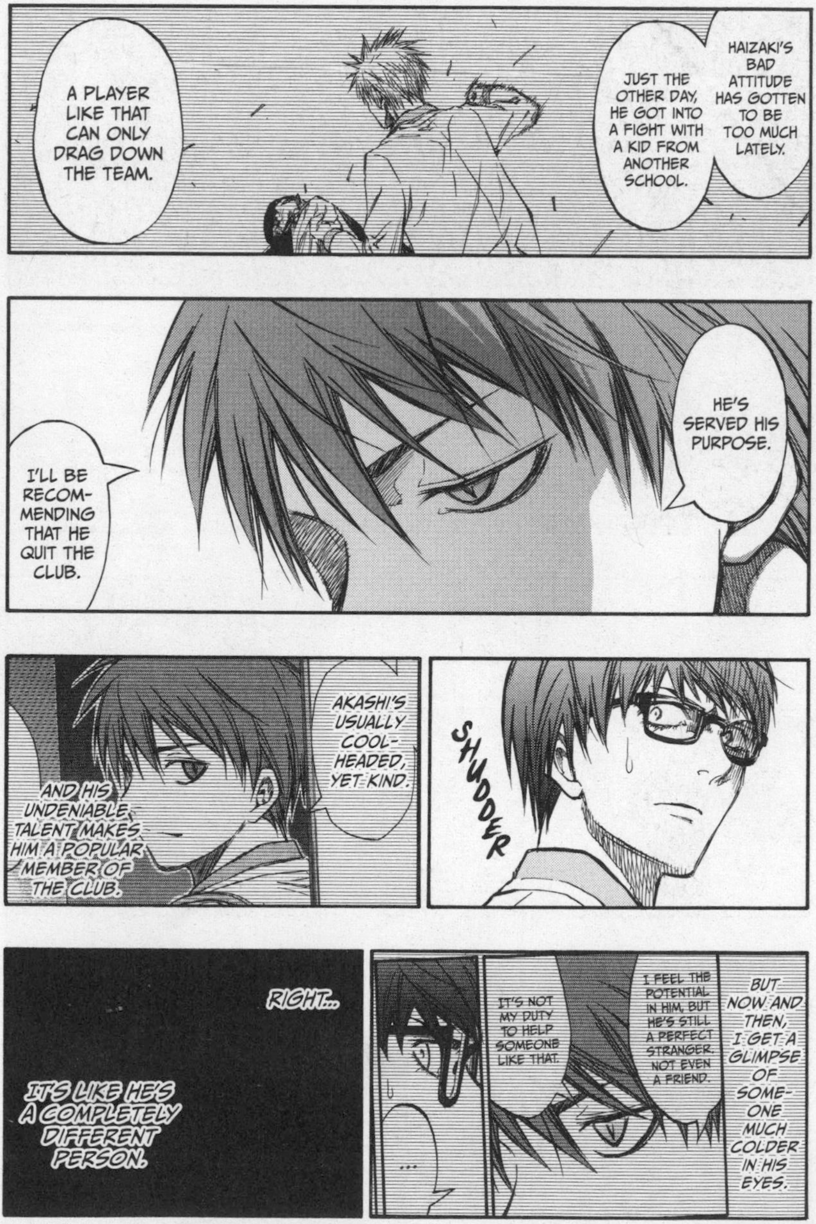
HAIZAKI'S BAD ATTITUDE HAS GOTTEN TO BE TOO MUCH LATELY.
JUST THE OTHER DAY, HE GOT INTO A FIGHT WITH A KID FROM ANOTHER SCHOOL.
A PLAYER LIKE THAT CAN ONLY DRAG DOWN THE TEAM.
HE'S SERVED HIS PURPOSE.
I'LL BE RECOMMENDING THAT HE QUIT THE CLUB.
SHUDDER
AKASHI'S USUALLY COOL-HEADED, YET KIND.
AND HIS UNDENIABLE TALENT MAKES HIM A POPULAR MEMBER OF THE CLUB.
BUT NOW AND THEN, I GET A GLIMPSE OF SOMEONE MUCH COLDER IN HIS EYES.
I FEEL THE POTENTIAL IN HIM, BUT HE'S STILL A PERFECT STRANGER. NOT EVEN A FRIEND.
IT'S NOT MY DUTY TO HELP SOMEONE LIKE THAT.
...
RIGHT...
IT'S LIKE HE'S A COMPLETELY DIFFERENT PERSON.

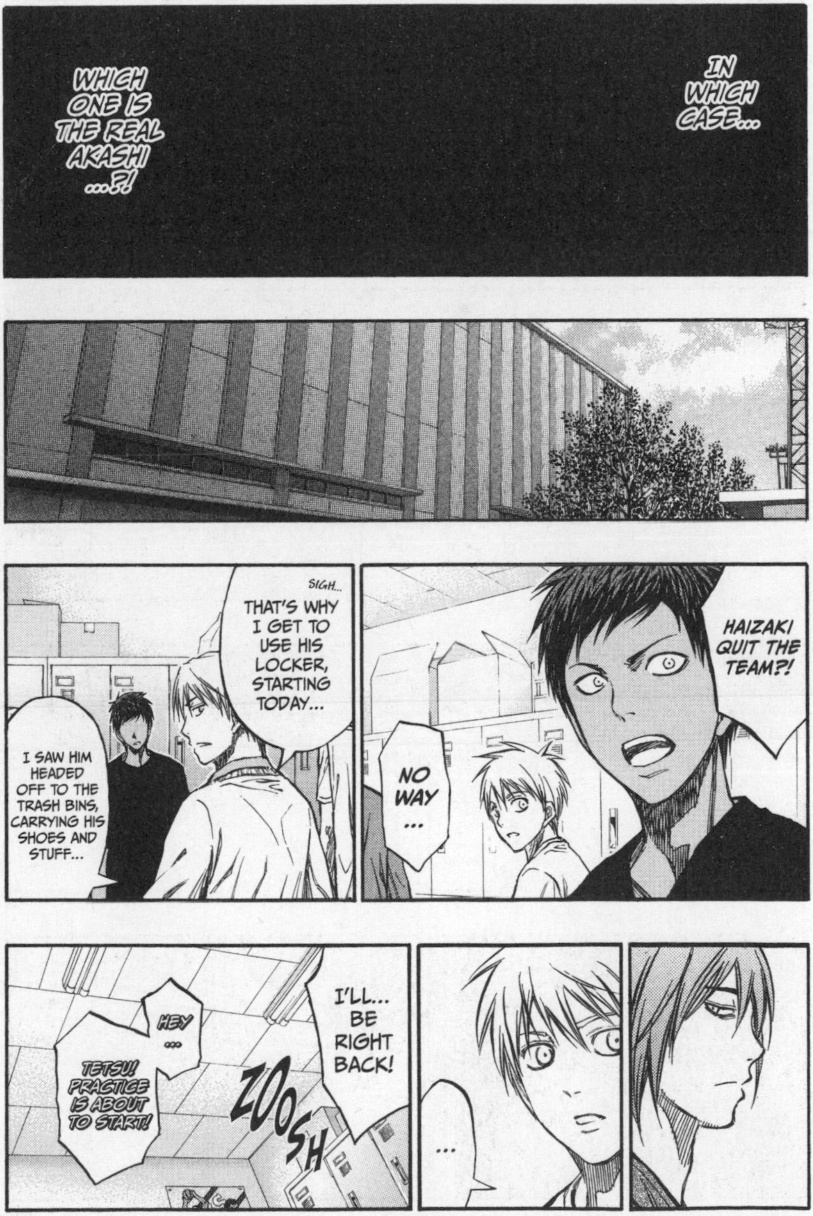
IN WHICH CASE...
WHICH ONE IS THE REAL AKASHI ...?!
HAIZAKI QUIT THE TEAM?!
NO WAY ...
SIGH...
THAT'S WHY I GET TO USE HIS LOCKER, STARTING TODAY...
I SAW HIM HEADED OFF TO THE TRASH BINS, CARRYING HIS SHOES AND STUFF...
...
I'LL... BE RIGHT BACK!
ZOOSH
HEY ...
TETSU! PRACTICE IS ABOUT TO START!

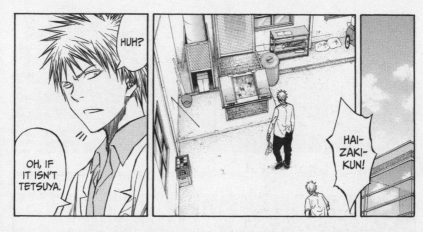

HAI-ZAKI-KUN!
HUH?
OH, IF IT ISN'T TETSUYA.
I HEARD YOU QUIT THE TEAM.
IS THAT TRUE?
YUP. SURE IS.
HA HA.
WHAT'D YOU COME HERE FOR ANYWAY, IDIOT?
IT'S NOT LIKE WE'RE FRIENDS OR ANYTHING.
THAT'S NOT WHY I'M HERE.
IT'S JUST THAT YOU HAVE A LOT OF TALENT, SO WHY WOULD YOU...?
SHADDUP.
I GOT BORED OF BASKETBALL.
THAT'S ALL IT IS, IDIOT.
GETTING ALL TIRED, STINKIN' OF SWEAT...
HANGING OUT WITH THE LADIES IS WAY MORE FUN.
IS THAT...
...HOW YOU REALLY FEEL, HAIZAKI-KUN?

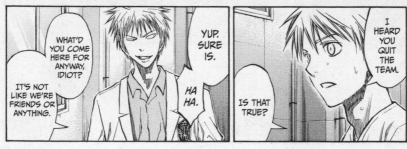

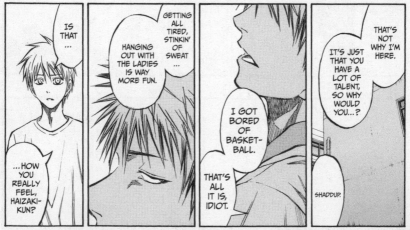

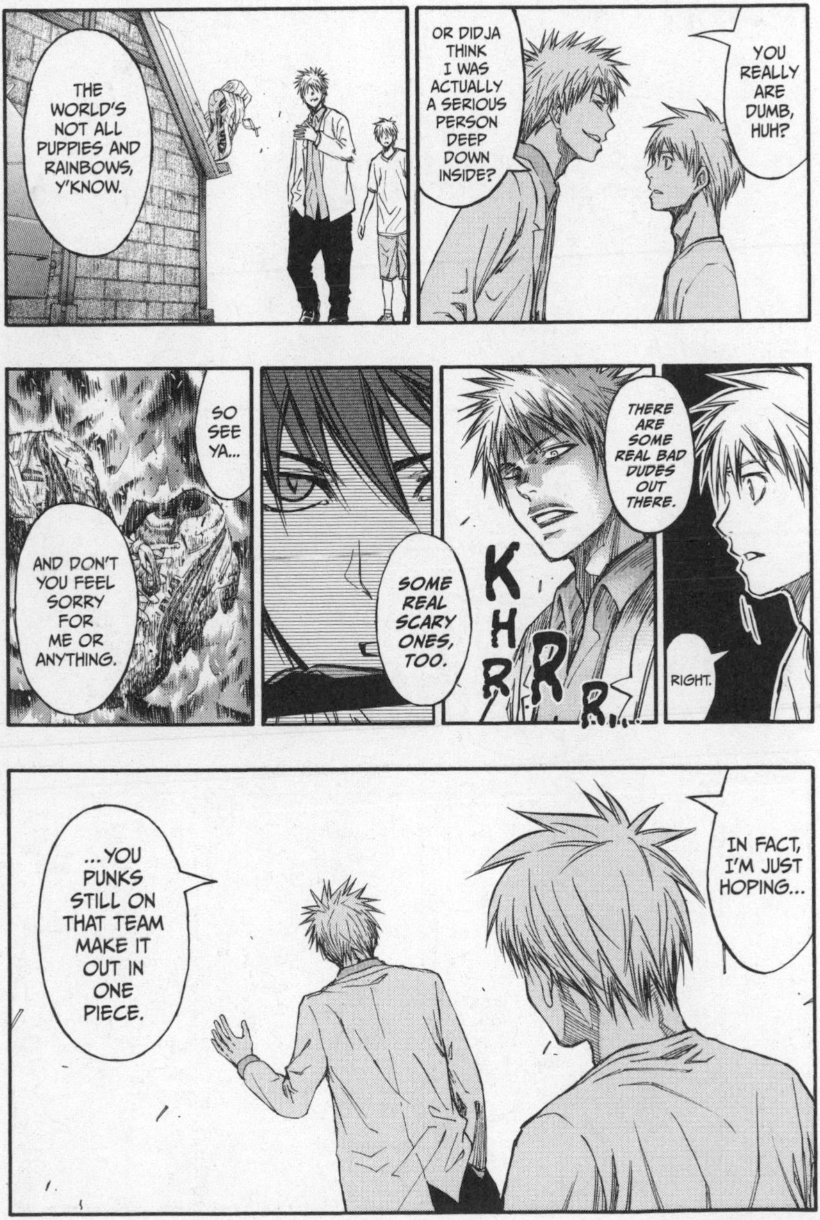
YOU REALLY ARE DUMB, HUH?
OR DIDJA THINK I WAS ACTUALLY A SERIOUS PERSON DEEP DOWN INSIDE?
THE WORLD'S NOT ALL PUPPIES AND RAINBOWS, Y'KNOW.
RIGHT.
THERE ARE SOME REAL BAD DUDES OUT THERE.
KHRRR...
SOME REAL SCARY ONES, TOO.
SO SEE YA...
AND DON'T YOU FEEL SORRY FOR ME OR ANYTHING.
IN FACT, I'M JUST HOPING...
...YOU PUNKS STILL ON THAT TEAM MAKE IT OUT IN ONE PIECE.

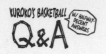

KUROKO'S BASKETBALL Q&A
W/ HALFWAY-DECENT ANSWERS

Q. **PLEASE STOP PICKING ON KISE-KUN.**
(XE from KYOTO PREFECTURE)

A. WHUUUT?!

KUROKO'S BASKETBALL BLOOPERS

TAKE 7

NON-SENSE.
HE EARNED OUR RESPECT A WHILE BACK.
MINE.
AND MURA-SAKI-BARA'S.
SWIP
SPLAT
MURA-SAKI-BARA?! WHAT HAP-PENED ?!
ADMINE

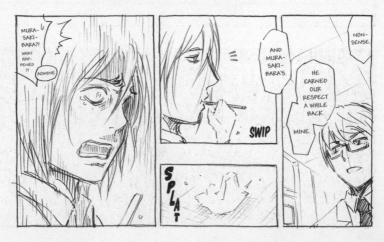

212TH QUARTER:

LIKE I CAN'T LOSE

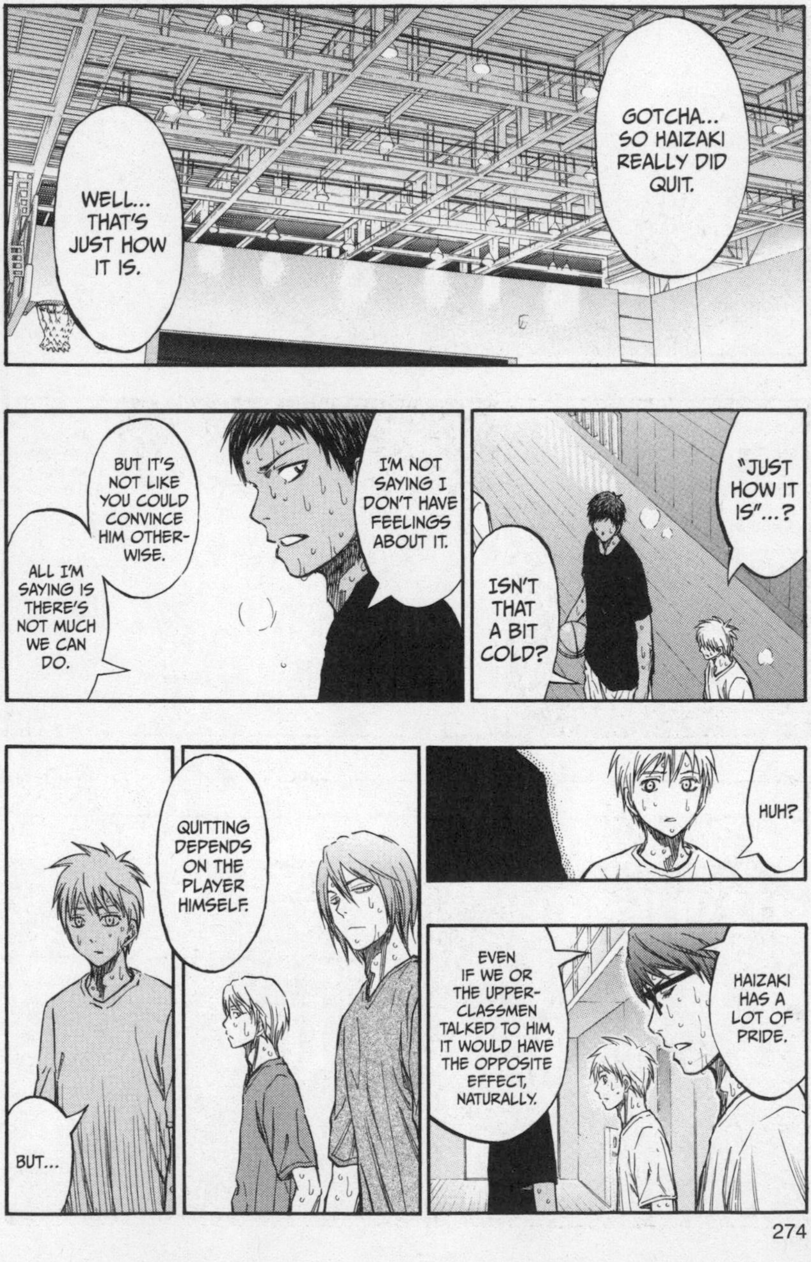
GOTCHA... SO HAIZAKI REALLY DID QUIT.
WELL... THAT'S JUST HOW IT IS.
"JUST HOW IT IS"...?
ISN'T THAT A BIT COLD?
I'M NOT SAYING I DON'T HAVE FEELINGS ABOUT IT.
BUT IT'S NOT LIKE YOU COULD CONVINCE HIM OTHER-WISE.
ALL I'M SAYING IS THERE'S NOT MUCH WE CAN DO.
HUH?
HAIZAKI HAS A LOT OF PRIDE.
EVEN IF WE OR THE UPPER-CLASSMEN TALKED TO HIM, IT WOULD HAVE THE OPPOSITE EFFECT, NATURALLY.
QUITTING DEPENDS ON THE PLAYER HIMSELF.
BUT...

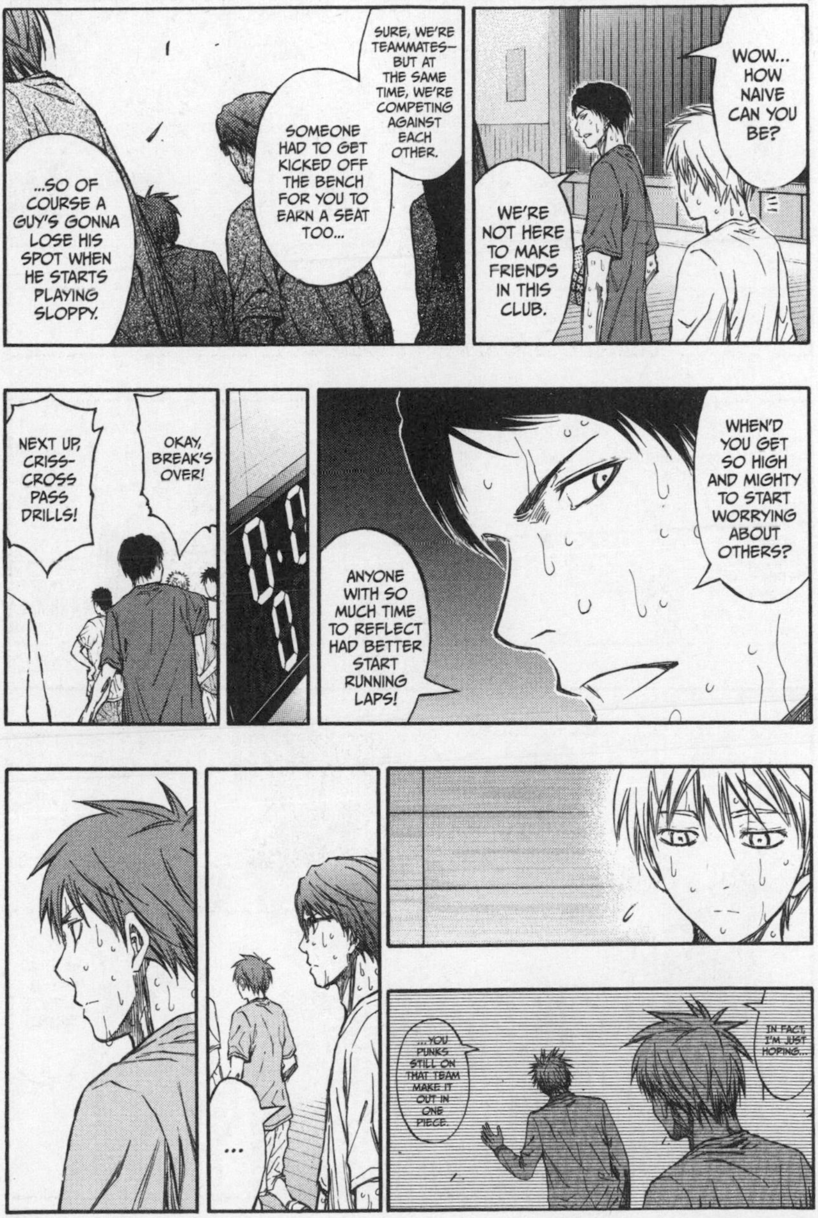
WOW... HOW NAIVE CAN YOU BE?
WE'RE NOT HERE TO MAKE FRIENDS IN THIS CLUB.
SURE, WE'RE TEAMMATES—BUT AT THE SAME TIME, WE'RE COMPETING AGAINST EACH OTHER.
SOMEONE HAD TO GET KICKED OFF THE BENCH FOR YOU TO EARN A SEAT TOO...
...SO OF COURSE A GUY'S GONNA LOSE HIS SPOT WHEN HE STARTS PLAYING SLOPPY.
WHEN'D YOU GET SO HIGH AND MIGHTY TO START WORRYING ABOUT OTHERS?
ANYONE WITH SO MUCH TIME TO REFLECT HAD BETTER START RUNNING LAPS!
OKAY, BREAK'S OVER!
NEXT UP, CRISS-CROSS PASS DRILLS!
IN FACT, I'M JUST HOPING...
...YOU PUNKS STILL ON THAT TEAM MAKE IT OUT IN ONE PIECE.
...

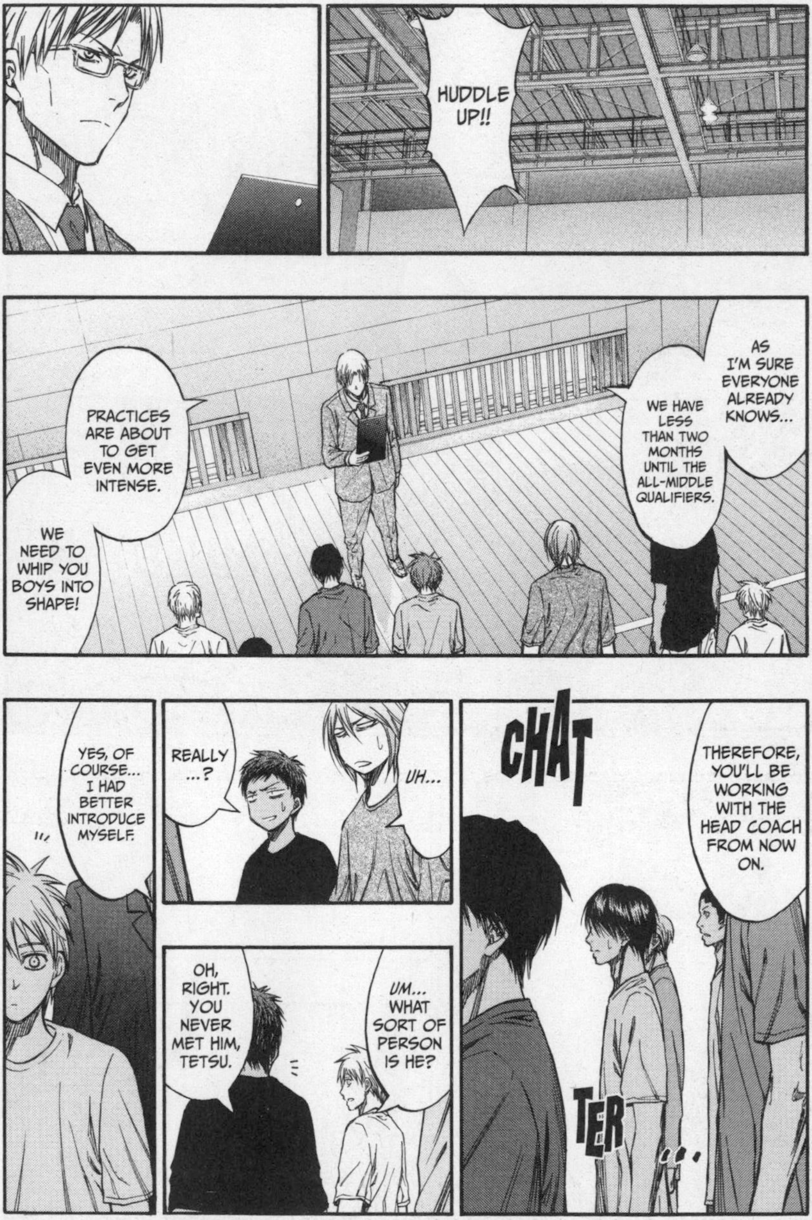
HUDDLE UP!!
AS I'M SURE EVERYONE ALREADY KNOWS...
WE HAVE LESS THAN TWO MONTHS UNTIL THE ALL-MIDDLE QUALIFIERS.
PRACTICES ARE ABOUT TO GET EVEN MORE INTENSE.
WE NEED TO WHIP YOU BOYS INTO SHAPE!
THEREFORE, YOU'LL BE WORKING WITH THE HEAD COACH FROM NOW ON.
CHAT
TER...
UH...
REALLY ...?
UM... WHAT SORT OF PERSON IS HE?
OH, RIGHT. YOU NEVER MET HIM, TETSU.
YES, OF COURSE... I HAD BETTER INTRODUCE MYSELF.

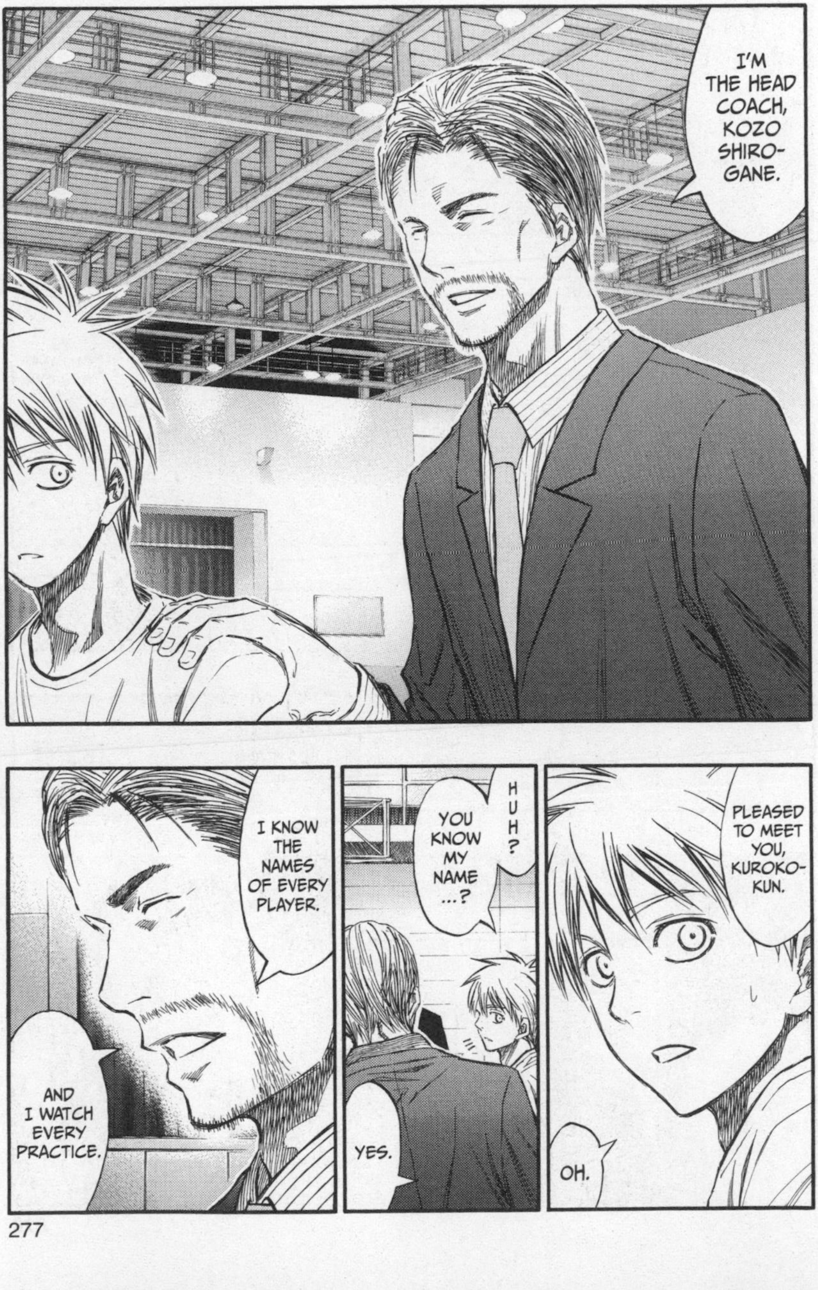
I'M THE HEAD COACH, KOZO SHIRO-GANE.
PLEASED TO MEET YOU, KUROKO-KUN.
OH.
HUH?
YOU KNOW MY NAME ...?
YES.
I KNOW THE NAMES OF EVERY PLAYER.
AND I WATCH EVERY PRACTICE.

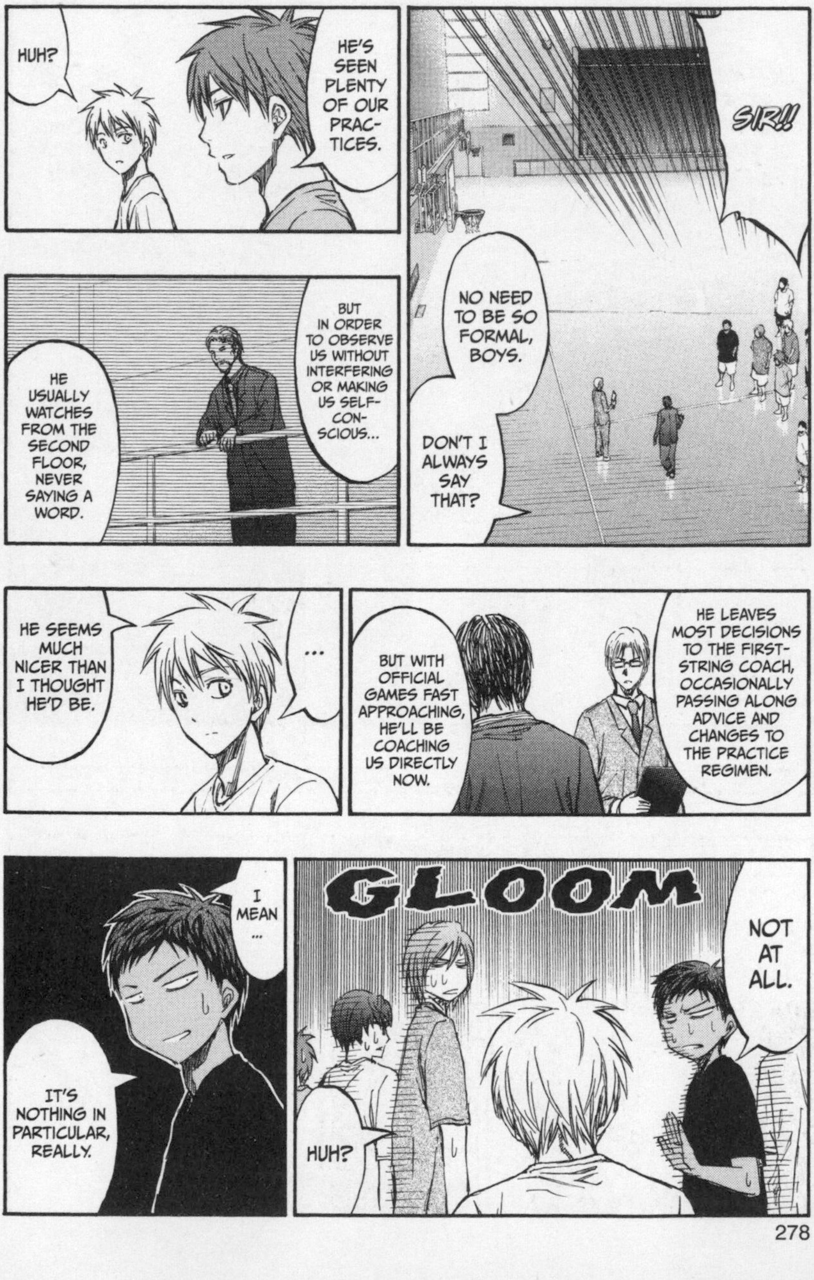
SIR!!
NO NEED TO BE SO FORMAL, BOYS.
DON'T I ALWAYS SAY THAT?
HE'S SEEN PLENTY OF OUR PRAC-TICES.
HUH?
BUT IN ORDER TO OBSERVE US WITHOUT INTERFERING OR MAKING US SELF-CON-SCIOUS...
HE USUALLY WATCHES FROM THE SECOND FLOOR, NEVER SAYING A WORD.
HE LEAVES MOST DECISIONS TO THE FIRST-STRING COACH, OCCASIONALLY PASSING ALONG ADVICE AND CHANGES TO THE PRACTICE REGIMEN.
BUT WITH OFFICIAL GAMES FAST APPROACHING, HE'LL BE COACHING US DIRECTLY NOW.
...
HE SEEMS MUCH NICER THAN I THOUGHT HE'D BE.
GLOOM
NOT AT ALL.
HUH?
I MEAN ...
IT'S NOTHING IN PARTICULAR, REALLY.

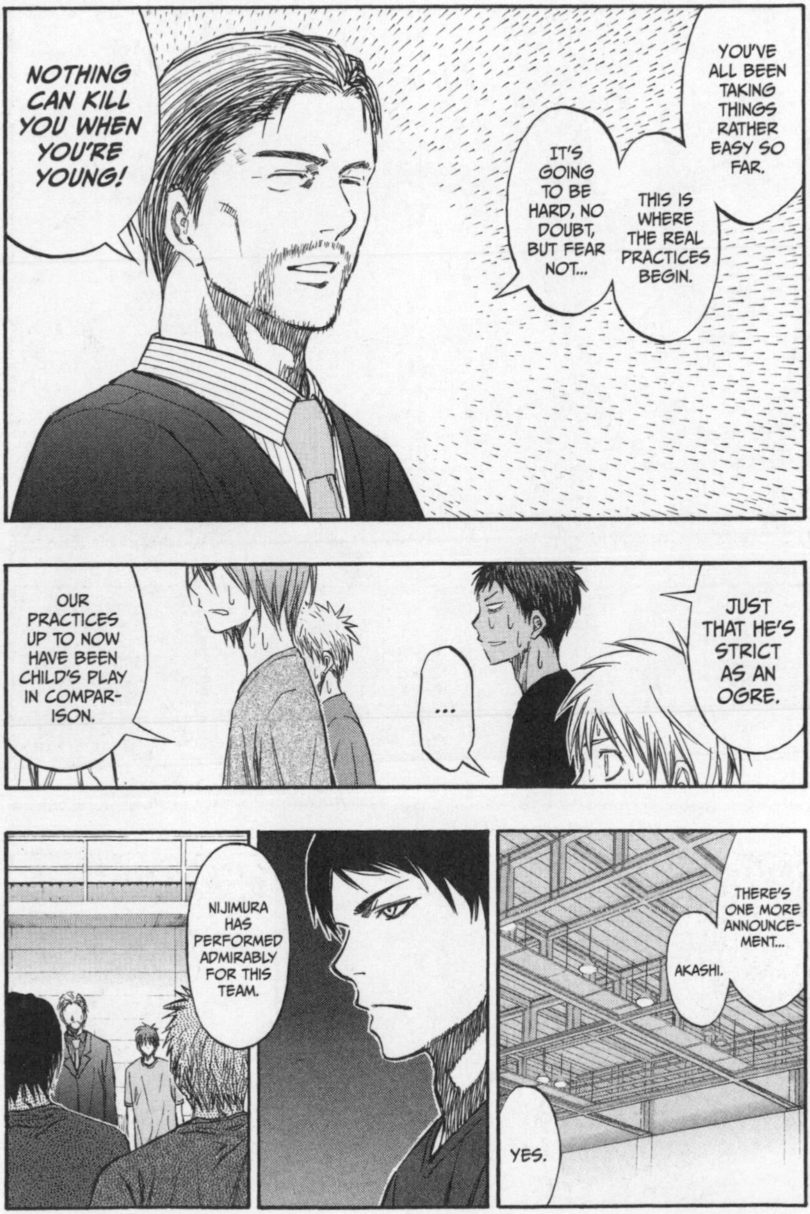
YOU'VE ALL BEEN TAKING THINGS RATHER EASY SO FAR.
THIS IS WHERE THE REAL PRACTICES BEGIN.
IT'S GOING TO BE HARD, NO DOUBT, BUT FEAR NOT...
NOTHING CAN KILL YOU WHEN YOU'RE YOUNG!
JUST THAT HE'S STRICT AS AN OGRE.
...
OUR PRACTICES UP TO NOW HAVE BEEN CHILD'S PLAY IN COMPAR-ISON.
THERE'S ONE MORE ANNOUNCE-MENT...
AKASHI.
YES.
NIJIMURA HAS PERFORMED ADMIRABLY FOR THIS TEAM.

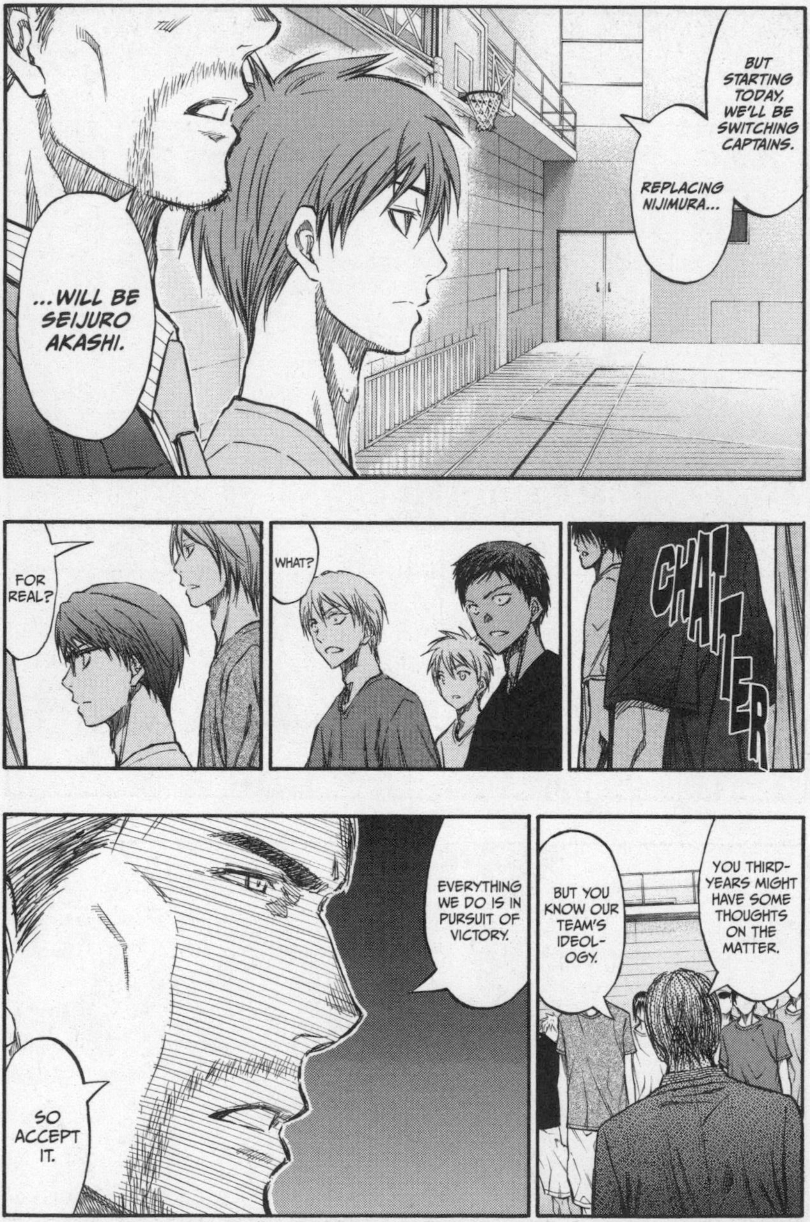
BUT STARTING TODAY, WE'LL BE SWITCHING CAPTAINS.
REPLACING NIJIMURA...
...WILL BE SEIJURO AKASHI.
CHATTER
WHAT?
FOR REAL?
YOU THIRD-YEARS MIGHT HAVE SOME THOUGHTS ON THE MATTER.
BUT YOU KNOW OUR TEAM'S IDEOL-OGY.
EVERYTHING WE DO IS IN PURSUIT OF VICTORY.
SO ACCEPT IT.

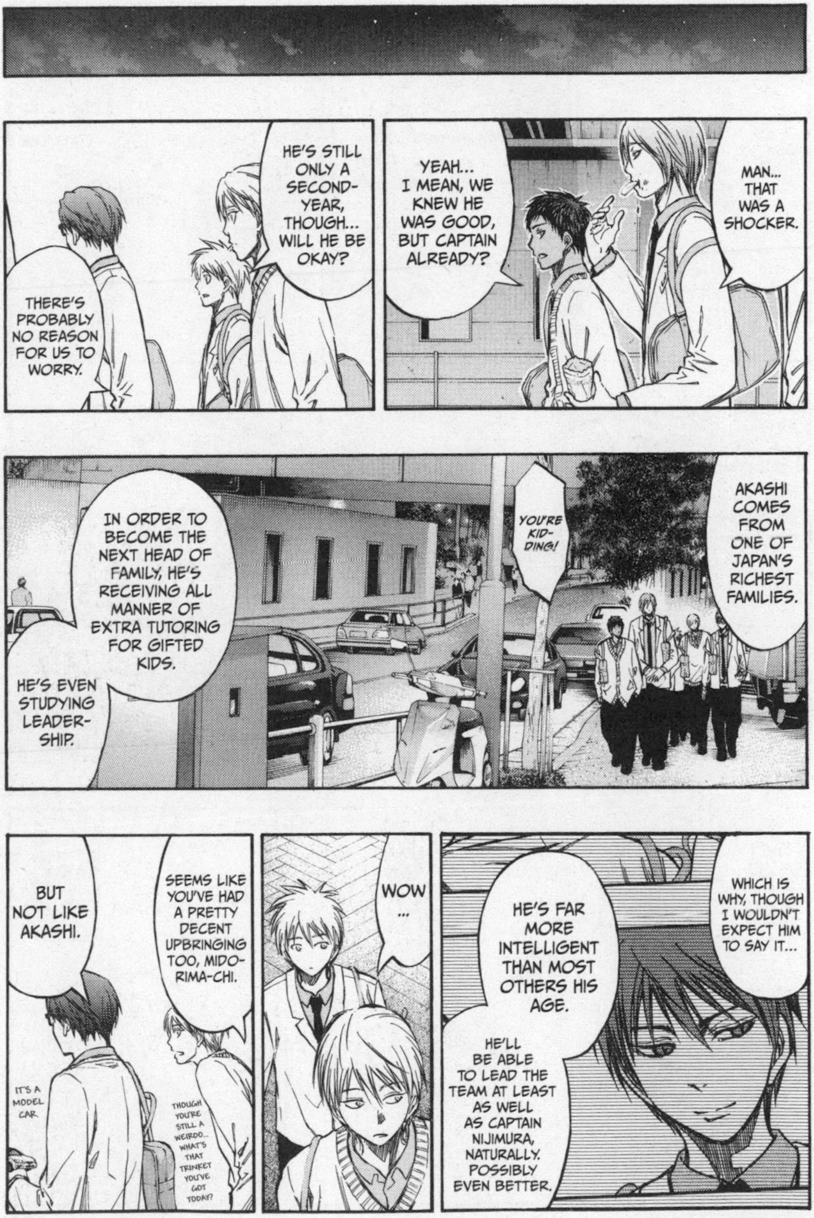
MAN... THAT WAS A SHOCKER.
YEAH... I MEAN, WE KNEW HE WAS GOOD, BUT CAPTAIN ALREADY?
HE'S STILL ONLY A SECOND-YEAR, THOUGH... WILL HE BE OKAY?
THERE'S PROBABLY NO REASON FOR US TO WORRY.
AKASHI COMES FROM ONE OF JAPAN'S RICHEST FAMILIES.
YOU'RE KID-DING!
IN ORDER TO BECOME THE NEXT HEAD OF FAMILY, HE'S RECEIVING ALL MANNER OF EXTRA TUTORING FOR GIFTED KIDS.
HE'S EVEN STUDYING LEADER-SHIP.
WHICH IS WHY, THOUGH I WOULDN'T EXPECT HIM TO SAY IT...
HE'S FAR MORE INTELLIGENT THAN MOST OTHERS HIS AGE.
HE'LL BE ABLE TO LEAD THE TEAM AT LEAST AS WELL AS CAPTAIN NIJIMURA, NATURALLY. POSSIBLY EVEN BETTER.
WOW ...
SEEMS LIKE YOU'VE HAD A PRETTY DECENT UPBRINGING TOO, MIDO-RIMA-CHI.
BUT NOT LIKE AKASHI.
THOUGH YOU'RE STILL A WEIRDO... WHAT'S THAT TRINKET YOU'VE GOT TODAY?
IT'S A MODEL CAR.

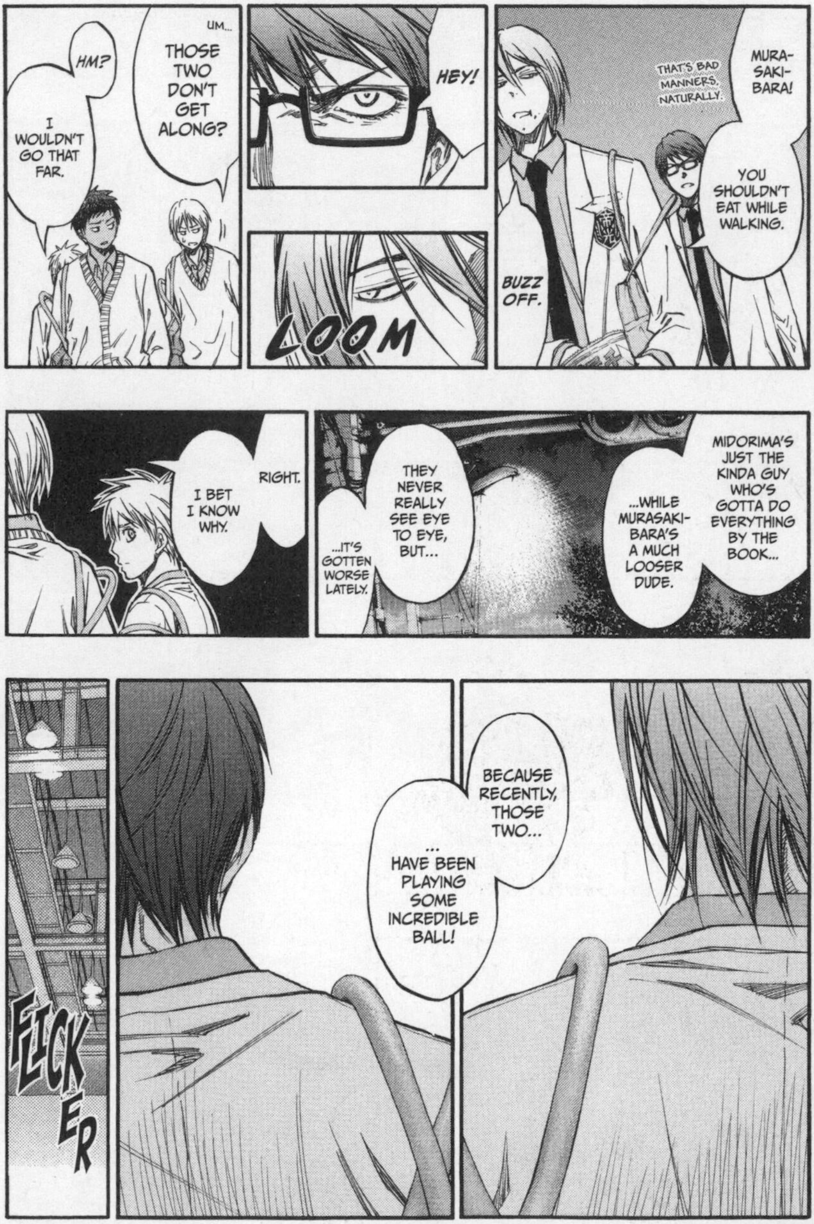
MURA-SAKI-BARA!
YOU SHOULDN'T EAT WHILE WALKING.
THAT'S BAD MANNERS, NATURALLY.
BUZZ OFF.
HEY!
LOOM
UM...
THOSE TWO DON'T GET ALONG?
HM?
I WOULDN'T GO THAT FAR.
MIDORIMA'S JUST THE KINDA GUY WHO'S GOTTA DO EVERYTHING BY THE BOOK...
...WHILE MURASAKI-BARA'S A MUCH LOOSER DUDE.
THEY NEVER REALLY SEE EYE TO EYE, BUT...
...IT'S GOTTEN WORSE LATELY.
RIGHT.
I BET I KNOW WHY.
BECAUSE RECENTLY, THOSE TWO...
... HAVE BEEN PLAYING SOME INCREDIBLE BALL!
FLICKER

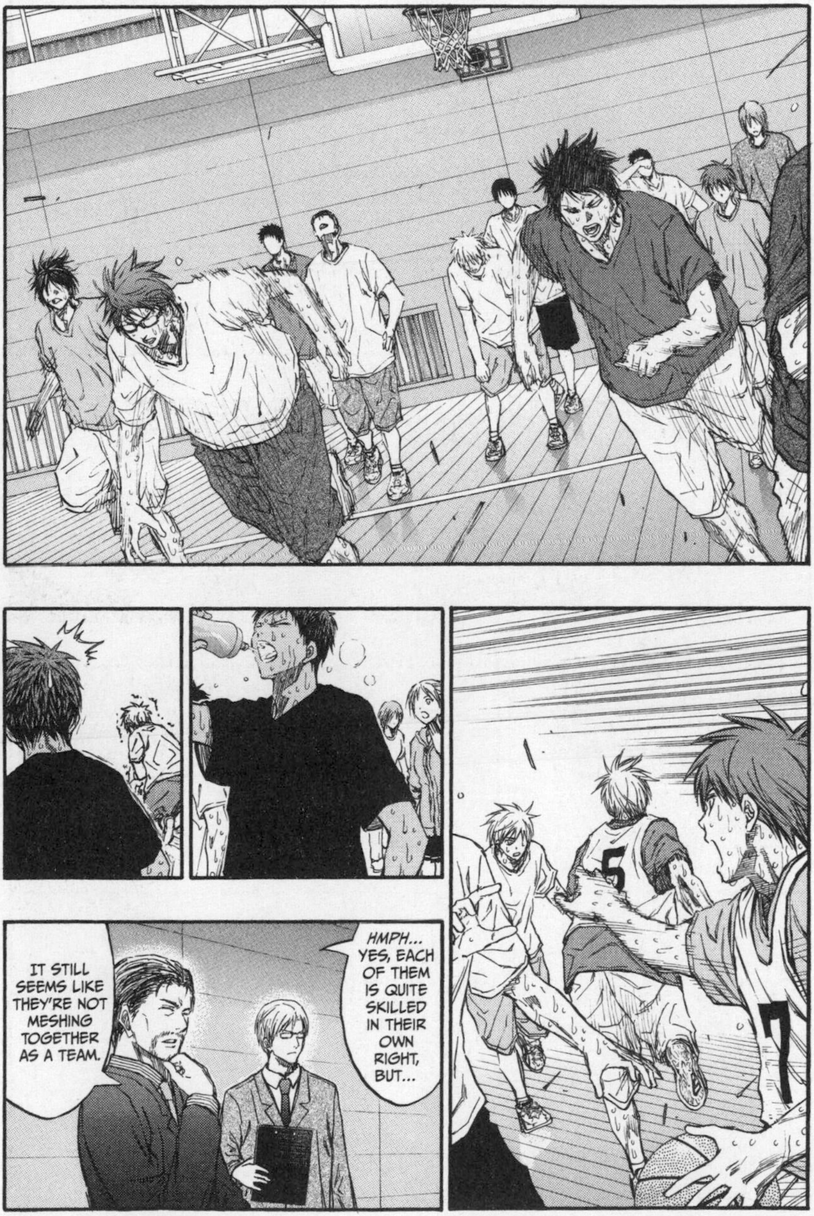
HMPH... YES, EACH OF THEM IS QUITE SKILLED IN THEIR OWN RIGHT, BUT...
IT STILL SEEMS LIKE THEY'RE NOT MESHING TOGETHER AS A TEAM.

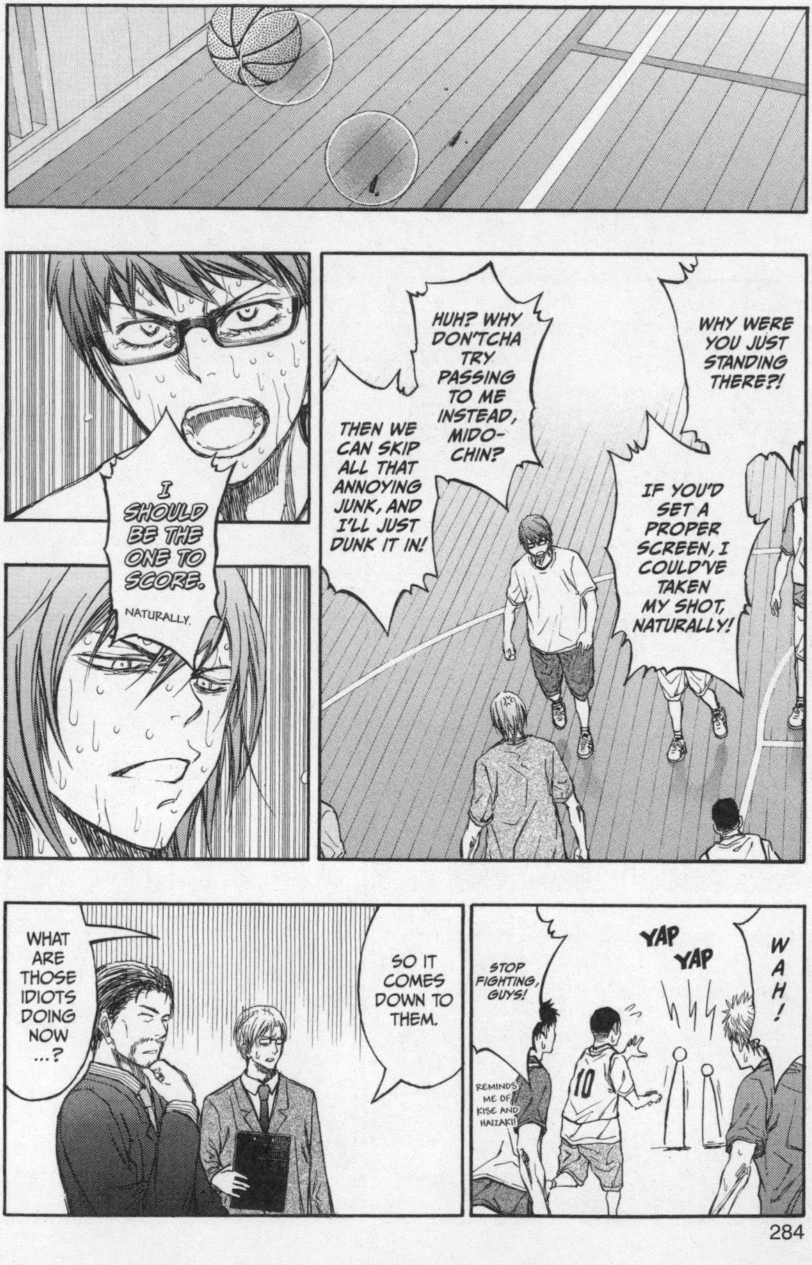
WHY WERE YOU JUST STANDING THERE?!
IF YOU'D SET A PROPER SCREEN, I COULD'VE TAKEN MY SHOT, NATURALLY!
HUH? WHY DON'TCHA TRY PASSING TO ME INSTEAD, MIDO-CHIN?
THEN WE CAN SKIP ALL THAT ANNOYING JUNK, AND I'LL JUST DUNK IT IN!
I SHOULD BE THE ONE TO SCORE.
NATURALLY.
WAH!
YAP YAP
STOP FIGHTING, GUYS!
REMINDS ME OF KISE AND HAIZAKI!
SO IT COMES DOWN TO THEM.
WHAT ARE THOSE IDIOTS DOING NOW ...?

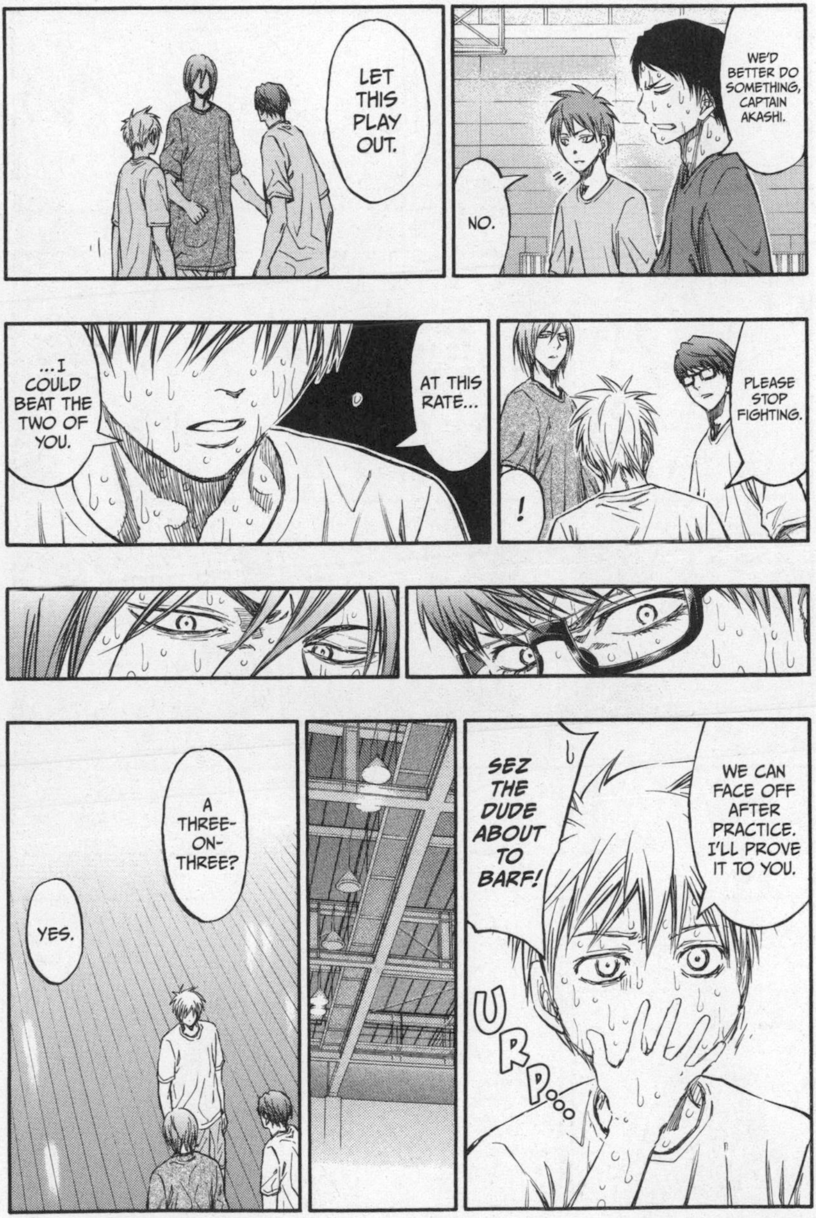
WE'D BETTER DO SOMETHING, CAPTAIN AKASHI.
NO.
LET THIS PLAY OUT.
PLEASE STOP FIGHTING.
!
AT THIS RATE...
...I COULD BEAT THE TWO OF YOU.
WE CAN FACE OFF AFTER PRACTICE. I'LL PROVE IT TO YOU.
SEZ THE DUDE ABOUT TO BARF!
URP...
A THREE-ON-THREE?
YES.

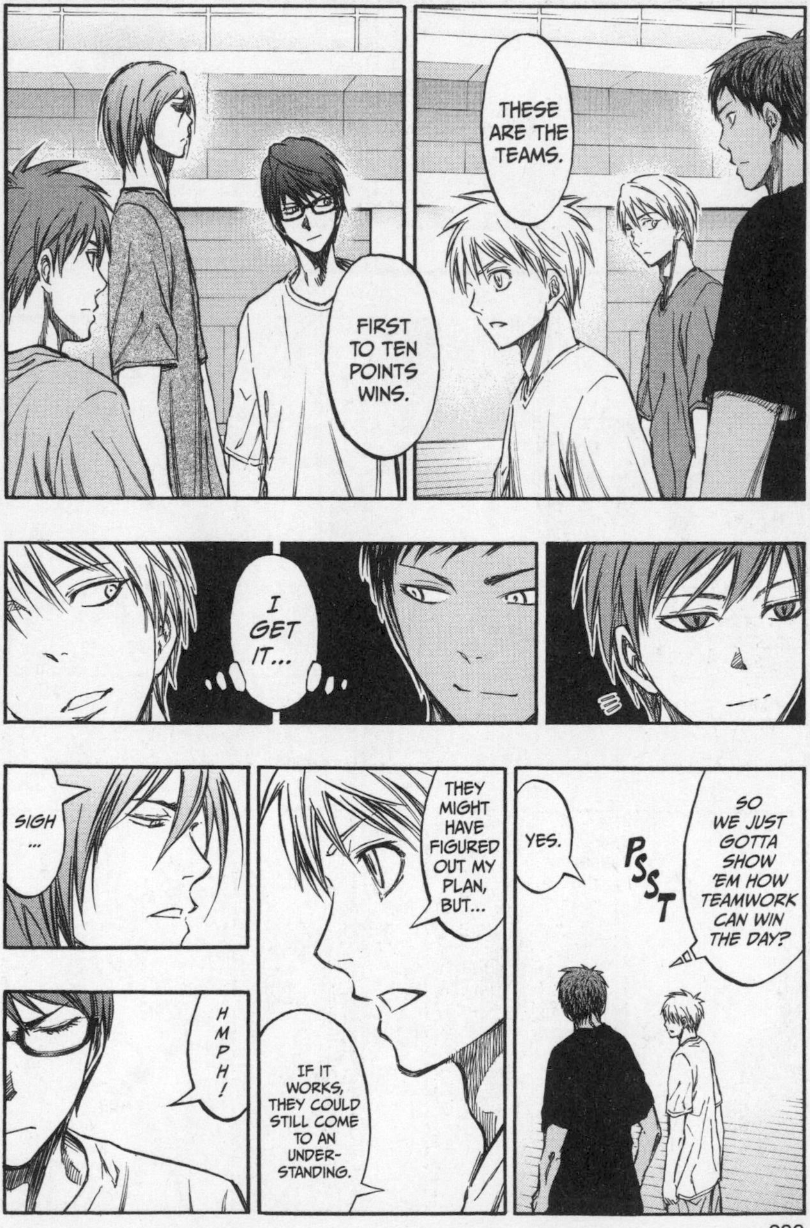
THESE ARE THE TEAMS.
FIRST TO TEN POINTS WINS.
I GET IT...
SO WE JUST GOTTA SHOW 'EM HOW TEAMWORK CAN WIN THE DAY?
PSST
YES.
THEY MIGHT HAVE FIGURED OUT MY PLAN, BUT...
IF IT WORKS, THEY COULD STILL COME TO AN UNDER-STANDING.
SIGH...
HMPH!

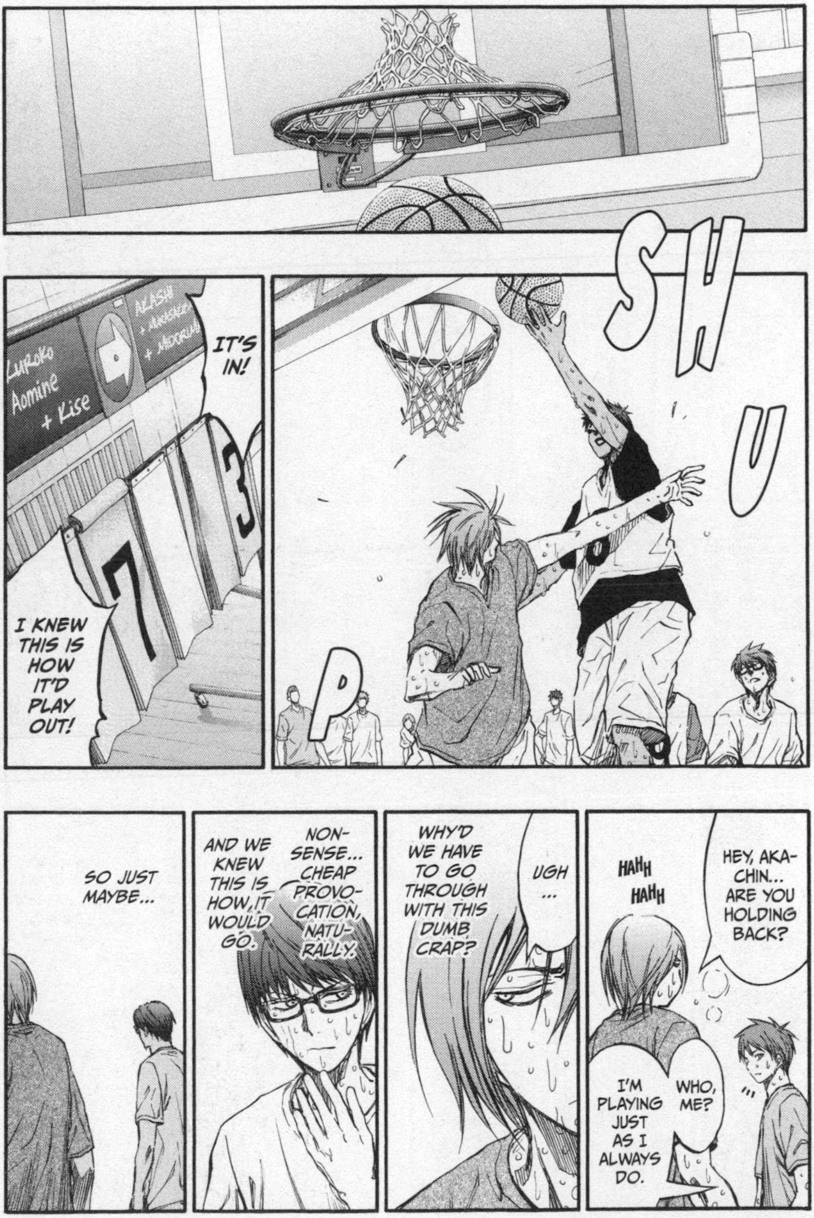
SHUP
Kuroko Aomine + Kise
IT'S IN!
I KNEW THIS IS HOW IT'D PLAY OUT!
HEY, AKA-CHIN... ARE YOU HOLDING BACK?
HAHH HAHH
WHO, ME?
I'M PLAYING JUST AS I ALWAYS DO.
UGH...
WHY'D WE HAVE TO GO THROUGH WITH THIS DUMB CRAP?
NON-SENSE... CHEAP PROVOCATION, NATURALLY.
AND WE KNEW THIS IS HOW IT WOULD GO.
SO JUST MAYBE...

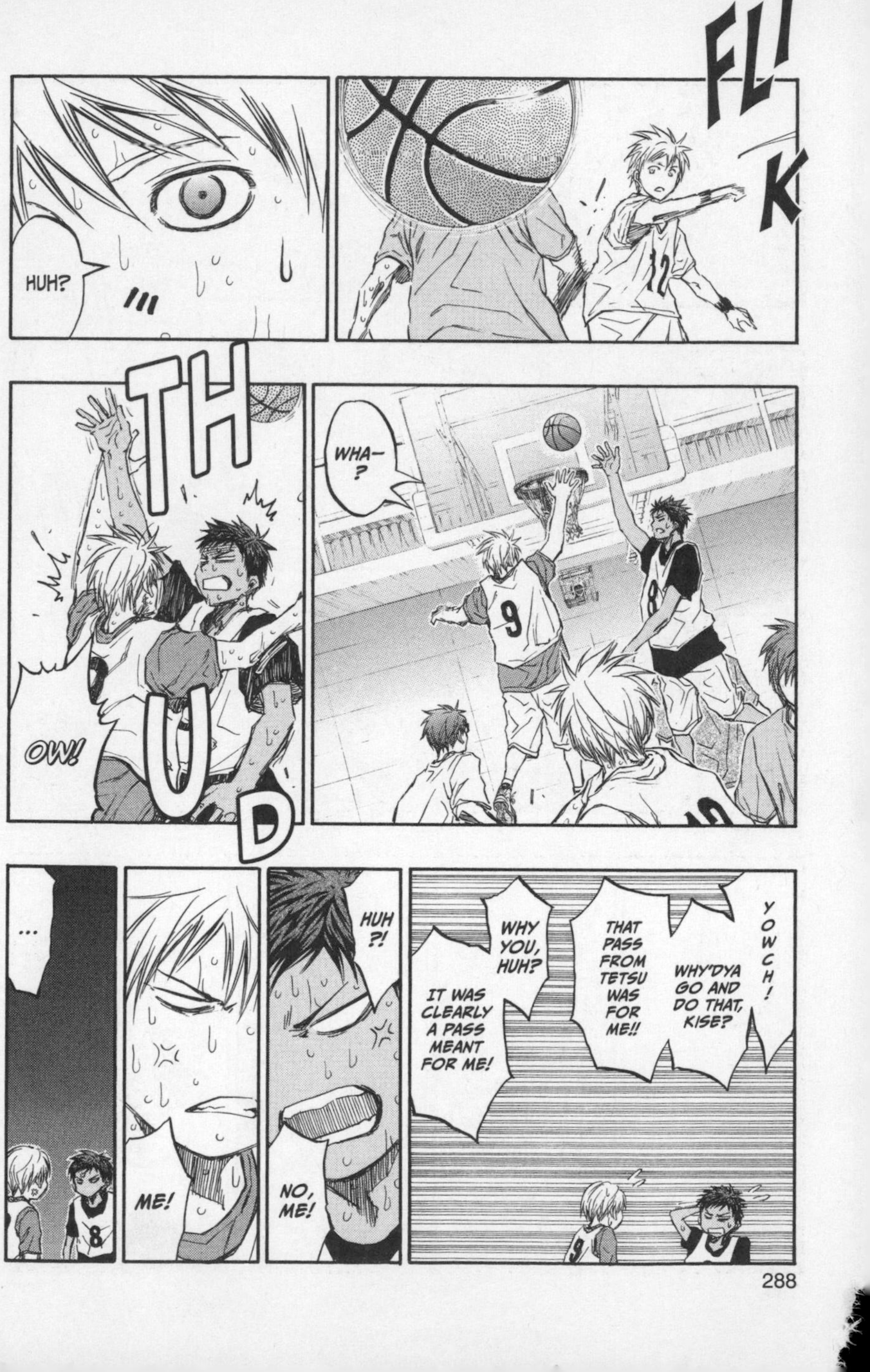
FLIK
HUH?
WHA-?
THUD
OW!
YOWCH!
WHY'DYA GO AND DO THAT, KISE?
THAT PASS FROM TETSU WAS FOR ME!!
WHY YOU, HUH?
IT WAS CLEARLY A PASS MEANT FOR ME!
HUH?!
NO, ME!
ME!
...

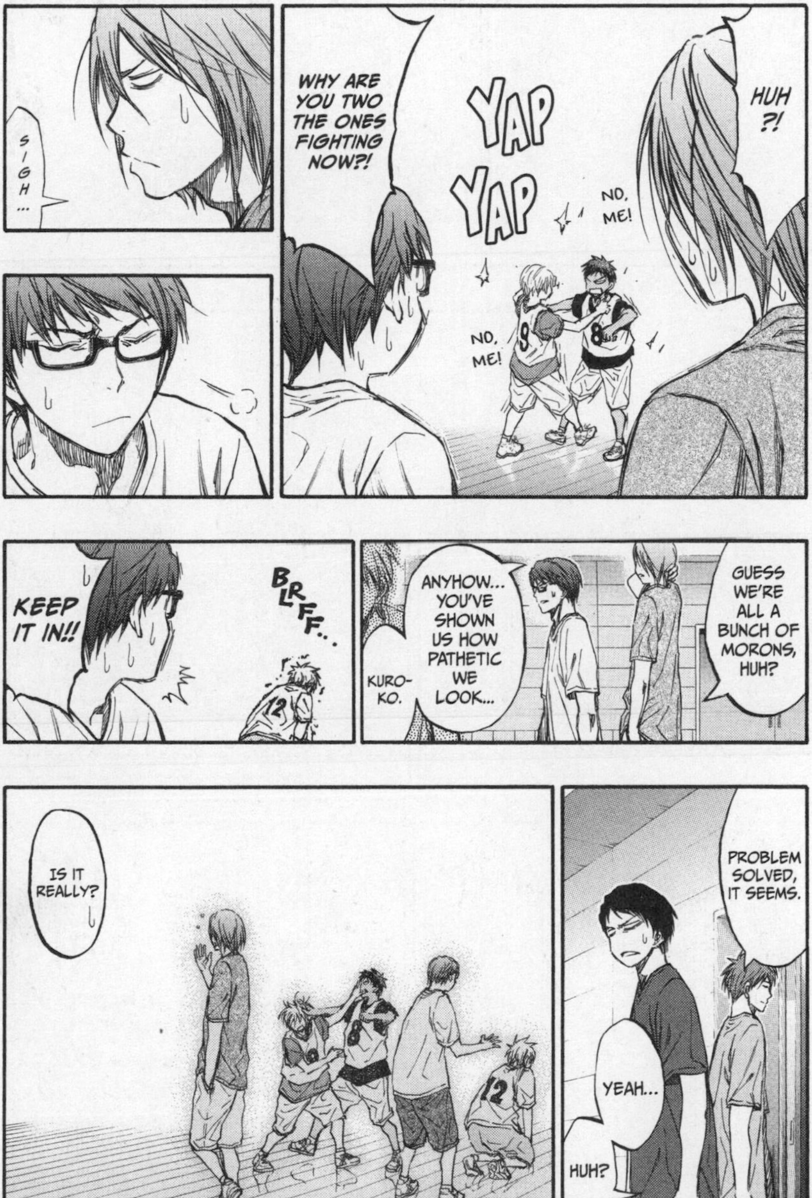
HUH ?!
NO, ME!
YAP YAP
WHY ARE YOU TWO THE ONES FIGHTING NOW?!
NO, ME!
SIGH...
GUESS WE'RE ALL A BUNCH OF MORONS, HUH?
ANYHOW... YOU'VE SHOWN US HOW PATHETIC WE LOOK...
KURO-KO.
BLRFF...
KEEP IT IN!!
PROBLEM SOLVED, IT SEEMS.
YEAH...
HUH?
IS IT REALLY?

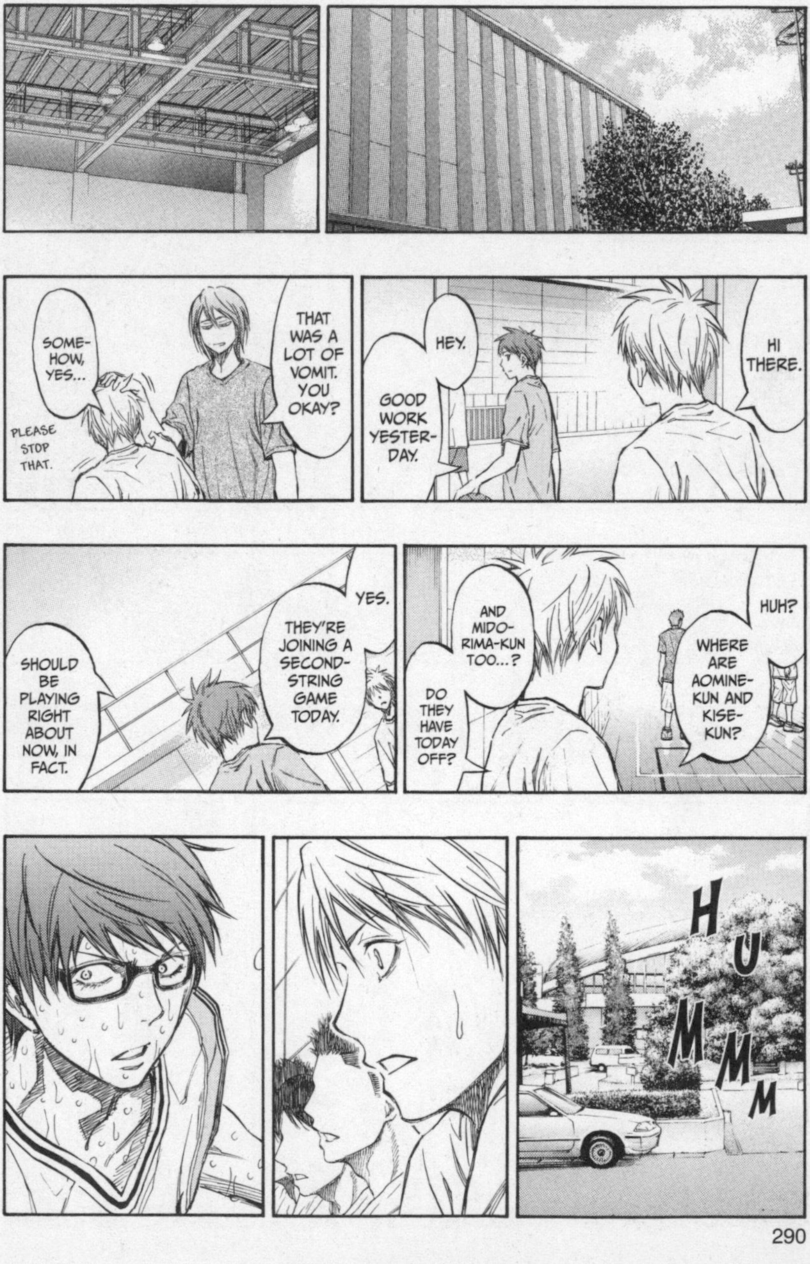
HI THERE.
HEY.
GOOD WORK YESTERDAY.
THAT WAS A LOT OF VOMIT. YOU OKAY?
SOMEHOW, YES...
PLEASE STOP THAT.
HUH?
WHERE ARE AOMINE-KUN AND KISE-KUN?
AND MIDORIMA-KUN TOO...?
DO THEY HAVE TODAY OFF?
YES.
THEY'RE JOINING A SECOND-STRING GAME TODAY.
SHOULD BE PLAYING RIGHT ABOUT NOW, IN FACT.
HUMMMM

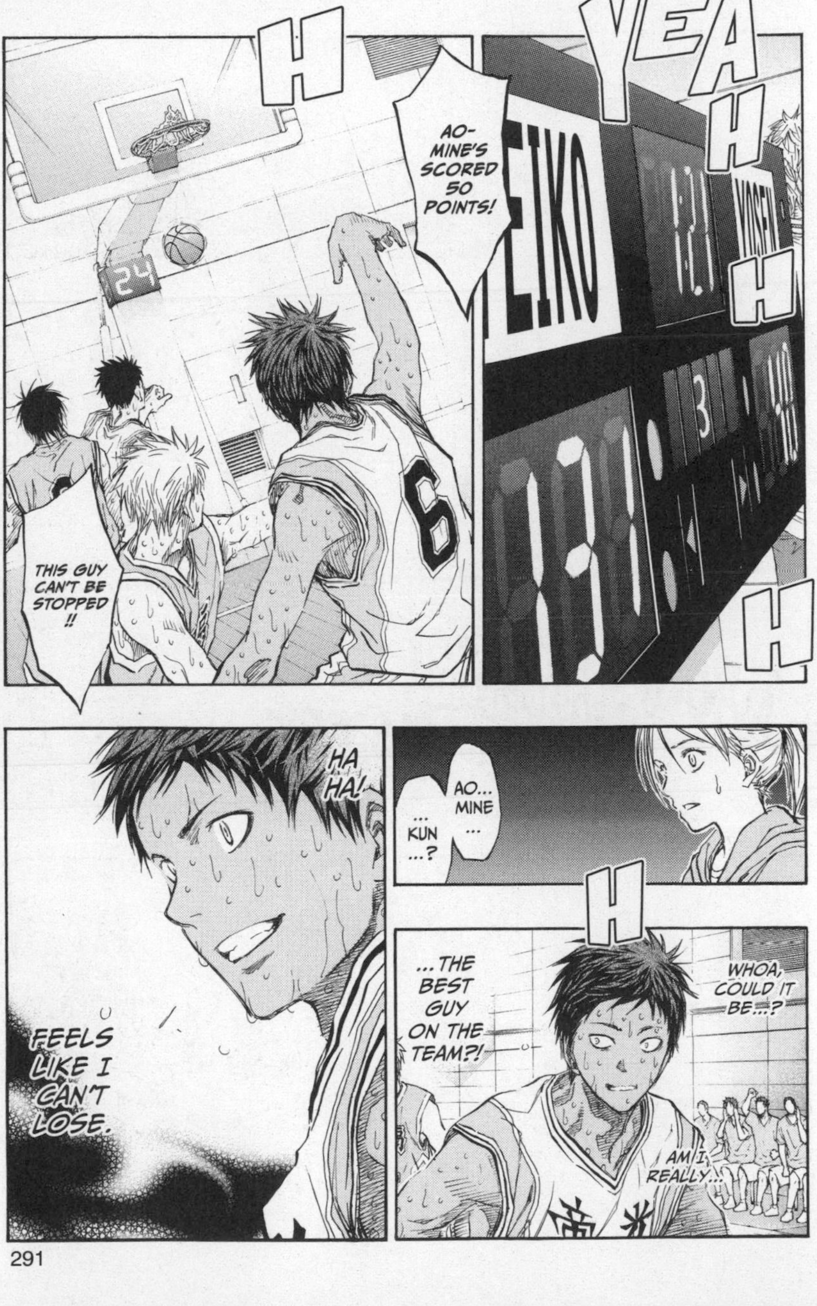
YEAH
H
H
H
EIKO
YOSEN
H
AO-MINE'S SCORED 50 POINTS!
THIS GUY CAN'T BE STOPPED!!
AO... MINE...
... KUN ...?
H
WHOA, COULD IT BE...?
...THE BEST GUY ON THE TEAM?!
AM I REALLY...
HA HA!
FEELS LIKE I CAN'T LOSE.

KUROKO'S BASKETBALL BLOOPERS

TAKE 9

JUST THAT HE'S STRICT AS AN OGRE.
OUR PRACTICES UP TO NOW HAVE BEEN CHILD'S PLAY IN COMPARISON.
...
CHILD'S PLAY... SO HOW ABOUT THE HEAD COACH'S PRACTICES?
!!!
UM ...
WHAD-DYA THINK, AKA-SHI?
I DUNNO ...
A 60-HOUR WORK WEEK...
HUH ?!
KURO-KO
I'M GOING TO DIE ...

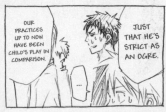

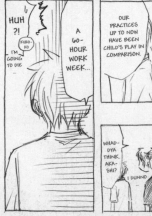

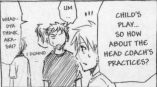

213TH QUARTER: LIONS TO THE RABBIT

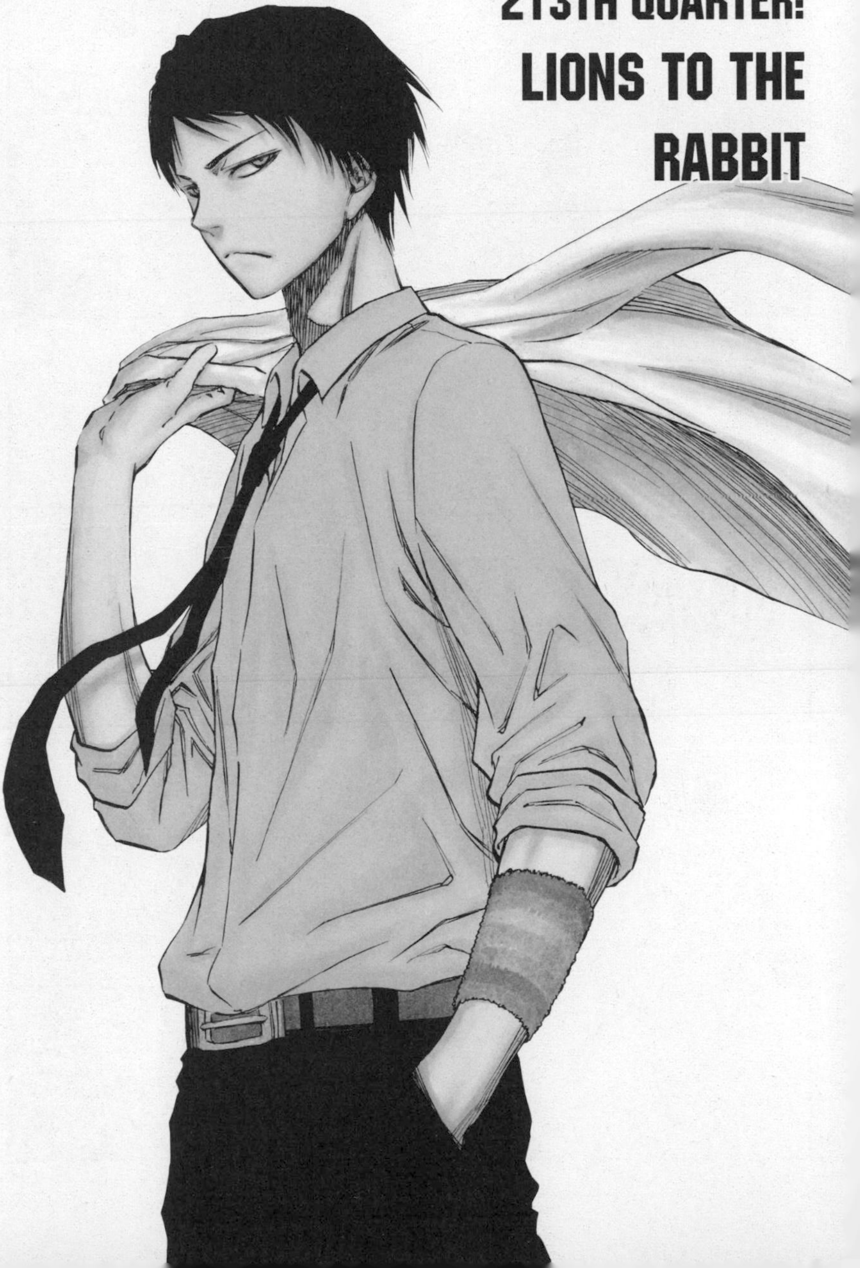

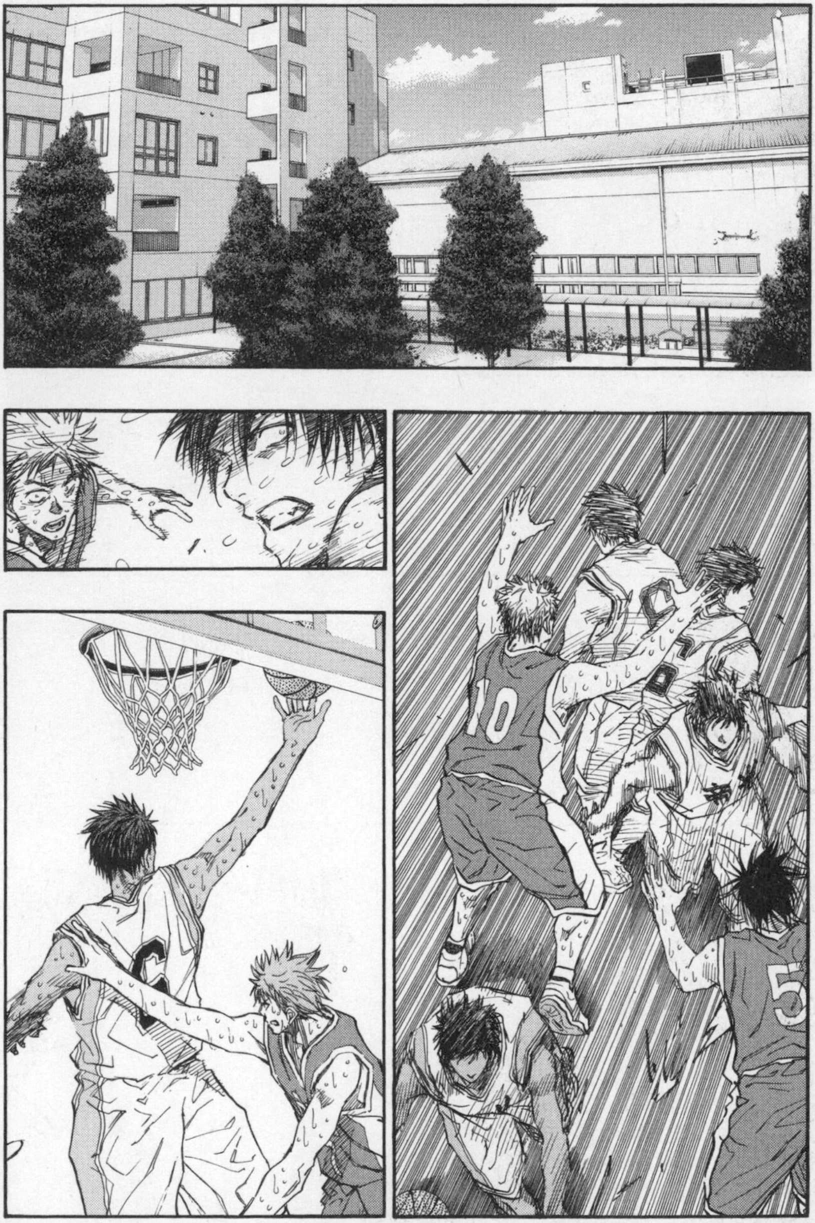

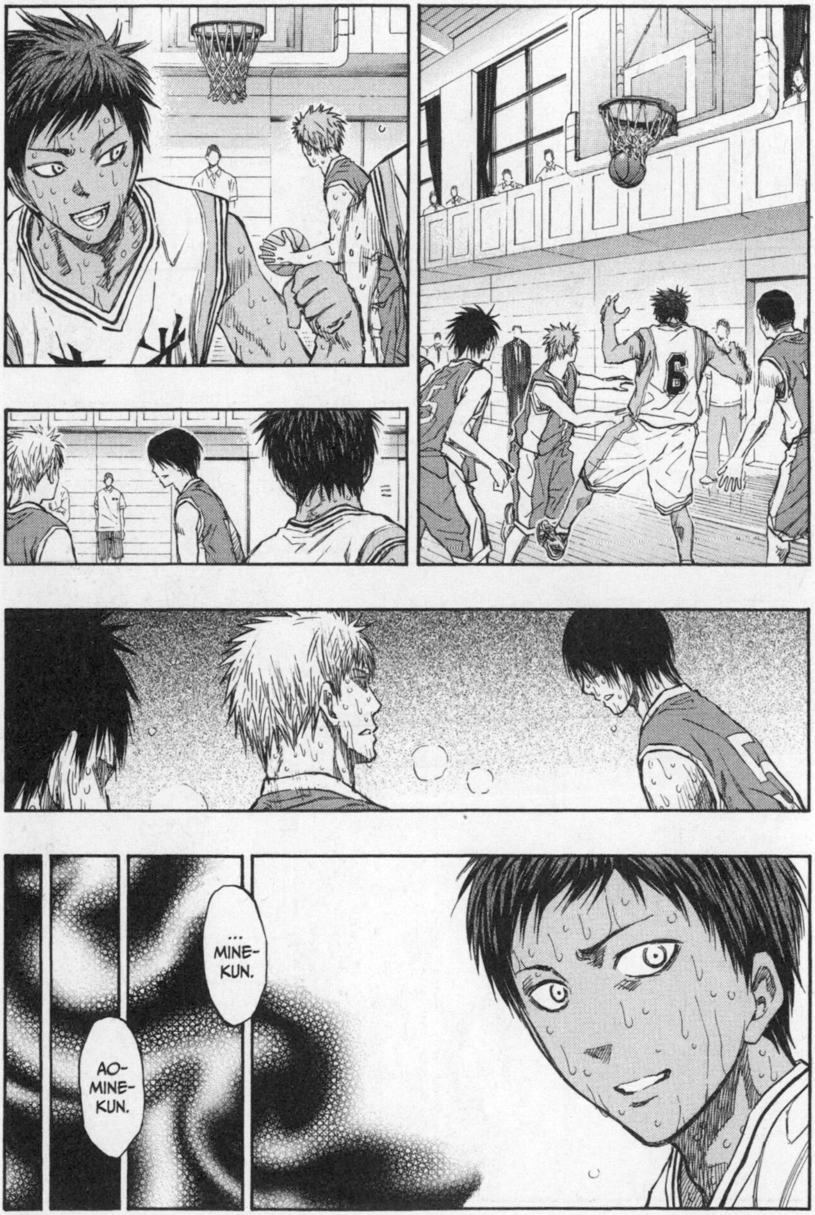

... MINE-KUN.
AO-MINE-KUN.

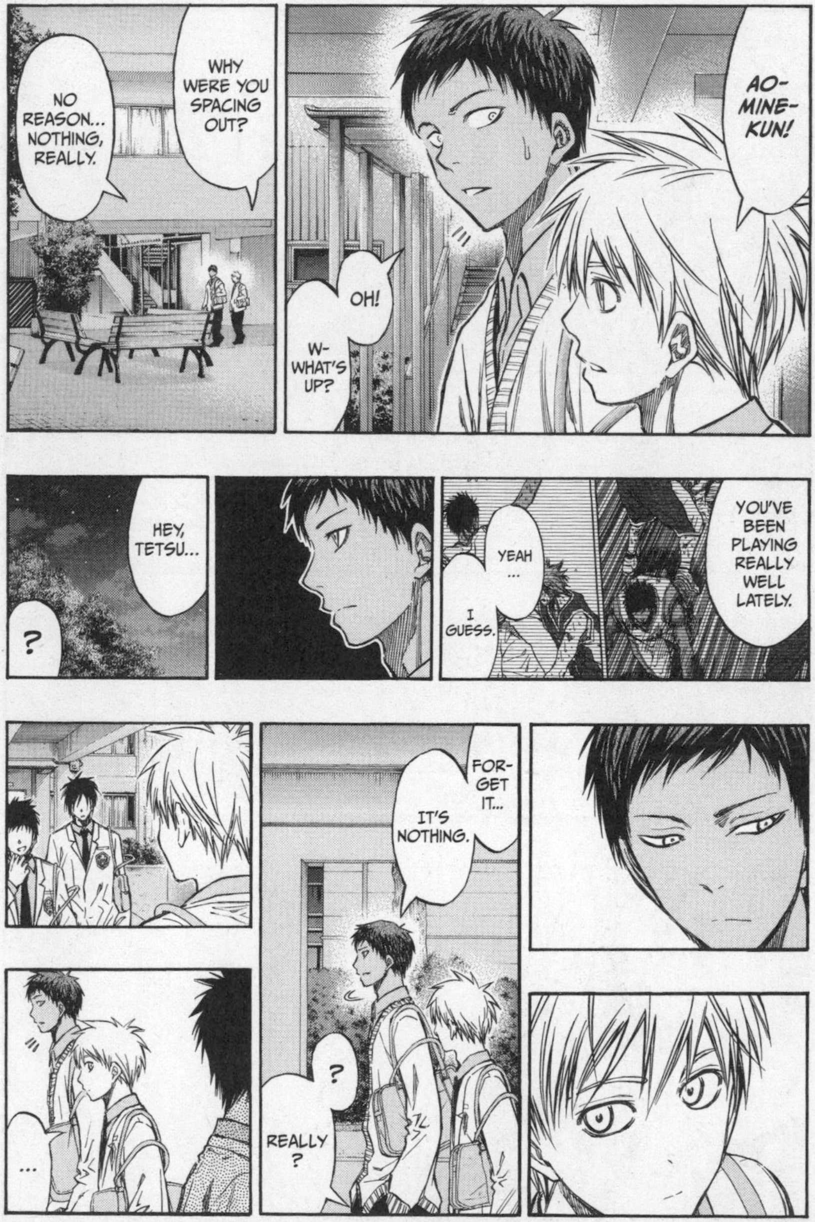
AO-MINE-KUN!
OH!
W-WHAT'S UP?
WHY WERE YOU SPACING OUT?
NO REASON... NOTHING, REALLY.
YOU'VE BEEN PLAYING REALLY WELL LATELY.
YEAH... I GUESS.
HEY, TETSU...
?
FOR-GET IT...
IT'S NOTHING.
?
REALLY?
...

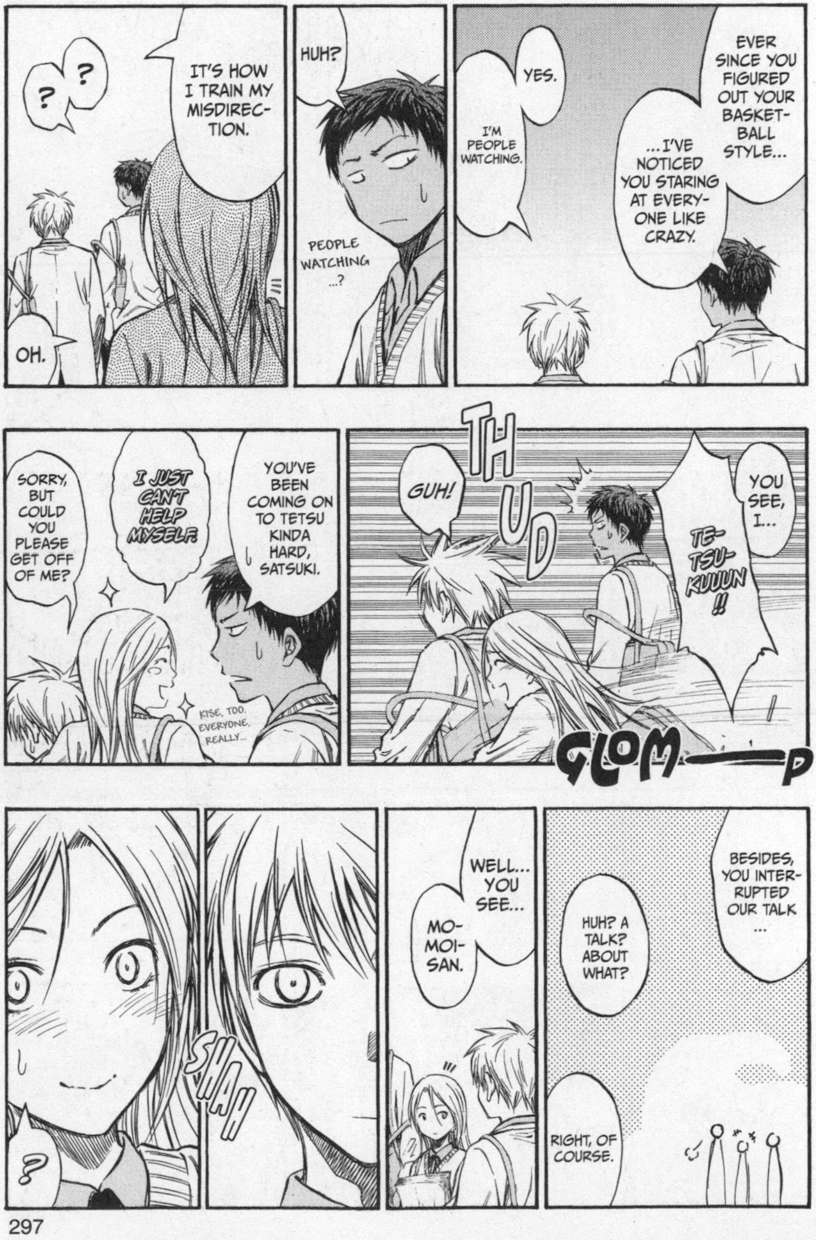
EVER SINCE YOU FIGURED OUT YOUR BASKET-BALL STYLE...
...I'VE NOTICED YOU STARING AT EVERY-ONE LIKE CRAZY.
YES.
I'M PEOPLE WATCHING.
HUH?
PEOPLE WATCHING ...?
IT'S HOW I TRAIN MY MISDIREC-TION.
? ?
OH.
YOU SEE, I...
TE-TSU-KUUUN!!
GLOM—P
THUD
GUH!
YOU'VE BEEN COMING ON TO TETSU KINDA HARD, SATSUKI.
I JUST CAN'T HELP MYSELF.
SORRY, BUT COULD YOU PLEASE GET OFF OF ME?
KISE, TOO. EVERYONE, REALLY...
BESIDES, YOU INTER-RUPTED OUR TALK ...
HUH? A TALK? ABOUT WHAT?
RIGHT, OF COURSE.
WELL... YOU SEE...
MO-MOI-SAN.
SHAH
?

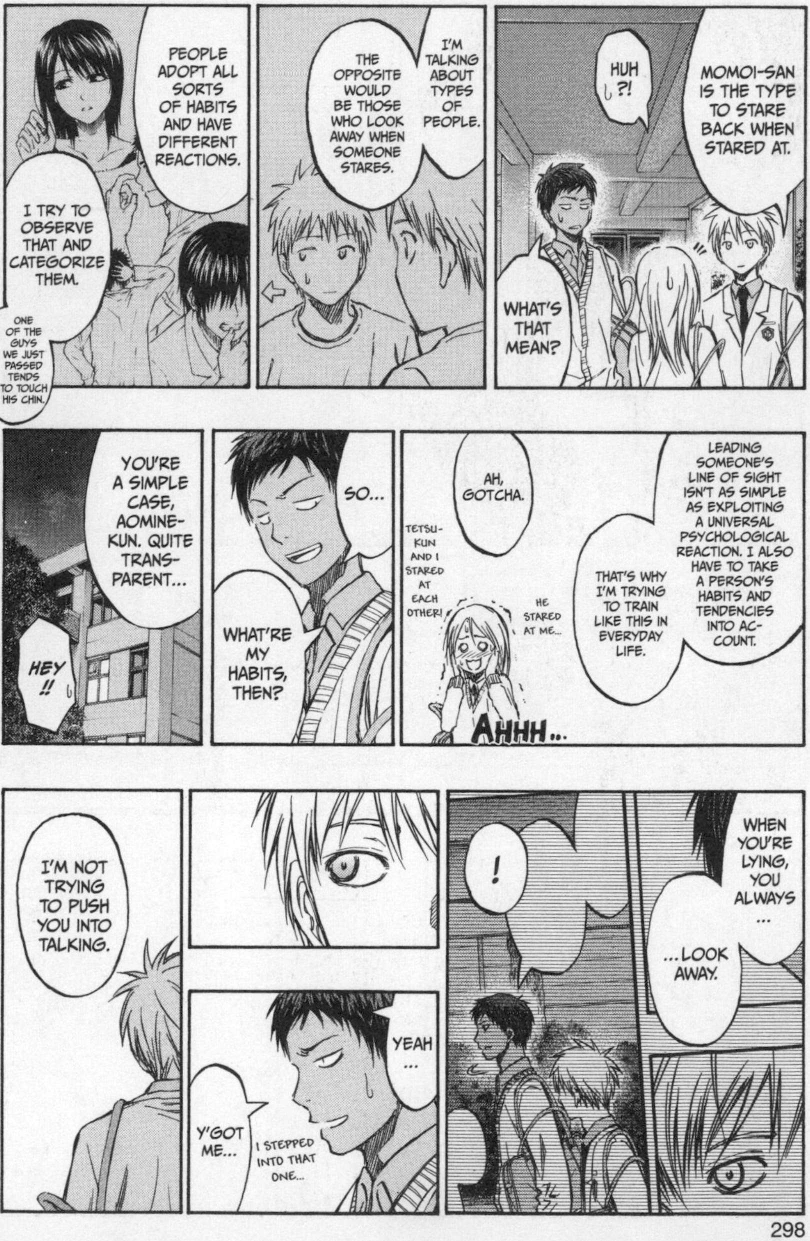
MOMOI-SAN IS THE TYPE TO STARE BACK WHEN STARED AT.
HUH ?!
WHAT'S THAT MEAN?
I'M TALKING ABOUT TYPES OF PEOPLE.
THE OPPOSITE WOULD BE THOSE WHO LOOK AWAY WHEN SOMEONE STARES.
PEOPLE ADOPT ALL SORTS OF HABITS AND HAVE DIFFERENT REACTIONS.
I TRY TO OBSERVE THAT AND CATEGORIZE THEM.
ONE OF THE GUYS WE JUST PASSED TENDS TO TOUCH HIS CHIN.
LEADING SOMEONE'S LINE OF SIGHT ISN'T AS SIMPLE AS EXPLOITING A UNIVERSAL PSYCHOLOGICAL REACTION. I ALSO HAVE TO TAKE A PERSON'S HABITS AND TENDENCIES INTO AC-COUNT.
AH, GOTCHA.
THAT'S WHY I'M TRYING TO TRAIN LIKE THIS IN EVERYDAY LIFE.
HE STARED AT ME...
TETSU-KUN AND I STARED AT EACH OTHER!
AHHH...
SO...
WHAT'RE MY HABITS, THEN?
YOU'RE A SIMPLE CASE, AOMINE-KUN. QUITE TRANS-PARENT...
HEY !!
WHEN YOU'RE LYING, YOU ALWAYS ...
...LOOK AWAY.
!
YEAH ...
Y'GOT ME...
I STEPPED INTO THAT ONE...
I'M NOT TRYING TO PUSH YOU INTO TALKING.

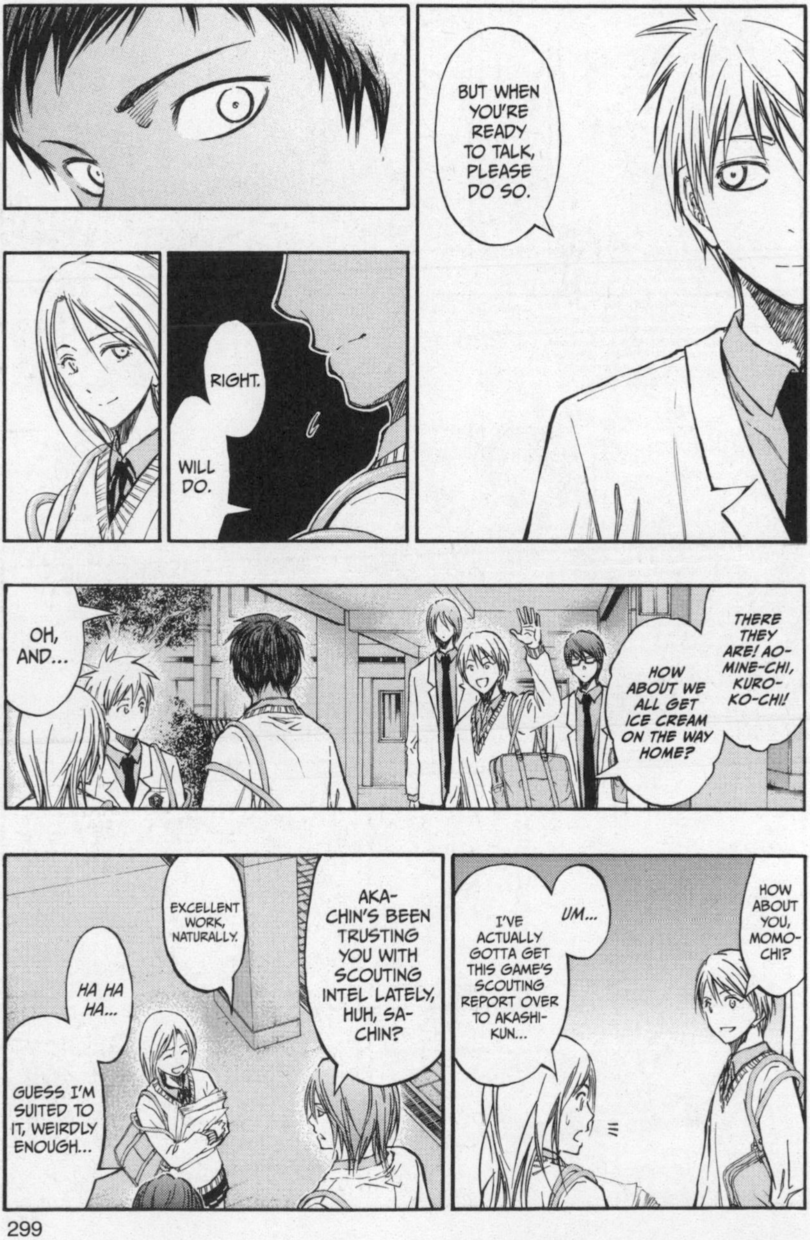
BUT WHEN YOU'RE READY TO TALK, PLEASE DO SO.
RIGHT.
WILL DO.
THERE THEY ARE! AO-MINE-CHI, KURO-KO-CHI!
HOW ABOUT WE ALL GET ICE CREAM ON THE WAY HOME?
OH, AND...
HOW ABOUT YOU, MOMO-CHI?
UM...
I'VE ACTUALLY GOTTA GET THIS GAME'S SCOUTING REPORT OVER TO AKASHI-KUN...
AKA-CHIN'S BEEN TRUSTING YOU WITH SCOUTING INTEL LATELY, HUH, SA-CHIN?
EXCELLENT WORK, NATURALLY.
HA HA HA...
GUESS I'M SUITED TO IT, WEIRDLY ENOUGH...

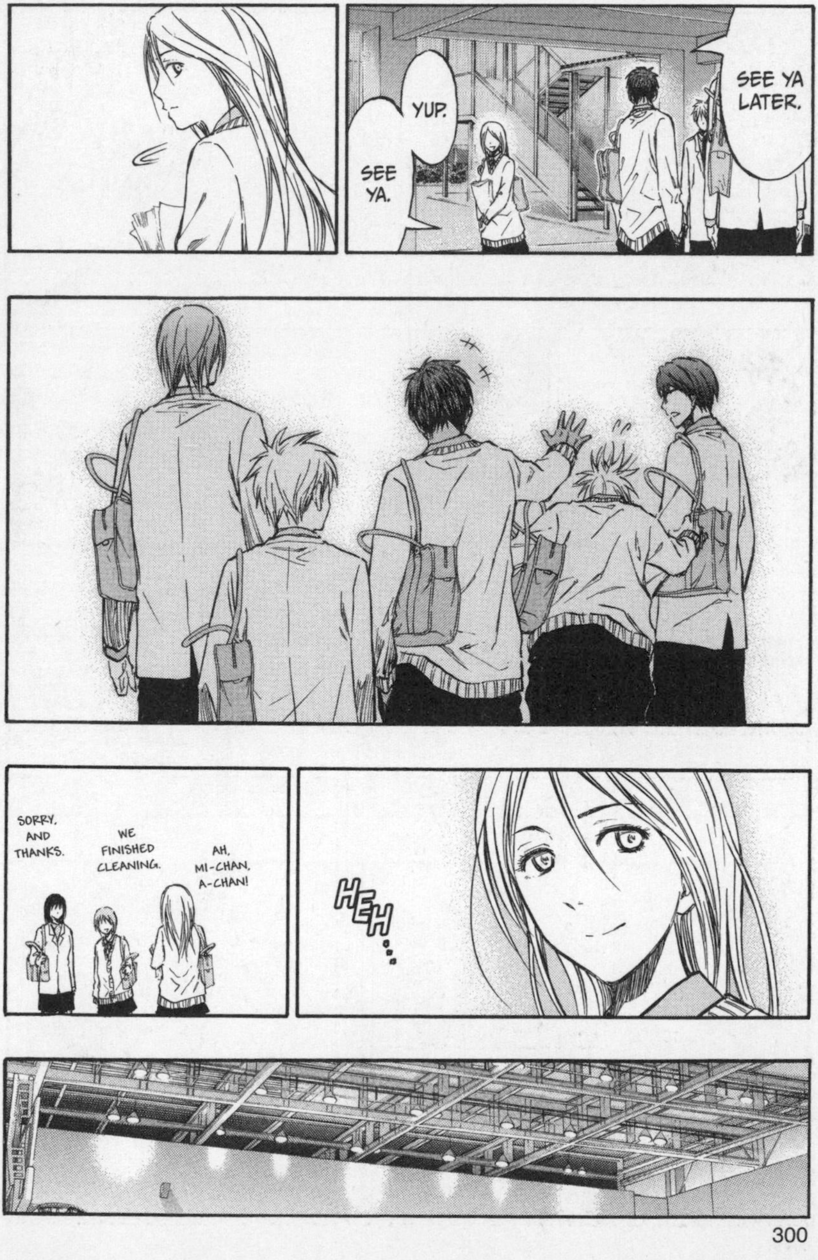
SEE YA LATER.
YUP.
SEE YA.
HEH...
AH, MI-CHAN, A-CHAN!
WE FINISHED CLEANING.
SORRY, AND THANKS.

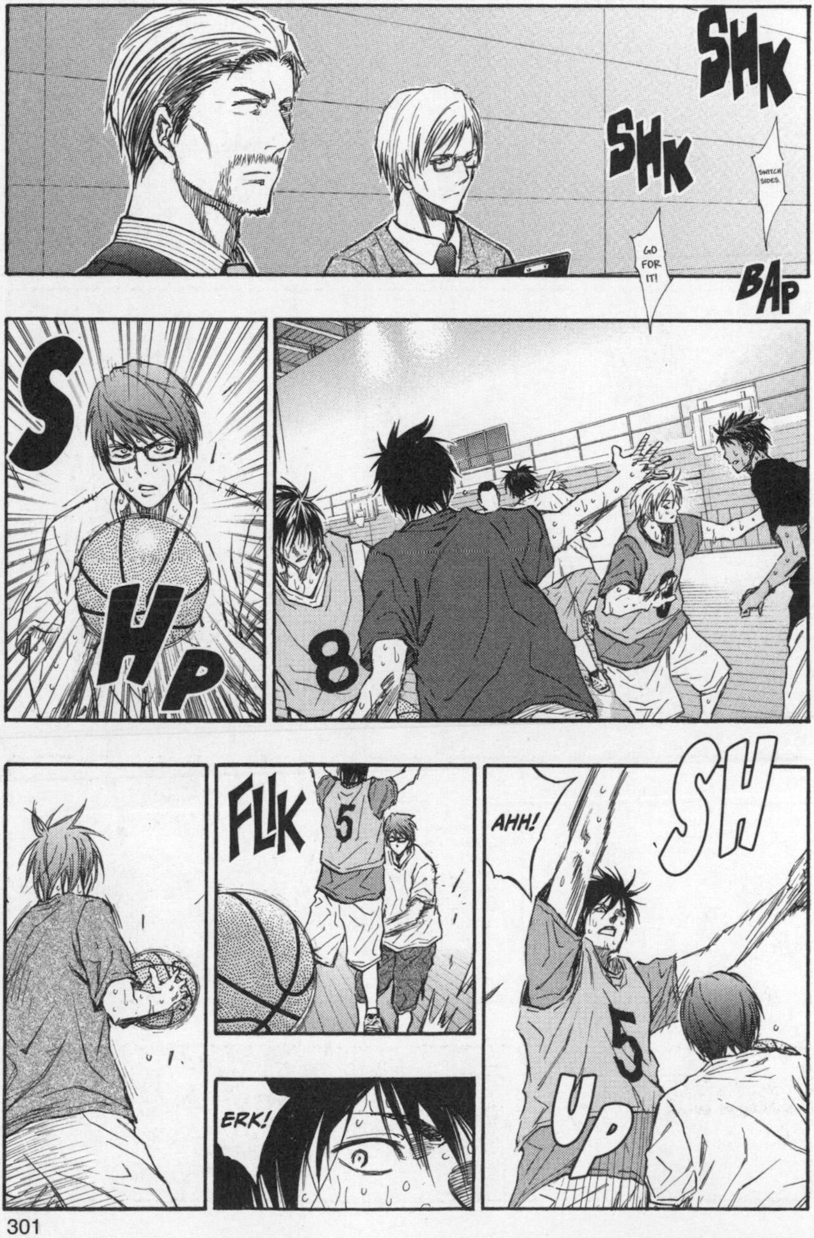
SHK
SHK
SWITCH SIDES.
GO FOR IT!
BAP
SHP
SH
AHH!
UP
FLIK
ERK!

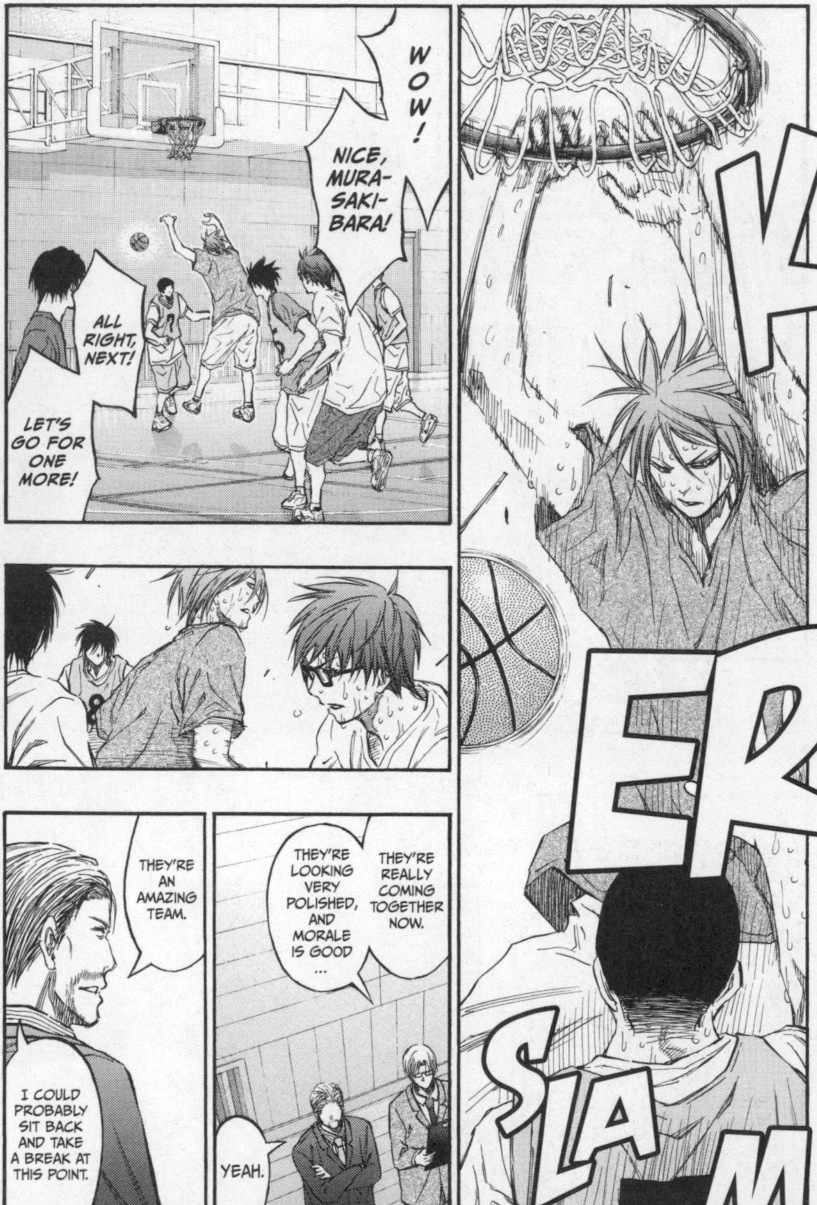
KER
SLAM
WOW!
NICE, MURASAKIBARA!
ALL RIGHT, NEXT!
LET'S GO FOR ONE MORE!
THEY'RE REALLY COMING TOGETHER NOW.
THEY'RE LOOKING VERY POLISHED, AND MORALE IS GOOD ...
YEAH.
THEY'RE AN AMAZING TEAM.
I COULD PROBABLY SIT BACK AND TAKE A BREAK AT THIS POINT.

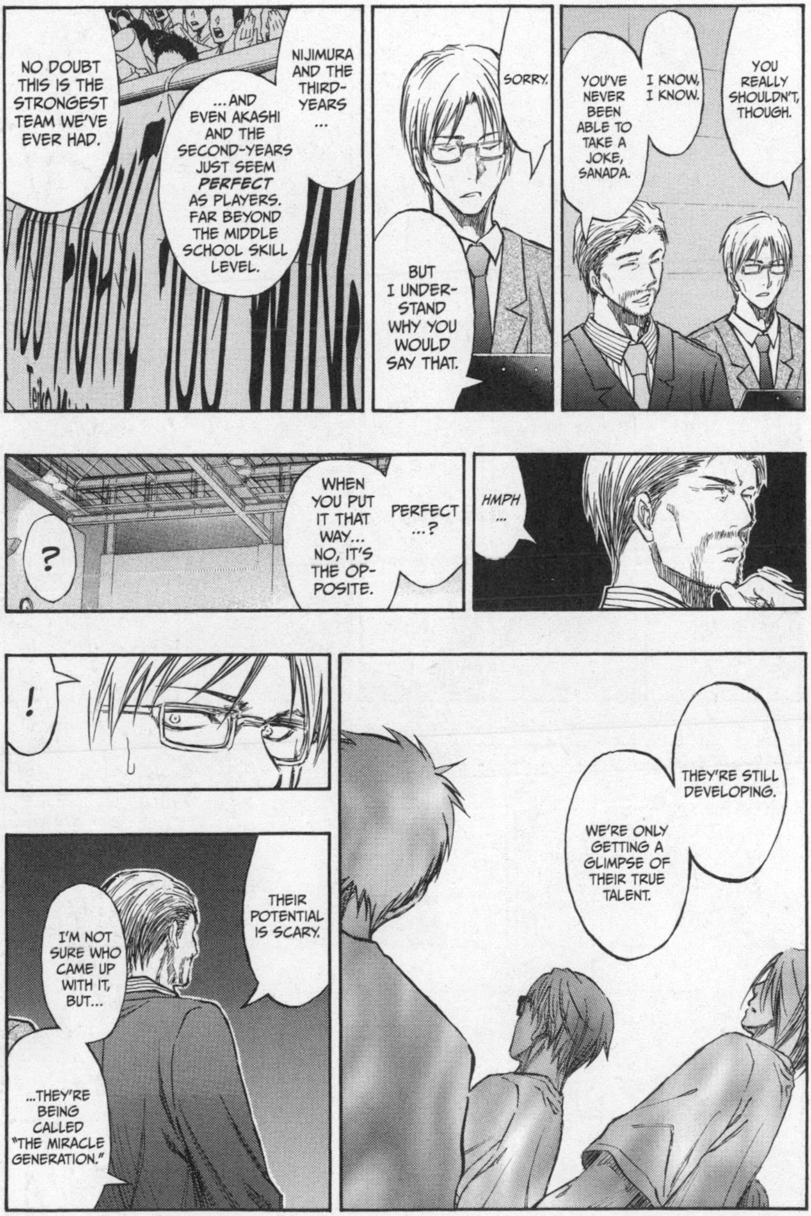
YOU REALLY SHOULDN'T, THOUGH.
I KNOW, I KNOW.
YOU'VE NEVER BEEN ABLE TO TAKE A JOKE, SANADA.
SORRY.
BUT I UNDERSTAND WHY YOU WOULD SAY THAT.
NIJIMURA AND THE THIRD-YEARS ...
...AND EVEN AKASHI AND THE SECOND-YEARS JUST SEEM *PERFECT* AS PLAYERS. FAR BEYOND THE MIDDLE SCHOOL SKILL LEVEL.
NO DOUBT THIS IS THE STRONGEST TEAM WE'VE EVER HAD.
HMPH ...
PERFECT ...?
WHEN YOU PUT IT THAT WAY... NO, IT'S THE OPPOSITE.
?
THEY'RE STILL DEVELOPING.
WE'RE ONLY GETTING A GLIMPSE OF THEIR TRUE TALENT.
!
THEIR POTENTIAL IS SCARY.
I'M NOT SURE WHO CAME UP WITH IT, BUT...
...THEY'RE BEING CALLED "THE MIRACLE GENERATION."

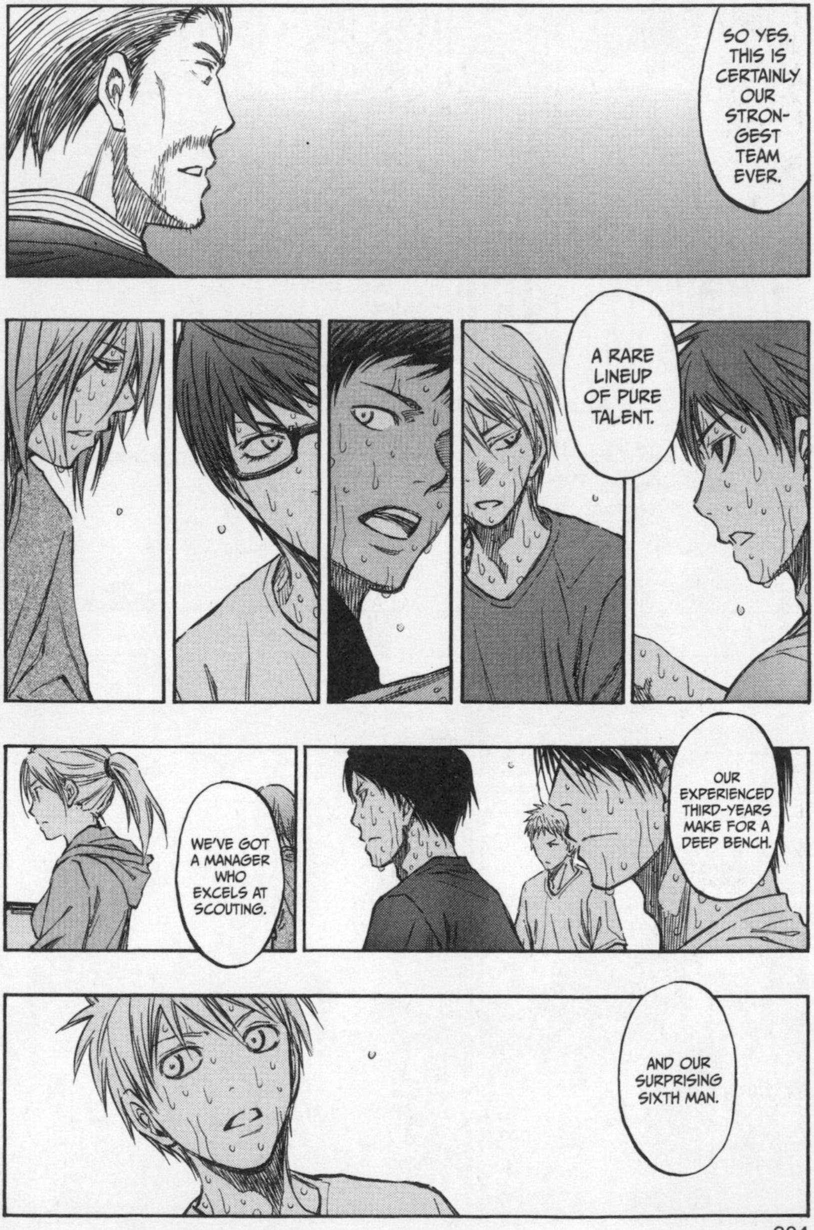
SO YES. THIS IS CERTAINLY OUR STRON- GEST TEAM EVER.
A RARE LINEUP OF PURE TALENT.
OUR EXPERIENCED THIRD-YEARS MAKE FOR A DEEP BENCH.
WE'VE GOT A MANAGER WHO EXCELS AT SCOUTING.
AND OUR SURPRISING SIXTH MAN.

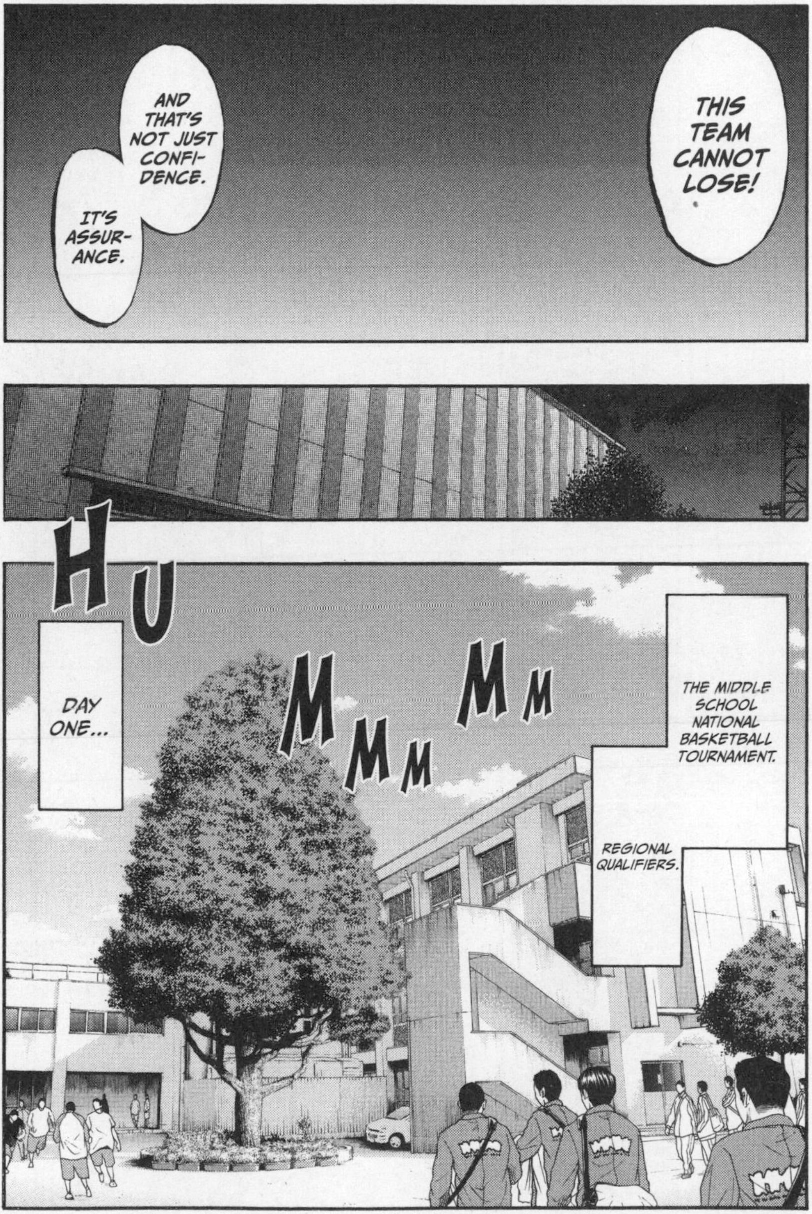
THIS TEAM CANNOT LOSE!
AND THAT'S NOT JUST CONFIDENCE.
IT'S ASSURANCE.
THE MIDDLE SCHOOL NATIONAL BASKETBALL TOURNAMENT.
REGIONAL QUALIFIERS.
HUMMMMMM
DAY ONE...

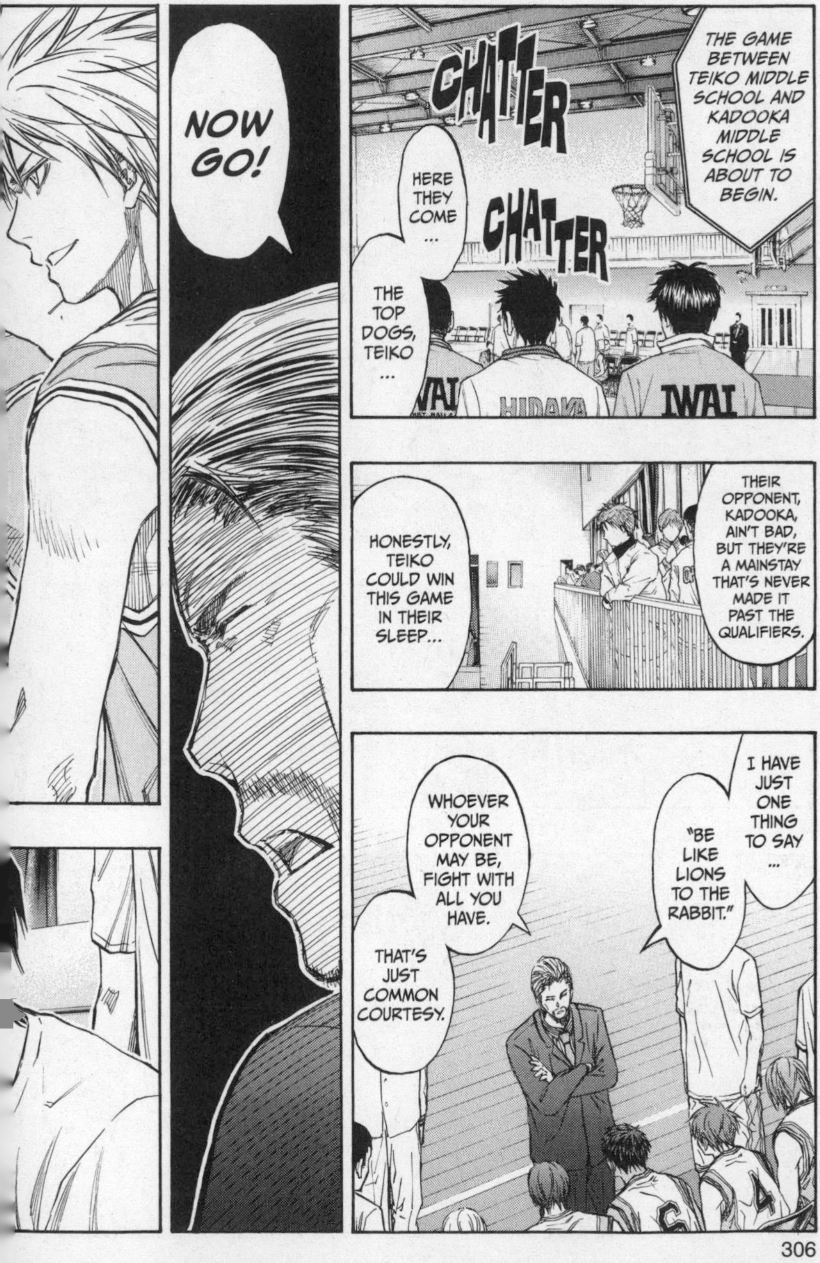
THE GAME BETWEEN TEIKO MIDDLE SCHOOL AND KADOOKA MIDDLE SCHOOL IS ABOUT TO BEGIN.
CHATTER
CHATTER
HERE THEY COME ...
THE TOP DOGS, TEIKO ...
IWAI
HIDAKA
IWAI
THEIR OPPONENT, KADOOKA, AIN'T BAD, BUT THEY'RE A MAINSTAY THAT'S NEVER MADE IT PAST THE QUALIFIERS.
HONESTLY, TEIKO COULD WIN THIS GAME IN THEIR SLEEP...
I HAVE JUST ONE THING TO SAY ...
"BE LIKE LIONS TO THE RABBIT."
WHOEVER YOUR OPPONENT MAY BE, FIGHT WITH ALL YOU HAVE.
THAT'S JUST COMMON COURTESY.
NOW GO!

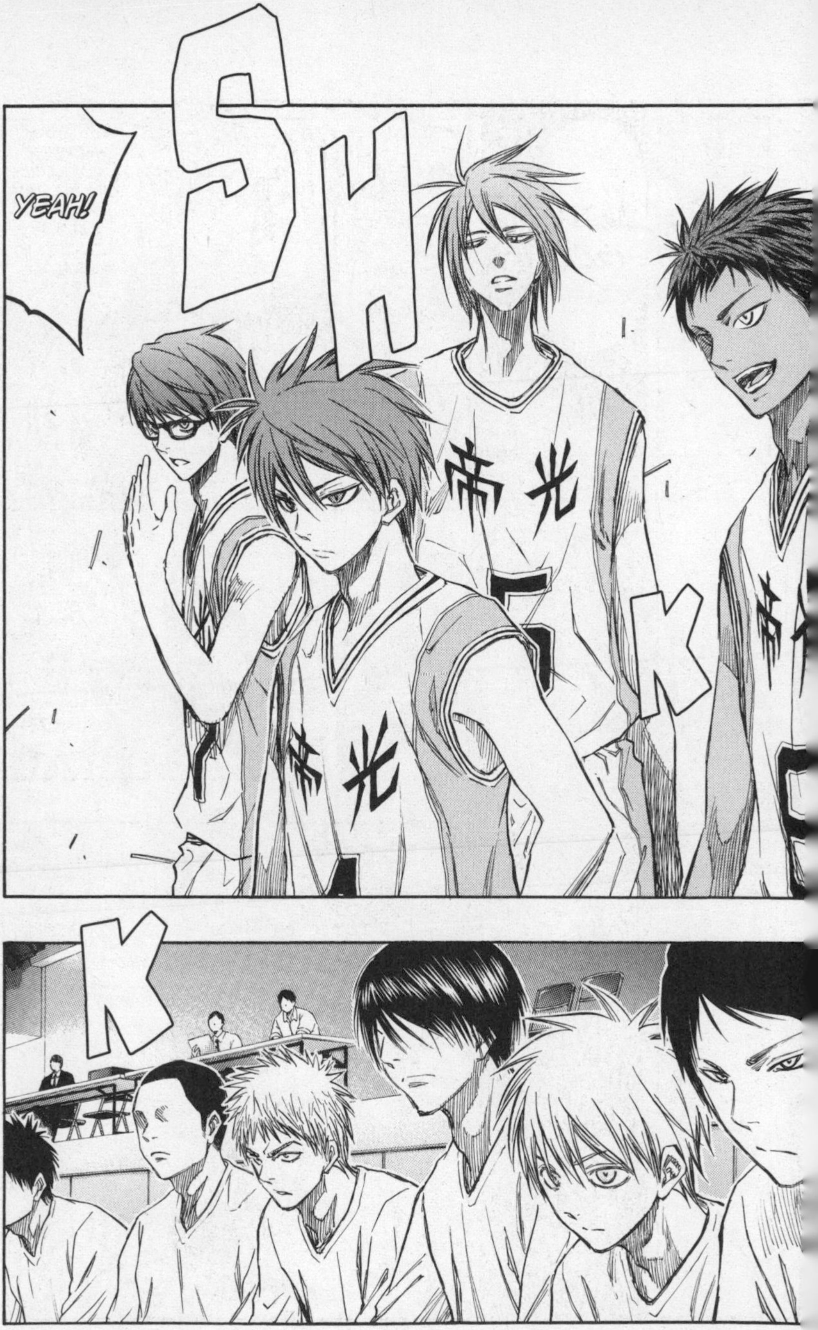
YEAH!
SHKK

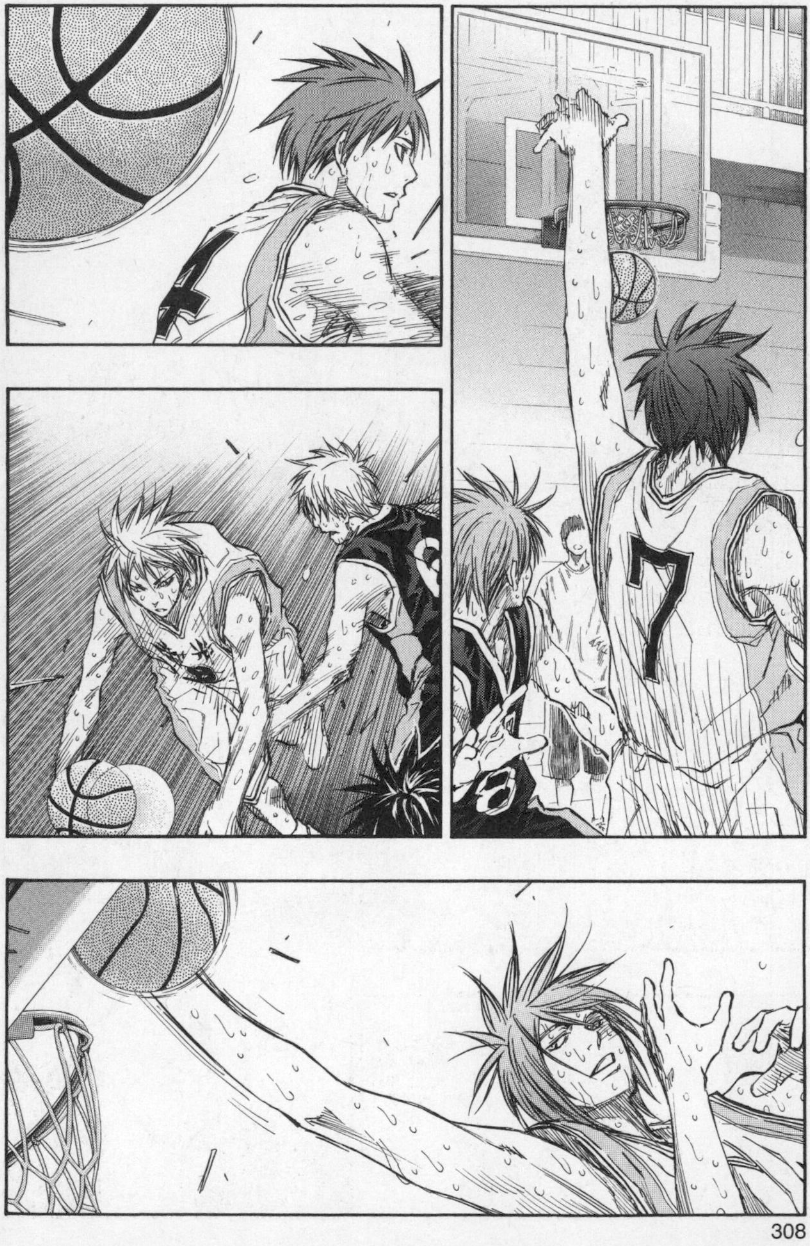

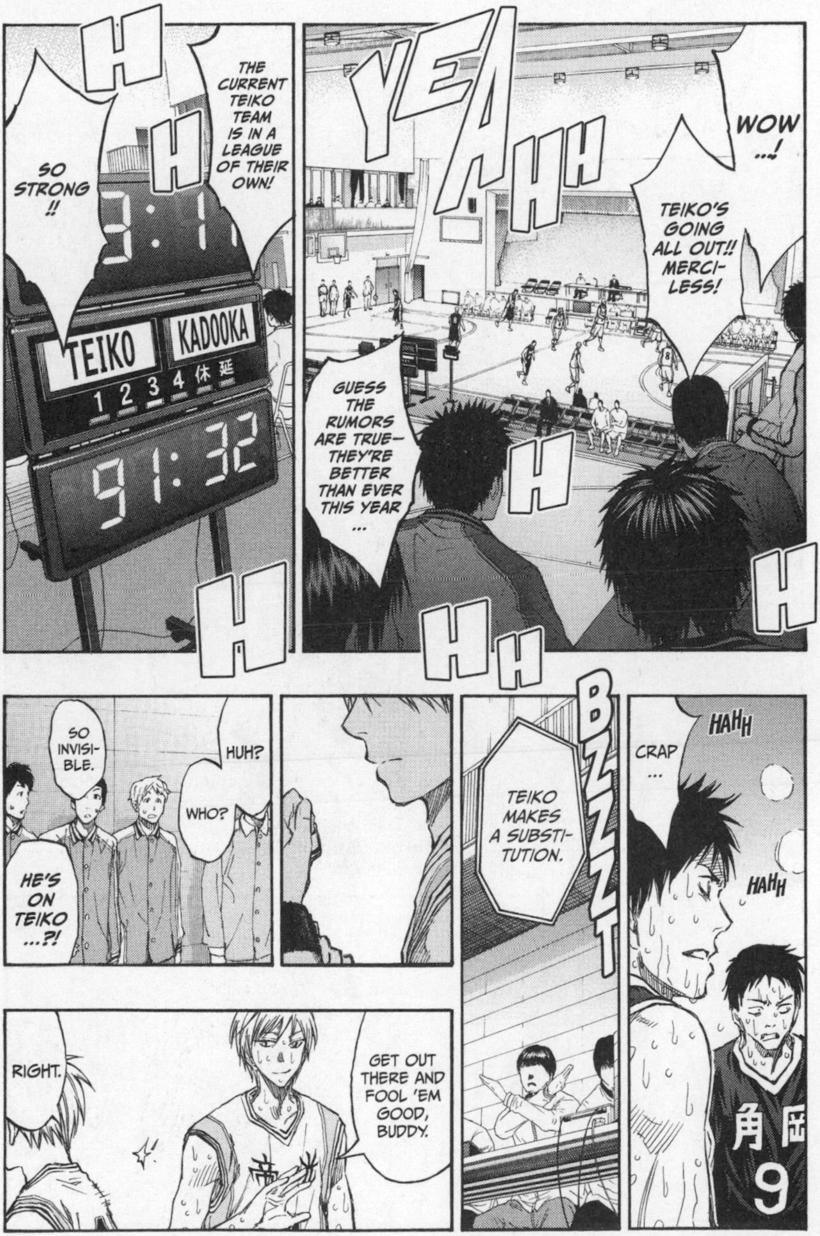
YEAHHHHHHH
WOW ...!
TEIKO'S GOING ALL OUT!! MERCILESS!
GUESS THE RUMORS ARE TRUE—THEY'RE BETTER THAN EVER THIS YEAR ...
THE CURRENT TEIKO TEAM IS IN A LEAGUE OF THEIR OWN!
SO STRONG !!
TEIKO
KADOOKA
1 2 3 4 休 延
91:32
HAHH
CRAP ...
HAHH
BZZZT
TEIKO MAKES A SUBSTITUTION.
HUH?
WHO?
SO INVISIBLE.
HE'S ON TEIKO ...?!
GET OUT THERE AND FOOL 'EM GOOD, BUDDY.
RIGHT.

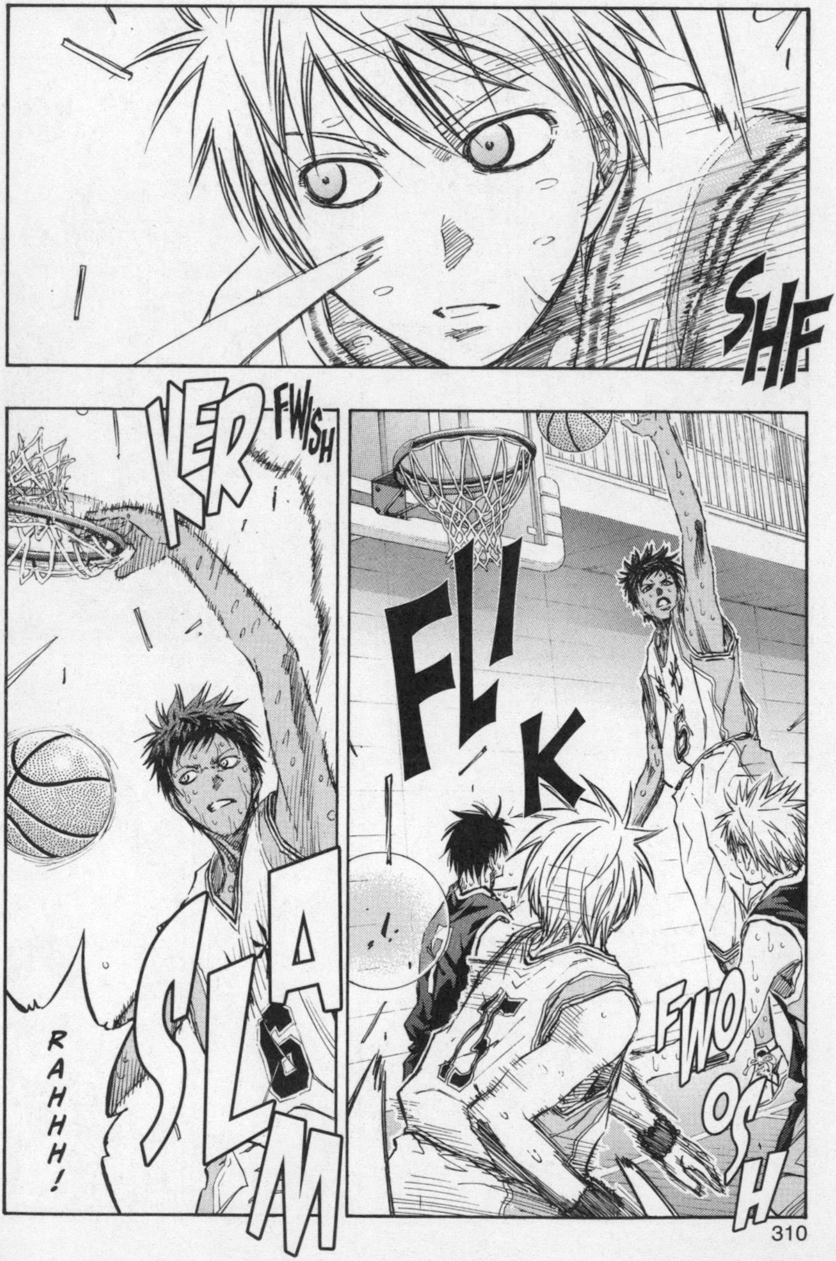
SHF
FLIK
FWOOSH
F-WISH
VER
SLAM
RAHHH!

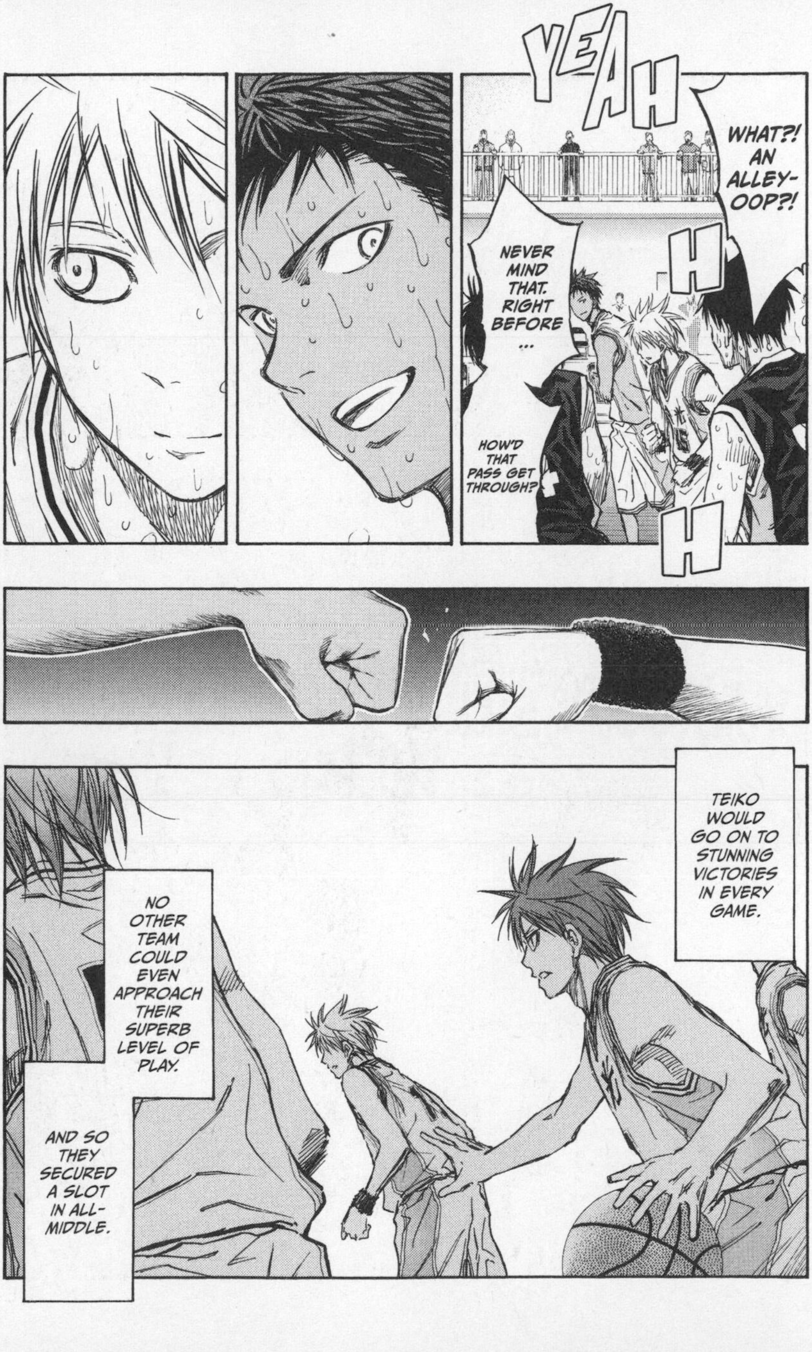
YEAH
WHAT?! AN ALLEY-OOP?!
NEVER MIND THAT. RIGHT BEFORE...
HOW'D THAT PASS GET THROUGH?
H
H
TEIKO WOULD GO ON TO STUNNING VICTORIES IN EVERY GAME.
NO OTHER TEAM COULD EVEN APPROACH THEIR SUPERB LEVEL OF PLAY.
AND SO THEY SECURED A SLOT IN ALL-MIDDLE.

KUROKO'S BASKETBALL BLOOPERS TAKE 2

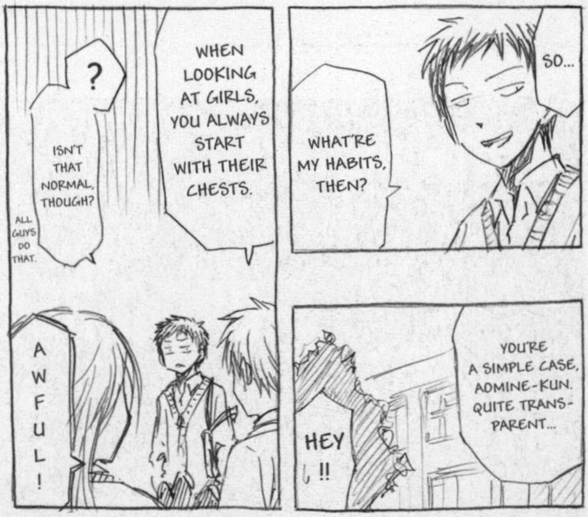
SO...
WHAT'RE MY HABITS, THEN?
WHEN LOOKING AT GIRLS, YOU ALWAYS START WITH THEIR CHESTS.
?
ISN'T THAT NORMAL, THOUGH?
ALL GUYS DO THAT.
YOU'RE A SIMPLE CASE, AOMINE-KUN. QUITE TRANS-PARENT...
HEY!!
AWFUL!

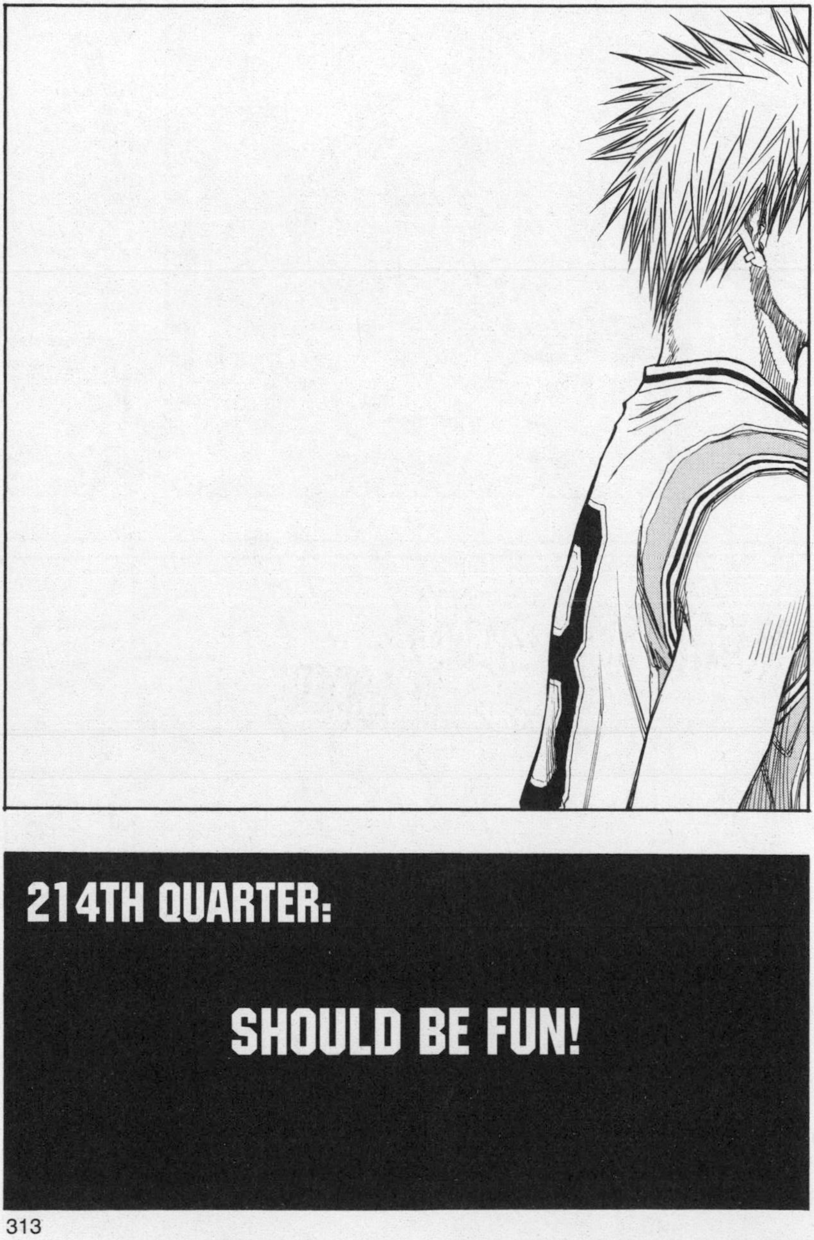

214TH QUARTER:

SHOULD BE FUN!

THE STARTING LINEUP OF TEIKO'S STRONGEST-EVER TEAM CONSISTED OF MIRACLE GENERATION MEMBERS, AND THEY BLASTED PAST THEIR FIRST GAME IN THE ALL-MIDDLE REGIONAL QUALIFIERS.

AFTERWARD, THEY WOULD CONTINUE TO RACK UP VICTORIES...

... SECURING A SPOT IN THE ALL-MIDDLE TOURNAMENT WITH EASE.

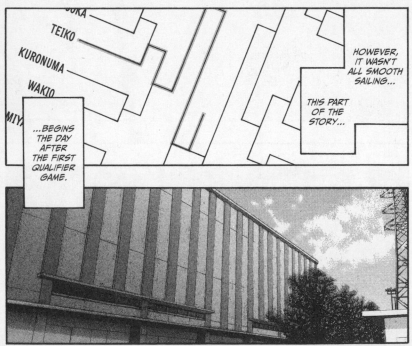

HOWEVER, IT WASN'T ALL SMOOTH SAILING...

THIS PART OF THE STORY...

...BEGINS THE DAY AFTER THE FIRST QUALIFIER GAME.

TEIKO

KURONUMA

WAKIO

314

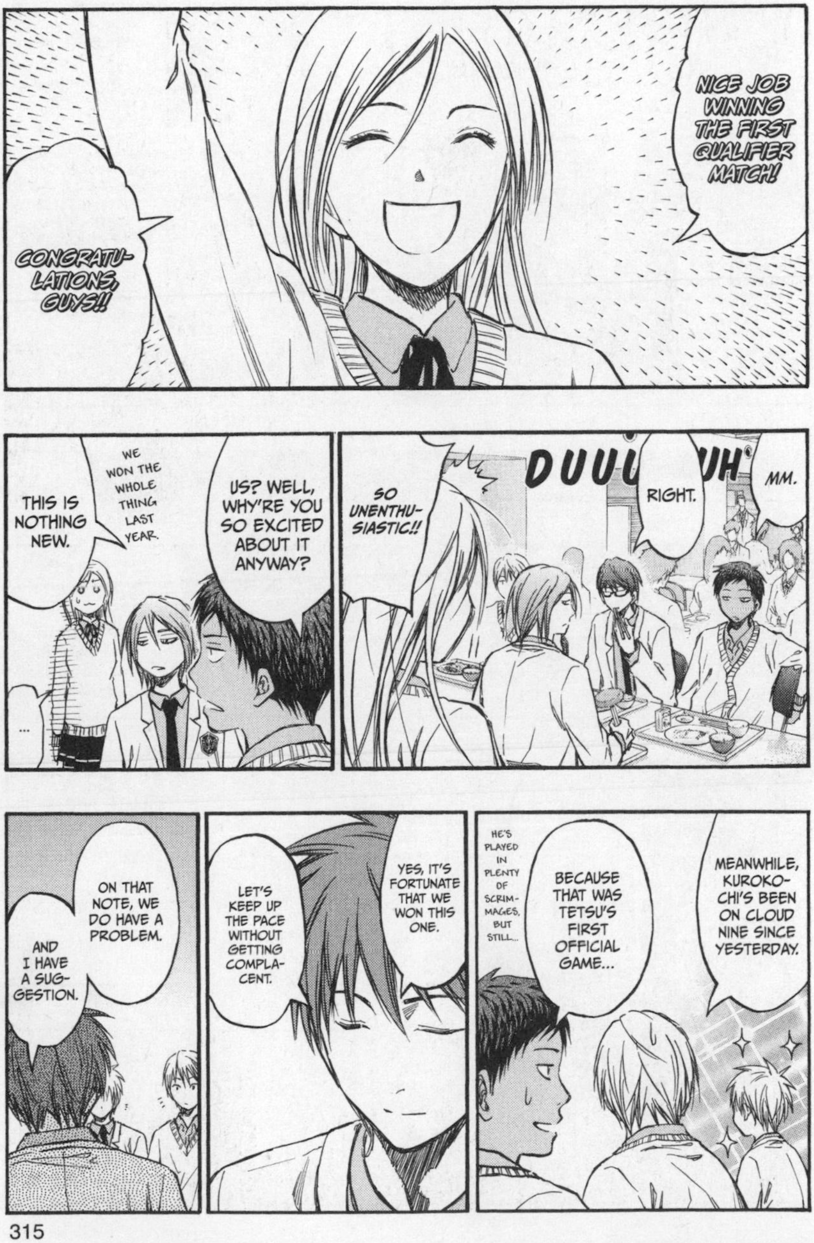

NICE JOB WINNING THE FIRST QUALIFIER MATCH!
CONGRATULATIONS, GUYS!!
MM.
RIGHT.
DUUU
UH
SO UNENTHUSIASTIC!!
US? WELL, WHY'RE YOU SO EXCITED ABOUT IT ANYWAY?
WE WON THE WHOLE THING LAST YEAR.
THIS IS NOTHING NEW.
...
MEANWHILE, KUROKOCHI'S BEEN ON CLOUD NINE SINCE YESTERDAY.
BECAUSE THAT WAS TETSU'S FIRST OFFICIAL GAME...
HE'S PLAYED IN PLENTY OF SCRIMMAGES, BUT STILL...
YES, IT'S FORTUNATE THAT WE WON THIS ONE.
LET'S KEEP UP THE PACE WITHOUT GETTING COMPLACENT.
ON THAT NOTE, WE DO HAVE A PROBLEM.
AND I HAVE A SUGGESTION.

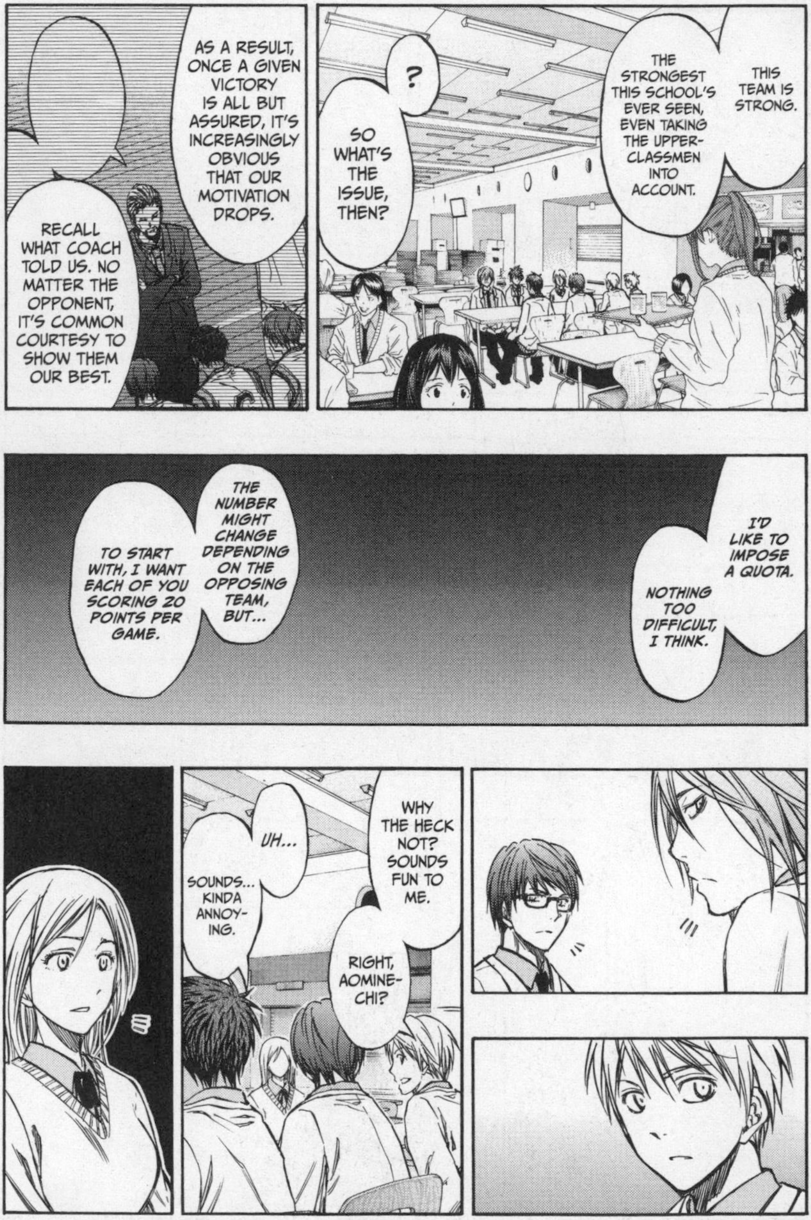
THIS TEAM IS STRONG.
THE STRONGEST THIS SCHOOL'S EVER SEEN, EVEN TAKING THE UPPER-CLASSMEN INTO ACCOUNT.
?
SO WHAT'S THE ISSUE, THEN?
AS A RESULT, ONCE A GIVEN VICTORY IS ALL BUT ASSURED, IT'S INCREASINGLY OBVIOUS THAT OUR MOTIVATION DROPS.
RECALL WHAT COACH TOLD US. NO MATTER THE OPPONENT, IT'S COMMON COURTESY TO SHOW THEM OUR BEST.
I'D LIKE TO IMPOSE A QUOTA.
NOTHING TOO DIFFICULT, I THINK.
THE NUMBER MIGHT CHANGE DEPENDING ON THE OPPOSING TEAM, BUT...
TO START WITH, I WANT EACH OF YOU SCORING 20 POINTS PER GAME.
WHY THE HECK NOT? SOUNDS FUN TO ME.
UH...
SOUNDS... KINDA ANNOY-ING.
RIGHT, AOMINE-CHI?

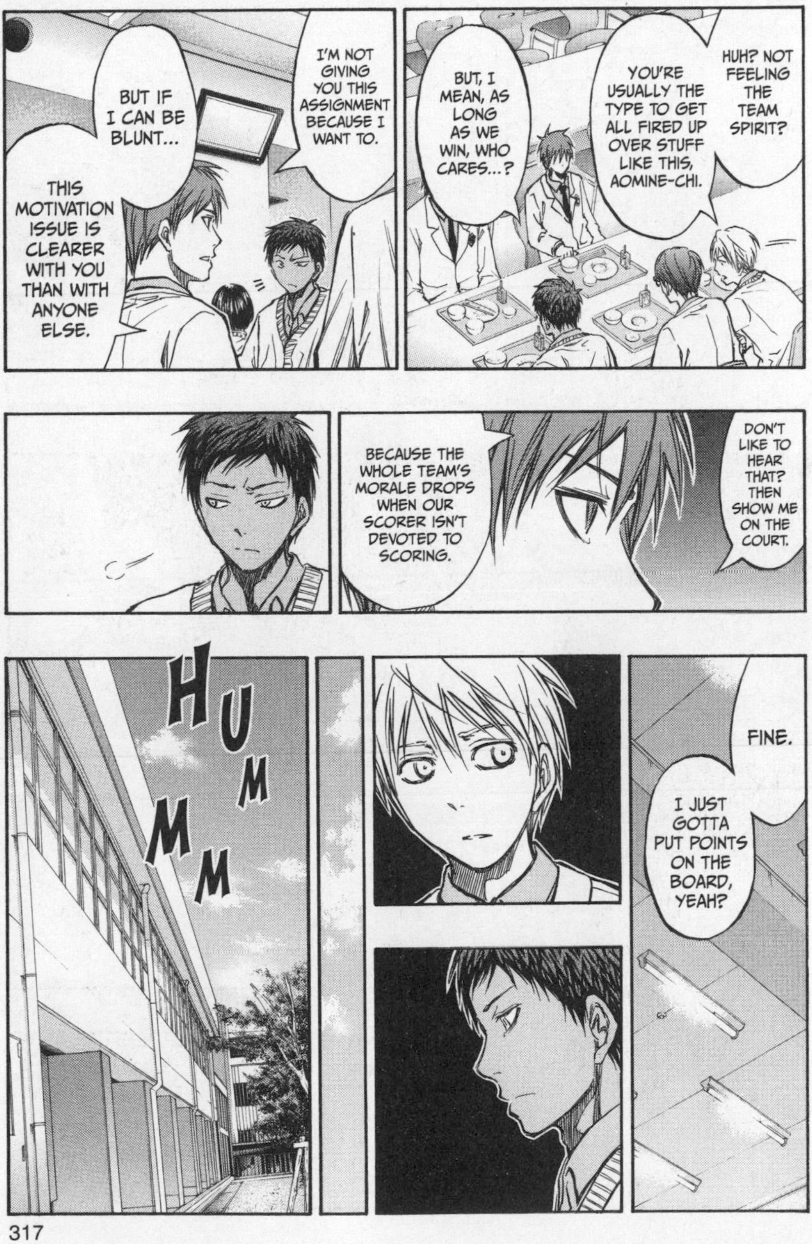
HUH? NOT FEELING THE TEAM SPIRIT?
YOU'RE USUALLY THE TYPE TO GET ALL FIRED UP OVER STUFF LIKE THIS, AOMINE-CHI.
BUT, I MEAN, AS LONG AS WE WIN, WHO CARES...?
I'M NOT GIVING YOU THIS ASSIGNMENT BECAUSE I WANT TO.
BUT IF I CAN BE BLUNT...
THIS MOTIVATION ISSUE IS CLEARER WITH YOU THAN WITH ANYONE ELSE.
BECAUSE THE WHOLE TEAM'S MORALE DROPS WHEN OUR SCORER ISN'T DEVOTED TO SCORING.
DON'T LIKE TO HEAR THAT? THEN SHOW ME ON THE COURT.
FINE.
I JUST GOTTA PUT POINTS ON THE BOARD, YEAH?
HUMMM

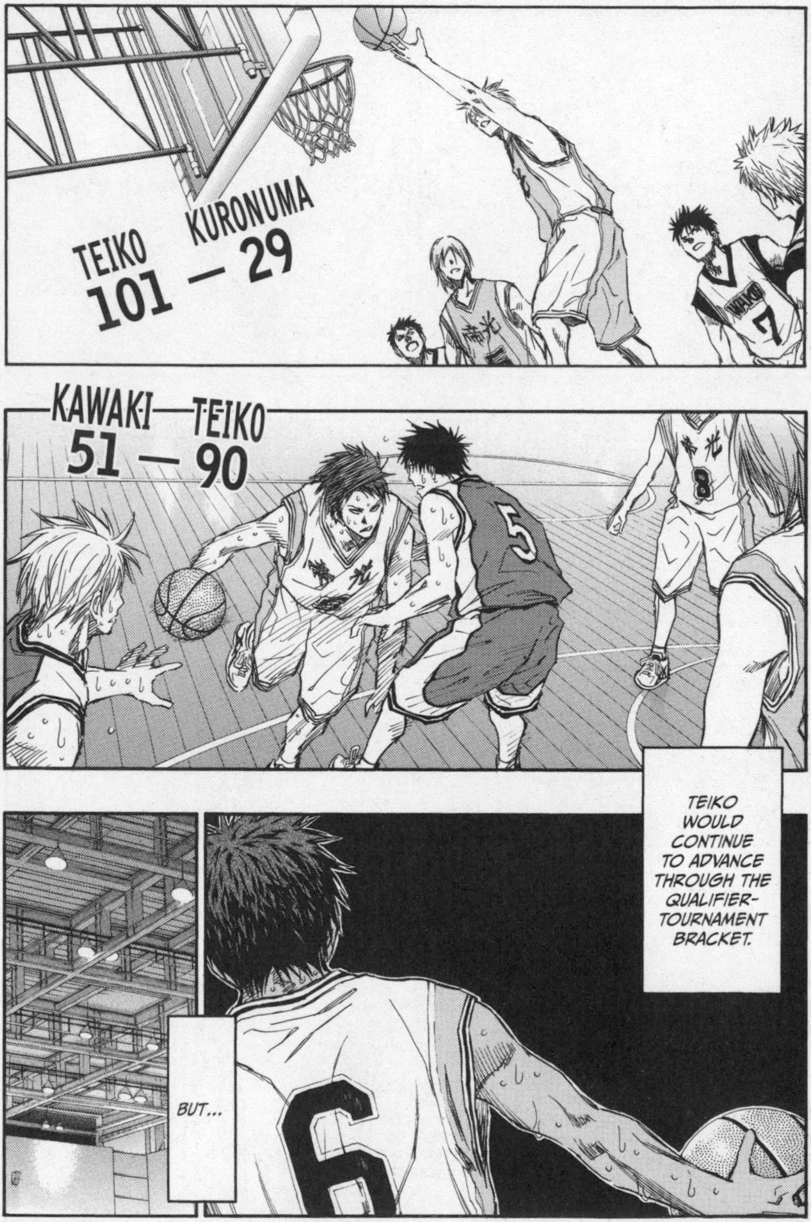
TEIKO 101 — 29 KURONUMA
KAWAKI 51 — 90 TEIKO
TEIKO WOULD CONTINUE TO ADVANCE THROUGH THE QUALIFIER-TOURNAMENT BRACKET.
BUT...

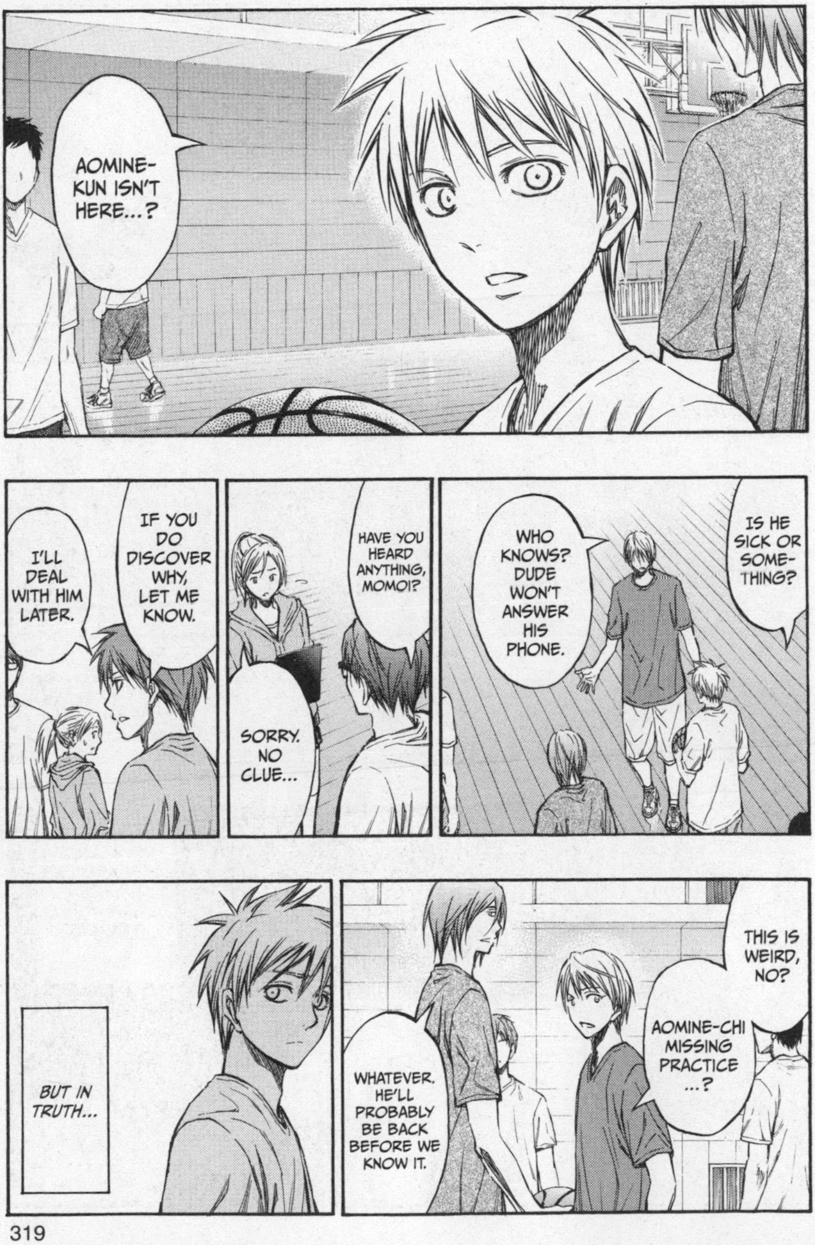
AOMINE-KUN ISN'T HERE...?
IS HE SICK OR SOMETHING?
WHO KNOWS? DUDE WON'T ANSWER HIS PHONE.
HAVE YOU HEARD ANYTHING, MOMOI?
SORRY. NO CLUE...
IF YOU DO DISCOVER WHY, LET ME KNOW.
I'LL DEAL WITH HIM LATER.
THIS IS WEIRD, NO?
AOMINE-CHI MISSING PRACTICE ...?
WHATEVER. HE'LL PROBABLY BE BACK BEFORE WE KNOW IT.
BUT IN TRUTH...

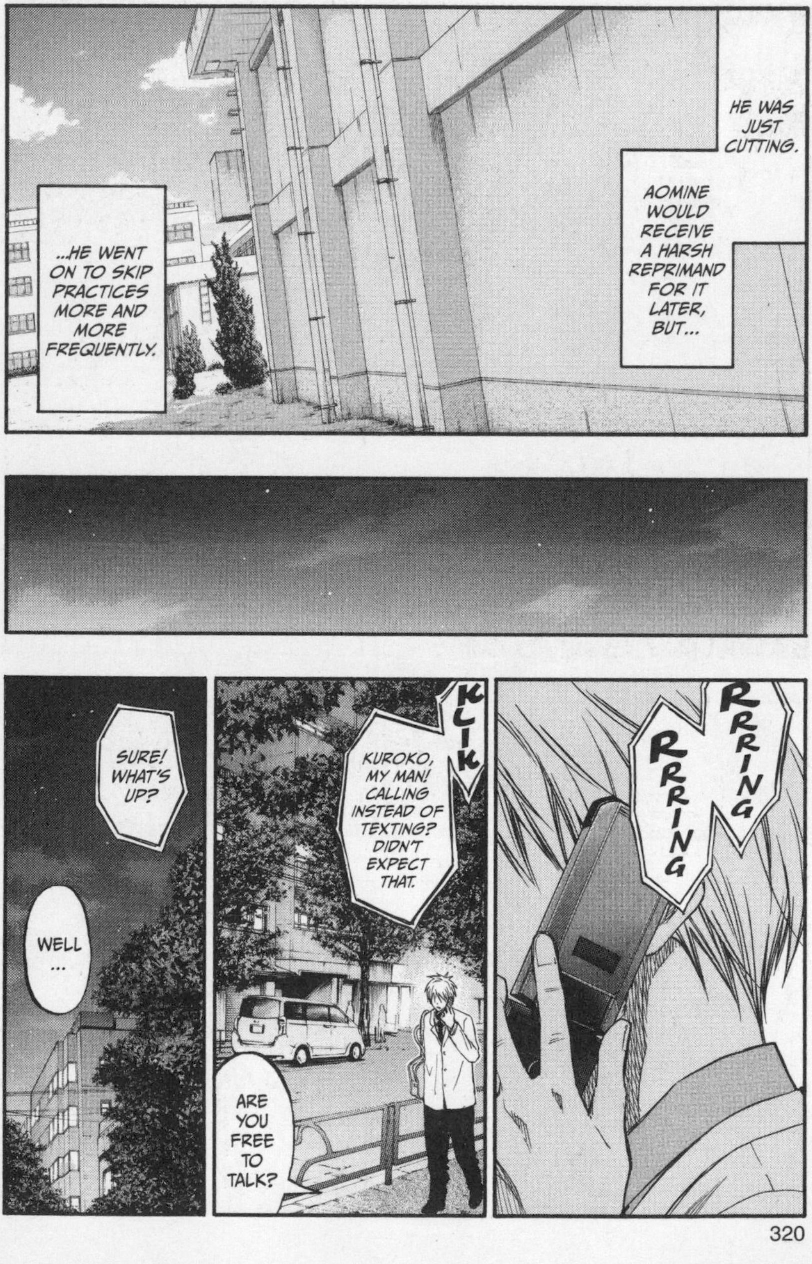
HE WAS JUST CUTTING.
AOMINE WOULD RECEIVE A HARSH REPRIMAND FOR IT LATER, BUT...
...HE WENT ON TO SKIP PRACTICES MORE AND MORE FREQUENTLY.
RRRING RRRING
KLIK
KUROKO, MY MAN! CALLING INSTEAD OF TEXTING? DIDN'T EXPECT THAT.
ARE YOU FREE TO TALK?
SURE! WHAT'S UP?
WELL...

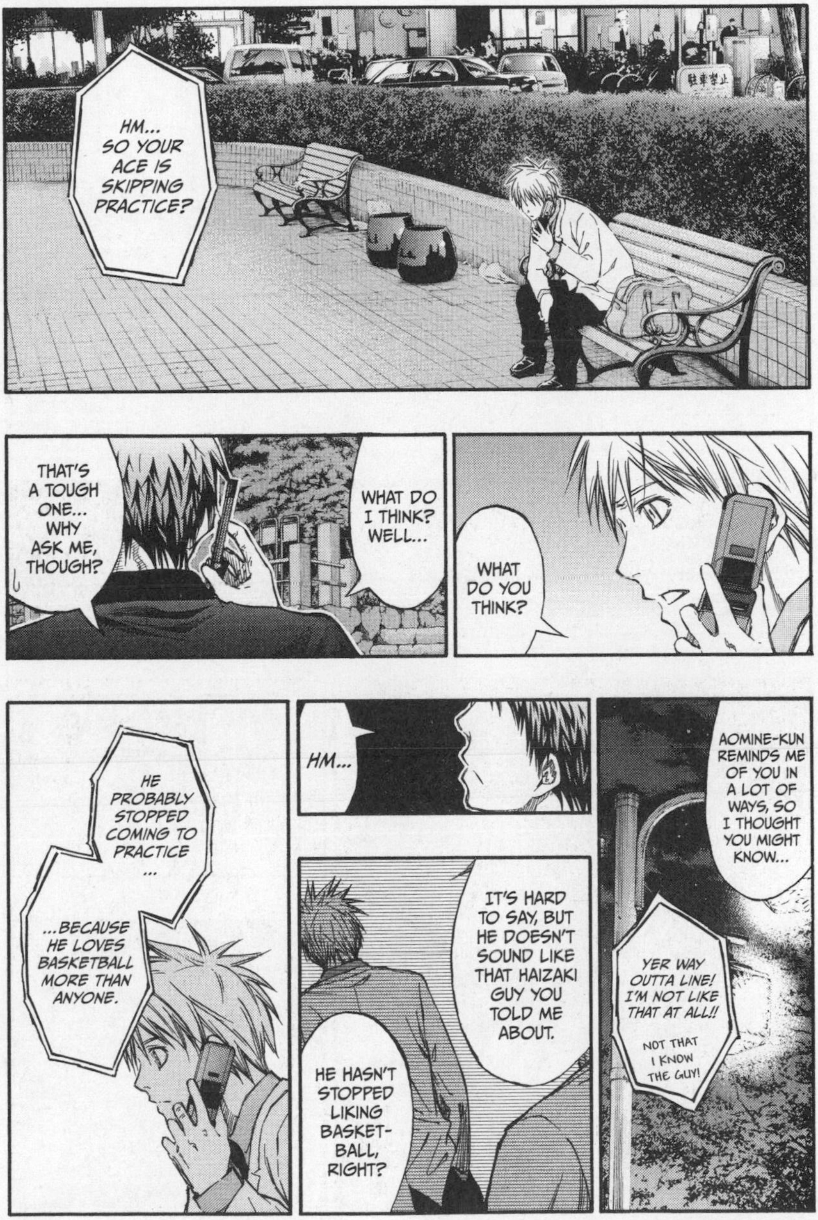
HM... SO YOUR ACE IS SKIPPING PRACTICE?
WHAT DO YOU THINK?
WHAT DO I THINK? WELL...
THAT'S A TOUGH ONE... WHY ASK ME, THOUGH?
AOMINE-KUN REMINDS ME OF YOU IN A LOT OF WAYS, SO I THOUGHT YOU MIGHT KNOW...
YER WAY OUTTA LINE! I'M NOT LIKE THAT AT ALL!!
NOT THAT I KNOW THE GUY!
HM...
IT'S HARD TO SAY, BUT HE DOESN'T SOUND LIKE THAT HAIZAKI GUY YOU TOLD ME ABOUT.
HE HASN'T STOPPED LIKING BASKET-BALL, RIGHT?
HE PROBABLY STOPPED COMING TO PRACTICE ...
...BECAUSE HE LOVES BASKETBALL MORE THAN ANYONE.

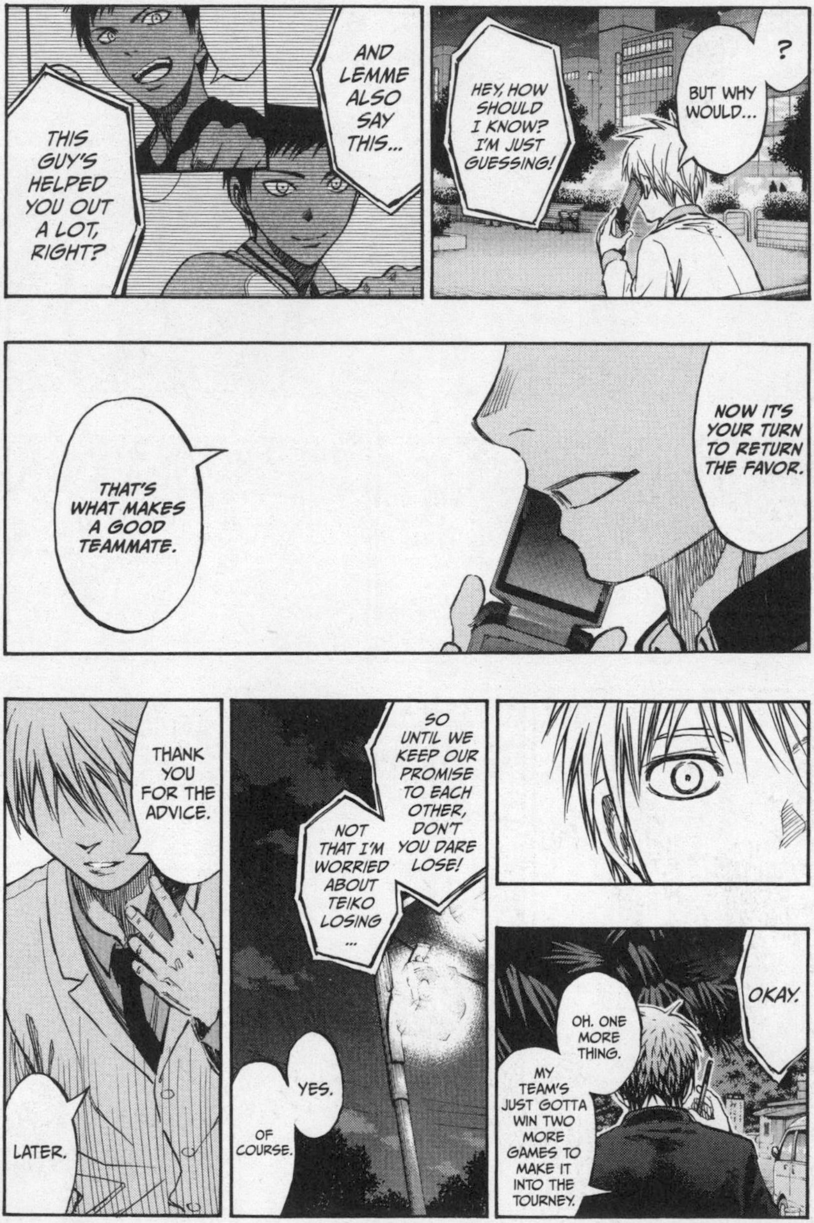
?
BUT WHY WOULD...
HEY, HOW SHOULD I KNOW? I'M JUST GUESSING!
AND LEMME ALSO SAY THIS...
THIS GUY'S HELPED YOU OUT A LOT, RIGHT?
NOW IT'S YOUR TURN TO RETURN THE FAVOR.
THAT'S WHAT MAKES A GOOD TEAMMATE.
OKAY.
OH. ONE MORE THING.
MY TEAM'S JUST GOTTA WIN TWO MORE GAMES TO MAKE IT INTO THE TOURNEY.
SO UNTIL WE KEEP OUR PROMISE TO EACH OTHER, DON'T YOU DARE LOSE!
NOT THAT I'M WORRIED ABOUT TEIKO LOSING ...
YES.
OF COURSE.
THANK YOU FOR THE ADVICE.
LATER.

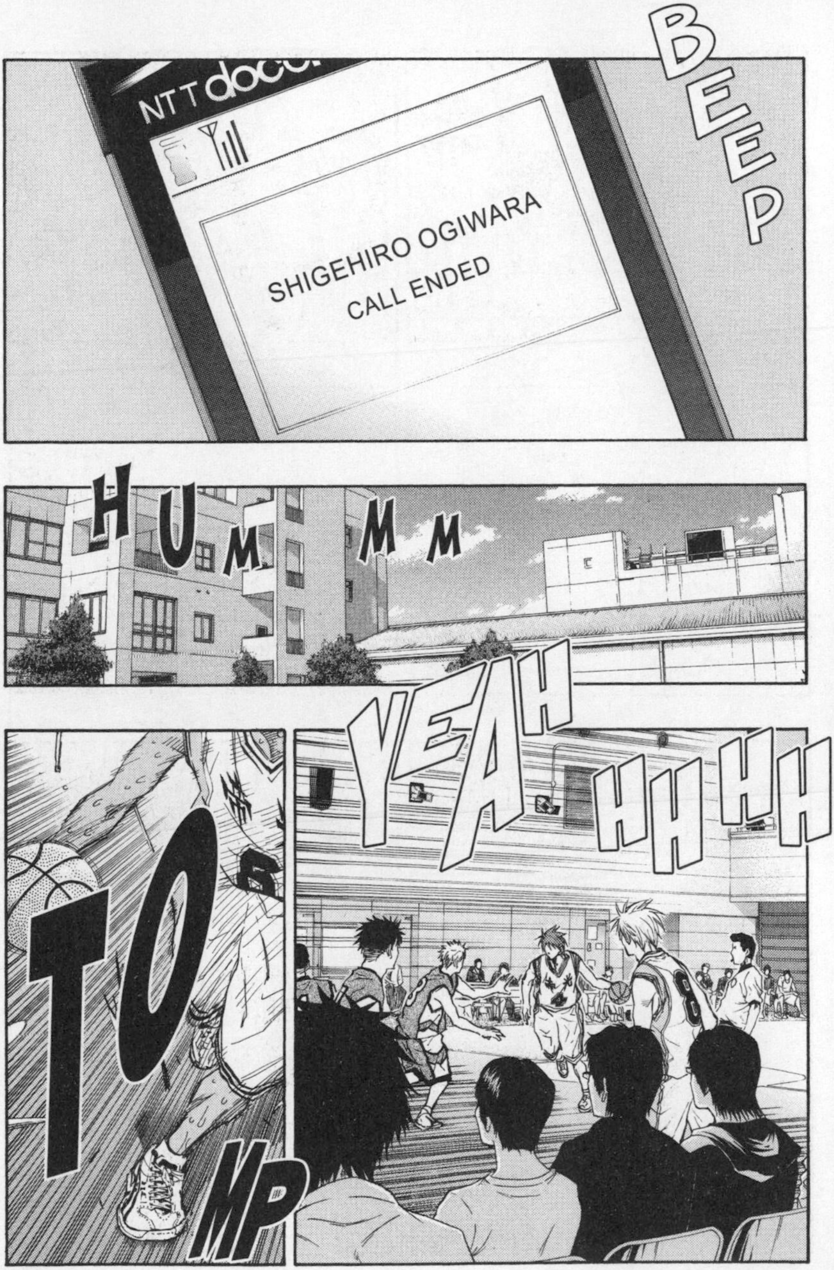
BEEP
NTT docomo
SHIGEHIRO OGIWARA
CALL ENDED
HUMMM
YEAHHHHH
TOMP

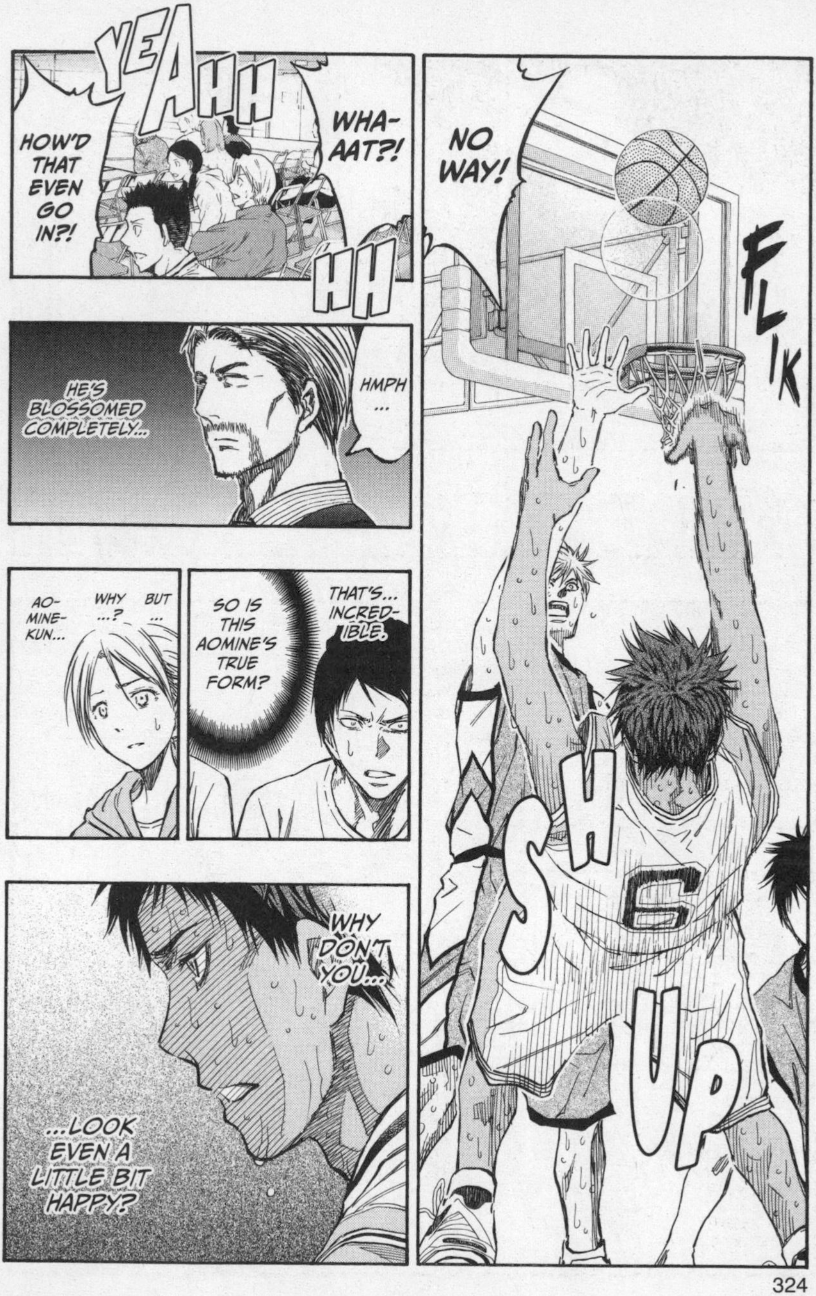
NO WAY!
FLIK
SHUP
YEAHHHH
WHA-AAT?!
HOW'D THAT EVEN GO IN?!
HMPH...
HE'S BLOSSOMED COMPLETELY...
THAT'S... INCREDIBLE.
SO IS THIS AOMINE'S TRUE FORM?
BUT...
WHY...?
AOMINE-KUN...
WHY DON'T YOU...
...LOOK EVEN A LITTLE BIT HAPPY?

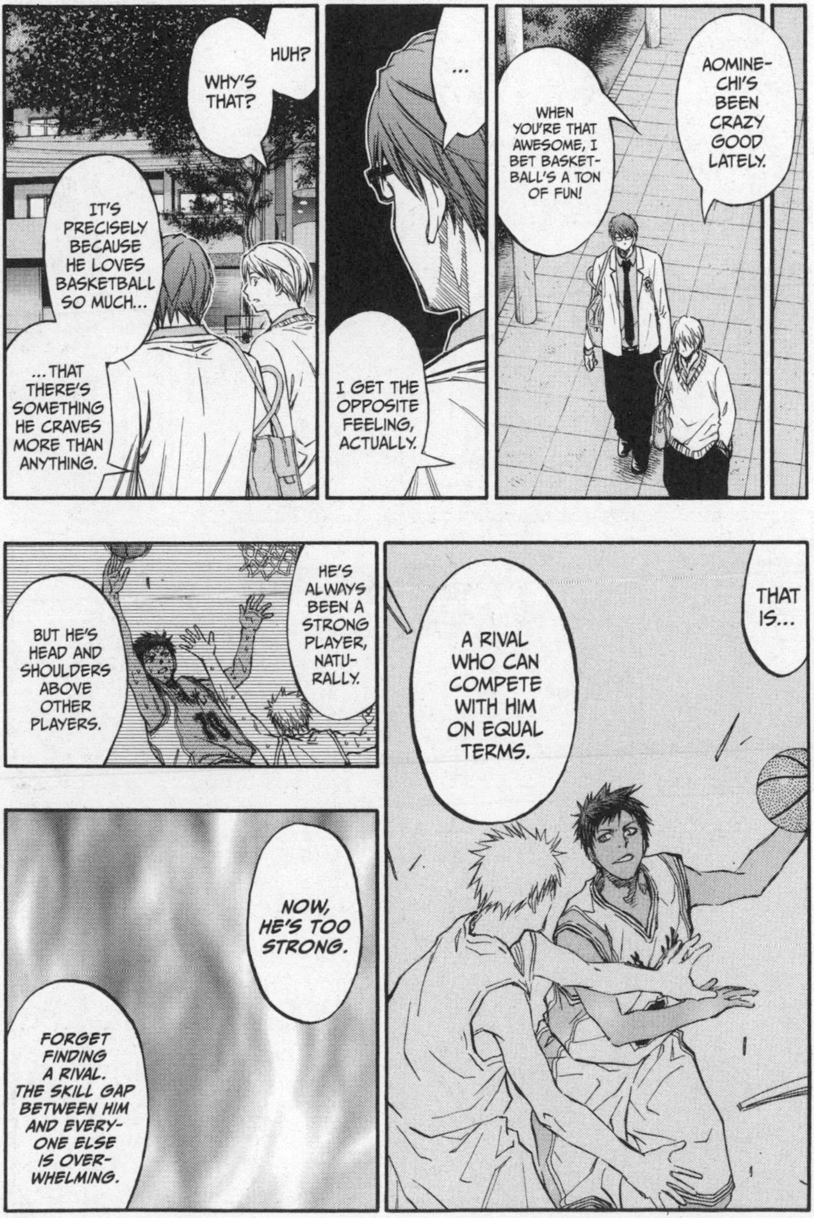
AOMINE-CHI'S BEEN CRAZY GOOD LATELY.
WHEN YOU'RE THAT AWESOME, I BET BASKETBALL'S A TON OF FUN!
...
I GET THE OPPOSITE FEELING, ACTUALLY.
HUH? WHY'S THAT?
IT'S PRECISELY BECAUSE HE LOVES BASKETBALL SO MUCH...
...THAT THERE'S SOMETHING HE CRAVES MORE THAN ANYTHING.
THAT IS...
A RIVAL WHO CAN COMPETE WITH HIM ON EQUAL TERMS.
HE'S ALWAYS BEEN A STRONG PLAYER, NATURALLY.
BUT HE'S HEAD AND SHOULDERS ABOVE OTHER PLAYERS.
NOW, HE'S TOO STRONG.
FORGET FINDING A RIVAL. THE SKILL GAP BETWEEN HIM AND EVERYONE ELSE IS OVERWHELMING.

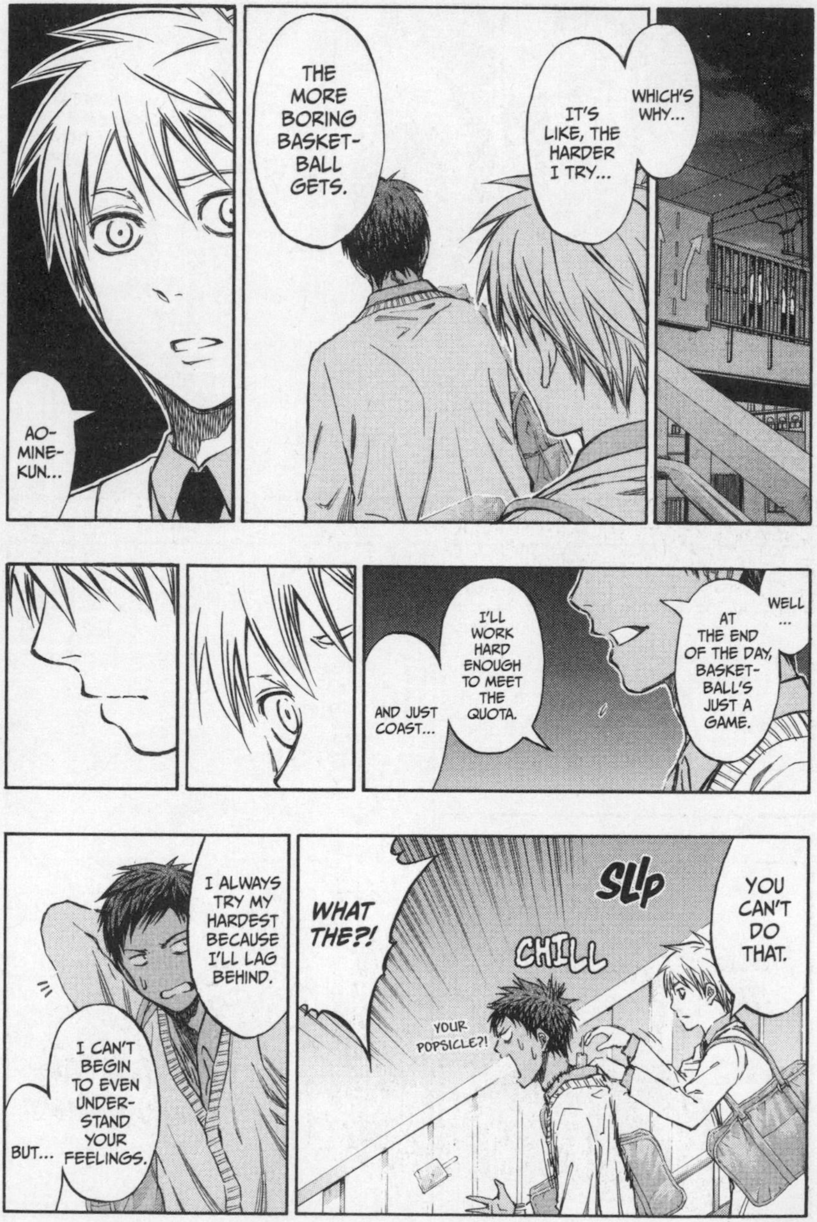
WHICH'S WHY...
IT'S LIKE, THE HARDER I TRY...
THE MORE BORING BASKETBALL GETS.
AO-MINE-KUN...
WELL...
AT THE END OF THE DAY, BASKETBALL'S JUST A GAME.
I'LL WORK HARD ENOUGH TO MEET THE QUOTA.
AND JUST COAST...
YOU CAN'T DO THAT.
SLIP
CHILL
WHAT THE?!
YOUR POPSICLE?!
I ALWAYS TRY MY HARDEST BECAUSE I'LL LAG BEHIND.
I CAN'T BEGIN TO EVEN UNDERSTAND YOUR FEELINGS.
BUT...

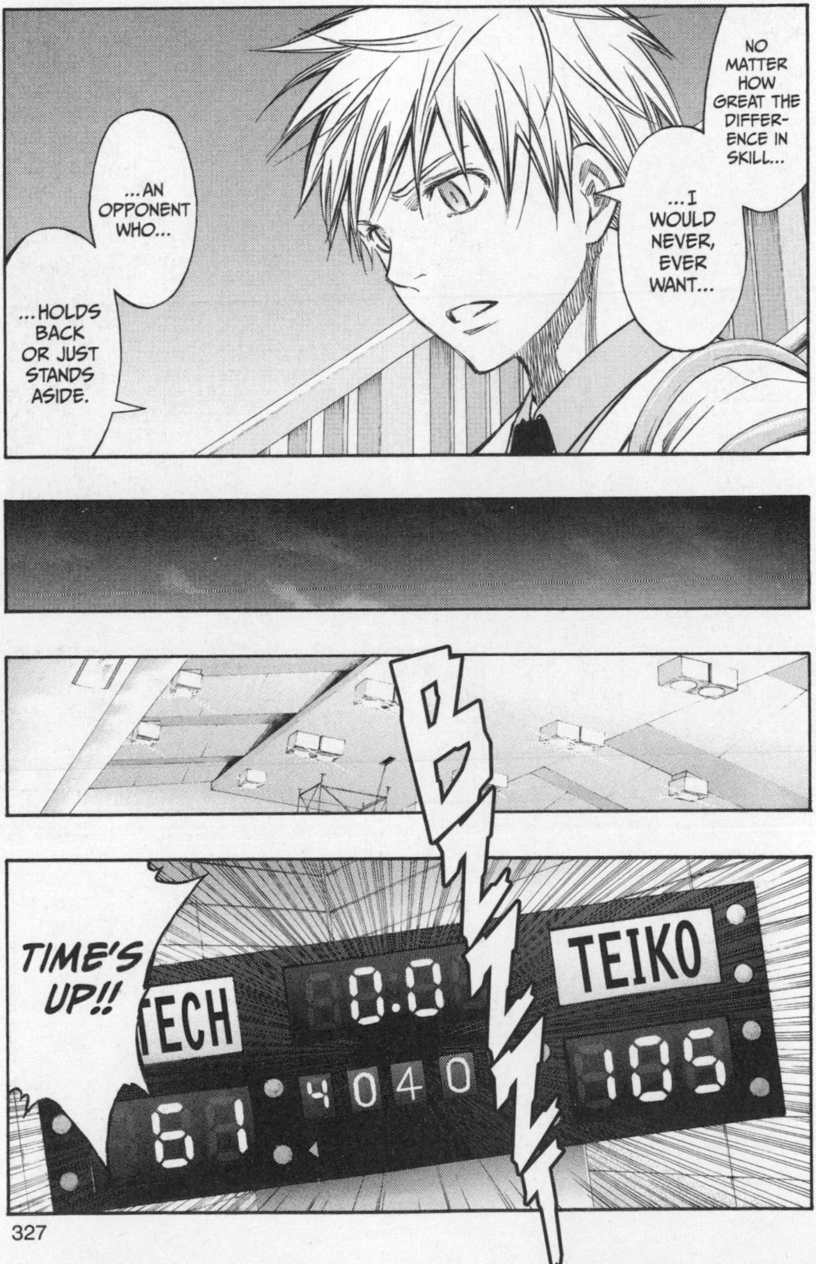
NO MATTER HOW GREAT THE DIFFERENCE IN SKILL...
...I WOULD NEVER, EVER WANT...
...AN OPPONENT WHO...
...HOLDS BACK OR JUST STANDS ASIDE.
TEIKO
0.0
TECH
105
61
TIME'S UP!!

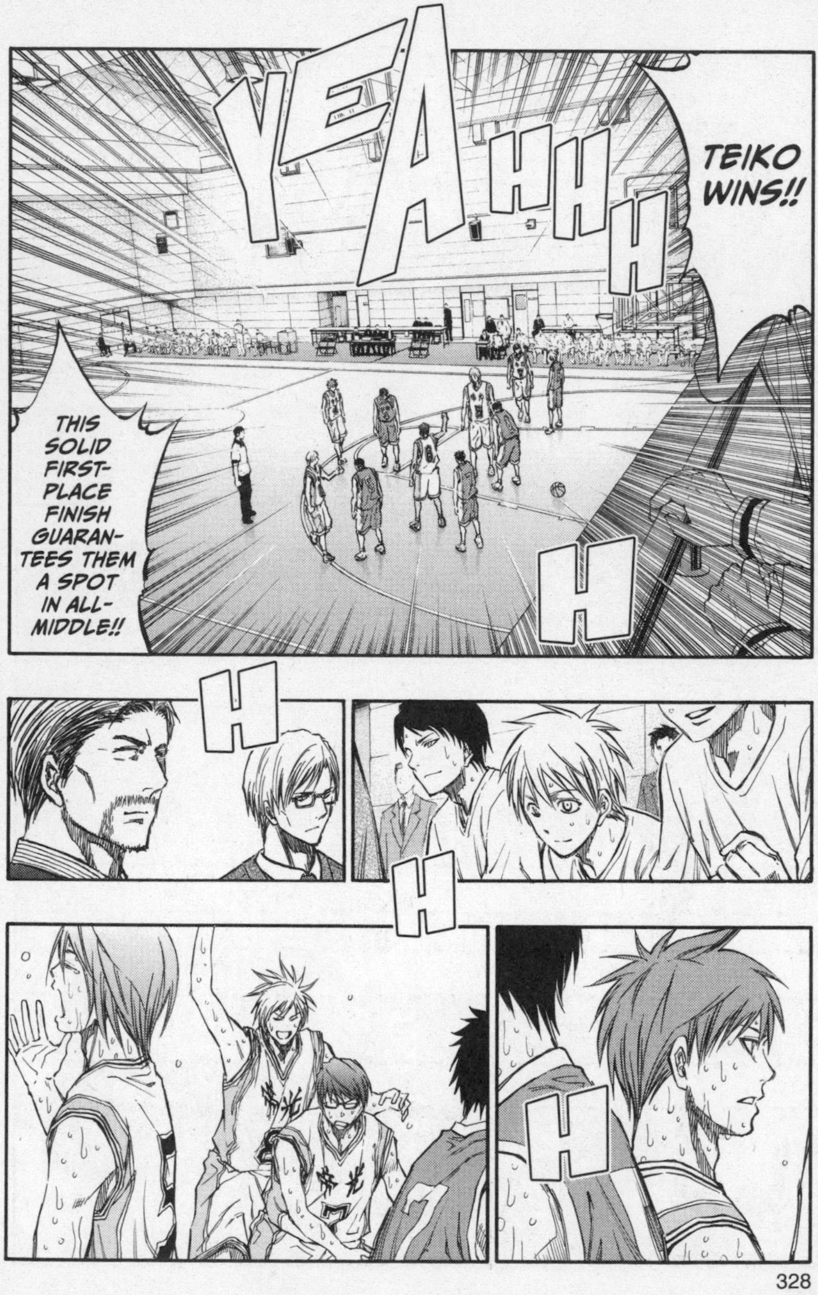
YEAHHHH
TEIKO WINS!!
THIS SOLID FIRST-PLACE FINISH GUARANTEES THEM A SPOT IN ALL-MIDDLE!!
H
H
H
H
H

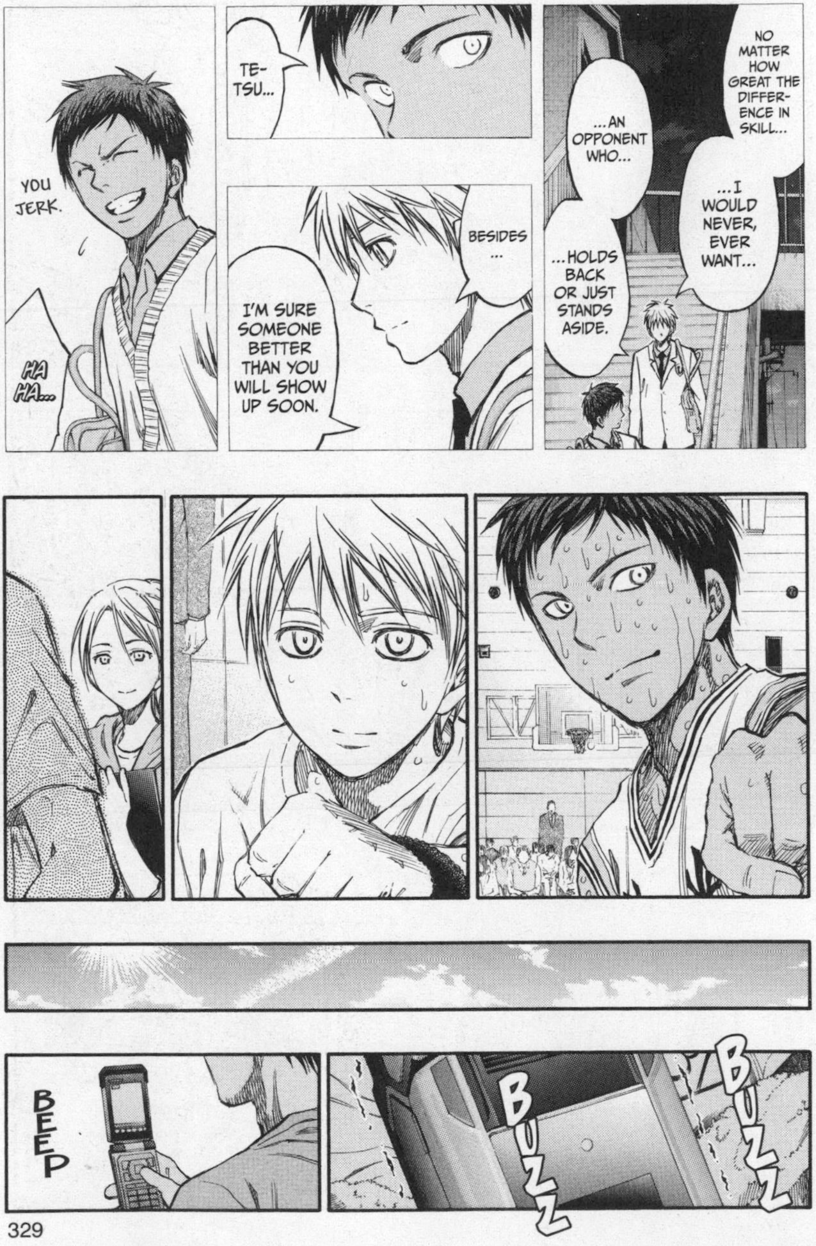
NO MATTER HOW GREAT THE DIFFERENCE IN SKILL...
...AN OPPONENT WHO...
...I WOULD NEVER, EVER WANT...
...HOLDS BACK OR JUST STANDS ASIDE.
TE-TSU...
BESIDES...
I'M SURE SOMEONE BETTER THAN YOU WILL SHOW UP SOON.
YOU JERK.
HA HA...
BUZZ
BUZZ
BEEP

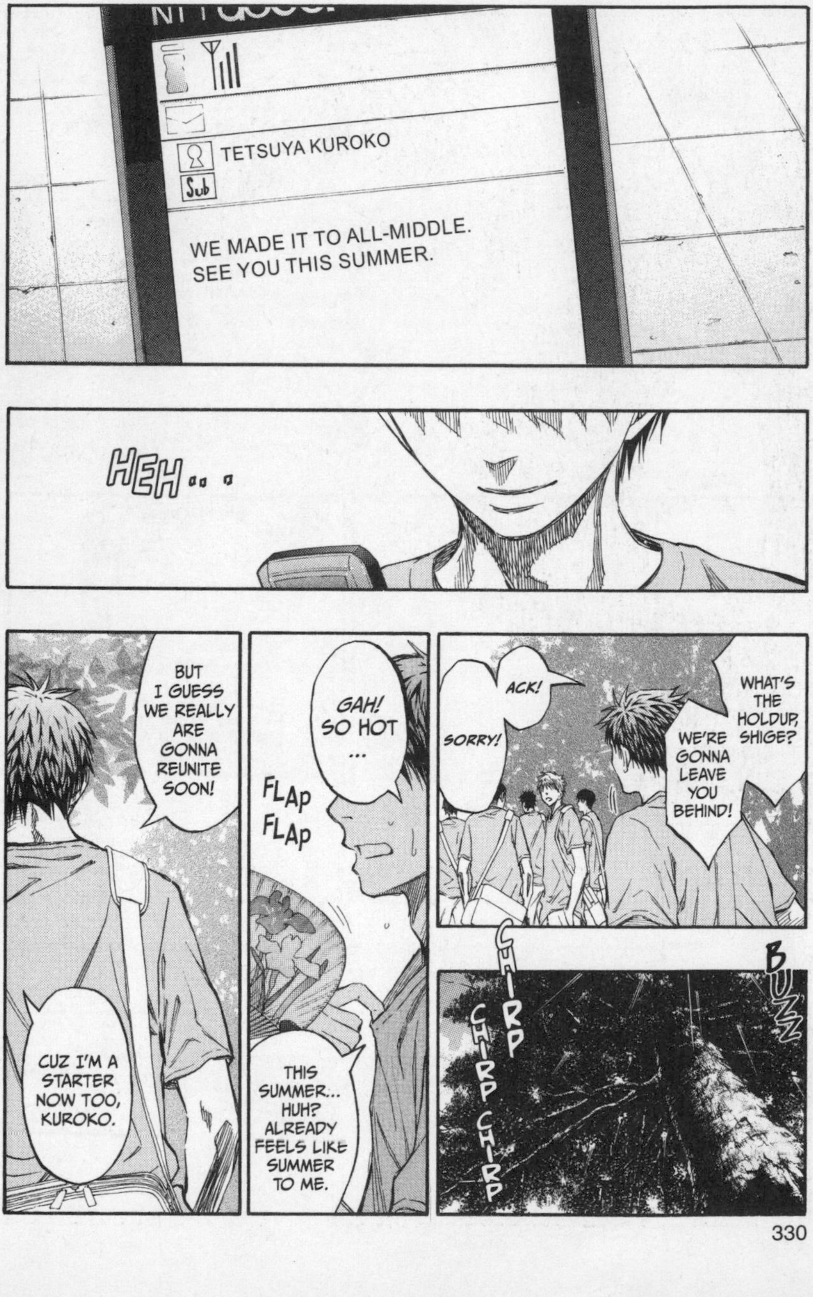
TETSUYA KUROKO
Sub
WE MADE IT TO ALL-MIDDLE. SEE YOU THIS SUMMER.
HEH...
WHAT'S THE HOLDUP, SHIGE?
WE'RE GONNA LEAVE YOU BEHIND!
ACK!
SORRY!
BUZZ
CHIRP CHIRP
CHIRP CHIRP
GAH! SO HOT...
FLAP FLAP
THIS SUMMER... HUH? ALREADY FEELS LIKE SUMMER TO ME.
BUT I GUESS WE REALLY ARE GONNA REUNITE SOON!
CUZ I'M A STARTER NOW TOO, KUROKO.

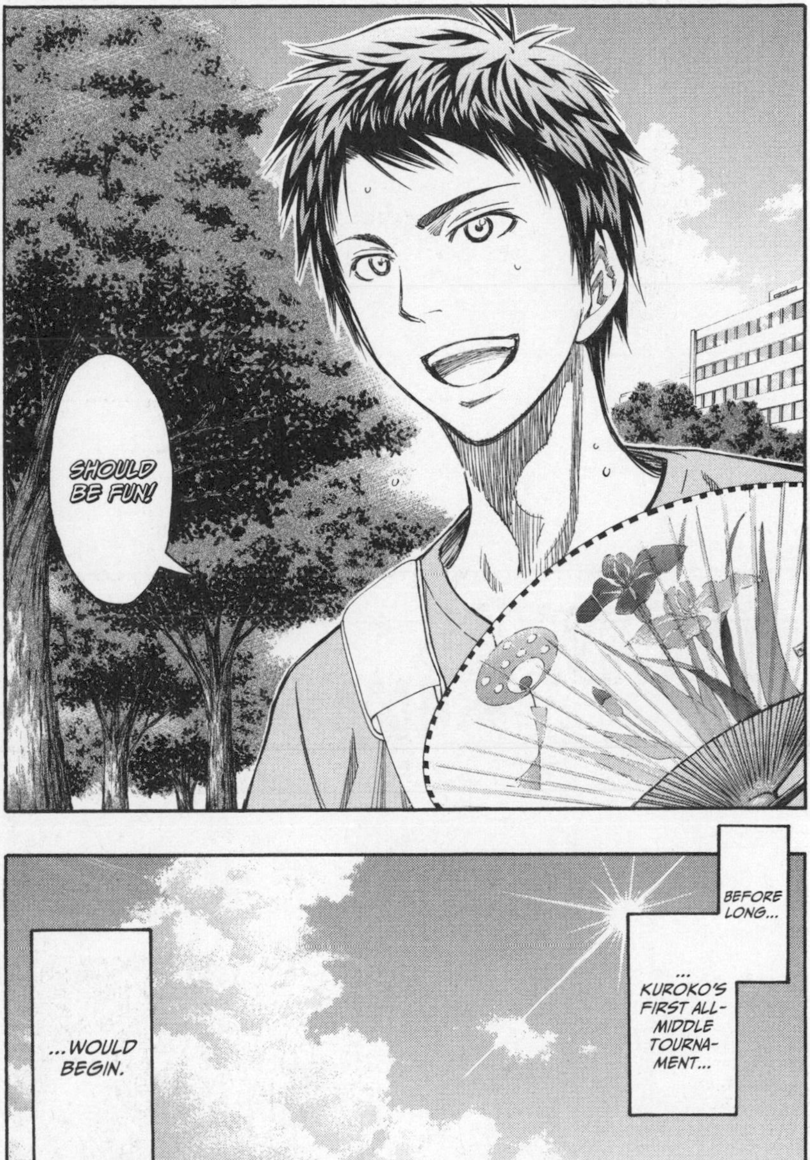
SHOULD BE FUN!
BEFORE LONG...
...KUROKO'S FIRST ALL-MIDDLE TOURNAMENT...
...WOULD BEGIN.

KUROKO'S BASKETBALL BLOOPERS
TAKE 7

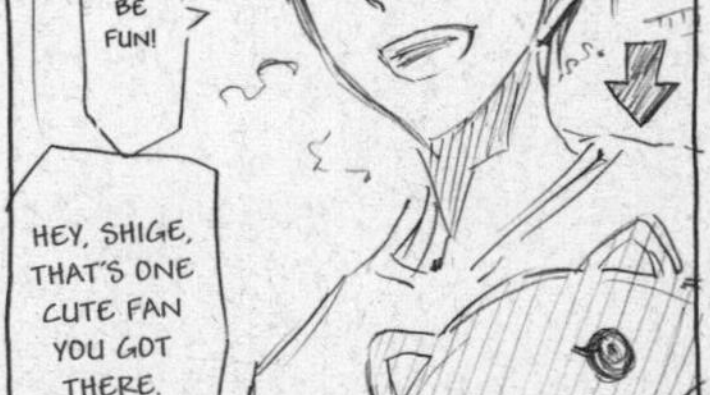
SHOULD BE FUN!
HEY, SHIGE, THAT'S ONE CUTE FAN YOU GOT THERE.
IS THAT A CAT?

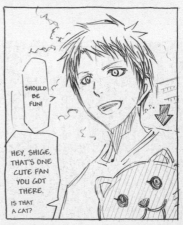

215TH QUARTER:

LET'S DO OUR BEST

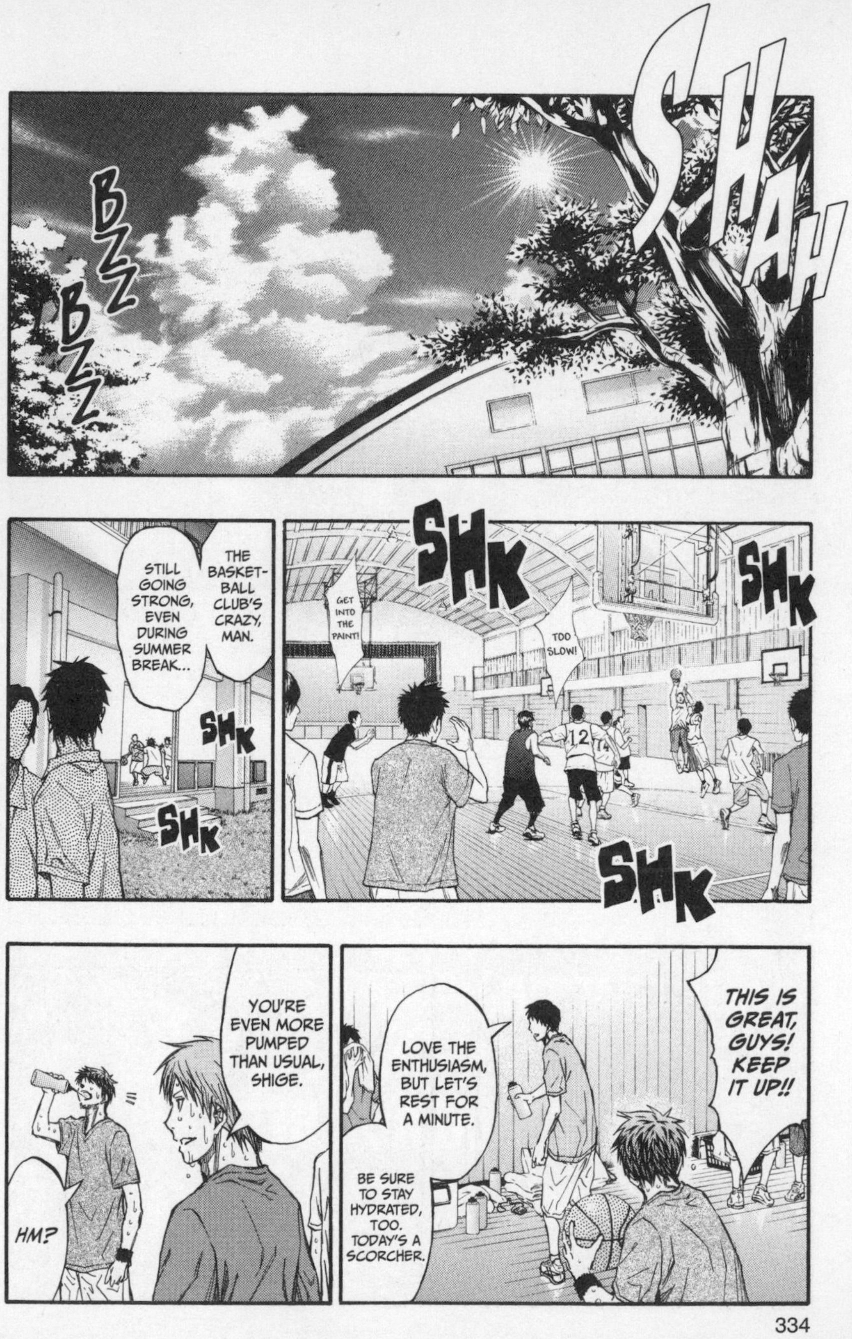
SHAH
BZZ
BZZ
SHK
SHK
TOO SLOW!
GET INTO THE PAINT!
SHK
THE BASKETBALL CLUB'S CRAZY, MAN.
STILL GOING STRONG, EVEN DURING SUMMER BREAK...
SHK
SHK
THIS IS GREAT, GUYS! KEEP IT UP!!
LOVE THE ENTHUSIASM, BUT LET'S REST FOR A MINUTE.
BE SURE TO STAY HYDRATED, TOO. TODAY'S A SCORCHER.
YOU'RE EVEN MORE PUMPED THAN USUAL, SHIGE.
HM?

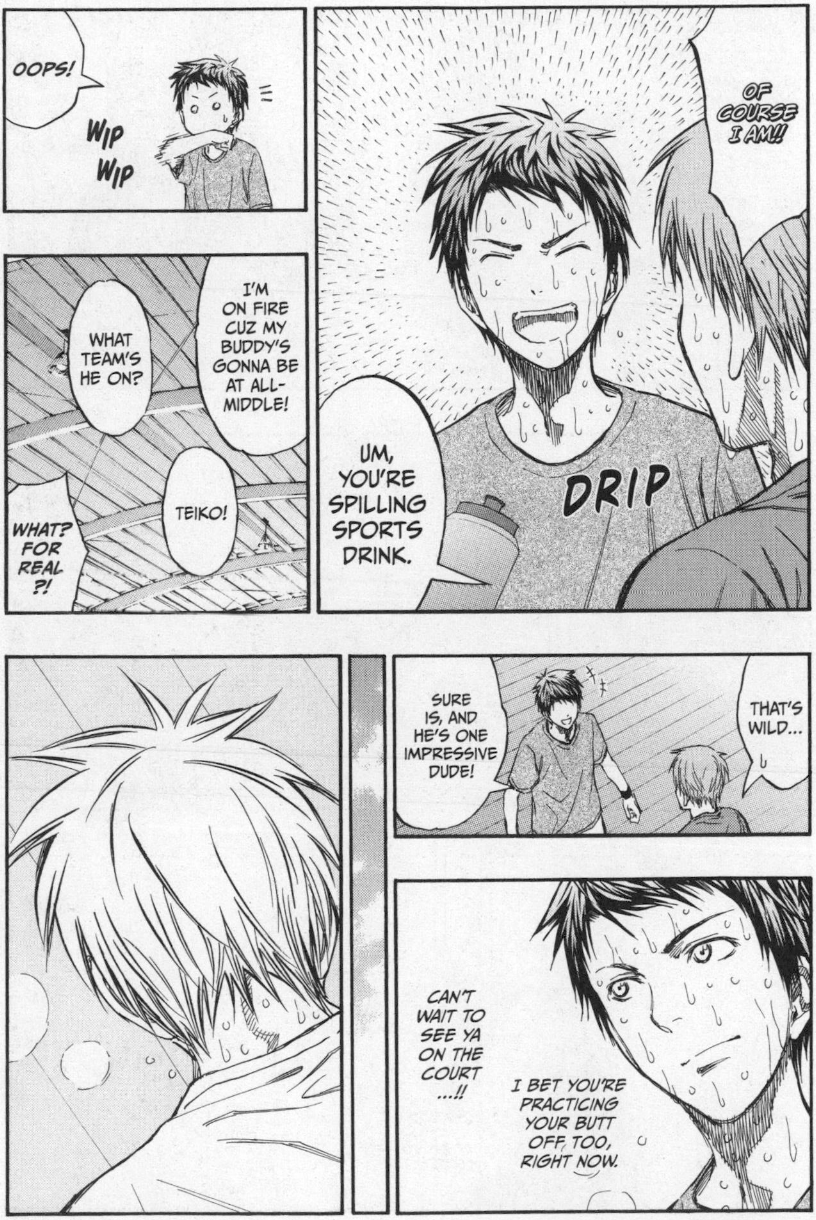
OF COURSE I AM!!
UM, YOU'RE SPILLING SPORTS DRINK.
DRIP
OOPS!
WIP WIP
I'M ON FIRE CUZ MY BUDDY'S GONNA BE AT ALL-MIDDLE!
WHAT TEAM'S HE ON?
TEIKO!
WHAT? FOR REAL?!
THAT'S WILD...
SURE IS, AND HE'S ONE IMPRESSIVE DUDE!
I BET YOU'RE PRACTICING YOUR BUTT OFF, TOO, RIGHT NOW.
CAN'T WAIT TO SEE YA ON THE COURT...!!

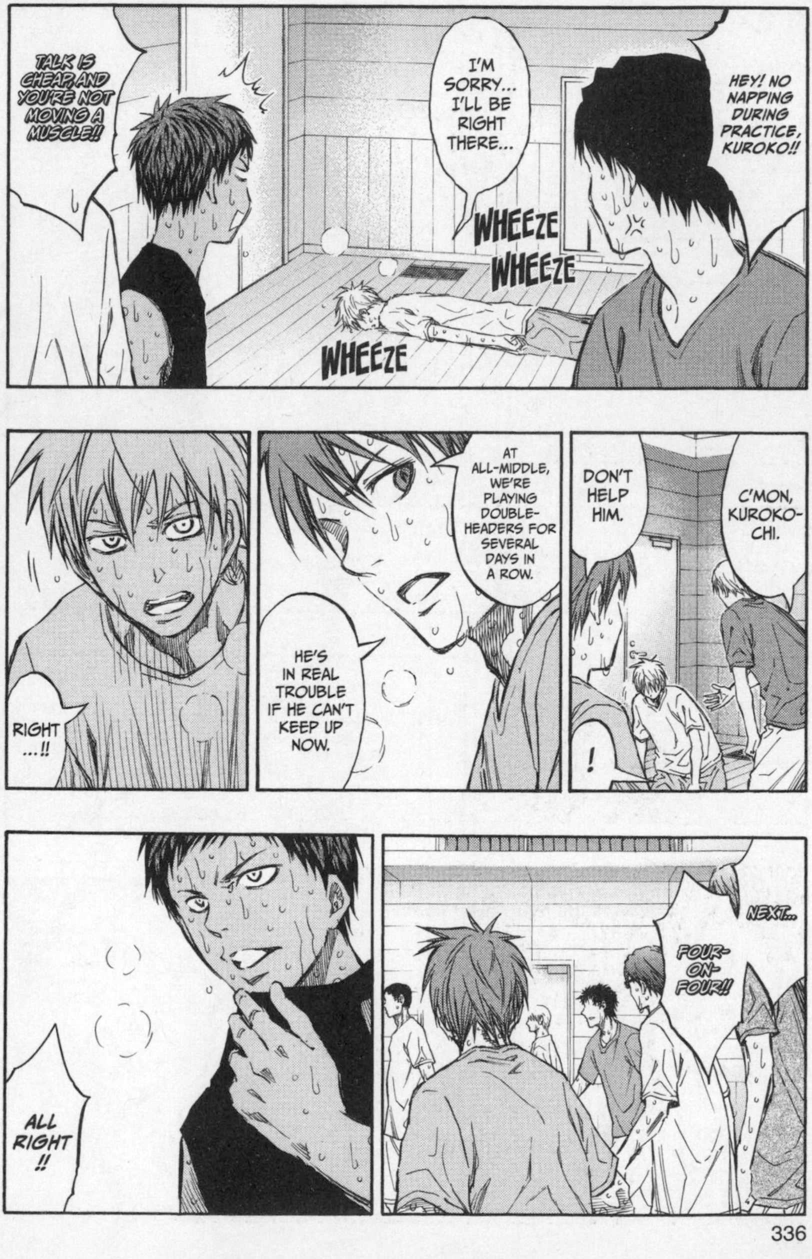
HEY! NO NAPPING DURING PRACTICE, KUROKO!!
I'M SORRY... I'LL BE RIGHT THERE...
WHEEZE
WHEEZE
TALK IS CHEAP, AND YOU'RE NOT MOVING A MUSCLE!!
WHEEZE
C'MON, KUROKOCHI.
DON'T HELP HIM.
!
AT ALL-MIDDLE, WE'RE PLAYING DOUBLEHEADERS FOR SEVERAL DAYS IN A ROW.
HE'S IN REAL TROUBLE IF HE CAN'T KEEP UP NOW.
RIGHT ...!!
NEXT...
FOUR-ON-FOUR!!
ALL RIGHT !!

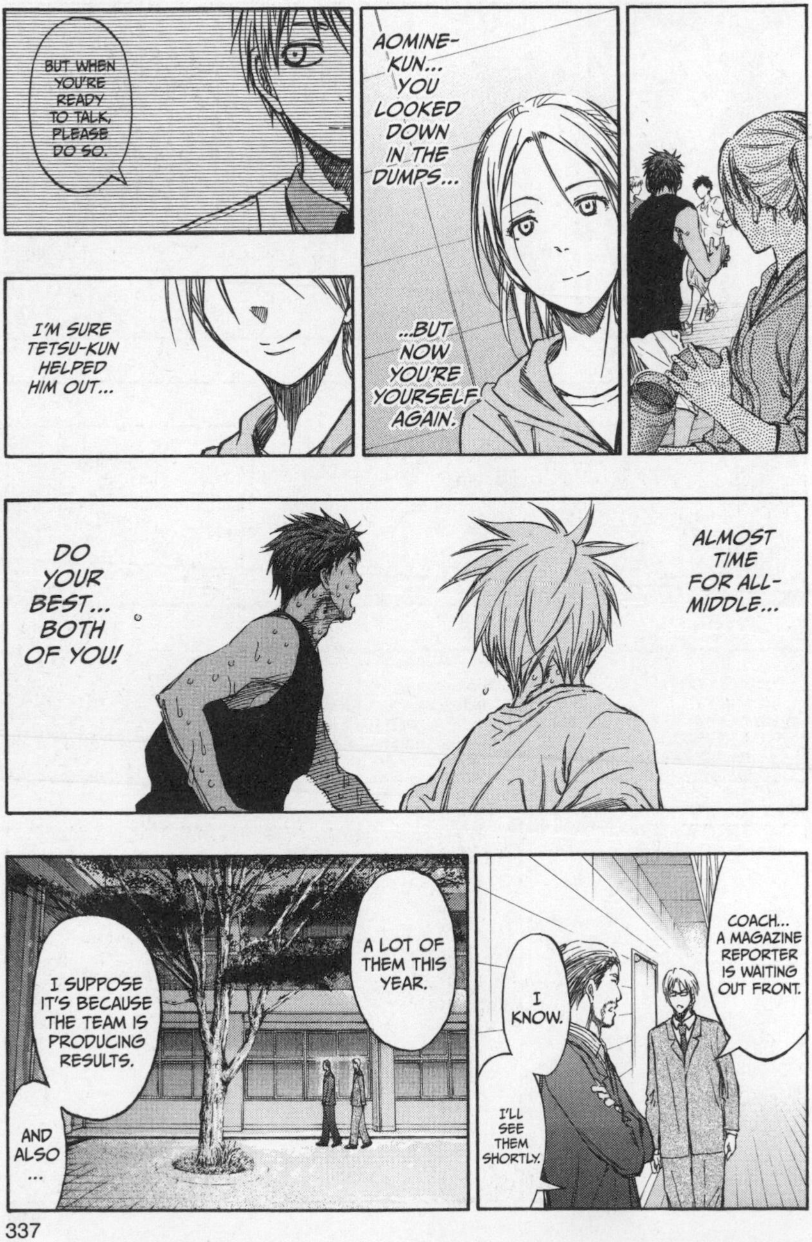
AOMINE-KUN... YOU LOOKED DOWN IN THE DUMPS...
...BUT NOW YOU'RE YOURSELF AGAIN.
BUT WHEN YOU'RE READY TO TALK, PLEASE DO SO.
I'M SURE TETSU-KUN HELPED HIM OUT...
ALMOST TIME FOR ALL-MIDDLE...
DO YOUR BEST... BOTH OF YOU!
COACH... A MAGAZINE REPORTER IS WAITING OUT FRONT.
I KNOW.
I'LL SEE THEM SHORTLY.
A LOT OF THEM THIS YEAR.
I SUPPOSE IT'S BECAUSE THE TEAM IS PRODUCING RESULTS.
AND ALSO ...

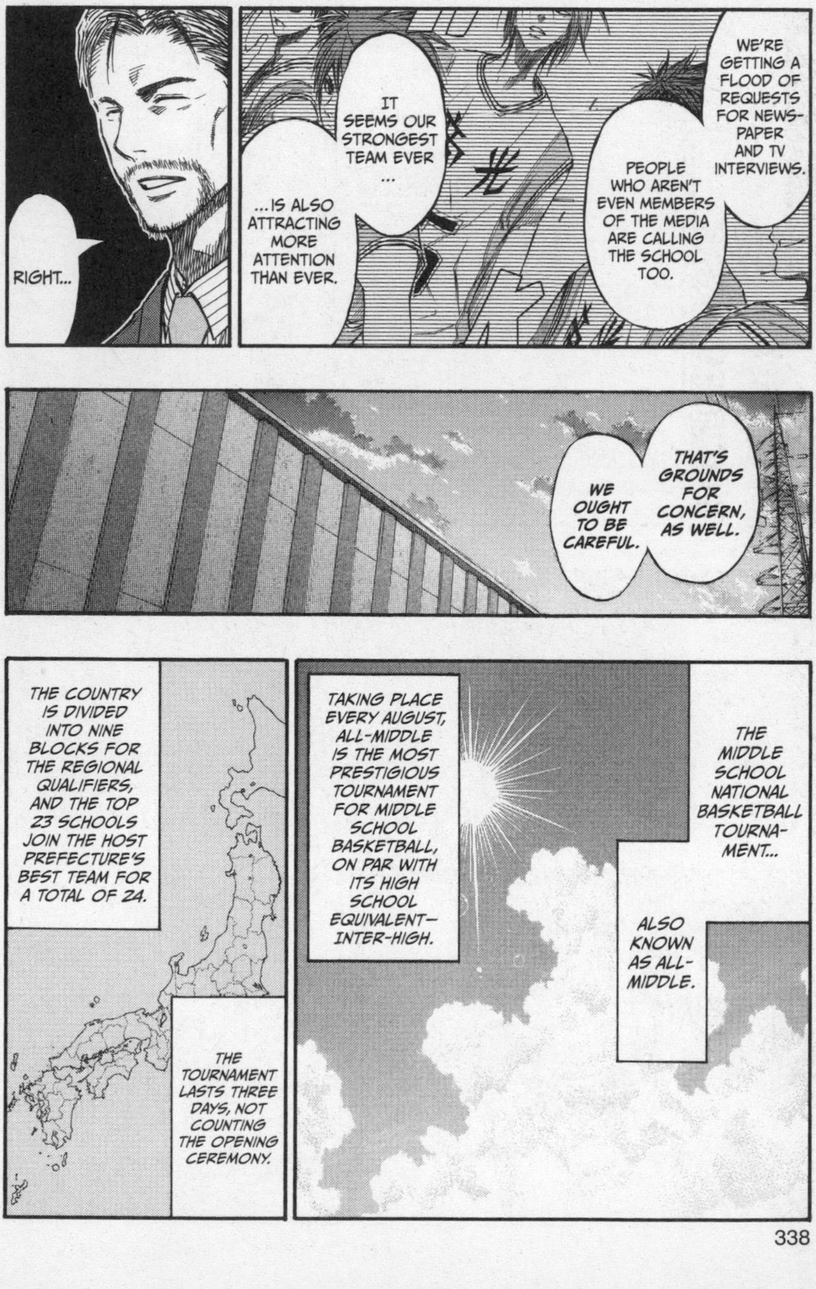
WE'RE GETTING A FLOOD OF REQUESTS FOR NEWS-PAPER AND TV INTERVIEWS.
PEOPLE WHO AREN'T EVEN MEMBERS OF THE MEDIA ARE CALLING THE SCHOOL TOO.
IT SEEMS OUR STRONGEST TEAM EVER ...
...IS ALSO ATTRACTING MORE ATTENTION THAN EVER.
RIGHT...
THAT'S GROUNDS FOR CONCERN, AS WELL.
WE OUGHT TO BE CAREFUL.
THE MIDDLE SCHOOL NATIONAL BASKETBALL TOURNA-MENT...
ALSO KNOWN AS ALL-MIDDLE.
TAKING PLACE EVERY AUGUST, ALL-MIDDLE IS THE MOST PRESTIGIOUS TOURNAMENT FOR MIDDLE SCHOOL BASKETBALL, ON PAR WITH ITS HIGH SCHOOL EQUIVALENT—INTER-HIGH.
THE COUNTRY IS DIVIDED INTO NINE BLOCKS FOR THE REGIONAL QUALIFIERS, AND THE TOP 23 SCHOOLS JOIN THE HOST PREFECTURE'S BEST TEAM FOR A TOTAL OF 24.
THE TOURNAMENT LASTS THREE DAYS, NOT COUNTING THE OPENING CEREMONY.

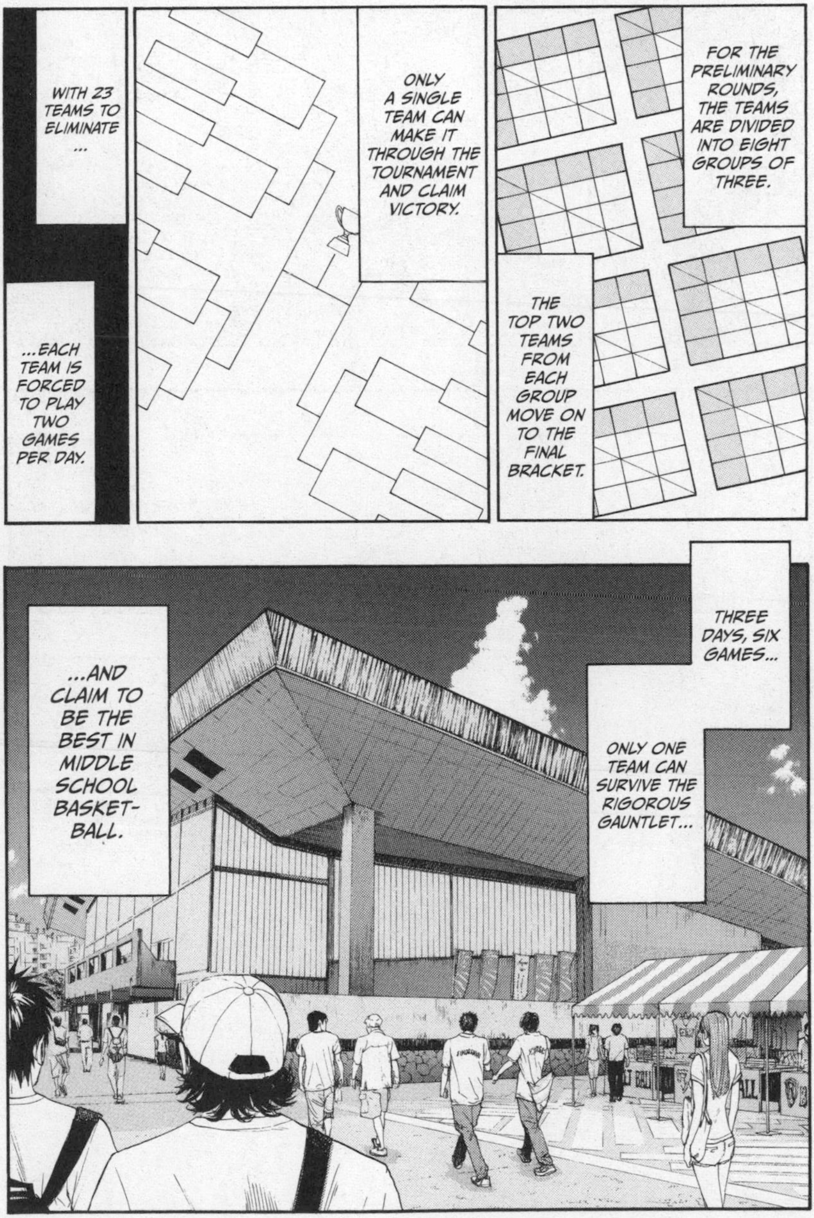
FOR THE PRELIMINARY ROUNDS, THE TEAMS ARE DIVIDED INTO EIGHT GROUPS OF THREE.
THE TOP TWO TEAMS FROM EACH GROUP MOVE ON TO THE FINAL BRACKET.
ONLY A SINGLE TEAM CAN MAKE IT THROUGH THE TOURNAMENT AND CLAIM VICTORY.
WITH 23 TEAMS TO ELIMINATE ...
...EACH TEAM IS FORCED TO PLAY TWO GAMES PER DAY.
THREE DAYS, SIX GAMES...
ONLY ONE TEAM CAN SURVIVE THE RIGOROUS GAUNTLET...
...AND CLAIM TO BE THE BEST IN MIDDLE SCHOOL BASKET-BALL.

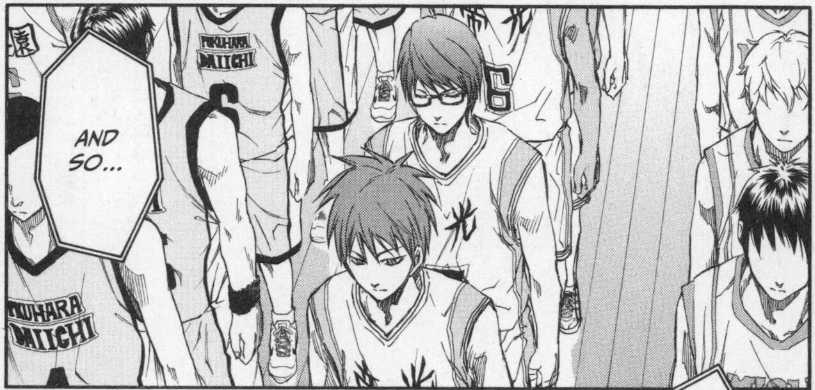
AND SO...
FUKUHARA DAIICHI
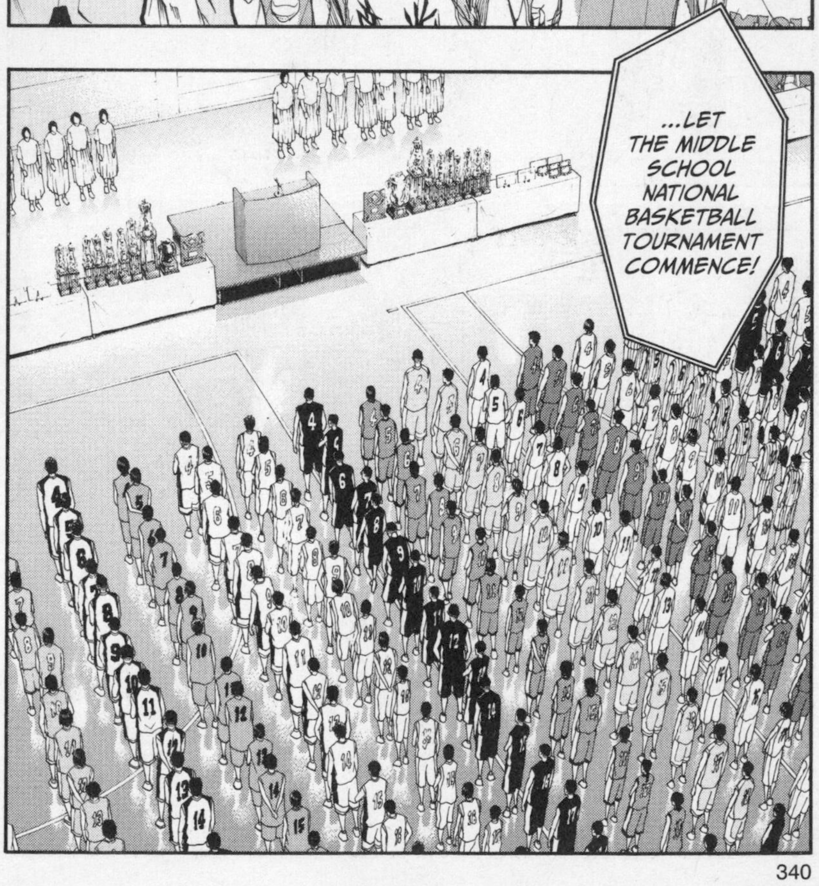
...LET THE MIDDLE SCHOOL NATIONAL BASKETBALL TOURNAMENT COMMENCE!

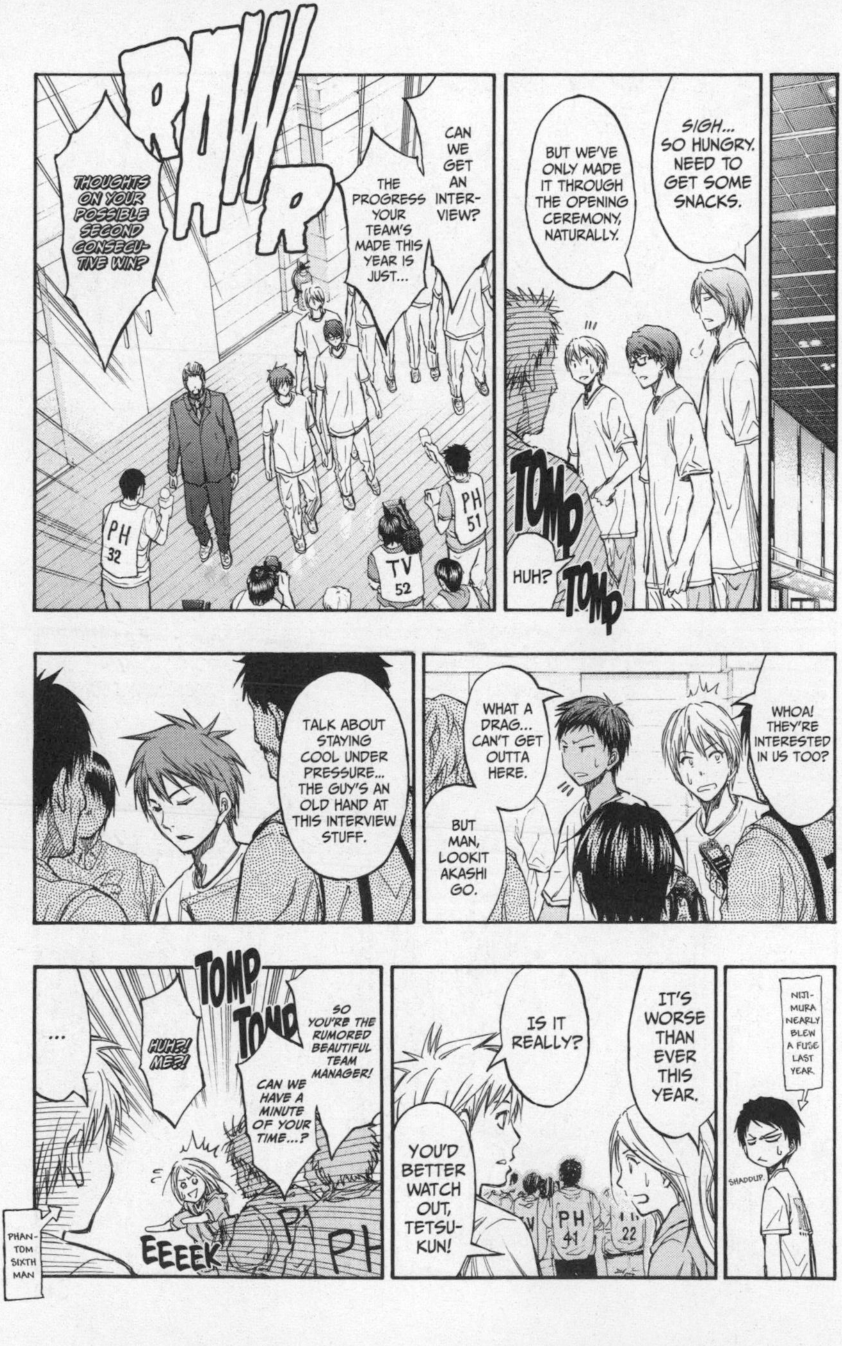
SIGH... SO HUNGRY. NEED TO GET SOME SNACKS.
BUT WE'VE ONLY MADE IT THROUGH THE OPENING CEREMONY, NATURALLY.
TOMP
HUH?
TOMP
RAWR
CAN WE GET AN INTER-VIEW?
THE PROGRESS YOUR TEAM'S MADE THIS YEAR IS JUST...
THOUGHTS ON YOUR POSSIBLE SECOND CONSECU-TIVE WIN?
WHOA! THEY'RE INTERESTED IN US TOO?
WHAT A DRAG... CAN'T GET OUTTA HERE.
BUT MAN, LOOKIT AKASHI GO.
TALK ABOUT STAYING COOL UNDER PRESSURE... THE GUY'S AN OLD HAND AT THIS INTERVIEW STUFF.
NIJI-MURA NEARLY BLEW A FUSE LAST YEAR.
SHADDUP.
IT'S WORSE THAN EVER THIS YEAR.
IS IT REALLY?
YOU'D BETTER WATCH OUT, TETSU-KUN!
TOMP TOMP
SO YOU'RE THE RUMORED BEAUTIFUL TEAM MANAGER!
CAN WE HAVE A MINUTE OF YOUR TIME...?
HUH?! ME?!
EEEEK
...
PHAN-TOM SIXTH MAN

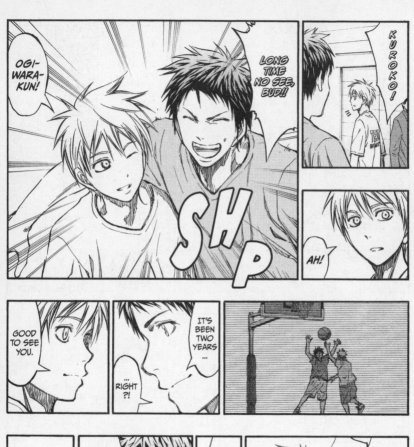

KUROKO!
AH!
LONG TIME NO SEE, BUD!!
OGI-WARA-KUN!
SHP
IT'S BEEN TWO YEARS...
...RIGHT?!
GOOD TO SEE YOU.
WHOA, THAT'S REALLY A TEIKO JERSEY!
IT'S ONLY JUST HITTING ME, SEEING IT IN PERSON!
AND SOME-THING ABOUT YOU SEEMS DIFFER-ENT...
YOU TOO, OGI-WARA-KUN...
AND, UM...
YOU HAVE SOME RICE ON YOUR FACE.
AH!
YIKES! MUST BE FROM LUNCH.
SAME AS EVER, I SEE.
PLUCK
MUNCH

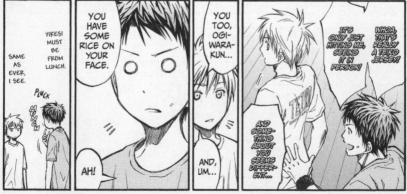

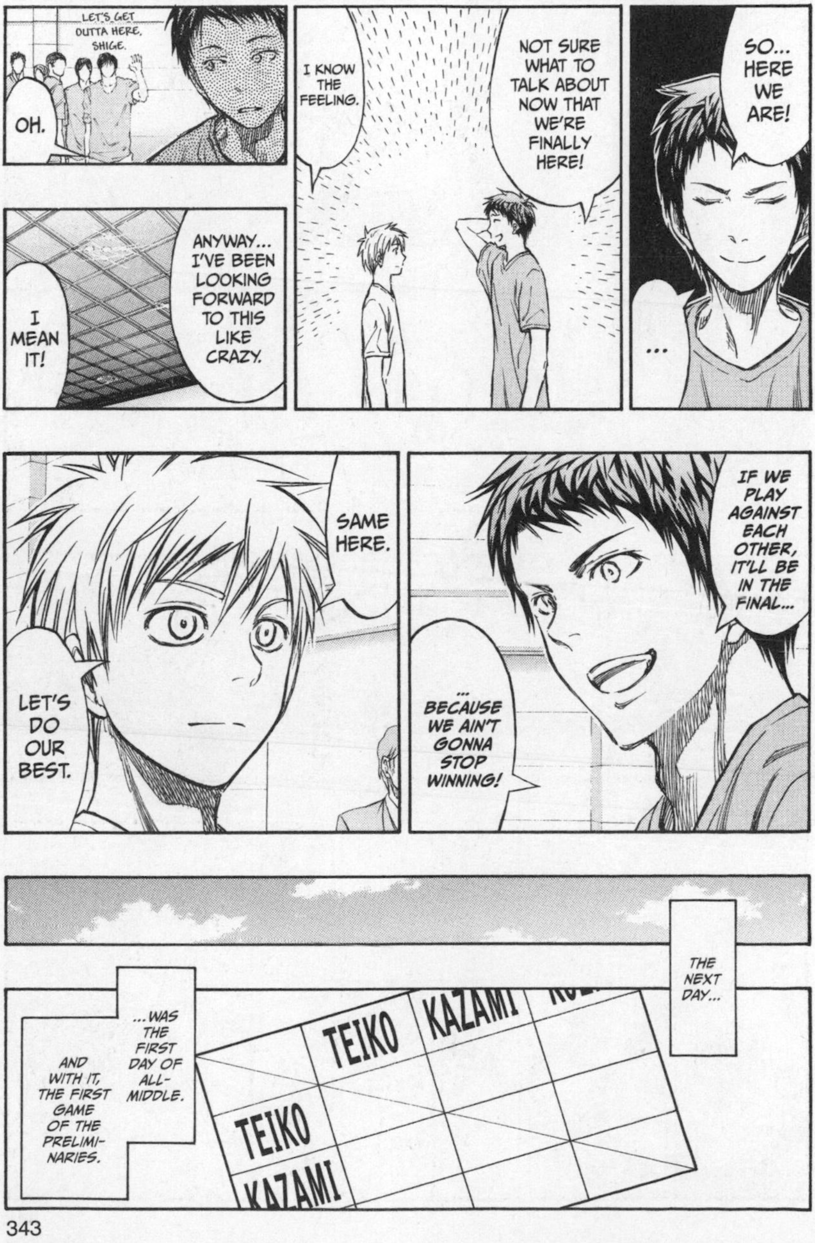
SO... HERE WE ARE!
...
NOT SURE WHAT TO TALK ABOUT NOW THAT WE'RE FINALLY HERE!
I KNOW THE FEELING.
LET'S GET OUTTA HERE, SHIGE.
OH.
ANYWAY... I'VE BEEN LOOKING FORWARD TO THIS LIKE CRAZY.
I MEAN IT!
IF WE PLAY AGAINST EACH OTHER, IT'LL BE IN THE FINAL...
...BECAUSE WE AIN'T GONNA STOP WINNING!
SAME HERE.
LET'S DO OUR BEST.
THE NEXT DAY...
...WAS THE FIRST DAY OF ALL-MIDDLE.
AND WITH IT, THE FIRST GAME OF THE PRELIMINARIES.
TEIKO
KAZAMI
TEIKO
KAZAMI

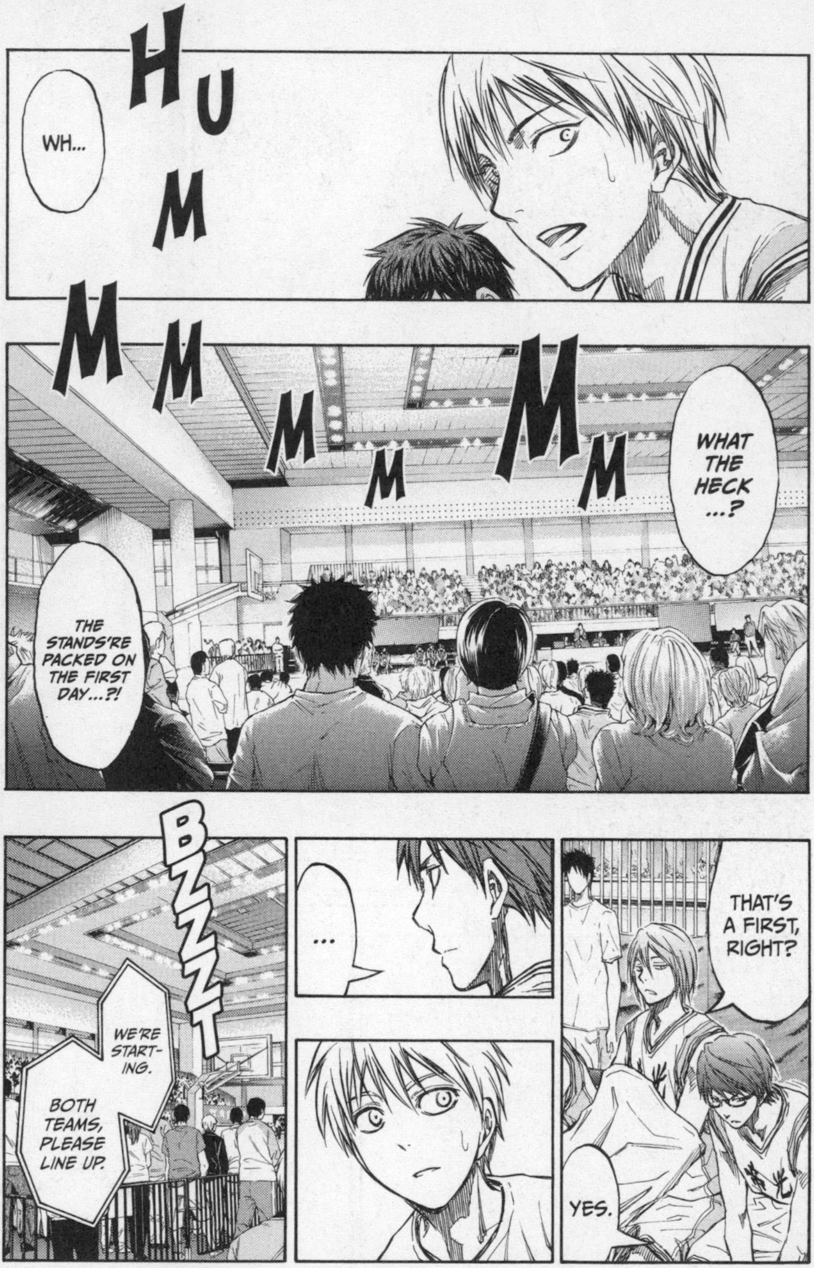
HUMMMMMMMM
WH...
WHAT THE HECK...?
THE STANDS'RE PACKED ON THE FIRST DAY...?!
THAT'S A FIRST, RIGHT?
YES.
...
BZZZT
WE'RE STARTING.
BOTH TEAMS, PLEASE LINE UP.

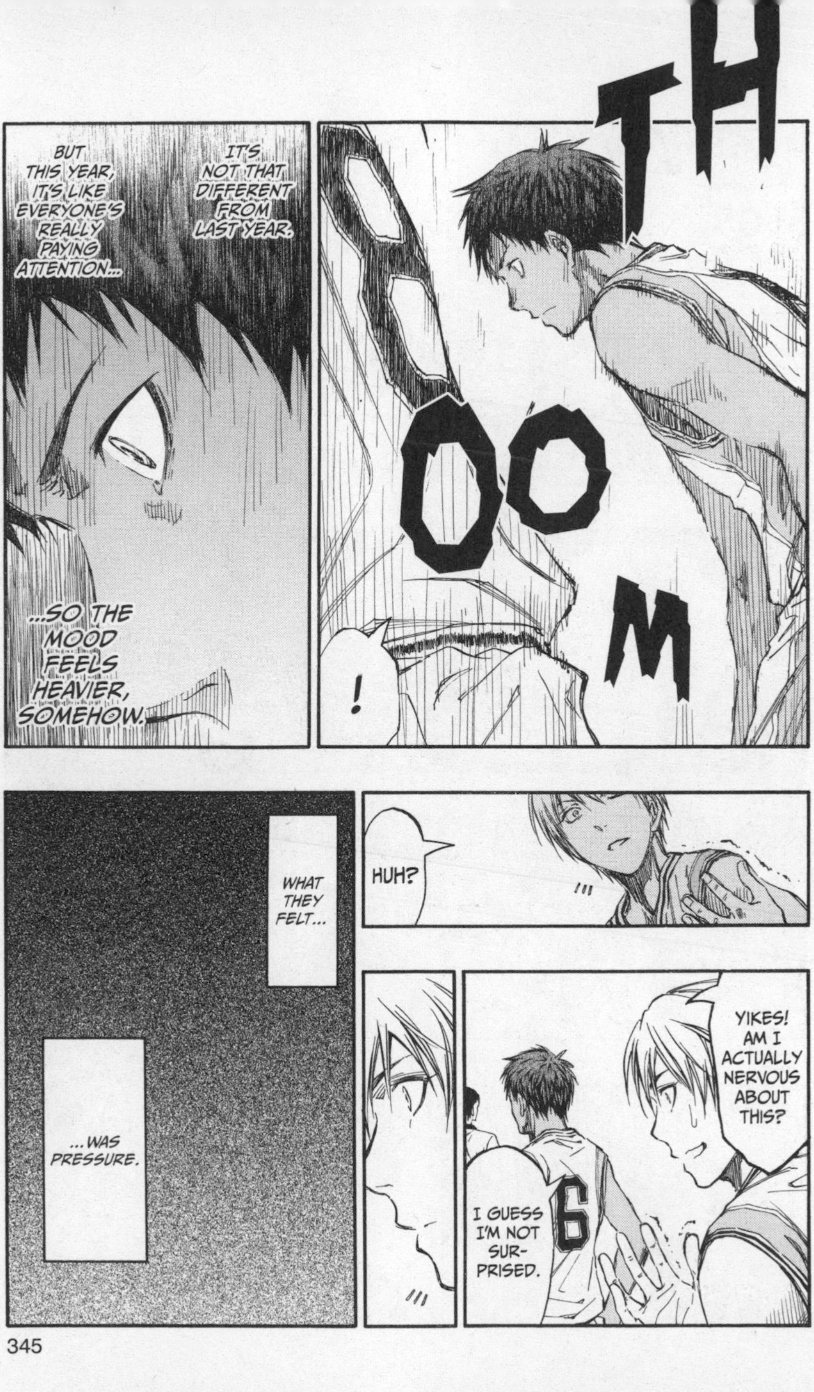
THOOM
!
IT'S NOT THAT DIFFERENT FROM LAST YEAR.
BUT THIS YEAR, IT'S LIKE EVERYONE'S REALLY PAYING ATTENTION...
...SO THE MOOD FEELS HEAVIER, SOMEHOW.
HUH?
YIKES! AM I ACTUALLY NERVOUS ABOUT THIS?
I GUESS I'M NOT SUR-PRISED.
WHAT THEY FELT...
...WAS PRESSURE.

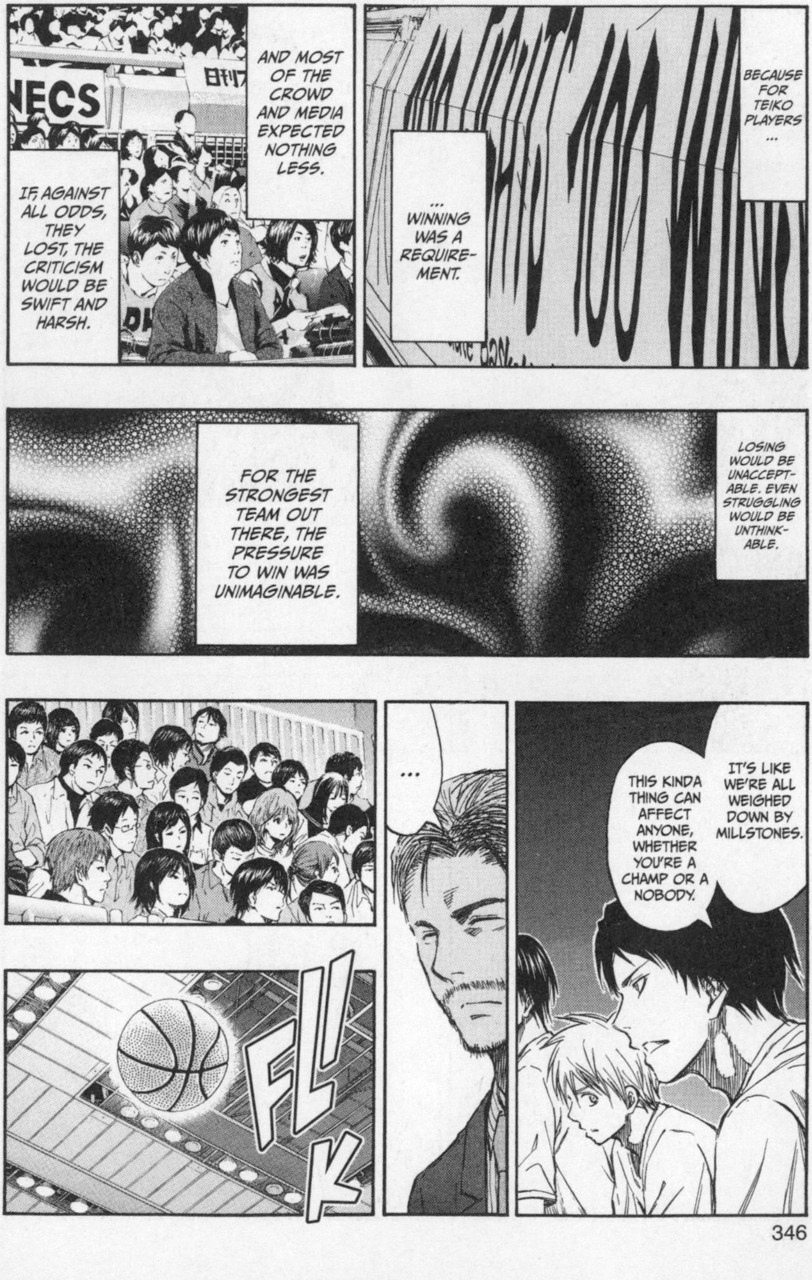
BECAUSE FOR TEIKO PLAYERS ...
... WINNING WAS A REQUIREMENT.
AND MOST OF THE CROWD AND MEDIA EXPECTED NOTHING LESS.
NECS
IF, AGAINST ALL ODDS, THEY LOST, THE CRITICISM WOULD BE SWIFT AND HARSH.
LOSING WOULD BE UNACCEPTABLE. EVEN STRUGGLING WOULD BE UNTHINKABLE.
FOR THE STRONGEST TEAM OUT THERE, THE PRESSURE TO WIN WAS UNIMAGINABLE.
IT'S LIKE WE'RE ALL WEIGHED DOWN BY MILLSTONES.
THIS KINDA THING CAN AFFECT ANYONE, WHETHER YOU'RE A CHAMP OR A NOBODY.
...
FLIK

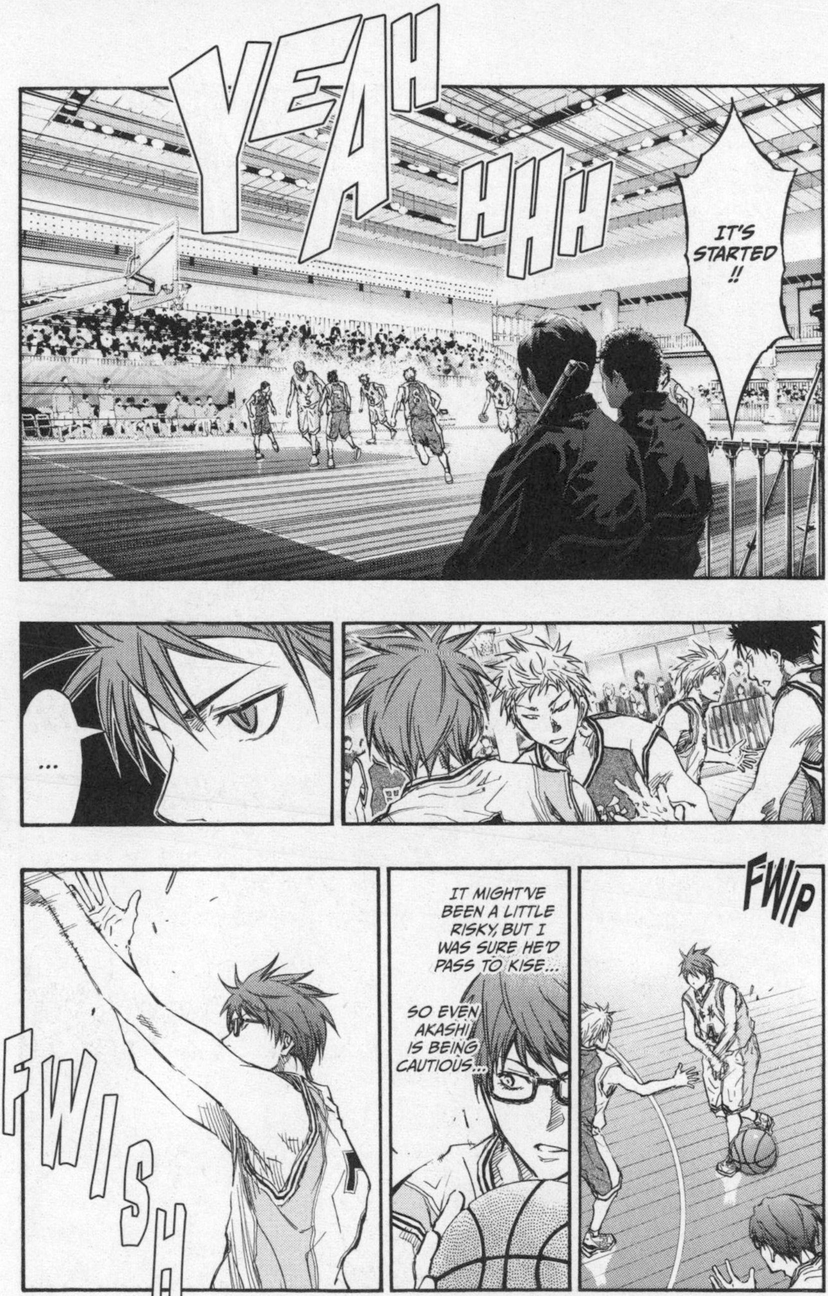
IT'S STARTED !!
YEAHHHHH
...
FWIP
IT MIGHT'VE BEEN A LITTLE RISKY, BUT I WAS SURE HE'D PASS TO KISE...
SO EVEN AKASHI IS BEING CAUTIOUS...
FWISH

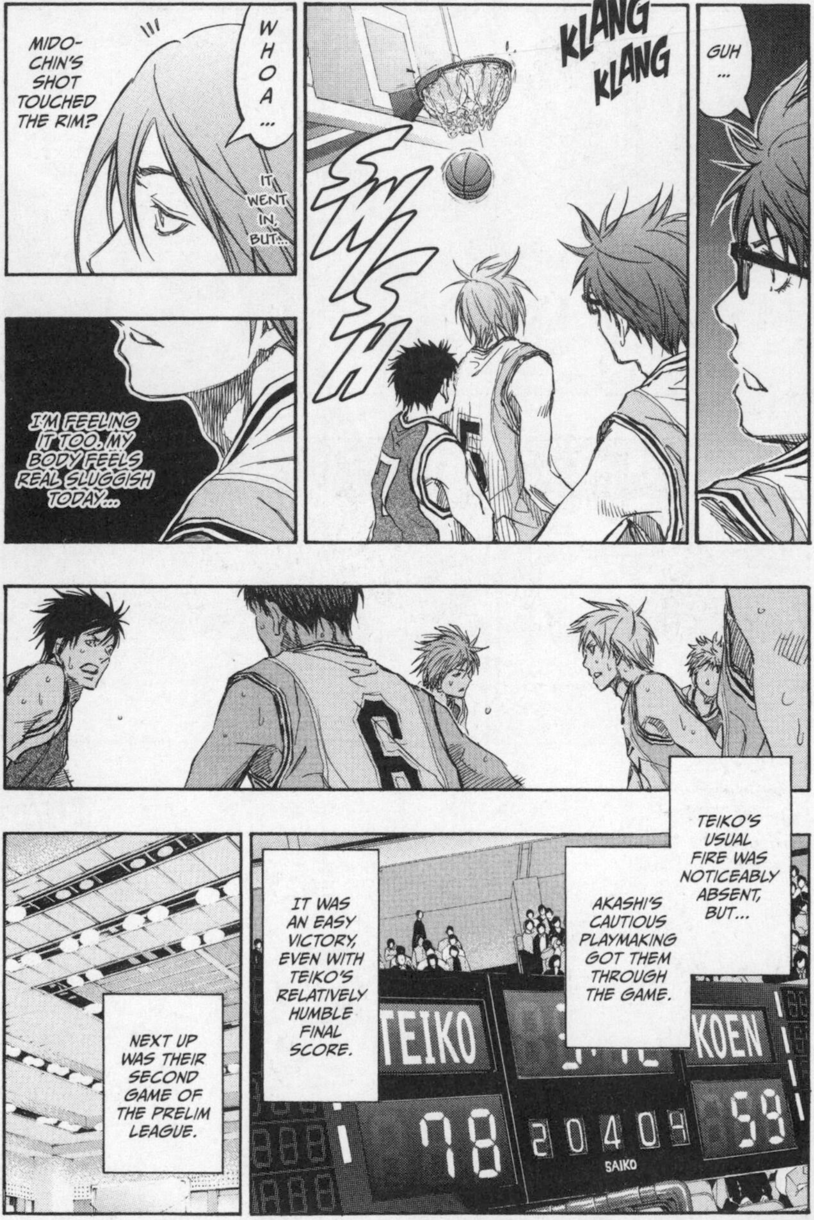
GUH ...
KLANG
KLANG
SWISH
WHOA ...
MIDO-CHIN'S SHOT TOUCHED THE RIM?
IT WENT IN, BUT...
I'M FEELING IT TOO. MY BODY FEELS REAL SLUGGISH TODAY...
TEIKO'S USUAL FIRE WAS NOTICEABLY ABSENT, BUT...
AKASHI'S CAUTIOUS PLAYMAKING GOT THEM THROUGH THE GAME.
IT WAS AN EASY VICTORY, EVEN WITH TEIKO'S RELATIVELY HUMBLE FINAL SCORE.
TEIKO
KOEN
78
59
SAIKO
NEXT UP WAS THEIR SECOND GAME OF THE PRELIM LEAGUE.

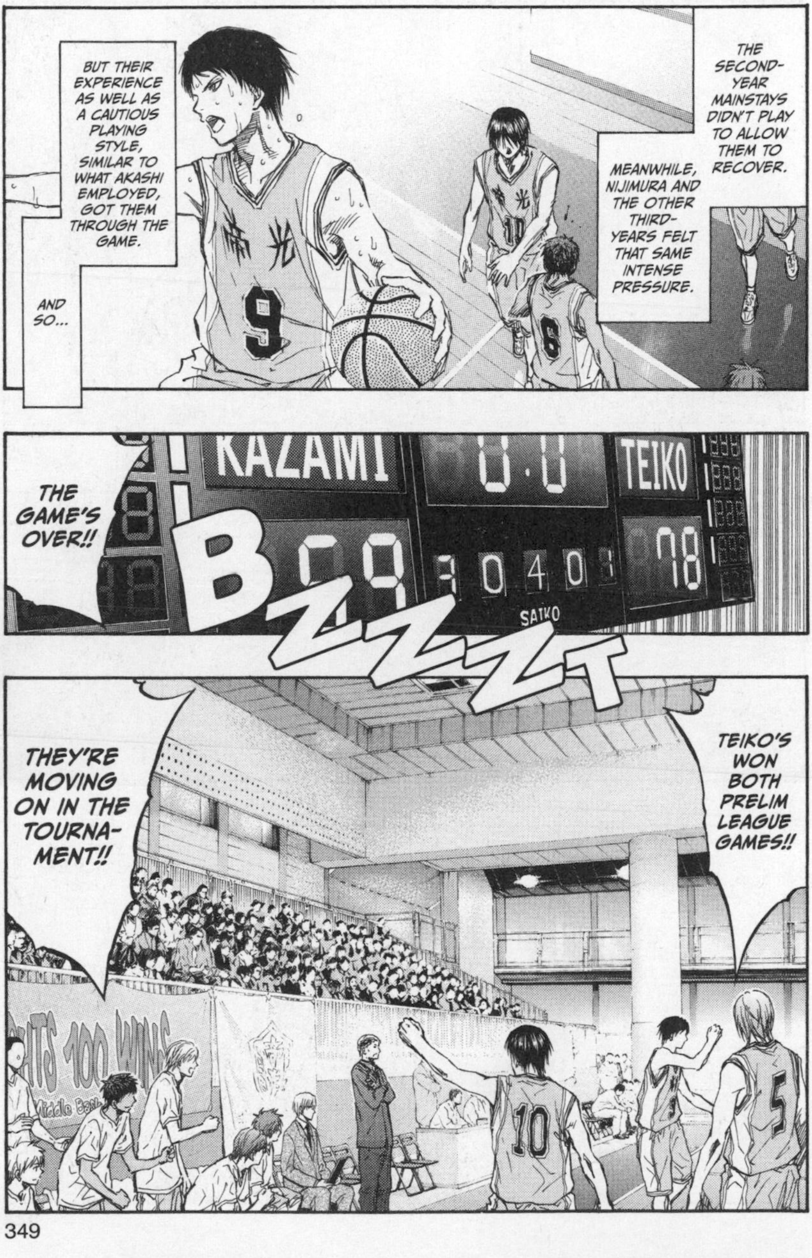
THE SECOND-YEAR MAINSTAYS DIDN'T PLAY TO ALLOW THEM TO RECOVER.
MEANWHILE, NIJIMURA AND THE OTHER THIRD-YEARS FELT THAT SAME INTENSE PRESSURE.
BUT THEIR EXPERIENCE AS WELL AS A CAUTIOUS PLAYING STYLE, SIMILAR TO WHAT AKASHI EMPLOYED, GOT THEM THROUGH THE GAME.
AND SO...
KAZAMI
TEIKO
78
THE GAME'S OVER!!
BZZZT
TEIKO'S WON BOTH PRELIM LEAGUE GAMES!!
THEY'RE MOVING ON IN THE TOURNAMENT!!

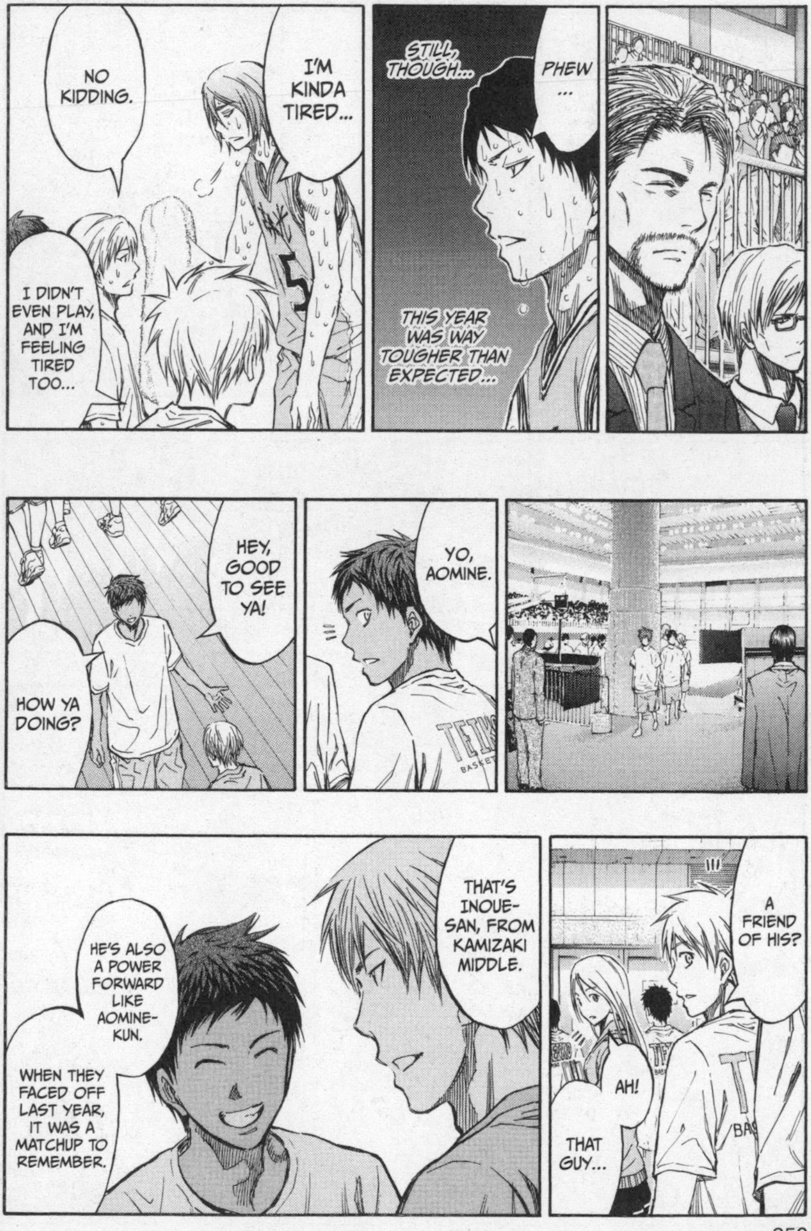
PHEW ...
STILL, THOUGH...
THIS YEAR WAS WAY TOUGHER THAN EXPECTED...
I'M KINDA TIRED...
NO KIDDING.
I DIDN'T EVEN PLAY, AND I'M FEELING TIRED TOO...
YO, AOMINE.
HEY, GOOD TO SEE YA!
HOW YA DOING?
A FRIEND OF HIS?
AH!
THAT GUY...
THAT'S INOUE-SAN, FROM KAMIZAKI MIDDLE.
HE'S ALSO A POWER FORWARD LIKE AOMINE-KUN.
WHEN THEY FACED OFF LAST YEAR, IT WAS A MATCHUP TO REMEMBER.

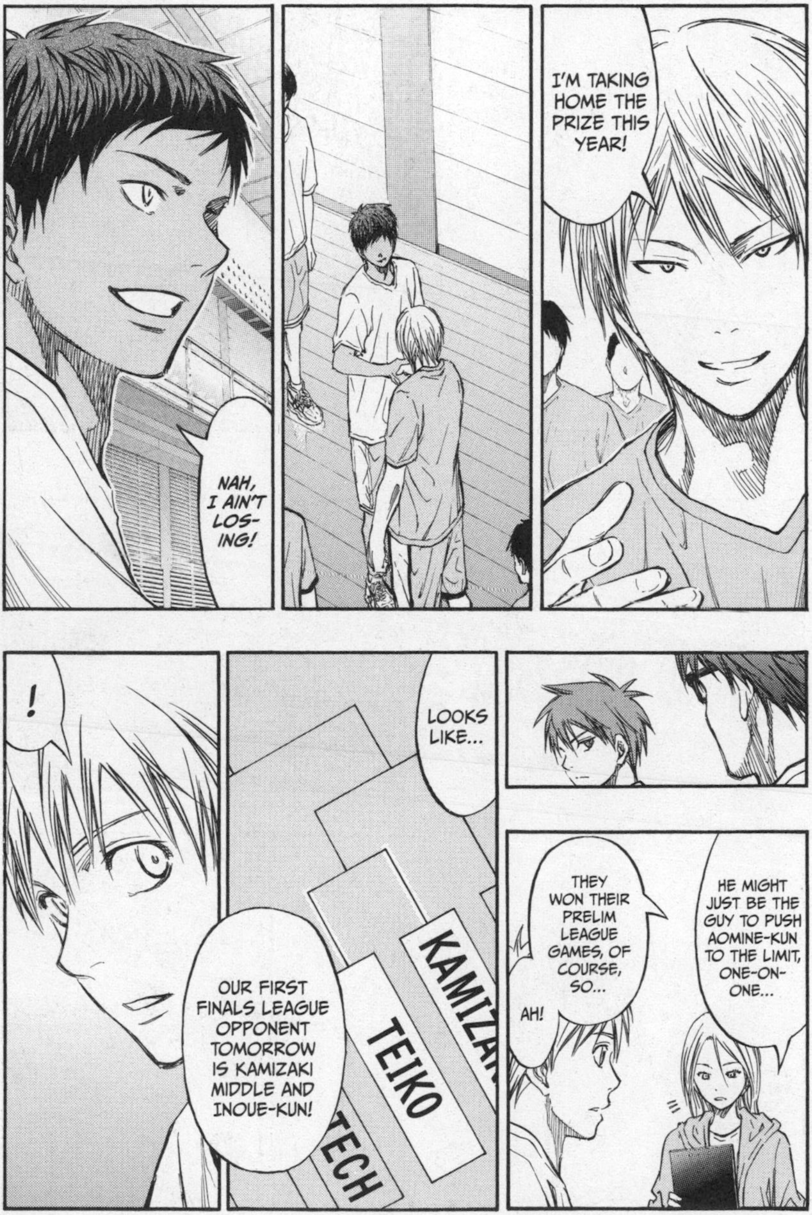
I'M TAKING HOME THE PRIZE THIS YEAR!
NAH, I AIN'T LOS-ING!
HE MIGHT JUST BE THE GUY TO PUSH AOMINE-KUN TO THE LIMIT, ONE-ON-ONE...
THEY WON THEIR PRELIM LEAGUE GAMES, OF COURSE, SO...
AH!
LOOKS LIKE...
TEIKO
TECH
OUR FIRST FINALS LEAGUE OPPONENT TOMORROW IS KAMIZAKI MIDDLE AND INOUE-KUN!
!

KUROKO'S BASKETBALL BLOOPERS

TAKE 12

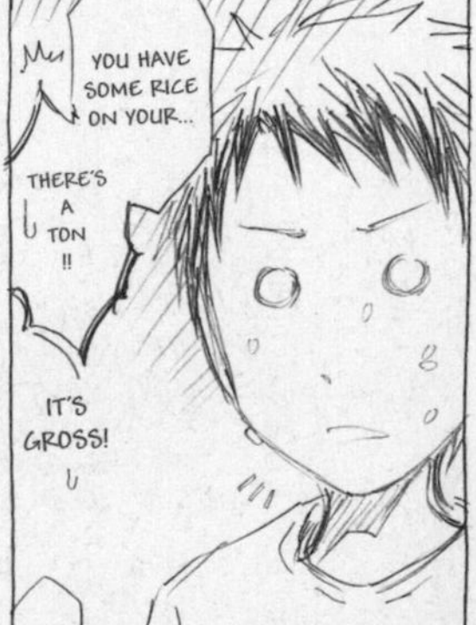
YOU HAVE SOME RICE ON YOUR...
THERE'S A TON !!
IT'S GROSS!
HUH?

216TH QUARTER:

SORRY

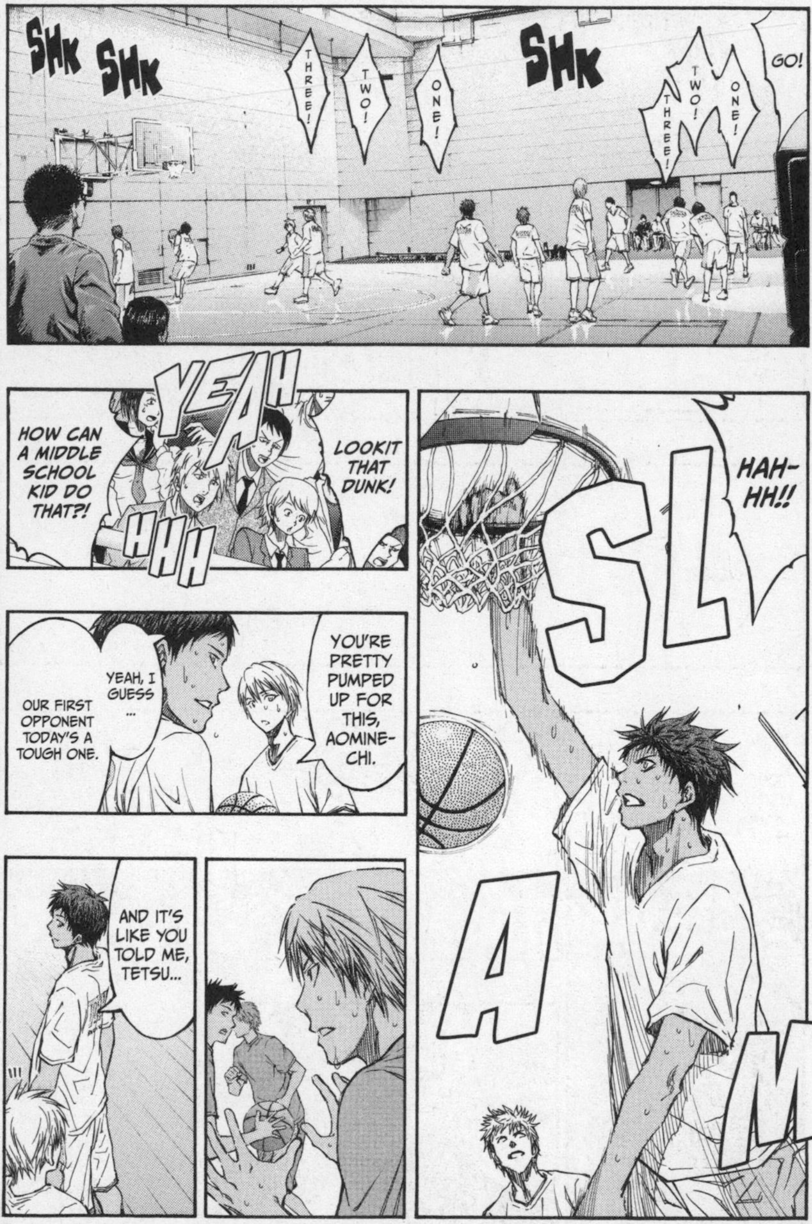
GO!
ONE!
TWO!
THREE!
SHK
ONE!
TWO!
THREE!
SHK
SHK
HAH-HH!!
SLAM
LOOKIT THAT DUNK!
YEAH
HOW CAN A MIDDLE SCHOOL KID DO THAT?!
HHH
YOU'RE PRETTY PUMPED UP FOR THIS, AOMINE-CHI.
YEAH, I GUESS ...
OUR FIRST OPPONENT TODAY'S A TOUGH ONE.
AND IT'S LIKE YOU TOLD ME, TETSU...
!!!

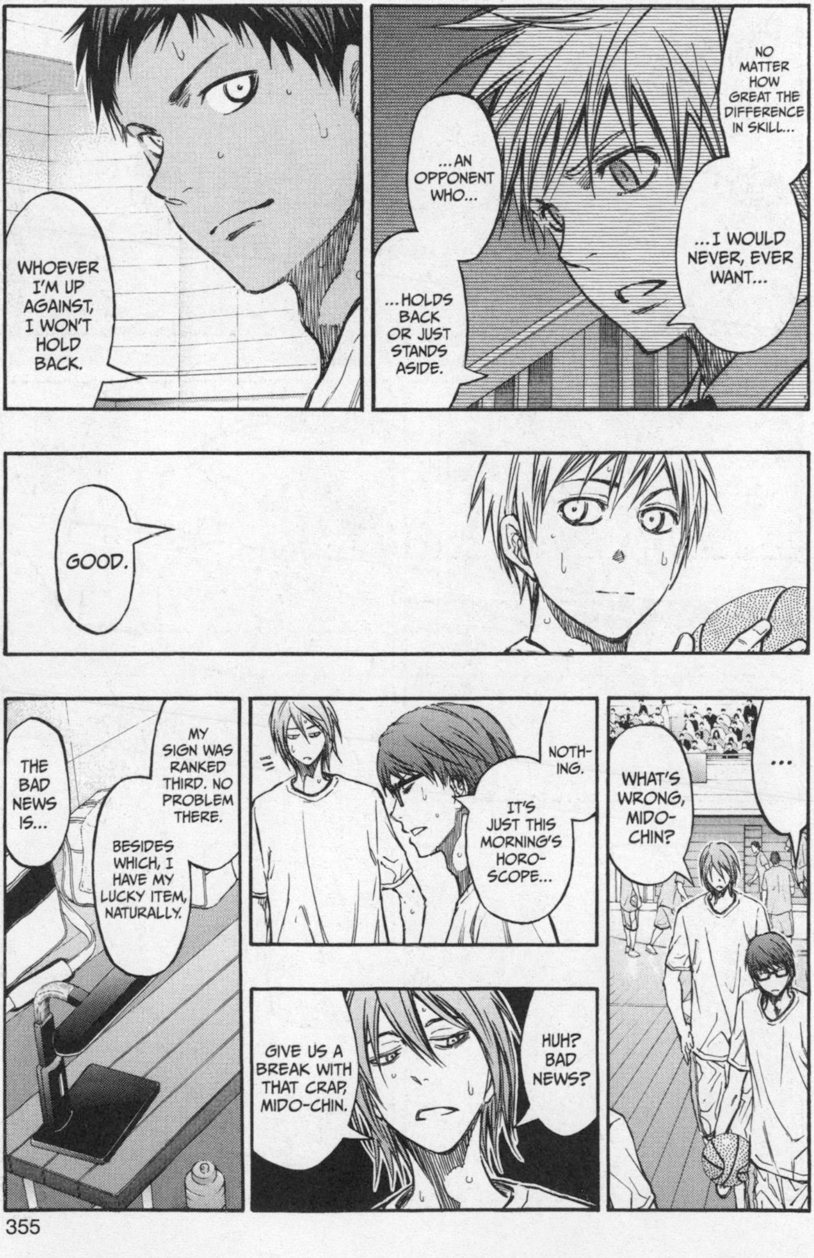
NO MATTER HOW GREAT THE DIFFERENCE IN SKILL...
...I WOULD NEVER, EVER WANT...
...AN OPPONENT WHO...
...HOLDS BACK OR JUST STANDS ASIDE.
WHOEVER I'M UP AGAINST, I WON'T HOLD BACK.
GOOD.
...
WHAT'S WRONG, MIDO-CHIN?
NOTHING.
IT'S JUST THIS MORNING'S HOROSCOPE...
HUH? BAD NEWS?
GIVE US A BREAK WITH THAT CRAP, MIDO-CHIN.
MY SIGN WAS RANKED THIRD. NO PROBLEM THERE.
BESIDES WHICH, I HAVE MY LUCKY ITEM, NATURALLY.
THE BAD NEWS IS...

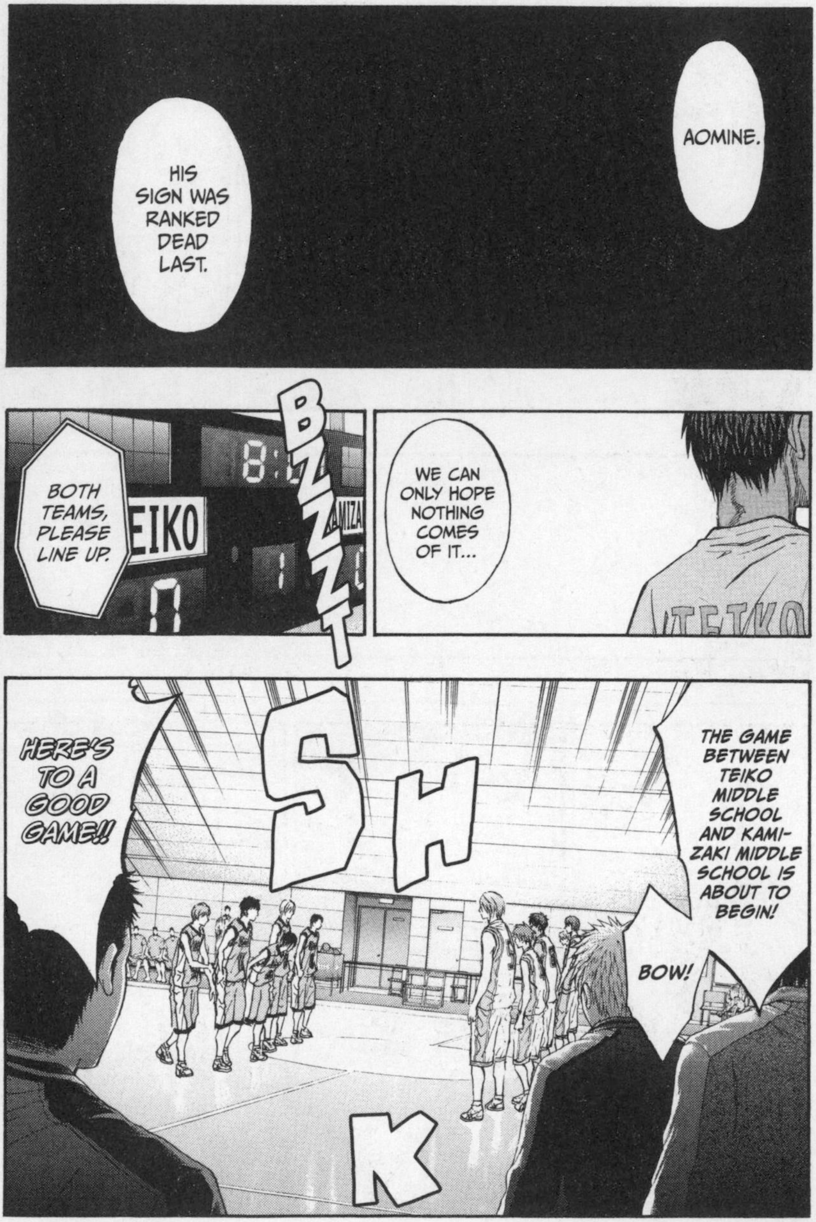
AOMINE.
HIS SIGN WAS RANKED DEAD LAST.
WE CAN ONLY HOPE NOTHING COMES OF IT...
BZZZT
BOTH TEAMS, PLEASE LINE UP.
THE GAME BETWEEN TEIKO MIDDLE SCHOOL AND KAMIZAKI MIDDLE SCHOOL IS ABOUT TO BEGIN!
BOW!
SHK
HERE'S TO A GOOD GAME!!

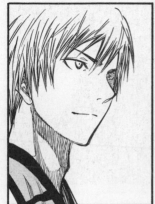

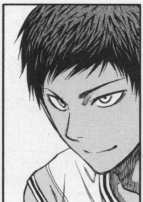

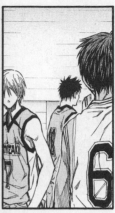

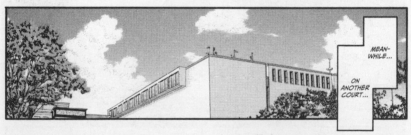

MEAN-WHILE...
ON ANOTHER COURT...
SHK
SHK
SHK
...?!
GAH!
WHAT'S UP, SHIGE?
UM... WE GOT ANY SPARE LACES...?
UH...
OH?!

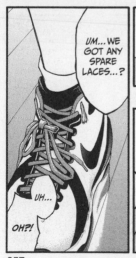

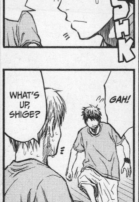

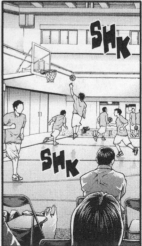

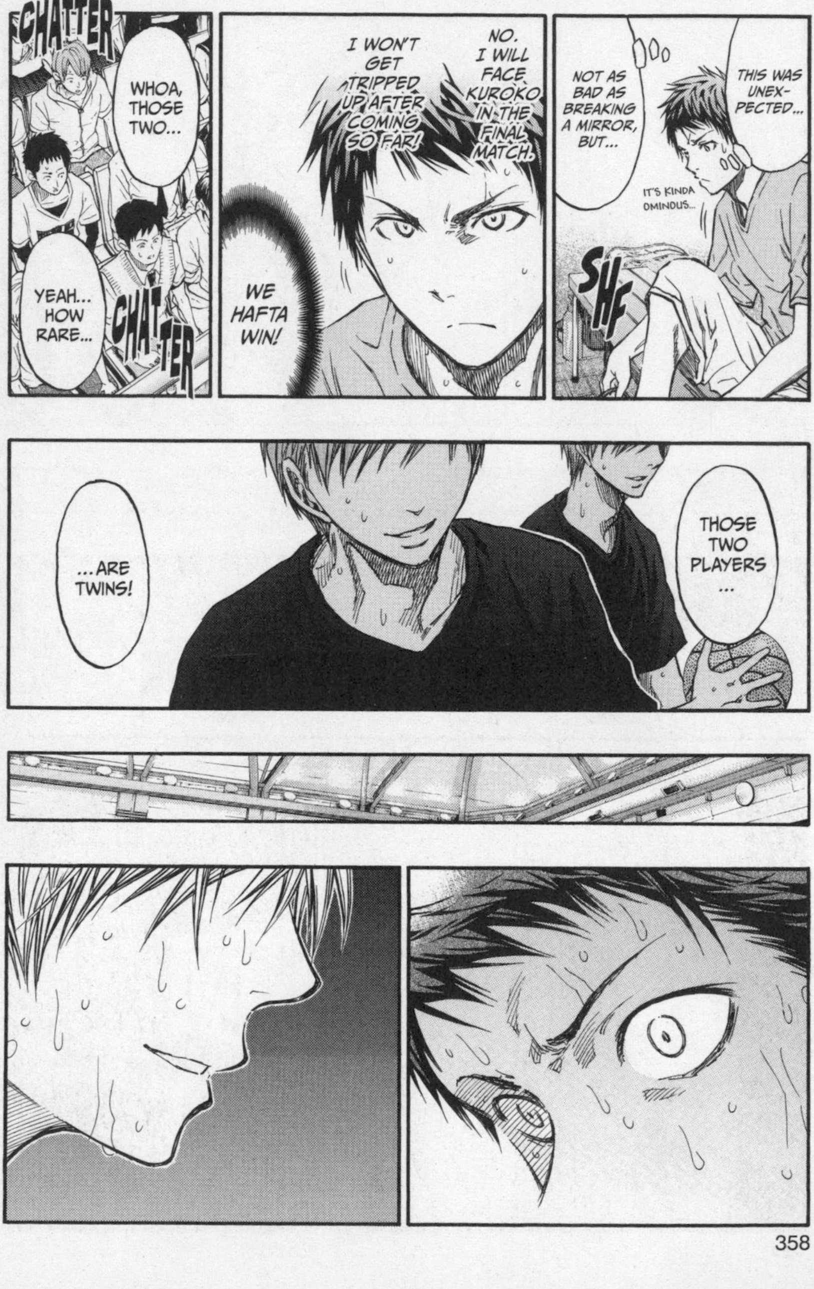
THIS WAS UNEXPECTED...
NOT AS BAD AS BREAKING A MIRROR, BUT...
IT'S KINDA OMINOUS...
SHF
NO. I WILL FACE KUROKO IN THE FINAL MATCH.
I WON'T GET TRIPPED UP AFTER COMING SO FAR!
WE HAFTA WIN!
CHATTER
WHOA, THOSE TWO...
YEAH... HOW RARE...
CHATTER
THOSE TWO PLAYERS...
...ARE TWINS!

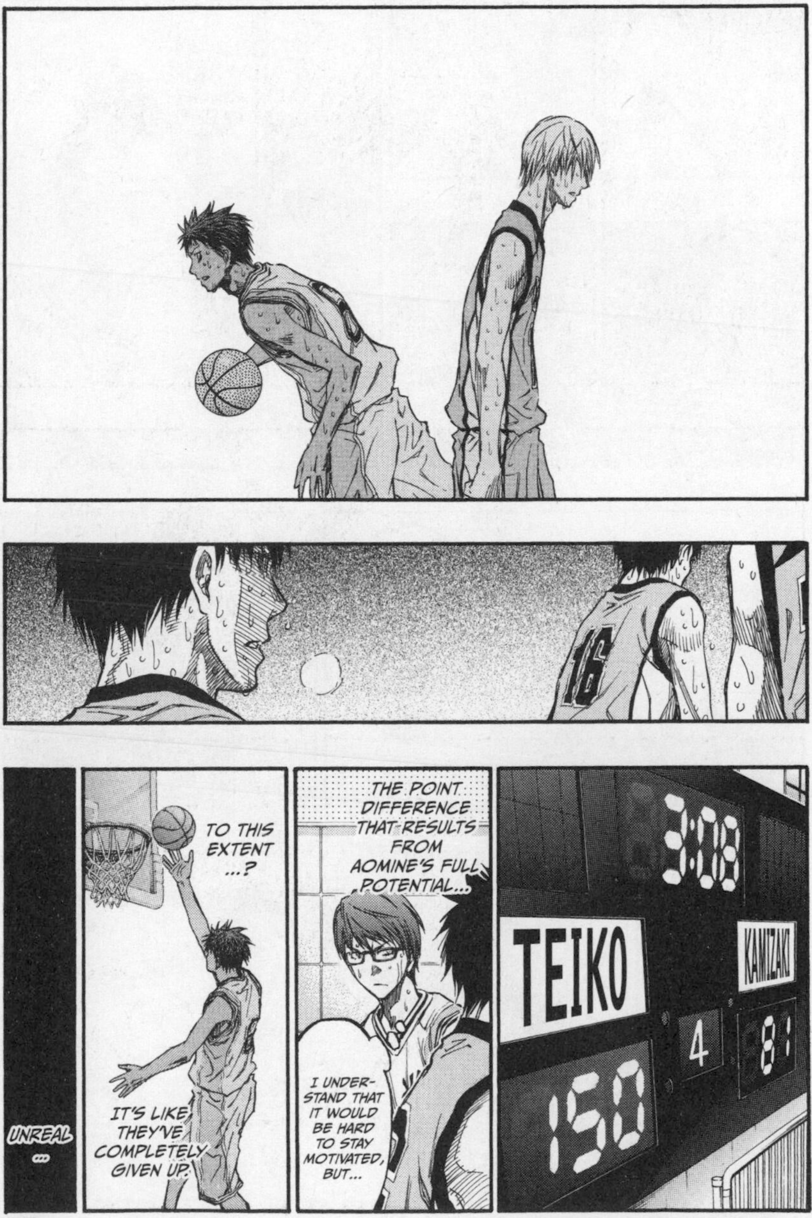
3:08
TEIKO
KAMIZAKI
4
150
THE POINT DIFFERENCE THAT RESULTS FROM AOMINE'S FULL POTENTIAL...
I UNDERSTAND THAT IT WOULD BE HARD TO STAY MOTIVATED, BUT...
TO THIS EXTENT ...?
IT'S LIKE THEY'VE COMPLETELY GIVEN UP.
UNREAL ...

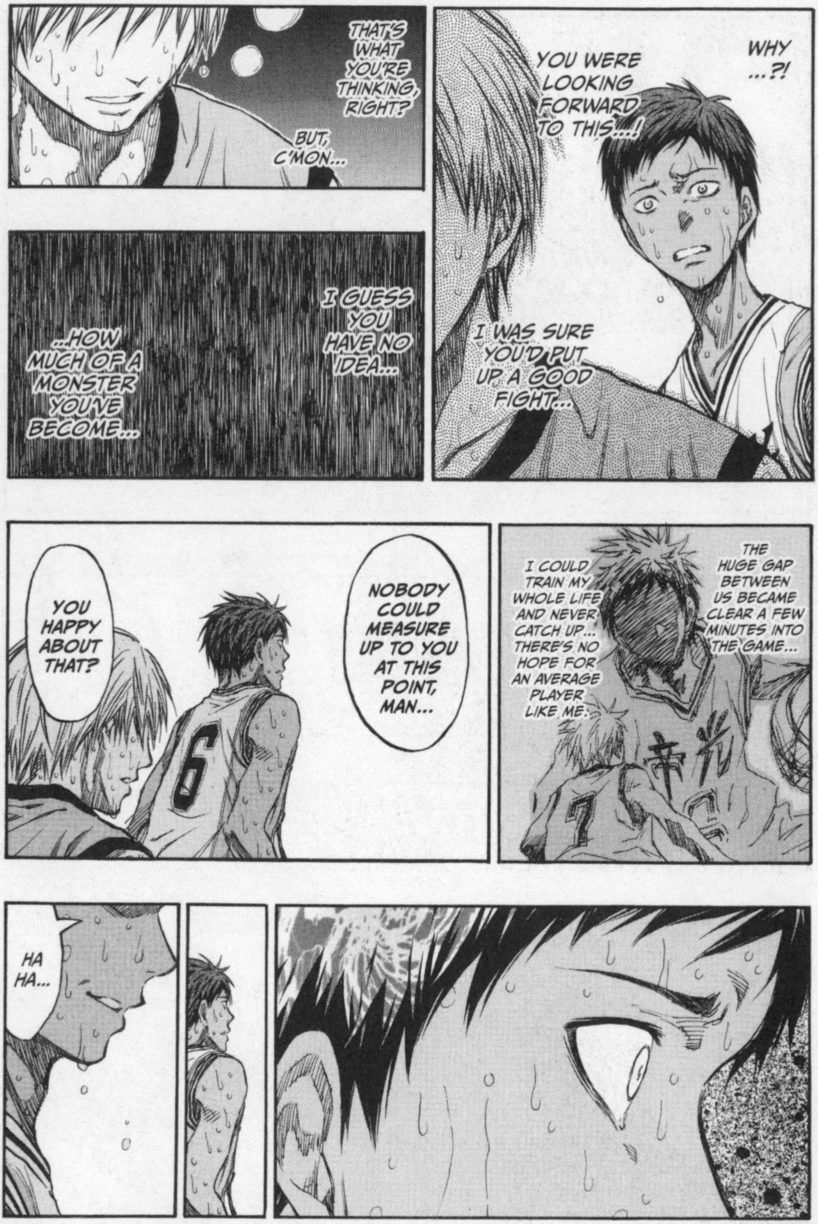
WHY ...?!
YOU WERE LOOKING FORWARD TO THIS...!
I WAS SURE YOU'D PUT UP A GOOD FIGHT...
THAT'S WHAT YOU'RE THINKING, RIGHT?
BUT, C'MON...
I GUESS YOU HAVE NO IDEA...
...HOW MUCH OF A MONSTER YOU'VE BECOME...
THE HUGE GAP BETWEEN US BECAME CLEAR A FEW MINUTES INTO THE GAME...
I COULD TRAIN MY WHOLE LIFE AND NEVER CATCH UP... THERE'S NO HOPE FOR AN AVERAGE PLAYER LIKE ME.
NOBODY COULD MEASURE UP TO YOU AT THIS POINT, MAN...
YOU HAPPY ABOUT THAT?
HA HA...

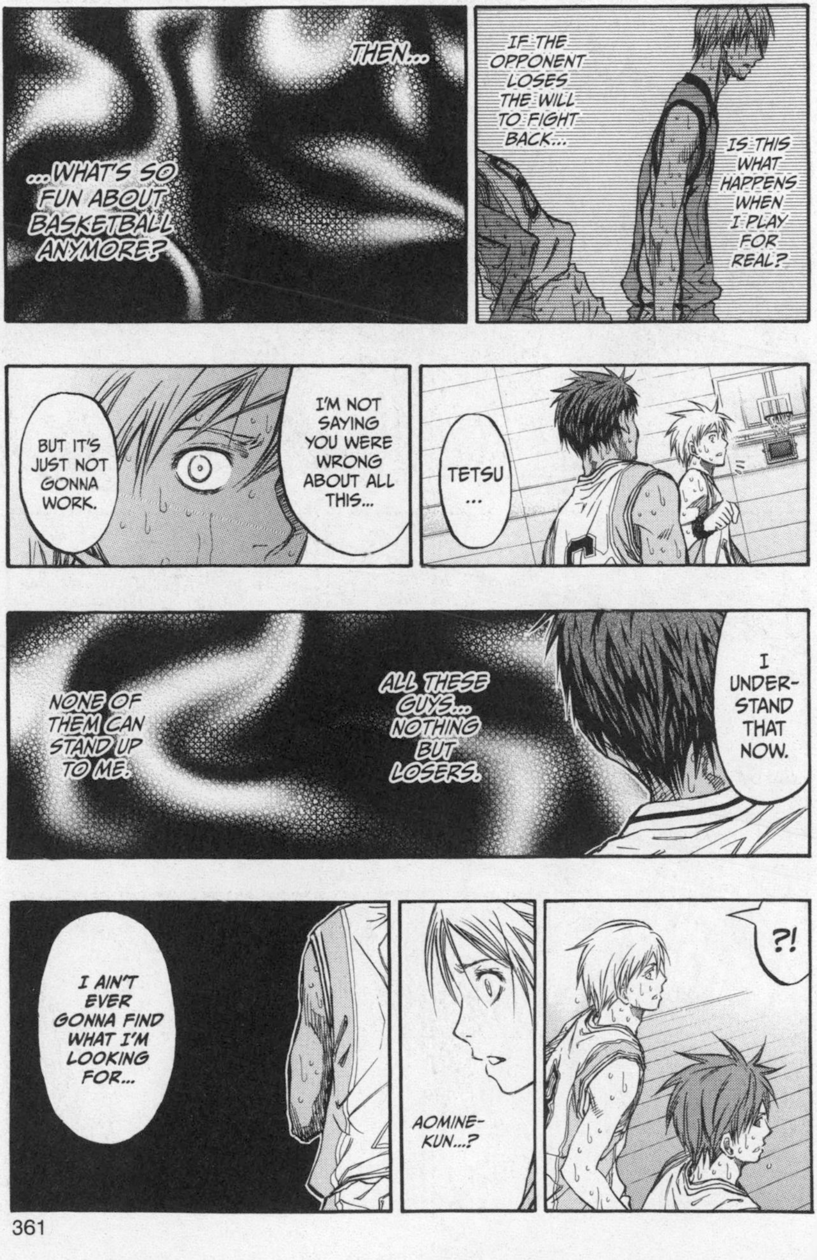
IF THE OPPONENT LOSES THE WILL TO FIGHT BACK...
IS THIS WHAT HAPPENS WHEN I PLAY FOR REAL?
THEN...
...WHAT'S SO FUN ABOUT BASKETBALL ANYMORE?
TETSU...
I'M NOT SAYING YOU WERE WRONG ABOUT ALL THIS...
BUT IT'S JUST NOT GONNA WORK.
I UNDERSTAND THAT NOW.
ALL THESE GUYS... NOTHING BUT LOSERS.
NONE OF THEM CAN STAND UP TO ME.
?!
AOMINE-KUN...?
I AIN'T EVER GONNA FIND WHAT I'M LOOKING FOR...

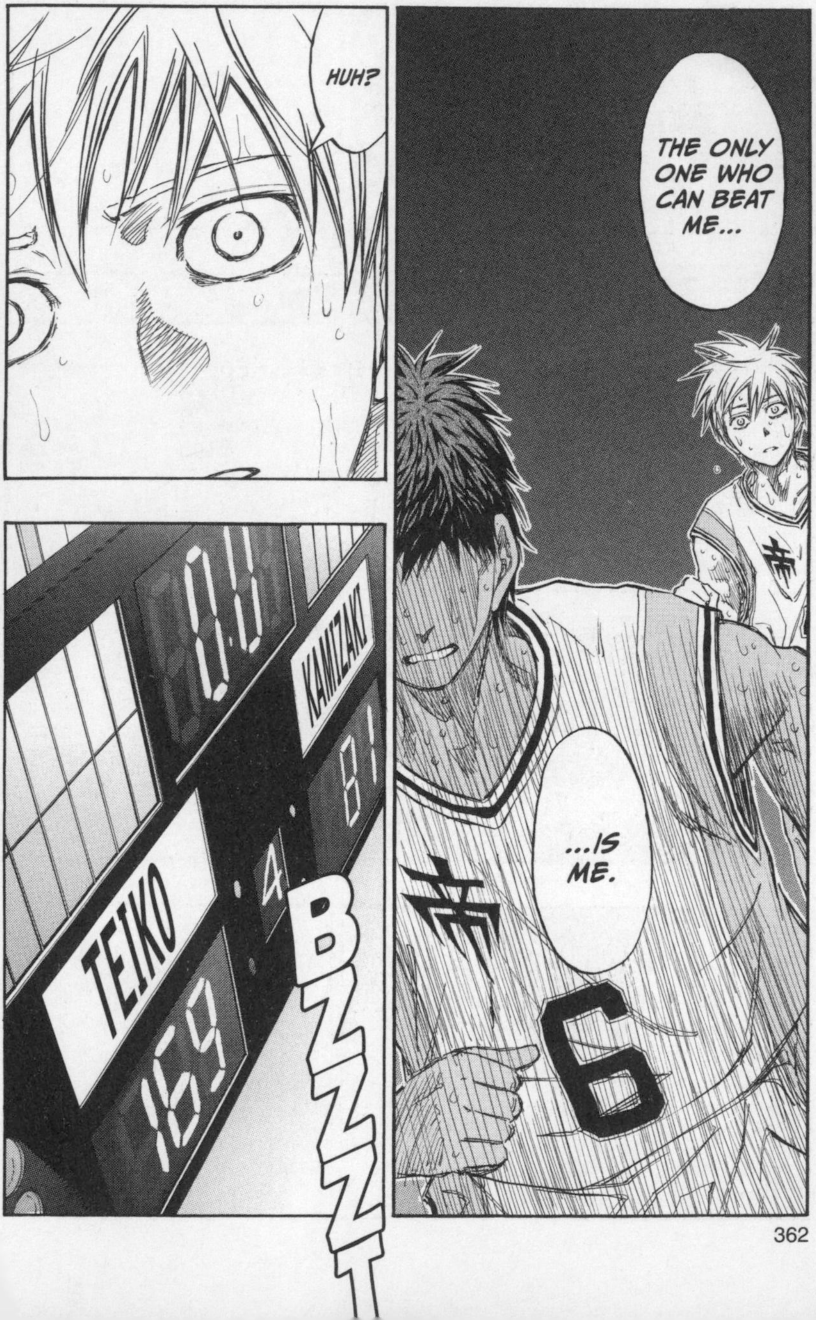
THE ONLY ONE WHO CAN BEAT ME...
...IS ME.
HUH?
KAMIZAKI
81
TEIKO
169
BZZZT

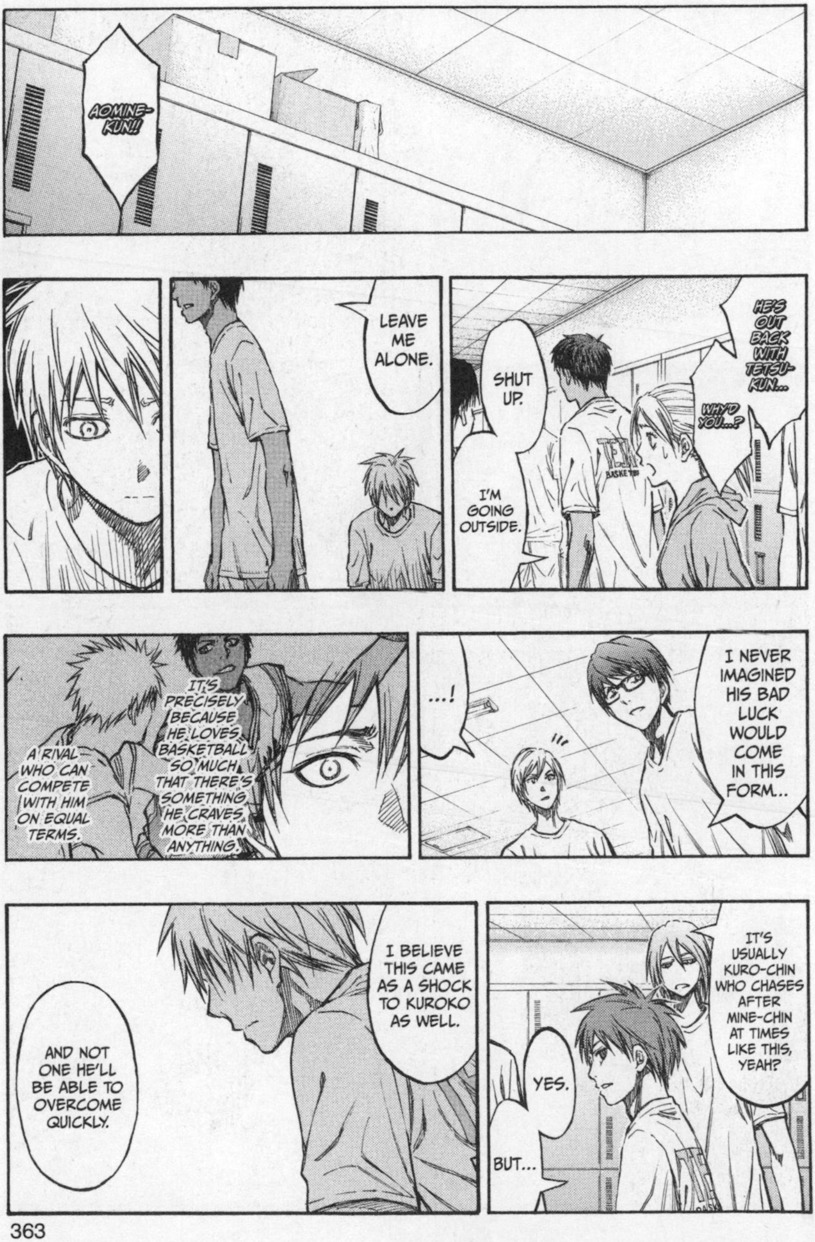
AOMINE-KUN!!
HE'S OUT BACK WITH TETSU-KUN...
WHY'D YOU...?
SHUT UP.
I'M GOING OUTSIDE.
LEAVE ME ALONE.
I NEVER IMAGINED HIS BAD LUCK WOULD COME IN THIS FORM...
...!
IT'S PRECISELY BECAUSE HE LOVES BASKETBALL SO MUCH THAT THERE'S SOMETHING HE CRAVES MORE THAN ANYTHING.
A RIVAL WHO CAN COMPETE WITH HIM ON EQUAL TERMS.
IT'S USUALLY KURO-CHIN WHO CHASES AFTER MINE-CHIN AT TIMES LIKE THIS, YEAH?
YES.
BUT...
I BELIEVE THIS CAME AS A SHOCK TO KUROKO AS WELL.
AND NOT ONE HE'LL BE ABLE TO OVERCOME QUICKLY.

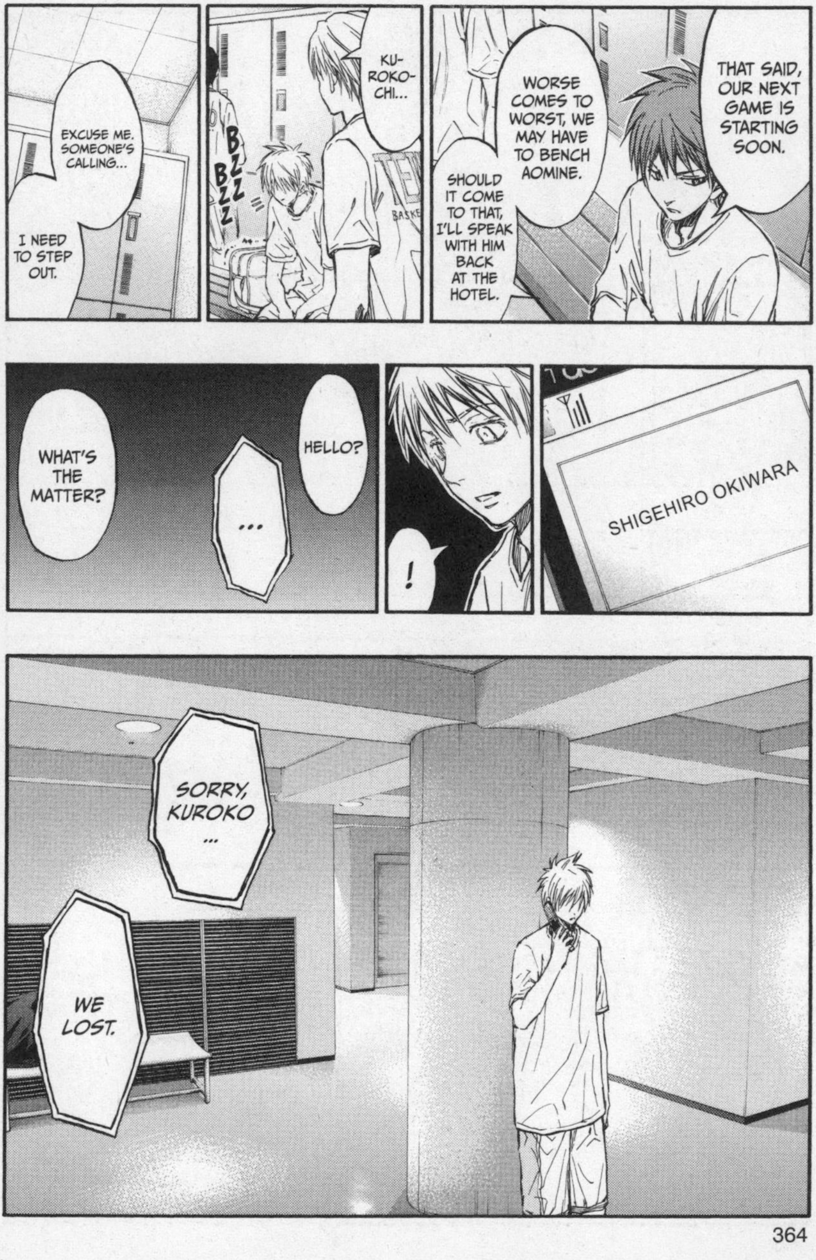
THAT SAID, OUR NEXT GAME IS STARTING SOON.
WORSE COMES TO WORST, WE MAY HAVE TO BENCH AOMINE.
SHOULD IT COME TO THAT, I'LL SPEAK WITH HIM BACK AT THE HOTEL.
KU-ROKO-CHI...
BZZ BZZ
EXCUSE ME. SOMEONE'S CALLING...
I NEED TO STEP OUT.
SHIGEHIRO OKIWARA
!
HELLO?
...
WHAT'S THE MATTER?
SORRY, KUROKO...
WE LOST.

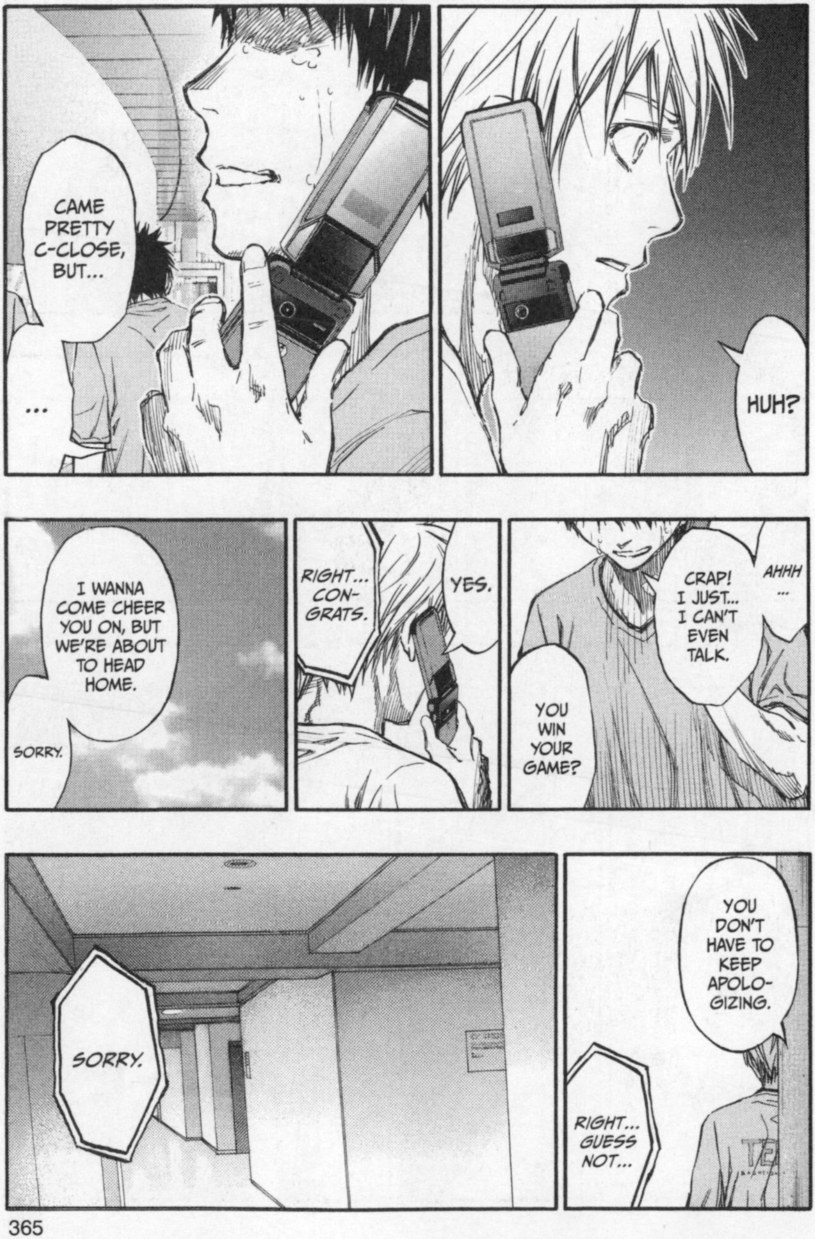
HUH?
CAME PRETTY C-CLOSE, BUT...
...
AHHH...
CRAP! I JUST... I CAN'T EVEN TALK.
YOU WIN YOUR GAME?
YES.
RIGHT... CON-GRATS.
I WANNA COME CHEER YOU ON, BUT WE'RE ABOUT TO HEAD HOME.
SORRY.
YOU DON'T HAVE TO KEEP APOLO-GIZING.
RIGHT... GUESS NOT...
SORRY.

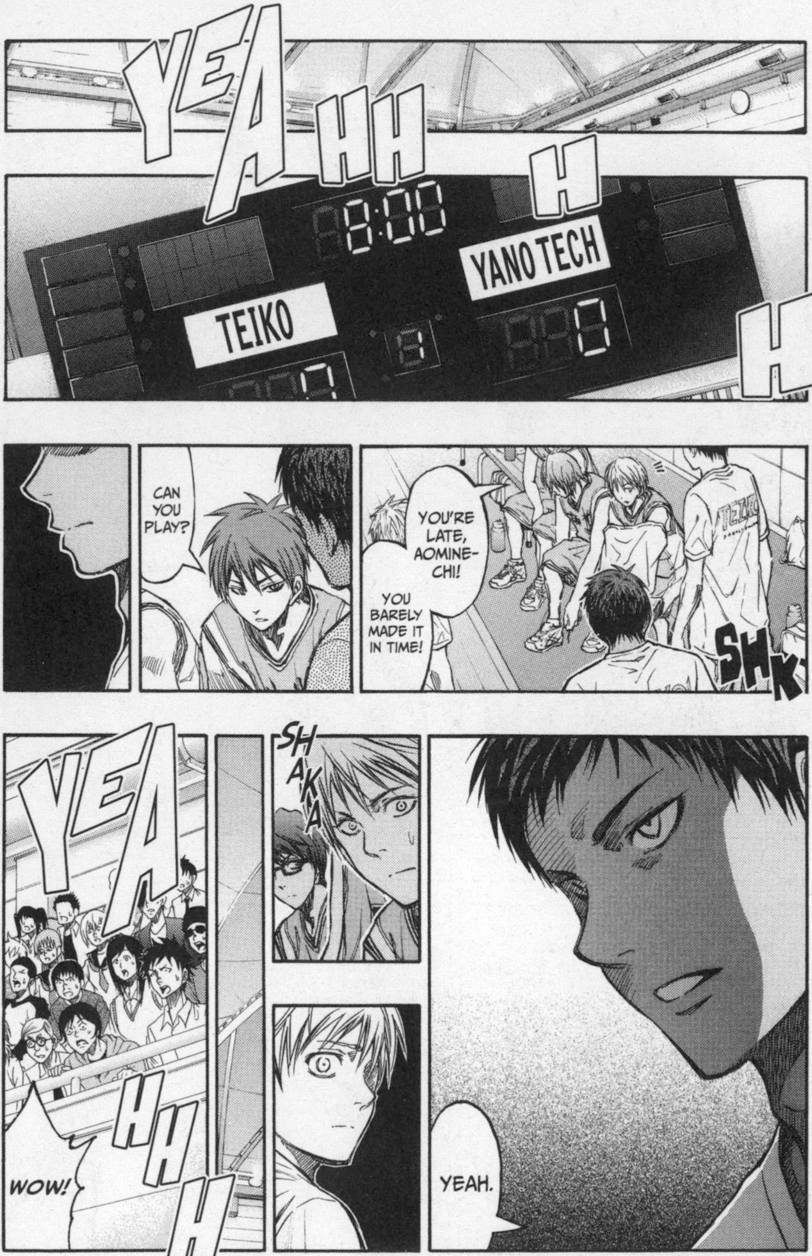
YEAHHHH
8:00
YANO TECH
TEIKO
YOU'RE LATE, AOMINE-CHI!
YOU BARELY MADE IT IN TIME!
SHK
CAN YOU PLAY?
YEAH.
SHAKA
YEAHHH
WOW!

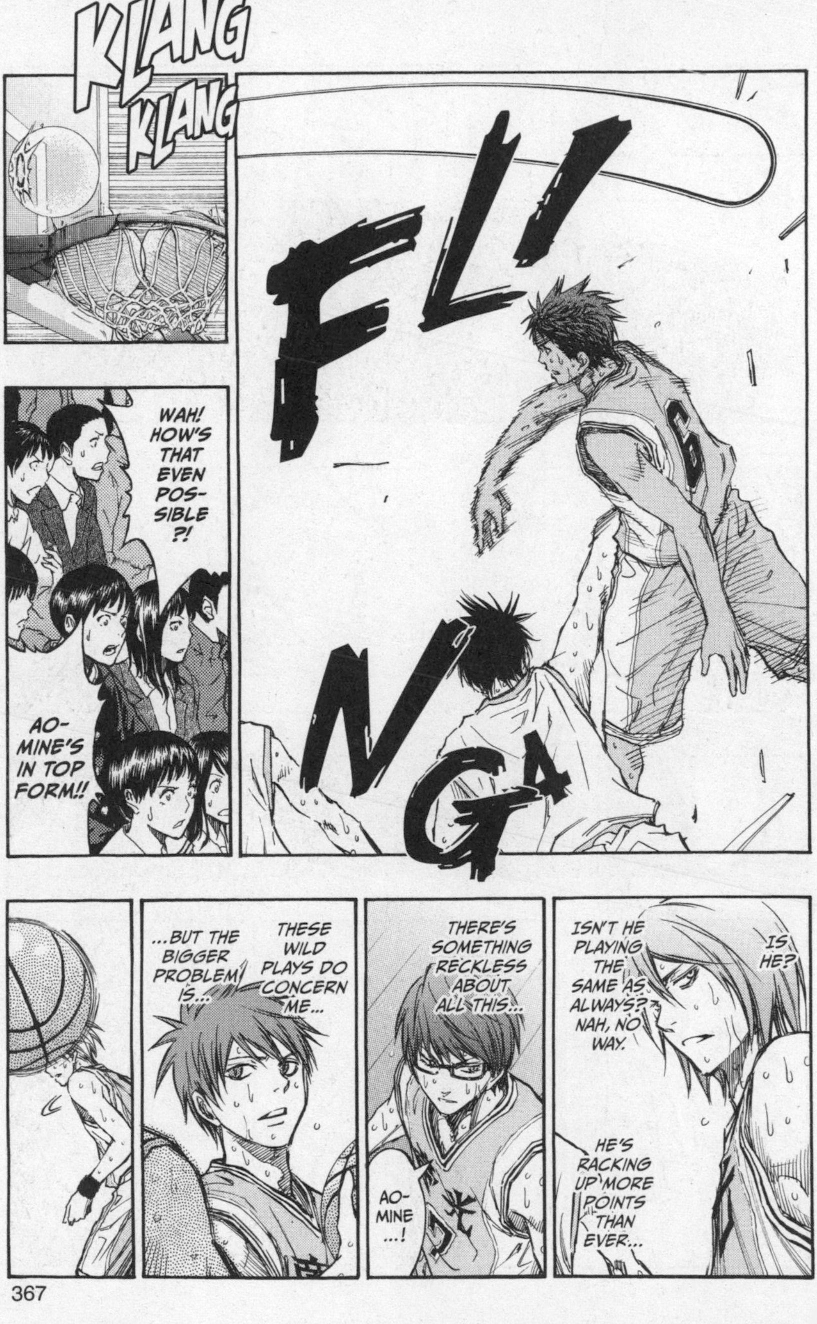
FLING
KLANG
KLANG
WAH! HOW'S THAT EVEN POS-SIBLE?!
AO-MINE'S IN TOP FORM!!
IS HE?
ISN'T HE PLAYING THE SAME AS ALWAYS? NAH, NO WAY.
HE'S RACKING UP MORE POINTS THAN EVER...
THERE'S SOMETHING RECKLESS ABOUT ALL THIS...
AO-MINE ...!
THESE WILD PLAYS DO CONCERN ME...
...BUT THE BIGGER PROBLEM IS...

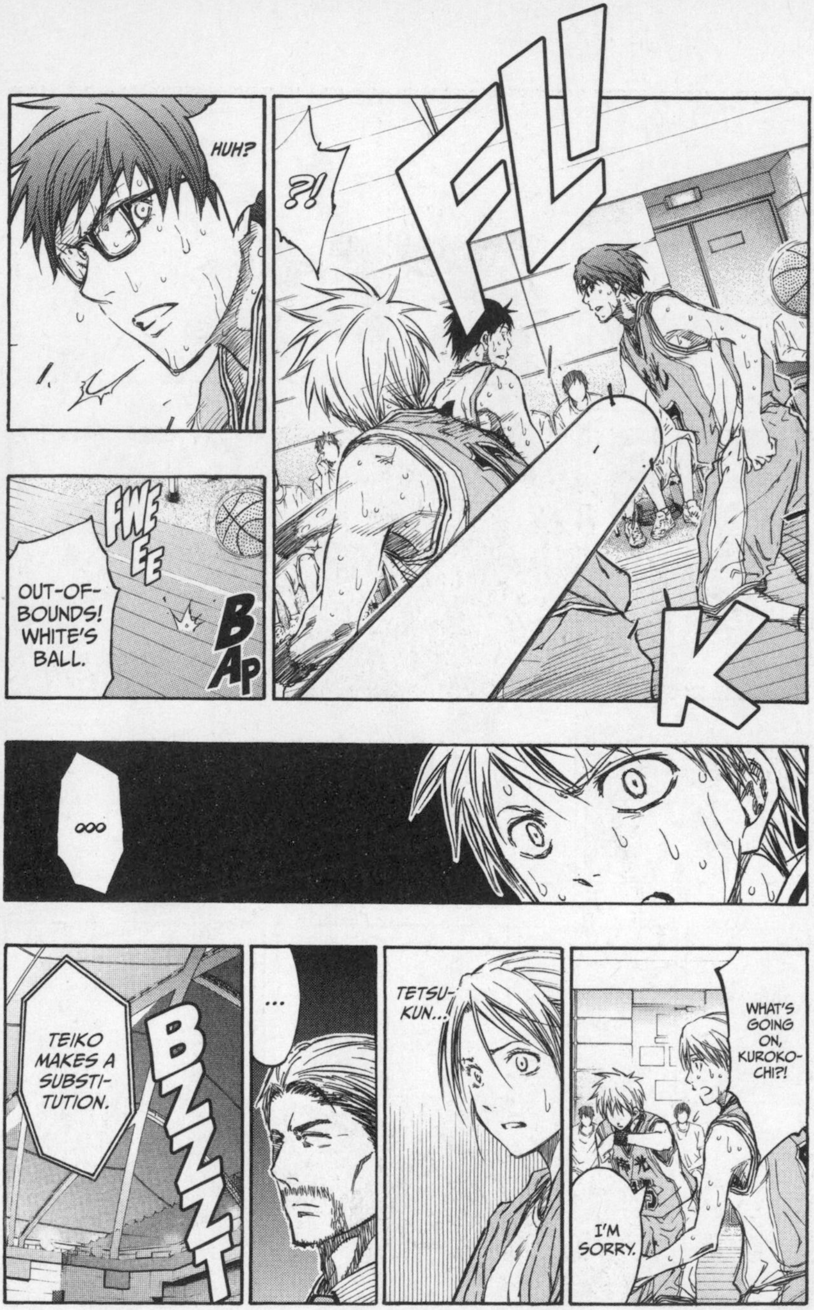
?!
FL!
K
HUH?
FWEEE
OUT-OF-BOUNDS! WHITE'S BALL.
BAP
...
WHAT'S GOING ON, KUROKOCHI?!
I'M SORRY.
TETSU-KUN...
...
TEIKO MAKES A SUBSTITUTION.
BZZZT

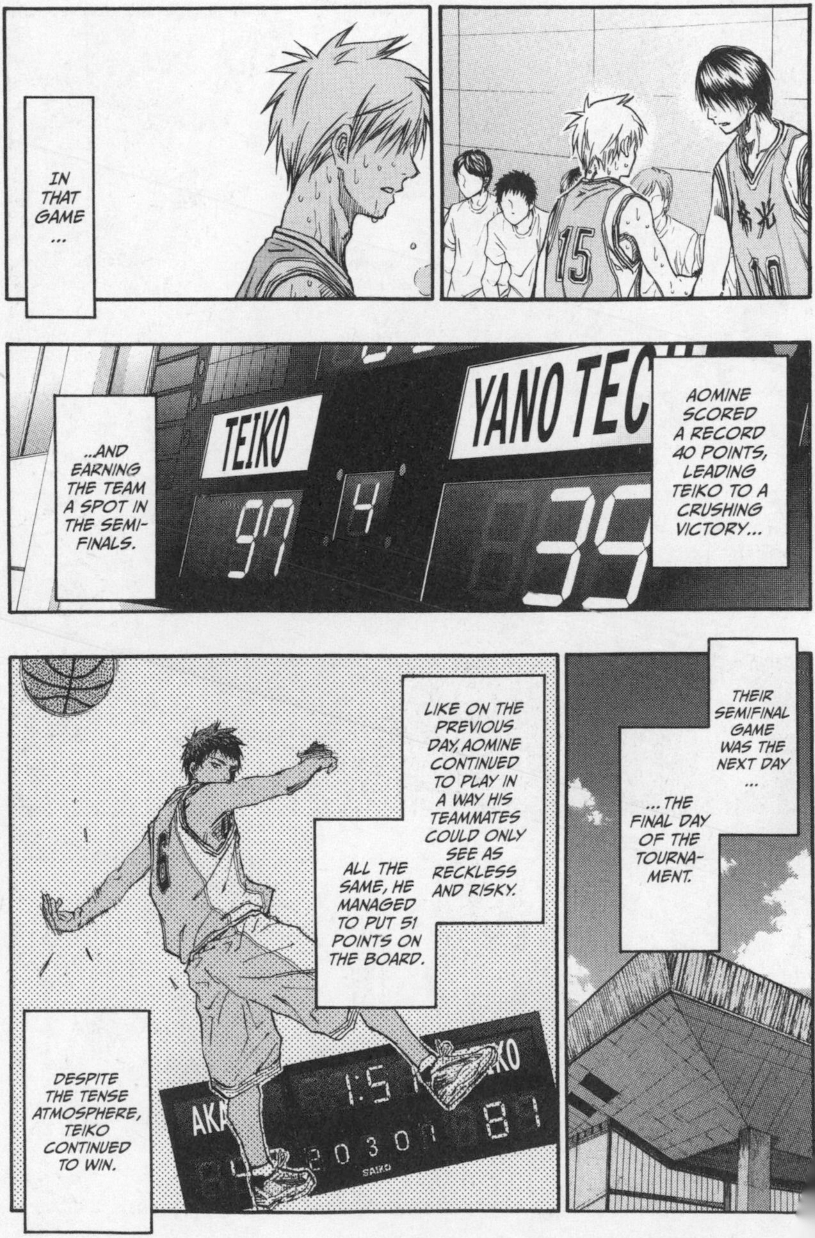
IN THAT GAME ...
AOMINE SCORED A RECORD 40 POINTS, LEADING TEIKO TO A CRUSHING VICTORY...
...AND EARNING THE TEAM A SPOT IN THE SEMI-FINALS.
THEIR SEMIFINAL GAME WAS THE NEXT DAY ...
...THE FINAL DAY OF THE TOURNAMENT.
LIKE ON THE PREVIOUS DAY, AOMINE CONTINUED TO PLAY IN A WAY HIS TEAMMATES COULD ONLY SEE AS RECKLESS AND RISKY.
ALL THE SAME, HE MANAGED TO PUT 51 POINTS ON THE BOARD.
DESPITE THE TENSE ATMOSPHERE, TEIKO CONTINUED TO WIN.

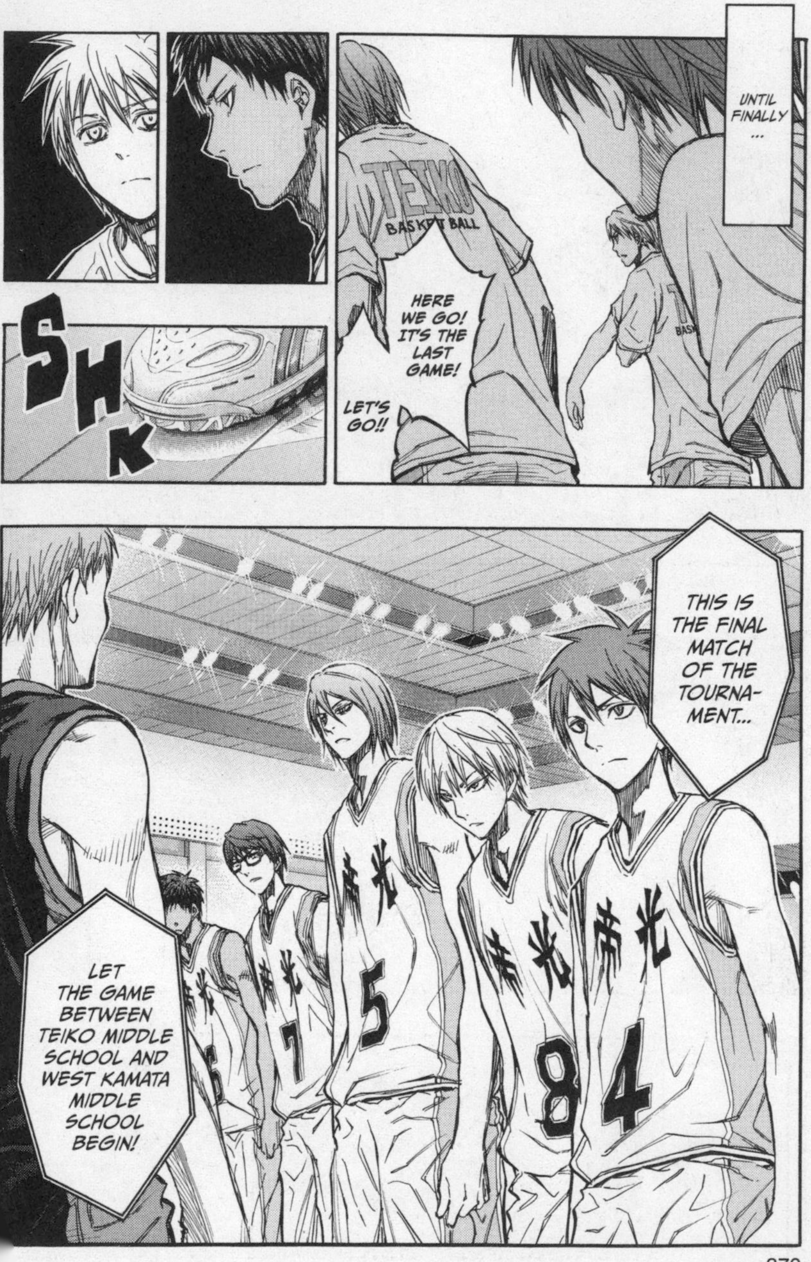
UNTIL FINALLY ...
HERE WE GO! IT'S THE LAST GAME!
LET'S GO!!
SHK
THIS IS THE FINAL MATCH OF THE TOURNA-MENT...
LET THE GAME BETWEEN TEIKO MIDDLE SCHOOL AND WEST KAMATA MIDDLE SCHOOL BEGIN!

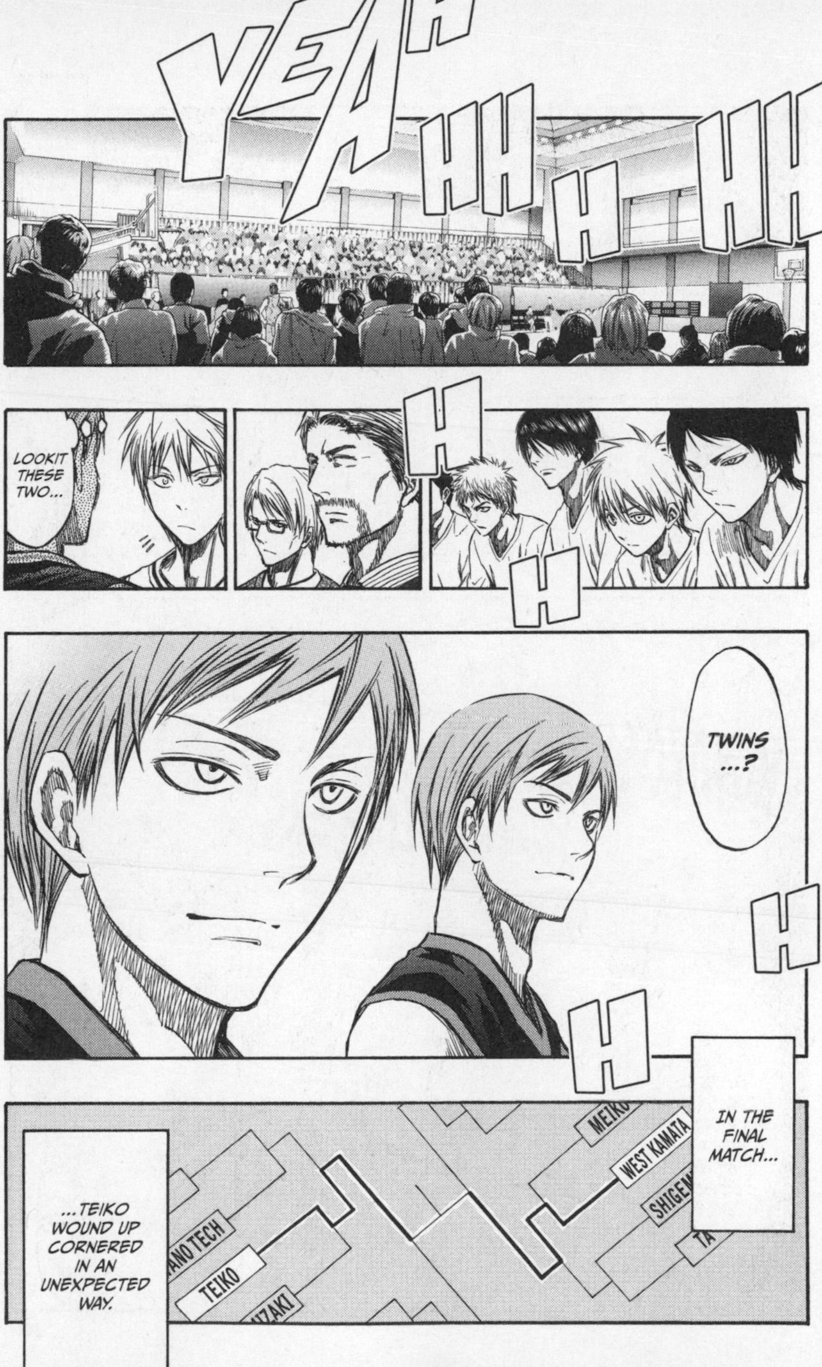
YEAHHHHHHHHH
LOOKIT THESE TWO...
TWINS ...?
IN THE FINAL MATCH...
...TEIKO WOUND UP CORNERED IN AN UNEXPECTED WAY.
MEIKO
WEST KAMATA
TEIKO

KUROKO'S BASKETBALL BLOOPERS TAKE 10

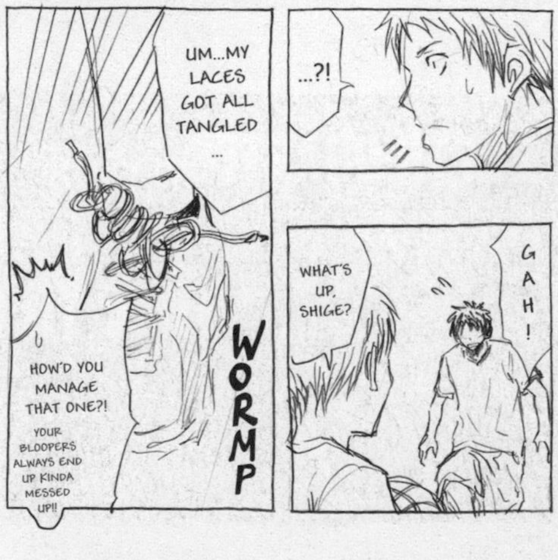
...?!
GAH!
WHAT'S UP, SHIGE?
UM...MY LACES GOT ALL TANGLED...
WORMP
HOW'D YOU MANAGE THAT ONE?!
YOUR BLOOPERS ALWAYS END UP KINDA MESSED UP!!

217TH QUARTER:

TIME TO GO

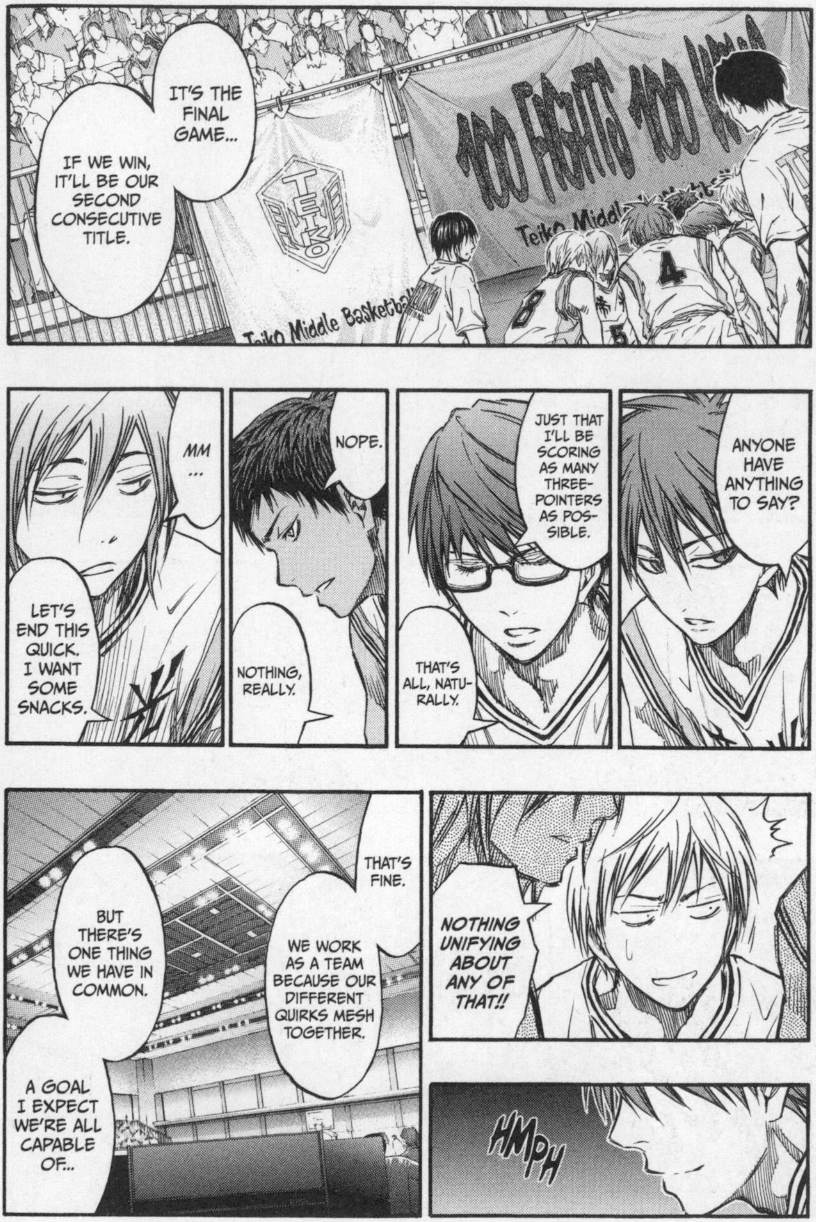
IT'S THE FINAL GAME...
IF WE WIN, IT'LL BE OUR SECOND CONSECUTIVE TITLE.
TEIKO
ANYONE HAVE ANYTHING TO SAY?
JUST THAT I'LL BE SCORING AS MANY THREE-POINTERS AS POSSIBLE.
THAT'S ALL, NATURALLY.
NOPE.
NOTHING, REALLY.
MM...
LET'S END THIS QUICK. I WANT SOME SNACKS.
NOTHING UNIFYING ABOUT ANY OF THAT!!
HMPH
THAT'S FINE.
WE WORK AS A TEAM BECAUSE OUR DIFFERENT QUIRKS MESH TOGETHER.
BUT THERE'S ONE THING WE HAVE IN COMMON.
A GOAL I EXPECT WE'RE ALL CAPABLE OF...

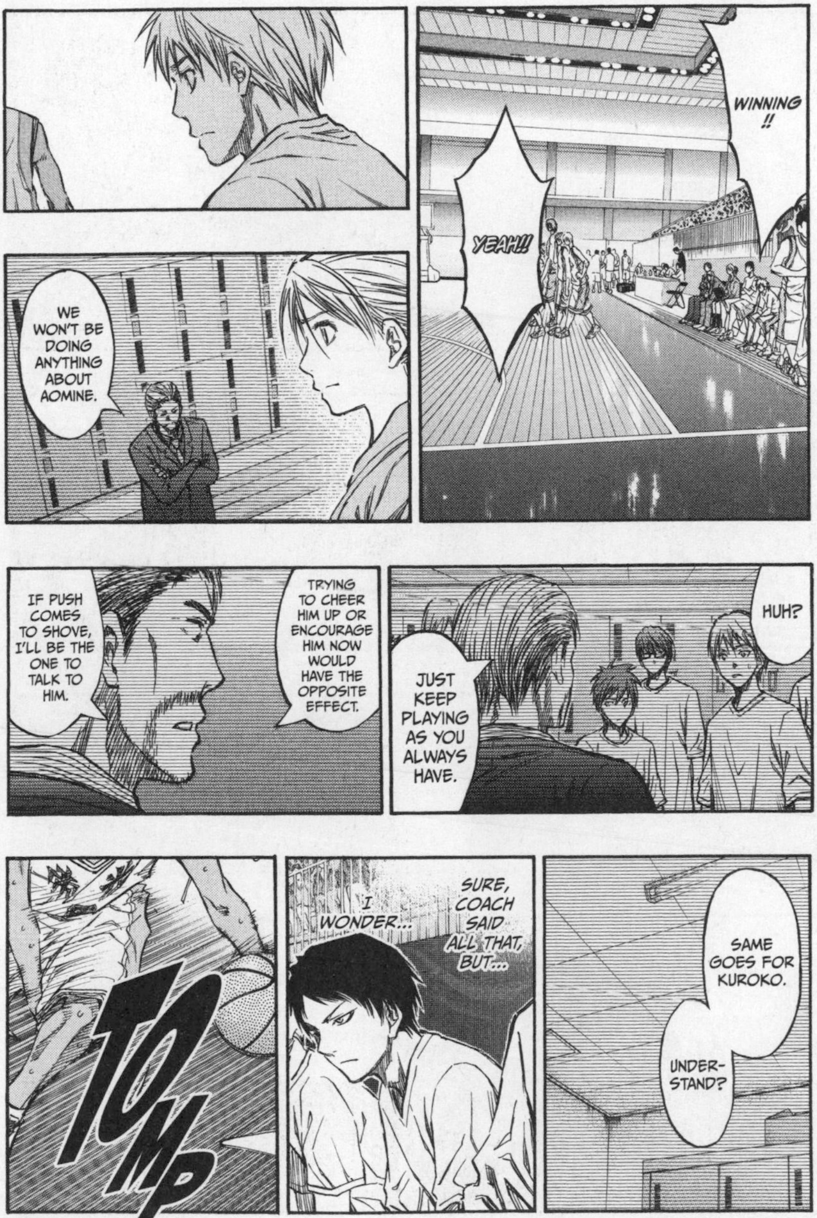
WINNING!!
YEAH!!
WE WON'T BE DOING ANYTHING ABOUT AOMINE.
HUH?
JUST KEEP PLAYING AS YOU ALWAYS HAVE.
TRYING TO CHEER HIM UP OR ENCOURAGE HIM NOW WOULD HAVE THE OPPOSITE EFFECT.
IF PUSH COMES TO SHOVE, I'LL BE THE ONE TO TALK TO HIM.
SAME GOES FOR KUROKO.
UNDER-STAND?
SURE, COACH SAID ALL THAT, BUT...
I WONDER...
TOMP

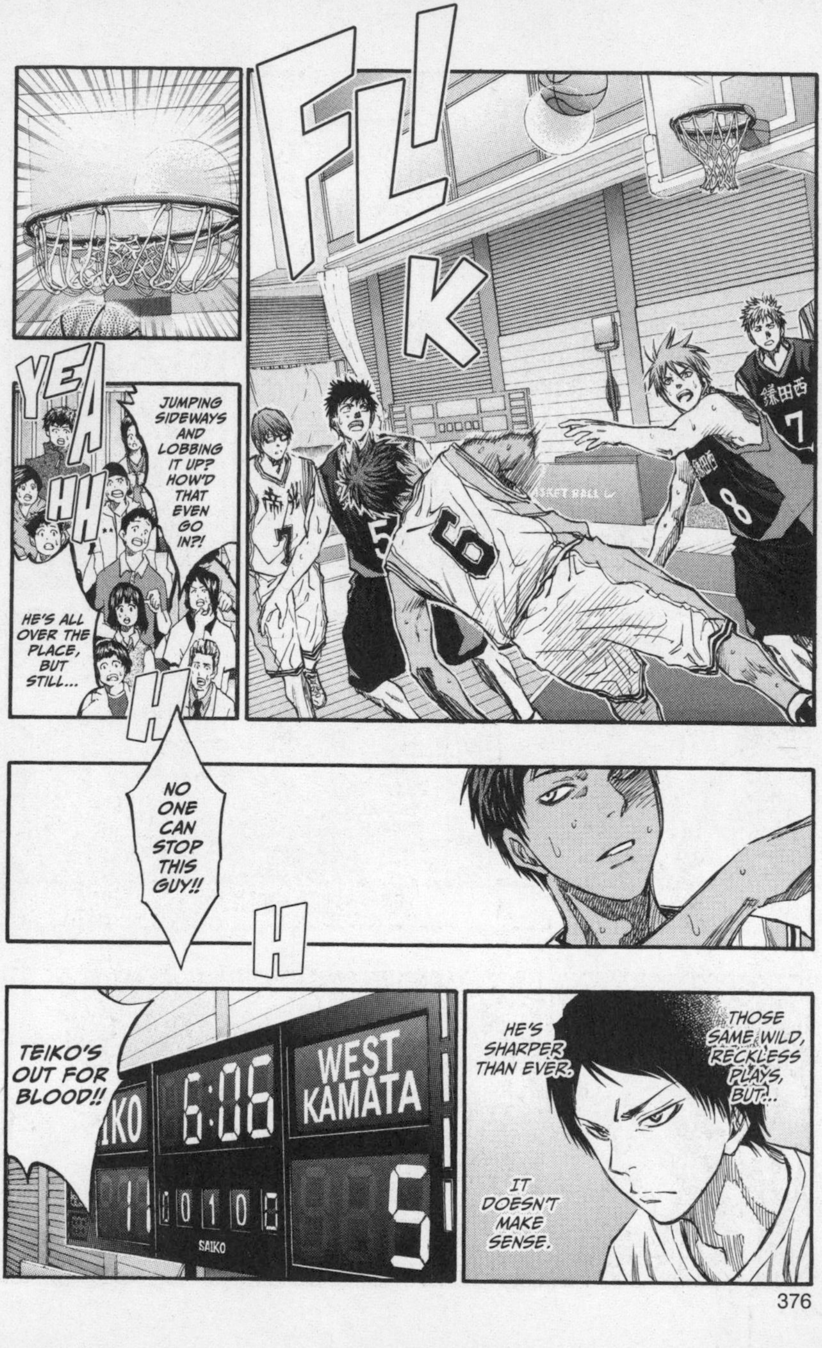
FLIK
YEAHHHH
JUMPING SIDEWAYS AND LOBBING IT UP? HOW'D THAT EVEN GO IN?!
HE'S ALL OVER THE PLACE, BUT STILL...
NO ONE CAN STOP THIS GUY!!
THOSE SAME WILD, RECKLESS PLAYS, BUT...
HE'S SHARPER THAN EVER.
IT DOESN'T MAKE SENSE.
TEIKO'S OUT FOR BLOOD!!
IKO
6:06
WEST KAMATA
11
5
SAIKO

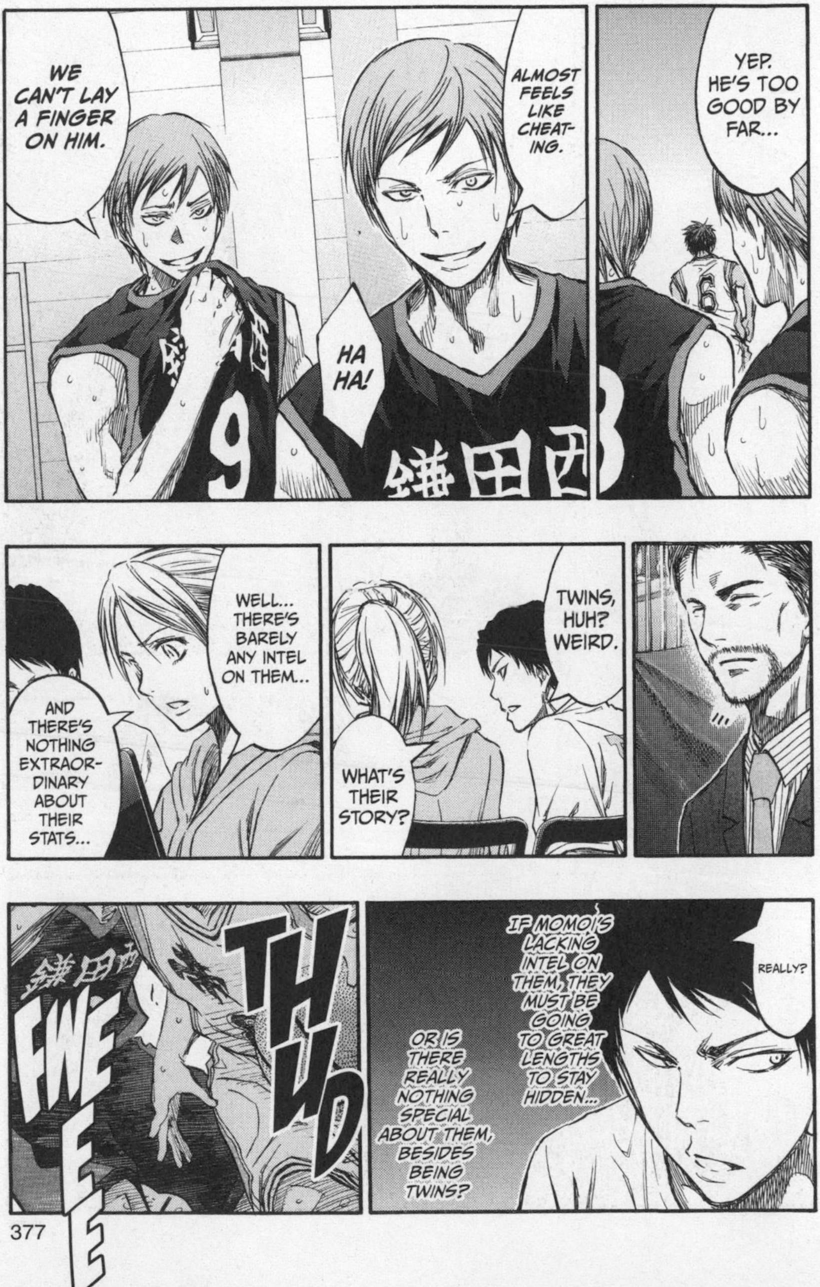
YEP. HE'S TOO GOOD BY FAR...
ALMOST FEELS LIKE CHEAT-ING.
WE CAN'T LAY A FINGER ON HIM.
HA HA!
TWINS, HUH? WEIRD.
WHAT'S THEIR STORY?
WELL... THERE'S BARELY ANY INTEL ON THEM...
AND THERE'S NOTHING EXTRAOR-DINARY ABOUT THEIR STATS...
REALLY?
IF MOMO'S LACKING INTEL ON THEM, THEY MUST BE GOING TO GREAT LENGTHS TO STAY HIDDEN...
OR IS THERE REALLY NOTHING SPECIAL ABOUT THEM, BESIDES BEING TWINS?
THUD
FWEEE

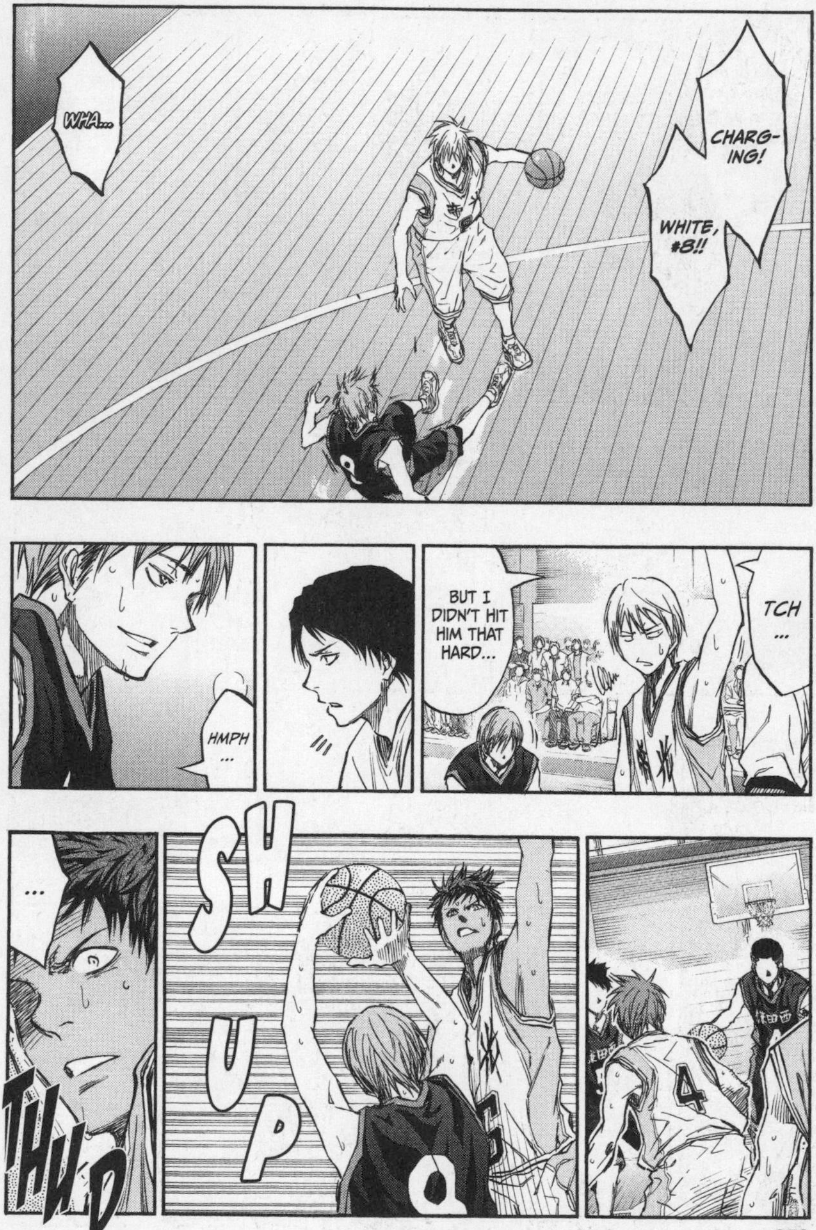
CHARG-ING!
WHITE, #8!!
WHA...
TCH ...
BUT I DIDN'T HIT HIM THAT HARD...
HMPH ...
SHUP
...
THUD

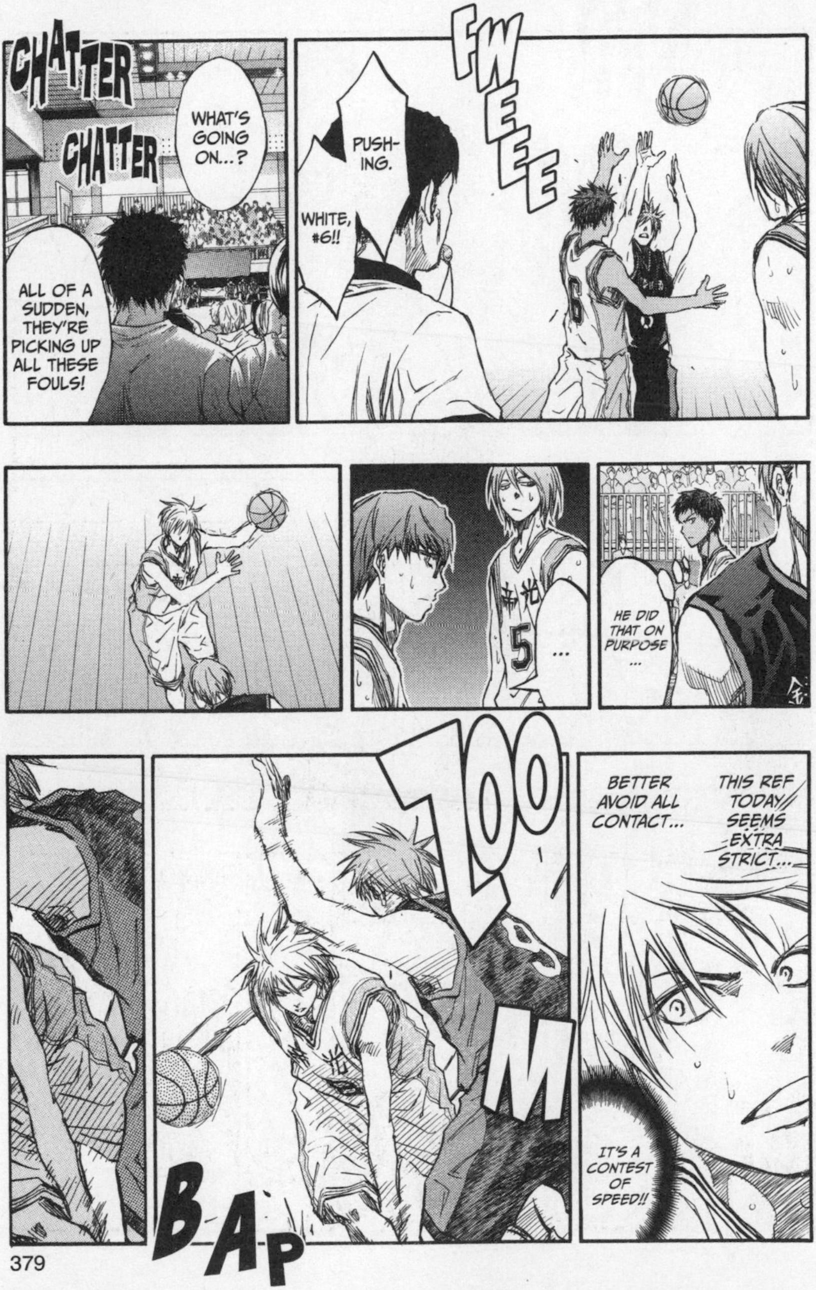
FWEEE
PUSHING.
WHITE, #6!!
CHATTER
CHATTER
WHAT'S GOING ON...?
ALL OF A SUDDEN, THEY'RE PICKING UP ALL THESE FOULS!
HE DID THAT ON PURPOSE...
...
THIS REF TODAY SEEMS EXTRA STRICT...
BETTER AVOID ALL CONTACT...
IT'S A CONTEST OF SPEED!!
ZOOM
BAP

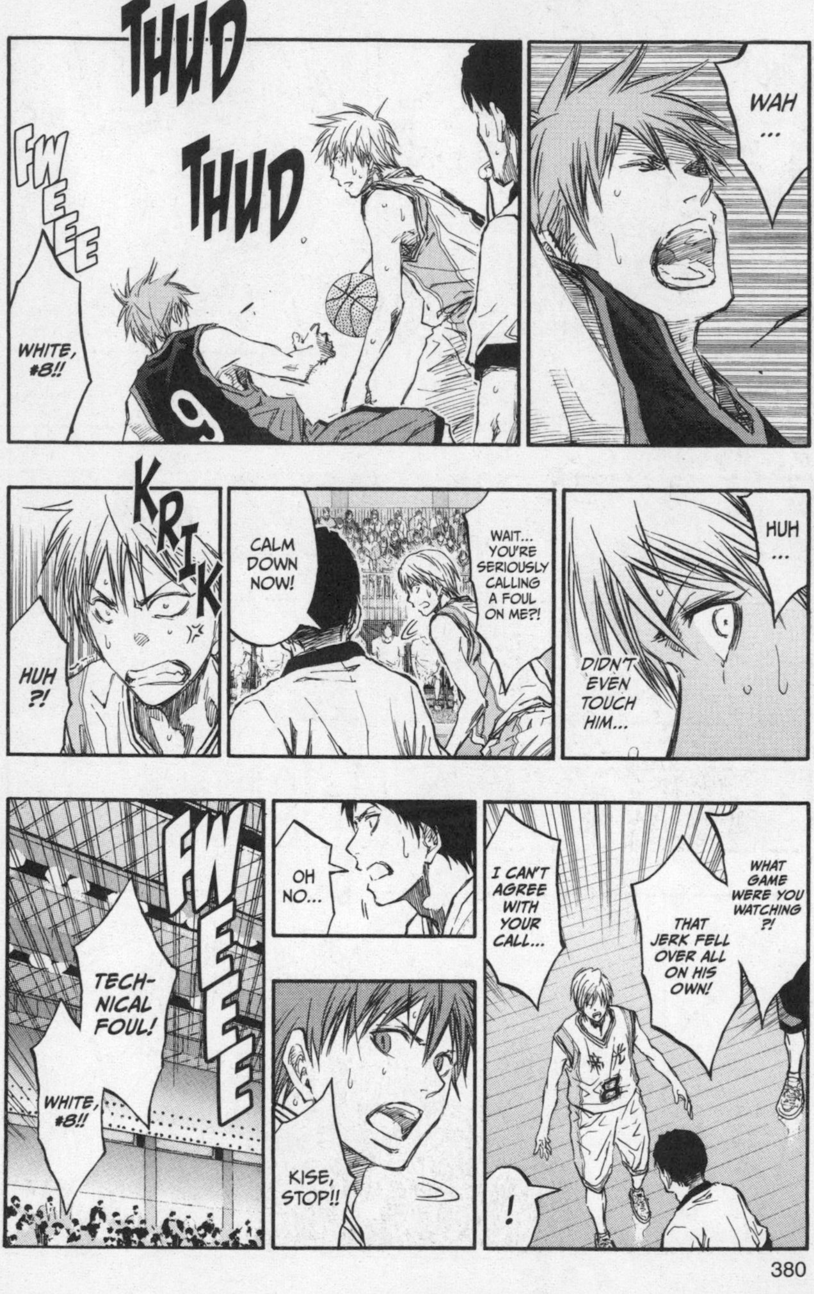
WAH ...
THUD
THUD
FWEEE
WHITE, #8!!
HUH ...
DIDN'T EVEN TOUCH HIM...
WAIT... YOU'RE SERIOUSLY CALLING A FOUL ON ME?!
CALM DOWN NOW!
KRIK
HUH ?!
WHAT GAME WERE YOU WATCHING ?!
THAT JERK FELL OVER ALL ON HIS OWN!
I CAN'T AGREE WITH YOUR CALL...
!
OH NO...
KISE, STOP!!
FWEEE
TECH-NICAL FOUL!
WHITE, #8!!

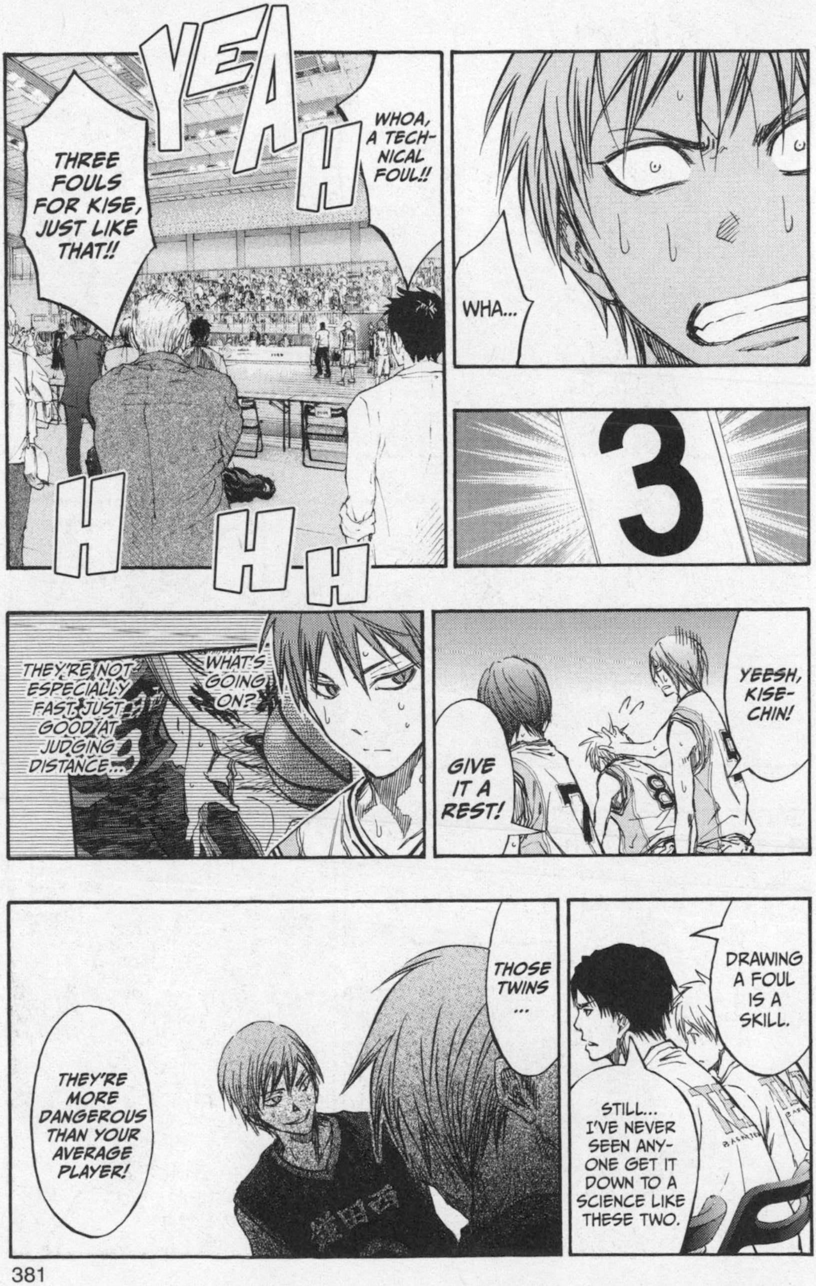
WHA...
3
YEAHHHH
WHOA, A TECHNICAL FOUL!!
THREE FOULS FOR KISE, JUST LIKE THAT!!
YEESH, KISE-CHIN!
GIVE IT A REST!
WHAT'S GOING ON?
THEY'RE NOT ESPECIALLY FAST. JUST GOOD AT JUDGING DISTANCE...
DRAWING A FOUL IS A SKILL.
STILL... I'VE NEVER SEEN ANYONE GET IT DOWN TO A SCIENCE LIKE THESE TWO.
THOSE TWINS...
THEY'RE MORE DANGEROUS THAN YOUR AVERAGE PLAYER!

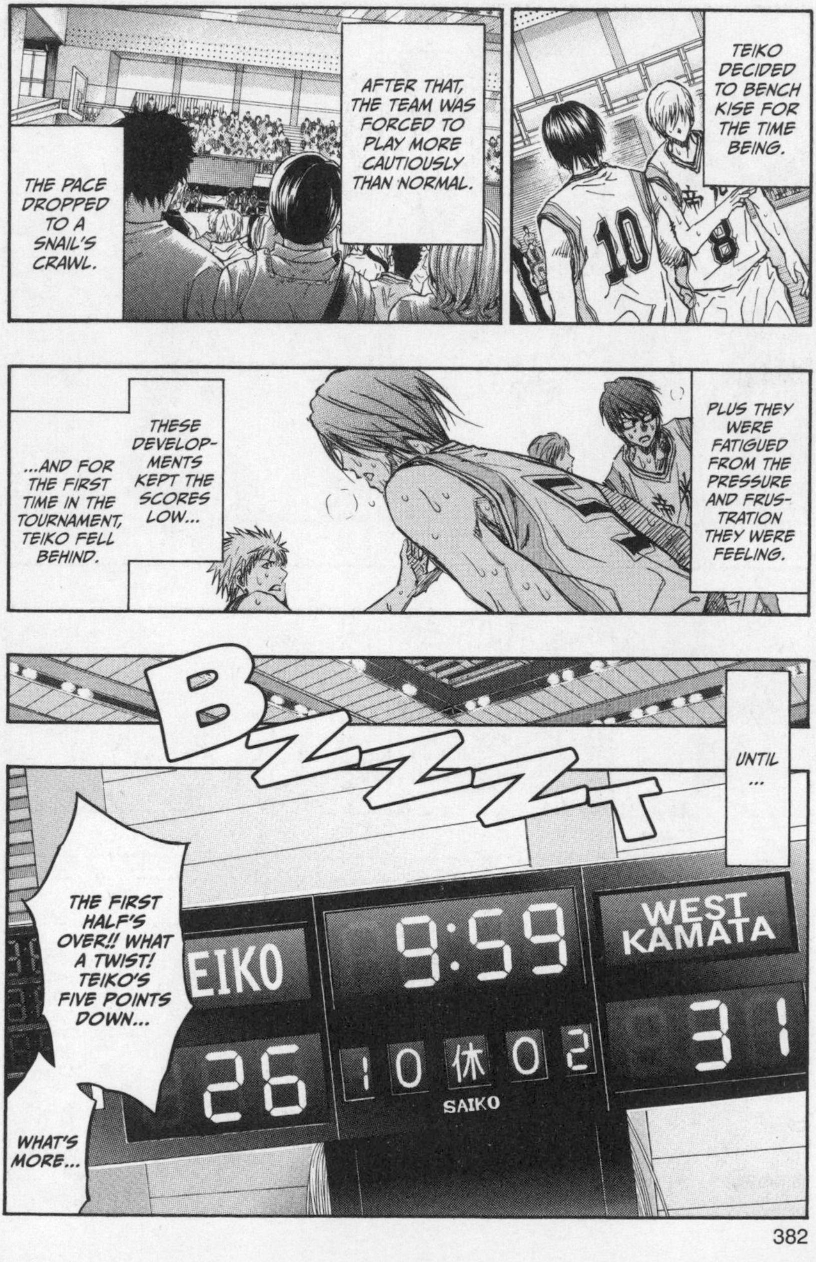
TEIKO DECIDED TO BENCH KISE FOR THE TIME BEING.
AFTER THAT, THE TEAM WAS FORCED TO PLAY MORE CAUTIOUSLY THAN NORMAL.
THE PACE DROPPED TO A SNAIL'S CRAWL.
PLUS THEY WERE FATIGUED FROM THE PRESSURE AND FRUSTRATION THEY WERE FEELING.
THESE DEVELOPMENTS KEPT THE SCORES LOW...
...AND FOR THE FIRST TIME IN THE TOURNAMENT, TEIKO FELL BEHIND.
BZZZZT
UNTIL...
THE FIRST HALF'S OVER!! WHAT A TWIST! TEIKO'S FIVE POINTS DOWN...
WEST KAMATA
9:59
EIKO
26
10 休 02
SAIKO
31
WHAT'S MORE...

HE'S ALL BUT USELESS IN THE SECOND HALF!!

THEIR ACE, AOMINE, HAS FOUR FOULS!!

					P	P	P	P	P
				6	⊗	⊘		⊗	
				7	⊗	⊗		⊗	

DAIKI AOMINE

SHINTARO MIDORIMA

RYOTA KISE

...

...AND HIS RECKLESS STYLE IS FINALLY GETTING THE BETTER OF HIM.

WE'VE TRIED TO BE CAREFUL WITH THESE FOULS, BUT AOMINE...

DON'T GO ANY-WHERE JUST YET.

AO-MINE.

Basketball

SANADA... TAKE THE BOYS BACK TO THE LOCKER ROOM.

I'LL HANDLE THIS.

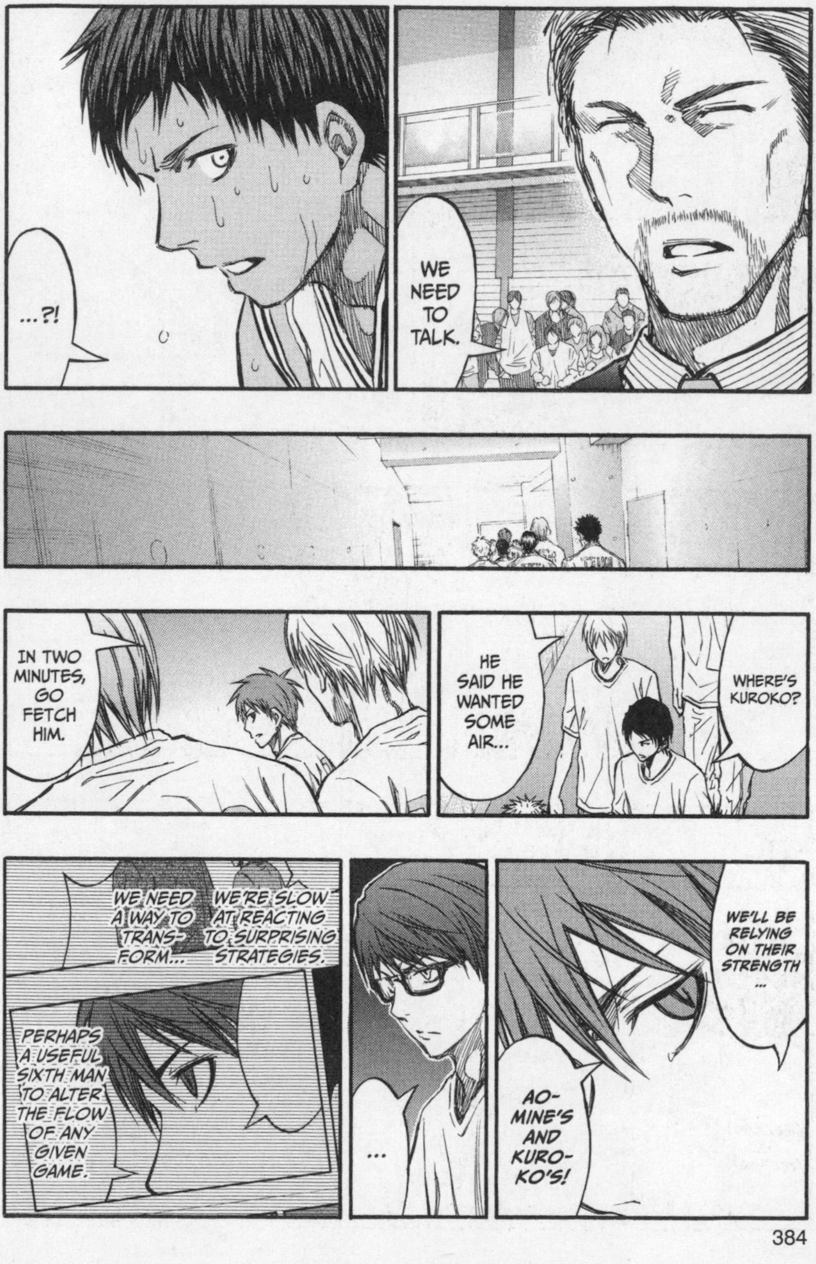
WE NEED TO TALK.
...?!
WHERE'S KUROKO?
HE SAID HE WANTED SOME AIR...
IN TWO MINUTES, GO FETCH HIM.
WE'LL BE RELYING ON THEIR STRENGTH...
AO-MINE'S AND KURO-KO'S!
...
WE'RE SLOW AT REACTING TO SURPRISING STRATEGIES.
WE NEED A WAY TO TRANS-FORM...
PERHAPS A USEFUL SIXTH MAN TO ALTER THE FLOW OF ANY GIVEN GAME.

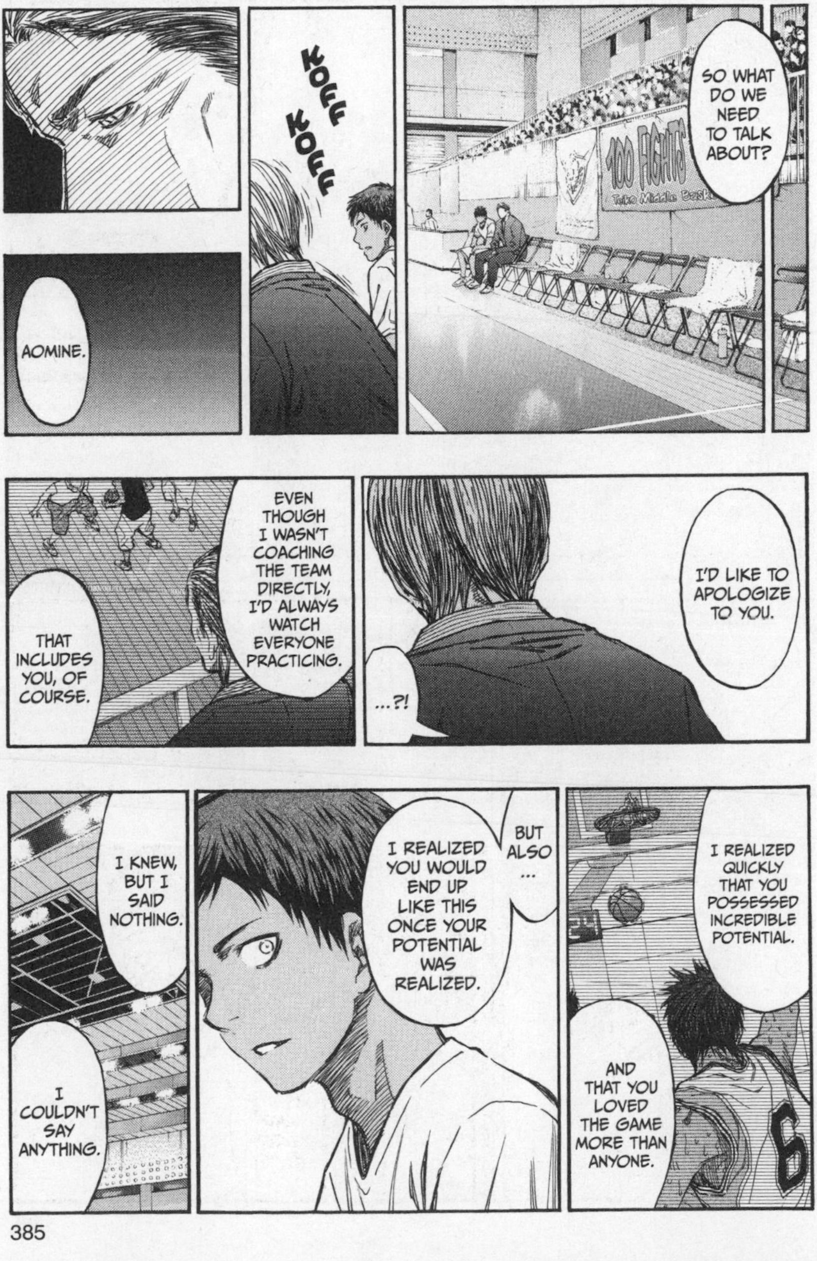
SO WHAT DO WE NEED TO TALK ABOUT?
100 FIGHTS
KOFF KOFF
AOMINE.
I'D LIKE TO APOLOGIZE TO YOU.
...?!
EVEN THOUGH I WASN'T COACHING THE TEAM DIRECTLY, I'D ALWAYS WATCH EVERYONE PRACTICING.
THAT INCLUDES YOU, OF COURSE.
I REALIZED QUICKLY THAT YOU POSSESSED INCREDIBLE POTENTIAL.
AND THAT YOU LOVED THE GAME MORE THAN ANYONE.
BUT ALSO...
I REALIZED YOU WOULD END UP LIKE THIS ONCE YOUR POTENTIAL WAS REALIZED.
I KNEW, BUT I SAID NOTHING.
I COULDN'T SAY ANYTHING.

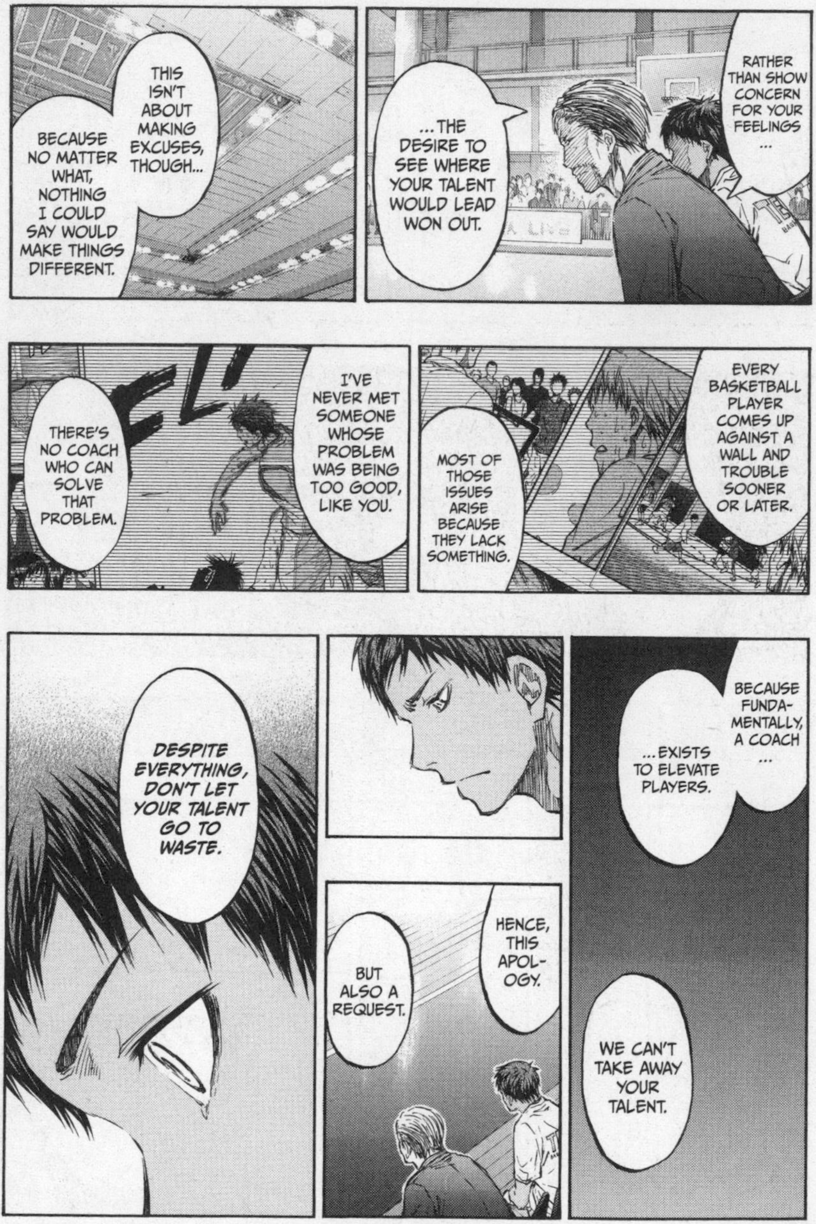
RATHER THAN SHOW CONCERN FOR YOUR FEELINGS ...
...THE DESIRE TO SEE WHERE YOUR TALENT WOULD LEAD WON OUT.
THIS ISN'T ABOUT MAKING EXCUSES, THOUGH...
BECAUSE NO MATTER WHAT, NOTHING I COULD SAY WOULD MAKE THINGS DIFFERENT.
EVERY BASKETBALL PLAYER COMES UP AGAINST A WALL AND TROUBLE SOONER OR LATER.
MOST OF THOSE ISSUES ARISE BECAUSE THEY LACK SOMETHING.
I'VE NEVER MET SOMEONE WHOSE PROBLEM WAS BEING TOO GOOD, LIKE YOU.
THERE'S NO COACH WHO CAN SOLVE THAT PROBLEM.
BECAUSE FUNDAMENTALLY, A COACH ...
...EXISTS TO ELEVATE PLAYERS.
WE CAN'T TAKE AWAY YOUR TALENT.
HENCE, THIS APOLOGY.
BUT ALSO A REQUEST.
DESPITE EVERYTHING, DON'T LET YOUR TALENT GO TO WASTE.

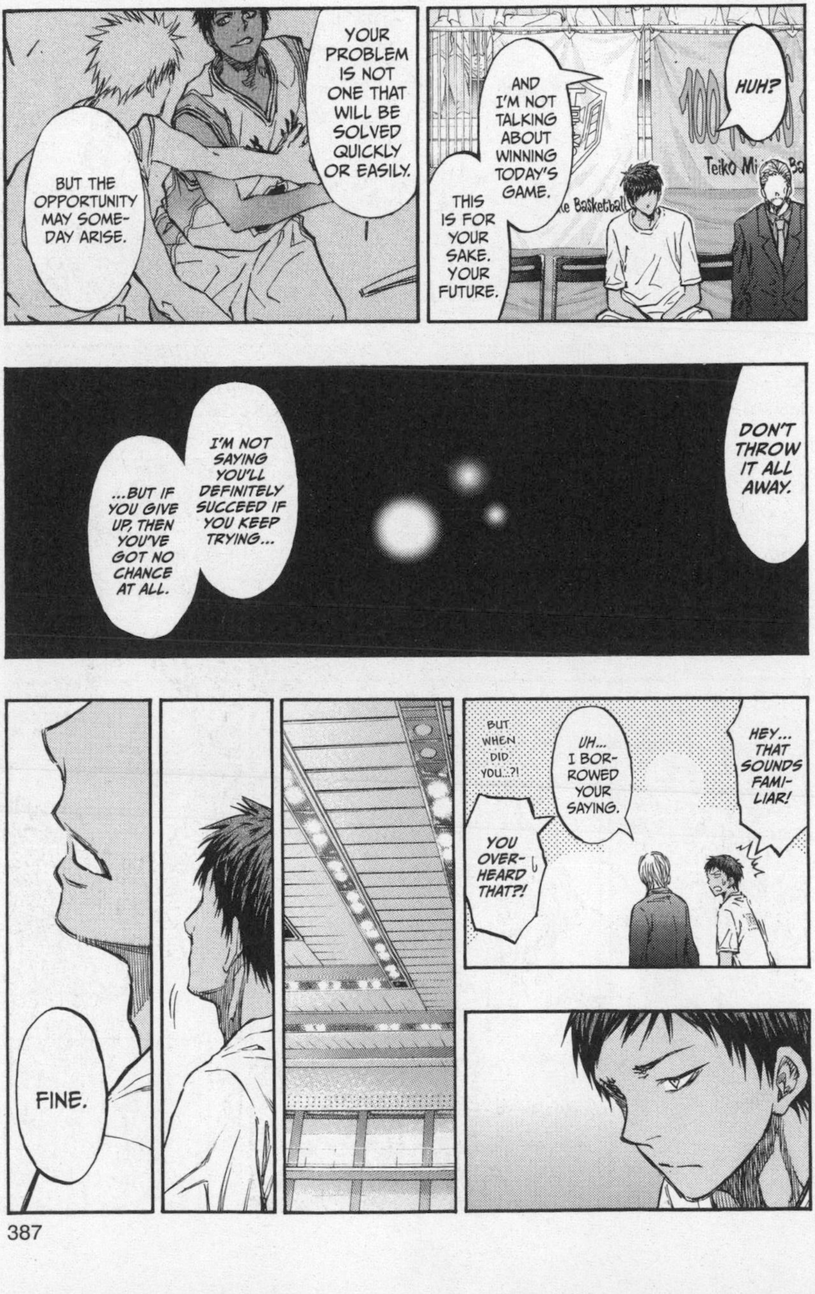
HUH?
AND I'M NOT TALKING ABOUT WINNING TODAY'S GAME.
THIS IS FOR YOUR SAKE. YOUR FUTURE.
YOUR PROBLEM IS NOT ONE THAT WILL BE SOLVED QUICKLY OR EASILY.
BUT THE OPPORTUNITY MAY SOME-DAY ARISE.
DON'T THROW IT ALL AWAY.
I'M NOT SAYING YOU'LL DEFINITELY SUCCEED IF YOU KEEP TRYING...
...BUT IF YOU GIVE UP, THEN YOU'VE GOT NO CHANCE AT ALL.
HEY... THAT SOUNDS FAMI-LIAR!
UH... I BOR-ROWED YOUR SAYING.
BUT WHEN DID YOU...?!
YOU OVER-HEARD THAT?!
FINE.

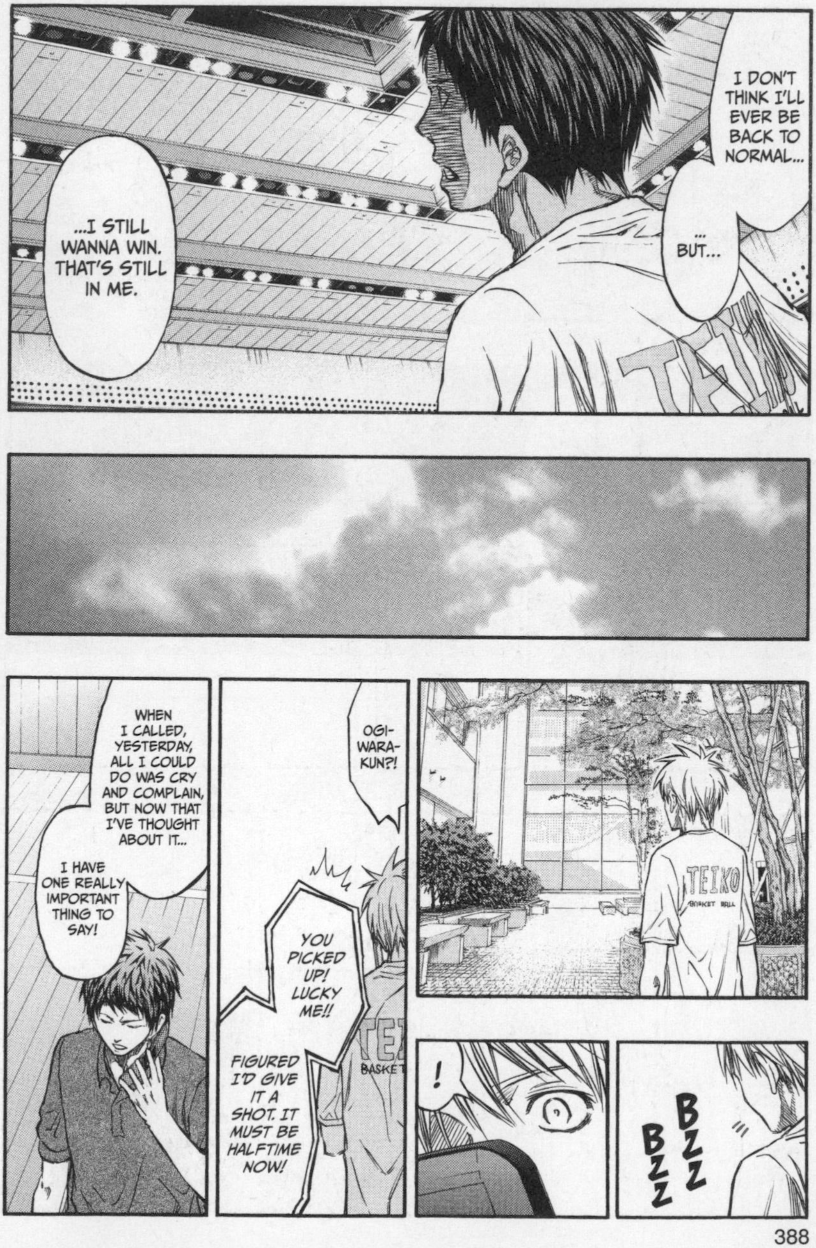
I DON'T THINK I'LL EVER BE BACK TO NORMAL...
... BUT...
...I STILL WANNA WIN. THAT'S STILL IN ME.
TEIKO
TEIKO BASKET BALL
BZZ BZZ
!
OGI-WARA-KUN?!
YOU PICKED UP! LUCKY ME!!
FIGURED I'D GIVE IT A SHOT. IT MUST BE HALFTIME NOW!
WHEN I CALLED, YESTERDAY, ALL I COULD DO WAS CRY AND COMPLAIN, BUT NOW THAT I'VE THOUGHT ABOUT IT...
I HAVE ONE REALLY IMPORTANT THING TO SAY!

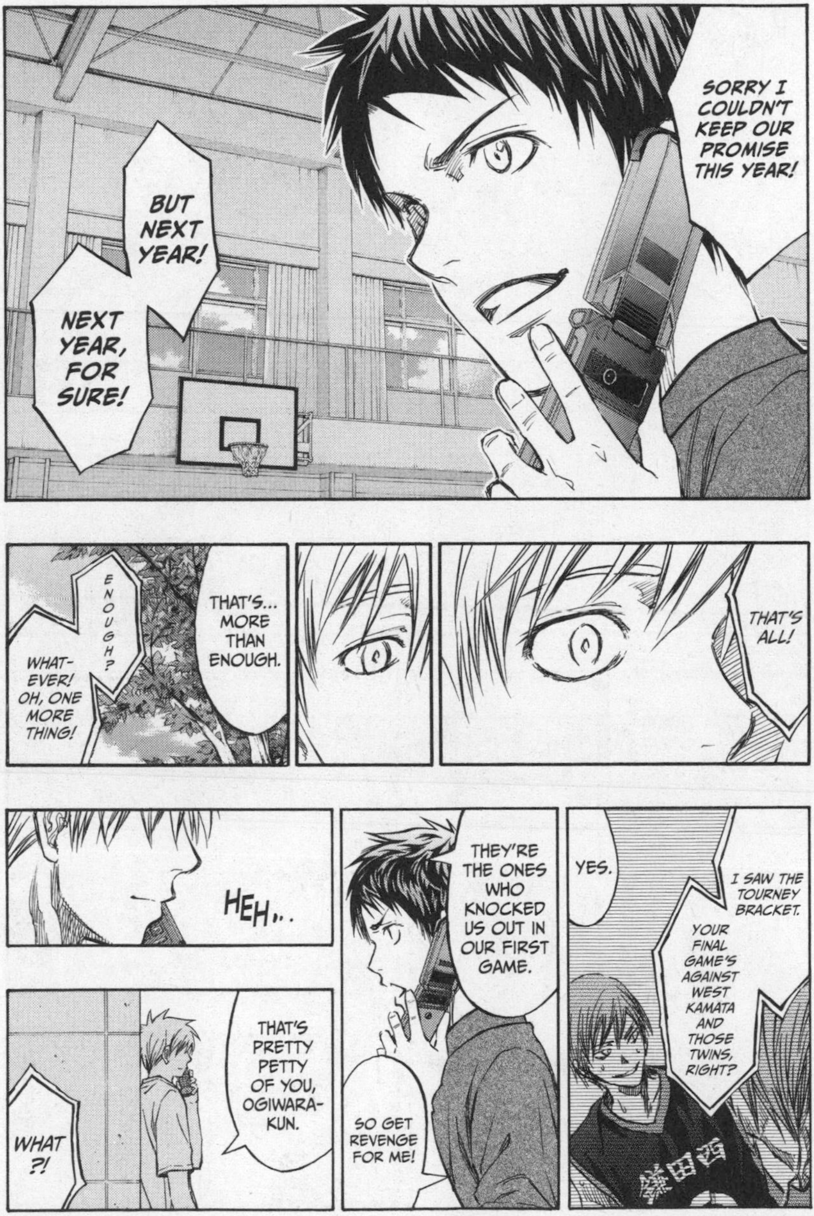
SORRY I COULDN'T KEEP OUR PROMISE THIS YEAR!
BUT NEXT YEAR!
NEXT YEAR, FOR SURE!
THAT'S ALL!
THAT'S... MORE THAN ENOUGH.
ENOUGH?
WHAT-EVER! OH, ONE MORE THING!
I SAW THE TOURNEY BRACKET.
YOUR FINAL GAME'S AGAINST WEST KAMATA AND THOSE TWINS, RIGHT?
YES.
THEY'RE THE ONES WHO KNOCKED US OUT IN OUR FIRST GAME.
SO GET REVENGE FOR ME!
HEH...
THAT'S PRETTY PETTY OF YOU, OGIWARA-KUN.
WHAT?!

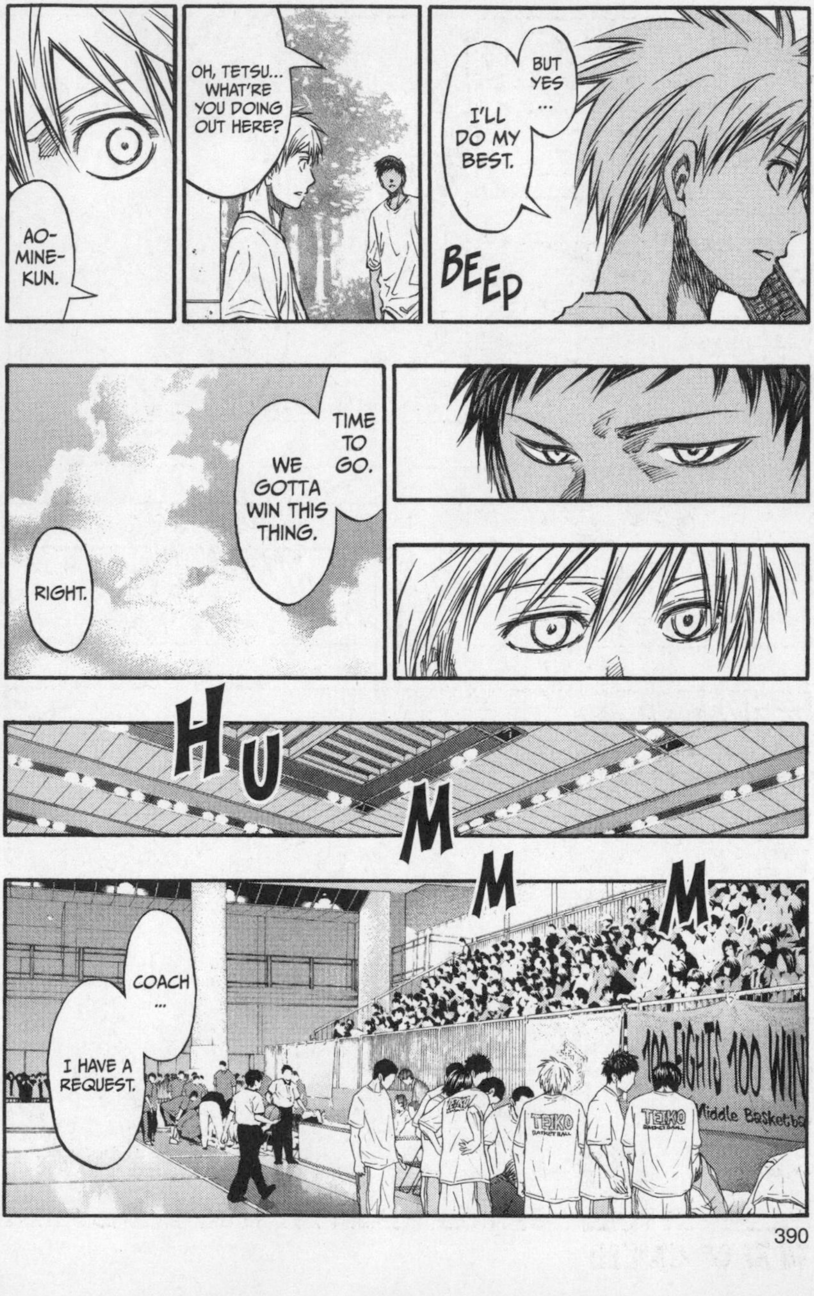
BUT YES ...
I'LL DO MY BEST.
BEEP
OH, TETSU... WHAT'RE YOU DOING OUT HERE?
AO-MINE-KUN.
TIME TO GO.
WE GOTTA WIN THIS THING.
RIGHT.
HUMMMM
COACH ...
I HAVE A REQUEST.
100 FIGHTS 100 WIN
Middle Basketba

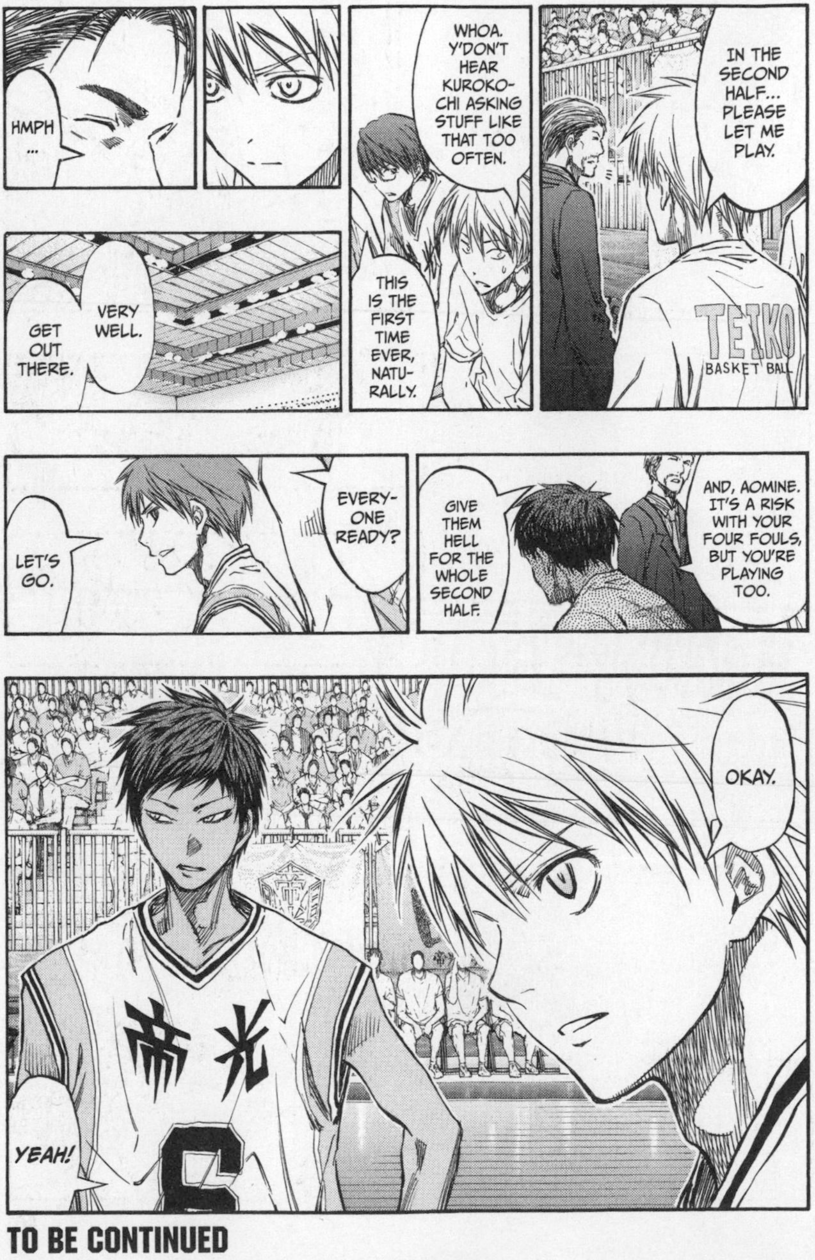
IN THE SECOND HALF... PLEASE LET ME PLAY.
WHOA. Y'DON'T HEAR KUROKO-CHI ASKING STUFF LIKE THAT TOO OFTEN.
THIS IS THE FIRST TIME EVER, NATU-RALLY.
TEIKO
BASKET BALL
HMPH ...
VERY WELL.
GET OUT THERE.
AND, AOMINE. IT'S A RISK WITH YOUR FOUR FOULS, BUT YOU'RE PLAYING TOO.
GIVE THEM HELL FOR THE WHOLE SECOND HALF.
EVERY-ONE READY?
LET'S GO.
OKAY.
YEAH!

TO BE CONTINUED

KUROKO'S BASKETBALL BLOOPERS

TAKE 5

REALLY?
IF MOMOI'S LACKING INTEL ON THEM, THEY MUST BE GOING TO GREAT LENGTHS TO STAY HIDDEN...
OR IS THERE REALLY NOTHING SPECIAL ABOUT THEM, BESIDES BEING TWINS?
AH! THERE'S ONE INTERESTING TIDBIT HERE!
WHAT?!
THEY'RE GREAT AT HAVING OUT-OF-BODY EXPERIENCES.
OUT-OF-BODY
ARE YOU FEELING ALL RIGHT, MOMOI?
DID YA THINK THIS BLOOPER WAS YOUR CHANCE TO GET WEIRD?

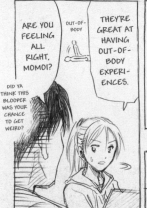

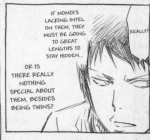

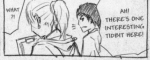

Coming Next Volume

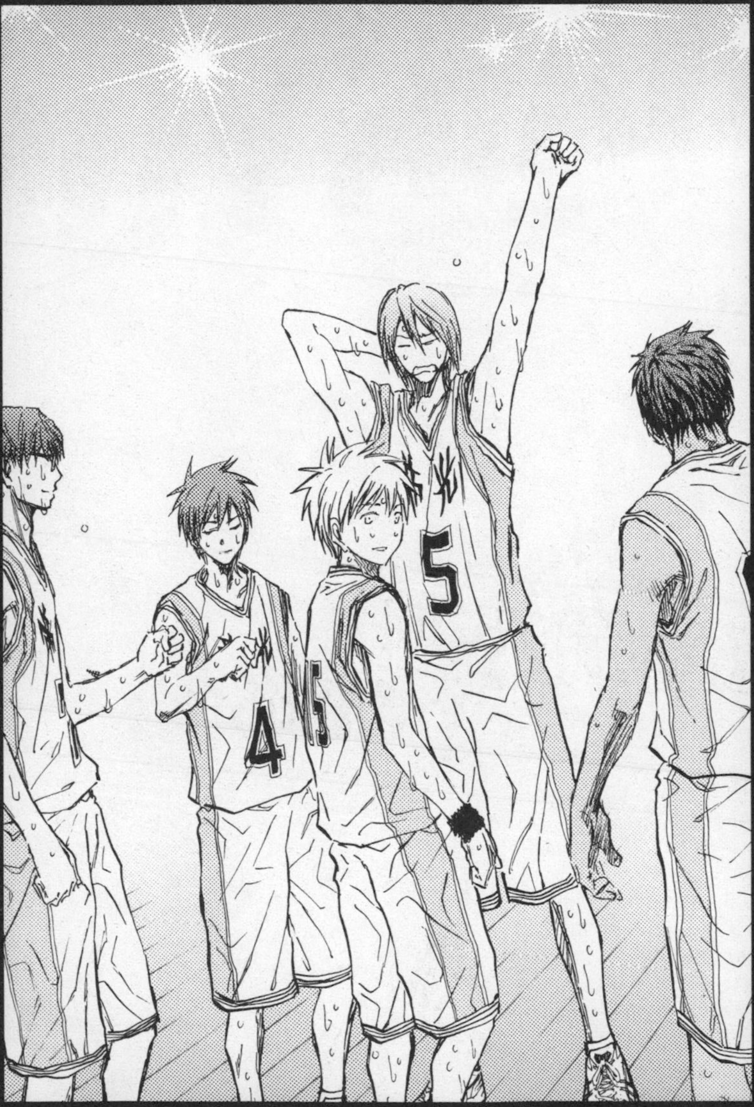

Teiko Middle School's basketball team is steamrolling the competition thanks to the Miracle Generation! But cracks in their armor are starting to show...

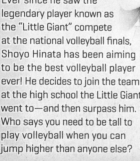

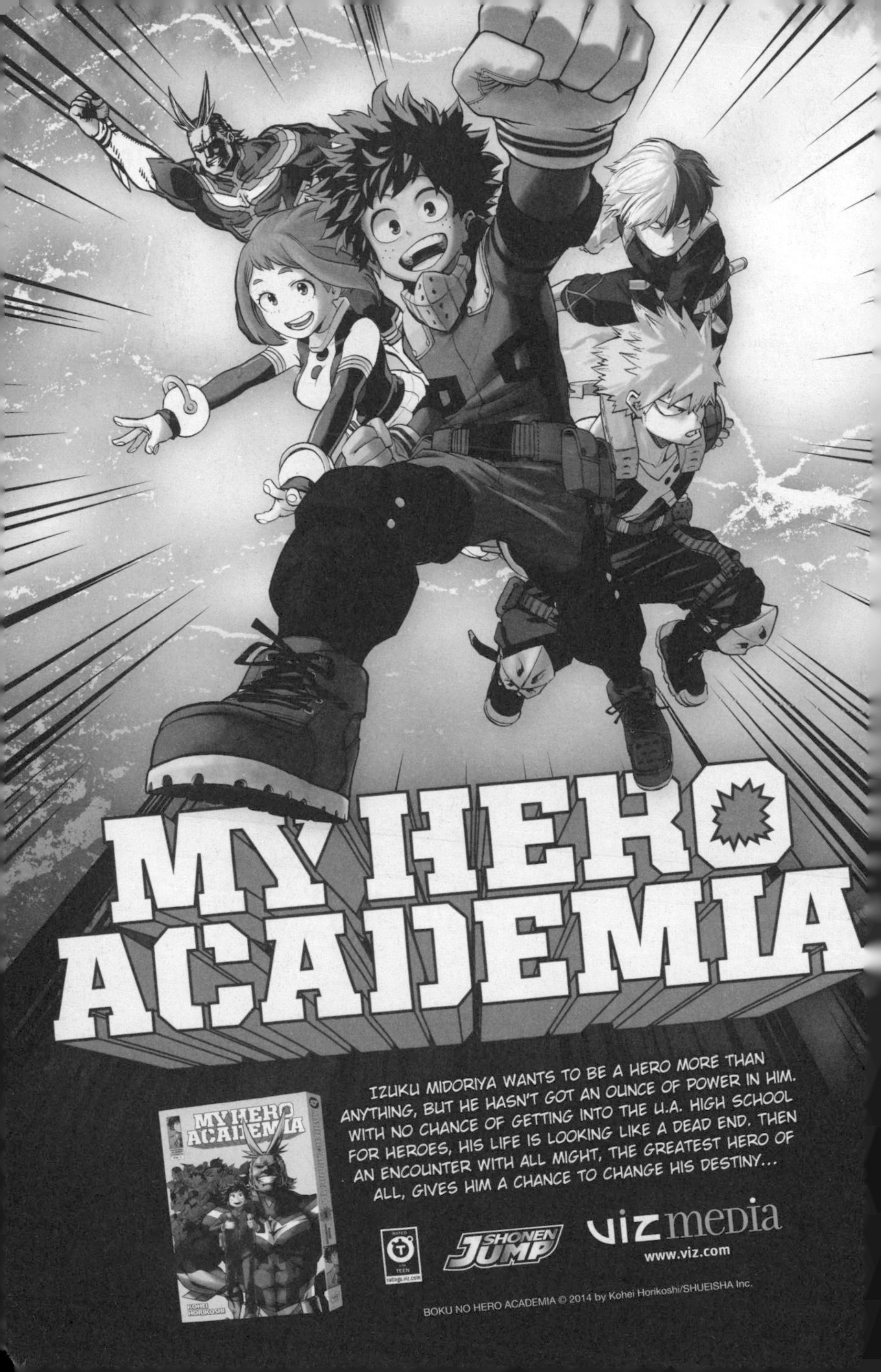
MY HERO ACADEMIA
IZUKU MIDORIYA WANTS TO BE A HERO MORE THAN ANYTHING, BUT HE HASN'T GOT AN OUNCE OF POWER IN HIM. WITH NO CHANCE OF GETTING INTO THE U.A. HIGH SCHOOL FOR HEROES, HIS LIFE IS LOOKING LIKE A DEAD END. THEN AN ENCOUNTER WITH ALL MIGHT, THE GREATEST HERO OF ALL, GIVES HIM A CHANCE TO CHANGE HIS DESTINY…
MY HERO ACADEMIA
KOHEI HORIKOSHI
TEEN
ratings.viz.com
SHONEN JUMP
viz media
www.viz.com
BOKU NO HERO ACADEMIA © 2014 by Kohei Horikoshi/SHUEISHA Inc.

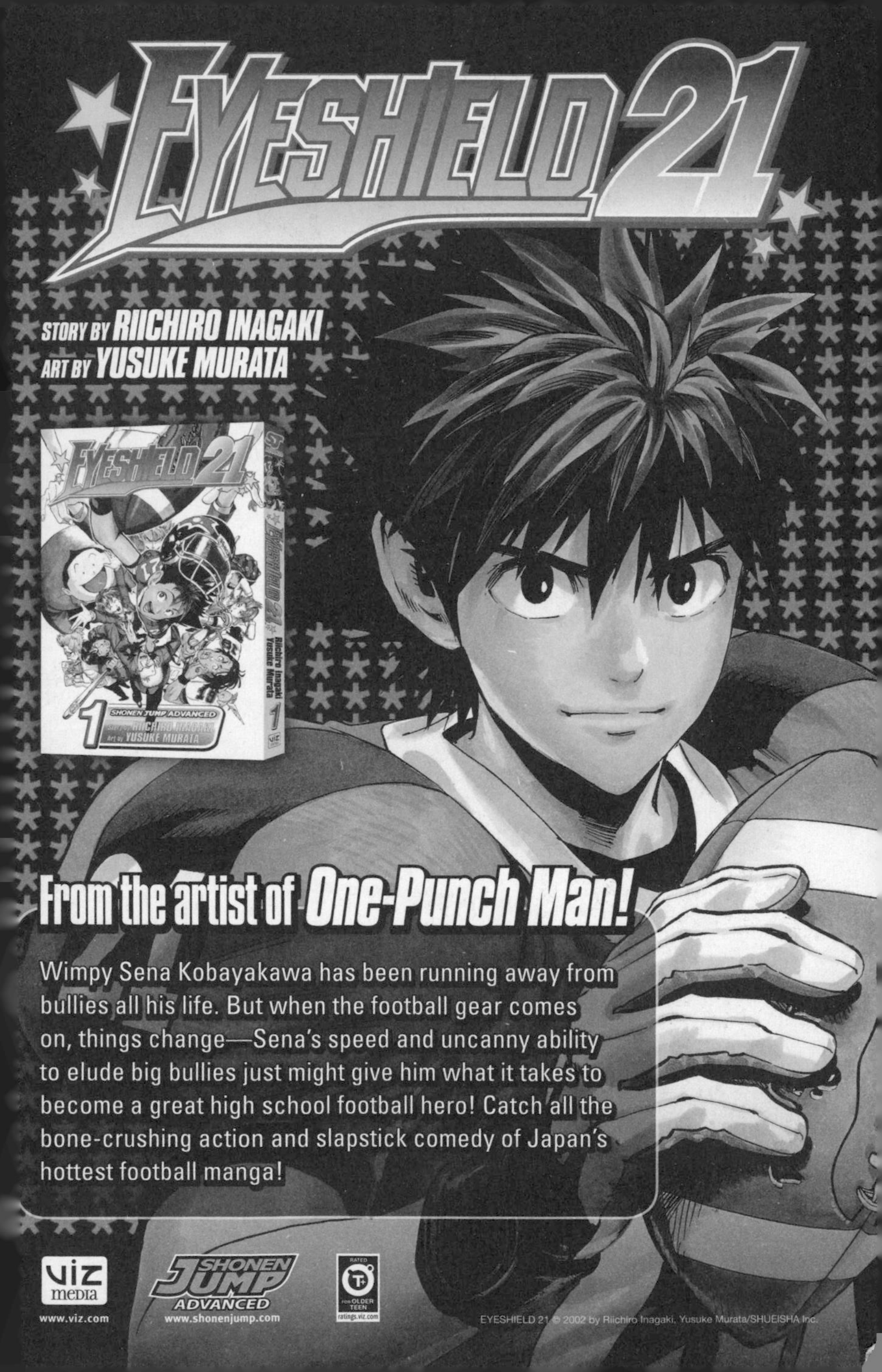
EYESHIELD 21
STORY BY RIICHIRO INAGAKI
ART BY YUSUKE MURATA
EYESHIELD 21
1
SHONEN JUMP ADVANCED
Story by RIICHIRO INAGAKI
Art by YUSUKE MURATA
From the artist of One-Punch Man!
Wimpy Sena Kobayakawa has been running away from bullies all his life. But when the football gear comes on, things change—Sena's speed and uncanny ability to elude big bullies just might give him what it takes to become a great high school football hero! Catch all the bone-crushing action and slapstick comedy of Japan's hottest football manga!
VIZ media
www.viz.com
SHONEN JUMP ADVANCED
www.shonenjump.com
RATED T+ FOR OLDER TEEN
ratings.viz.com
EYESHIELD 21 © 2002 by Riichiro Inagaki, Yusuke Murata/SHUEISHA Inc.

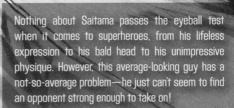
  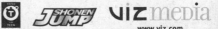

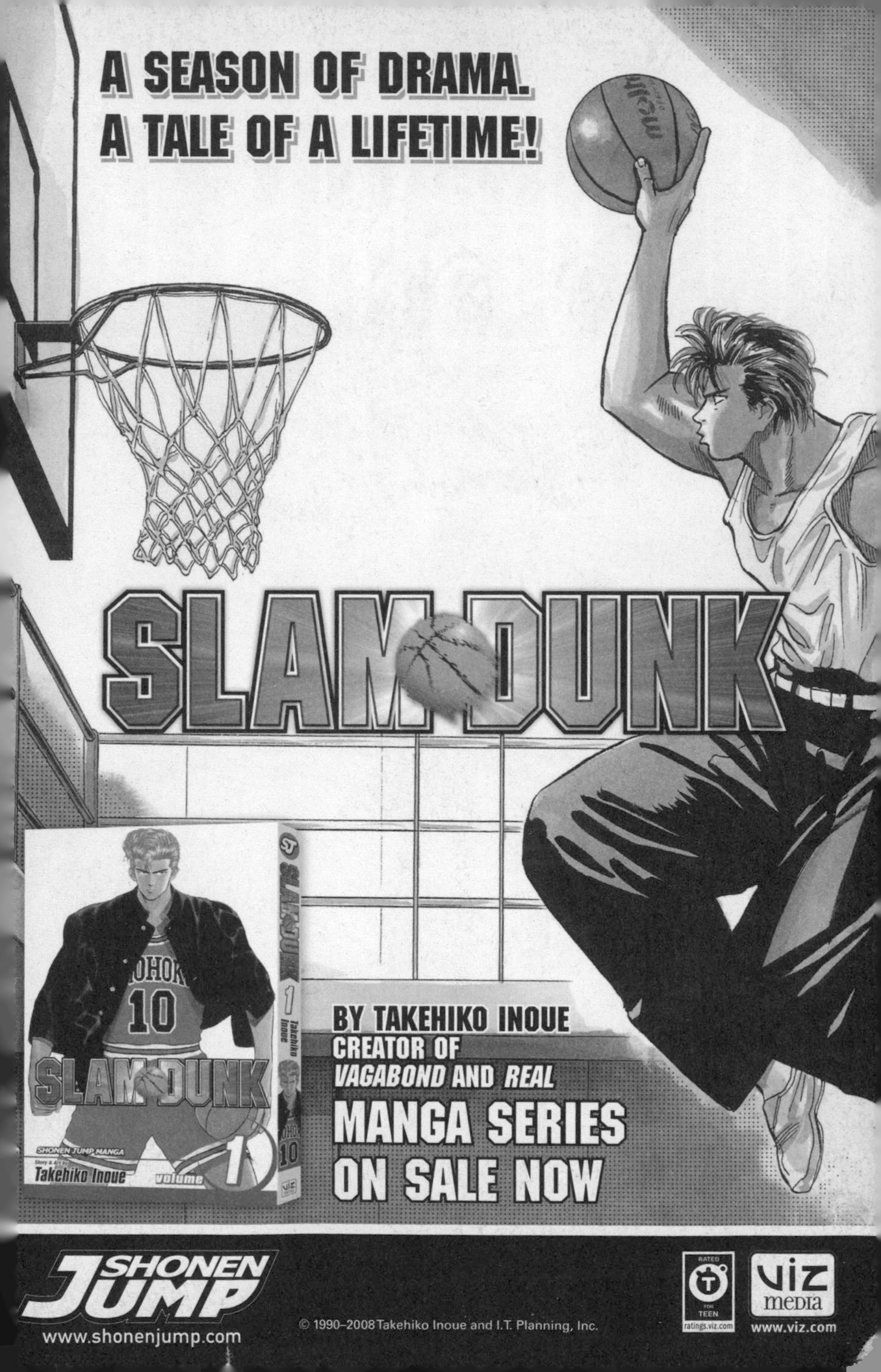
A SEASON OF DRAMA.
A TALE OF A LIFETIME!
SLAM DUNK
SLAM DUNK
SHONEN JUMP MANGA
Story & Art by
Takehiko Inoue
volume 1
BY TAKEHIKO INOUE
CREATOR OF
VAGABOND AND *REAL*
MANGA SERIES
ON SALE NOW
SHONEN JUMP
www.shonenjump.com
© 1990–2008 Takehiko Inoue and I.T. Planning, Inc.
RATED T FOR TEEN
ratings.viz.com
VIZ media
www.viz.com

YOU'RE READING THE WRONG WAY!

KUROKO'S BASKETBALL reads from right to left, starting in the upper-right corner. Japanese is read from right to left, meaning that action, sound effects and word-balloon order are completely reversed from English order.

1
2
1
3
4
2
5
6
3
7
8
4
9
5
142

FLIP IT OVER TO GET STARTED!

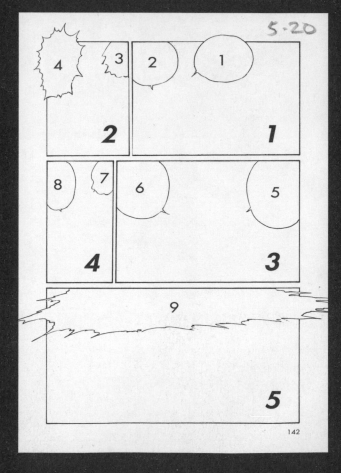